$ 10.50

D1498601

THIRD EDITION

ARCHITECTURAL AND BUILDING TRADES DICTIONARY

R. E. PUTNAM   **G. E. CARLSON**

 American Technical Society   Chicago 60637

Contents

Copyright, © *1950, 1955, 1974 by*
AMERICAN TECHNICAL SOCIETY

THIRD EDITION
12th Printing 1974

*No portion of this publication may be reproduced
by any process such as photocopying, recording,
storage in a retrieval system, or transmitted by any
means without permission of the publisher.*

*Library of Congress Catalog Card Number: 74-75483
ISBN 0-8269-0402-5*

Printed in the United States of America

A

ASTM: American Society for Testing and Materials.

Aaron's-rod: An architectural ornament consisting of a straight molding or rounded section from which a design of scrollwork or leafage emerges, representing a rod with a serpent twined about it. Sometimes confused with the *caduceus of Mercury;* however, there is a distinction between the two —Aaron's-rod has only one serpent while the caduceus has two serpents twined in opposite directions.

abacus: A slab forming the uppermost member or division of the capital of a column, either curved or square, and supporting the architrave. See Fig. 1.

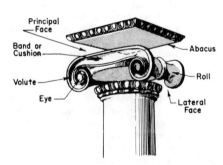

Fig. 1. Abacus.

abatement: In carpentry, the wasting of timber when shaping it to size; hence, a decrease in its strength.

abatjour (a-ba-zhoor'): In building, a device for admitting daylight and deflecting it downward when it enters a window, as a sloping soffit of a lintel or arch; also, a movable slat or screen; a skylight.

abattoir (a-ba-twar'): A public slaughter house for cattle, sheep, and hogs.

abbreviations: See *symbols and abbreviations,* page 443.

abrasion: The process of wearing away by friction. The act of reducing material by *grinding* instead of cutting with tools.

abrasion resistance: Ability of a surface to resist being worn away by rubbing and friction.

abrasive: A substance used for wearing away or polishing a surface by friction. A grinding material, such as emery, sand, and diamond. Other abrasives include: crushed garnet and quartz, pumice or powdered lava, also decomposed limestone, known as *tripoli.* There are other abrasives which are made artificially and sold under various trade names.

abrasive paper: Paper, or cloth, covered on one side with a grinding material glued fast to the surface, used for smoothing and polishing. Materials used for this purpose include: crushed flint, garnet, emery, or corundum.

abrasive tools: All implements used for wearing down materials by friction or rubbing are known as *abrasive tools;* these include: grindstones which are made of pure sandstone, whetstones, emery wheels, sandpaper, and emery cloth.

abreuvoir (a-bru-vwar'): In masonry, the mortar joint between stones in a wall or between two arch stones.

1

absolute: In the trades, a term often used to designate perfection or exactness; anything which is complete in its own character.

absolute humidity: The weight of water vapor per unit volume, pounds per cubic foot, or grams per cubic centimeter; or a mass of water vapor present in unit volume of the atmosphere, usually measured as grams per cubic meter. It may be expressed also in terms of the actual pressure of the water vapor present.

absolute volume: The amount of space a material would take up if all its air spaces were removed and it was just one solid block.

absolute zero: The point at which all thermal motion ceases and from which absolute temperature is reckoned, which is approximately —273.1° C. or —458.8° F. References to the absolute-temperature scale may be indicated, as 20° *absolute,* or 20° A.

absorption: The action or process by means of which a material extracts one or more substances present in an atmosphere or mixture of gases or liquids. This process is accompanied by physical change, chemical change, or both, of the sorbent. The process by which a liquid is drawn into and tends to fill pores in a porous solid body.

absorption bed: A pit of relatively large dimensions filled with coarse aggregate, containing a distribution pipe system which allows absorption of septic tank effluent.

absorption field: A system of trenches containing coarse aggregate and distribution pipe through which the septic tank effluent may seep into the surrounding soil.

abut: To meet or touch with an end, as one construction member meeting another.

abutment: The masonry, timber, or timber and earth structure supporting the end of a bridge or arch.

abutment piece: In framing a building, the lowest structural member which receives and distributes the thrust of an upright or strut; the *soleplate* of a partition to which studding is nailed. Same as *foot plate* or *solepiece.* See *mudsill.*

abutting joint: A joint produced by the meeting of two pieces end on, with the grain of one piece forming an angle with the grain of the other piece. See *butt joint.*

acanthus: An architectural ornament patterned after the leaves of the acanthus, a plant native to the Mediterranean regions. A well-known example of the use of the acanthus ornamentation is the Corinthian capital. See Fig. 2.

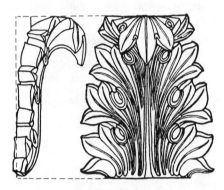

Fig. 2. Acanthus.

accelerator: Any substance added to gypsum plaster during the mixing process, which will speed up its natural set; material added to Portland cement concrete during the mixing to hasten its natural development of strength. In heating, a centrifugal pump located in the return circuit of a central heating system, by means of which it is possible to increase the flow.

access: A passageway or means of approach to a room or building; a corridor between rooms; also, a term used in building construction referring to points at which concealed equipment may be reached for inspection and repair.

access court: An area which permits entrance to a group of clustered residences.

access door: Any door which allows access to concealed equipment or parts of a building not often used, such as a door to concealed plumbing parts.

accordion doors: Folding doors supported by carriers with rollers which run on a track. The doors fold up in a manner similar to the bellows of an accordion. See Fig. 3.

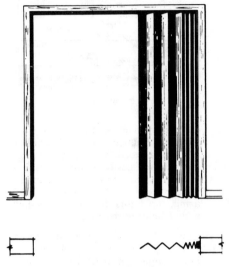

Fig. 3. Accordion door.

accouple: To join or couple; to bring together as ties or braces joined together in building construction.

accouplement (a-kup′l-ment): In carpentry, a tie or brace of timber; in architecture, the placing of two columns, or pilasters, close together, as in pairs of columns forming a colonnade.

acoustic jars: Large, earthenware jars found under the choir stalls of some medieval churches, their purpose apparently being to increase the sound of the singing; also called *resonators.*

acoustical board: Any type of special material, such as insulating boards used in the control of sound or to prevent the passage of sound from one room to another.

acoustical materials: Sound absorbing materials for covering walls and ceilings; a term applied to special plasters, tile, or any other material for wall coverings composed of mineral, wood, or vegetable fibers; also, cork or metal used to control or deaden sound. See Fig. 4.

acoustical plaster: Any finishing plaster used with an aggregate designed to reduce the reflection and reverberation of sound.

Fig. 4. Acoustical tile being applied to ceiling. (Celotex Corp.)

Vermiculite and other porous materials, having the property of absorbing sound waves, have been used successfully for *acoustical plaster.*

acoustical tile: Any tile composed of materials having the property of absorbing sound waves; hence, reducing the reflection and reverberation of sound; any tile designed and constructed to absorb sound waves. See Fig. 4.

acoustics: Science of sound. A study of the effects of sound upon the ear. The sum of the qualities that determines the value of an auditorium as to distinct hearing. The acoustics are said to be *good* or *bad* according to the ease of clearness with which sounds can be heard by the audience. The main factors influencing acoustical conditions are reverberation, extraneous noises, loudness of the original sound, and the size and shape of the auditorium.

acrophobia: A fear of heights.

acropolis (a-krop'o-lis): The name given to the citadel or fortified section of cities in ancient Greece and Asia Minor. Intended originally as a strong point, the acropolis developed as the cultural center of the city. The most important of these was at Athens. Because of its historical associations and the famous buildings to be found on it, it is usually referred to as *The Acropolis.*

across: A term used in carpentry when cutting or sawing *across* a board at approximately a right angle to the length of the piece.

acroter (ak'ro-ter): A small pedestal placed on the apex or at the basal angle of a pediment to support a statue or other ornament; a statue or ornament placed on such a pedestal. See Fig. 5.

acroteria (ak-ro-te'ri-a): In modern architecture, small pedestals placed at the apex and at the extremities of a pediment, usually without bases or plinths; also, the pedestals alone.

acrylic plastic glaze: A synthetic material which comes in sheets for use on windows in high breakage areas. Results in a comparatively shatterproof window.

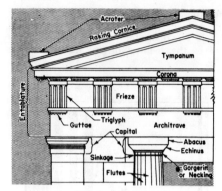

Fig. 5. Acroter.

acrylic plastics: Noncrystalline *thermoplastics* with optical clarity, excellent weather resistance, and good shatter resistance. They are soft and easily scratched, with a slow-to-fast burning rate and maximum use temperatures of 150° to 200° F. Used for glazing, top lights, hardware, window frames, and lighting fixtures.

acrylic resin: A synthetic material such as Lucite, which comes in flat, shaped, or corrugated panels of extruded sheeting. Used for lighting fixtures, skylights, and in other areas where translucence and diffusion of light are desired.

addition: Any construction or change in a building which increases its cubic contents by increasing its exterior dimensions; also, the original designing of a building with one or more rooms joined to the main structure so as to form one architectural whole, with each part a necessary adjunct of the other, and both parts constituting in use and purpose one and the same building.

addition: In cement making, a chemical material ground into the cement at the time of manufacture; like an admixture, this material improves one of the properties of concrete, such as accelerating the hydration process of fresh concrete.

adherence: The property of unlike particles for sticking together; a clinging quality, as in a glutinous substance.

adhesion: 1. Act or state of adhering; a sticking fast. 2. The attraction that holds molecules together.

adhesive: A substance capable of holding materials together by surface attachment. This is a general term and includes cements, mucilage, and paste as well as mastic and glue. A mastic or glue is used to hold materials on a smooth under surface, such as ceiling tile. Where nailing of material in place is not desirable or practical, a glue or resin adhesive is often used, as for holding wallboard, flooring, or roofing. The two kinds of adhesives used are glues and mastics. *Glues* are obtainable in either liquid or dry form. The dry form is commonly used and mixed on the job into a liquid. In mixing glues, *mastics* are much thicker than glues and usually have an asphalt, rubber, or resin base. They commonly come already mixed. Table 1, page 7, lists common adhesives.

adjacent: Near to, touching, or adjoining, as *adjacent* angles.

adjust: To make right, to arrange exactly, to bring into a true relative position, as the structural members of a building.

adjustable clamp: Any type of clamping device that can be adjusted to suit the work being done, but particularly clamps used for holding column forms while concrete is poured.

adjustable key: A key with an adjustable shank or stem, so the length of the key can be adapted to doors of various thicknesses; a key for a sliding-door lock.

adjustable pipe hanger: In plumbing, a pipe hanger consisting of a beam clamp, an adjustable rod, and an adjustable ring. See *strap pipe hanger,* page 435.

adjustable triangle: This drafting and lettering triangle can be adjusted to any de-

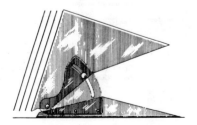

Fig. 6. Adjustable triangle.

sired angle by means of a movable arm which pivots from the base arm at one end. See Fig. 6.

adjustable wrench: A wrench similar to an open-end wrench, except that it has an adjustable jaw which can be moved to fit various sized bolts. See Fig. 7.

Fig. 7. Adjustable wrench.

adjusting lever: In a carpenter's plane, a lever for adjusting the bit so it will cut shavings of uniform thickness.

adjusting nut: Any button or nut by means of which adjustments may be made on tools or other devices.

adjusting plane: A carpenter's plane having attachments which provide for the adjustment of the bit so it will cut shavings to any thickness desired.

adjusting screw: A type of set screw used to adjust instruments, tools, or devices.

adjustment: In construction work, the process of placing and fixing of structural members in a related position.

admixture: A material other than water, aggregates, and hydraulic cement, used as an ingredient of concrete or mortar. It is added to the batch immediately before or during its mixture. It may add coloring or control strength or setting time.

adobe (a-do'bi): An aluminous earth from which unfired brick is made, especially in the western part of the United States; an unfired brick dried in the sun.

adobe (a-do'bi) construction: Any building constructed of unburnt, sundried bricks which are made out of adobe soil found in the arid regions of the southwestern part of the United States, where this type of construction is in common use.

5

TABLE I. ADHESIVES: TYPES AND PROPERTIES*

(1) ANIMAL GLUES. Solvents: Water. **Nature:** Melted and applied hot. Some are liquids applied cold. **Bonds:** Excellent for wood, leather, glass, paper. Poor for metals. **Strength:** Very high on wood. Up to 10,000-12,000 psi in shear. **Temperature resistance:** Medium for heat, good for cold. **Creep resistance:** Good. **Water resistance:** Very poor. **Cure:** Initial gel and then air-drying @ room temperature.

(2) ASPHALTIC MIXTURES. Solvents: Water, aromatics, carbon tetrachloride and disulphide. **Nature:** Thermo-plastic. Natural asphalts usually hard and brittle when cold. **Bonds:** Good for metals, rubber, or glass, floor coverings, roofing felts. **Strength:** Low to fair, depending upon grade and temperature. **Temperature resistance:** Poor for heat, good for cold. Melting point may be as high as 200°F., or as low as 50°F. **Creep resistance:** Very poor. **Water resistance:** Good to excellent. **Cure:** Elevated temperatures or cooling to room temperature.

(3) BLOOD ALBUMIN GLUES. Solvents: Water. **Nature:** Usually dry powder. **Bonds:** Fair for wood. Good for leather and paper. Poor for metals or glass. **Strength:** Good. **Temperature resistance:** Fair for both heat and cold. **Creep resistance:** Good. **Water resistance:** Poor. **Cure:** Dries at room temperature or low heat, 150-200°F.

(4) CASEIN GLUES. Solvents: Water. **Nature:** Usually dry powder. Sometimes called thermo-plastic. **Bonds:** Good to medium for wood to wood, or paper. **Strength:** Up to 1650 psi in shear, on wood. **Temperature resistance:** Medium resistant to both heat and cold. **Creep resistance:** Good. **Water resistance:** Very good. **Cure:** Air drying or chemically reacted.

(5) CELLULOSE CEMENTS. Solvents: Water emulsion, ethyl acetate or acetone. **Nature:** Thermo-plastic. Fused by heating. **Bonds:** Good for glass, wood, paper, leather. Not for rubber. **Strength:** good. 1000-1400 psi on wood, in shear. **Temperature resistance:** Fair to good for both heat and cold. **Creep resistance:** Good. **Water resistance:** Water mixed, poor. Other solvents, fair to medium. **Cure:** Air drying and setting.

(6) CHLORINATED RUBBER. Solvents: Ketones or aromatics. **Nature:** Usually liquid. **Bonds:** Medium for wood, metals or glass. Good for paper. **Strength:** No data. **Temperature resistance:** Medium for both heat and cold. **Creep resistance:** Poor. **Water resistance:** Medium to good. **Cure:** Dries at room temperature.

(7) EPOXY RESIN. Solvents: No solvent needed. **Nature:** Thermo-setting.

Bonds: Excellent for wood, metal, glass, masonry. **Strength:** High. 1000-7000 psi on wood. **Temperature resistance:** Excellent for both heat and cold. **Creep resistance:** Good to poor, depending upon compounding. **Water resistance:** Fair to excellent, depending upon compounding. **Cure:** Catalyst and hot-press (up to 390°F.) or strong catalyst @ room temp.

(8) MELAMINE RESINS. Solvents: Water, alcohol. **Nature:** Thermo-setting. Powder with separate catalyst. Applied cold. Colorless, non-staining. **Bonds:** Excellent for paper or wood. Poor for metals or glass. **Strength:** No data. **Temperature resistance:** Excellent for both heat and cold. **Creep resistance:** very good. **Water resistance:** Excellent. **Cure:** Hot-press @ 300°F.

(9) UREA RESINS. Solvents: Water; alcohol, or alcohol hydrocarbons blends. **Nature:** Thermo-setting. **Bonds:** Excellent for wood, leather, paper. Poor for metals or glass. **Creep resistance:** Good. **Water resistance:** Fair. **Cure:** some heat desirable, but some types will cure @ room temperature.

(10) NEOPRENE RUBBER ADHESIVES. Solvents: Water emulsions or volatile solvents. **Nature:** Thermo-plastic, with some thermo-setting characteristics. **Bonds:** Excellent for wood, asbestos board, metals, glass. **Strength:** Up to 1200 psi in shear. **Temperature resistance:** Good for heat or cold. 100 to 400 psi @ 180°F. **Creep resistance:** Fair to good. **Water resistance:** Excellent. **Cure:** Some heat desirable.

(11) NITRILE RUBBER ADHESIVES. (Sometimes called Buna N rubber.) Solvents: Water emulsions or volatile solvents. **Nature:** Both thermo-plastic and thermo-setting types available. **Bonds:** Wood, paper, porcelain enamel, polyester skins. **Strength:** Thermo-setting, to 4000 psi shear, thermo-plastic, to 600 psi. **Temperature resistance:** Good for both heat and cold. **Creep resistance:** Good to fair. **Water resistance:** Excellent. **Cure:** heat cure preferable.

(12) PHENOLIC RESINS. Solvents: Water, alcohol, ketones. **Nature:** Dry or liquid. **Bonds:** Good to excellent for wood, paper. Medium to poor for glass and metals. **Strength:** Good. **Temperature resistance:** Excellent for both heat and cold. **Creep resistance:** Excellent. **Water resistance:** Excellent. **Cure:** Some set @ room temperature, some require hot-press.

(13) POLYVINYL RESINS: Solvents: Water, ketones. **Nature:** Liquid, usually

an emulsion. **Bonds:** Good for wood or paper. **Strength:** Up to 950 psi in shear on wood. **Temperature resistance:** Fair for heat, good for cold. Fuses @ 220-350°F. **Creep resistance:** Fair to poor. **Water resistance:** Fair to medium. **Cure:** Air drying and setting @ room temperature.

(14) RESORCINOL RESINS. Solvents: Alcohol, water, ketones. **Nature:** Thermo-setting. Usually liquid with separate catalyst. **Bonds:** Wood, paper. Poor for glass or metals. **Strength:** On wood, up to 1950 psi in shear. **Temperature resistance:** Excellent for cold. More heat resisting than wood. **Creep resistance:** Very good. **Cure:** Room temperature or moderate (200°F.) heat.

(15) SODIUM SILICATE. Solvents: Water. **Nature:** Liquid. **Bonds:** Good for wood, metals. Excellent for paper, or glass. **Strength:** No data. **Temperature resistance:** Excellent for heat or cold. **Creep resistance:** Good. **Water resistance:** Poor. **Cure:** Dries at room temperature or moderate (150-200°F) heat.

(16) SOY-BEAN GLUE. Solvents: Water. **Nature:** Dry or water mixed. **Bonds:** Fair for wood or glass; poor for metals or rubber. **Strength:** No data. **Temperature resistance:** Fair for heat, poor for cold. **Creep resistance:** Good. **Water resistance:** Poor. **Cure:** Dries at room temperature.

(17) STARCH AND DEXTRIN GLUES. Solvents: Water. **Nature:** Dry and liquid available. **Bonds:** Wood, leather, paper. **Strength:** Fair to medium for wood or paper; poor for metals or glass. **Temperature resistance:** Fair for both heat and cold. **Creep resistance:** Fair. **Water resistance:** Poor. **Cure:** Dries @ room temperature.

(18) NATURAL RUBBER ADHESIVES. Solvents: Water emulsions, aromatics, various hydrocarbons. **Nature:** Latex emulsions or dissolved crepe rubber. **Bonds:** Good for rubber, glass or leather. Fair for wood or ceramics. **Strength:** Rather low, 340 psi in tension, on wood. **Temperature resistance:** Fair for both heat and cold. **Creep resistance:** Poor. **Water resistance:** Good. **Cure:** Dries @ room temperature.

SOURCE: PROFESSIONAL BUILDER

adsorption: The property of certain substances to condense water vapor without themselves being changed physically or chemically; the action, associated with surface adherence, of a material in extracting one or more substances present in a mixture of gases and liquids unaccompanied by chemical or physical change. *Silica gel* is an example of such a substance.

adze: A cutting tool resembling an ax. The thin arched blade is set at right angles to the handle. The adze is used for rough-dressing timber. See Fig. 8. Sometimes spelled "adz".

adze block: In a wood-planing machine, that part which carries the cutter.

adze eye: A type of *eye* used on a carpenter's hammer, where the eye is extended to give the handle a longer bearing than is possible without such an extension. See Fig. 9.

adze-eye hammer: A claw hammer with the eye extended. This gives a longer bearing on the handle than is the case in hammers not having an extended eye. See Fig. 9.

aerated concrete: A lightweight material made from a specially prepared cement, used for subfloors. Due to its cellular structure, this material is a retardant to sound transmission.

aerograph: A spray gun used in the application of paint. The paint passes from an

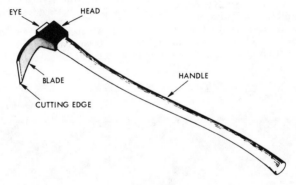

Fig. 8. Adze.

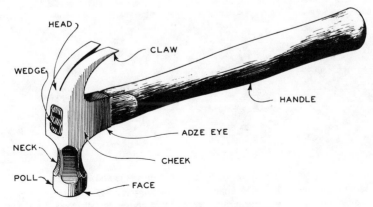

Fig. 9. Adze eye in claw hammer.

attached container to a small nozzle, where it is blown by compressed air into a fine spray which can be directed easily onto the surface to be covered.

aggregate: A collection of granulated particles of different substances into a compound or conglomerate mass. In mixing concrete, the stone or gravel used as a part of the mix is commonly called the *coarse aggregate,* while the sand is called the *fine aggregate.* Most aggregates contain varying degrees of moisture. To prevent an excessive amount of water from finding its way into the concrete, the amount held by the aggregate must be determined and this amount subtracted from that specified from the batch. See Fig. 10. In plastering, in addition to sand aggregate, lightweight aggregates are used. Three types of lightweight aggregates are in common use: vermiculite, perlite, and pumice. Also, in plastering, exposed aggregates are used on the actual plastered surface. These exposed aggregates are made from crushed rock and are blown on the surface with an *aggregate gun.* See Fig. 11.

aggregate gun: The aggregate gun is used to apply aggregates to a surface. It consists of a hopper attached to a short round pipe. See Fig. 11. This pipe is connected to a blower which is turned by an electric motor. This machine operates by the aggregates feeding into the round pipe by gravity and then being forced out the muzzle end by air from the blower.

aggregate seeder gun: The aggregate seeder gun is similar to the aggregate gun and is used to apply aggregates to a surface. It consists of a hopper attached to an electric motor which has an oscillating gear attachment. The machine operates by having the aggregates feed into the pan by gravity and the sponge oscillating enough to push the aggregates onto the surface.

aging: A process used by builders to make materials appear old, or ancient, by artificial means.

Fig. 10. Coarse aggregate for concrete. Good concrete gravel is shown at top. Note the variety of sizes, the smaller stones filling in spaces between larger ones. The three samples below were obtained by screening the natural mixture of gravel above. Smallest sizes are ¼" to ⅜"; next are ⅜" to ¾"; largest are ¾" to 1½ inches. (Courtesy of Portland Cement Association)

agreement: A contract between two or more parties, either written or verbal; an understanding regarding mutual interests.

aiguille (a'gwel): In masonry, an instrument for boring holes in stone or other masonry material.

air brick: A hollow or perforated brick specially prepared for ventilating purposes; also, a box of brick size made of metal with grated sides which allows air to enter a building where ventilation is otherwise restricted.

air brush: In painting, any of several different types of devices for spraying paint onto a surface by means of compressed air. See *aerograph,* page 6.

air cleaner: A device designed to remove air-borne impurities such as dust, cinders,

Fig. 11. Aggregate gun.

fumes, gases, vapors, and smoke from a stream of air. *Air cleaners* include air washers, air filters, electrostatic precipitators, and charcoal filters. See *air washer*.

air conditioner: A specific air-treating combination consisting of means for ventilation, air circulation, air cleaning, and heat transfer, with means for controlling room temperature and humidity, within limits determined according to current engineering standards and practices.

air conditioning: The process of heating or cooling, cleaning, humidifying or dehumidifying, and circulating air throughout the various rooms of a house or public building. The system may be designed for summer air conditioning or for winter air conditioning or for both.

air conditioning condenser: A unit which is either air or water cooled, the function of which is to condense hot, compressed refrigerant gases. Within the air conditioning system, the hot, compressed refrigerant moves from the compressor to the condenser, where it is cooled and condensed into the liquid refrigerant state. The large amounts of air necessary to operate air-cooled condensers limit their usage to units of less than three tons capacity. In the water-cooled condensing units, a *cooling tower* is commonly used to cool the water within the condenser system.

air content: The proportional volume of air voids in concrete. This is expressed as a percentage of the volume of the hardened concrete.

air-cooled slag: The product of relatively slow-cooling molten blast-furnace slag, resulting in a solid mass of tough, durable material which is excavated, crushed, and screened for commercial purposes, such as concrete and bituminous aggregate.

air drain: A flue or passageway for conveying fresh air to foundation walls to keep them dry; to woodwork, to preserve it; or to a fireplace.

air dried: A term used when referring to lumber or wood which has been dried or seasoned by exposure to the atmosphere without artificial heat.

air-dried lumber: Lumber that has been piled in yards or sheds for any length of time. Generally, the minimum moisture content of thoroughly air-dried lumber is 12 to 15 percent; the average is somewhat higher. Any lumber which is seasoned by drying in the air instead of being dried in a kiln or oven.

air dry: A term applied to wood or lumber in which the moisture content is in approximate equilibrium with the local atmospheric conditions.

air drying: The process of seasoning lumber or wood in the air instead of in a kiln.

air duct: A pipe for conducting air for ventilating the rooms of a house or to a furnace, sometimes applied to light or temporary construction as opposed to an *air drain* of masonry.

air-entrained concrete: Concrete containing the addition of an air-entraining agent which causes millions of minute bubbles of air to be trapped within the concrete. Air-entrained concrete is more resistant to freeze-thaw cycles than non-air-entrained concrete. On specifications this type of cement is designated by the letter "A" after type, such as Type IA, Type IIA, etc.

air-entraining cement: Portland cement containing an extra ingredient that causes billions of tiny air bubbles in a controlled amount which improves the workability of the concrete and its resistance to freezing and thawing.

air entrainment: A process whereby billions of air bubbles are uniformly produced throughout concrete. The purpose of the air bubbles is to improve the workability and frost resistance of the concrete.

air escape: In plumbing, a contrivance for discharging excess air from a water pipe. It consists of a *ball cock* which opens the discharging air valve when sufficient air has collected and closes it in time to prevent loss of water.

air flue: A flue which is usually fitted with a special type of valve built into a chimney stack so as to withdraw vitiated air from a room.

air grating: A perforated iron grating across an air duct which is built into the wall of a structure to admit air and provide ventilation.

Fig. 12. Air gun used for fireproofing of structural steel building.

air gun: In the building trades, a specially constructed gun in which the elastic force of condensed air projects atomized adhesive materials onto the surface of a wall for insulating purposes. See Fig. 12.

air locking: A term applied to material used to make parts of a building airtight, as the weather stripping used on revolving doors.

air locks: A term applied to the checking of the flow of water, in a low-pressure water system, caused by the trapping of air in the supply lines.

air pocket: An air space which accidentally occurs in concrete work.

air-seasoned lumber: Lumber seasoned by exposure to the atmosphere until there is

no further appreciable loss in weight due to evaporation of moisture. See *air drying.*

air slaking: In masonry, the process of exposing quicklime to the air, as a result of which it will gradually absorb moisture and break down into a powder.

air space: A cavity or space in walls or between various structural members.

airtight construction: In building, any structure so constructed and tight that air cannot pass through it.

air trap: A water-sealed trap which prevents foul air or foul odors from rising from sinks, wash basins, drain pipes, and sewers. See Fig. 13.

Fig. 13. Air trap.

air void: A small space enclosed by the cement paste in concrete and occupied by air. The term refers to both entrapped and entrained air voids.

air washer: A device consisting of an enclosed chamber where air is forced or drawn through a spray of water or is passed over thoroughly wetted plates to regulate the heat and moisture content of the air. Such a device cleans, purifies, and freshens the air by removing dust particles, bacteria, and foul odors. It may be used as a humidifier or as a dehumidifier.

airway: A space between roof insulation and roof boards for the movement of air.

aisle: A passageway by which seats may be reached, as the *aisle* of a church.

akroterion (ak-ro-te′ ri-on): On classical buildings, one of the angles of a pediment; also, a statue or other ornament placed at one of these angles, especially at the apex. Same as *acroter* or *acroterium.*

alabaster: A fine-grained gypsum, usually white but sometimes delicately tinted, often carved for mantel ornaments or other decorative construction features.

alburnum (al-bur' num): In trees, the living tissues of soft wood surrounding the heartwood; same as *sapwood.*

alcove: Any recess cut in a room.

alette (a-let): In architecture, a wing of a building; a buttress; a pilasterlike *abutment* of an arch seen on either side of a large engaged column, or pilaster, which carries the *entablature.*

align (a-lin): To adjust or arrange in a line.

aligning punch: A type of punch used by steel workers to bring a joint into such a position that the rivet holes will be in a straight line.

alignment: The adjustment or formation of a straight line through two or more points; the course or location of the elements of construction or design in relation to a predetermined line.

alkali: A water soluble salt already present in concrete. Alkalies from the concrete or in the ground soil where cement may be placed can react with some aggregates to form the damaging effect of expansion.

alkyd plastics: These *thermoset* plastics are fast-curing, dimensionally stable, have good heat and electrical insulation properties, low impact strength, and are self-extinguishing, with maximum use temperatures of 300° to 400° F. Used for paints, lacquers, and molded ignition parts.

alkyd resins: In painting, a modified form of *glyptal resin,* used principally for lacquer, paints, varnishes, and metal finishes.
all-heart: Heartwood throughout; that is, free of sapwood.

all-rowlock wall: In masonry, a wall built so that two courses of stretchers are standing on edge alternating with one course of headers standing on edge.

alley: A narrow passageway between houses or rows of seats; a covered passage under a house affording access directly to an inner court or yard without entering the house; especially in American cities, a thoroughfare through the middle of a square or block, giving access to the rear of buildings.

alligatoring: A defect in a painted surface, resulting from the application of a hard finishing coat over a soft primer coat. The pattern of this defect has the appearance of alligator hide. The checking pattern is caused by the slipping of the new coat over the old coat. The old coat can be seen through the cracks.

allure: A walk along the top of a castle wall.

alluvial (a-lu'vi-al) soil: Soil, sand, or gravel deposited by flowing water, especially during times of floods. Such soil is not stable enough to insure a firm foundation for heavy structures.

almery or ambry: A cupboard in the thickness of a wall, especially popular in medieval times; also, in churches, a high cupboard to contain a processional cross.

alphaduct: In electricity, a flexible nonmetal conduit.

altar: In Christian churches a table or elevated structure used in connection with the worship service; the communion table.

altar rail: The rail in front of an altar, separating the chancel from the body of the church.

alteration: A building-code term which varies slightly in meaning according to the community requirements: as, any change in a structure which does not increase any of its exterior dimensions; or any modification in construction or grade of occupancy; also, any change or rearrangement in the structural parts of a building or in the facilities, or any enlargement whether by extension on any side or by increase in height or by the moving from one location to another.

alternating current (a.c.): Current in which the flow of electricity (electrons) is reversed in direction at regular intervals as it passes through the circuit. Usually this is the type of current supplied by power companies for use in the home and on the farm and in industry. Generally, a 60-cycle (Hertz) current is supplied.

altitude: The perpendicular distance from a specified level, as the elevation above sea level.

alto-relievo (al-to-re-le′vo): Sculptures in high relief, in which at least one half of the figure projects, from the surface of the background on which they are carved.

aluminum conduit: Aluminum tube or underground passage for electric wires.

aluminum foil insulation: A type of metallic insulation consisting of thin sheets of aluminum which is mounted on another material; used in one or more layers with air spaces between each pair of layers. See Fig. 14. The following types are used: heavy flat foil mounted on one or both sides of heavy kraft paper with asphalt; a plaster base consisting of steel reinforcing wire, backed with metalated (aluminum foil) kraft paper; and an aluminum-colored paper. There is also aluminum foil-backed gypsum board and blanket insulation with an aluminum reflective foil or coating. Aluminum foil insulations are usually installed in much the same manner as other flexible insulations: either between and fastened to the sides of framing members or fastened to the edges of framing members. To be effective, air spaces are needed on both sides of the insulation.

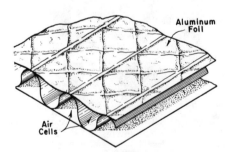

Aluminum Foil

Air Cells

Fig. 14. Aluminum foil.

aluminum molding: Insulating strips of pressed or molded aluminum made into a great variety of patterns for building purposes; especially used for installing linoleum tops for worktables in kitchens, around kitchen sinks, or in the installation of fiber and adhesive tile-design wainscoting on kitchen and bathroom walls.

aluminum nails: Nails made of this metal are lightweight, stainless, rustless, and sterilized.

aluminum paint: A paint containing aluminum alloys, effective in preventing discoloration of painted surfaces in regions where combating the effect of mildew growth presents a painting problem; also effective as a corrosive resistant when applied to steel or other metal construction. It has also been used with satisfactory results on asbestos-cement siding.

ambient temperature: Temperature of the surrounding air.

ambo (am′bo): In early Christian or Eastern churches, a raised platform, a pulpit, or reading desk used when reading the epistles and gospels or when making announcements to the people.

ambulatory (am′bu-la-to-ri): A covered passage or sheltered walk, generally located just within the main walls of a building; a passageway around the choir in the apse or chancel of a cathedral or between the columns and walls of a circular building.

American National Standards Institute (ANSI): Publishes the American National Standards, approved standards and specifications in all areas of building construction, safety, testing, drafting, manufacturing, engineering, etc.

American National Thread Series: The old thread series which has been generally replaced by the *Unified Thread Series*.

American softwood lumber standards: "American lumber standards embody provisions for softwood lumber dealing with recognized classifications, nomenclature, basic grades, sizes, description, measurements, tally, shipping provisions, grade marking, and inspection of lumber. The primary purpose of these standards is to serve as a guide or basic example in the preparation or revision of the grading rules of the various lumber manufacturers' associations. A purchaser must, however, make use of association rules, as the basic standards are not in themselves commercial rules." (PS 20-70)

American standard wire gage: A system of designating the diameters of wires of non-ferrous metals by the use of numbers. See Fig. 15.

ammonia: A colorless, pungent gas soluble in either water or alcohol. In liquefied form, *ammonia* is used as a refrigerant in ice-making plants, in air-conditioning systems, and in other mechanical refrigerators.

ampacity: Current carrying capacity expressed in amps.

ampere (amp): The rate at which a given quantity of electricity flows through a conductor or circuit.

ampere-hour: The quantity of electricity delivered by a current of one ampere flowing for one hour. Used in rating storage batteries for doorbells.

ampere-hour meter: An instrument which registers or records the number of ampere-hours of electrical energy which have passed through a circuit.

amphiprostyle (am-fip'ro-stil): Provided with a row of columns at each end, but with none on the sides; having a columned portico at each end.

amphitheater (am-fi-the'a-ter): A structure whose plan is laid out on a system of curves around a central pit or arena, with seats in oval or circular tiers rising one behind another, and usually intended for exhibition purposes.

analysis: In construction work, the simple process of reducing a problem to its primary parts, as the finding of the forces, or stress and strain, in the various members of a loaded structure; also, the resolving of a compound into its various elements or parts.

anchor: In building, a special metal form used to fasten together timbers or masonry. See Fig. 16. Also, an egg-shaped ornament alternating with a dartlike tongue used to enrich a molding; different names have been given to this type of molding which is sometimes called *egg-and-dart molding, egg-and-tongue molding,* or *egg-and-anchor molding.*

anchor blocks: Blocks of wood built into masonry walls to which partitions and fixtures may be secured.

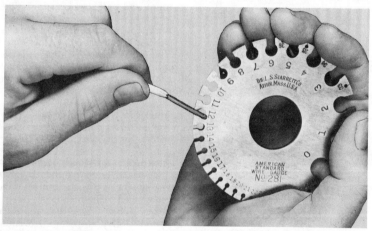

Fig. 15. Using a wire gage to determine the size of a wire. The size of wire is found by placing the wire between the slots on the outside edge of the gage. The slot in which the wire fits snugly indicates the gage of the wire. The round hole at the bottom of the slot makes it easier to remove the wire after checking for size.

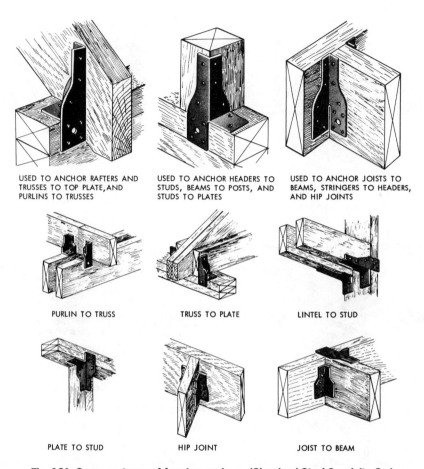

USED TO ANCHOR RAFTERS AND TRUSSES TO TOP PLATE, AND PURLINS TO TRUSSES

USED TO ANCHOR HEADERS TO STUDS, BEAMS TO POSTS, AND STUDS TO PLATES

USED TO ANCHOR JOISTS TO BEAMS, STRINGERS TO HEADERS, AND HIP JOINTS

PURLIN TO TRUSS

TRUSS TO PLATE

LINTEL TO STUD

PLATE TO STUD

HIP JOINT

JOIST TO BEAM

Fig. 16A. Common types of framing anchors. (Cleveland Steel Specialty Co.)

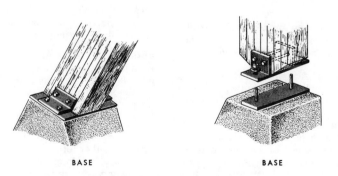

BASE

BASE

Fig. 16B. Methods of anchoring large beams.

15

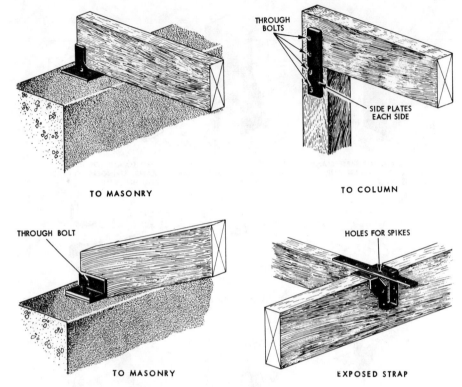

TO MASONRY

THROUGH BOLTS

SIDE PLATES EACH SIDE

TO COLUMN

THROUGH BOLT

TO MASONRY

HOLES FOR SPIKES

EXPOSED STRAP

Fig. 16C. Methods of anchoring large beams.

anchor bolts: Bolt which fastens columns, girders, or other members to concrete or masonry. Fig. 17 illustrates anchor bolts used to anchor sills to masonry foundations.

anchor dart: A term applied to the dartlike member of an egg-and-anchor, or egg-and-dart, molding. See Fig. 223, page 169.

anchor nailing: A method of driving nails at opposite angles through two or more boards.

anchor plates: Small flat pieces, often made of perforated metal, through the center of which various types of hangers may be inserted. Adhesive is then applied to the back of the piece, which is pressed against a surface forcing the adhesive up around

the edges and through the perforations, if any, to form a key, which will support the weight then placed on the protruding hanger.

anchor ties: Any type of fastener used to secure the parts of a wall to some stable object, such as another wall.

anchorage: The permanent placement, or foundation, to which the lower members of a building may be attached to secure greater stability for the entire structure. In concrete, the securing of bars by hooks, bends or embedment length.

anchored: A term used in referring to the tying together of the various structural parts of a building, especially when walls and floor joists are tied together by means of metal ties.

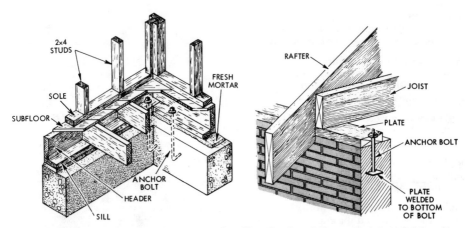

Fig. 17. Anchor bolts are used to secure the sill to the foundation and plate to brick wall.

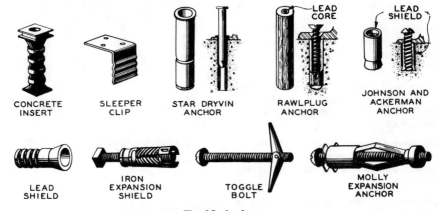

Fig. 18. Anchors.

anchors: In building construction, devices used to give stability to one part of a structure by securing it to another part (see Fig. 621, page 476); metal ties, such as concrete inserts or toggle bolts, used to fasten any structural wood member to a concrete or masonry wall. See Fig. 18. (See Fig. 47, page 362.)

ancon (an'kon); pl., ancones: A boss or projection left on a block of masonry to serve as a console or small bracket; a vertical corbel supporting a cornice. *Ancones* are sometimes used to support busts or other figures.

andiron: One of a pair of metallic supports for wood burning in a fireplace; also called a *firedog;* any metal device for supporting wood in a fireplace.

angle: The inclination of one straight line to another, or the space between two straight lines which either meet or would meet if extended. An angle is measured in degrees or radians.

angle bar: In building construction, a vertical bar between two faces of a polygonal, or bow, window.

angle bead: A molded strip used in an angle, usually where two walls meet at right angles. See *corner bead,* page 123.

angel beam: In architecture, a horizontal member of a medieval roof truss, usually decorated with figures representing angels carved on the member or beam.

angle block: In woodwork, a small wooden block used in making joints, especially right-angled points, more rigid.

angle board: A board which is used as a gage by which to plane other boards to a required angle between two faces.

angle bonds: In masonry work, brick or metal ties used to bind the angles or corners of the walls together.

angle brace: In building construction, any bar fixed across the inside of an angle in a framework in order to stiffen the framework of the structure; also, a special tool for drilling in corners where there is not room enough to use the cranked handle of the ordinary brace.

angle bracket: A type of support which has two faces usually at right angles to each other. To increase the strength, a web is sometimes added.

angle cleat: In building, a small bracket which is formed of angle iron used to support or locate a member in a structural framework.

angle closer: In masonry, a portion of a whole brick which is used to close up the bond of brickwork at corners. See *closer,* page 103.

angle dividers: A tool primarily designed for bisecting angles. It can be used also as a *try square.* See Fig. 612, page 465.

angle float: A plasterer's trowel which is specially shaped to fit into the angle between adjacent walls of a room. See Fig. 19. A wooden handle is attached in the center between the flanges (such as 9″ x 4″ x ¾″ flanges). There are three types of material used to make angle floats. They are plexiglass, stainless steel, and aluminum. The plasterer uses this tool to apply finishes to inside angles. Also called *inside angle tool.*

Fig. 19. Angle float for finished surface.

angle gage: A tool used to set off and test angles in work done by carpenters, bricklayers, and masons.

angle iron: A section of a strip of structural iron bent to form a right angle; used for lintels to support masonry over openings, such as doors and windows. Also used for anchoring walls to foundations. See Fig. 20, left. Also, straps of metal which are cut or bent to form a 90° angle for use in reinforcing the right-angle corners of frames, boxes, etc. These and other similar fastenings are shown in Fig. 20, right.

angle joint: Any joint formed where two construction members meet at an angle.

angle newel: In stair building, a newel post located at the angle of a well.

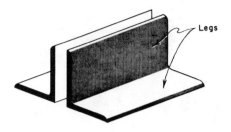

Fig. 20. Angle irons.

angle of repose: The maximum angle to the horizontal or greatest slope at which a heap of any loose, solid material, as earth, will stand without sliding; also, the greatest angle at which the bed joints of an arch will remain supported by friction. Sometimes called the *angle of rest.*

angle paddle: A plastering tool used to clean out and, in most cases, to finish the angle or corner after it has been floated. The finished result, however, is not comparable to the properly troweled out angle. They are made of aluminum, rubber and plastic. See Fig. 21.

angle plane: A plastering tool used for preparing the surfaces (after brown coat has set) for a finish coat by knocking down high spots, cleaning angles, and scraping. The angle plane is much easier to use for this work than an old trowel. See Fig. 22. In carpentry, a plane whose cutting iron shapes an internal angle.

angle plow: A plastering tool is used to apply pressure and finish setting materials, such as putty coat materials, in place of using the angle float. It is used primarily to apply finishes to inside angles. See Fig. 23.

angle post: An angle newel located in the angle of a stairway.

angle rafter: In carpentry, the rafter at the hip of a roof. It receives the jack

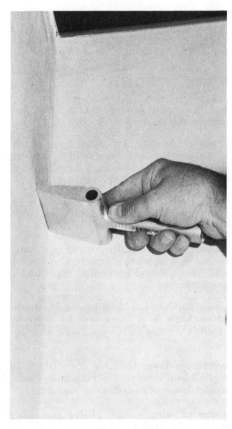

Fig. 21. Angle paddle.

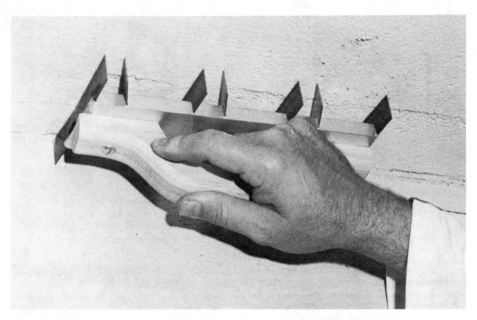

Fig. 22. Plasterer using an angle plane.

rafters. Same as *hip rafter*. It is sometimes called *angle ridge*.

angle reinforcing: The reinforcing of all angles at the inner corners of a wall or ceiling by use of a wire-mesh fabric applied over insulating boards or rock lath.

angle shaft: A corner bead enriched with a capital or base, or both; same as an *angle bead*.

angle staff: A decorative corner bead consisting of a slender column with a capital and base; a round angle staff is called an *angle bead*.

angle tie: Any bar fixed across the inside of an angle in a framework in order to render the latter more rigid. Same as *angle brace*.

anhydrous lime: Unslaked lime which is made from almost pure limestone. Same as *quicklime*. Also called *common lime*.

annealed wire: A soft, pliable wire used extensively in the building trade for tie wires, especially for wiring concrete forms.

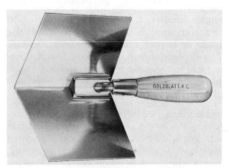

Fig. 23. Plows. (Top) Wide blade angle plow. (Bottom) Angle plow.

annealing: Annealing is a heating and cooling process used to relieve stresses, to add toughness, and to remove brittleness. *Annealing* builds up *malleability.*

annual ring: The arrangement of the wood of a tree in concentric rings, or layers, due to the fact that it is formed gradually, one ring being added each year. For this reason, the rings are called *annual rings.* Note that the ring includes both *springwood* (light and porous) and *summerwood* (dark and dense). The rings can easily be counted in a cross section of a tree trunk. If a tree is cut close to the ground, the age of the tree can be estimated by the number of annual growth rings. See Fig. 24.

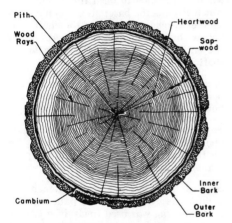

Fig. 24. Annual rings.

annular ball-bearing: A bearing in which the balls are contained in a ringlike holder, as in a ball-bearing butt hinge.

annular bit: A carpenter's tool which cuts a ring-shaped (annular) channel and leaves intact a central cylindrical plug.

annular nails: Nail with circular ridges on the shank. Ridges give greater holding power. See *ratchet nail,* Fig. 390, page 296.

annular vault: The same as a *barrel vault,* which is a vault rising from two parallel walls. See *barrel arch,* Fig. 45, page 38.

annulated column or shaft: A type of column much used in English architecture; a shaft made up of two or more long, superimposed cylinders having an annular band at each point appearing to retain the shaft, but the ring, or band, is commonly worked on an interposed stone plate whose edge projects slightly. This form of column is most common in clustered piers of Gothic churches.

annulet: A small ring or band of molding encircluing a capital or column; also a square molding used to separate the parts at the top of a column, as in the Doric capital.

annunciator wire: A soft copper wire having two layers of cotton threads wound about it in opposite directions and the thread covered with paraffin wax.

anodizing: Coating aluminum parts with a hard surface film of aluminum oxide through an electric process in a chrome-acid solution. The film acts as a protective coating and serves as an excellent paint base.

anta: A rectangular pier or pilaster formed by thickening a wall at its extremity; often furnished with a capital and base; also, a special type of pier formed by thickening a wall at its termination. A pilaster opposite another, as on a door jamb.

anta cap. The top or capital of an *anta.*

antae: Plural of *anta.*

antechamber: An outer chamber before the chief apartment and leading into it; a relatively small room, or vestibule, where people wait for an audience in the chief chamber.

antefix (an'te-fiks); pl., antefixes: In classical architecture, the upright ornaments placed at regular intervals along the eaves or cornices to conceal the termination of the tiling ridges.

antemion: An ornamental palm-leaf pattern used in decorative designs. The design arranged in a flat, radiating cluster is used in architectural designs; also on vases.

ante-solarium: In building construction, a balcony which faces the sun.

antichecking iron: In lumbering, a term applied to a piece of flat iron driven into the end of a piece of timber to prevent checking or splitting of the wood. The iron piece is sharpened on one edge and bent to the shape of the letter *C,* the letter *S,* or the letter *Z,* hence, called a *C-iron,* an *S-iron,* or a *Z-iron.*

anti-freeze: A substance added to liquid to prevent it from freezing.

antisiphon trap: A device designed to increase resealing quality in the trap of a *drain pipe.* The additional reseal is obtained by enlarging the volume of water in the trap, by building a bowl of increased diameter into the outlet leg of the trap. Two types of antisiphon traps are shown in Fig. 25.

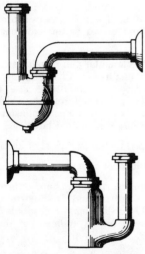

Fig. 25. Antisiphon traps.

antisiphonage pipe: A small escape pipe connecting the outer side of a waste trap to the open air to prevent opening of the trap when other fixtures connected to the same waste pipe are in use; a pipe leading into the vent stack and carrying off foul gases from a sanitary fixture. Same as *vent pipe.*

apartment: A room, or suite of two or more rooms, suitable as a residence for one or more persons. Generally used in connection with multi-family buildings.

aperture: In building, an opening left in a wall for a door or window or for ventilating purposes.

apex: In architecture, the topmost feature of any structure.

apex stone: A triangular stone at the top of a gable wall, often decorated with a carved trefoil. Sometimes called a *saddle stone.*

apophyge (a-pof'i-je): The small curvature, or outward spread, given to the bottom of a shaft of an Ionic or Corinthian column where it expands to form the cincture by which it joins the base; also, a similar but slighter spread at the top of the shaft. The hollow, or *scotia,* beneath the *echinus* of the earliest Doric capitals, leading to the shaft.

appendage: In building, any structure appended or attached to the outer wall of a building but not necessary to its stability.

appliance: A broad category of electrically operated household appliances used for heating, cooling, cooking, cleaning, repairing, etc.

applied molding: The arrangement of molding to give the effect of paneling. *Applied molding* was used freely in a type of architecture of the seventeenth century known as *Jacobean architecture.*

apprentice: One who enters upon an agreement to serve an employer or with a Joint Apprenticeship and Training Committee for a stated period of time for the purpose of receiving instruction and learning a trade. The apprentice is free to leave the employer. Generally, the apprentice's employment is subject to collective bargaining agreements. The employer is at liberty to lay off or to discharge the apprentice. Related instruction is provided by the Joint Apprenticeship and Training Committee (JATC). Apprentices are protected by Federal, State and the local JATC in regard to hours of work, wages, and conditions of employment, and there is no control over the apprentices outside of the working hours. Also, apprentices are now selected from applicants who meet the standards of the local JATC. In most cases today the apprentice is indentured to the JATC and they assign him to a contractor. If the contractor runs out of work, the JATC will place him with another contractor. This permits the JATC to control the training and handle the federal and veteran's paperwork.

Start of the short arc cycle. High temperature electric arc melts advancing wire electrode into a drop of liquid metal. Wire is fed mechanically through the welding torch. Arc heat is regulated by the power supply.   (A)

Molten electrode moves toward workpiece. Note cleaning action. Argon gas mixture, developed for short arc, shields molten wire and seam, insuring regular arc ignition, preventing spatter, and weld contamination.   (B)

Electrode makes contact with workpiece, creating short circuit. Arc is extinguished, allowing to cool. Frequency of arc extinction in short arc varies from 20 to 200 times per second, according to job requirements.   (C)

Drop of molten wire breaks contact with electrode, causing arc to reignite. Electrode is broken by pinch force, a squeezing power common to all current carriers. Amount and suddenness of pinch is controlled by power supply.   (D)

With arc renewed, short arc cycle begins again. Because of precision control of arc characteristics and cool, uniform operation, short arc produces perfect welds on metals as thin as .030-In. carbon or stainless steel.   (E)

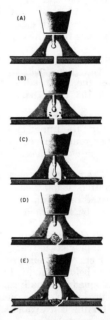

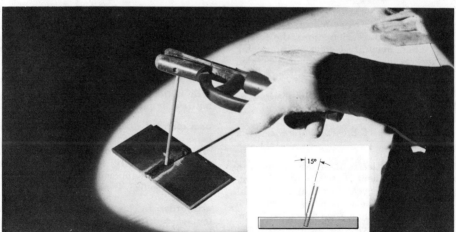

Fig. 26. (Top). Typical mode of metal transfer in the short arc (MIG). (Bottom). Position of the electrode for welding a butt joint (Shielded Metal). (The Lincoln Electric Co.)

apprenticeship: Apprenticeship is training for those occupations commonly known as skilled crafts or trades that require a wide and diverse range of skills and knowledge. As practiced today apprenticeship is a system of training in which the young worker is given thorough instruction and experience, both on and off the job, in all the practical and theoretical aspects of the work in a skilled trade. Apprenticeship usually lasts from three to four years.

apron: In building, a plain or molded finish piece below the stool of a window put on to cover the rough edge of the plastering. See Fig. 198, page 154.

apron piece: A beam or horizontal timber supporting the upper ends of the carriage pieces or rough strings in a staircase. Also called a *pitching piece.*

apse: The projecting part of a building, as of a church, usually semicircular in plan; the curved or angular and vaulted end of a church back of the altar.

aqueduct (ak'we-dukt): An engineering work employed to carry a conduit for water from one point to another, either above or below ground. In crossing a valley, an aqueduct usually consists of a series of arches resting on piers; an artificial canal for the conveyance of water.

arabesque: A fantastic combined pattern of interwoven flowers, foliage, fruits, and geometrical figures. Sometimes the foliage and other fancifully combined interlacing of various designs include figures of men and animals.

arbor: A type of detached latticework or an archway of latticework.

arc: Any part of the *circumference* of a circle.

arc welding: Electrical welding process in which intense heat is obtained by the arcing between the welding rod and the metal to be melted. The molten metal from the tip of the electrode is then deposited in the joint and, together with the molten metal of the edges, solidifies to form a sound and uniform connection. Fig. 26 illustrates arc welding. See *gas welding* types, page 214.

arcade: An arched roof or covered passageway; a series of arches supported either on piers or pillars. An *arcade* may be attached to a wall or detached from the wall.

arch: A curved or pointed structural member supported at the sides or ends. An *arch* is used to bridge or span an opening, usually a passageway or an open space. Also, an arch may be used to sustain weight, as the arch of a bridge. See Fig. 27.

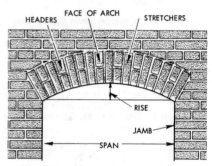

Fig. 27. Face of an arch.

arch bar: A support for a flat arch. The support may be a strip of iron or a flat bar.

arch brace: A curved brace in a wooden frame.

arch brick: Special wedge-shaped brick used in the building of an arch, also suitable for other circular work; a term also applied to brick which have been overburned by being placed in contact with the fire in the arch of the kiln.

arch buttress: An arch springing from a buttress or pier; a flying buttress.

arch center: Usually, a substructure of timbers, or planks, on which a masonry arch or vault rests during the process of its erection and until it is completed and becomes self-supporting. See *centers for arches,* page 92.

arch order: In classical architecture, a system of construction in which arches are framed with columns and entablatures.

arch rib: In vaulting, a projecting band on the line of an arch.

arch ring: In an arched structure, the curved member which is the main supporting element; the body of the arch between the *intrados* and the *extrados*. See *arch,* Fig. 27. See *column,* Fig. 137, page 108.

arch stone: A stone shaped like a wedge for use in an arch. Same as *voussoir,* page 473.

arched beam: In building, any beam which is formed into an arched shape to support such as a roof.

architect: One who designs and oversees the construction of a building; anyone skilled in methods of construction and in planning buildings; a professional student of architecture.

architect's scales: See scales.

Architectural Graphic Standards. A publication put out by the American Institute of Architects (A.I.A.) to provide authoritative practice aids.

architectural models: See *models,* page 288.

architectural orders: See *orders of architecture,* page 305.

architecture: The art or science of constructing houses, churches, schools, office buildings, warehouses, bridges, or any other structure for human use; in a restricted sense, a fine art, a method of erecting an edifice characterized by peculiarities of ornamentation and design especially pleasing to the eye.

architrave: The lowest part of an entablature. It is beneath the frieze and is the part which rests upon the capital of a column. See Fig. 137, page 108.

architrave cornice: An entablature of only two members, an architrave and a cornice, the frieze being omitted.

architrave of a door: The molded band, group of moldings, or other finished work above and on both sides of a door opening, especially if square in form. The upper part, or lintel, of the door aperture is known as the *traverse,* the lining at the sides of the opening is called the *jamb.*

archives (ar'kivz): A closet, or repository, for keeping and preserving public records and other documents.

archivolt: An ornamental band surrounding a curved member such as an arch over a space or passageway; also a series of such members forming the inner contour of an arch; the molding or other adornment on the wall face of the stone of an archway is commonly known as the *archivolt.* See *column,* Fig. 137, page 108.

archway: The passageway under an arch.

area: An uncovered space, such as an open court; also, a sunken space around the basement of a building, providing access and natural lighting and ventilation. Same as *areaway.* See Fig. 28. This term is currently used in connection with a term to indicate function: as sleeping, living, working, utility, kitchen, laundry, storage, and outdoor and play areas. Its extended use is due to open planning principles, in which large rooms, or even whole floors of a house, are separated into activity areas without the use of ceiling-to-floor, load-bearing walls, which usually created separate rooms for each in the past. Often, too, a roofless area, such as a *patio,* is considered part of the house and designated by function.

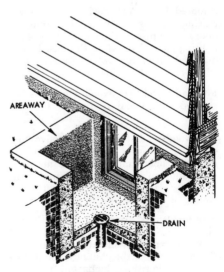

AREAWAY

DRAIN

Fig. 28. Areaway.

area drain: A drain set in the floor of a basement areaway, any depressed entry way, a loading platform, or a cemented driveway which cannot be drained otherwise. See Fig. 28.

area wall: A wall surrounding an areaway which is provided to admit light and air to a basement or cellar. See *areaway,* Fig. 28.

areaway: An open subsurface space, around a basement window or doorway, adjacent to the foundation walls. An *areaway* provides a means of admitting light and air for ventilation and also affords access to the basement or cellar. See Fig. 28.

areaway wall: Any wall built to hold back or support earth around an areaway; the same as *window wall.* Usually, these walls are constructed of building materials such as concrete, concrete blocks, brick, rubble stone, or steel. See Fig. 28.

armored cable: Rubber-insulated wires which are wrapped with a flexible steel covering. Often called BX. See Fig. 406, page 310.

armored concrete: Concrete which has been strengthened by reinforcing with steel rods or steel plates. See *reinforced concrete,* page 364.

armored front: Any device fastened with machine screws to the regular front of a door lock to protect the lock while the door is being painted or while the lock is being mortised; also, to protect the set screw which checks the cylinder.

armored wood: Any wood which has been covered with metal to protect the wood fibers.

arnott valve: A type of flap valve fitted near the ceiling in a room to permit the escape of hot vitiated air. The air passes away into an air flue or chimney, while back flow is prevented automatically by the closing of the flap.

arresters (spark arresters): A cage-like device of rust-resistant perforated sheets, wire, or expanded metal installed in the flue at the top of the chimney, the purpose of which is to reduce the hazard from flying sparks.

arris: An edge or ridge where two surfaces meet. The sharp edge formed where two moldings meet is commonly called an *arris.* See Fig. 29 and Fig. 547, page 414.

arris fillet: A triangular piece of wood for raising the slates or tiles of a roof, near the eaves, to throw off rain water; a sort of *canting* strip.

arris gutter: A gutter shaped like the letter V, usually made of wood, fastened to the eaves of a roof in such a way that it will carry off rain water.

arrisways: In building, a term used when referring to tile or slates laid diagonally; also, in carpentry, the sawing of square timbers diagonally. Sometimes called *arriswise.*

art metal: Any metal shaped into artistic forms and used for ornamental purposes, such as the ironwork on hinges and door knockers. See *ironwork,* page 247.

articulation: In architectural design, a systematic arrangement, in a design or plan, of related parts which are clearly distinguishable. In structural engineering, the process of constructing movable joints, usually with joint pins.

artificial: A term applied to works of art or the skill of man-made products as opposed to the products of nature. See *artificial marble.*

artificial marble: A kind of building material manufactured in imitation of natural marble.

artificial seasoning of wood: Removing moisture from wood by some means other than air drying.

artificial stone: A special kind of manufactured product resembling a natural stone. A common type is made from pulverized quarry refuse mixed with Portland cement (sometimes colored) and water. After being pressed into molds, the mixture is allowed to dry out. Then it is seasoned in the open air for several months before being used.

artisan: A skilled craftsman; an artist; one trained in a special mechanical art or trade; a handicraftsman who manufactures articles of wood or other material.

Fig. 29. Stripping an arris (external corner) using a wood strip to act as a guide. (Dahlhauser; Keystone Steel & Wire Co.)

asbestine (as-bes'tin): A silicate of magnesium much used in paint, serving as an aid in holding paint pigment in solution and in binding paint films together. Also marketed under such names as *talc* and *French chalk.*

asbestos (as-bes'tos): A variety of mineral fiber occurring in long and delicate fibers or fibrous masses. It is a poor conductor of heat and can withstand high temperatures.

asbestos cement: A fire-resisting, waterproofing material made by combining Portland cement with asbestos fibers.

asbestos cement sheeting: A weatherproof building material made of Portland cement and asbestos. It is also fire resistant.

asbestos curtain: A curtain made of asbestos and other fire-resisting materials; designed to close the proscenium opening of a theater stage, in case of fire, thus protecting the audience.

asbestos lumber: A fire-resisting material consisting of asbestos fiber and Portland cement, made in sheets for use in building construction.

asbestos paper: A fire-resisting paper made of asbestos combined with other suitable materials which are incombustible.

asbestos plaster: A type of combustible fire-resisting plaster, especially used for wrapping pipes. Usually, it consists of asbestos, infusorial earth, and a binding material.

asbestos roofing: A roof covering made of Portland cement and asbestos, obtainable in sheets or in the form of shingles.

asbestos shingles: A type of shingle made for fireproof purposes. The principal composition of these shingles is *asbestos,* which is incombustible, non-conducting, and chemically resistant to fire. This makes *asbestos shingles* highly desirable for roof covering.

ash dump: A cast-iron frame having one or two counterbalanced iron leaves placed in the floor of a fireplace through which ashes may be disposed of by dumping them into the *ashpit* in the base of the chimney. See Fig. 245, page 188.

ash pan: A metal container under a grate for the collection and removal of ashes.

ash pit: A pit under a grate or at the bottom of a chimney for ashes. See Fig. 245, page 188.

ash pit door: A cleanout door of cast iron or pressed steel with a frame, built in the base of a fireplace through which ashes may be removed from the *ash pit;* also, a door used in the bottom of a chimney for the removal of soot.

ashlar: One of the studs or uprights between floor beams and rafters in a garret. A short stud cutting off the angle between floor and roof in an attic, thus affording a wall of some height. Also, squared stone used in foundations and for facing of certain types of masonry walls. See Fig. 30.

ashlar brick: A brick that has been rough hackled on the face to make it resemble stone.

ashlar line: The outer edge or line of an exterior wall which projects above any base.

ashlar masonry: Masonry work of sawed,

dressed, tooled, or quarry-faced stone with proper bond. See Fig. 30.

ashlaring: The process of facing a well with ashlar; ashlar masonry; also, a term sometimes applied to the upright boarding placed across the acute angle formed where the roof and floor meet in an attic.

asphalt: A mineral pitch insoluble in water and used extensively in building for waterproofing roof coverings of many different types, for exterior wall coverings, flooring tile, and in paints.

asphalt cement: A cement prepared by refining petroleum until it is free from water and all foreign material, except the mineral matter naturally contained in the asphalt. It should contain less than one percent of ash.

asphalt mastic: A mixture of asphalt and mineral materials used especially for roofing and for *dampproofing.*

asphalt paint: An asphaltic product in liquid form, sometimes containing small amounts of other materials such as lampblack and mineral pigments.

asphalt roofing: A roofing and waterproofing material composed of saturated asbestos or rag felt cemented together with asphalt or tar pitch.

asphalt shingles: A type of composition shingles made of felt saturated with asphalt or tar pitch and surfaced with mineral granules. There are many different patterns, some individual and others in strips, Fig. 31.

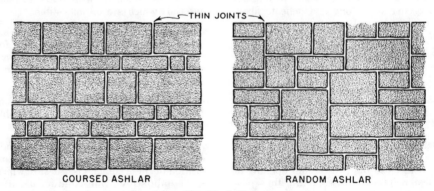

COURSED ASHLAR   RANDOM ASHLAR

Fig. 30. Ashlar.

2 AND 3 TAB SQUARE BUTT

2 AND 3 TAB HEXAGONAL

Fig. 31. Common asphalt roof shingles.

asphaltum (as-fal'tum): A mineral pitch found in natural beds but also obtained as a residue from petroleums and coal tar. It is a form of brittle and glossy bitumen, black or brown in color, used extensively as a cement. The terms *asphaltum* and *asphalt* are used interchangeably.

assize: In masonry, a cylinder-shaped block of stone which forms part of a column or a layer of stone in a building.

astragal: A small semicircular molding, either ornamental or plain, used for covering a joint between doors. For decorative purposes it is sometimes cut in the form of a string of beads. See Fig. 32.

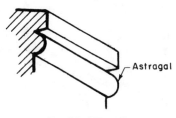

Astragal

Fig. 32. Astragal.

atmosphere: The air surrounding the earth. A pressure of one atmosphere is 14.7 pounds to the square inch.

atmospheric pressure: The pressure due to the weight of the atmosphere and indicated by a barometer. *Standard Atmospheric Pressure* or *Standard Atmosphere* is the pressure of 76 cm. of mercury having a density of 13.5951 grams per cubic centimeter, under standard gravity of 980.665

cm. per second. It is equivalent to 14.696 lbs. per square inch or 29.921 in. of mercury at 32° F.

atrium: Also the entrance hall and chief apartment of an ancient Roman house. A large hallway or lobby with galleries at each floor level on three or more sides.

attached column: A column projecting three-fourths of its diameter from the wall to which it is attached.

attached garage: See *garage,* page 213.

attenuation: Tapering off and gradually narrowing to a point.

attic: A garret; the room or space directly below the roof of a building. In modern buildings, the *attic* is the space between the roof and the ceiling of the upper story. In classical structures, the *attic* is the space, or low room, above the entablature or main cornice of a building.

attic floor: The flooring of an attic, including the joists which support the floor. See *braced framing,* Fig. 82, page 65.

attic frames and sash: Windows especially designed for admitting light to attics.

attic louver: An opening for ventilating a closed attic. See Fig. 364, page 274.

attic room: Attic space which is finished as living accommodations but which does not qualify as a half story. See *half story.*

attic ventilators: In home building, any mechanical wind-driven device; also, the use of power-driven fans for ventilating purposes. See also *louver,* Fig. 364, page 274.

auger: A wood-boring tool used by the carpenter for boring holes larger than can be made with a gimlet. The handle of an *auger* is attached at right angles to the tool line. There are several different types of augers made for various purposes.

auger bit: An auger without a handle to be used in a brace. Such a bit has square tapered shanks made to fit in the socket of a common brace. This combination tool is known as a *brace and bit.* See Fig. 59, page 50.

autoclaves: A strong, covered vessel used for sterilizing, cooking, or steam curing small concrete products.

autogenous healing: A longtime natural process of closing and filling of cracks in concrete or mortar of the structure.

automatic: A device which is operated by certain changes or conditions in an electric circuit and which is not controlled by a person; anything which has an inherent power of action, as a mechanism which is self-regulating.

automatic grouter: A pressurized steel form, faced with foam rubber, which forces grout in and around stones, or brick, after it has been poured in from the top of stonework.

automatic heat: The regulation of room temperature and the control of the heating plant by thermostats, making it unnecessary to attend the plant by hand, the fuel being fed to the furnace or boiler mechanically, as in coal stokers, oil burners, and automatic gas-burning and electrical installations.

automatic time switch: A switch operated at certain intervals by a timepiece or clock.

auxiliary switch: In electricity, a switch operated or controlled by the action of another circuit.

avoirdupois weight: A system of weights in common use in English-speaking countries for weighing all commodities except precious stones and metals, also precious drugs. In this system, 16 ounces equal one pound; 2,000 pounds equal one *short ton;* a *long ton* contains 2,240 pounds.

awl: A small, sharp-pointed instrument used by the carpenter for making holes for nails or screws. The carpenter often uses an *awl* to mark lines where pencil marks might become erased. See Fig. 33.

Fig. 33. Awl.

awl haft: The handle of an *awl*.

awning: A rooflike cover of canvas or metal placed over a window, slanting outward to exclude the direct rays of the sun.

awning type window: A type of window in which each light opens outward on its own hinges, which are placed at its upper edge. Such windows are often used as ventilators in connection with fixed picture windows. See Figs. 34 and 634, page 484.

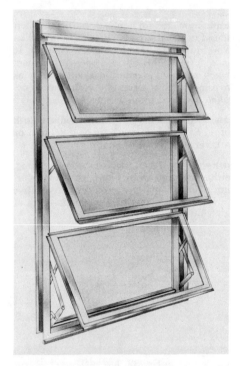

Fig. 34. Metal awning type windows are designed to open simultaneously. (Reynolds Aluminum Co.)

axhammer or ax: A type of cutting tool, or ax, having two cutting edges, or one cutting edge and one hammer face, used for dressing or spalling the rougher kinds of stone.

axial: Situated in an axis or on the axis.

axis: *pl. axes.* A line about which a body turns or rotates.

axis of symmetry: A line, imaginary or real, about which a geometrical figure or drawing is symmetrically developed and in which the center of gravity is located.

azimuth. The term "azimuth" refers to a compass reading in degrees and minutes from north reading clockwise from 0 to 360 degrees.

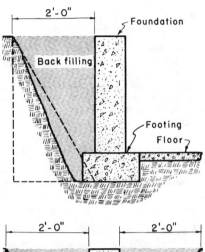

B

back: In carpentry, the top or upper side of a dome rib, a handrail, or a roof rafter. In window construction, the part between the sill of the sash frame and the floor is called the *back*. In masonry, that part of a dressed stone opposite to its face; also, the *extrados* of an arch or of a vault.

back band: In carpentry, the outer molding of the inner trim of a window or door casing.

back bar: A horizontal bar in the chimney of an open fireplace on which kettles and other cooking utensils may be hung; sometimes called *randle bar*.

back catch: A type of fastener, attached to an outside wall, for catching and holding in an open position a shutter, window blind, or a door.

back edging: A method of chipping away the *biscuit* below the glazed face of a brick or tile, the front itself being scribed.

back fillet: The edge or fillet by which a slightly projecting structural part returns to the face of the wall, as a *quoin* or *architrave*.

back filling or backfill: Coarse dirt, broken stone, or other material used to build up the ground level around the basement or foundation walls of a house to provide a slope for drainage of water away from the foundation. Areas requiring back filling are shown in Figs. 35 and 202, page 158.

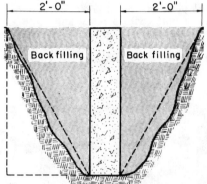

Fig. 35. Back filling.

back-flap hinge: In building, a term applied to a hinge in two leaves, screwed to the face of a door which is not thick enough to permit the use of a *butt hinge*.

back flow: In plumbing, the flow of water or sewage in the direction opposite to its normal flow.

back-flow valve: In plumbing, a contrivance inserted in the drain of a house or other building to prevent a reversal of the flow of sewage. Its chief function is to prevent a flood and the resulting damage which might be caused by the overflowing of a combination type of public sewerage.

back hearth: In a hearth to a fireplace, the fire-proof floor under the grate upon which the fire is built.

31

back of an arch: In building, the *extrados* of an arch or vault. See Fig. 45.

back plastering: For insulating purposes, the installing of lath and plaster in the stud space midway between the outside sheathing and the inside lath and plaster of an exterior wall, thus providing a double air space in the wall. Also, the application of a 3/8″ thick mortar coat on the back of the facing tier for purposes of moisture proofing and air proofing. Also called *parging*. See Fig. 411, page 315.

back pressure: In plumbing, air pressure in pipes when it is greater than the atmospheric pressure.

back-puttying: In a window sash, the forcing of putty with a putty knife into any space that may be left between the edges of the rebate and the glass on the back of the sash after the sash has been face puttied.

back vent: A pipe for ventilating purposes, attached to a waste pipe on the sewer side of its trap to prevent siphonage of waste or superfluous fluid.

backhoe: An excavating machine which has a loading bucket in front which is drawn toward the machine when in operation. See Fig. 36.

backing: In masonry, rubble or broken stones used at the back of facing. In carpentry, strips nailed at angles of walls and partitions to provide solid corners for nailing the ends of lath. Also, the bevel on the top edge of a hip rafter that allows the roofing board to fit the top of the rafter properly. See Fig. 38.

backing brick: The inner part of a brick wall which is often of a cheaper and less perfect brick than that used for the face

Fig. 36. An excavation with a 14 foot backhoe. (J. I. Case Co.)

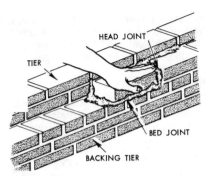

Fig. 37. Backing brick.

of the wall. Bed and head joints for backing tier of brick are shown in Fig. 37.

backing hip rafter: A beveling arris, as at corners of hip rafters, to tie up with adjacent roof surfaces. See Fig. 38.

backing of a joist or rafter: The blocking used to bring a narrow joist up to the height of the regular width joists. The widths of joists or rafters may vary, and in order to assure even floors or roofs some of the joists or rafters must be blocked up until all the upper surfaces are of the same level.

backing of a wall: The rough inner face of a wall; the material which is used to fill in behind a retaining wall.

backing tier: In masonry, the tier of rough brickwork which backs up the *face tier* of an exterior wall for a residence or other well-built brick structure. This part of a brick wall is often of a cheaper grade of brick than that used for the face tier. See Fig. 37.

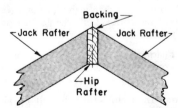

Fig. 38. Backing hip rafter.

backing-up: The process of laying the backing of a masonry wall; also, the use of a cheaper grade brick for the inner face of a wall.

backplate: A backpiece, or plate, used on the inside of a door for framing an opening for a letter drop on the front door; any piece or plate used as backing for any construction member.

backsaw: Any saw with its blade stiffened by an additional metal strip along the back. The *backsaw* is commonly used in cabinet work as a bench saw. See Fig. 39.

Fig. 39. Backsaw.

backset: The horizontal distance from the front of a door lock to a center line through the keyhole or through the door knob.

backup: That part of a masonry wall behind the exterior facing and consisting of one or more withes or thicknesses of brick or other masonry material.

backup brick: The brick used on the inside of the wall.

backup strips or lathing boards: Narrow strips of wood nailed at the angles of walls and partitions to provide solid corners for nailing the ends of lath. The same as *backing.*

backwater flap: In plumbing, a type of valve in which back flow of a liquid is prevented by a hinged metal flap fitted in an intercepting chamber, so as to allow the flow of water in one direction only. See Fig. 203, page 158.

backwater valve: An automatic valve placed in the sewer lateral to keep sewerage from backing into the basement or into plumbing fixtures during times of heavy rains and flood periods. See *backwater flap,* Fig. 203, page 158.

badger: An implement used to clean out the excess mortar at the joints of a drain after it has been laid.

badger plane: In carpentry work, a wide rabbet plane having a skew mouth with iron flush at one side. This plane is used to facilitate close working into a corner when making a rebate or for other purposes where the use of such a plane is advantageous.

badigeon (ba-dij'un): In building, a kind of cement or paste made by mixing suitable materials for filling holes or covering defects in stones or wood.

baffle or baffle plate: An artificial surface, usually a plate or wall, for deflecting, retarding, or regulating the flow of fluids or gasses (see Fig. 290, page 222); also a portable screen for absorbing or deflecting sound so as to improve its quality or characteristics, as in motion picture studios.

bague (bag): The ring of a plate of an annulated column.

balance: In building construction, the equilibrium between opposing forces, such as the stress and strain in various parts of a building due to the loads carried by its structural members.

balanced circuit: In electricity, a three-wire circuit having the same load on each side of the neutral wire.

balanced load: In electricity, a load connected in such a way that the currents taken from each side of a three-wire system are equal.

balanced step: In a flight of stairs, any one of a series of winders so arranged that the small ends of the steps are not much narrower than the parallel steps or fliers.

balcony (bal'ko-ni): A platform, enclosed by a railing or balustrade, projecting from the face of either an inside or outside wall of a building. Usually an inside balcony is supported by *columns* or *consoles,* while an outside balcony is often supported by *brackets;* also, a gallery in a theater.

balk: A large, squared timber or beam.

ball-bearing butt: A butt hinge equipped with ball bearings to prevent wearing of the butts at the joints and to insure the operation of doors without noise. Designed especially for inside doors of hospitals, schools, and office buildings.

ball catch: A type of door fastening in which a spring-controlled metal ball projecting through a smaller hole engages with a striking plate.

ball chain: See *bead chain,* page 43.

ball cock: In plumbing, a self-regulating faucet which is opened or closed by the rising and falling of a hollow ball floating on the surface of the water.

ball-flower: A decorative feature carved in the hollow of a molding; an ornament resembling a ball arranged in the hollow of a flowerlike adornment; an enrichment of molding characteristic of English Gothic during the thirteenth century and later.

ball peen hammer: A hammer having a peen which is hemispherical in shape, used especially by metal workers and stone masons. See Fig. 40.

Fig. 40. Ball peen hammer.

ball valve: A type of water valve which regulates the flow of water in a tank by means of a floating ball. This ball fits on the end of a lever, and by its rise and fall, due to suction and its own weight, allows water to flow; then shuts it off when it reaches a certain height.

balled (slang): This refers to no threads in pipe work—or to bell and spigot connection.

balloon: In architecture, a ball or globe crowning a pillar, pier, or _other similar structural members.

balloon framing: A type of building construction in which the studs extend in one piece from the first floor line or sill to the roof plate. In addition to being supported by a ledger board, the second-floor joists are nailed to the studs. See Fig. 41.

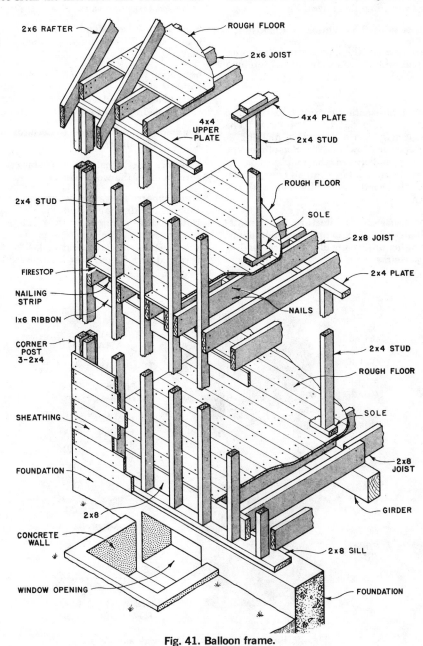

Fig. 41. Balloon frame.

baluster: One of a series of small pillars, or units, of a balustrade; an upright support of the railing for a stairway. See *closed-string stair,* Fig. 130, page 103.

baluster shaft: The column of a baluster.

balustrade: A railing consisting of a series of small columns connected at the top by a coping; a row of balusters surmounted by a rail.

band: A horizontal decorative feature of a wall, such as a flat frieze or fascia. The *band* usually has a projecting molding at the upper and lower edges. Sometimes the flat portion between the moldings is ornately decorated, but in small frame structures the band is usually flat and unadorned.

band course: In architecture, a horizontal band around a column or around a building, serving as an ornamental feature; and as a *belt course.*

band saw: A saw in the form of an endless serrated steel belt running on revolving pulleys; the saw is used in cutting woodwork; also used for metal work. See Fig. 42.

band shell: A bandstand having a sounding board, shaped like a huge sea shell, at the rear.

bandage: In architecture, a strengthening band or strip, as of stone or iron; a metal band placed around a tower or dome to prevent spreading and to give added strength.

banding: In architecture, to decorate with a band, strip, or stripe.

banister: The balustrade of a staircase; a corruption of the word *baluster.*

banjo tapers: There are two types of banjo tapers: the dry taper and the wet taper. Both of these are used by the plasterer for taping seams. A roll of tape is placed inside the case at the round end. The tape is then drawn to and past the tapered end,

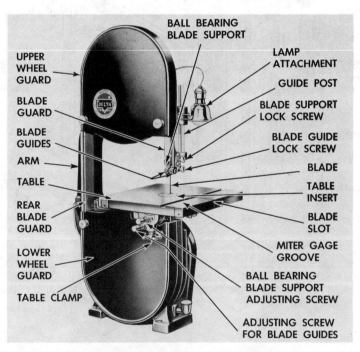

Fig. 42. Band saw and parts. (Rockwell Mfg. Co.)

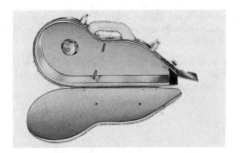

Fig. 43. Wet tape banjo taper. (Goldblatt Tool Co.)

and the tape is released as the banjo taper is run along the seam. See Fig. 43.

bank of transformers: A number of transformers located at one place and connected to the same circuit.

banker: In masonry, a type of workbench on which bricklayers and stonemasons work when shaping arches or other construction requiring shaped materials.

bar: In architecture, a *sash bar;* a slender strip of wood which separates and supports the panes in a window sash. A round or square rod used to reinforce concrete. In masonry, a shortened term for *reinforcing bar, rod steel,* etc. Also see *rebar,* page 363, *deformed bar,* page 140.

bar chairs: A manufactured device used to hold up the welded wire fabric at one-half the thickness of the concrete slab during the time of placing.

bar chart or graph: A graph used by builders for scheduling construction work. Each part of the job is represented by a bar or line with one end representing the starting date and the other the completion date. The progress of the job is, therefore, visually represented.

bar clamp: A device consisting of a long bar and two clamping jaws used by woodworkers for clamping large work.

bar handle: A door handle which consists of a horizontal bar mounted on one or more brackets.

bar list: Bill of materials, where all quantities, sizes, lengths and bending dimensions are shown.

bar number: A number (approximately the bar diameter in eighths of inches) used to designate the bar size. For example: A #5 bar is approximately 5/8 in. in diameter.

bar placing subcontractor: A contractor or subcontractor who handles and places reinforcement and bar supports, often colloquially referred to as a "bar placer" or "placer."

bar sash lift: A sash lift which consists of a bent bar, fastened at each end to the sash with screws, forming a handle by means of which the sash can be lifted. See Fig. 44.

Fig. 44. Bar sash lift.

bar spacing: Spacing of reinforcing bars measured from center to center of the bars.

bar supports: Devices, usually of formed wire, to support, hold, and space reinforcing bars.

barbed dowel pin: A short, headless nail with a sharp point on the lower end and barbs between the two ends, used largely for fastening the mortise-and-tenon joints in a window sash and for door work.

barefaced tenon: In carpentry, a tenon which is shouldered on one side only.

barefoot: In architecture, a term applied to a joint which is set up and fastened without a mortise-and-tenon, as in a balloon frame where one member, as a post or stud, butts against another and is held in position by *toenailing.*

barge course: A part of the tiling which usually projects beyond the principal rafters or *bargeboards,* along the sloping edge of a *gable roof;* also, a course of brick laid on edge to form the coping of a wall. See *bargeboard.*

barge spike: A square spike with a chisel point used extensively in heavy timber construction. See *boat spike,* page 57.

barge stone: In masonry, one of the stones which form the sloping edge of a *gable roof.*

bargeboard: The decorative board covering the projecting portion of a gable roof; the same as a *verge board;* during the late part of the nineteenth century, bargeboards frequently were extremely ornate.

bark: The rough outer covering of a tree trunk, sometimes used for decorative effect. See Fig. 24, page 21.

bark pockets. A patch of bark nearly, or wholly, enclosed in the wood is known as a *bark pocket.*

barn: A building used to house domestic animals, also used for storing feed, such as grain and hay, to feed the animals.

barn boards: Softwood lumber commonly used for barn siding. See *barn siding.*

barn-door hanger: A device consisting of a sheave mounted in a frame fastened to a sliding door traveling on an overhead track, or rail, which carries the door. Suitable for any extra heavy sliding doors, such as those used for barns, garages, warehouses, and freight cars.

barn-door latch: A heavy thumb latch.

barn-door pull: Any large door pull suitable for extra heavy doors, as barn doors, garages, warehouses, and freight cars.

barn-door roller: A device consisting of a sheave mounted in a frame fastened to the bottom of a barn door or any other extra heavy door which travels on a track or rail on the floor which carries the door.

barn-door stay: A device consisting of a small roller, sometimes mounted on a screw or spike, for guiding any sliding door, such as those for barns, garages, and freight cars.

barn siding: Drop siding of wood or tongue-and-groove boards used for enclosing a barn or other farm building.

barrel arch: An arch which resembles a segment of a barrel and having a length much greater than its span. See Fig. 45.

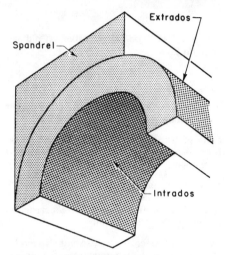

Fig. 45. Barrel arch.

barrel bolt: A round bolt, for fastening a door or a window sash, made to slide into a cylindrical socket or barrel; mounted on a frame projecting from its surface to hold the bolt in place and to guide it. See Fig. 46.

Fig. 46. Barrel bolt (Stanley Works)

barrel drain: A drain which is cylindrical in form.

barrel roof: One similar to the interior of a barrel in shape, or like a *barrel vault.* See *barrel arch,* Fig. 45.

barrel vault: One semicylindrical in form having parallel abutments and the same section throughout. See *barrel arch,* Fig. 45.

bas-relief (ba-re-lef′): Sculpture in low relief in which the figures project only slightly from the face of the background.

basal angle: An angle situated at the base of a structural member.

base: The lowest part of a wall, pier, monument, or column; the lower part of a complete architectural design.

base beads: See *grounds,* page 225.

baseboard: A board forming the base of something; the finishing board covering the edge of the plastered wall where the wall and floor meet; a line of boarding around the interior walls of a room next to the floor. For three members of the *baseboard* see Fig. 47.

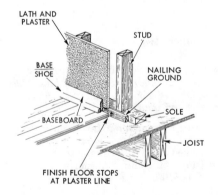

LATH AND PLASTER

STUD

BASE SHOE

NAILING GROUND

BASEBOARD

SOLE

JOIST

FINISH FLOOR STOPS AT PLASTER LINE

Fig. 47. Baseboard.

base coat: A substance, composed of equal parts of raw linseed oil and turpentine, applied as a base for any wood finish or stain which does not obscure the grain of the wood.

base course: A footing course, as the lowest course of masonry of a wall or pier; the foundation course on which the remainder rests.

base-court: In medieval times, the outer, lower, or inferior court of a castle or mansion; also, the rear courtyard of a farmhouse.

base line: In construction work, a definitely established line from which measurements are taken when laying out building plans or other similar working plans. In a perspective drawing, the line formed by the intersection of the ground plane and the picture plane. In surveying, the term *base line* refers to lines running due east and west (true parallels of latitude). These serve as reference for positions north and south. The positions of the base lines can be secured from survey offices.

base metal or parent metal: This is the metal to be welded.

base molding: The molding above the plinth of a wall, pillar, or pedestal; the part between the shaft and the pedestal or, if there is no pedestal, the part between the shaft and the plinth. In carpentry, the molding at the top of a baseboard. See Fig. 47.

base of a column: That part of a column upon which the shaft rests; the part between the shaft and the *plinth;* sometimes the *base* is considered as including all of the lower members of the column together with the plinth. See *column,* page 108.

base plate: A plate or steel slab upon which a column stands. See Fig. 16, bottom, page 15.

base shoe: For interior finish, a strip of molding nailed to the baseboard close to the floor. See Fig. 47 and 48.

base trim: The finish at the base of a piece of work, as a board or molding used for finishing the lower part of an inside wall, such as a *baseboard;* the lower part of a column which may consist of several decorative features, including various members which make up the base as a whole; these may include an ornate pedestal and other decorative parts. See Figs. 47 and 48.

basement: The story of a building next below the main floor; a story partly or wholly

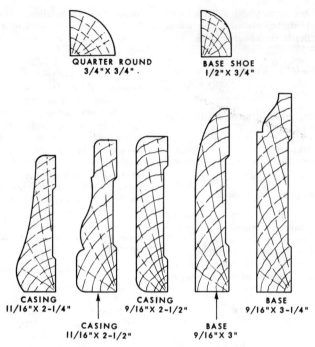

Fig. 48. Typical base trim moldings.

below the ground level; the finished portion of a building below the main floor or section; also, the lowest division of the walls of a building. Usually contains the heating plant. See Fig. 259, page 199.

basement space: See *crawl space,* page 129.

basement window frames and sash: Frames and sash, of either wood or metal, for use in basement openings. Usually, such windows do not have more than two or three lights. For an illustration of a portion of a *basement window and frame,* see *areaway,* Fig. 38, page 25.

basic stress: See *stresses,* page 436.

basil: (baz′il): The beveled edge of a cutting tool, such as a drill or chisel. Same as *bezel.*

basso-relievo (bas-o-re-le vo): Bas-relief in which the figures are projected from a background but not detached from it.

bastard sawed: Hardwood lumber in which the annual rings make angles of 30° to 60°

with the surface of the piece, midway between true *quartersawed* and true *plainsawed.* (See Fig. 434, page 330, for plainsawed and quartersawed.)

bastard tuck pointing: In masonry, a type of pointing of joints whereby a wider ridge is formed along the center of the joints than in true tuck pointing of mortar joints. See *tuck pointing,* page 465.

bat: A piece of brick with one end whole, the other end broken off.

batch: The amount of concrete mixed at one time—it could be a bucketful, a wheelbarrow full, or a mixer full.

batch meter: A device that controls mixing time by locking the discharge mechanism so the mixer cannot be discharged until the pre-set mixing time has expired.

batching: Measuring the ingredients for a batch of concrete or mortar by weight or volume and introducing them into the mixer.

40

batt insulation: A type of small-sized blanket insulating material, usually composed of mineral fibers and made in relatively small units for convenience in handling and applying. The sizes of batt insulation vary from 2 to 3 inches in thickness, with widths from 15 to 23 inches, and in lengths from 8 to 48 inches. Typical *batt insulation* is shown in Fig. 49.

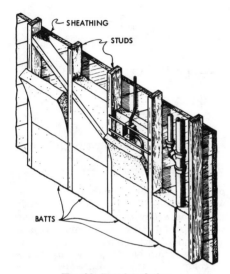

Fig. 49. Batt insulation.

batten: A thin, narrow strip of board used for various purposes; a piece of wood nailed across the surface of one or more boards to prevent warping; a narrow strip of board used to cover cracks between boards; a small molding used for covering joints between sheathing boards to keep out moisture. When sheathing is placed on walls in a vertical position and the joints covered by battens, a type of siding is formed known as *boards and battens*. This form of siding is commonly used on small buildings, farm structures, and railroad buildings. A cleat is sometimes called a *batten*. Squared timbers of a special size used for flooring are also known as *battens*. These usually measure 7 inches in width, 2½ inches in thickness, and 6 feet, or more, in length.

batten door: A door made of sheathing boards reinforced with strips of boards nailed crossways and the nails clinched on the opposite side.

batten plate: A spacer plate to hold component parts of a member at the correct distance apart.

batten strap: A metal strip, usually of copper, used for securing a batten or nailing strip to the top of edge of a copper roof gutter.

battening: In plastering, the application of wood strips or battens to which laths or other material may be attached.

batter: A receding upward slope; the backward inclination of a timber or wall which is out of plumb; the upward and backward slope of a retaining wall which inclines away from a person who is standing facing it. A wall is sometimes constructed with a sloping outer face while the inner surface is perpendicular; thus, the thickness of the wall diminishes toward the top. See Fig. 50.

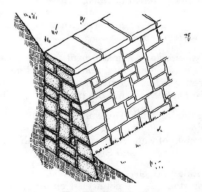

Fig. 50. Batter.

batter board: Usually, one of two horizontal boards nailed to a post set up near the proposed corner of an excavation for a new building. The builder cuts notches or drives nails in the boards to hold the stretched building cord which marks the outline of the structure. The boards and strings are used for relocating the exact corner of the building at the bottom of the finished excavation. See Fig. 51 and Fig. 445, page 341.

41

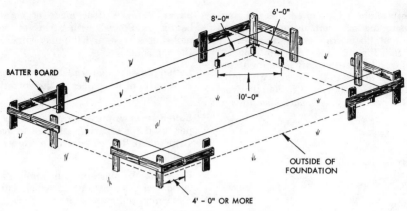

Fig. 51. Batter board.

batter brace: In construction work, an inclined brace set at the end of a truss to give added strength and support.

batter post: An inclined post set as a brace at the end of truss or other structural member to give added strength and support. See *batter brace.*

batter rule: An instrument which consists of a rule, or frame, and a plumb line and bob by which the batter, or slope of a wall, is regulated during the process of building.

battering wall: Any wall with a sloping face used for sustaining the pressure of the weight of water or of a bank of earth. Same as *retaining wall.* See Fig. 50.

battery: In electricity, a number of primary or storage cells connected either in series or in parallel, as a source of electric current; also, a combination of apparatus for producing a united electrical effect.

battlement: A low wall made up of a series of solid parts alternating with open spaces; a low railing at the edge of a platform or bridge; a decorative feature of massive types of architecture; the indented, or notched, wall of a parapet used as an ornamental design on furniture; in ancient times, a parapet, with open spaces, surmounting the walls of a fortified building. The soldiers defending the building could shoot through the open spaces and at the same time be protected by the masonry of the parapet.

bay (ba): A recessed space projecting outward from the line of a wall for a window known as a *bay window;* also, a window with its usual setting or framing, as jambs and window backing; a space or division of a wall within a building between two rows of columns, piers, or other architectural members, or a space between a row of columns and a bearing wall; also, a compartment in a barn where grain in the stalk and hay may be stored.

bay stall: A window seat built into the opening of a bay window. See *carol,* page 86.

bay window: A window, either square, rectangular, polygonal, or curved in shape projecting outward from the wall of a building, forming a recess in a room; a window supported on a foundation extending beyond the main wall of a building; a projecting window similar to a bay window, but carried on brackets or *corbels;* the term *bay window* may also be applied to an *oriel window* which projects over the street line.

bayonet socket: In electric lighting, a lamp socket which has two lengthwise slots in the sides of the socket, and at the bottom the slots make a right-angle turn. The lamp base has two pins in it that slide in the slots in the socket. The lamp is held in the socket by being given a slight turn when the pins reach the bottom of the slots.

bead: A circular or semicircular molding; a beaded molding is known as *beading;* when the beads are flush with the surface and separated by grooves, this type of molding is called *quirk bead.* See *bead molding,* Fig. 52. Also, in welding, narrow layer or layers of metal deposited on the base metal as the electrode melts. See Fig. 476, page 368.

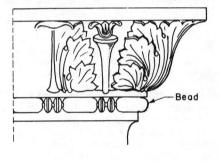

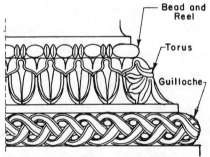

Fig. 52. Bead molding.

bead and butt: In carpentry, a term applied to a type of framing for panelwork in which the panels come flush with the frame and have beads run on the adjoining edges with a *sticker machine.* The beads run with the grain of the wood and butt against the *rail.*

bead and reel (bed and rel): A commonly used decorative molding consisting of a small sphere and one or two circular disks,

alternating singly or in pairs with oblong, olive-shaped beads. Also called *reel and bead molding.* See Fig. 52.

bead chain: In plumbing and electrical work a chain of alternating metal spheres and wires. Used for chain pulls for electric switches, key chains, etc.

bead molding: In carpentry, any molding carved to resemble a bead, as a *cock bead, quirk bead, bead and butt, bead and reel,* and others. See Fig. 52.

bead plane: A special type of plane used for cutting beads.

beaded joint: A joint which has a bead cut on the edge of one or both adjoining members to conceal the joint and to give it a more pleasing appearance.

beader: A tool for cutting beads. See *bead plane.*

beadflush: A term applied to a panel or to paneling work in which a panel is surrounded by a bead which usually is worked in the edges of the frame, so that the frame, bead, and panel are flush along their front faces.

beading: In architecture, a kind of molding, or rounded projecting band, used as a decorative feature. See *bead.* In sheet metal a type of depression made in the metal. The shape of the bead varies. Fig. 53 shows the three basic sheet metal beads.

beading machine: Machine used for making beads in sheet metal.

beading tool: A carpenter's tool having a concave edge used to cut beads on boards. Same as *bead plane.*

beadwork: In architecture, ornamental molding cut with a beading tool; also called *beading.*

beak: In architecture, a slight continuous projection which ends in an arris or a narrow fillet; also, the part of a drip from which rain water is thrown off from a roof. A term sometimes applied to the crooked end of a bench holdfast.

beak molding: A molding with a downward projecting part, the whole outline some-

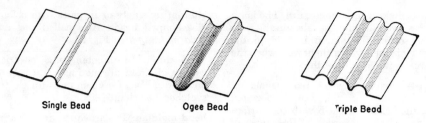

Single Bead   Ogee Bead   Triple Bead

Fig. 53. Types of beads made in beading machine.

what resembling a bird's beak, to make a drip for rain water and prevent the water from working back against the face of the wall below.

beakhead: A drip mold on the extreme lower edge of the lowest member of a cornice. See *beak molding.*

beakhead ornament: An ornament consisting of a series of grotesque figures resembling heads with beaks, used to enrich moldings. A decorative feature often used in Romanesque architecture; also, a method of decorating Norman doorways.

beaking joint: In carpentry, a joint formed by the meeting of a number of adjacent heading joints in the same straight line.

beam: Any large piece of timber, stone, iron, or other structural material used to support a load over an opening, or from post to post; one of the principal horizontal timbers, relatively long, used for supporting the floors of a building. An inclusive term for joists, girders, rafters, and purlins. Fig. 54 illustrates a large, laminated beam. For typical *reinforced concrete beams,* see Fig. 473, page 364. See *simple beam,* page 404.

beam anchor: In building construction, a type or form of anchor used for tying the walls firmly to the floors. See *wall anchor,* page 474.

beam and slab floor construction: A reinforced concrete floor system in which a solid slab is supported by beams or girders of reinforced concrete.

beam bolster: Continuous bar support used to support the bars in the bottom of beams.

beam ceiling: A type of construction in which the beams of the ceiling, usually placed in a horizontal position, are exposed to view. The beams may be either true or false, but if properly constructed the appearance of the ceiling will be the same whether the beams are false or true.

beam fill: Masonry or concrete used to fill the spaces between joists and also between a basement or foundation wall and the framework of a structure to provide fire stops in outside walls for checking fires which start in the basement of a building. See Fig. 237, page 181.

beam girder: Two or more beams fastened together by cover plates, bolts, or welds to form a single structural member.

beam hanger: A wire, strap, or other hardware device that supports formwork from structural members.

beam pocket: Opening left in a vertical member in which a beam is to rest; also an opening in the column or girder from where forms for intersecting beams will frame in.

beam schedule: List in working drawing, giving number, size and placement of steel beams used in a structure. See *column schedule,* page 108.

bearer: In architecture, any small member which is used primarily to support another member or structure, as one of the short pieces of quartering used to support the winders in winding stairs.

bearing: That portion of a beam or truss which rests upon a support; that part of

Fig. 54. Laminated beam being slipped into place in a hanger which is attached to a girder. (West Coast Lumbermen's Association)

any member of a building that rests upon its supports. The term *bearing* refers to a compass reading to indicate the angle in degrees and minutes from north to south. This means that the reading will approach ninety degrees in four quadrants. The reading N 35 degrees E means that the property line with such a marking is in the direction 35 degrees east of north.

bearing plate: A plate placed under a heavily loaded truss beam, girder, or column to distribute the load so the pressure or its weight will not exceed the bearing strength of the supporting member.

bearing value: The load a soil will sustain without substantial deformation.

bearing wall or partition: A wall which supports the floors and roof in a building;

a partition that carries the floor joists and other partitions above it.

beating out: A term sometimes applied to the cutting of a mortise.

bed: In masonry, a layer of cement or mortar in which the stone or brick is embedded, or against which it bears; either of the horizontal surfaces of a stone in position as the *upper* and *lower beds;* the lower surface of a brick, slate, or tile. Also, the recess formed by the mold to hold plaster ornament.

bed dowel: A dowel placed in the center of a stone bed.

bed in putty: Working putty into a rabbet of a sash before the glass is inserted or set.

bed joint: In brickwork, the horizontal joint upon which the bricks rest (see Fig.

45

37); also, the radiating joints of an arch.

bed molding: Finish molding used where the eaves of a building meet the top of the outside walls (see Fig. 48, page 40); the moldings, in any architectural order, used as a finish immediately beneath the corona and above the frieze; any molding in an angle, as between the projection of the overhanging eaves of a building and the sidewalls.

bed of a slate: The under side.

bed of a stone: The under surface of a stone; when the upper surface is prepared to receive another stone it is called the *top bed,* and the natural stratification of the stone is called the *natural bed.*

bed plate: A foundation plate used as a support for some structural part; a metal plate used as a bed, or rest, for a machine; a foundation framing forming the bottom of a furnace.

bed puttying: The process of placing a thin layer of putty or bedding compound in the rabbet of a window sash and pressing the glass onto this bed. Glazing points are then driven into the wood, and the sash is face puttied. Then the window is turned over, and the excess putty or glazing compound which emerges on the other side is cleared away by running a putty knife around the perimeter of the glass opening.

bed stone: A large foundation stone, as one used to support a girder.

bed timber: A timber serving as a foundation or support for other work.

bedding: A filling of mortar, putty, or other substance in order to secure a firm bearing.

bedrock: Solid rock which underlies any superficial formations; hence, a firm foundation on which to erect a building, especially a heavy structure.

belfry: A tower in which a bell is hung, the separate or attached bell tower of a church.

bell: A metal device, usually cup-shaped, mechanically equipped for producing a ringing sound when in operation; a common example is the electric doorbell.

In plumbing, that part of a pipe which, for a short distance, is enlarged sufficiently to receive the end of another pipe of the same diameter in order to make a joint. See Fig. 347, page 263.

bell-and-spigot joint: In plumbing, a common type of joint for cast-iron pipes, each length of pipe being made with an enlarged or bell end and a plain or spigot end; the spigot end of one length fitting into the bell end of the next length, the joint made tight by calking. Sometimes called *spigot-and-socket joint,* Fig. 347, page 263.

bell-hanger's bit: A long, slim, wood bit used for drilling through the frame of a building when installing door bells.

bell or hub: In plumbing, the enlarged end of a pipe into which the end of another pipe of the same diameter may be fitted to form a joint between the two lengths. The joint thus formed is secured by calking. Also called *socket.*

bell push: A button which is pushed to ring a bell.

bell trap: A type of bell-shaped stench trap consisting of a covered iron receptacle set in concrete floors and fastened to drainage pipe lines for carrying away water from a floor.

belled: Having a butt or bottom end shaped like a bell, often used on concrete piers or caissons.

belt: In masonry, a band course, or courses, of brick or stone projecting from a brick or stone wall, usually placed in line with the sills of the windows. It may be molded, fluted, plane, or enriched at regular intervals, or a course may be of a different kind of brick or stone.

belt conveyor: An endless belt passing over pulleys, providing a track on which loose materials or small articles are carried from one point to another. *Conveyor belts* are used extensively in large post offices for handling mail and packages.

belt course (kors): A layer of stone or molded work carried at the same level across or around a building. Also, a decorative feature, as a horizontal band around a building or around a column.

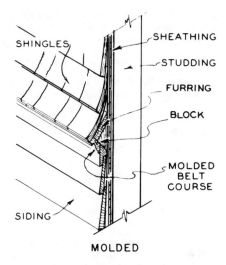

MOLDED

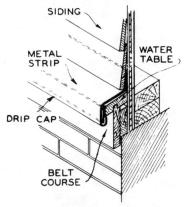

WITH METAL FLASHING

Fig. 55. Belt courses.

Two types of belt courses are shown in Fig. 55.

belt dressing: Any of various substances used to prolong the life of a belt or to improve its frictional grip and prevent slipping.

belt lacing: Narrow strips of rawhide with which belts are laced together. The term *belt lacing* should not be applied to wire hooks and other types of fasteners sometimes used to hold the ends of belts together.

bench apron: A covering board or facing used along the front of a workbench.

bench dog: A wooden or metal peg placed in a hole near the end of a workbench to prevent a piece of work from slipping out of position or off the bench.

bench hook: A hook-shaped device used to prevent a piece of work from slipping on the bench during certain operations; a flat timber or board with cleats nailed on each side and one on each end to hold a piece of work in position and to prevent slipping, which might cause injury to the top of the workbench.

bench marks (b.m.) A basis for computing elevations by means of identification marks or symbols on stone, metal, or other durable matter, permanently fixed in the ground, and from which differences of elevations are measured. A bench mark could serve as a datum (reference position) on a building site. The U.S. Geological surveys provide bench marks with the elevation *(related to sea level)* given at intervals across the country.

bench plane: Any plane used constantly and kept handy on the bench; a plane used on the bench as a jack plane, a truing plane, or a smoothing plane.

bench stop: An adjustable metal device, usually notched, attached near one end of a workbench to hold a piece of work while it is being planed.

bench table: A course of projecting stones forming a stone seat running around the walls at the base of a building, such as a large church; a projecting course around the base of a pillar sufficient to form a seat.

bench vise: An ordinary vise used by carpenters and other woodworkers to hold material which is being worked on at a bench to which the vise is attached.

benchwork: In carpentry, work which is done with small hand tools at a workbench, as distinct from work done with machines.

47

bend: A short piece of curved pipe, as an *elbow,* used to connect two adjacent straight lengths of a conduit.

bending: Fig. 56 shows how compression, tension, and sliding shear occur together in bending. Compression occurs along the *inner* edge of the bend, tension occurs along the *outer* edge of the bend, and sliding shear occurs *inside* the bending member.

Fig. 56. Bending a length of wood sets up multi-stresses: compression, shear, and tension.

bending moment: The tendency of a structural member to rotate about an axis; for example, the midsection of a beam has a tendency to bend downward.

bending pin or iron: In plumbing, a tool used to expand or straighten lead pipe.

beneficiation: Improvement of the chemical or physical properties of a raw material (e.g., aggregates) or intermediate product by the removal of undesirable components or impurities.

bent: A framework transverse to the length of a structure usually designed to carry lateral as well as vertical loads. A self-supporting frame having at least two legs and usually placed at right angles to the length of the structure it supports. Example: the columns and cap supporting the spans of a bridge is called a bent.

bent bar: A reinforcing bar bent to a prescribed shape such as a truss bar, hook bar, stirrup, or column tie.

bent cap: A concrete beam or block: extending across and encasing the heads of piles or columns, comprising the top of a bent for the bridge span above. (See also *pile cap,* page 325.)

bent wood: Wood formed by curved wood members by steaming or boiling the wood and bending it to a form.

berm: The dirt shoulder alongside a road.

bevel: One side of a solid body which is inclined in respect to another side, with the angle between the two sides being either greater or less than a right angle; a sloping edge. See *T bevel,* page 448.

bevel board (pitch board): A board used in framing a roof or stairway to lay out bevels.

bevel of door: The angle of the bevel for the front edge of a door; usually the bevel is from $\frac{1}{8}''$ to $2''$.

bevel of lock: A term used when describing the direction of the bevel of the latch bolt. Usually, *regular bevel* indicates a lock that functions on a door opening in, and *reverse bevel* indicates a lock for a door opening out.

bevel siding: A board used for wall covering, as the shingle, which is thicker along one edge. When placed on the wall, the thicker edge overlaps the thinner edge of the siding below to shed water. The face width of the bevel siding is from $3\frac{1}{2}''$ to $11\frac{1}{4}''$ wide. See Fig. 57.

bevel square. The bevel square is a combination square and 45° angle. The shape is triangular. The square corner of the triangle forms a 90° angle; the other two corners form 45° angles. The plasterer uses the bevel square to miter cuts and also to mark off 45° or 90° lines as he might need them.

bevel washer: In structural work, a type of washer frequently used to give a flat bearing for the nut when a threaded rod passes through a beam at an angle.

bevel weld: A bevel weld involves preparation of one of the members prior to the welding operation. When both sides are prepared, the term to call for the weld is V *weld.* See Fig. 58.

beveled halving: In carpentry, a halving joint where the meeting surfaces are not cut parallel to the plane of the timbers

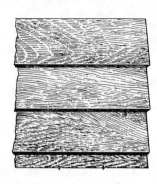 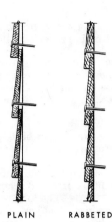

PLAIN   RABBETED

Fig. 57. Bevel siding: A traditional siding pattern. A strong shadow line is produced. (California Redwood Assoc.)

but are cut at an angle so that, when forced together, the timbers may not be pulled apart by a force in their own plane.

bezel: In cutting tools, such as a chisel or drill, the sloping cutting edge of the tool. Also spelled *basil*.

bias: In carpentry, a line or cut at the oblique or diagonal angle.

bib: In plumbing, a faucet or tap. A water faucet threaded so a hose may be attached to carry water. Also sometimes spelled *bibb*.

bib nozzle: A faucet or stopcock bent or curved downward. Same as *bibcock*.

bib valve: A draw-off tap of the type used for a domestic water supply. It is closed by the screwing down of a leather-washered disc onto a seating in the valve body.

bibcock: In plumbing, a faucet fitted with a nozzle curving downward, used as a draw-off tap. Same as *bib nozzle*. Also called *stopcock*.

bid: An offer by the contractor to his client to construct a structure meeting the conditions specified in the bid for a given price.

bidet: A bathroom fixture similar to a sitz bath; also used for bathing the lower part of the body.

bifolds: Doors, usually on closets, wherein doors are hinged to each other, hang from an overhead track, and fold to one or both sides.

bill of materials: A list of materials needed in the structure giving quantities, description, and sizes of each.

binder: In building, a timber or steel beam supporting the bridging joists in a double or framed floor.

In earthwork, the material which enables the fill material to stick together.

In painting, that nonvolatile portion of the paint that provides cohesion, that is, the oil and resin.

In masonry, a bond used to tie parts of a wall together.

binding: In carpentry, a term applied to some moving part, such as a window or

Fig. 58. Single bevel and V groove joints.

door, that does not move freely because of some defect or improper installation.

binding joists: In carpentry, a support, such as a timber or steel beam, for the bridging joists in a double or framed floor. Same as *binder.*

bird peck: A small hole or patch of distorted grain resulting from birds pecking through the growing cells in the tree.

bird's-eye: In lumber, a small central spot with the wood fibers arranged around it in the form of an ellipse so as to give the appearance of an eye, such as is seen in bird's-eye maple.

bird's-eye maple: A variety of the wood of the sugar maple in which the wavy grain causes eyelike markings, producing effective patterns making this a highly prized wood for decorative and finishing purposes.

bird's-mouth: A cutout near the bottom of a rafter which fits over the rafter plate. See *roof members,* Fig. 483, page 371.

bisect: To divide or cut a line, plane, or solid into two equal parts.

bit: That part of a key which projects and enters a lock contacting the bolt or tumblers (or both); also, a term applied to a cutting tool. See *bits,* Fig. 59.

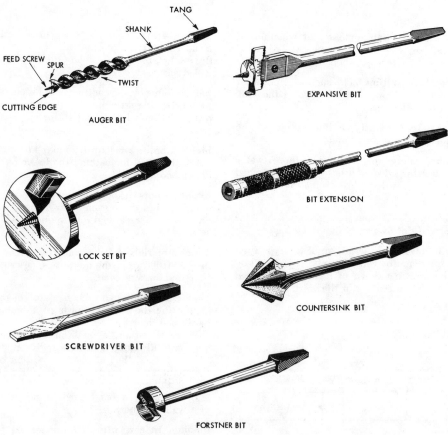

Fig. 59. Bits used by the carpenter.

bit brace or bit stock: A curved device used for holding boring or drilling tools; a bit stock, with a curved handle, designed to give greater leverage than is afforded by a boring tool with a straight handle. See Fig. 81, page 64.

bit extension: An attachment for an auger bit which extends the bit so the user can bore through walls and floors. The extension has a relatively long shank, a tang, and jaws for holding the bit. See *bits*, Fig. 59.

bit gage: An attachment to a bit which controls the drilling or boring to a given depth. Same as *bit stop*. See Fig. 60.

Fig. 60. Bit gage.

bit stop: A device attached to a bit to limit the drilling or boring to a desired depth. See *bit gage*, Fig. 60.

bitch: In carpentry, a type of *dog*, or steel fastening piece, in which the ends are bent so as to point in opposite directions.

bits: Cutting tools for boring holes used in combination with a *brace*, the combined tool being known as *brace and bit*. See Figs. 59 and 81, page 64.

bitting: An indentation or cut on that portion of a door-lock key which sets the tumblers.

blade: The longer of the two extending arms of the *framing square*, usually 24 inches long and 2 inches wide. The *tongue* of the square forms a right angle with the *blade*. *Rafter framing tables* and *essex board measure tables* appear on the faces of the blade of the square. Also called *body*. See Fig. 570, page 431.

blank flue: If the space on one side of a fireplace is not needed for a flue, a chamber is built in and closed off at the top in order to conserve material and labor and to balance weight. See Fig. 61.

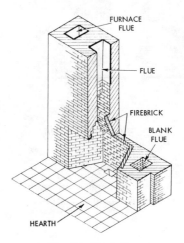

FURNACE FLUE

FLUE

FIREBRICK

BLANK FLUE

HEARTH

Fig. 61. Blank flue.

blanket insulation: A flexible type of lightweight blanket for insulating purposes, supplied in rolls, strips, or panels; sometimes fastened to heavy paper of an asphalt-treated or vapor-barrier type. These blankets may be composed of various processed materials, as mineral wool, wood fibers, glass fiber, cotton, eel grass, or cattle hair. Thicknesses vary from $\frac{1}{2}$ inch to 2 inches. The thicker types have a flange for stapling. Standard width is 15 inches to fit between studding set 16 inches on center. Obtainable also in 23-inch width for studding set 24 inches on center and in a 19 inch width for 20 inch spacing. See Fig. 62.

blast heater: A set of transfer coils or sections used to heat air by drawing or forcing the air through the coils by means of a fan.

bleaching: In wood finish, cleansing or whitening by the use of oxalic acid or some substance with similar properties.

bleed: To exude a liquid as in a minute leak. Also used to describe a paint base

Fig. 62. Applying fiberglas insulation blanket. (Owens-Corning Fiberglas Corp.)

breaking through the finish coat of paint. To leak an iron-stained liquid, as the seams of a boiler.

bleeder tile: Tile pipe placed in the foundation walls of a building to allow the surface water accumulated by the outside tile drain to pass into the drain provided on the inside of the foundation wall. Sometimes called *bleeder pipe*. See Fig. 63.

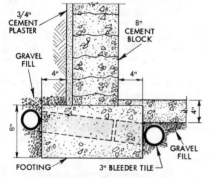

Fig. 63. Bleeder tile.

bleeding: In wood finishing, often a term applied to the use of mahogany and red dye stains. Unless some quick-setting material, such as shellac, is used as a finish coat, the coloring from the wood or the undercoat may work up into intermediate and top coats, coloring them. This is called *bleeding*. In concrete work, the exuding of water from concrete. The water either rises to the surface and weakens the slab or escapes through the forms, sometimes carrying cement along.

bleeding of wood: The exuding of preservative from a treated timber or board.

blemish: Any imperfection which mars the appearance of wood.

blend: In painting, to obtain a desired shade or color by mixing two different colored pigments; also, to apply paint to a surface so one shade will gradually pass into another shade.

blending: In painting, the mixing of two pigments and then applying the finish paint to a surface so that one shade passes into the other to produce a desired color effect.

blind: A covering for a window, consisting of a light wooden section in the form of a door to shut out light, give protection to the glass, or to add temporary insulation. In recent times, often used only for ornamental purposes. Same as *shutter,* page 402.

blind arcade: In architecture, an arcade which is closed at the back and serves only as a decorative feature.

blind arch: In architecture, a closed arch used for ornamentation to make one portion of a building harmonize with another part in which there are actual arched openings. A *blind arch* does not penetrate the structure.

blind area: A wholly or partly covered area outside of a building to keep moisture away from the walls.

blind casing: A kind of rough casing for a box-window frame; the inside piece of a window frame; a subcasing. See Fig. 198, page 154.

blind catch: A type of window-blind fastener, consisting of a hooklike contrivance used for holding a blind in place when it is in a closed position.

blind floor: A floor which serves as a base for a finish floor; the *rough floor,* or subfloor. See *balloon frame,* Fig. 41, page 35.

blind header: In masonry work, stones or bricks having the appearance of headers; they really are only short blocks of stone or the ends of bricks.

blind hinge: A type of hinge made especially for use on outside blinds or shutters; also, a concealed hinge.

blind mortise: Any mortise which does not pass entirely through the material in which it is cut; a mortise that is cut only part way through a board.

blind nailing: Driving nails in such a way that the holes are concealed. Sometimes called *secret nailing.* See Fig. 64.

blind stop: A rectangular molding used in the assembly of a window frame; usually a piece measuring ¾" x 1⅜". See *double-hung window,* Fig. 198, page 154.

blind tenoned: Any paneled assembly having tenons on the ends of the rails which are mortised into, but extend only part way through, the stile. See *mortise-and-tenon,* page 294.

blister: A defect in a painted surface which may be caused by the application of direct heat to the surface. See *blistering.* Also a puffing out of a plaster coat.

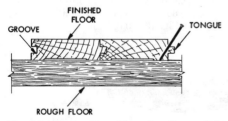

Fig. 64. Blind nailing drives flooring up tight and hides nails.

blistering: In painting, a defect arising on a painted surface due to one of a number of different causes, such as subjecting the surface to direct heating which causes the painted surface to swell up locally to form blisters; blistering or air pockets may also be caused by the sealing in of moisture, to hand smears, or to a difference in temperature of surface and finishing materials. This also occurs in plastering.

blistery: A term applied to defects in glass, such as air bubbles, or a painted surface which swells up to form blisters.

block: In building construction, a small piece of wood glued into the interior angle of a joint to strengthen and stiffen the joint (Fig. 330, page 252); a piece of wood placed back of a wainscot for support and to hold it away from the wall; a building unit of terra-cotta or cement which differs from brick in being larger and sometimes hollow. Device through which rope, cable, or chain is run to obtain mechanical advantage. See Fig. 65. See: *block and tackle.*

block and tackle: These are chain hoists, windlasses, and winches, or a combination of these, used to give mechanical advantage for lifting or pulling. Fig. 66 shows rope used in single blocks. Double and triple blocks are often used with the rope reeved or "threaded" through the blocks in various arrangements to give mechanical advantage or to multiply the force in making available power move a greater load than the same power could do directly. The increase in power is equal in ratio to the number of strands supporting the load.

block bridging: In building construction, blocks or short pieces of wood nailed between joists or between studding to serve as bridging braces. In case of fire, such blocks also help to check the fire and prevent its spreading to other parts of the structure. Also called *fire blocks.*

block flooring of wood: Small squares of flooring cut from narrow, short strips of regular flooring or made in solid blocks of wood. The sizes and thickness vary with the end use desired.

block-in-course: A kind of masonry used for heavy engineering construction, in which the stones are carefully squared and fin-

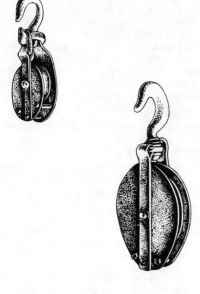

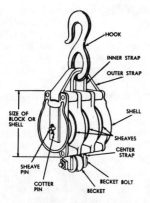

Fig. 65. Two single blocks in common use are shown (top). The parts of a block are labeled on a triple block (bottom). (Dept. of the Army)

ished to make close joints and the faces are dressed with a hammer.

block-in-course bond: In masonry, a bond used for uniting the concentric courses of an arch by inserting transverse courses, or *voussoirs,* at intervals.

block plan: The plan for a building site showing the outlines of existing and proposed buildings.

block plane: A tool used for working end grain. This type of plane is usually small in size, measuring from 5 to 7 inches in length. The cutting bevel is placed up instead of down and has no cap iron. Designed to use in one hand when in operation. See Figs. 67A and 67B.

Fig. 67A. Low-angled steel block plane; operated with one hand. (Stanley Works)

block tin: In plumbing, pure tin.

blocking: In carpentry, the process of fastening together two pieces of board by gluing blocks of wood in the interior angle. Also, the use of wood blocks as filler pieces, etc. See Fig. 165, page 130.

Fig. 66. Block and tackle. An arrangement of rope and tackle blocks which supplies the mechanical advantage for hoisting timbers.

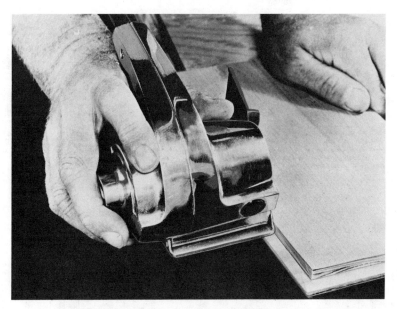

Fig. 67B. Power block plane. (Porter-Cable Machine Co.)

blocking course: In masonry, a finishing course of stones on top of a cornice, showing above the cornice and crowning the walls, usually serving as a sort of solid parapet forming a small architectural attic.

bloom: An efflorescence which sometimes appears on masonry walls, especially on a brick wall. This occurs most often within the first year after building. Also, a defect on a varnished surface usually caused by a damp atmosphere.

blow-hole: Hole where air and gas can escape.

blown joint: In plumbing, a joint in soft metal, such as lead, made by the use of a blowpipe.

blowtorch: A portable device which is used by plumbers, painters, and electricians to apply intense local heat.

blub: In building, a swelling or bulging out of newly plastered work.

blue stain: A discoloration of lumber due to a fungus growth in the unseasoned wood.

Although *blue stain* mars the appearance of lumber, it does not seriously affect the strength of the timber.

blueprint: A working plan used on a construction job by tradesmen; an architectural drawing made by draftsmen, then transferred to chemically treated paper by exposure to sunlight or strong artificial light. The sensitized paper, to which the drawing is transferred, turns blue when exposed to light. Fig. 68 illustrates a typical first floor plan for a residence. While the old standard type of blueprints is still in use, more and more industry and the trades are using prints on white paper printed in blue, black, and sepia ink. The basic reason for this change (which is not new) is that dark ink on white paper is easier to read, to indicate change, and to make corrections.

bluestone: A grayish-blue sandstone quarried near the Hudson River, much used in the East as a building stone, especially for window and door sills; also used for lintels.

blushing: In painting, a condition in which a bloom or gray cloudy film appears on a newly finished surface on hot humid days,

Door Schedule

Mark	Size	Am't Req'd	Remarks	Mark	Size	Am't Req'd	Remarks
A	3'-0"x6'-8"x1¾"	1	Exterior Flush Door	D	2'-4"x6'-8"x1⅜"	4	Flush Doors
B	2'-8"x6'-8"x1¾"	7	Flush Doors 1-Sliding 1-Metal Cover'd	D₁	2'-4"x6'-8"x1⅜"	1	Louvered
				E	1'-3"x6'-8"x1⅜"	1	Bi-Fold Louvered
C	2'-6"x6'-8"x1⅜"	4	Flush Doors	F	2'-10"x6'-8"x1¾"	2	Exterior 2-Lights
C₁	2'-6"x6'-8"x1⅜"	2	Louvered	G	2'-8"x6'-8"x1¾"	1	Exterior 2-Lights

Note: All Exterior Wall Dimensions are to Outside Face of Studs and Centerlines of Windows and Doors Interior Dimensions are to Centerlines of Partitions.

Publisher's Note: This drawing was originally drawn to the scale shown. The drawing was reduced to fit the page and can no longer be scaled.

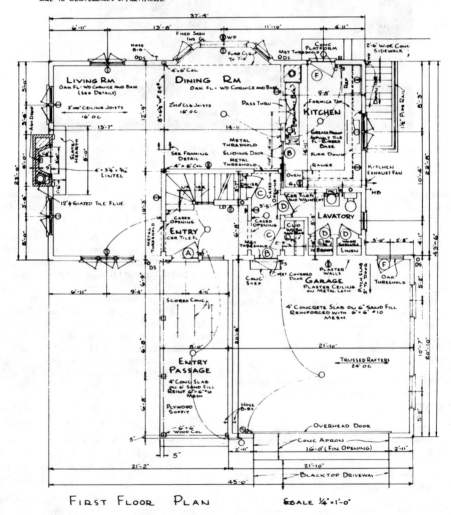

First Floor Plan   Scale ¼"=1'-0"

Fig. 68. First floor plan.

usually caused by the condensation of moisture or by the too rapid evaporation of the solvents.

board: A piece of sawed timber of a specified size, usually 1 inch thick and from 4 to 12 inches wide. Narrower material is usually referred to as *strips.*

board and batten: A type of siding composed of wide boards and narrow battens. The boards (generally twelve inches wide) are nailed to the sheathing so there is one-half inch space between them. The battens (generally three inches wide) are nailed over the open spaces between the boards. See Fig. 69.

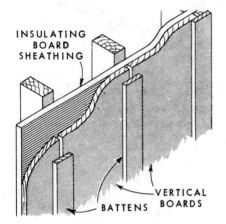

INSULATING BOARD SHEATHING

VERTICAL BOARDS

BATTENS

Fig. 69. Board and batten.

board foot: The equivalent of a board 1 foot square and 1 inch thick. See *board measure.* See Fig. 70.

board lath: In building construction, a thin, narrow piece of wood about four feet long nailed to wall studding as a support for plastering; also, a type of lath produced in large sheets sometimes called plaster board and usually intended as a base for plastering.

board measure: A system of measurement for lumber. The unit of measure being one board foot which is represented by a piece of lumber 1 foot square and approximately 1 inch thick. Quantities of lumber are des-

ignated and prices determined in terms of *board feet,* see Fig. 70.

board-measure scale: A scale found on the back of the body of a steel framing square; also called *essex board measure.*

board rule: A measuring device with various scales for finding the number of board feet in a quantity of lumber without calculation; a graduated scale used in checking lumber to find the cubic contents of a board without mathematical calculation. See Fig. 71. Also called a *tally stick.*

board sheathing: A term commonly applied to a waterproofed, insulating, composition board which is made in large sheets of various dimensions. It can be used as the base for any kind of exterior surface treatment.

boarding: A covering made of boards, as box sheeting of a building.

boarding-in: The process of nailing boards on the outside studding of a house.

boards: Yard lumber eight inches or more in width and less than two inches thick.

boasted work: In masonry, a dressed stone having a finish on the face similar to tooled work. *Boasting* may be done by hand or with a machine tool.

boaster: In stone masonry, a chisel used to smooth the surface of hard stone or to remove tool marks.

boasting: In masonry, the dressing of stone with a broad chisel and mallet.

boat lumber: A term commonly applied to wide boards (12″ to 16″ in width) of light-weight clear wood, such as cedar, redwood, or white pine.

boat spike: A long, square spike used in heavy timber construction. Same as *barge spike.*

body coat: That coat of paint between the first (priming) coat and the last (finish) coat of paint.

body of framing square: The blade or longer portion of a framing square.

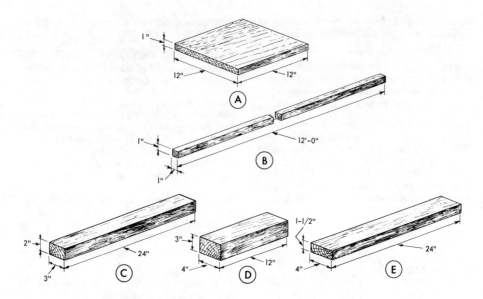

Fig. 70. The unit of measure for lumber is the board foot. Each of the above pieces is one board foot.

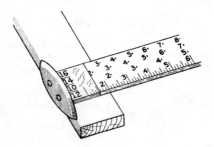

Fig. 71. Using a board rule. In this case if this board were 12' long it would have 2 board feet. (Read scale to right of the 12 on rule.)

boiled oil: Linseed oil, which, in painting, is heated to a temperature of from 400° to 600° F. to which is added a small quantity of a drier, such as lead monoxide or manganese dioxide; used extensively to promote the quick drying of a newly painted surface.

boiler-heating surface: That part of the surface of the heat-transfer apparatus which is in contact, on one side, with the fluid which is being heated and, on the other side, with the gas or refractory which is being cooled, and in which the fluid that is being heated forms part of the circulat-

| CARRIAGE BOLT | MACHINE BOLT | LAG BOLT | FLAT HEAD STOVE BOLT | ROUND HEAD STOVE BOLT | HANDRAIL BOLT |

Fig. 72. Types of commonly used bolts.

ing system. This surface should be measured on the the side receiving the boiler, water walls, water floor, and water screens.

boiler horsepower: The equivalent evaporation of 34.5 pounds of water per hour from and at 212° F. This is equal to a heat output of $970.3 \times 34.5 = 33,475$ B.t.u. per hour.

bolster: A short horizontal timber resting on the top of a column for the support of beams or girders. A crosspiece on an arch centering, running from rib to rib; the bearing place of a truss bridge upon a pier.

bolt: A fastener, usually consisting of a piece of metal having a head and a threaded body for the receptacle of a nut. For common types of bolts, see Fig. 72. Also, a short section of a tree trunk. A short log suitable for peeling for veneer.

bolts and angle irons: In form building, the column forms are held in place by means of angle irons which are held together firmly at the corners by the use of long bolts.

bond: In masonry and bricklaying, the arrangement of brick or stone in a wall by lapping them upon one another to prevent vertical joints falling over each other. As the building goes up, an inseparable mass is formed by tying the face and backing together. Various types of bond are shown in Fig. 73. Also means to stick or adhere, as concrete can bond to old concrete, masonry, reinforcing steel, etc.

bond breaker: A material, such as form oil, used to prevent adhesion or sticking of newly placed concrete and the forms, wall, etc.; sometimes a bond breaker is not desired such as hardened mortar on the form and reinforcement.

bond course: In masonry, a course of headers or bond stones.

bond stones: In masonry, stones running through the thickness of a wall at right angles to its base to bind the wall together.

bond timber: In a brick wall, a timber used as a bond by placing it in a horizontal position. Battens and laths are secured to these timbers which are arranged in tiers.

bonding: Any material used to join two surfaces and tie them together.

bonnet: In building, a wire netting used to cover the top of a ventilating pipe or a chimney; also, in plumbing, a cover for guiding and enclosing the tail end of a valve spindle.

boom: In building, any long beam, especially the upper or lower flange of a built-up girder. See *chord,* page 99. A spar or beam projecting from the mast of a derrick, supporting or guiding the weights to be lifted.

border: A finishing strip near or along the edge of a surface, usually distinctive and ornamental.

bore: The internal diameter for a pipe, cylinder, or a hole for a shaft, either machined or rough finished.

59

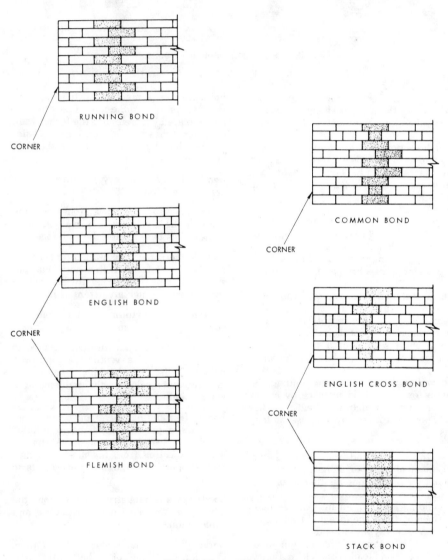

Fig. 73. Typical brick bonds.

boring: The process of making holes in wood or metal for the insertion of bolts or other fasteners used in building construction.

borrow soil: Soil borrowed from another location to be used in construction.

boss: An ornamental, projecting, knob-like block, as the carved keystone at the intersection of the ribs in Gothic vaulting.

bossage: In masonry, stones which are roughly dressed, such as corbels and quoins built in so as to project and then are finish-dressed in position.

bossing: In plumbing, the process of shaping malleable metal, especially sheet lead, to make it conform to the irregularities of the surface it is covering. The operation is accomplished by tapping the metal with a special mallet. See *bossing mallet.*

bossing mallet: In plumbing, a mallet specially shaped for use in the process of dressing sheet lead to a required form by *bossing.*

bossing stick: In plumbing, a wooden tool used to shape sheet lead for tank lining.

Boston hip roof: A method of shingling used to cover the joint, or hip, of a hip roof. To insure a watertight job, a double row of shingles or slate is laid lengthwise along the hip. See Fig. 74, left.

Boston ridge: A finish for the ridge of a roof, consisting of shingles saddled over the ridge and intersecting with the courses of shingles from both sides of the roof; a shingle ridge finish. For a Boston-type of hip roof, see Fig. 74.

bottom rail: The lowest horizontal member of a window sash or a door.

bottombolt: A bolt on the bottom of a door, so designed that friction prevents the bolt from dropping until released into the locking position.

boulder wall: In masonry, a type of rustic wall composed of boulders, usually undressed, and mortar.

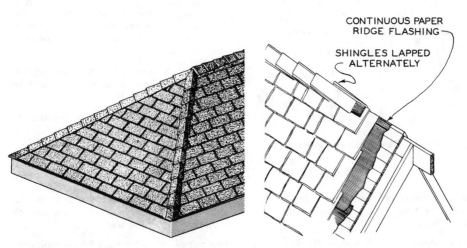

Fig. 74. (Left) Boston hip and ridge requires overlapping strips for asphalt shingled roof. (Right) Boston ridge.

boulders and cobbles: Stone material over three inches in size.

bounding wall: A wall enclosing any area or defining a boundary.

bow: Any part of a building which projects in the form of an arc or of a polygon. In lumber, a defect consisting of a deviation flatwise from a straight line drawn from end to end of a piece. See *warp.*

bow compass: An instrument used by draftsmen for drawing circles or arcs having a radius of less than ¾ inch. The *bow compass* consists of two legs joined at the top. One leg carries a pencil or pen point. The other leg is fitted with a needle point which is placed at the center of the circle. See Fig. 75.

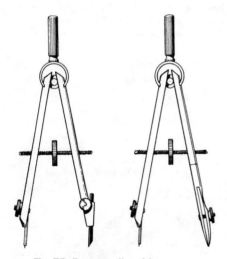

Fig. 75. Bow pencil and bow pen.

bow dividers: A draftsman's instrument used for transferring measurements. See Fig. 76.

bow window: A window in the bow of a building, such as a bay window, especially a bay with a curved ground plan.

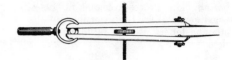

Fig. 76. Bow dividers.

bowled floor: In building construction, a special type of floor which slopes downward toward the stage or altar, as in a theater or church. The inclination usually is about ½ inch to the foot.

box beam: In building construction, a term sometimes applied to a box girder; also, a hollow beam formed like a long box. See Fig. 77.

box bolt: A bolt similar to the *barrel bolt* except that the box bolt is square or flat.

box casing: In window framing, the inside piece forming a sort of blind casing, sometimes called *subcasing* or *inside casing.*

box column: A type of built-up hollow column used in porch construction; it is usually square in form.

box connector: In electricity, an attachment used for fastening the ends of a cable to a box.

box cornice: A type of cornice which is completely inclosed by means of the *shingles, fascia,* and *plancier.* In cross section shaped like a box. Same as *closed cornice.* See Fig. 78.

box drain: A drain with a flat top and bottom, and upright sides, usually built in brickwork or concrete.

box frame: A window frame containing boxes for holding the sash weights.

box girder: In building construction, a girder of cast iron having a hollow rectangular section; also, a girder or beam made of wood formed like a long box. Also, a bridge span having a top and bottom slab with two or more walls forming one or more rectangular spaces.

box gutter: A gutter built into a roof, consisting of a horizontal trough of wood construction lined with galvanized iron, tin, or

Fig. 77. Box beams made of 2 X 4 frames with plywood webs are used in an experimental house. (Douglas Fir Plywood Assoc.)

Fig. 78. In the box or closed cornice the plancier and fascia conceal the rafter end.

(Note the soffit screen in the plancier to ventilate the cornice and attic space.)

copper to make it watertight. Sometimes called *concealed gutter.* See Fig. 79.

box nails: These are similar in appearance to *common nails.* However, they are not quite so thick and are obtainable only from 2*d* to 40*d* in size. They are used on wood that splits easily. See Fig. 419, page 320 for sizes.

box out: To form an opening or pocket in concrete by a box-like form.

box sill: A header nailed on the ends of joists and resting on a wall plate. It is used in frame-building construction. See Fig. 80.

box staple: The box on a doorpost into which the bolt of the lock engages.

box strike: A door strike with the opening for receiving the bolt enclosed, or boxed, to prevent access from the rear or to make access from the rear impossible. See *strike,* page 436.

boxed cornice: A closed-in cornice which in cross section appears boxlike, the enclosing members being the wall of the building, the roof, the fascia, and the plancier. Same as *closed cornice.* Fig. 78.

boxed pith: When a piece of lumber contains the *pith* of a tree.

boxing up: In building, a term used when referring to the operation of applying a rough covering, such as sheathing boards, to a house or other structure.

brace: A piece of wood or other material used to resist weight or pressure of loads; an inclined piece of timber used as a support to stiffen some part of a structure (see Fig. 82). A support used to help hold parts of furniture in place giving strength and durability to the entire piece.

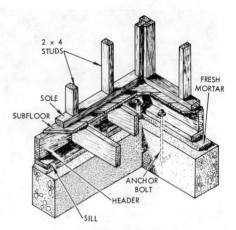

Fig. 80. Box sill.

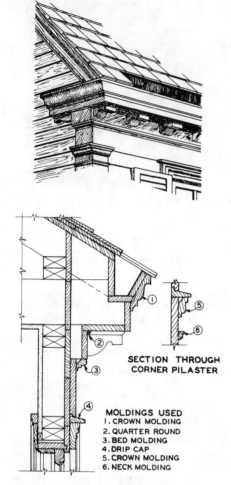

**SECTION THROUGH
CORNER PILASTER**

MOLDINGS USED
1. CROWN MOLDING
2. QUARTER ROUND
3. BED MOLDING
4. DRIP CAP
5. CROWN MOLDING
6. NECK MOLDING

Fig. 79. Box gutter.

brace jaws: The parts of a bit brace which clamp around the tapered shank of a bit. See Fig. 86.

brace measure: A table which gives the lengths of a large number of different length braces. It is usually found on the center of the back of the tongue of a steel framing square. Also called *brace scale* and *brace table*. See Fig. 83.

brace piece: The shelf of a mantel. Same as *mantelpiece*.

A term also applied to a tool with which *auger bits* are turned for boring holes in wood. A bit brace is shown in Fig. 81.

brace bit: A tool used for boring holes in wood. An ordinary bit has square, tapered shanks to fit into the socket of a common brace. See Fig. 60.

brace frame: A type of framework for a building in which the corner posts are braced to sills and plates. See Fig. 82.

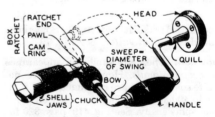

Fig. 81. Ratchet brace and parts.

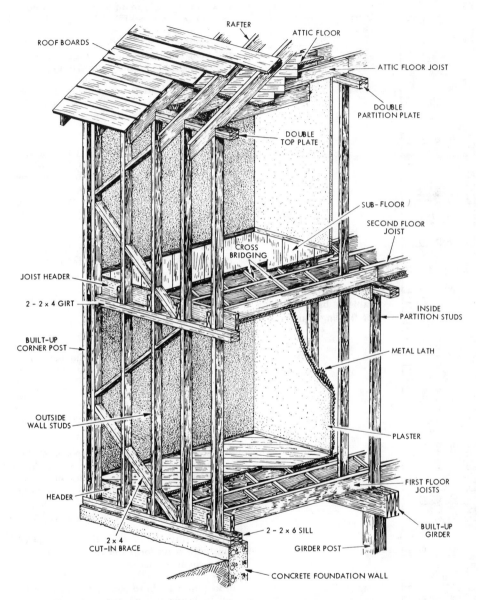

RAFTER

ROOF BOARDS

ATTIC FLOOR

ATTIC FLOOR JOIST

DOUBLE
PARTITION PLATE

DOUBLE
TOP PLATE

SUB-FLOOR

SECOND FLOOR
JOIST

CROSS
BRIDGING

JOIST HEADER

2 - 2 x 4 GIRT

INSIDE
PARTITION STUDS

BUILT-UP
CORNER POST

METAL LATH

OUTSIDE
WALL STUDS

PLASTER

HEADER

FIRST FLOOR
JOISTS

BUILT-UP
GIRDER

2 x 4
CUT-IN BRACE

2 - 2 x 6 SILL

GIRDER POST

CONCRETE FOUNDATION WALL

Fig. 82. Braced framing. Braced frame construction is extremely rigid but it is seldom used because of the size of the framing members and the cost involved. This modified braced framing is very satisfactory where strong winds are encountered. Notice the girt at the second level.

65

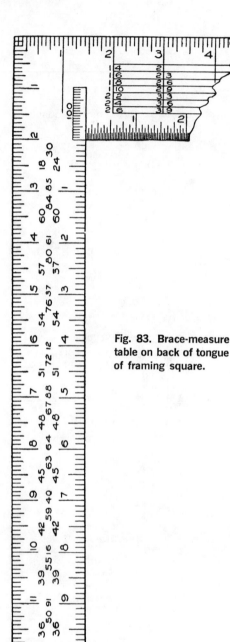

Fig. 83. Brace-measure table on back of tongue of framing square.

brace scale: A table which gives the lengths of a large number of different length braces. See *brace measure,* Fig. 83.

brace table: A scale or measure giving the different lengths of braces. Same as *brace scale.* Also called *brace measure,* Fig. 83.

braced arch: A structure or member framed so as to form an arch and arranged so the end reactions will be inclined for supporting a vertical load.

braced framing: In building construction, a type of heavy-timber framing in which the frame is formed and stiffened by the use of posts, girts, and braces, as opposed to the less-rigid type known as *balloon framing.* A *Braced Frame* is shown in Fig. 82.

braces: Pieces fitted and firmly fastened to two others at any angle in order to strengthen the angle.

bracing: The ties and rods used for supporting and strengthening the various parts of a building, such as between studs or joists. See *bridging,* page 70.

bracket: A projection from the face of a wall used as a support for a cornice or some ornamental feature (see Fig. 401, page 304); a support for a shelf.

bracket cornice: A series of exposed brackets supporting a cornice.

bracketing: In building, the wooden skeleton pieces to which are fastened the lath and plaster forming the surface of a cornice; also, the shaped timber supports which form a basis for the plasterwork and moldings of ceilings and parts near ceilings.

brad: A thin, usually small, nail made of wire with a uniform thickness throughout and a small head.

brad punch or **brad setter:** A tool used to set the heads of brads below the surface of wood; also called *nail set.*

bradawl: A short, straight awl with a chisel or cutting edge at the end; a non-tapering awl.

braided wire: In electricity, a conductor composed of a number of small wires twisted or braided together.

branch: In plumbing, the inlet or outlet of a pipe fitting which is set at an angle with the run. See Fig. 620, page 473. A pipe into which no other branch pipes discharge.

branch circuit: That part of a wiring system between the final set of fuses protecting the circuit and the place where the lighting fixtures or appliances are connected. See Fig. 84.

branch control center: An assembly of circuit breakers for the protection of branch circuits feeding from the control center. See Fig. 84.

branch cutout: In electricity, the holder for the branch-circuit fuse.

branch drain: In plumbing, the drainpipe which communicates between a gulley, soil pipe, or sanitary fitting and the main drainpipe.

branch ell: In plumbing, an elbow having a back outlet in line with one of the outlets of the *run;* also called a *heel outlet elbow.*

branch pipe: In plumbing, a special type of pipe having one or more branches.

brandering: In plastering, the operation of nailing furring strips to girders, joists, or a solid surface. The furring, to which the lath are nailed, provides a key for the plaster and also takes it away from the wall surface.

brandreth: Any wooden framework for support, as a stand for a cask; also, a fence or railing around a well. Same as *brandrith.*

brashness: A condition of wood which is characterized by a low resistance to shock and by an abrupt failure across the grain without the normal splintering of the wood.

brattishing: A kind of cresting, as an ornamental parapet of a wall; a row of upright foliage, or leaves, on the cornice of a screen.

braze: To solder with an alloy relatively infusible as compared to common solder; a high temperature solder.

brazier: In building, a portable iron container or pan for holding burning coals of fire, used to dry off work during the process of constructing a building.

brazing: Brazing is similar to welding: a metal rod (*bronze filler rod*) is used with a lower melting point than the metals being joined (*base metals*). The rod melts to join the metals; base metals do not melt.

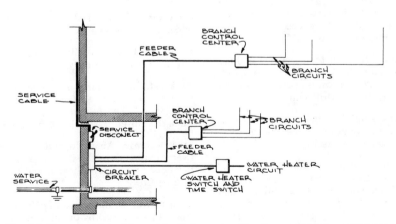

Fig. 84. There is a trend in residential construction to use branch control centers.

break: A lapse in continuity; in building, any projection from the general surface of a wall; an abrupt change in direction as in a wall.

break ground: In construction, the first work performed when excavation is begun for a new building.

break iron: An iron fastened to the top of the bit of a plane. The purpose of the iron is to curl and break the shavings.

break joint: The principle of placing the parts of a structure together so the joints will not form a vertical line. To arrange joints so they do not come directly under or over the joints of adjoining pieces, as in shingling, siding, etc. See *breaking of joints*.

breakfast nook: A dinette, or small cozy room near to the kitchen in which breakfast is served.

breakfast room: A small room in which breakfast is served. See *breakfast nook*.

breaking of joints: A staggering of joints to prevent a straight line of vertical joints. The arrangement of boards so as not to allow vertical joints to come immediately over each other.

breaking radius: The limiting radius of curvature to which wood or plywood can be bent without breaking.

breaks: In plastering, to arrange and nail the laths so the joints are staggered; that is, the joints do not all occur one above another in the same vertical line.

breast drill: A small tool used for drilling holes by hand in wood or metal. A hand-turned crank transmits power through bevel gears to the drill chuck.

breast of a window: The backing of the recess and the parapet under the window sill, composed of masonry.

breastsummer: A heavy timber, or *summer,* placed horizontally over a large opening; a beam flush with a wall or partition which it supports; a lintel over a large window of a store, or shop, where the lintel must support the superstructure above it.

breezeway: A covered passage, open at each end, which passes through a house, or between two structures, increasing ventilation and adding an outdoor living effect.

brick: Block of material used for building or paving purposes. Bricks are made from clay or a clay mixture molded into blocks which are then hardened by drying in the sun or baking in a kiln. American-made brick average 2½ x 4 x 8 inches in size. See Fig. 85.

brick beam: A lintel made of brick, with iron straps.

brick cement: A waterproofed masonry cement employed for every kind of brick, concrete brick, tile, or stone masonry and also in stucco work.

brick construction: A type of building construction where the exterior walls are bearing walls, built of brick or a combination of brick and tile masonry.

brick corbeling: In brick walls, a corbeling composed of brick.

brick facing: The same as *brick veneer.*

brick hammer: A tool used by bricklayers for dressing brick or for breaking them. Same as *bricklayer's hammer*. See Fig. 86.

brick nogging: In a wood-framed wall or partition, brickwork used to fill in the spaces between studs or timbers. Also called *brick-and-stud work.*

brick pier: A detached mass of masonry which serves as a support.

brick seat: Ledge on wall or footing to support a course of masonry.

brick set: In masonry, a tool used to cut bricks when exact surfaces are required. See Fig. 87. The *brick hammer* is used to force the chisel-like brick set into the brick.

brick trimmer: An arch built of brick between trimmers in the thickness of an upper floor to support a hearth and to guard against fire.

brick trowel: In masonry, a flat triangular-shaped trowel used by bricklayers for picking up mortar and spreading it on a wall.

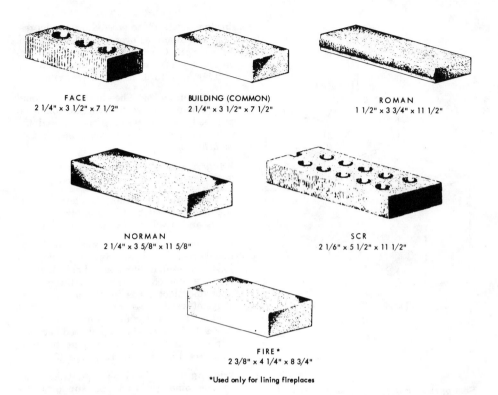

FACE
2 1/4" x 3 1/2" x 7 1/2"

BUILDING (COMMON)
2 1/4" x 3 1/2" x 7 1/2"

ROMAN
1 1/2" x 3 3/4" x 11 1/2"

NORMAN
2 1/4" x 3 5/8" x 11 5/8"

SCR
2 1/6" x 5 1/2" x 11 1/2"

FIRE*
2 3/8" x 4 1/4" x 8 3/4"

*Used only for lining fireplaces

Fig. 85. These six standard brick types are used in residential construction. Sizes may vary in different localities.

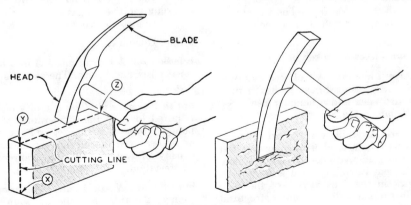

Fig. 86. Brick hammer.

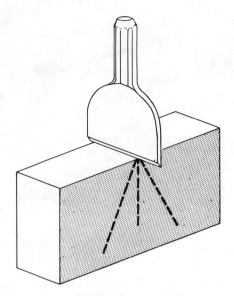

Fig. 87. Brick set.

See *buttering trowel,* page 78. See *head joint,* page 234. Fig. 37, page 32, for an illustration of how a trowel is used.

brick veneer: A brick facing applied to the surface of the walls of a frame structure or other types of structures. See Fig. 88.

brick-veneer construction: A type of building in which a wood frame has an exterior surface of brick applied as a veneer. See Fig. 88.

brickbat: Pieces of broken bricks.

bricklayer's hammer: A tool used by bricklayers for dressing brick. It has both a sharpened peen and a hammer head. See *brick hammer,* Fig. 86.

brickwork: Anything constructed of bricks which have been used as building material since the primitive ages of civilized man. The ancient Egyptians used a crude kind of brick in the construction of the arch and the vault as well as for other structural purposes.

bridge: A structure erected over a depression or stream, as over a highway, chasm, or river, to provide a passageway for vehicles or pedestrians; also, any structure similar in form or use, as a *bridging joist.*

bridge measure: The line or diagonal which connects two figures, one taken on the body of the framing square and the other on the tongue, is sometimes known as *bridge measure.*

bridge socket: See *cable attachments,* page 80.

bridgeboard: The string of a stair, consisting of a notched board for supporting the risers and treads of a wooden stairway.

bridging: Arrangement of small wooden or metal pieces between timbers, such as joists, to stiffen them and hold them in place; a method of bracing partition studding and floor joists by the use of short strips of wood; cross bridging used between floor joists; usually a piece of 1 x 3, 2 x 2, or 2 x 4. Solid wood bridging used between partition studs is the same size as the studding. See Figs. 89 and 168, page 132.

bridging joist: A beam, or joist, which rests on the binding joists and supports the flooring.

bridle joint: A type of joint which is the reverse of a *mortise-and-tenon joint.* Instead of a tongue and mortise being cut in the centers of two adjoining pieces, two tongues are cut along the outside edges of the tenoned piece, and the two corresponding mortises are cut at the edges of the other piece to receive them.

bright: Unstained.

brindle iron: A hanger made of iron to receive joists and beams. The same as *stirrup.*

British thermal unit: The quantity of heat required to raise the temperature of one pound of pure water one degree Fahrenheit at or near the temperature of maximum density of water 39 degrees Fahrenheit. Abbreviation: B.t.u.

broach post: Vertical timber tie used to connect the ridge and the tie beam of a roof, shaped at its lower end so as to afford

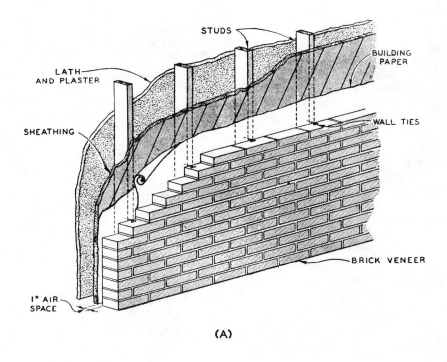

(A)

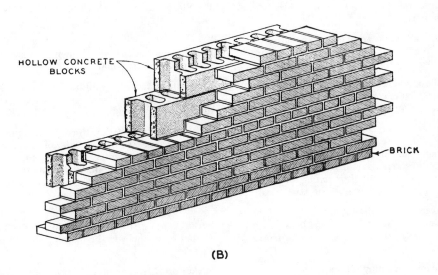

(B)

Fig. 88. Pictorial views of brick veneer on frame and on concrete block walls.

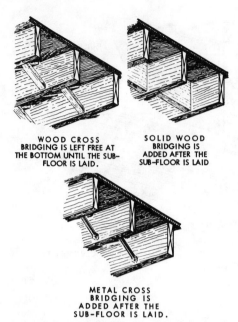

WOOD CROSS BRIDGING IS LEFT FREE AT THE BOTTOM UNTIL THE SUB-FLOOR IS LAID.

SOLID WOOD BRIDGING IS ADDED AFTER THE SUB-FLOOR IS LAID

METAL CROSS BRIDGING IS ADDED AFTER THE SUB-FLOOR IS LAID.

Fig. 89. Various types of bridging are used to strengthen floors and distribute the load.

bearing to two struts which support the middle points of the rafter. Also called *king post.*

broached work: In masonry, broad grooves which give a finish to a building stone made by dressing the stone with a punch.

broken and dotted line: In drawing, any line which is composed of a dot and a dash in consecutive order used for indicating projections. Also known as a *dot-and-dash line.*

broken joints: In building construction, joints are arranged so they will not fall in a straight line. *Broken joints* tend to add strength and stiffness to the structure.

broken line: In drawing, any line which is composed of a series of long dashes used to indicate the points from which measurements are taken.

bronze: An alloy of copper and tin; a term applied sometimes to other alloys which do not contain tin.

broom closet: A small recess or separate cabinet for keeping brooms and cleaning materials.

brown coat: A coat of plaster which is applied with a fairly rough finish to receive the finish coat; in two-coat work, the term refers to the base coat of plaster which is applied over the lath; in three-coat work it is the second coat applied over a *scratch coat.* See Fig. 579, page 438.

browning brush: The browning brush is used to throw water on the surface of applied mortar to provide "slip" or lubrication to the tools used to straighten the surface. See Fig. 90.

Fig. 90. Browning brush. (Goldblatt Tool Co.)

brownstone: A reddish-brown sandstone used as a building material.

brownstone front: A building which has a facing or front of brownstone. A mark of distinction and wealth during the 1800's.

brush or spray coat: A waterproofing application of one or more coats of asphalt, pitch, or a commercial waterproofing on the exterior of the foundation, below the grade line, with a brush, trowel, or by spraying. May be used where subgrade moisture problems are not severe.

buck: Framing around an opening in a wall. A door buck encloses the opening in which a door is placed.

bucker-up: Member of a riveting team who holds rivet in place with steel bar while the riveter hammers it down.

bucket trap: In a steam-heating system, a kind of valve for eliminating air and condensed moisture from pipes and radiators without allowing steam to escape. A discharge tube is actuated by a bucket attached to a valve.

buckle: To twist or bend out of shape permanently; a term commonly applied to a plate or any other structural member which crumples and becomes deformed or distorted under a compressive load.

buckled: A term applied to a construction member which has crumpled, bent, or warped.

buckling: In painting, a condition caused by the shrinking of a pyroxylin lacquer film over an oil-base undercoater when full drying time has not been given to the undercoater.

buggy: A manual or powered vehicle used to transport fresh concrete from the mixer to location where the concrete is to be placed.

builder's acid: A combination of hydrochloric acid (1 part by volume) and water (4 parts by volume) used to remove mortar stains from brick.

builder's level: A telescope-like instrument incorporating a bubble level that mounts on a tripod. It is used in laying out stakes and string lines particularly on larger jobs. It is used to establish height and slope of flatwork and structures, Fig. 91. See *level*, page 266.

builder's staging: A sturdy kind of scaffolding formed of square timbers strongly braced together and capable of being used for the handling of heavy materials.

builder's tape: Steel measuring tape, usually 50 or 100 feet in length, contained in a circular case. Sometimes *builder's tape* is made of fabricated materials.

building: A structure used especially for a dwelling, barn, factory, store, shop or warehouse; the art, or work, of assembling materials and putting them together in the form of a structure; the act of one who builds.

building area: The total ground area of each building and accessory building. Does not include uncovered entrances, terraces, and steps.

building block: Any hollow rectangular block of burnt clay, terra cotta, concrete,

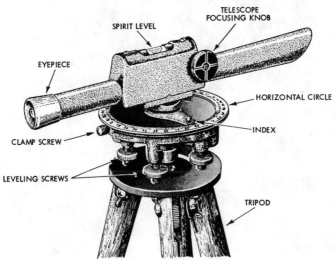

Fig. 91. The builder's level is an accurate instrument used for determining points in a horizontal plane. (David White Instruments, Div. of Realist, Inc.)

cement, or glass manufactured for use as building material.

building brick: A *solid masonry unit* made primarily for building purposes and not especially treated for texture or color. Formerly called common brick. Its nominal dimensions (which include the thickness of the mortar joint used with it) are 4" x 2⅔" x 8". See Fig. 85.

building code: A collection of regulations adopted by a city for the construction of buildings and to protect the health, morals, safety, and general welfare of those within or near to the buildings.

building drain: The part of the piping of a plumbing drainage system which receives discharge from soil, waste and other stacks inside a building. Also called *house drain.*

building line: The line, or limit, on a city lot beyond which the law forbids the erection of a building; also, a second line on a building site within which the walls of the building must be confined; that is, the

outside face of the wall of the building must coincide with this line.

building materials. The wide variety of materials which enter into building construction.

building materials dealer: A supplier of a specific kind of construction material such as wood, stone, brick, etc.

building paper: A form of heavy paper prepared especially for construction work. It is used between rough and finish floors and between sheathing and siding as an insulation and to keep out vermin. It is used, also, as an undercovering on roofs as a protection against weather.

building permits: Permits required from state and local governments for building any kind of a permanent structure. A fee is usually required to obtain such permits.

building stone: An architectural term applied in general to any kind of stone which may be used in the construction of a build-

Fig. 92. A counter top lavatory with a cabinet below is an interesting and practical feature of a modern bathroom. (Rheem Mfg. Co.)

ing, such as limestone, sandstone, granite, marble, or others.

building trades: All trades which belong to the building industry and have a part in the construction of a building, including carpentry, masonry, painting, plumbing, electricity, and heating.

built-in: A builder's term for furniture which is fitted or *built in* a special position in a house. When drawing plans, the architect must make provision for all built-in furniture.

built-in bathtub: A bathroom fixture intended for bathing purposes; designed to fill a special position, such as in a recess where the tub is fastened to remain permanently. See Fig. 92.

built-in cupboard: Any cupboard which is permanently fixed in its position by being

built into the wall of the room in which it is located.

built-in furniture: Any furniture, such as a cabinet, cupboard, or bookcase which is permanently fastened to a building by being built into the wall of the room in which it is located.

built-in nailing blocks: In construction work, a wood block built into a wall for use as a *nailing block* or *anchor block*.

built-in oven: Any of various new ovens designed for installation in a wall at a level which eliminates stooping. Such ovens may be heated by gas or electricity. Some of these units have glass panels in their doors, allowing inspection of cooking foods. Electric control panels for such ovens sometimes include controls for *built-in stoves*. See Fig. 93.

Fig. 93. Counter top ranges and built-in ovens are features of modern kitchens. (Kitchen Kompact.)

built-in seat: A type of built-in chest which also serves as a seat. See *window seat,* page 484.

built-in stove: Stoves are often designed for counter top installation in the kitchen. Such units are sometimes mounted rigidly in counter tops, while at other times they are mounted on a pivoted base which folds the entire unit into the wall when not in use. Heating controls for such stoves are found with the stove unit, or they may be located in an integrated control panel located in *built-in oven* units. See Fig. 93.

built-up: A term used in the building trades when referring to a structural member made up of two or more parts fastened together so as to act as a single unit.

built-up beam: A beam formed by bolting or nailing two or more planks together to add strength to the structural timbers. Same as *built-up girder.* Typical built-up wood beams are shown in Fig. 94.

built-up column: In architecture, a column which is composed of more than one piece.

built-up girder: A girder formed by the bolting or nailing together of two or more planks. See *built-up beam,* Fig. 94.

built-up roof: A roofing material applied in sealed waterproof layers where there is only a slight slope or pitch to the roof.

built-up timber: A timber made by fastening several pieces together and forming one of larger dimension.

bulge: In architecture, a term applied to a slight swelling outward, as a graceful swelling on columns; also, a term applied to a defect, as the bending outward of a wall.

bulkhead: In building construction, a box-like structure which rises above a roof or floor to cover a stairway or an elevator shaft. Also: a partition blocking fresh concrete from a section of the forms or closing the end of a form, such as at a construction joint.

bulking: In building construction, the increase in the size of material due to the absorption of moisture. Same as *moisture expansion.*

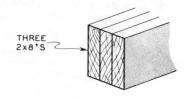

BUILT-UP 6x8 BEAM

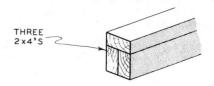

BUILT-UP 4x6 BEAM

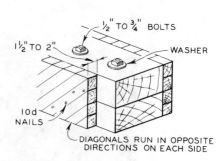

CLARKE BEAM

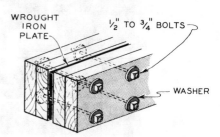

FLITCH BEAM

Fig. 94. Built-up beams.

bull dozer: A tractor with caterpillar tread which is used to push away debris for clearing an area.

bull floating: First stage in the final finishing of concrete flatwork after screeding; sometimes substituted for darbying. Smooths and levels hills and voids left after *screeding.*

bull header: In masonry, a brick having one rounded corner, usually laid with the short face exposed to form the brick sill under and beyond a window frame; also used as a *quoin* or around doorways.

bull nose: An exterior angle which is rounded to eliminate a sharp or square corner. In masonry, a brick having one rounded corner; in carpentry, a stair step with a rounded end used as a starting step. Also called *bull's nose.*

bull stretcher: A brick with one corner rounded and laid with the long face exposed, as a *quoin.*

bull-nose plane: A small plane which can be used in corners or other places difficult to reach. The mouth can be adjusted for coarse or fine work. See Fig. 95.

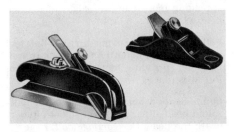

Fig. 95. Bull-nose rabbet plane for working close into corners. (Stanley Works)

bull-nose starting step: In stair building, a step which is rounded at the outer corner, as the starting step which extends beyond the newel post.

bullet catch: A type of door fastener that has a spring catch. See Fig. 96.

Fig. 96. Bullet catch.

bullhead tee: In plumbing, a tee with a branch longer than the run; also, one having an outlet larger than the opening on the run.

bull's-eye arch: In building, a circular opening, such as a circular or oval window.

bulwark: Defensive structure; a solid wall or rampart for protective purposes.

bumper: In building, a knoblike *doorstop* attached to a wall against which a door bumps; any device used as an obstruction for a swinging door or for a sliding door. Also, a term applied to a workman who molds handmade brick.

bumping: This term is applied to the process of raising or bumping flat metal so as to form ornaments for cornice work, curved moldings, sheet metal balls, and covers for various objects. The operation is performed by a raising hammer and a raising block. See *raising,* page 359.

bungalow: A one-story house with low, sweeping lines and a wide veranda; sometimes the attic is finished as a second story.

bungalow siding: A name sometimes applied to bevel siding of eight inches or more in width. See *siding,* page 403; also *bevel siding,* page 48.

burglar alarm: In building construction, any contrivance, fastened to a window or door, which sounds an alarm when the window or door is opened.

burl: An abnormal growth on the trunks of many trees; an excrescence often in the form of a flattened hemisphere; veneer made from these excrescences. An especially beautiful *burl* veneer is cut from the stumps of walnut trees.

burnett's process: The infusion of timber with chloride of zinc as a preservative.

burning in: In plumbing, the process of fastening the edge of a lead flashing into a stone wall by turning it into a dovetail groove which has been cut in the stone; then filling the groove with molten lead and calking it.

burnisher: A tool of hardened steel used for finishing and polishing metal work by friction. The *burnisher* is held against the revolving metal piece which receives a smooth, polished surface due to the compression of the outer layer of the metal. This tool is used, also, to turn the edge of a scraper.

burr: Ragged, sharp projecting edges of particles of material produced by the use of a cutting tool.

burrs: In brick making, lumps of brick which have fused together during the process of burning; often misshapen and used for rough walling.

bus bar: A copper strip run on a switch and panel board from which all circuits are tapped; also, a large copper bar to which the main feeders or circuits are connected.

bushing: In plumbing, a screwed piece, or plug, for connecting two pipes of different sizes in the same line. The plug which serves as a reducing adapter is designed to receive a pipe of smaller diameter than that of the pipe into which it is screwed. In electricity, an insulating tube or sleeve which protects a conductor where it passes through a hole in a building or apparatus.

butt: A hinge of any type except a strap hinge.

butt gage: A type of marking gage used to indicate the depths and widths of mortises for butts. See Fig. 97.

butt hinge: A hinge secured to the edge of a door and the face of the jamb it meets when the door is closed, as distinguished from the strap hinge. Usually mortised into the door and jamb. See Fig. 98.

butt joint: Any joint made by fastening two parts together end to end without overlapping. See Fig. 99.

butt stile: In building, the stile of a door to which the butts are attached.

butt strap: In a butt joint, a plate or strap which is fastened to both pieces and covers the joint.

butt weld: A butt weld is a weld where two pieces are butted together and fused.

butt-welded splice: A reinforcing bar splice made by welding the butted ends.

butterfly roof: A roof constructed so as to appear as two shed roofs connected at the lower edges. See Fig. 100.

buttering: In masonry, the process of spreading mortar on the edges of a brick before laying it.

buttering trowel: In masonry, a flat tool similar to but smaller than the brick trowel, used for spreading mortar on a brick before it is placed in position.

button-headed bolt: A bolt having a half-round head either square or smooth underneath the head. See *carriage bolt,* page 87.

buttress: A projecting structure built against a wall or building to give it greater strength and stability. See Fig. 101. See also, *flying buttress,* page 201.

buzz saw: A circular saw.

buzzer: An electric call signal, consisting of a *door bell* with the hammer and gong removed. It operates on the same principle as a vibrating bell.

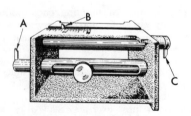

Fig. 97. Butt gage.

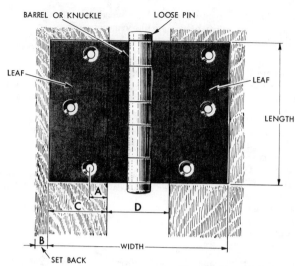

BARREL OR KNUCKLE   LOOSE PIN

LEAF

LEAF

LENGTH

(A) Keep this distance sufficient to prevent splitting
(B) Set back enough to prevent splitting when chiseling
(C) Width of the gain
(D) Maximum clearance when door is open

A

C   D

B

WIDTH

SET BACK

Fig. 98. Butt hinge.

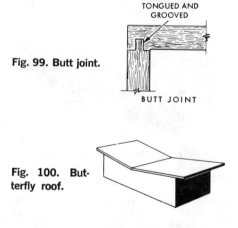

TONGUED AND GROOVED

Fig. 99. Butt joint.

BUTT JOINT

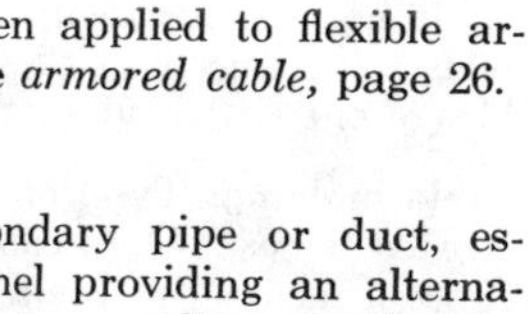

Fig. 100. Butterfly roof.

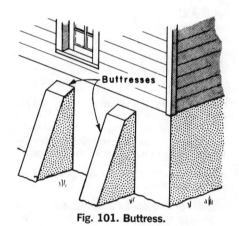

Buttresses

Fig. 101. Buttress.

bx: A term often applied to flexible armored cable. See *armored cable,* page 26.

by-pass: A secondary pipe or duct, especially a channel providing an alternative deflected route, usually controlled by a damper or valve, and connected with a main passage for conveying a fluid around an obstruction.

C

CBR: California Bearing Ratio, the ratio of force required for a given penetration of a compacted soil sample compared to well-graded crushed stone.

CRSI: Concrete Reinforcing Steel Institute.

CSI specifications format: See *Construction Specifications Institute.*

cabin: In construction work, a wooden hut near a building-works area used as an office by the general foreman or by the clerk of works.

cabin hook: A type of fastener, consisting of a small hook and eye, used on the doors of cabinets.

cabinet: Piece of furniture, fitted with shelves or drawers, sometimes both, and enclosed with doors, as a *kitchen cabinet* for holding small kitchen equipment; a case with shelves or drawers used as a depository for various articles, such as jewels or precious stones. The doors for such cases are often made of glass, especially when the cases are used for display purposes. In electricity, an iron box containing fuse, cutouts, or switches.

cabinet burnisher: A tool, variously shaped with a hard, smooth rounded end or surface used to turn over the edge of scrapers, etc.

cabinet file: A thin half-round tool used by cabinetmakers and joiners for smoothing joints.

cabinet finish: In building, a term applied to any interior finish in hardwoods which is varnished or polished like cabinet work.

cabinet latch: Name applied to various kinds of catches. These range from the type of catch used on refrigerator doors to the horizontal spring-and-bolt latch operated by turning a knob, as on kitchen cabinets.

cabinet lock: Any device designed for fastening the doors of cabinets.

cabinet projection: In drawing, a method of representing a solid object as parallel to the observer and the faces perpendicular thereto are drawn at an angle, usually of 45°, the slant edges being drawn to half scale.

cabinet scraper: A tool, made of a flat piece of steel, designed with an edge in such a shape that when the implement is drawn over a surface of wood any irregularities or uneven places will be removed, leaving the surface clean and smooth. The *cabinet scraper* is used for final smoothing of surfaces before sandpapering.

cabinet trim: Hardwood trim for interior finish treated like cabinetwork.

cabinet window: A type of bay window formerly used extensively in shops for the display of goods; also, an imitation of a cabinet window sometimes used in elegant establishments, such as a governor's mansion.

cabinetwork: The work of one who makes fine furniture or beautifully finished woodwork of any kind.

cable: In electricity, a conductor composed of a number of wires twisted together. See Fig. 102.

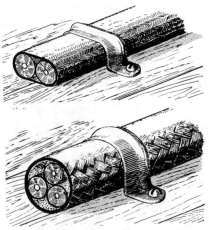

Fig. 102. Cable—nonmetallic sheathed.

cable attachments: Since steel cable will kink if tied in knots, various means are used to attach it to loads. See Fig. 103.

cable box: In electricity, a box which protects the connections or splices joining cables of one circuit to another.

cable molding: Type of molding which is twisted to resemble a cable or rope; sometimes a member in the form of a cable, as a twisted shaft.

cable rack: A frame for supporting electric cables.

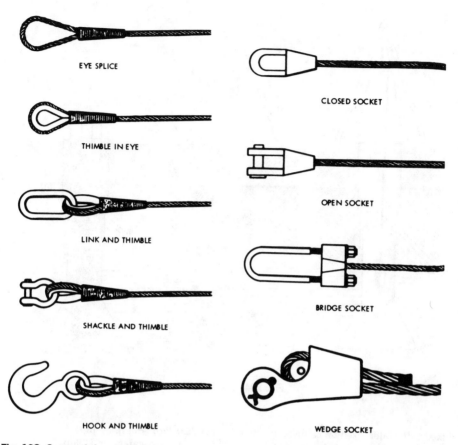

EYE SPLICE

THIMBLE IN EYE

LINK AND THIMBLE

SHACKLE AND THIMBLE

HOOK AND THIMBLE

CLOSED SOCKET

OPEN SOCKET

BRIDGE SOCKET

WEDGE SOCKET

Fig. 103. Some of the attachments commonly used with cables are shown. (Dept. of the Army)

cable splice: In electrical work, a connection between two cables. In construction, the joining of two wire rope cables by interweaving the wire strands. *See splice,* page 419.

cage: In building, any timber construction which encloses another.

caisson (ka'son): A deeply recessed panel sunk in a ceiling or soffit. A watertight box used for surrounding work involved in laying a foundation of any structure below water.

caisson pile: A type of pile which has been made watertight by surrounding it with concrete, as shown in Fig. 104. The diameter of a caisson pile usually is larger than 2 feet; a smaller diameter pile is called a *pier.*

calcareous: Containing calcium carbonate or, less generally, containing the element calcium.

calcimine (kal'si-min): In painting, a white or tinted wash made of whiting and glue

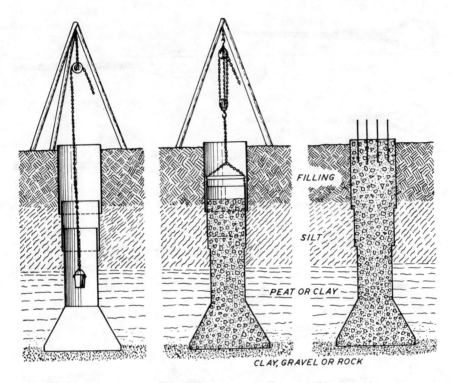

Fig. 104. Caisson piles.

mixed with water, used on ceilings or other plaster as a finish coat. Also spelled *kalsomine*.

calcining: A term applied to the process of producing lime by the heating of limestone to a high temperature. The same as *lime-burning*.

calcium carbonate: A pure variety is found in marble. Chalk, shells, and coral are composed mainly of calcium carbonate. The most abundant variety is found in limestone which, however, is never pure.

calcium chloride: A salt granulate sometimes used with water in mixing concrete and mortar to accelerate the setting time of concrete. See *accelerator*.

caliber (kal'i-ber): The diameter of a round or cylindrical body, especially the interior diameter of a hollow cylinder.

caliduct (kal'i-dukt): A pipe for conveying hot air, hot water, or steam for heating purposes.

caliper: An instrument for measuring circular objects, usually consisting of two legs, often bent, fastened together at the top with a hinge or spring.

calk: In plumbing, to drive oakum, or other material suitable for the purpose, into joints to make them airtight and watertight.

calk joint: In plumbing, a joint packed with *oakum* and finished with molten lead. See Fig. 105.

calked ends: In construction work, the ends of built-in iron ties which have been split and splayed to give more secure anchorage.

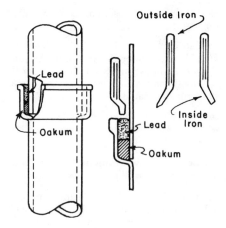

Fig. 105. Calk joint.

calking: The process of driving tarred oakum or other suitable material into seams to make the joints watertight, airtight, or steamtight; to fill the seams of a ship to prevent leaking; to close or fill seams or crevices with rust cement; to make weathertight the joints made by a glass block panel and the wall (see Fig. 286, page 218). Calking compounds are applied with a putty knife or calking gun.

calking compound: A mastic substance designed and used especially to seal the exterior edges of window and door frames against the weather.

calking gun: Tool used to apply waterproofing material.

calking mallet: A specially made wooden mallet used to drive a *calking tool.*

calking tool: A tool used for driving tarred oakum, cotton, and other materials into seams and crevices to make joints watertight and airtight. The *calking tool* is made of steel and in appearance somewhat resembles a chisel. See Fig. 105.

call bell: An electric bell, which calls or summons a person wanted, as an attendant or an operator; also, a bell which sounds an alarm.

calorie: The amount of heat required to raise the temperature of one gram of water one degree centigrade.

calotte (ka-lot′): A small dome in the ceiling of a room to increase the headroom.

calyon: In building, flint or pebble stone used in wall construction.

calyx (ka′liks): The outer covering of a carved flower ornament.

camber: A slight arching or convexity of a timber or beam; the amount of upward curve given to an arched bar, beam, or girder to prevent the member from becoming concave due to its own weight or the weight of the load it must carry.

camber beam: A beam with an arched upper surface or a beam sloping down toward each end to serve as a support for the roof covering on a flat roof.

camber slip: A frame of wood with its upper surface having a slight convex upward curve, upon which the brickwork of a flat arch is laid, so that, after setting, the soffit will be straight. Also called *camber piece.*

cambium (kam′bi-um) layer: In a tree, the sheathlike layer of soft tissue or cells between the solid wood and the bark. The cells of this soft tissue are capable of division and from them new tissues arise to form the wood and bark of the tree. Hence, the new growth takes place in this layer.

came (kam): A slender, suitably grooved rod or bar of cast lead for connecting and holding adjacent panes of glass in a window; used especially in casements and stained-glass windows.

camp ceiling: In architecture, a type of ceiling often used in attic rooms and garrets, in which the two opposite side walls slope in at the top, in line with the rafters, to meet the plane surface of the upper, or middle section, which is horizontal.

campanile: A bell tower, usually detached from the main building, especially a bell tower separated from a church building.

candle: In electricity, one unit of light intensity.

candle power: The illuminating power or the amount of light for a source such as a lamp, when compared to the light of a standard candle.

canopy: A rooflike structure projecting from a wall or supported on pillars, as an ornamental feature; in electricity, the exterior part of a lighting fixture which fits against the wall or ceiling, thus covering the outlet box.

canopy switch: In electricity, a switch fastened to the canopy and used to turn on and off the light in the fixture.

cant: To incline at an angle; to tilt; to set up on a slant, or at an angle; also a molding formed of plain surfaces and angles rather than curves. In building, a term applied to a bay window having three sides, the outer two being splayed from the wall face, commonly known as a *cant bay.*

cant board: A board which slopes, as the boards laid on each side of a valley gutter, to support the sheet lead.

cant brick: In masonry, a purpose-made brick with one side beveled. See *splayed brick,* page 419.

cant hook: A stout, wooden lever with an adjustable steel or iron hook near the lever end. The *cant hook* is used to turn round or square timbers. See Fig. 106.

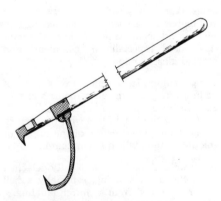

Fig. 106. The cant hook is used to handle rough timber on land.

cant molding: A beveled molding. See *canting strip.*

cant strip: A beveled piece of lumber used at gable ends under shingles or at the junction of the house and a flat deck under the roofing. It is used to establish the correct slant for the shingles.

canted column: In architecture, a column which has faceted sides instead of curved flutes.

canted wall: A wall built at an angle to the face of another wall.

cantilever: A projecting beam supported only at one end; a large bracket, usually ornamental, for supporting a balcony or cornice; two bracketlike arms projecting toward each other from opposite piers or backs to form the span of a bridge, making what is known as a *cantilever bridge.*

cantilever joists: Short joists used to support a projecting balcony or cornice where the *overhang* is parallel to the second-story joists. *Cantilever joists* are also used to support a *bay window* which has no supporting foundation. See Fig. 107.

canting strip: A projecting molding near the bottom of a wall to direct rain water away from the foundation wall; in frame buildings, the same as a *water table.*

cantling: In masonry, the lower of two courses of burnt brick enclosing a clamp for firing brick.

canton: In building, a pilaster or *quoin* which forms a salient corner projecting from a wall face.

canvas walls: Various grades of canvas are pasted over plastered walls, to serve as a base for paint application and wallpaper.

cap: The top parts of columns, doors, and moldings; the coping of a wall; a cornice over a door; the lintel over a door or window frame; a top piece. In plumbing, a threaded fitting used to close a pipe end.

cap iron: The stiffening plate screwed to the cutting iron of a jack plane. Sometimes called *back iron.*

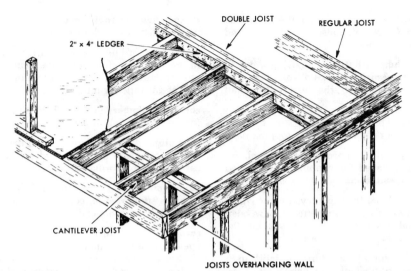

DOUBLE JOIST

REGULAR JOIST

2" x 4" LEDGER

CANTILEVER JOIST

JOISTS OVERHANGING WALL

Fig. 107. Cantilever joists rest on the wall plate and are fastened to a double joist and ledger.

cap stone: Stone used for the crown or top part of a structure.

Cape Cod style: This style is derived from the one-story or story-and-a-half cottages which were built primarily in the Cape Cod district of Massachusetts. See Fig. 108 for an example of the Cape Cod house. The principal characteristics are the rather steeply pitched roof with gable ends and with the eave line down low near the ground at about the level of the first-floor ceiling.

capillary action: In hardened concrete or mortar, the seepage of moisture through the material due to incomplete or faulty surface finishing. Same as *capillary flow.*

capillary water: Water capable of moving in any direction in the soil by capillary action.

capital: The upper part of a column, pilaster, or pier; in Greek architecture, three distinct types of capitals were used—*Corinthian, Doric,* and *Ionic;* in Roman archi-

Fig. 108. Cape Cod style. (Samuel Cabot, Inc.)

tecture, five types were used, the three used by the Greeks and also the *Tuscan* and *Composite* types.

capped butt: A butt hinge having a cap to cover the securing screws of each leaf. The cap is fastened to the butt with small screws.

capping: The uppermost part on top of a piece of work; a crowning or topping part.

capping brick: In masonry, brick which are specially shaped for capping and exposed top of a wall. Same as *coping brick.*

capping plane: In carpentry, a plane which gives a slightly rounding effect to a wooden handrail; used especially for working the upper surface of staircase rails.

caracole (kar'a-kol): Staircase built in a spiral form; a winding or helical staircase.

carbolineum (kar-bo-lin'e-um): A name applied to an oily, dark-brown substance consisting of antracene oil (obtained from coal tar) and zinc chloride. It is used as a preservative for wood or timber.

carbon dioxide: Odorless gas present in the air.

carborundum: An abrasive made from a combination of carbon and silicon and sometimes used instead of emery.

carborundum cloth or paper: An abrasive cloth or paper made by covering the material with powdered carborundum held in place by some adhesive such as glue.

carborundum stone: An abrasive stone, made of carborundum, used for sharpening tools such as plane bits and chisels.

carcase: The frame of a house; the unfinished framework, or skeleton, of a building or ship. Also *carcass.*

carcass floor or roof: In architecture, the uncovered framework of a floor or roof.

carcassing: In building, the work involved in erecting or constructing the framework of a structure; also, the layout and installation of gas pipe for a building.

carcassing timber: The structural members for the framework of a building.

card plate: A metal plate used on drawers of cabinets or on doors to hold a label or card carrying information.

carnarvon arch: In architecture, a lintel which is supported on corbels or is shaped into shoulders at its end.

carol: In architecture, a seat built into the opening of a bay window; also, a small inclosure in a cloister built against a window on the inner side and serving as a study. See *bay stall,* page 42.

carpenter: A craftsman who builds with wood; a worker who builds with the heavier forms of wood, as with lumber in the structural work of a building.

carpenter's finish: A term applied to practically all finish work performed by a carpenter, except that classed as *rough finish.* It includes casings, laying finish flooring, building stairs, fitting and hanging doors, fitting and setting windows, putting on baseboards, and installing all other similar finish material.

carpenter's level: A bubble level mounted in a metal or wooden beam. Used in leveling vertical or horizontal surfaces. See Fig. 109.

carpentry: Work which is performed by a carftsman in cutting, framing, and joining pieces of timber in the construction of ships, houses, and other structures of a similar character.

Fig. 109. Levels are available in either aluminum or wood.

carpet strip: A piece beneath a door attached to the floor.

carport: A garage, built into a house, which has a roof but only one or two side walls. Generally found in mild climates. See Fig. 110.

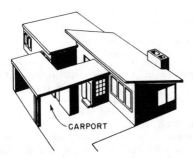

Fig. 110. Carport.

carrell (kar'el): A small room designed as a place for individual study or reading in the stack room of a library.

carriage: The support for the steps of a wooden stairway; these supports may be either of wood or steel.

carriage bolt: A round-headed bolt, usually square, directly underneath the head to prevent the bolt from turning while the nut is put on or taken off. Same as *buttonheaded bolt.* See *bolts,* Fig. 72, page 59.

carriage piece: A wood joist giving intermediate support between the wall string and outer string to the treads of wide wooden staircases. Same as *roughstring.*

carrying capacity: In electricity, the amount of current a wire can carry without becoming overheated.

cartoon (kar-toon): Large design made on strong paper to serve as a model, as of a fresco; a design made on paper to be transferred to the fresh plaster of a wall to be painted in fresco later.

cartridge fuse: In electricity, a fuse enclosed in an insulating tube in order to confine the arc or vapor when the fuse blows.

carving: Ornaments on furniture or woodwork executed by cutting or chiseling designs on a surface.

case: The framework of the structure in building construction. In masonry, the external facings of a building when these are of better material than the backing.

case bay: In carpentry, the space between two binders under a floor. See *binder,* page 47.

cased: A building term used to describe a structural member or part covered with a different material, usually of a better quality.

cased opening: Any opening finished with jambs and trim, but without doors.

casement: Window hinged to open about one of its vertical edges. See *casement window,* Fig. 111.

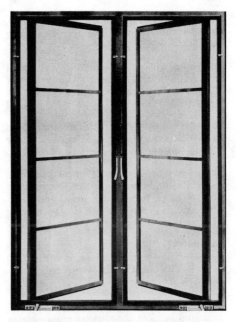

Fig. 111. Metal casements provide maximum ventilation and light. (Republic Steel Corp.)

casement adjuster: A handle or rod for adjusting and securing the sash of a casement or French window.

casement frames and sash: Frames of wood or metal enclosing part or all of the sash which may be opened by means of hinges attached to the vertical edges. See Fig. 111.

casement molding: Shallow concave molding similar to a *cavetto* (see Fig. 114) or *scotia* (see Fig. 509, page 390.)

casement window: Window with sash that open on hinges; a window sash made to open by turning on hinges attached to its vertical edge. See Fig. 111.

casement-window fastener: Catch for securing a casement or French window.

casing: The framework around a window or door. See Fig. 190, page 150. Also the finished lumber around a post or beam.

casing knife: In building, a knife used by paper hangers for trimming wallpaper at baseboards and around window and door frames.

casing nail: A wire nail with a flaring head, used for outside finish and also for nailing flooring.

cassoon or caisson (ka'son): A sunken panel in a ceiling, vault, or soffit, usually one of many sunken panels forming a continuous pattern.

cast: An impression or mold; an impression taken in wax, plaster of Paris, or other plastic substance.

caster: A wheel, or set of wheels, set in a swivel frame attached to the feet or base of a piece of furniture, trucks, and portable machines. Casters help in the moving of furniture without injury to the floor.

cast-in-place: Mortar or concrete which is deposited in the place where it is required to harden as part of the structure, as opposed to precast concrete.

cast-iron pipes: In plumbing, pipes made of cast iron to meet the various requirements of a sewerage or drainage system. Typical cast-iron pipes appear in Fig. 112.

casting plaster: This is a fine plaster used to give smoother castings for plaques and art statuary. It is highly plastic and has great surface hardness and strength. Only water is needed for application.

catalyst additive gun: The catalyst additive gun is used by plasterers for special veneers where a catalyst is required. (Note: A catalyst is used to accelerate the set of the material.)

catch: A spring bolt used to fasten or secure a door when it is shut.

catch basin: A cistern, or depression, at the point where a gutter discharges into a sewer to catch any object which would not readily pass through the sewer; a reservoir to catch and retain surface drainage; a receptacle at an opening into a sewer to retain any matter which would not easily pass through the sewer; a trap to catch and hold fats, grease, and oil from kitchen sinks to prevent them from passing into the sewer. See Fig. 113.

catch bolt: Door lock with a spring-loaded bolt which normally is extended in the locking position but which automatically and momentarily is retracted in the process of shutting the door.

catenarian arch: In building, an arch which has the shape of an inverted catenary or hanging chain. See *catenary*.

catenary (kat'e-nar-i): The shape assumed by a perfectly flexible slender cord suspended at its ends from two supports in equilibrium under given forces.

catherine-wheel window: A circular window with mullions radiating from the center, representing a wheel with spikes projecting from the rim; also called a *rose window* or a *wheel window*.

catwalk: A narrow passageway for pedestrians along a bridge.

caul: A tool used in forming veneer to the shape of a curved surface.

caulking: See *calking*, page 83.

cavetto: Quarter round, concave molding; a concave ornamental molding opposed in

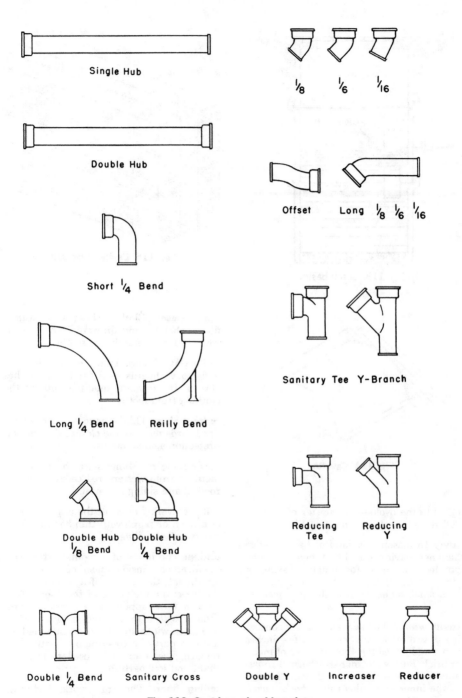

Single Hub

⅛ ⅙ 1/16

Double Hub

Offset   Long ⅛ ⅙ 1/16

Short ¼ Bend

Long ¼ Bend   Reilly Bend

Sanitary Tee Y-Branch

Double Hub   Double Hub
⅛ Bend   ¼ Bend

Reducing   Reducing
Tee   Y

Double ¼ Bend   Sanitary Cross   Double Y   Increaser   Reducer

Fig. 112. Cast-iron plumbing pipes.

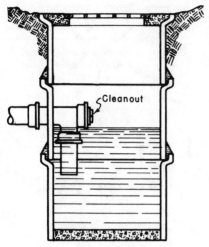

Fig. 113. Catch basin.

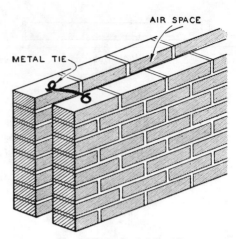

Fig. 115. Cavity brick wall.

Fig. 114. Cavetto.

cedar closet: Clothes closet with lining, floors, shelves, and drawers of red cedar, whose odor is offensive to moths.

cedar closet-lining: Thin red-cedar tongue-and-groove boards used for lining clothes closets. Its aromatic qualities protect the clothing from moths.

cedar lining: Thin tongue-and-groove cedar boards used to line clothes closets as a protection against moths.

cedar shingles: Shingles which are manufactured from western red cedar; used for roofing and siding material.

ceil: To overlay or cover the upper surface of a room or porch with thin boards. Commonly called *ceiling*.

effect to the ovolo—the quarter of a circle called the quarter round. See Fig. 114.

cavil: In masonry, a kind of heavy sledge hammer having one blunt end and one pointed end, used for rough dressing of stone at the quarry; a term also applied to a small stone ax resembling a *jedding ax*.

cavity wall: A hollow wall, usually consisting of two brick walls erected a few inches apart and joined together with ties of metal or brick. Such walls increase thermal resistance and prevent rain from driving through to the inner face. Also called *hollow wall*. See Fig. 115.

ceiling: The lining of a room, particularly the overhead inside finish of a room or apartment; the surface of a room opposite the floor; the underside of the floor above. Also, a term applied to a narrow board, usually with a tongue-and-groove, worked to a given width and thickness intended for use as a part of a covering or sheathing to replace plaster or to be used to frame a slight and low partition.

ceiling floor: The framework, including joists and covering, which supports the overhead interior lining of a room, when the ceiling is framed separately from the floor of the story above it.

ceiling joists: The joists which support the overhead interior lining of a room. In some cases, ceiling joists serve as floor joists for a story above. In other cases, the floor of an upper story is supported by a separate set of joists.

ceiling light: Any light fixture attached to the ceiling of a room; a term commonly applied to an electric light.

ceiling outlet: In electric wiring, an outlet placed in the ceiling of a room.

cellar: A room or set of rooms partly or wholly below the surface of the ground, used especially for keeping provisions and other stores; a room beneath the main portion of a building. See *basement,* page 39.

cellar frames and sash: Window frames of wood or metal, usually having two or three lights, designed for use in basement openings. Same as *basement frames and sash.*

cellulose: The principal component of wood; it forms the framework of the wood cells.

cement: In building, a material for binding other material or articles together, usually plastic at the time of application but hardens when in place; any substance which causes bodies to adhere to one another, such as Portland cement, stucco, and natural cements; also, mortar or plaster of Paris.

cement-base waterproof coating: Compounds which seal the pores in basement walls or floors, providing protection against water pressure and dampness in the ground. These compounds usually come in a cement base, but some can be purchased in paste, powder, or liquid form, to be mixed with cement before application.

cement-coated nails: Nails which have been covered with cement by a special process; used principally in the laying of parquetry floors in the building industry.

cement colors: A special mineral pigment used for coloring cement used for floors. In addition to the natural coloring pigment

obtained from mineral oxides, there are manufactured pigments produced especially for cement work.

cement gun: A mechanical device used for spraying fine concrete or cement mortar by means of pneumatic pressure.

cement joggle: In masonry construction, a key which is formed between adjacent stones by running mortar into a square-section channel which is cut equally into each of the adjoining faces, thus preventing relative movement of the faces.

cement mortar: A building material composed of Portland cement, sand, and water.

cement paste: A mixture of cement and water which fills the spaces between the aggregates and holds them together to form a solid mass.

cement plaster: Gypsum plaster which is prepared to be used, with the addition of sand, as a base-coat plaster.

cement stucco dash brush: This brush is used to give a stucco effect to a plaster wall. The brush is dipped into the material and it is thrown onto the surface with varying techniques. See Fig. 116.

Fig. 116. Cement stucco dash brush.

cementation: A term applied to the setting of a plastic; also, the process of uniting and binding articles or materials together so they will adhere firmly, by using an adhesive such as asphalt or Portland cement. See *grouting,* page 226.

cementing trowel: A trowel similar to the plasterer's trowel, but often of a heavier gauge stock.

center: A fixed point about which the radius of a circle, or of an arc, revolves; the point about which any revolving body rotates or revolves, as the middle, or center, of activity.

center line: A broken line, usually indicated by a dot and dash, showing the center of an object and providing a convenient line from which to lay off measurements.

center matched: Tongue-and-groove lumber with the tongue and groove at the center of the piece rather than offset as in standard matched.

center punch: A steel hand tool, ground to a conical point of about 90°, used to make a small dent in a metal surface, the purpose of which is to establish the starting point for a drilled hole. See Fig. 455, page 351.

center stringer: The center horse in a flight of stairs. The same as carriage or roughstring.

center to center: In taking measurements, a term meaning on *center* as in the spacing of joists, studding, or other structural parts.

centering: The frame on which a brick or stone arch is turned; the false work over which an arch is formed. In concrete work, the *centering* is known as the *frames*.

centerpiece: An ornament placed in the middle of a ceiling; also, an ornament for the middle of a table.

centers for arches: Temporary structures, consisting of parallel frames or ribs, usually of timbers or planks placed at convenient distances apart, for supporting the *voussoirs* during the construction of masonry arches. A *center* must be curved on the outside to a line parallel to that of the soffit of the arch.

centigrade: Thermometer whose scale at the freezing point is zero and one-hundred at the boiling point of water.

centimeter: A measure of length in the metric system equal to the one-hundredth part of a meter or .3937 inch.

central mixed concrete: Ready mix concrete which is completely mixed in a stationary mixer and then delivered to the site in agitating or fixed trucks.

ceramic mosaic: A collective term applied to floor tiles which are marketed in sheet units. The individual units are spaced properly and mounted on sheets of paper. The tiles are produced in a variety of sizes, shapes, and colors used extensively for shower-bath floors; also for regular bathroom floors.

ceramic tile: A thin, flat piece of fired clay, usually square. These pieces of clay are attached to walls, floors, or counter tops with cement or other adhesives, creating durable, decorative, and dirt-resistant surfaces. Tiles may be plastic process (formed while clay is wet) or dust-pressed process (compressed clay powder). They may be glazed (vitrified coating); unglazed (natural surface); nonvitrified, semivitrified, and vitreous (porous, semiporous, or relatively nonporous).

ceramic veneer: A fired, glazed-clay veneer for facing buildings; made in sheets, moldings, corners, and varied shapes. There is also a spray-on wall finish with ceramic or vitreous surface qualities that is resistant to temperature, acid, and alkali.

cesspipe: In plumbing, a discharge pipe for waste water, especially from a cesspool.

cesspool: In plumbing, a pit or cistern in a drain for the reception or detention of sewage. Also, a small square wooden box, lined with lead, which serves as a cistern in the gutter of a parapet at a point where the roof water is discharged into a down pipe.

chafe: To wear away as by friction.

chain: In construction, a flexible linkage of metal, used for its strength in tension for hoisting or transmission of force or power. Several widely varying types are used in construction.

chain bolt: A bolt designed to be attached to the top of a door, with a chain attached for actuating the bolt against the pressure of a spring which holds the bolt in a locking position.

chain bond: In masonry, the bonding to-gether of a stone wall by the use of a built-in chain or iron bar.

chain door-fastener: A substantially built chain which has one end secured to a plate which is to be attached to the opening edge of a door. The other end of the chain car-ries a hook or ball to be inserted in a slid-ing slot only a few inches; the chain is re-leased by lifting the ball or hook from the slide. See Fig. 117.

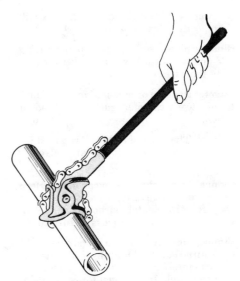

Fig. 117. Chain door fastener.

Fig. 118. Chain tongs.

chain-pipe vise: When fitting steam pipes, a portable vise which utilizes a heavy chain to fasten the pipe in the jaw.

chain timbers: In building construction, bond timbers, as the strengthening timbers used in building brick walls which are cir-cular in plan.

chain tongs: In plumbing or electrical wir-ing a pipe or conduit turning appliance consisting of a heavy bar with sharp teeth near one end, which are held against the pipe by a chain wrapped around the pipe and secured to the bar. See Fig. 118.

chain wrench: A pipe wrench used in close quarters; chain is provided for ratchet-like action.

chair rail: A wooden molding around the wall of a room at chair-back height to af-ford protection against damage when chairs are pushed back or rubbed against the wall.

chalk line: Length of string which has been thoroughly filled with chalk dust, used to strike a straight guide line on work, such as on boards or shingles. The chalked string is held taut close to the work, by nails at each end of the string, which is

then plucked with the fingers to strike a line; also, the line which is made with a chalking line. See Figs. 119 and 445, page 341.

chalking: A painting term defining a com-mon effect of weathering on paint surfaces in which the surface oils are destroyed, leaving loose color particles or powder.

chamfer: A groove, or channel, as in a piece of wood; a bevel edge; an oblique surface formed by cutting away an edge or corner of a piece of timber or stone. Any piece of work that is cut off at the edges at a 45 degree angle so that two faces meeting form a right angle are said to be *cham-fered*.

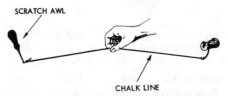

SCRATCH AWL

CHALK LINE

Fig. 119. The chalk line is used for long straight lines. Be sure to snap the taut line square to the surface. (Stanley Works)

93

chamfer bit: A bit so formed that it will chamfer the edges of a hole.

chamfer plane: A carpenter's plane having a V-grooved bottom which is used for beveling the edges of woodwork.

chamfer stop: An ornamental feature which terminates a chamfer, such as a bead or trefoil.

chancel: That part of a church reserved for the clergy, including the altar and choir proper.

channel: A concave groove cut in a surface as a decorative feature; a grooved molding used for ornamental purposes; a decorative concave groove on parts of furniture.

channel iron: A rolled iron bar with the sides turned upward forming a rim, making the *channel iron* appear like a channel-shaped trough. In sectional form, the *channel iron* appears like a rectangular box with the top and two ends omitted. See Fig. 120.

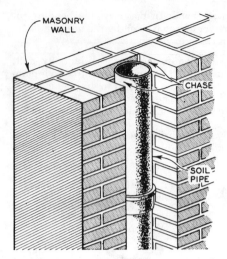

Fig. 121. Chase in masonry wall.

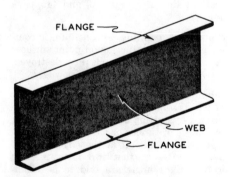

Fig. 120. Channel iron.

chaplet: In architecture, a small ornamental molding carved into beads or other decorative designs; an ornamental *astragal.*

chaptrel: The capital of a column, or pier, which receives an arch, in Gothic architecture; an *impost*. See *column,* Fig. 137, page 108.

charging: Putting materials into the mixer.

chase: In masonry, a groove or channel cut in the face of a brick wall to allow space for receiving pipes, ducts, or conduits; in building, a trench dug to accommodate a drainpipe; also, a recess in a masonry wall to provide space for pipes and ducts. See *wall chase,* Fig. 121, page 475.

chase wedge: In plumbing, a wooden wedge fastened to a handle, used for bossing sheet lead. See *bossing,* page 60.

chaser: A threading tool, many toothed or with a single cutting edge, shaped especially for cutting or finishing external or internal screw threads or specified pitch and standard. Usually used on work revolving in a lathe.

chasing: The decorative features produced by grooving or indenting metal.

chatter: In carpentry or other mechanical work the operation of a cutting tool improperly so that it cuts and skips intermittently.

check: An ornamental design of inlaid squares; a small hairlike split, usually occurring only in finely figured crotches and burls, caused chiefly by strain in the seasoning of the wood. In highly figured veneers, these checks add beauty and character to the figure and are not considered defects.

Also, a blemish in wood or in a board caused by the separation of wood tissues during seasoning, usually across the rings of annual growth. See Fig. 122. *Surface check* occurs on a surface of a piece. *End check* occurs on an end of a piece. *Through check* extends from one surface through the piece to the opposite surface or to an adjoining surface.

check list: A detail list of the elements of a particular construction job which is used to insure that no details are overlooked in preparing the estimate.

check rail: The middle horizontal member of a double-hung window, forming the lower rail of the top sash and the top rail of the lower sash.

check stop: A molding for holding the bottom sash of a double-hung window in place in a window frame.

check valve: In plumbing, a valve preventing the backflow of water or other liquid by automatically closing.

checkerboard placement: The practice of planning a concrete job so that adjacent slabs of concrete can be placed at separate times. This is handy when special colors or finishes are used and creates a control joint without sawing or jointing.

checkerwork: Any work arranged like or resembling a checkerboard in pattern. Sometimes spelled *chequerwork*.

checking: Cracks that appear in many exterior paint coatings. In time they may penetrate entirely through the coating.

checking of wood: Cracks or blemishes in timber due to uneven seasoning. *Checking* may be caused by the shrinking of the wood more rapidly around the circumference of a log than along the radial lines. See Fig. 122.

cheek: One of the solid parts on each side of a mortise; also, one of the parts removed on either side of a timber to form a tenon; one of the sides of an opening, as of a door or window opening.

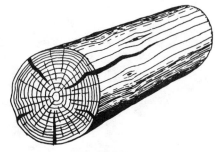

Fig. 122. Check.

cheek cut: A beveled cut on the edge of a hip, jack, valley, or cripple rafter; also, a side cut on any of such rafters.

cheek of hammer: The flat side of the *head* of a claw hammer. See Fig. 127, page 101.

chemical plaster: A type of plastering material which has been patented by the manufacturers, who produce the material by a secret process. Same as *patented plaster*.

cheneau (sha'no): A cresting or ornamental motive on the upper part of a cornice. The gutter and also the projecting pipe to carry water from the gutter.

chequer: A decorative feature used in furniture making, consisting of an ornamental arrangement of squares; much used in inlay work.

chest pull: Any device, such as a knob or handle, used as a means for pulling open a drawer or door of a chest, box, or any similar container.

chevron: The meeting place of rafters at the ridge of a gable roof; a zigzag pattern used as an ornamentation in Romanesque architecture.

chimes: In building, a mechanical device used in place of a *doorbell*. Instead of a ringing noise, the *chimes* sound a musical note or tune. Also called *door chimes*.

chimney: That part of a building which contains the flues for drawing off smoke or fumes from stoves, furnaces, fireplaces, or some other source of smoke and gas. See Fig. 123.

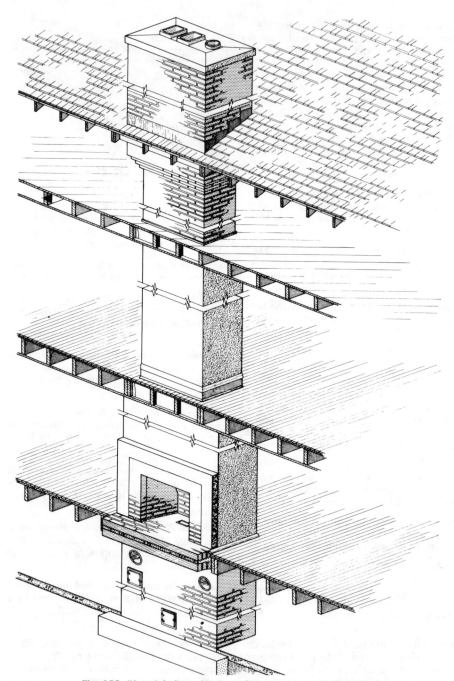

Fig. 123. Pictorial view of a three-flue chimney with fireplace.

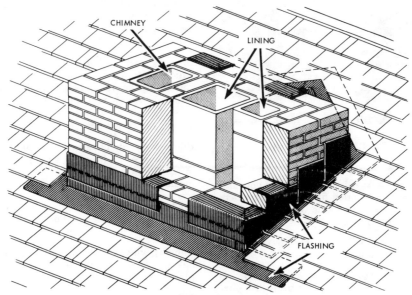

Fig. 124. Method of flashing chimney.

chimney arch: The arch above a fireplace opening.

chimney back: That portion of the wall of a chimney at the back of a fireplace. See *fireback,* page 187.

chimney bar: An iron bar supporting the masonry of the arch above a fireplace opening.

chimney blocks: Cement blocks designed so as to form a continuous round flue when placed in position one on top of another.

chimney board: Fender before an open fire, as an open fireplace.

chimney bond: In masonry, a form of bond commonly used for the internal division walls of domestic chimneys as well as for the outer walls. The surface of this type of wall is made up of stretchers which break joints at the center with a header on each alternate course at the corner.

chimney breast: That part of a chimney which projects from a wall where the chimney passes through a room. When the chimney is a part of a fireplace, usually the breast of the chimney is built much wider than the chimney itself to provide for a mantel or to improve the appearance of the room.

chimney cap: A cover for a chimney; a device especially designed to improve the draft by presenting an exit opening to leeward.

chimney cricket: A small false roof built on the main roof behind a chimney to throw off rain water and prevent the roof's leaking at this point.

chimney flashing: Any kind of metal or composition material placed around a chimney shaft to protect the roof against moisture from rain water or snow. See Fig. 124.

chimney head: The upper end or top of a chimney.

chimney hood: A covering for a chimney to make it more ornamental; also, to prevent rain water from entering the flues. The design of the *hood* may be circular in form or it may be flat. See Fig. 125.

97

WITHE

Fig. 125. Chimney hoods.

chimney hook: A hook for holding pots and kettles over an open fire, as in a fireplace; also, a hook at the side of a chimney for holding the tongs.

chimney jambs: The upright pieces or sides of a fireplace opening.

chimney lining: Rectangular or round tiles placed within a chimney for protective purpose. The glazed surface of the tile provides resistance to the deteriorating effects of smoke and gas fumes. See Fig. 124.

chimney lug: A metal pole or bar on which a kettle or pot is hung over an open fire, as in a fireplace. See *chimney hook.*

chimney piece: Any ornamental construction placed over or around the opening of a fireplace; often, a mantel or shelf over a fireplace.

chimney pot: Pipe of tile or sheet metal placed at the top or head of a chimney to improve the draft and carry off the smoke. See Fig. 126.

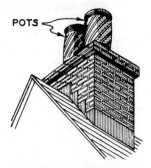

POTS

Fig. 126. Chimney pot.

chimney shaft: That part of a chimney which extends above a roof; also, a chimney, such as a factory chimney, which stands isolated.

chimney stack: A flue or shaft of a chimney which contains more than one flue, often containing several flues, especially a shaft rising above a roof; a term sometimes loosely applied to a *chimney shaft* containing only one flue.

chimney throat: That part of a chimney directly above the fireplace where the walls of the flue are brought close together as a means of increasing the draft.

chimney tun: A chimney stack, or the unit containing a number of flues grouped together.

chimney wing: One of the sides of a chimney where it is narrowed above the fireplace.

China cupboard: A dining-room fixture, often built in, for holding plates, glassware, silverware, tablecloths, and napkins.

chink: In building, a crack or small fissure in a wall surface.

chip: In structural work, a small piece of stone, wood, or other material cut off from a larger piece by means of a quick blow with a cutting instrument such as a *chip ax.*

chip ax: Small, sharp cutting tool used in the building trades for cutting and shaping structural stone or timbers.

chipping: A process of cutting off small pieces of metal or wood with a cold chisel and a hammer.

chisel: A cutting tool with a wide variety of uses. The cutting edge on the end of the tool usually is transverse to the axis. The cutting principle of the *chisel* is the same as that of the wedge. See: *wood chisel,* page 487.

choker: A sling hitch that is self-tightening.

chop inlay: A type of inlay used in furniture making in early times when ornamental pieces were fitted into a solid surface.

chord: In building construction, the bottom beam of any truss; in a Howe truss, where two parallel beams are placed one above the other, both beams are called *chords*. See: *truss,* page 464.

chord of an arch: The span of an arch.

chuck: Any contrivance for holding work, as a *vise chuck;* also, a part of a tool for holding, as that portion of a brace which holds the bit. See *brace,* Fig. 82, page 65.

churn molding: A zigzag molding often used in early Norman architecture.

chutes: Made of metal, wood, or rubber and used to place fresh concrete in hard-to-reach areas such as in tall structural forms or over distances where the transporting vehicle can't approach close enough.

ciborium (si-bo'ri-um): A vaulted canopy, resembling an inverted cup, supported on four columns, and covering a high altar; usually standing free.

cincture: An encircling fillet which separates the shaft of a column from the capital or from the base; a decorative feature in the form of a ring or girdle at the top and bottom of a column between the shaft and the capital and between the shaft and the pedestal.

cinder blocks: Building blocks in which the principal materials are cement and cinders.

cinder concrete: A type of concrete made from Portland cement mixed with clean, well-burned coal cinders which are used as coarse aggregate.

cinder fill: A fill of cinders, from three to six inches deep, under a basement floor as an aid in keeping the basement dry; also, a fill of cinders outside of a basement wall to a depth of twelve inches over drain tile to facilitate drainage. Sometimes pebble gravel is used instead of cinders.

cinders: The residue which remains after any material, such as coal, has been burned; the *clinkers* which remain after coal is burned; slag from a metal furnace; fragments of unburned lava from a volcano.

cinquefoil (sink'foil): A decorative design; an ornament having five cusps sometimes in the form of a circle and sometimes forming the cusping of a head.

circuit: In electricity, the path taken by an electrical current in flowing through a conductor (two or more wires) from one terminal of the source of supply to the other.

circuit breaker: A switch which stops the flow of current by opening the circuit automatically when more electricity flows through the circuit than the circuit is capable of carrying. Resetting may be either automatic or manual.

circuit vent: In plumbing, the extension of a horizontal soil pipe beyond the connection at which liquid wastes enter the soil or waste pipe. See *loop vent,* page 273.

circular and angular measure: A standard measure expressed in degrees, minutes, and seconds, as follows:

$$
\begin{aligned}
60 \text{ seconds } ('') &= 1 \text{ minute } (') \\
60 \text{ minutes } &= 1 \text{ degree } (°) \\
90 \text{ degrees } &= 1 \text{ quadrant} \\
4 \text{ quadrants } &= 1 \text{ circle or circumference}
\end{aligned}
$$

circular arch: An arch having a radius which measures one-half of the length of the span. See *elliptical arch,* page 172.

circular mil: The area of a circle one mil in diameter or one-thousandth of an inch in diameter. The area in a circular mil equals the diameter in mils squared or multiplied by itself. The *circular mil* is used as a unit in measuring the cross section of wire.

circular saw: A saw with teeth spaced around the edge of a circular plate, or disc, which is rotated at high speed upon a central axis, or spindle, used for cutting lumber or sawing logs.

circular stairs: A stairway having steps which, in plan, radiate from a common center; a *winding stair.* See Fig. 563, page 426.

circulation: In planning the passage from one room to another; in heating the movement of air.

circumference: The perimeter of a circle; a line that bounds a circular plane surface.

circumscribe: The process of drawing a line to enclose certain portions of an object, figure, or plane; to encircle; to draw boundary lines; to enclose within certain limits.

cistern: An artificial reservoir or tank, often underground, for the storing of rain water collected from a roof.

Civil Rights Act of 1964: This act makes unlawful the practice of discrimination, in matters of employment, education, housing, and voting, against any individual because of his race, color, religion, sex, or national origin. The Civil Rights Act requires affirmative nondiscriminatory selection of apprentices by industry joint committees.

clamp: A device for holding portions of work together, either wood or metal; an appliance with opposing sides or parts that may be screwed together to hold objects or parts of objects together firmly.

clamp nail: An invisible fastening for miter and butt joints. A saw cut is made in each of the pieces of wood to be joined. Glue is applied where the pieces join. The pieces are then held together and the clamp nail driven in place. The flanges on the nail draw the wood together, making a tight joint. See Fig. 373, page 282.

clamping plate: A timber connector. See Fig. 595, page 455.

clamping screw: A screw used in a clamp; a screw used to hold pieces of work together in a clamp.

clamshell: Two similar pieces hinged together to form a gate.

clapboard: A long, thin board, graduating in thickness from one end to the other, used for siding, the thick end overlapping the thin portion of the board.

clapboard gage: A type of siding gage, used for spacing courses when applying siding.

clarke beam: A type of built-up wood beam, formed of two or more joists bolted together, and reinforced with short diagonal pieces placed solidly along the length of the beam on each side. See Fig. 94, page 76.

classic molding: A type of molding similar to that used in classic orders of architecture.

classical: Pertaining to a style of architecture modeled upon principles embodied in the early types of Greek and Roman structures.

claw: Anything which resembles an animal's claw, as the forked end of the head of a hammer used for drawing nails from a board. See Fig. 127.

claw bar: A kind of *crowbar* or lever having one end bent and split so as to form claws which are used for pulling nails, especially large nails and spikes. Also called *wrecking bar* or *pinch bar*. See Fig. 425, page 325.

claw hammer: A carpenter's tool having one end curved and split for use in drawing nails by giving leverage under the heads. See Fig. 127.

claw hatchet: A carpenter's hatchet with a notch on one side of the blade for use in pulling out nails. A kind of *shingling hatchet,* see Fig. 307, page 233.

claw of hammer: The part of the head of a carpenter's hammer which is bent and split so it can be used to extract nails from wood. See Fig. 127.

claw plate: A timber connector. See Fig. 595, page 455.

claw tool: A stonemason's tool having teeth or claws; used for dressing soft stone. Sometimes called *tooth chisel.*

clay: In masonry, a common type of soil which is compact and brittle when dry but plastic when wet; used in the manufacture of brick.

clay mill: A mill where clay is mixed and tempered; a *pugmill.*

clay shale: Clay which has a laminated structure, used as one of the ingredients in making clay tile.

cleanout: A unit with removable plate or plug affording access into plumbing or other drainage pipes for cleaning out ex-

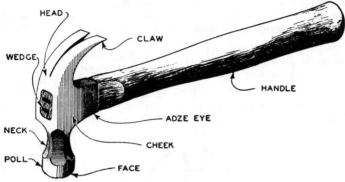

HEAD

CLAW

WEDGE

HANDLE

ADZE EYE

NECK

CHEEK

POLL

FACE

Fig. 127. Claw hammer.

traneous material. See Figs. 128 and 113, page 90. Also, the pocket or door at the foot of a chimney by means of which soot and ashes may be removed. See Fig. 245, page 188. In masonry, an opening in the forms for removal of refuse; they are closed before the concrete is placed.

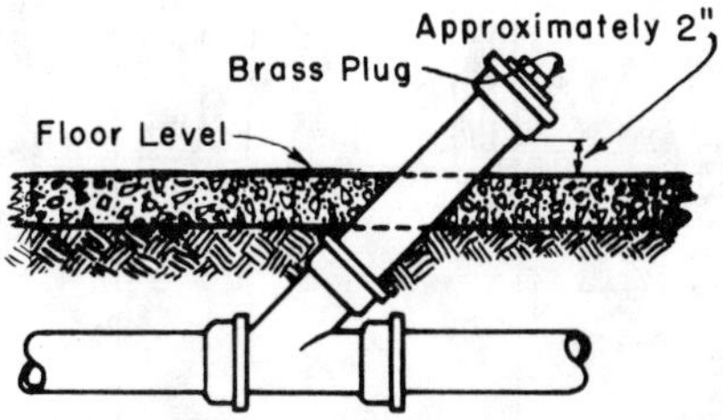

Approximately 2"

Brass Plug

Floor Level

Fig. 128. Cleanout.

cleanout door: A door and frame of cast iron placed near the base of smoke flues and ash pits to allow for the removal of ashes. See Fig. 245, page 188.

cleanout for house drain: A branch pipe which leads from the main drain pipe through the floor of a building. The cleanout pipe is equipped with a removable brass cover, making access to the main pipe possible when it becomes necessary to remove waste material which clogs the system. See Fig. 128.

clear angle of vision: An area which the human eye perceives without any distortion. This approximate angle, 30°, originates from the *station point,* extends to, and includes the object. The angle will govern the plan location of the station point.

clear lumber: Any lumber which is free of knots or other blemishes.

clearance: The amount of space between the cutting edge of a tool and the vertical position of the surface of the work.

clearstory or clerestory (kler'sto-ri): The portion of a multistory room extending above the single-story height. It contains windows for lighting and ventilation purposes. A style of architecture especially used in church buildings or similar structures.

cleat: A strip of wood or metal fastened across a door or other object to give it additional strength; a strip of wood or other material nailed to a wall usually for the purpose of supporting some object or article fastened to it. Small board used to connect formwork members or used as a brace. In electricity, a piece of ceramic insulating material used to fasten wires to flat surfaces.

cleat wiring: In electricity, an older system of wiring in which the wires are attached to a wall or other surface by ceramic cleats.

101

click test: Rough estimate of the hydration of a material by knocking two pieces together and noting the clarity of the sound.

clinch: The process of securing a driven nail by bending down the point; to fasten firmly by bending down the ends of protruding nails.

clinkers: A vitrified stony material which is fused together and remains in a furnace after coal containing stony impurities has been burned; also, unburned lava from a volcano; slag from a metal blast furnace.

clip: A kind of metal fastener used in places where penetrating or adhesive fasteners reduce the efficiency of the construction. Clips of various kinds hold members together directly or hold them together by tension in opposing clips. Clips may be

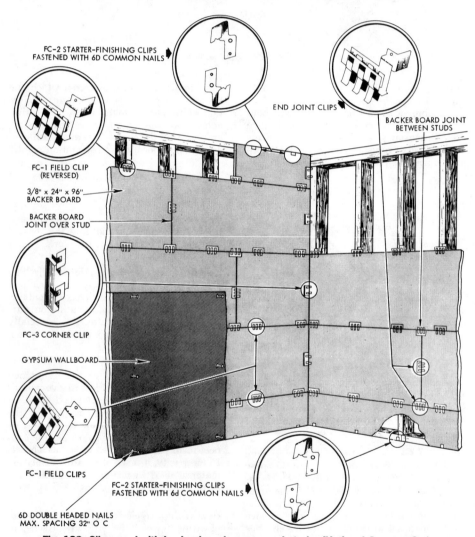

FC-2 STARTER-FINISHING CLIPS
FASTENED WITH 6D COMMON NAILS

END JOINT CLIPS

BACKER BOARD JOINT
BETWEEN STUDS

FC-1 FIELD CLIP
(REVERSED)

3/8" x 24" x 96"
BACKER BOARD

BACKER BOARD
JOINT OVER STUD

FC-3 CORNER CLIP

GYPSUM WALLBOARD

FC-1 FIELD CLIPS

FC-2 STARTER-FINISHING CLIPS
FASTENED WITH 6d COMMON NAILS

6D DOUBLE HEADED NAILS
MAX. SPACING 32" O C

Fig. 129. Clips used with backer boards over wood studs. (National Gypsum Co.)

used where there is no overlapping of members and where it is desirable to have semi-independent members in construction to minimize stresses, as well as for other purposes. Fig. 129 illustrates various clips.

cloak rail: Type of *hook strip,* or rail, with or without hooks, on which garments are hung.

cloak room: A small room, or closet, where coats, especially overcoats, are temporarily deposited.

clockwise: Moving in the same direction as the rotation of the hands of a clock; with a right-hand motion.

clockwise rotation: Anything which turns in the same direction as the hands of a clock; a right-handed rotation.

close: A narrow entry; an alley; a plot of enclosed land about a building; the enclosure about an abbey or cathedral; also an enclosure bounded by an imaginary line.

close fit: A term applied to a type of machine thread used on structural parts where accuracy is essential.

close grain: Lumber which has narrow and inconspicuous annual rings. The term is also used sometimes to indicate wood which has small closely spaced pores, but in this sense the term *fine textured* is more often used.

close nipple: In plumbing, a nipple twice as long as standard pipe thread, with no shoulder between the two sets of threads.

close string: A method of stair building in which a kind of curb string (on which the balusters are set) has a straight upper edge that usually is parallel with the lower edge, so the outer ends of the steps are entirely covered. Sometimes called a *closed string* stair. See Fig. 130.

closed cornice: A cornice which is entirely enclosed by the *roof, fascia,* and the *plancher.* Same as *boxed cornice.* See Fig. 131.

closed socket: See *cable* attachments, page 80.

closed stairway: A stairway which is completely closed on both sides by walls.

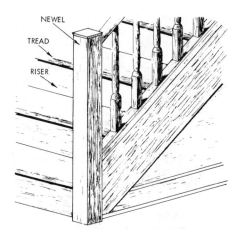

Fig. 130. Closed string stairs.

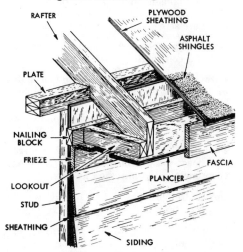

Fig. 131. Closed cornice.

closed-string stairs: Stairs in which the treads are not visible in a side view of the staircase. Also called *close-string stairs.* See Fig. 130.

closed valley: In building construction, a valley in which the courses of shingles meet and completely cover the lining of tin or other material.

closer: In constructing a masonry wall, any portion of a brick used to close up the bond next to the end brick of a course; the last stone, if smaller than the others, in a horizontal course, or a piece of brick which finishes a course; also, a piece of brick in each alternate course to enable a bond to be formed by preventing two headers from exactly superimposing on a stretcher. Same as *closure.*

closet: A small room or recess, usually enclosed, for storing articles, especially clothing; also, see *water-closet,* page 476.

closet knob: A kind of doorknob consisting of a spindle having a knob on one end and a metal plate on the other end, for securing the spindle to the door, for use on closet doors.

closet pole: A round molding on which clothes hangers may be suspended in clothes closets or elsewhere. Lead or steel pipes are sometimes used as closet poles.

closure: Part of a brick used to close the end of a course. See *closer.*

clothes chute: In building, a kind of slide or ductlike conductor through which soiled clothes are carried from various rooms, such as the kitchen or bathroom, to the laundry.

clout nail: In building, a nail with a large flat head, used principally for fastening sheet metal and nailing on gutters.

cluster: In lighting, a fixture having two or more lamps on it.

clustered: Grouped together; a number of similar objects brought together in a cluster such as a group of houses. In architecture, a *clustered column* is one which appears to consist of several columns or shafts. See *clustering.*

clustered columns: A group of columns arranged so as to form a single column or pier; same as *clustered pier.*

clustered pier: A pier composed of several piers or columns; also, called *clustered columns.*

clustering: Placing houses closer together; all residents use a common park. Fig. 132 illustrates a development that follows the clustering concept.

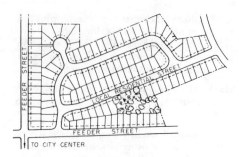

Fig. 132. Minor streets connect clusters of houses. (United States Savings and Loan League).

coak: A kind of tenon or projection on one of the surfaces of a scarfed joint, fitting into a corresponding recess in the other surface; also, a dowel pin of hard wood or metal which is let into timbers to unite them or keep them from slipping. See *scarf joint,* page 387, Fig. 506, page 389.

coarse aggregate: Crushed stone or gravel used to reinforce concrete; the size is regulated by building codes. See *rubble concrete,* page 377.

coarse grain: Wood or lumber having wide and conspicuous annual rings in which there is considerable difference between springwood and summerwood. Sometimes the term is used to designate wood having large pores, but in this sense the term *coarse textured* is more often used.

coarse textured: Wood or lumber having large pores; also, often called *coarse grain.*

coarse threads: Screw threads designated as *UNC,* these are used for the bulk production of screws, bolts, and nuts for general applications requiring rapid assembly or disassembly.

coat: A layer of any substance or material which covers another, as one, two, or three coats of paint or plaster.

coat and hat hook: A hook for holding coats and hats. Such a hook usually has two or more projecting prongs; the longest is intended for holding a hat, and the shorter hooks are for coats or other garments.

cob: A small mixture of unburned clay usually with straw as a binder. Used in building walls known as *cob walls.*

cob wall: A wall built of clay blocks made of unburnt clay or chalk mixed with straw; also, a wall constructed of *cobs,* such as clay bats.

cobwork: A type of work which consists of logs laid horizontally with the ends joined so as to form an enclosure, often rectangular in shape, as for a log house. See *quoins,* page 355.

cock: In plumbing, a type of valve with an opening to permit the passage of liquids; a faucet or tap, as over a kitchen sink. Same as *spigot.*

cock bead: In carpentry, a *bead molding* which projects beyond the surface of a wall or structural member to which it is applied.

cock beading: A type of molding used as a decorative feature in furniture making; a small semicircular molding raised above the surface, providing an ornamental trim for the edges of the drawers of bureaus or cabinets.

cocking: In carpentry, a type of jointing used to connect one beam to another across which it is bearing. See *cogging.*

cockle stairs: In carpentry, a term sometimes applied to *winding stairs.* See Fig. 563, page 426.

code: Any systematic collection or set of rules pertaining to one particular subject and devised for the purpose of securing uniformity in work or for maintaining proper standards of procedure, as a *building code.*

coefficient heat transmission: A term applied to any one of a number of coefficients which may be used to calculate heat transmission by either conduction, convection, or radiation through various materials and structures.

coefficient of thermal expansion: Change in linear dimension per unit length, or change in volume per unit volume per degree of temperature change.

coffer: An ornamental recessed panel in a ceiling or soffit. A coffer is a cast unit of plain or ornamental plaster. A number of units are cast to cover the required ceiling area. Coffers are made up in the shop by modelers and cast by the caster. The plasterer hangs the coffers in place on the job. See Fig. 133.

cofferdam: A watertight enclosure usually built of piles or clay, within which excavating is done for foundations; also, a watertight enclosure fixed to the side of a ship for making repairs below the water line.

cog: In carpentry, the solid middle portion which remains in a structural timber after two notches have been cut to form a *cogged joint.* See *cogging.*

cogged joint: A joint having one member notched so as to form a cog and the other member notched to fit over the cog.

Fig. 133. Single coffer hung in place.

cogging: In carpentry, a method of jointing in which one beam is connected to another across which it is bearing. Notches which are as long as the top beam is wide are cut in the top surface of the lower beam opposite one another, leaving a solid part. The upper beam has a small transverse groove cut in it to fit over the solid middle part. Also called *calking*.

cohesion: The mutual attraction of particles of soil caused by molecular cohesion and moisture films. The cohesion of a particular soil will vary with the moisture content.

coign or coin (koin): A wedge; also, a projecting corner. Often used in the expression, *coign of vantage,* meaning a position advantageous for observation or action.

coil heating: In building, a type of *panel heating.*

cold-air duct: In heating and ventilating systems, a pipe which carries cold air.

cold chisel: A name applied to a chisel made of tool steel of a strength and temper that will stand up under the hardest usage. A chisel suitable for cutting and chipping cold metal, such as nails. See Fig. 134.

Fig. 134. Cold chisel.

cold-drawn steel: Steel rolled to final shape at relatively low temperatures.

cold flow: In plastics, a term used to designate a change of dimension or distortion caused by a sustained application of a force greater than the elastic limit.

cold glue: Liquid glue used in a cold form; any glue used direct from a container without heating.

cold joint: A joint or discontinuity formed when a concrete surface hardens before the

next batch is placed against it. See: *construction joint,* page 117.

cold molding: In plastics, a process whereby a composition is shaped at ordinary temperatures; then hardened by baking.

cold weather concreting: The process of preventing fresh concrete from freezing during the winter months (40 degrees F or lower).

collar: In carpentry, an encircling band resembling a *collar;* a molding extending around a leg of furniture.

collar beam: A horizontal tie beam, in a roof truss, connecting two opposite rafters at a level considerably above the wall plate.

collar-beam roof: A roof composed of two rafters tied together by a horizontal beam connecting points about halfway up the rafters. The collar beams tend to stiffen the roof. See Fig. 135.

collection line: That part of a plumbing system which receives the discharge of all soil and waste stacks within the building and conveys it to the house sewer. It may be installed under ground or it may be suspended from the basement ceiling. See *house drain,* page 240.

collective bargaining: Union and employer representatives meet together to negotiate contracts.

college: A building, or group of buildings, used by an institution of higher learning.

cologne (ko-lon′) earth: In painting, a lignite which yields a deep-brown transparent earth.

colonial: A style of architecture used in America during Colonial times and sometimes used by builders as late as 1840; also, a type of furniture in vogue in early America before the American Revolution and applied to this type of furniture as late as the nineteenth century.

colonial architecture: A phrase applied to the style of architecture in America before The Revolution (1775); it was chiefly a modification of the English Georgian style of the corresponding period. Fig. 136 illustrates a period New England Colonial.

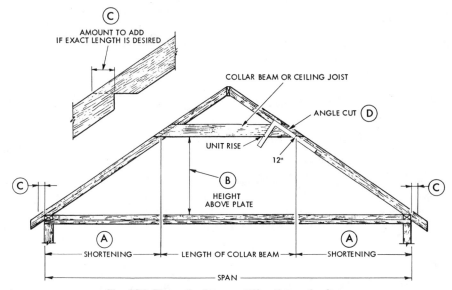

Fig. 135. The collar beams stiffen the roof rafters.

Fig. 136. The New England Colonial has very little overhang at the eaves or gable. Note the six-light transom above the door, the paneled pilasters flanking the door, and the decorative window cap. The Barnaby house was built in Freetown, Massachusetts, before 1740. (Historic American Building Survey, Library of Congress, Washington, D.C. Photo by Arhur C. Haskell)

colonnade: A series of columns at regular intervals, usually carrying an architrave.

color: Any one of the hues of the spectrum; also the tints or shades produced by the blending of any two or more of the hues seen in the spectrum.

coloring pigment: In painting, a pigment or stainer which is added to paint when a final color is required, different from that of the base used. Sometimes called *stainer*.

column: A perpendicular supporting member, circular or rectangular in section; a vertical shaft which receives pressure in the direction of its longitudinal axis. The parts of a column are: the *base* on which the *shaft* rests, the body, or shaft, and the head known as the *capital*. See Fig. 137.

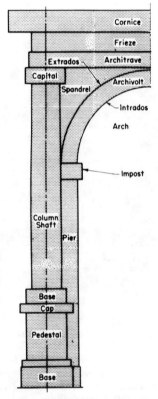

Fig. 137. Column and arch.

column anchorage: Anchors used so that the column base is several inches above the floor level where moisture may collect. See Fig. 138.

column schedule: List on working drawings giving number, size, and placement of steel columns used in a structure. See *beam schedule,* page 44.

column ties: Bars bent into square, rectangular, circular or U shapes for the purpose of holding column vertical bars laterally secure for the placement of concrete. See Fig. 139.

column verticals: Upright or vertical bars in a column. See Fig. 139.

columniation: Arrangement of columns where their placing and relation to each other form a principal feature of a design.

comb: In carpentry, the ridge of a roof; a *comb board;* in masonry, a tool used to give a finish to the face of stone, a *drag;* in house painting, an instrument used for graining surfaces.

comb board: The ridge board of a roof; the board at the ridge of a roof to which the rafters are nailed.

comb grain: In quarter-sawed lumber, grain with narrow, nearly parallel stripes of plainly marked dark and light colors.

comb roof: A double-sloping, or gable, roof.

combination doors: Doors having an inside removable section so the same frame serves both summer and winter. A screen door is inserted in warm weather and a storm door may be inserted in winter.

combination lock: A lock which has changeable tumblers whose mechanism is controlled by means of a movable dial inscribed with letters or figures. The bolt of the lock cannot be moved until after the dial has been turned so as to combine the characters in a certain order or succession.

combination pliers: A pincerlike tool, with long, flat, roughened jaws adjustable for size of opening by means of a slip joint. The inner grip is notched for grasping and holding round objects; the outer grip is

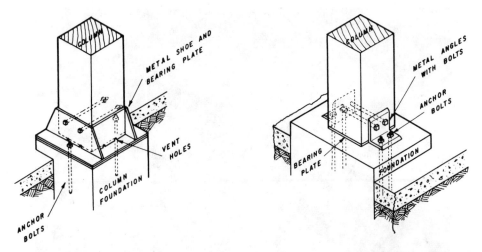

Fig. 138. Typical methods of anchoring column bases to concrete foundations. (National Lumber Manufacturer's Assoc.)

scored. The tool is used for cutting or bending wire. See Fig. 442, page 339.

combination square: Tool which combines in handy compact form the equivalent of several tools, including an inside try square, outside try square, mitre square, plumb, level, depth gage, marking gage, straight edge, bevel protractor, and center head in addition to square head. See Fig. 140.

combination trap: In plumbing, a P-type floor drain trap constructed in two pieces so as to allow some latitude for adjustment during installation. See Fig. 257, page 193.

combination windows: Windows having an inside removable section so the same frame serves both summer and winter. In warm weather a screen may be inserted and in winter a storm window is used.

combined escutcheon plate: Metal plate, for a door, with both a knob socket and a keyhole.

combined store-door lock: A lock with a heavy dead bolt as well as a latch bolt operated by thumb handles instead of knobs.

combing: To rake or scrape damp plaster with a *scarifier* or *scratcher.*

comfort air conditioning: A process for maintaining, within required limits, the quality of air necessary for the comfort of people in inclosed spaces, such as ventilation, movement or circulation of the air, air cleaning, temperature, and humidity.

common bond: In masonry, a form of bond in which every sixth course is a header course and the intervening courses are stretcher courses. Sometimes varied so a header bond is used every fourth or fifth course. See Fig. 73, *brick bonds,* page 60.

common brick: See *building brick,* page 74. See Fig. 85, page 69.

common catenary: The curve assumed by a chain or heavy cord hanging freely between two points of supports, when the forces are parallel and proportional to the length of the chain or cord. See *catenary,* page 88.

common lime: A material produced by the burning of limestone to the proper degree, used for making mortar for plastering and masonry work. Same as *quicklime,* page 354.

109

Fig. 139. Reinforced column. Square ties hold the four column bars in place.

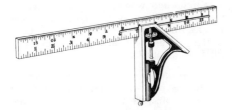

Fig. 140. Combination square.

common nails: These are available from 2d to 60d in length. As their name implies, they are the most commonly used kind of nail and will usually be supplied if no other specification is made. They are used when the appearance of the work is not important; for example, in the framing-in of houses and building of concrete forms. See Fig. 141. See Fig. 419, page 320 for sizes.

Fig. 141. Common nail.

common rafter: One of a series of rafters extending from the rafter plate of a roof to the ridge pole. See Fig. 483, page 371.

common wall: A wall jointly used by two parties, one or both of whom are entitled to such use under the provisions of a lease.

communicating-door lock: A type of lock especially designed for use on doors between connecting rooms, usually equipped with a knob latch which has a thumb bolt.

compact: To increase the firmness or weight supporting ability of the subgrade by pounding or compressing it with hand or power equipment.

compacting: A process of packing the material into as dense a state as possible.

compass: An instrument with two legs joined at the top, used to describe circles and curves when laying out work on building plans. See Fig. 142.

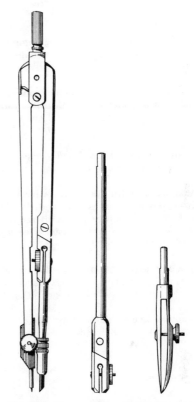

Fig. 142. Compasses and attachments.

compass brick: In masonry, a curved or tapering brick for use in curved work, such as in arches.

compass plane: A cutting tool used for smoothing concave or convex surfaces; a plane with an adjustable sole.

compass roof: A roof having its rafters bent to the shape of an arc; also, a timber roof in which each truss has its rafters, collar beams, and braces combined into an arched form.

compass saw: See *keyhole saw,* page 256.

component. A part of a house assembled before delivery to the building site. See *prefabricate,* page 347.

composite arch: A pointed arch with curves struck from different centers; the *lancet arch.*

composite deck: Bridge decking composed of material other than wood, usually asphalt or concrete.

composition roofing: A roofing consisting of asbestos felt saturated with asphalt and assembled with asphalt cement. Also called *prepared roofing* and *roll roofing.*

composition shingles: Shingles made, or formed, from composition roofing material.

compound: A term applied to a base coat plaster to which sand is to be added on the job. In some localities the term refers to neat goods or to cement plaster. See *neat plaster,* page 299.

compound arch: An arch made up of a number of concentric archways placed successively within and behind each other.

compound beam: A built-up beam or a beam composed of two or more members.

compregnated wood: An assembly of veneer impregnated with liquid resin and bonded under high pressure, with the grain of the various layers of veneer usually parallel. Also called *compreg.*

compression: Squeezing together; making smaller by pressure. Compression stress is the result of squeezing or crushing. It may be *parallel* to the grain or *perpendicular* to the grain. See Fig. 143. The most familiar example of compression parallel to the grain is the stress in a post or column. Compression perpendicular to the grain occurs, for example, in the bearing parts of a beam and in flooring. See Fig. 143, right. The weight of a superstructure on a concrete foundation is a compressive stress or load. (See also Fig. 532, page 404.)

compression bars: Steel used to resist compression forces.

compression "blow out": The result of excessive restraint on a heated concrete member when internal pressure exceeds the compressive strength.

compression failure: Deformation of the wood fibers resulting from excessive compression along the grain either in direct end compression or in bending. In surfaced lumber, compression failures appear as fine wrinkles across the face of the piece.

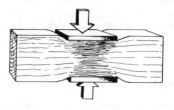

Fig. 143. (Left) Compression of wood parallel to the grain. (Right) Compression of wood perpendicular to the grain.

compression set: Remaining smaller after pressure.

compression wood: Abnormal wood that forms on the lower side of branches and leaning and crooked softwood trees. It is hard and brittle and has a lifeless appearance; it shrinks lengthwise more than normal wood.

compressive strength: Maximum compressive stress a material will bear without fracture. In masonry, the measured resistance of concrete or mortar to forces that are pressing it or sqeezing it together. It is expressed in pounds per square inch (psi).

compressor: One of the main parts of an air conditioning system required in the cooling cycle.

concave: A curved recess; hollowed out like the inner curve of a circle or sphere; the interior of a curved surface or line; a bowl-shaped depression.

concave joint: In masonry, a mortar joint formed with a special tool or a bent iron rod. This type of mortar joint is weather resistive and inexpensive. See Fig. 333, page 254.

concealed gutter: In building, a gutter which is constructed in such a manner that it cannot be seen. Sometimes called a *hidden gutter* or a *concealed box gutter*. See Fig. 79, page 64.

concealed heating: Method of heating a building by the installation of heating units, consisting of pipes which are concealed in floors, ceilings, or walls. Also called *panel heating*.

concealed light: Any artificial light source, concealed behind a decorative facing, which allows the light to diffuse over its edges and through it if the facing is translucent. This type of lighting can be recessed into ceiling or wall; can be direct, indirect, or semidirect. Cove and valance lighting are examples of concealed light.

concentrated load: The weight localized on, and carried by, a beam, girder, or other supporting structural part.

concentric: Having a common center, as the annual growth rings of a tree.

concentric arch: An arch which is laid in several courses whose curves have a common center.

concha (kong'ka): In architecture, the smooth concave surface of a vault.

concrete: In masonry, a mixture of cement, sand, and gravel with water in varying proportions according to the use which is to be made of the finished product. *Plain concrete* is without reinforcement or with only minimal reinforcement. *Reinforced concrete* has reinforcement imbedded so that concrete and steel work together to resist forces.

concrete-bent construction: A system of construction in which precast concrete bent framing units are the basic load-bearing members. The principal advantages and problems are similar to those in *post and beam* construction. A concrete bent consists of a vertical and a horizontal load-bearing member, which are cast in one piece and designed on the cantilever principle.

concrete blocks: In masonry, precast, hollow, or solid blocks of concrete used in the construction of buildings. Typical concrete blocks used in building trade are shown in Fig. 144.

concrete cover: The clear distance from the face of the concrete to the reinforcing steel. Also referred to as *fireproofing, clearance,* or *concrete protection.*

concrete form: Wooden or metal mold into which concrete is poured. See *forms,* page 204.

concrete insert: A type of metal anchor used to secure structural wood parts to a concrete or masonry wall. See *anchors,* Fig. 18, page 17.

concrete mixers. Mechanical mixers for mixing concrete ingredients; they may be either stationary or mobile. Concrete is often delivered to the job site in truck mixers. See Fig. 145.

concrete nail: A hardened-steel nail used for fastening wood, etc., to masonry work. See Fig. 389, page 296.

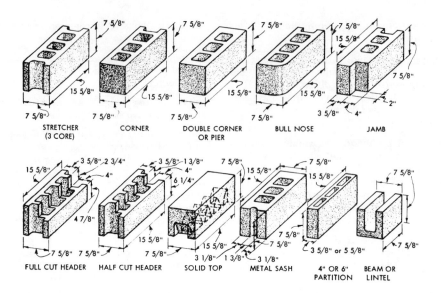

STRETCHER (3 CORE) CORNER DOUBLE CORNER OR PIER BULL NOSE JAMB

FULL CUT HEADER HALF CUT HEADER SOLID TOP METAL SASH 4" OR 6" PARTITION BEAM OR LINTEL

(IN SOME AREAS THE ABOVE UNITS ARE AVAILABLE IN 4" NOMINAL HEIGHTS)

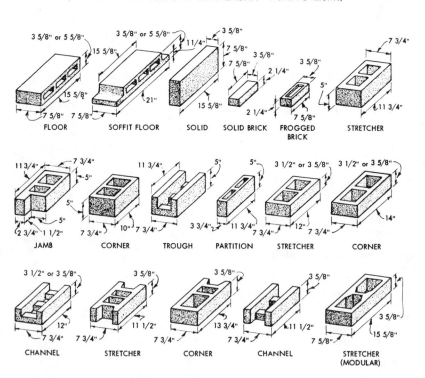

FLOOR SOFFIT FLOOR SOLID SOLID BRICK FROGGED BRICK STRETCHER

JAMB CORNER TROUGH PARTITION STRETCHER CORNER

CHANNEL STRETCHER CORNER CHANNEL STRETCHER (MODULAR)

Fig. 144. Concrete blocks.

Fig. 145. A heavy-duty truck mounted mixer. (International Harvester Co.)

concrete paint: A specially prepared thin paint, consisting of a mixture of cement and water, applied to the surface of a concrete wall to give it a uniform finish and to protect the joints against weathering by rain or snow.

concrete, reinforced: See *reinforced concrete,* page 364.

concrete slab on the ground: A concrete structure such as a patio, a driveway, a floor, pavement, etc.

concrete wall: In building construction, any wall made of reinforced concrete, such as a basement wall.

condensate: In steam heating, water condensed from steam; in air conditioning, water extracted from air, as by condensation on the cooling coil of a refrigeration machine; any liquid formed by the condensation of vapor.

condensation: The act or process of changing a substance from a vapor to a liquid state due to cooling. Also, beads or drops of water, and often frost, in cold weather, which accumulate on the inside of the exterior covering of a building, when warm, moisture-laden air, from the interior, reaches a point where the temperature no longer permits the air to sustain the moisture it holds. Use of louvers will reduce moisture condensation in attics.

condensation pump: In fitting steam pipes, a device for removing liquid condensation from steam returns.

condominium: Individual ownership of a unit in a multi-unit structure (as an apartment building).

conduction: Transfer of heat by contact; if the end of an iron rod is held in the fire, some heat will flow to the hand by conduction.

conductor: In plumbing, a pipe for conveying rain water from the roof gutter to the drain pipe. Also called *leader, downspout,* or *down pipe.* In electricity, a wire or path through which a current of electricity flows; a rod used to carry lightning to the ground, called a *lightning rod.*

conductor head: An enlargement at the top of a conductor, or leader, to receive rain water in large quantities at a narrow opening where a gutter is not practical. See *leader head,* page 264.

conduit: A natural or artificial channel for carrying fluids, as water pipes, canals, and aqueducts; a tube, or trough, for receiving and protecting electric wires. For conduit and fittings see Fig. 146.

conduit bender: A device for making bends and elbows in rigid conduits. When there are many bends to be made, a type of bender called an *elbow-former* should be used for this purpose. See *hickey,* page 236; *roll type hand benders,* page 370.

conduit box: In electricity, an iron or steel box located between the ends of the conduit where the wires or cables are spliced; or the box to which the ends of a conduit are attached and which may be used as an outlet, junction, or pull box. See *outlet box,* page 306; *pull box,* page 351.

conduit bushing: In electricity, a short threaded sleeve fastened to the end of the conduit inside the outlet box. The inside of the sleeve is rounded out on one end to prevent injury to the wires. See Fig. 146.

conduit coupling: A short metal tube threaded on the inside and used to fasten two pieces of conduit end to end. See Fig. 146.

conduit elbow: In electric wiring, a short piece of tubing bent to an angle, usually of 45 or 90 degrees. See Fig. 146.

conduit fittings: In electric wiring, a term applied to all of the auxiliary items, such as boxes and elbows used or needed for the conduit system of wiring.

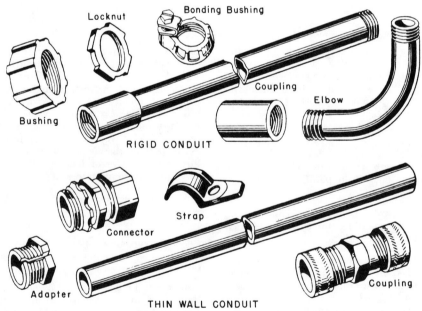

Fig. 146. Conduit and fittings.

conduit, rigid: A mild steel tubing used to enclose electric light and power wires.

conduit rod: A short rod, coupled to other rods, pushed through a large conduit to remove obstructions and to pull a cable into the conduit.

conduit system: In electricity, a system of wiring in which the conductors are contained in a metal tubing.

conduit wiring: Electric light wires which are placed inside a tubing.

cone: In solid geometry, a figure, the bottom of which is a circle, the sides tapering evenly upward to a point.

congé (kon'ha): Molding in the form of a quarter-hollow or a *cavetto;* an *apophyge.* Often used at the junction of a column with its base; also, a kind of finish molding placed at the top of fixtures. See Fig. 147.

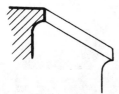

Fig. 147. Congé.

conifers: See *softwoods,* page 414.

conoid: A cone-shaped geometrical figure or solid.

consistency: Degree of firmness or stiffness. The wetness or ability of freshly mixed concrete to flow; measured by the *slump.*

consolidating: Molding fresh concrete within the forms and around reinforcement in order to eliminate voids other than entrained air.

construction: The process of assembling materials and erecting a structure; also, that which is built; the style or medium in which a building is built, as of wood, steel, or masonry.

construction, frame: A type of construction in which the structural parts are of wood or depend upon a wood frame for support. In building codes, if masonry veneer is applied to the exterior walls the classification of this type of construction is usually unchanged.

construction joint: A rigid, immovable joint where two slabs or parts of a structure are joined firmly to form a solid, continuous unit. In masonry, the surface where two successive placements of concrete meet; a temporary joint employed when the placing must be interrupted because of weather, time, etc.

Construction Specifications Institute (C.S.I.): This organization has established a format for construction specifications. The format is comprised of four major groupings:

Bidding Requirements
Contract Forms
General Conditions
Specifications (Technical)

Within this last grouping of *Specifications,* 16 permanent *divisions* are found.

Division 1—General Requirements
Division 2—Site Work
Division 3—Concrete
Division 4—Masonry
Division 5—Metal
Division 6—Wood and Plastics
Division 7—Thermal and Moisture
 Protection
Division 8—Doors and Windows
Division 9—Finishes
Division 10—Specialties
Division 11—Equipment
Division 12—Furnishings
Division 13—Special Construction
Division 14—Conveying Systems
Division 15—Mechanical
Division 16—Electrical

consulting engineer: A person retained to give expert advice in regard to all engineering problems; supposedly an experienced engineer of high rating in his profession.

contemporary: Living, occurring, or existing at the present period of time.

continuous: A term applied to a structural member having three or more supports, or extending over two or more panels, as a *continuous beam, span, truss, panel.* See *continuous girder.*

continuous beam: A timber that rests on more than two supporting members of a structure.

continuous girder: A girder or beam supported at more than three points and extending over the supports as distinct from a series of independent girders or beams.

continuous header: The top plate is replaced by 2 x 6's turned on edge and running around the entire house. This header is strong enough to act as a lintel over all wall openings, eliminating some cutting and fitting of stud lengths and separate headers over openings. This is especially important because of the emphasis on one-story, open planning houses. See Fig. 148.

continuous high chairs: Welded wire bar supports consisting of a top supporting

Fig. 148. Continuous header. (Professional Builder)

wire with evenly spaced legs welded on. Used to support bars near the top slabs. See also *high chairs,* page 237.

continuous hinge: A long strip hinge used in furniture making; an example is the hinge on the lid which covers the keyboard of a piano.

continuous vent: In plumbing, the extension of a vertical waste pipe above the connection at which liquid wastes enter the waste pipe to a point above all windows. The extension may or may not continue in a vertical length.

contour: The outline of a figure, as the profile of a molding; also, a term applied to a line joining points having the same elevation above or below some given level, such as *sea level.* See Fig. 149.

contour lines: Contour lines are lines that identify the level or elevation of the ground by identifying the lines with their elevation value. See Fig. 149.

contraction: In terms of fresh or hardened concrete, the shrinkage or squeezing of the concrete, especially due to the thaw of the weather during a freeze-thaw cycle.

contraction joint: A control joint; tooled groove made to allow for shrinkage in a concrete shaft. See *control joint.*

contractor: One who agrees to supply materials and perform certain types of work for a specified sum of money, as a *building contractor* who erects a structure according to a written agreement or *contract.*

contractor's bond: A bond required by the client to insure that the contractor fulfills his obligations.

control center, main: The assembly of circuit breakers for the protection of feeders and branch circuits.

control joint: In concrete flatwork, a groove cut or tooled into the top of the slab, usually to about 1/5 the thickness of the slab. The groove predetermines the location of natural cracking caused by shrinkage as the concrete hardens. In concrete block masonry, a continuous vertical joint without mortar. Such material as rubber, plas-

tic, or building paper is used to key the joint which is then sealed with calk. Control joints are used in very long walls where thermal expansion and contraction may cause cracking in the mortar joints.

convection: The motion which results in a fluid from the difference in density and the action of gravity. In heat transmission, this meaning has been extended to include both *natural* and *forced* circulation or motion.

convector: A type of heat dispenser used when heating is accomplished by convection. See Fig. 150.

convector radiator: A type of heating in which steam or hot water runs through a pipe core, heating metal plates or fins attached to it at short intervals. Air passed over these fins picks up heat and distributes it through vents in an enclosure to the area to be heated. See Fig. 150.

convenience outlet: An electrical outlet in the wall which can be used for plugging in electrical devices. See *receptacle,* page 363.

conventions: In building, a pictorial representation of numerous items which cannot be shown by symbols on the plan views for a house or other structure. Typical plan-view *conventions* are shown in Fig. 151.

convex: An outward curve, as the surface of a sphere.

conveyors: Mechanical devices used to carry material from one place to another.

cooked glue: Any type of dry glue requiring heating before it can be used; also, glue used in a hot form.

coolant: A solution used to cool machinery.

cooling tower: A device, usually placed outdoors, for cooling the water used in an air conditioner's condenser, so that it may be re-used, thus conserving water. The heated water is carried to the cooling tower and the cooled water away from it by extensions of the pipes used in the condenser.

coopered joints: The joining of curved parts in such a way as to make the joints resemble those used in the construction of barrels. Such joints are used especially in furniture making.

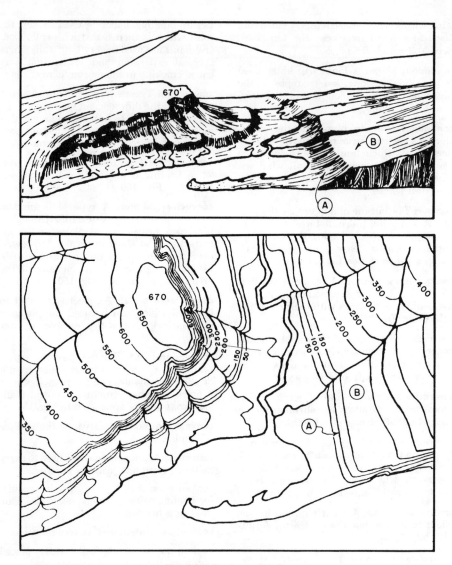

Fig. 149. Contour sketch.

copal (ko'pal): A term used in painting for a class of various resins derived from tropical trees or from material of recent fossil origin which furnish raw materials for the varnish and lacquer industries.

copal varnish: Varnish in which copal is the chief ingredient. See *copal*.

cope: To remove part of the flange at the end of a beam to avoid interference.

coped joint: The seam, or juncture, between molded pieces in which a portion of one piece is cut away to receive the molded part of the other piece. See Fig. 152.

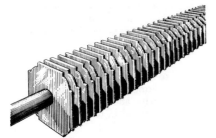

Fig. 150. Convector radiator.

coping brick: In masonry, brick having special shapes for use in capping the exposed top of a wall. It is sometimes used with a creasing and sometimes without. In the latter case, the brick is wider than the wall and has drips under its lower edges.

coping frame: The bow frame which carries the narrow blade of a coping saw. See Fig. 153.

coping saw: A saw which is used for cutting curves and hollowing out moldings. The narrow blade of the *coping saw,* carried on pins set in a steel bow frame, is from 1/16″ to 1/8″ wide and 6-1/2″ long. See Fig. 153.

coping: A covering or top for brick walls. The cap or top course of a wall. The coping frequently is projected out from the wall to afford a decorative as well as protective feature.

copper clout nail: A fastening device designed to be clinched and to withstand corrosion, used especially in boat building and in the construction of garden trellises and porch furniture. See Fig. 390, page 296.

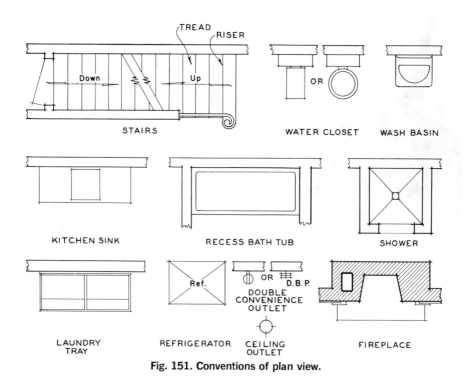

Fig. 151. Conventions of plan view.

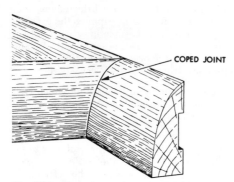

Fig. 152. One piece of a coped joint is cut to fit the profile of the other piece.

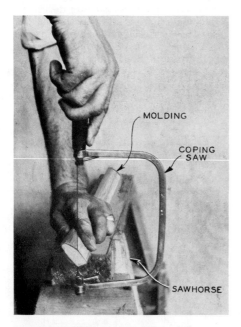

Fig. 153. Coping saw is used to follow profile of miter cut to make coped joint.

copper tubing: See *tubing,* page 464.

copperlite glazing: A term applied to glazing when a number of individual lights or panes are separated by strips of copper.

copperplating: The depositing of a copper coating on the surface of another metal by any one of several formulas, the principal ingredient of which is *cyanide of potassium.* The plating can be accomplished by either the dipping method or by the electrolytic method.

coquina (ko'ke-na): A soft, whitish rock or limestone formed by the cementing together of marine shells and corals; used as a building material in the southern part of the United States.

corbel: A short piece of wood or stone projecting from the face of a wall to form a support for a timber or other weight; a bracketlike support; a stepping out of courses in a wall to form a ledge; any supporting projection of wood or stone on the face of a wall. See Fig. 154.

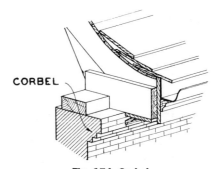

Fig. 154. Corbel.

corbel out: The building of one or more courses of masonry out from the face of a wall to form a support for timbers. See Fig. 154.

corbel table: A horizontal row of corbels supporting lintels or small arches; a projecting course, as of masonry, which is supported by a series of corbels; a cornice supported by corbels.

corbel vault: A vault which has been corbeled.

corbeled chimney: A chimney which is supported by a brickwork projection from a wall, forming a sort of bracket, or corbel; also, a chimney erected on a bracket constructed of wood members.

corbeling: In building, a projecting course of brick or stone which forms a ledge for supporting a load. See Fig. 154.

corbie (kor-bi): A series of steplike projections on the sloping sides of a gable; also called *crowstepped.*

corbie gable: A gable finished with corbie-steps.

corbie stones: Stones used for covering the steps of a crowstepped gable wall.

corbiestep gable: A gable which has a series of regular steps up each slope. Same as *corbie gable.* See *crowstep gable,* page 133.

corbiesteps: A series of steplike projections along the slope of a gable wall; also called *crowsteps.*

cord: Wood cut in four-foot lengths, usually for firewood. A pile of wood measuring four feet in width, four feet in height, and eight feet in length. In electricity, two insulated flexible wires or cables twisted or held together with a covering of rubber, tape, or braid.

core: In building, the material removed from a mortise; the central part of anything; the wood center or base; usually of soft wood, on which veneers are glued; the center stock of a plywood panel. Also, the central part of the stiles and rails of a door (see Fig. 189, page 149); and the central part of the hollow core flush door.

Corinthian: Pertaining to the most ornate of the three Greek orders of architecture. It is characterized by the distinguishing feature of its bell-shaped capital adorned with rows of conventionalized acanthus leaves. See *acanthus,* Fig. 2, page 2.

Corinthian bracket: Projection from the face of a wall, used to support a cornice or shelflike feature, ornamented with an *acanthus* leaf design. See Fig. 155.

Corinthian order: One of the five conventional orders of architecture. See *Corinthian.* See Fig. 403, page 306.

cork tiles: Tiles made from pressed cork and used as flooring.

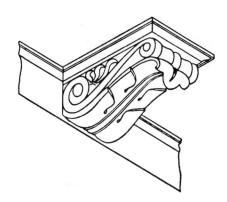

Fig. 155. Corinthian bracket.

corking: In carpentry, a method of connecting one beam to another across which it is bearing. See *cogging,* page 106.

corner: The intersection of two adjacent faces.

corner angles: Fasteners used for either inside or outside corners, depending upon which side of the angle is countersunk for the screw heads. Sizes range from 1 inch to 8 inches. See Fig. 156.

Fig. 156. Corner angle iron.

corner bead: A small projecting molding, or bead, built into plastered corners to prevent accidental breaking of the plaster; such a *bead* usually is of metal. See Fig. 157.

corner bead metal: Strip of formed galvanized iron which is sometimes combined with a strip of metal lath, placed on corners before plastering, to reinforce the corners.

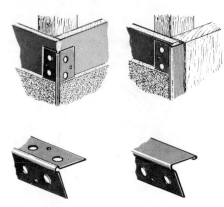

Fig. 158. Corner tape creaser. (Goldblatt Tool Co.)

Fig. 157. Metal corner beads. (Bestwall Gypsum Co.)

corner bit brace: Specially designed *bit brace* for use in positions where it is difficult for a workman to operate the regular bit brace; a corner brace useful for tradesmen who have occasion to work close to perpendicular surfaces and in corners.

corner boards: Boards used to finish the corner of a building; any board used on a corner. See Fig. 160.

corner braces: Diagonal braces at the corners of frame structure to stiffen and strengthen the wall.

corner chisel: A special type of carpenter's chisel, having two straight cutting edges meeting at right angles; used for cutting the corners of mortises.

corner clamp: A clamp used in holding mitered joints in place for gluing or nailing.

corner posts or studs: The two or three studs spiked together to form a corner in a frame structure. See Fig. 41, page 35.

corner tape creaser: The corner tape creaser is used to apply tape to inside and outside corners before plastering. See Fig. 158.

corner trowel: Special type of plasterer's trowel having a V-shaped blade made for working corners. These trowels are made in two patterns, one for inside corners, another for outside corners.

cornerite: Metal mesh lath cut into strips and bent to form a right angle for use in interior corners of walls and ceilings to prevent cracks in plaster.

corners: See *corner bead.*

cornice: Projection at the top of a wall; a term applied to construction under the eaves or where the roof and side walls meet; the top course, or courses, of a wall when treated as a crowning member. See Fig. 159. (See also Figs. 131, page 103, and 230, page 174.)

cornice return: A type of cornice trim where the sloping line of a gable roof meets the vertical line of the wall of the building. In this type of finish, the fascia is started across the face of the gable end of the building and then is returned on itself about two feet from the intersection of the roof line with the vertical line of the wall. See Fig. 160.

cornice trim: The exterior finish on a building where the sloping roof meets the vertical wall. See Fig. 160.

corona: That part of a cornice supported by and projecting beyond the bed molding. It is surmounted by the cymatium, or crowning molding, of a cornice. The corona serves as a protection to the walls by throwing off rain water. See *entablature,* Fig. 230, page 174.

corporation cock: In plumbing, a device installed to serve as a control stop for the city-water service, when the main is tapped

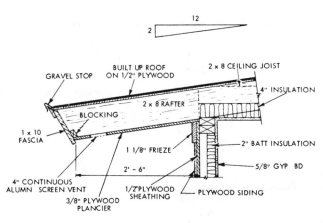

Fig. 159. The detail of the cornice shows the builder how to prepare and assemble the framing and how to trim members.

without shutting off the city-water supply. Sometimes called *corporation stop*.

corridor: A passageway in a building into which several apartments open; a gallery or passage, usually covered, into which rooms open, as the *corridor* of a hotel or of an art gallery.

corrosion: The oxidation, or rusting, of metals caused by contact and chemical union with oxygen in a damp atmosphere.

corrugated: A surface formed of parallel ridges and depressions, alternately convex or concave.

corrugated glass, plastic, or metal: Corrugated panels, sheets, or rolls of various materials are available for decorative partitions, doors, or other surfaces. The glass, or plastic, is often used in front of light sources to aid diffusion. Corrugated metal forms reflective surfaces and air spaces for insulating purposes. There are many other older or less common uses for corrugated materials.

corrugated iron: Sheet iron, usually galvanized, shaped into straight, parallel, regular, and equally curved ridges and grooves; used on the sides and roofs of buildings.

corrugated iron fasteners: A device used for corner jointing in wood construction, as in window screens, where strength and a finished appearance are unimportant. See Fig. 161.

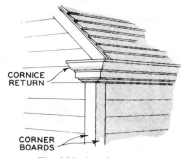

Fig. 160. Cornice return.

Fig. 161. Corrugated iron fastener.

125

cottage latch: A small lift latch for use on light cupboard or cabinet doors.

coulisse (koo-les): In construction work, a piece of timber having a groove in which another member slides, the groove serving as a guide. Also called *cullis*.

counterbore: Increasing the size of a hole through part of its length by boring a hole of greater diameter, usually at one end of the original hole.

counterbracing: A type of diagonal bracing which transmits a strain in an opposite direction from the main bracing; in a truss or girder, bracing used to give additional support to the beam and to relieve it of transverse stress.

counterclockwise: Motion in the direction opposite to the rotation of the hands of a clock.

counterclockwise rotation: Anything which turns in a direction opposite to that of the hands of a clock; a lefthanded rotation. See *clockwise rotation,* page 103.

counterflashing: Sheet metal incorporated in the masonry of a chimney where it passes through the roof for the purpose of protecting the exposed ends of the roof flashing. See Fig. 165, page 130.

countersink: To make a depression in wood or metal for the reception of a plate of iron, the head of a screw, or bolt, so the plate, screw, or bolt will not project beyond the surface of the work; to form a flaring cavity around the top of a hole for receiving the head of a screw or bolt. A countersunk bit is shown in Fig. 59, page 50.

countersink bit: A drill, or other tool, for cutting a flaring enlargement in the upper part of a hole in which a screw is to be driven below the surface of the material. See Fig. 59, page 50.

countersunk: In carpentry, a term applied to a screw, bolt, or other fastener having the head sunk below the surface.

couple-close: A pair of rafters which are framed together with a tie fixed at the foot or with a *collar beam*.

coupled: Meaning linked together. "Coupled columns" are arranged in pairs, with their bases and capitals touching and with a correspondingly wider span between the grouping pairs.

coupled column: One of a pair of columns set nearer together than others of the same order or forming one of many groups of two. In the classical orders they are one half of a diameter apart.

coupling: In plumbing, a short collar, with only inside threads at each end, for receiving the ends of two pipes which are to be fitted and joined together.

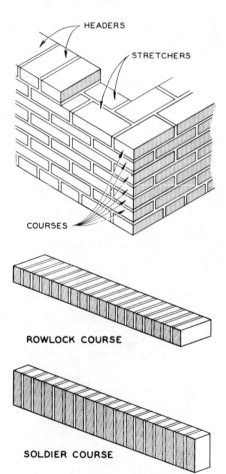

Fig. 162. Courses in brickwork.

course: A continuous level range or row of brick or masonry throughout the face or faces of a building; to arrange in a row. A row of bricks when laid in a wall is called a *course*. See Fig. 162.

coursed ashlar: In masonry, a type of ashlar construction in which the various blocks of structural material have been arranged according to height to form regular courses in the face of walls. See Fig. 30, page 28.

coursed rubble masonry: Masonry composed of roughly shaped stones fitting approximately on level beds and well bonded.

court: An open space surrounded partly or entirely by a building; an open area partly or wholly enclosed by buildings or walls.

cove: A concave molding; an architectural member, as a ceiling, which is curved or arched at its junction with the side walls: also, a large, hollow cornice; a niche. See Fig. 291, page 222.

cove bracketing: The lumber skeleton, or framing, for a cove: a term applied chiefly to the *bracketing* of a cove ceiling.

cove ceiling: A ceiling which rises from the walls with a concave curve.

cove molding: A quarter round or concave molding; sometimes called the *cavetto*. See *cavetto,* page 88, Fig. 114, page 90. Fig. 163 shows a typical mold used in plastering to make a cove molding.

Fig. 163. A two member cove mold showing basic construction. Notice nibs or shoes on the slipper and ceiling line of the horse or stock.

Fig. 164. Special cranes being used in heavy construction. (Medusa Portland Cement Co.)

coved and flat ceiling: A ceiling in which the coved section forms the quadrant of a circle, rising from the walls and intersecting in a flat surface.

coved ceiling: A ceiling which is constructed in a curve or arch where it joins the side walls.

cover plate: A plate fastened to the flanges of a girder to increase area of cross section.

covered joint: In carpentry, any joint which is formed by having a rebate cut on each of the joining edges. Same as a *shiplap joint.*

coving: The scotia inverted on a large scale; a concave molding often found in the base of a column. See *scotia,* Fig. 509, page 390.

cracking: In painting, a term applied to deep checks in film occurring in the filler coats of paint or lacquer but which later also affect the color coats. Such *cracking* is the result of improper mixing of materials.

cradling: Lumber work, or framing, for sustaining the lath and plaster of vaulted ceilings.

craft: Manual skill; a trade; an occupation; skill in the execution of manual work; special skill in a manual art or handiwork.

cramp: In masonry, a contrivance consisting of iron rods or bars with the ends bent to a right angle; used to hold blocks of stone together.

crane: A hoisting device equipped with a boom and cables which will pick up a load, move it to another position and set it down again. A great variety of types have been built, many of which are designed for specific needs and specific operations. Fig. 164 shows specialized cranes being used in high level construction.

crank brace: A brace having a bent handle by means of which the tool may be rotated.

crawl space: In cases where houses have no basements, the space between the first floor and the surface of the ground is made large enough for a man to crawl through for repairs and installation of utilities.

crawling: In painting, a defect appearing during the process of applying paint in which the film breaks, separates, or raises, as a result of applying the paint over a slick or glassy surface. Such defects may also be due to surface tension caused by heavy coatings or the use of an elastic film over a surface which is hard and brittle.

crazing: In painting, a minute cracking of a finish coat of paint due to uneven shrinking of paint. In masonry, the appearance of very fine cracks while the concrete surface is drying because of uneven contraction.

creep: The tendency of hardened concrete to bend more and more under load as time passes.

cremorne bolt: A bolt consisting of a sliding rod, fastened at the top and bottom of a casement or French window with strikes or plates. A knob or handle at the center of the bolt, when turned, causes the rods to move in opposite directions, thus either locking or unlocking the window.

crenel (kre-nel′): A notch or indentation; one of the open spaces between the merlons of an embattlement. See *crenelated molding.*

crenelated molding: Embattled or adorned with an indented pattern. See *embattled,* page 172.

creosote: As used for a wood preservative, a distillate of coal tar produced by high-temperature carbonization of bituminous coal; *creosote* is heavier than water and consists principally of liquid and solid aromatic hydrocarbons containing an appreciable quantity of tar acids and tar bases.

creosoting: The process of injecting creosote into timber as a means of increasing its durability when it is to be exposed to the weather.

crest: The ridging of a roof, especially a ridging which is ornamental; the same as *cresting;* a type of ridge tiling.

cresting: An ornamental finish of the wall or ridge of a building. The *cresting* of shingle roofs is generally of sheet metal.

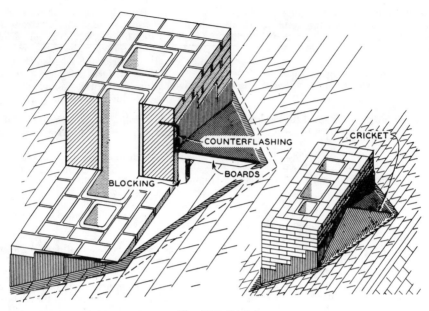

Fig. 165. Cricket.

crib: A cratelike framing used as a support for a structure above; any of various frameworks, as of logs or timbers, used in construction work; the wooden lining on the inside of a shaft; openwork of horizontally cross-piled, squared timbers, or beams, used as a retaining wall.

cricket: In architecture, a small false roof or the elevation of part of a roof behind an obstacle as a watershed built behind a chimney or other roof projection. Same as *saddle*. See Fig. 165.

crimp: To offset the end of an angle or metal strip so it can overlap another piece. Also: to indent the ends of pipes, tubing, flanges, etc. Fig. 166 shows a metal flange being crimped to steel studding.

cripple: In building construction, any part of a frame which is cut less than full size, as a *cripple studding* over a door or window opening.

Fig. 166. Crimping.

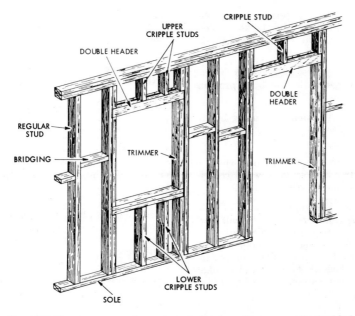

CRIPPLE STUD

UPPER
CRIPPLE STUDS

DOUBLE HEADER

DOUBLE
HEADER

REGULAR
STUD

TRIMMER

BRIDGING

TRIMMER

LOWER
CRIPPLE STUDS

SOLE

Fig. 167. Members around openings in frame walls are usually doubled.

cripple jack rafter: A *jack rafter* that is cut in between a hip and valley rafter. A *cripple jack* touches neither the ridge nor the plate but extends from a valley rafter to a hip rafter.

cripple rafter: A rafter extending from a hip to a valley rafter.

cripple studding: In framing, a studding which is less than full length, as a studding cut short to be used over a door or window opening. See 167.

cripple timbers: In building construction, timbers which are shortened for some reason, as the *cripple rafters* in a hip roof. See *jack timbers.*

critical path method (CPM): A graphic scheduling method using arrows to show the relationship between elements of a construction project. This chart makes clear what critical jobs must be completed before another job can start; identifies the "critical" path to follow and the most economical scheduling.

crocket: An ornament along the slope of a gable, spire, or pinnacle, resembling bent or curved foliage; usually in the form of a winding stem, like a creeping plant with flowers projecting at intervals.

crook: Warping in wood or boards, resulting in distortion of the material causing the edge to become either convex or concave lengthwise. See *warp,* page 475.

cross: In plumbing, a special fitting with four branches arranged in pairs, each pair on one axis and axes at right angles. It is used as a junction at the intersection of two pipe lines; also, a religious symbol placed on church gables, sometimes richly floriated in a great variety of forms; any ornament in the form of a modified cross used for decorative purposes.

cross aisle: The part of a cruciform church which crosses at right angles to the greatest length between the nave and the apse or choir; the transept.

cross banding: In veneering, the veneer sheet between the core and the face veneer whose grain runs at right angles to the grain of the core.

cross brace: Any crosspiece which diverts, transmits, or resists the weight or pressure of a load.

cross bracing: A system of bracing by the use of cross struts or ties; see *cross bridging;* also *counterbracing,* page 126.

cross break: A defect in timber which is caused by the separation of wood cells in a piece of lumber across the grain.

cross bridging: Bridging especially in floors consisting of transverse rows of small diagonal braces or struts set in pairs and crossing each other between the timbers. Cross bridging may be used in place of bracing set into the face of the stud and in place of wood bracing between joists. Fig. 168 illustrates cross bridging.

cross section: A transverse section cut at right angles to the longitudinal axis of a piece of wood, drawing, or other work.

cross springer: A diagonal springer, or rib, as the transverse ribs of a vault.

cross-vaulting: A vaulting formed by the intersection of two or more simple vaults.

cross ventilation: Producing a flow of air across a room by means of windows, doors, or other openings on opposite sides of the room.

crossband: To place the grain of layers of wood at right angles in order to minimize shrinking and swelling, such as in the plies of plywood.

crosscut saw: A saw which is made to cut transversely, as across the grain of wood. See Fig. 169.

crosscutting: Cutting with a saw across the width.

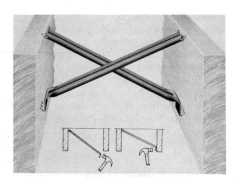

Fig. 168. Steel cross budging.

cross grain: A section of wood cut at right angles to the longitudinal fiber. Also, in wood, when the cells, or fibers, of wood do not run parallel with the axis or sides of a piece of timber, the result is a twisting and interweaving of the wood fibers known as *cross grain.* See *grain,* page 221.

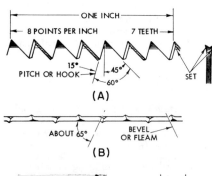

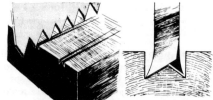

Fig. 169. Crosscut saw teeth which cut like two rows of knife points.

crossette: A projection or ear at a corner of the architrave of a door or window. Sometimes called *ancon* or *elbow*.

crosshatching: The marking or shading produced when a series of parallel lines cross each other; used to indicate or emphasize certain parts of a design. See *hatching,* page 233.

crosslap: A joint where two pieces of timber cross each other. This type of joint is formed by cutting away half the thickness of each piece at the place of joining so that one piece will fit into the other and both pieces will lie on the same plane. See Fig. 329, page 251.

crossover: In plumbing, a U-shaped fitting having the ends turned outward. It is used for passing the flow of one pipe past another when the two pipes lie in the same plane.

crotch: A veneer which has been cut from a piece of wood taken from a tree where a limb meets the trunk. See *crotch veneer.*

crotch veneer: A type of veneer cut from the crotch of a tree forming an unusual grain effect; also, veneer cut from wood of twin trees which have grown together, likewise forming an unusual grain effect.

crotchwood: A name which is applied to a highly figured veneer produced from that portion of a tree where two limbs unite.

crow foot: In electricity, a small fitting, fastened in an outlet box, to which fixtures are fastened.

crowbar: A heavy *pinch bar* made of a piece of rounded iron which is flattened to a chisellike point at one end. It is used as a lever. See Fig. 425, page 325.

crown: In architecture, the uppermost member of the cornice. Also, in road or driveway construction, the upward curve at the middle of a roadway built to allow for water run-off.

crown molding: A molding at the top of the cornice and immediately beneath the roof. See Fig. 79, page 64.

crown of an arch: In architecture, the highest point in an arch; the point at which the *keystone* is placed. Also called *vertex.*

crowning: The upper member of a cornice or other architectural form; the finishing at the top of a member.

crowstep: One of the steps with which a gable wall is often finished instead of a straight, continuous slope; also called *corbiestep.*

crowstep gable: In architecture, a term applied to a gable wall finished in steps instead of a continuous slope. Also called a *corbiestep gable.*

crumb: A soil texture resembling bread crumbs.

crush plate: A strip of wood attached to the edge of a form or intersection of fitted forms to protect the form from damage during stripping operations. The term is also used to designate a *wrecking strip.*

crushing strain: In structural work, the strain which causes the failure of the material by compression.

cube: In solid geometry, a solid consisting of six equal, square sides.

cube root: A given number which taken three times as a factor produces a number called its *cube,* $3 \times 3 \times 3$ equals 27. Hence, *3,* the given number, is the *cube root* of 27.

cubic content: In building construction, the number of cubic feet contained within the walls of a room or combination of rooms and used as a basis for estimating cost of materials and construction; cubic content is also important when estimating cost of installing heating, lighting, and ventilating systems.

cubic measure: The measurement of volume in cubc units, as follows:

1,728 cubic inches	= 1 cubic foot
27 cubic feet	= 1 cubic yard
231 cubic inches	= 1 gallon
128 cubic feet	= 1 cord

cul-de-sac: Street, road, or alley with only one outlet, one end being closed.

133

culls: In building construction, pieces of material which have been rejected and discarded as not suitable for good construction, such as the lowest grade of lumber.

cup: In lumber, a form of warp resulting in distortion of a board in which the face is convex or concave across the grains or width of a piece. See *warp,* page 475.

cup base: One of two types of base furnished with the Lally column.

cup chuck: In wood working, a lathe chuck with a deep recessed face, used in end-grain turning.

cup escutcheon: A plate for use on sliding doors with a recessed panel to provide a finger hold as well as to provide space for the knob or latch control, all of which does not project beyond a line flush with the edge of the door.

cup joint: In plumbing, a socket joint formed between two small pipes in the same line, by opening out the end of one pipe to receive the tapered end of the other. The joint is then made firm by filling the space surrounding the lapped ends with molten solder. See *bell-and-spigot joint,* page 46.

cup shake: A defect in wood where annual rings separate from each other, thus forming a semicircular flaw. Such flaws may occur between two or more concentric layers of wood. Because of their appearance, such defects are known as *cup shake,* but since they are caused by the wind they are also known as *windshake.* See Fig. 635, page 485.

cupboard button: A small bar which turns, designed to fasten a door; a *turn button.*

cupboard catch: Small spring catch which is designed for securing a lightweight door. The catch is operated by a thumb piece or slide knob. See *cupboard turn,* Fig. 170.

cupola: Small vaulted structure attached to the roof of a building, usually hemispherical in shape, covering a circular or polygonal area and supported either upon solid walls or upon four arches.

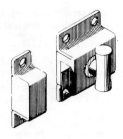

Fig. 170. Cupboard turn.

curb: In architecture, a wall plate which carries a dome at the springings.

curb box: In plumbing, a contrivance which usually consists of a tubelike casting or a long piece of pipe, placed over a *curb cock,* through which a key is inserted to permit the turning of the curb cock. See Fig. 171.

Fig. 171. Curb cock or stop.

curb cock: In plumbing, a control stop installed in a water service pipe between the curb and the sidewalk. Such a device makes it possible to shut off the water supply from a building if it is to be closed for any reason, or in time of an emergency such as a flood. Sometimes called *curb stop.* See Fig. 171.

curb edger: In masonry and cement work, a tool specially designed for shaping curved sections which must be finished smooth and true, such as the borders of driveways or pavements.

curb joint: The center joint of one side of a *gambrel roof.* Also called a *knuckle joint.*

curb plate: In building, the wall plate which supports a dome. See *curb.*

curb roof: The mansard roof taking its name from the architect who designed it. This type of roof has a double slope on each side, with the lower slope almost vertical. Frequently, the lower slope contains dormer windows, which make possible the addition of another story to the house. See *mansard roof,* page 276, Fig. 368, page 277.

curb stop: In plumbing, a valve placed in a service pipe at a point near the curb. Same as *curb cock,* Fig. 171.

curb-stop box: In plumbing, a cast iron box brought up to grade level and equipped with a removable iron cover through which the plumber gains access to the *curb cock;* also called curb stop. Same as *curb box* or *buffalo box.*

curb stringer: In stair building, the three-member assembly sometimes used in an open stair, consisting of one faced stringer, surmounted with a shoe rail to receive balusters, and one housed stringer.

curdling: In painting, a term applied to the thickening of varnish in the can; also, the incorporating into lacquer enamel, a fast-drying, weak solvent thinner, of an inferior quality.

curing: In mortar and concrete work, the drying and hardening process. Fresh concrete should be kept warm and moist to keep water present so it hydrates properly. See *hydration,* page 241.

curl: A spiral or curved marking in the grain of wood; a feather-form mark in wood.

current: In building, the inclination at which any surface is laid, such as a roof, in order to provide for the carrying away of rain water; also, the flow of electrical energy through a circuit.

curtail: A scroll termination on any architectural member.

curtain wall: A thin wall, supported by the structural steel or concrete frame of the building, independent of the wall below.

curve: A line which changes its direction continuously. See *flexible curves,* page 195, *irregular curves,* page 247.

curvilinear: Bounded by curved lines.

cushion head: In foundation construction, a capping to protect the head of a pile which is to be sunk into the ground with a *pile driver.* Such a cushion usually consists of a cast-iron cap. See Fig. 172.

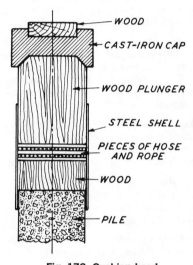

Fig. 172. Cushion head.

cusp: The intersecting point of the small arcs decorating the internal curves of Gothic foils; also the figure formed by the intersection of such arcs.

cut-in: A device operating in an electric circuit which connects two circuits.

cut nail: A square, tapered wood fastening used especially in heavy timber construction where great holding power is desired. No longer in common use, the cut nail has been largely replaced by the wire nail. See Fig. 389, page 296.

cutout box: In electricity, the box in which fuse-holder blocks, fuses, and circuit breakers are located.

cutter: In masonry, a brick made soft enough to cut with a trowel to any shape desired; then rubbed to a smooth face. Sometimes called *rubbers.* The same as *seconds.*

cutting gage: A gage similar in construction to the regular marking gages except that it has an adjustable blade for slitting thin stock instead of the marking pin.

cutting pliers: A type of pliers which, in addition to the flat jaws, has a pair of nippers placed to one side for cutting wires.

cycle: The flow of alternating current, first in one direction and then in the opposite direction, in one cycle; also referred to as *Hertz.* In a 60 cycle circuit, for example, direction change would occur 60 times every second.

cyclone cellar: A cellar or excavation, as a specially designed cave which serves as a refuge from severe windstorms, cyclones, or tornadoes. See *storm cellar,* page 434.

cyclostyle: When a structure is composed of a circular range of columns without a core, it is said to be *cyclostylar* in form; with a core, it is a *peristyle.*

cylinder: Any geometrical solid bounded by a curved surface and two equal parallel planes.

cylinder lock: A lock with the keyhole and tumbler mechanism contained in a cylinder which is separate from the lock case. See Fig. 173.

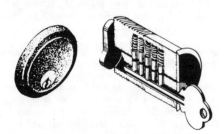

Fig. 173. Cylinder lock.

cylinder ring: A washer placed under the head of a cylinder lock to allow for the use of a long cylinder in a thin door.

cylindrical: A section having an extended convex surface or having the form of a cylinder.

cyma: A molding in common use, with a simple waved line concave at one end and convex at the other end, similar in form to an italic *f.* When the concave part is uppermost the molding is called *cyma recta;* but if the convexity appears above and the concavity below the molding is known as *cyma reversa.* See Figs. 174 and 230, page 174.

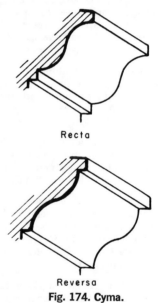

Recta

Reversa

Fig. 174. Cyma.

cymatium: In classic architecture, the crowning molding of an entablature when in the form of a cyma is known as the *cymatium.*

D

dado: The vertical face of an insulated pedestal between the base and surbase or between the base and cornice; a plain, flat surface at the base of a wall as in a room; sometimes such a surface is ornamented.

dado and rabbet: A joint formed by a rabbeted edge or end of one piece fitted into a groove or dado in another piece.

dado joint: A joint formed by the intersection of two boards, usually at right angles, the end of one of which is notched into the side of the other for a distance of half the latter's thickness. See Fig. 330, page 252.

dado rail: A horizontal rail or wide molding around the walls of a room dividing the walls horizontally into upper and lower panels. Sometimes called a *chair rail.*

dais: A platform at one end of a hall or large room raised above the level of the rest of the floor. The purpose of a *dais* is to give prominence to those who occupy it.

damper: A device used for regulating the draft in the flue of a furnace; also, a device for checking vibrations. See *fireplace,* page 189. Fig. 245, page 188.

dampproofing: The special preparation of a wall to prevent moisture from oozing through it; material used for this purpose must be impervious to moisture.

dampproofing agent: An admixture very similar to a permeability agent; used to reduce the capillary flow of moisture through concrete that is in contact with water or damp earth.

dap: To notch; also, a notch cut in one timber to receive another.

dap joint: A joint made by dapping two structural timbers.

dapping: In carpentry, the process of cutting notches in structural timbers.

darby: A flat tool used by plasterers to level the surface of plaster, especially on ceilings. The *darby* is usually about three and one-half inches wide, ½ inch thick, and forty-four inches long, with two handles on the back. See Fig. 175. In concrete flatwork, a smoothing tool used immediately after screeding. See *bullfloating,* page 77.

datum level: A basic level or line used as a reference for reckoning heights and depths of points or surfaces in building-construction work. Within the limits of any given city, the established *datum level* is recorded in the building codes which control the building standards for that city.

datum point: A point of elevation reference established by the city from which levels and distances are measured.

daubing: The process of giving a rough-stone finish to a wall by throwing a rough coating of plaster upon it; also, a term applied to the dressing of a stone surface with a special hammer so as to cover the surface with small holes.

dead bolt: In a door lock, a bolt with a square head controlled directly by the key when moved in either direction.

dead end: In plumbing, the extended portion of a pipe between a closed end and the connection nearest to it, forming a *dead* pocket in which there is no circulation; hence, permitting the stagnation of water or air contained in the extended and closed end of the pipe.

dead latch: A door lock having a spring bolt which cannot be operated on the outside except by the use of a key. Same as *night latch.*

dead level: An emphatic statement used to indicate an absolute level.

dead load: A permanent, inert load whose pressure on a building or other structure is steady and constant, due to the weight of its structural members and the fixed loads they carry, imposing definite stresses and strains upon it. See *live load,* page 270.

dead lock: A door lock equipped with a *dead bolt.*

deadening: The use of insulating materials made for the purpose of preventing sounds passing through walls and floors.

deadman: An anchor for a guy line, usually a beam, block, or other heavy item buried in the ground, to which the line is attached. In pipe work, anchor used to keep the sections of pipe from separating.

deal: A board or plank cut to a standard size, in US and Canada 11″ wide x 12′ long x 2½″ thick.

Fig. 175. Darbying on acoustical plaster.

decay: In timber, a disintegration of wood fiber due to the action of wood destroying fungi; also called *dote* or *rot*.

decibel: A unit used to express the relation between two amounts of power; a unit for measuring sound intensity. When sound or noise is created it gives off energy or power which is measured in *decibels*. The *decibel* is used as a measure of response in all types of electrical communication circuits. It is named in honor of Alexander Graham Bell.

deciduous: Pertaining to trees which shed their leaves annually.

decimal: A fractional part of a number, proceeding by tenths, each unit being ten times the unit next smaller.

decimal equivalent: The value of a fraction expressed as a decimal, as 1/4 equals .25.

deck: In building, the flat portion of a roof or floor roadway. In reinforced concrete construction, the formwork upon which the concrete floor is placed. See Fig. 176. In bridge building, the roadway or top which may be of planking, asphalt, concrete, girders, steel mesh, etc. See *composite deck*, page 112.

deck paint: Enamel paint very resistant to mechanical wear; used on such surfaces as porch floors.

deck roof: In architecture, a nearly flat roof with little inclination and without a *fire wall*.

decking: See *deck*.

decorated style: Pertaining to the pointed or Gothic style of architecture prevalent in Europe during the greater part of the 14th century; characterized by elaborate decorations and considered the most complete de-

Fig. 176. Decking being laid.

velopment of Gothic architecture. The best examples are found in England. Sometimes called the *Decorated Period.*

deep-seal trap: In plumbing, a water-seal trap which has twice the depth of a *common-seal trap.* The *deep-seal trap,* having a water column of four inches in depth, is used ordinarily for only abnormal conditions. See Fig. 177.

deeping: In carpentry, the cutting out of a structural member to the depth comparatively far below the surface of the piece being worked.

defect: In lumber, an irregularity occurring in or on wood that will tend to impair its strength, durability, or utility value.

deflection: A deviation, or turning aside, from a straight line; bending of a beam or any part of a structure under an applied

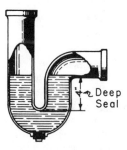

Fig. 177. Deep-seal trap.

139

load. In beams, the deflection is limited to a certain designated fraction of the span, usually about 1/360th. In highway bridges, the *deflection ratio* (deflection divided by span) may be 1/200, while in railroad bridges the ratio may vary from 1/200 to 1/300. Fig. 178 illustrates deflection in a wood beam.

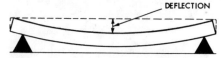

Fig. 178. The amount of bending that occurs in a wood member is called the deflection.

deformation: Act of deforming or changing the shape; alteration in form which a structure undergoes when subjected to the action of a weight or load.

deformed bar: A reinforcing bar made with lugs or ridges to produce a better bond between the bar and the concrete. Two types of *deformed bars* are shown in Fig. 179.

Bethlehem Bar

Courtesy of Bethlehem Steel Company

Ryerson Bar

Courtesy of Joseph Ryerson & Son, Inc.

Fig. 179. Deformed bars.

degrades: Pieces which, on reinspection, prove of lower quality than the grade in which they were classified.

degree: A unit of angular measurement. One 360th part of a circumference of a circle. Also a unit of temperature measurement, such as degree Fahrenheit or degree Centigrade.

degree-day: A unit employed in estimating fuel consumption and specifying the nominal heating load of a building in winter. It is based upon the temperature difference and time. For any one day, when the mean temperature is less than 65°F., there exists as many degree-days as there are Fahrenheit degree difference in temperature between the mean temperature for the day and 65°F.

degree of saturation: The ratio of the volume of water to the volume of the voids, that is, the amount of water in a material.

dehumidifier: In air conditioning, the washing screen of the fine water which cools the air extracted by the air-conditioning plant from an auditorium and, under certain conditions, reduces the water content of the output air while adjusting the dew point. Also a device used in homes to extract excess moisture from the air in summer to prevent "sweating" of cold surfaces.

dehumidify: To reduce by any process the quantity of water vapor or moisture content of air within a given space.

dehydrate: To take moisture from materials.

delamination: Coming apart layer by layer; separation of plies.

demarcation: In masonry, a fixed line for marking a boundary limit. Also, the marking off or separation by distinct boundaries.

density: The standard unit weight per unit volume of a material usually expressed as pounds per cubic foot.

denticular: Cut into dentils; containing dentils; when applied to an order, a course of small rectangular blocks in the cornice.

dentil: In Corinthian architecture, a cog or toothed member, such as a rectangular supporting block commonly used in the bed mold of the entablature. Each cog or tooth is called a *dentil*. See Fig. 230, page 174.

dentil band: In architecture, molding in the bed molding of a cornice, resembling a *dentil* or row of dentils. See Fig. 230, page 174.

depressed plaster ceiling panel: A sunken panel produced by furring down on the ceiling joists all the way around a room before the lathing is done. The sunken panel is effected usually with 2 x 2 strips which project approximately 18 inches from the side walls.

depth gage: A measuring instrument used for testing the depth of holes or recessed portions of any structural work. It consists of a narrow rule which slides through a crosspiece.

derrick: Any hoisting device used for lifting or moving heavy weights; also, a structure consisting of an upright or fixed framework, with a hinged arm which can be raised and lowered and usually swings around to different positions for handling loads. See Fig. 180.

Fig. 180. Derrick at work lifting timber members for a trestle. (West Coast Lumbermen's Assoc.)

describe: To give an account or represent by words; to trace, or draw, an outline of an object, as to *describe* an arc.

desiccate: To dry thoroughly or to make dry by removing the moisture content, as the seasoning of timber by exposing it in an oven to a current of hot air.

design: A drawing showing the plan, elevations, sections, and other features necessary in the construction of a new building. As used by architects, the term *plan* is restricted to the horizontal projection, while *elevation* applies to the vertical or exterior views.

design load: The capacity required of air-conditioning apparatus to produce specified conditions inside when specified conditions of temperature and humidity prevail outside and when all sources of load are taken at the maximum which then occur coincidentally. Air-conditioning equipment should have a capacity equal to the design load. Also, the load for which structural members such as beams, columns, girders, etc., are designed.

designer: Someone qualified to lay out or design a product which is to be manufactured for commercial use. Also called a *layout man.*

detail: A term in architecture applied to the small parts into which any structure or machine is divided. It is applied generally to moldings or other decorative features and to drawings showing a special feature of construction. In structural work it also applies to joints, hangers, angles, special columns and beams, ducts, conduits, etc.

detail drawing: A separate drawing showing a small part of a machine or structure in detail; a drawing showing the separate parts of a machine or other object with complete tabular data, such as dimensions, materials used, number of pieces, and operations to be performed; also, a drawing showing the position of the parts of a machine or tool and the manner in which the various parts are placed in assembling them. The cornice detail in Fig. 159, page 125, is a typical example of an architectural detail.

detailer: One who prepares small drawings for shop use; a draftsman who makes detailed drawings.

deterioration: A worsening or lowering in quality.

determine: In building, to find the bounds or dimensions of an area, building, or structural material by taking measurements.

dew point: The temperature at which a given sample of moist air will become saturated and deposit dew; the point at which dew begins to form. See *dew-point temperature.*

dew-point temperature: The temperature at which the condensation of water vapor in a space begins for a given state of humidity and pressure as the temperature of the vapor is reduced. The temperature corresponding to saturation (100 percent relative humidity) for a given absolute humidity at constant pressure.

diagonal: A straight oblique line connecting two nonadjacent angles of a quadrilateral, polygon, or polyhedron; a straight line which divides a rectangle into two equal triangles. The struts, ties, and braces of a lattice girder are its *diagonals.*

diagonal bond: In masonry, a form of bond sometimes used in unusually thick walls. The bricks are laid diagonally across the wall, with successive courses crossing each other in respect to rake.

diagonal grain: Lumber in which the annual rings are at an angle with the axis of a piece, as a result of the lumber being sawed at an angle with the bark of the tree.

diagonal pliers: These are used for cutting wires where it is difficult to use side cutting pliers. For example, as for cutting armored cable conductors after the metal armor has been cut. See Fig. 181.

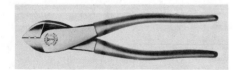

Fig. 181. Diagonal pliers.

diagonal rib: The rib which crosses the bay diagonally in Gothic vaulting.

diagram: A figure which gives the outline or general features of an object; a line drawing, as a chart or graph used for scientific purposes; a graphic representation of some feature of a structure.

dial lock: A lock having changeable tumblers which may be set by a dial on the face or door of the lock. Same as *combination lock.*

diameter: A straight line passing through the center of a circle or sphere and terminating in the circumference.

diaper: A pattern or type of ornament used in decorating a wall, panel, or other plane surface with a continuous design of flowers or geometrical figures. The surface is entirely covered with a succession of units, the outline of one forming part of the adjoining unit.

diastyle: A term used to describe a classic arrangement of columns, having the space of four diameters from center to center of their shafts and where the intercolumniation measures three diameters.

diatomaceous earth: A fine siliceous earth composed chiefly of cell walls of diatoms; used in filtration, as an abrasive, etc.

die: The dado of a pedestal; the cubical part of a pedestal between its base and cap.

dies: Tools for bending and threading metal conduits for electrical conductors or wires; also used for threading plumbing pipes and rods.

diffuser: An air register for spreading the flow of air as from a duct to the room.

dimension: The measured distance between two points; a definite measure shown on a drawing; the size of a room or building, as the length, width, and height; also, the size of building material given in length, width, and thickness.

dimension lumber: Lumber as it comes from the saws, commonly called *dimension stuff,* 2 inches thick and from 4 to 12 inches wide. See *scantlings* and *planks;* also, lumber cut to standard sizes or to sizes ordered.

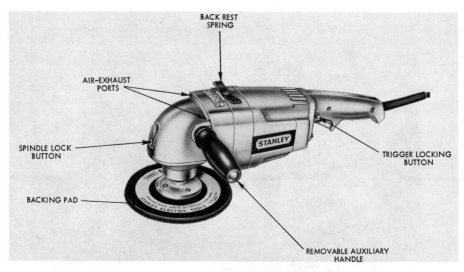

BACK REST
SPRING

AIR-EXHAUST
PORTS

SPINDLE LOCK
BUTTON

TRIGGER LOCKING
BUTTON

BACKING PAD

REMOVABLE AUXILIARY
HANDLE

Fig. 182. Portable disc sander. (Stanley Works)

dimension shingles: Shingles cut to a uniform size as distinguished from *random shingles.*

diminution: Tapering; the gradual reduction in size toward the end of an object or column.

dipping solution: In the process of heating a soldering iron, the tinned part of the point becomes discolored and should be cleaned off before beginning the soldering operation. This is done by plunging the point of the soldering iron into a solution composed of ½ ounce of powdered sal ammoniac and one quart of clean water immediately after removing it from the fire.

direct current (d.c.): Current in which the electricity (electrons) flows in one direction only. Examples, a dry cell, an automobile battery.

direct nailing: Nailing perpendicular to the initial surface or to the junction of the pieces joined. Also called *face nailing.*

direction: The position, or location, of one point in relation to another, as the points indicated by the needle of a surveyor's compass.

disappearing stair: A specially constructed stairway which can be folded and swung upward into a space in the ceiling when not in use.

disc sander: A motor driven portable tool designed to edge finish floors, etc. Also, a larger machine mounted on a stand, used in carpentry to sand end grain of objects. Fig. 182 illustrates a portable disc sander.

discharging arch: Any architectural member, or strut, designed to resist pressure and to distribute the weight of a wall above an opening, such as over a door or window.

disintegration: In masonry, the gradual wasting away or crumbling of building stone.

dispersing agent: An addition or admixture capable of increasing the fluidity of pastes, mortars, or concrete by reduction of inter-particle attraction.

display model: In architecture, a greatly reduced, scale model of a structure as it would appear with landscaping, people, automobiles, etc. See Fig. 183.

disposal field: See *absorption field,* page 2.

143

Fig. 183. Models placed in their topographic setting with scale figures give a realistic atmosphere.

dissolve: To liquefy or cause to pass into solution; to melt or change from a solid to a fluid state by the addition of some other substance.

distemper: A term applied to a composition used for painting walls; a paint in which the colors are tempered or mixed with any of various glutinous substances, such as size, glue, or the white of eggs.

distributed load: In building, a load spread evenly over an entire surface, or along the length of a girder, expressed in pounds or tons per foot.

distribution box: In electricity, a small metal box in a metallic tubing or conduit installation which permits accessibility for connecting branch circuits. In septic systems the concrete box from which effluent is distributed to the field tiles.

distribution line: In electricity, the main feed line of a circuit to which branch circuits are connected.

distribution panel: In electricity, an insulated board from which connections are made between the main feed lines and branch lines.

distribution tile: Concrete or clay tile without bell mouths. These tiles are laid with a little space at each joint, in lines which fan out from a septic tank distribution box.

distyle: Pertaining to a structure with two columns across the front, as a portico having two columns between antae.

divide: To separate into parts; to cut apart into two or more pieces; to separate as by a partition.

divided bathroom: A bathroom in which the bath area is separated from the wash bowl and water closet areas by a partition. This arrangement facilitates use of the bathroom by two persons at the same time, assuring privacy and conserving time.

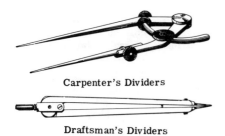

Carpenter's Dividers

Draftsman's Dividers

Fig. 184. Dividers.

divided light: In architecture, a window composed of small panes of glass.

dividers: A measuring device consisting of two metal points with hinged legs, used for setting off distances, dividing into equal units, etc. The *carpenter's dividers* are also used for scribing irregular surfaces. See Fig. 184, top. The *draftsman's dividers* are similar to a compass except they have no drawing point. See Fig. 184, bottom.

Fig. 185 illustrates some of the common uses of the *carpenter's dividers,* used by carpenters, masons, plasterers, tile setters, etc.

division wall: Usually an interior bearing wall which separates a building into several rooms or compartments; also, a masonry wall which completely separates one building from another. Division walls may be either bearing walls or self-supporting walls.

dog: In building, a piece of metal for binding pieces of wood or two timbers together, for which purpose the metal is hooked at each end at right angles to the length, so the hooked ends may be driven into the timbers or wood. The term is also applied to a great variety of gripping implements.

dog anchor: An iron rod or bar with the ends bent to a right angle, used for holding pieces of timber together.

dog-eared fold: In plumbing, a folding joint formed at the corner of a sheet-lead tray.

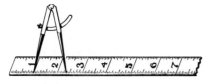

TO SET DIVIDERS HOLD BOTH POINTS ON THE MEASURING LINES OF THE RULE.

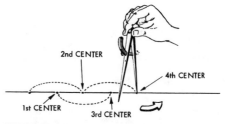

DIVIDERS ARE USED TO STEP OFF A MEASUREMENT SEVERAL TIMES ACCURATELY

DIVIDERS MAY BE USED TO SCRIBE A LINE TO MATCH AN IRREGULAR SURFACE MASONRY OR WOODWORK.

DIVIDERS ARE USED FOR SCRIBING CIRCLES OR AN ARC. ALSO FOR COMBINATIONS OF CIRCLES AND ARCS FOR MAKING LAYOUTS FOR CURVED DESIGNS, ETC.

Fig. 185. Carpenter's divider used on the job.

145

dog iron: A short iron strap or bar having the ends bent to a right angle; used as a *cramp* or joggle for holding timbers or stone together; a short iron bar with an eye in one end, used for driving or fitting into a timber or stone to lift it into position; also, a *firedog*.

dog-legged stairway: A term applied to stairs consisting of two or more successive flights, rising in opposite directions, and having platforms, or landings, but without a *wellhole*.

dog nail: In carpentry, a large nail with a head which projects over one side.

dog's ear: In plumbing, the corner of a sheet-lead tray, formed with a folding joint.

dog's tooth: In masonry, a string course where the bricks are laid so that one corner projects.

dogtooth: In architecture, a toothlike ornament or a molding cut into projecting teeth; a type of early architectural decoration in the form of a four-leafed flower, probably so named from its resemblance to a dog-toothed violet.

dolly: In building construction, a small truck used for moving heavy timbers of structural members, such as beams, girders, and columns. There are two types, one using a single roller and one having two wheels on an axle. See Fig. 186.

Fig. 186. A dolly used for moving timbers over level surfaces.

doloment: In building, a name applied to a composition used in making floors without joints.

dome: A large, vaulted structure generated by a vertical arch rotated about its vertical axis to form a circular, hexagonal, octagonal, etc., pattern as its base; the vaulted roof of a rotunda.

dome damper: A damper with a cast-iron frame placed at the bottom of the smoke chamber of a fireplace above the brick arch.

door: An opening in the wall of a house or other building which affords access to the building, an apartment, or a room, a *doorway;* also, the structural member which closes the doorway. Various designs for both outside and inside doors are shown in Fig. 187.

doorbell: A bell that rings inside a building when its control, located outside adjacent to an entrance door, is activated.

door bolt: A door fastener, consisting of a sliding bar or rod which is mounted and attached to a door so as to lock it.

doorbrand: A bar for a door; also, a term applied to a strap hinge which holds door planks together.

door buck: In building, a rough doorframe set in a partition or wall, especially a masonry wall. The doorframe is attached to the *door buck* which butts against the wall. The *door buck* may be of either metal or wood. See Fig. 188.

doorcase: The visible or inner frame of a door, including the finished trim with the two jamb pieces.

door casing: The finish material around a door opening.

door check: A device used to retard the movement of a closing door and to guard against its slamming, or banging, but also insures the closing of the door.

door chimes: In building, a mechanical device which takes the place of a *doorbell* or buzzer. Instead of a ringing or buzzing sound, the chimes sound a musical note or tune.

door closer: A device to check a door and to prevent its slamming when it is being closed. Same as *door check*.

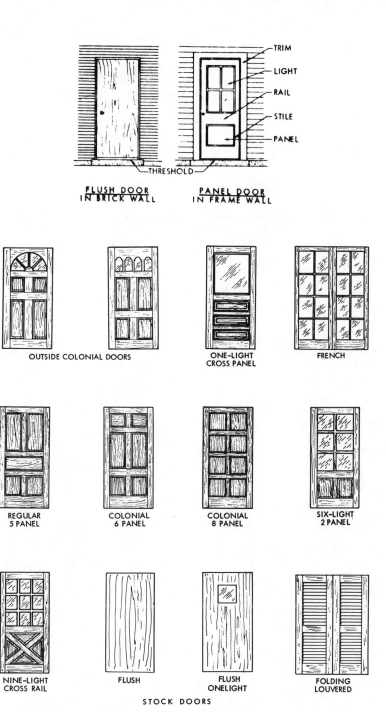

FLUSH DOOR
IN BRICK WALL

PANEL DOOR
IN FRAME WALL

TRIM
LIGHT
RAIL
STILE
PANEL

THRESHOLD

OUTSIDE COLONIAL DOORS

ONE-LIGHT
CROSS PANEL

FRENCH

REGULAR
5 PANEL

COLONIAL
6 PANEL

COLONIAL
8 PANEL

SIX-LIGHT
2 PANEL

NINE-LIGHT
CROSS RAIL

FLUSH

FLUSH
ONELIGHT

FOLDING
LOUVERED

STOCK DOORS

Fig. 187. Designs of stock doors.

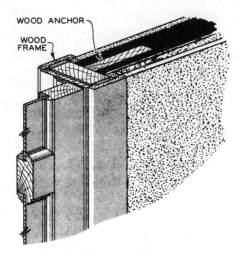

WOOD ANCHOR

WOOD FRAME

Fig. 188. Door buck.

door details: In carpentry, those parts of the building plans which pertain to the framing and finishing of the door, including the jamb and head details. See Figs. 189 and 190.

door frame: The case which surrounds a door and into which the door closes and out of which it opens. The frame consists of two upright pieces called *jambs* and the *lintel* or horizontal piece over the opening for the door. See Fig. 190.

door frame details: In carpentry, the special features, or structural details, of the door frame, including the head, sills, and jambs. See Fig. 190.

door head: The upper part of the frame of a door.

door holder: A device used for holding or fastening a door in an open position. See Fig. 191.

door jack: A frame used by carpenters for holding a door while it is being planed and the edges fitted to the size of a door opening. See Fig. 192.

door jamb: Two upright pieces fitted and held together by a head to form the lining for a door opening. See *door details*, Figs. 189 and 190.

doornail: A large-headed nail which is easily clinched; used for nailing a door through battens.

door plate: A metal plate on the door of a house or apartment carrying the name of the occupant.

door post: The jamb or sidepiece of a doorway.

door pull: A handle which is commonly mounted on a metal plate, designed for attaching to a door to facilitate the opening and closing of the door.

door schedule: A table, usually located on elevation drawing, which gives the symbols (number or letter) used for each type of door. The quantity, type, and size are given. See Fig. 68, page 56.

door sill: The sill or threshold of a door.

door step: A step before an outer door; also, one of several steps leading from an outer door to the ground or a street level.

door stone: The stone which forms the threshold of a door.

door stop: A device used to hold a door open to any desired position; a device usually attached near the bottom of a door to

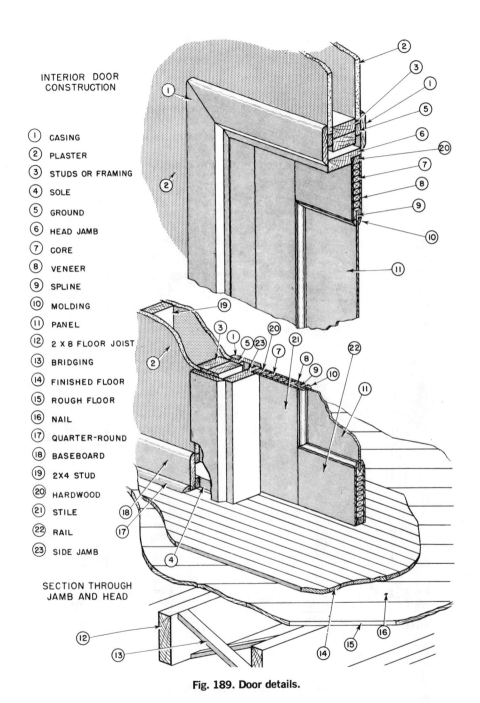

INTERIOR DOOR
CONSTRUCTION

① CASING
② PLASTER
③ STUDS OR FRAMING
④ SOLE
⑤ GROUND
⑥ HEAD JAMB
⑦ CORE
⑧ VENEER
⑨ SPLINE
⑩ MOLDING
⑪ PANEL
⑫ 2 X 8 FLOOR JOIST
⑬ BRIDGING
⑭ FINISHED FLOOR
⑮ ROUGH FLOOR
⑯ NAIL
⑰ QUARTER-ROUND
⑱ BASEBOARD
⑲ 2X4 STUD
⑳ HARDWOOD
㉑ STILE
㉒ RAIL
㉓ SIDE JAMB

SECTION THROUGH
JAMB AND HEAD

Fig. 189. Door details.

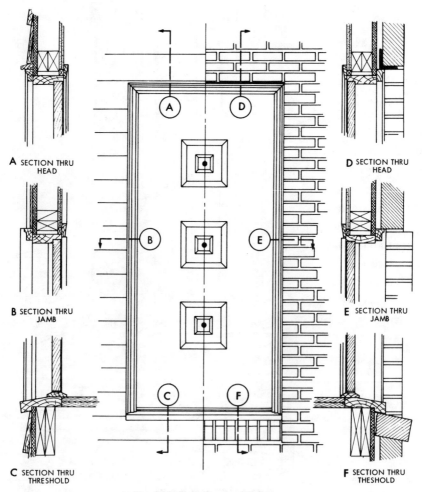

A SECTION THRU
HEAD

B SECTION THRU
JAMB

C SECTION THRU
THRESHOLD

D SECTION THRU
HEAD

E SECTION THRU
JAMB

F SECTION THRU
THESHOLD

Fig. 190. Door frame details.

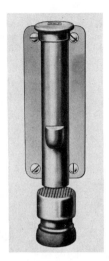

Fig. 191. Door holders.

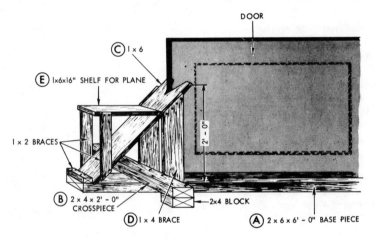

Fig. 192. Door jack for holding door while fitting it.

hold it open and operated by the pressure of the foot; a device placed on a baseboard to keep an open door from marring the wall. The *door stop* may or may not be attached to the door. The strip against which a door closes on the inside face of a door frame is also known as a *door stop*. A typical door stop is shown in Fig. 193.

Fig. 193. Door stop.

151

door strip: A strip of material, often flexible, attached to a door to cover the space between the bottom of the door and the threshold.

door switch: In electricity, a type of snap switch mounted on or in a door frame so that the opening or closing of the door operates the switch.

door trim: The casing around an interior door opening, to conceal the break between the plaster, or other wall covering, and the door frame or jamb. See *door details*, Fig. 189.

doorway: The opening or passageway which a door closes; an entranceway into a room or house; a portal.

dope: In building, a preparation which serves as a *retarder*.

doping: In building, any process which involves treatment with *dope*, a retarding preparation.

doric frieze: That part of the entablature between the cornice and the architrave in Doric architecture. See *column*, Fig. 137, page 108.

doric order: Pertaining to the oldest and simplest of the three Greek orders of architecture. It is distinguished by the absence of a base to the column.

dormer: In architecture, a dormer window, the vertical framing of which projects from a sloping roof; also, the *gablet*, or houselike structure in which it is contained. There are various types of dormers, one of the most common of these being the *gable dormer* shown in Fig. 194.

dormer window: A vertical window in a projection built out from a sloping roof; a small window projecting from the slope of a roof. See Fig. 194.

dote: *Dote, doze,* and *rot* are terms for *decay*; any form of wood decay.

dots: Small spots of plaster set plum with the grounds or level on a ceiling. See Fig. 195

Fig. 195. Establishing wall dots, using rod and level.

Fig. 194. Dormer.

dotted line: In drawing, a line consisting of short dashes indicating some concealed member represented on the drawing.

double-acting butt: A type of butt hinge which allows a door to swing in either of two directions; commonly used between a kitchen and dining room.

double-acting hinge: A hinge which permits motion in two directions, as on a swinging door, or on folding screens. See Fig. 196.

Fig. 196. Double-acting hinge.

double-acting spring hinge: A door hinge having two sets of springs which have tension in opposite directions, so as to push or move the door toward a closed position but at the same time allowing it to be opened in either direction.

double-bitted key: A lock key having bittings on both edges, so that either or both edges may move or turn the tumblers.

double-door bolt: A device with two sliding bars, one mounted at the top and the other at the bottom of a door, and moving in opposite directions, so as to lock the door at both the top and bottom simultaneously.

double end trimmed: Trimmed square by a saw on both ends.

double Flemish bond: A bond in which both the inner and outer faces of an exposed masonry wall are laid in *Flemish bond,* with all headers true or *full headers.*

double floor: A floor where binding joists support flooring joists above and ceiling joists below.

double-framed floor: A double floor with girders, into which the binding joists are framed.

double framing: The doubling of joists, trimmers, or other construction members to add strength to a building where stiffness is especially needed, as around stair openings and similar places.

double-gable roof: A type of roof which has two gables side by side on the same side of the building. Since the roof represents the letter **M** it is sometimes called an **M** roof.

double glazing: A double-glass pane in a door or window, with an air space between the two panes, which are sealed hermetically to provide insulation, and usually built into the sash. The term is occasionally used when referring to storm sash.

double header: A structural member made by nailing or bolting two or more timbers together for use where extra strength is required in the header, as around stair openings. See Figs. 107, page 85, and 167, page 131.

double head nails: Special nails used in temporary construction such as form work and scaffolds. They have an extra head or collar about a half-inch below the first. The collar keeps the head away from the wood, and the claws of a hammer can easily engage the head for removal. This eliminates the need to strike pieces of lumber to get them apart. See Fig. 197.

Fig. 197. Double headed nail.

double hung window: A window with an upper and lower sash, each carried by sash cords and weights. Fig. 198, left, shows the window; Fig. 198, right shows the details.

double jack rafter: A rafter which extends from a valley to a hip.

double pitch: Sloping in two directions, as a gable roof. See *double-pitch skylight.*

double pitch roof: A roof having two slopes, sometimes called a *saddleback roof.* Same as a *gable roof.*

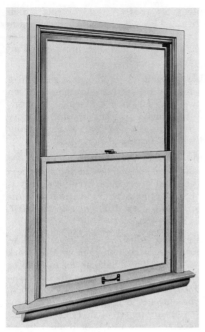

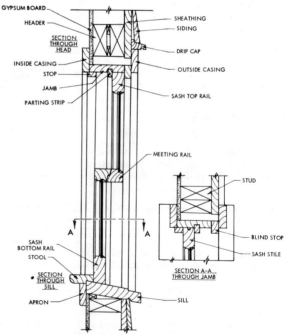

GYPSUM BOARD

HEADER

SECTION
THROUGH
HEAD

INSIDE CASING

STOP

JAMB

PARTING STRIP

SHEATHING

SIDING

DRIP CAP

OUTSIDE CASING

SASH TOP RAIL

MEETING RAIL

STUD

A

A

SASH
BOTTOM RAIL

STOOL

SECTION
THROUGH
SILL

APRON

BLIND STOP

SASH STILE

SECTION A-A
THROUGH JAMB

SILL

Fig. 198. **Double hung window and details. (Andersen Corp.)**

154

double pitch skylight: A skylight designed to slope in two directions.

double pole switch: A switch to connect or break two sides of an electric circuit.

double throw switch: In electricity, a switch which is arranged so the moving blade can be closed to either of two sets of contacts.

double vault: A vault with a duplicate wall, such as is sometimes found in wine cellars.

double window: A window with two sets of glazed sashes and an air space between them.

dovetail: In carpentry, an interlocking joint; a joint made by angle cutting two boards or timbers to fit into each other. A common type of joint used in making boxes or cases. See Fig. 330, page 252.

dovetail cramps: A device, usually of iron bent at the ends, or of dovetail form, used to hold together structural timbers or stone.

dovetail cutter: A tool used for cutting the inner and outer dovetails for joints.

dovetail dado: A groove cut so that the base is wider than the face of the opening to resist pull perpendicular to the face of the board. See *router,* Fig. 491, page 376.

dovetail-halved joint: A joint which is halved by cuts narrowed at the heel, as in a dovetail joint.

dovetail lap joint: Same as dovetail-halved joint.

dovetail saw: A small saw similar to a hacksaw, with smaller teeth and a different-shaped handle.

dovetail seam: In sheet metal work, a method of joining collars to flanges. There are three types dovetails: the plain dovetail, the beaded dovetail, and the flange dovetail. The dovetail seam is principally used on round or elliptical pipe and seldom on rectangular duct. See Fig. 199.

dovetailing: A method of fastening boards or timbers together by fitting one piece into the other as with dovetail joints. See Fig. 330, page 252.

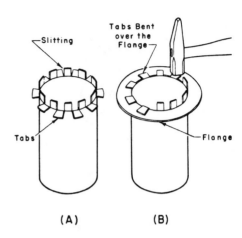

Fig. 199. Plain dovetail seam.

dowel: A pin of wood or metal used to hold or strengthen two pieces of timber where they join; a pin or tenon fitting into a corresponding hole and serving to fasten two pieces of wood together. See Fig. 329, page 251.

doweling: The method of fastening two pieces of timber together by the use of dowels; butt joints are sometimes secured by the use of glue and dowel pins.

dowel pin: A deformed or barbed, pointed, metal pin used to fasten mortise and tenon joints in sash and door work.

down draft: Flow of air downward, as a current of air down a chimney usually due to improper operation of furnace or fireplace from improper design.

down pipe: A spout or pipe, usually vertical, to carry rain water from a roof to the drain. See *downspout, leader,* page 263.

downspout: Any connector, such as a pipe, for carrying rain water from the roof of a building to the ground or to a sewer connection. See *down pipe, conductor,* page 116, and *leader,* page 263.

draft: A term used in reference to the pressure difference which causes a current of air or gases to flow through a flue, chimney, heater, or space; hence, a current of air.

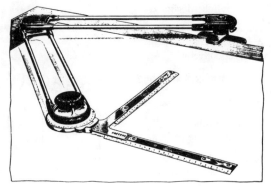

KEUFFEL & ESSER CO.; HOBOKEN, NEW JERSEY.

Fig. 200. The drafting machine is useful for doing large blueprints and drawings.

drafting machine: Machine used in some architectural drafting offices. The drafting machine combines the T-square, triangles, protractor, and scales. See Fig. 200.

draftsman: One who draws plans or sketches; usually a term applied to one who uses mechanical aids or instruments for preparing drawings for tradesmen.

draftsman's scale: A measuring scale used by draftsmen, flat with two edges or triangular with six edges. One edge is graduated in inches divided into sixteenths. Other edges are divided into fractional or decimal parts of an inch which represent feet to facilitate reducing measurements. Almost all scales have from two to eleven graduated faces that enable the draftsman to reduce or enlarge a distance to fit the drawing sheet. See Fig. 201.

draftstop: See *firestops,* page 190.

drag: In masonry, a tool which has steel teeth, used for dressing the surface of stone. Also called a *comb.*

drain: Any pipe, channel, or trench by means of which waste water or other liquid is carried off, as to a sewer pipe. See Fig. 202.

drainage: In plumbing, a system of drains; the process or means of draining; also, that which is disposed of by draining, as waste water or sewerage.

drain cock: In plumbing, a small valve placed at a low point in a pipe line to allow for draining.

draintile: A tile used in making drainpipes or in building drains. See Fig. 202.

draintile receptor: In plumbing, a device consisting of a **P** trap or deep seal, into which an ordinary cast-iron tee is calked. The top opening of the tee may be provided with either a cleanout plug or a floor-drain strainer. See Fig. 203.

drain trap: Any type of air trap used in drain pipes to shut off or carry off foul air or gas from waste pipes or sewers. Same as *stench trap.*

draw bolt: Any ordinary bolt, such as is used for latching doors.

drawbore: A hole bored through a mortise-and-tenon joint so that, when a pin is driven in, it will draw the shoulders of the tenon down upon the abutment cheeks of the mortise and make a tighter joint.

drawbridge: A type of bridge so constructed that it may be raised up or turned aside to allow for the passage of boats.

drawer pull: A handle or grip designed to fit the fingers, for opening or closing cupboard or closet drawers.

drawer slip: A guide or strip on which a drawer moves when it is opened.

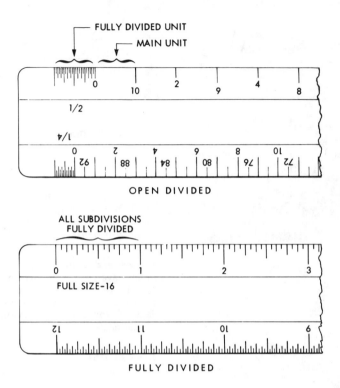

FULLY DIVIDED UNIT

MAIN UNIT

1/2

1/4

OPEN DIVIDED

ALL SUBDIVISIONS
FULLY DIVIDED

0   1   2   3

FULL SIZE-16

FULLY DIVIDED

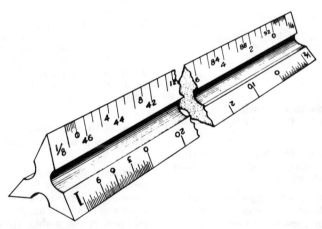

Fig. 201. The triangular architect's scale is made in 6″ and 12″ lengths. Scale graduations may be open or fully divided. (Top: Frederick Post Co.)

157

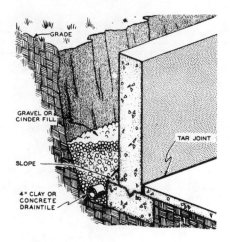

Fig. 202. Drains.

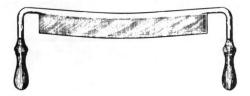

Fig. 204. Draw knife or drawshave.

dress: To smooth or finish a wood surface by the use of a carpenter's plane; also, to cut or trim to shape, as the shaping of stone by use of a stonecutter's ax.

dressed and matched: Boards or planks which have been machined in such a manner that there is a groove on one edge and a corresponding tongue on the other edge. Same as *tongue-and-groove* material. Abbreviation *D & M.*

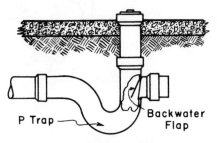

Fig. 203. Draintile receptor.

dressed lumber: In construction work, lumber machined and surfaced at a mill.

dressed masonry: Masonry work which has been given a smooth finish.

dressed-size lumber: A term commonly used when referring to the dimensions of lumber after planing; usually a planed piece is ½ or ¾ of an inch less than the nominal, or rough, size. For example, a 2x4 stud actually measures 1½x3½ inches; a 2x12 would measure 1½x11¼ inches; a 1x10, though, would measure ¾x9½ inches.

drawing: A sketch made with pen, pencil, or crayon representing by lines some figure or object.

drawing board: The board to which a draftsman attaches his paper preparatory to making a drawing.

drawknife: A woodworking tool with a blade and a handle at each end. The handles are at right angles to the blade which is long and narrow. It is used to smooth a surface by drawing the knife over it. See Fig. 204.

dresser: In plumbing, a tool used for straightening lead pipe and sheet lead.

dressing: Any decorative finish, as molding around a door; also, in masonry, all those stone or brick parts distinguished from the plain wall of a building, such as ornamental columns, jambs, arches, entablatures, copings, quoins, and string courses. The process of smoothing and squaring lumber or stone for use in a building.

158

drier: A substance, often a metal compound, which accelerates the drying of oil, paint, varnish, ink, etc.

drift plug: In plumbing, a wooden plug driven through a lead pipe to straighten out a kink.

driftpins: Steel pins used to hold steel beams in place temporarily.

drill: In building, a small tool used to bore holes in wood or metal for fastening builders' hardware and other similar purposes. Fig. 205 illustrates common hand drills and bits and a portable electric drill commonly used on construction jobs.

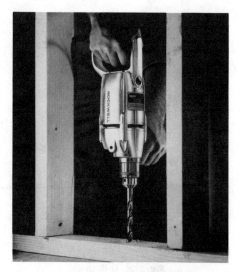

Fig. 205A. Portable electric drill.

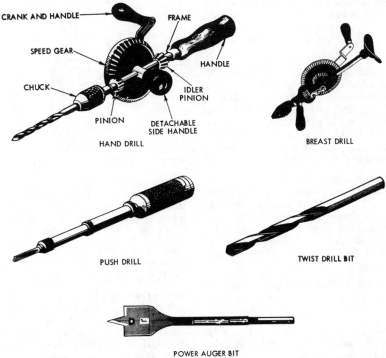

CRANK AND HANDLE

FRAME

SPEED GEAR

HANDLE

CHUCK

IDLER PINION

PINION

DETACHABLE SIDE HANDLE

HAND DRILL

BREAST DRILL

PUSH DRILL

TWIST DRILL BIT

POWER AUGER BIT

Fig. 205B. Drills and bits.

drill bit: A cutting tool for making round holes in wood, metal, or other hard materials by being rotated in a drill. Also called *drill point*. See *bits,* Fig. 60, page 51.

drill point: A tool used to drill holes in iron and other metals. Same as *drill bit*. See Figs. 60 and 205.

drill saw: A drill-like tool with a toothed surface used for cutting or enlarged holes of various shapes, such as for receptacles or switch boxes. See Fig. 206.

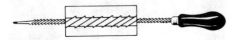

Fig. 206. Drill saw.

drinking fountain: In building construction, a small fixture which supplies drinking water for the public, especially in business offices, industrial plants, and store buildings.

drip: A construction member, wood, plastic or metal, which projects to throw off rain water; a channel cut on the underside of a sill (see Fig. 286, page 218); a pipe or a steam trap and a pipe, considered as a unit, which conducts condensation from the steam side of a piping system to the water or return side of the system.

drip cap: A molding placed on the exterior top side of a door or window so as to cause rain water to run off, or drip, on the outside of the frame of the structure. See Figs. 190 and 198, page 154. Also, a molding where the sheathing and foundation meet which throws water away from the foundation. See Fig. 55, page 47.

drip mold: A molding designed to prevent rain water from running down the face of a wall.

dripstone: In architecture, a stone drip placed over a window to throw off rain water; a label molding sometimes called a *weather molding*.

drive screw or screw nail: A type of screw which can be driven in with a hammer but is removed with a screw driver.

driveway: A private way for the use of vehicles.

driving home: In shopwork, the placing of a part, a nail, or screw in its final position by driving it with the blows of a hammer or screw driver.

drop chute: Chute sometimes used when fresh concrete is dropped for more than 4 feet. Prevents separation of concrete.

drop cord: In electricity, a flexible cord run down from the ceiling outlet box, with a socket attached at the desired height for a light bulb. See Fig. 207.

Fig. 207. Drop cord.

drop curtain: A curtain which drops in front of a stage, as between the acts of a play, to shut off the stage of the theater from the view of the audience.

drop-drawer pull: A handle which is pivoted at the ends, where it is attached to the plate fastened to a drawer.

drop elbow: In plumbing, an elbow used for joining pipes, having one or two ears or lugs for attachment to a wall; also, a small ell frequently used where gas is put into a building. Such fittings have wings cut on each side to permit fastening to a wall or framing timbers.

drop ell: In plumbing, an ell with ears or lugs in the sides by means of which it may be attached to a support.

drop escutcheon: A piece of metal, forming a pivoted drop, attached to an escutcheon for covering the *keyhole.*

drop handle: In furniture making, any type of handle, or drawer pull, which hangs pendantlike. Such handles are of various designs.

drop key plate: A key plate with a swinging cover for protecting the keyhole.

drop panel: The structural portion of a flat slab which is thickened (by lowering the form) throughout an area surrounding a column, column capital, or bracket.

drop-point slating: In building construction, a method of laying asbestos slates with one diagonal horizontal.

drops: Ornamental cylindrical guttae, such as those below the triglyphs which adorn the Doric entablature. See *guttae,* page 226, Fig. 5, page 4.

drop siding: A special type of weatherboarding used on the exterior surface of frame structures. See Fig. 243, page 186.

drop table: A table top hinged to a wall bracket which supports the table when the top is lowered to a horizontal position.

drop tee or T: In plumbing, a small tee piece which has the same type of wings as a *drop elbow.*

drop window: A type of window that is lowered into a pocket below the sill.

drop wire: In electricity, a feed wire to the building being supplied with electricity from the nearest pole of the supply line. The *drop wire* connects to the *service drop.*

drum: One of the cylindrical, or nearly cylindrical, blocks of which the shafts of the Composite and Corinthian columns are composed; a vertical wall, circular or polygonal, on which a dome or cupola rests.

drum trap: In plumbing, a trap closed at the lower end with a fitted screw cap at the top. See Fig. 208.

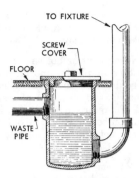

Fig. 208. Drum trap.

dry: In lumber, seasoned, not green. See *dry lumber.*

dry-bulb temperature: The temperature of a gas or mixture of gases indicated by an accurate thermometer after correction for radiation.

dry-bulb thermometer: An ordinary thermometer of standard type, used to find the dry-bulb temperature.

dry cell: A primary source of electric current, consisting of three elements—a zinc cylinder, a paste electrolyte, and a carbon rod in the center.

dryer: A mechanical drying machine used to take moisture out of veneer.

drying shrinkage: In concrete, reduction in size of concrete caused mainly by loss of water content during drying and hardening. Shrinkage begins immediately after placement and continues after hardening.

dry kiln: An ovenlike chamber in which wood is seasoned artificially, thus hastening the process of drying.

dry lumber: Under present standards, lumber which has been seasoned or dried to a moisture content (MC) of 19 percent or less.

dry masonry: Any type of masonry work laid up without the use of mortar.

dry mortar: In masonry, mortar which contains enough moisture to cause it to set properly but is not wet enough to cause it to be sticky; also, mortar which still retains a granular consistency.

dryout: When heat or hot winds cause water moisture in plaster mortar to be removed before the chemical reactions of setting have taken place, the plaster cannot set hard. Therefore, it returns to its original condition before it was mixed; in other words, it is not mortar at all but calcined gypsum.

dry rot: Various types of decay in timber, all of which reduces the wood to a fine powder.

dry rubble. Rough stone placed in a wall without mortar.

dry shrinkage: Shrinkage occurring in kiln-dried lumber after removal of the surface, as by planing; shrinkage of lumber occurring after seasoning in a kiln.

dry steam: A term applied to saturated steam which is free from water, or contains no entrained moisture. Sometimes called *dry saturated steam.*

dry stone wall: A masonry wall laid up without the use of mortar; *dry masonry.*

drywall: A system of interior wall finish using sheets of gypsum board and taped joints. Also, a wall laid without the use of mortar. Fig. 209 shows a common use of gypsum board for drywall construction.

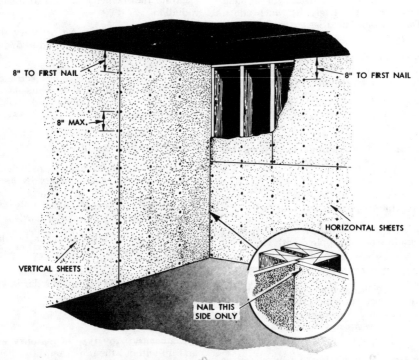

Fig. 209. One layer application of gypsum drywall shows nailing pattern for horizontal or vertical sheets. (United States Gypsum Co.)

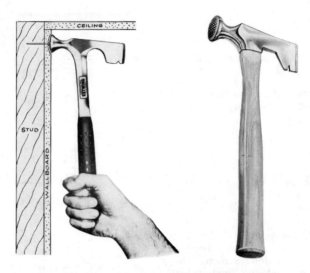

Fig. 210. Drywall hammers. (Goldblatt Tool Co.)

drywall hammers: Special hammers used for nailing up gypsum board for drywall construction. See Fig. 210.

drywall joint tool. The drywall joint tool is constructed like the regular plastering trowel except for the shape of the blade, which is made of flexible steel with approximately $\frac{3}{16}''$ concave bow. See Fig. 211.

drywall mud masher: This is the lightweight tool for mixing small amounts of the joint cement evenly. Shaped much like the familiar potato masher, it is made of steel wire with a wooden handle and has a 5″ diameter head. Its overall length is 24″. Fig. 212 shows two types in general use. Use of this tool is limited to small work.

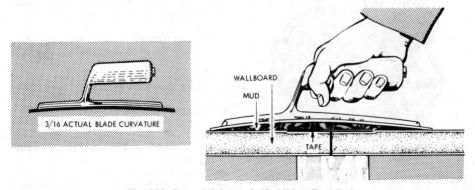

Fig. 211. Drywall joint tool. (Goldblatt Tool Co.)

163

Fig. 212. Mashers. (Left) Round head drywall masher. (Right) Square head drywall masher. (Goldblatt Tool Co.)

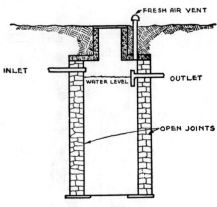

Fig. 214. Dry well.

drywall tool pouch: Leather bag used to hold drywall tools while working on the job. See Fig. 213.

drywall tools: Tools specially designed for the installation of gypsum board or other drywall panels in finishing a room. They include such materials as mixing hoppers and pumps, special drywall hammers, squares, tape dispensers, knives, spreading and finishing tools. See *drywall tool pouch*, Fig. 213, for typical tools used on the job. See also: *banjo tapers, corner tape creaser, drywall hammers, drywall joint tool, drywall mud masher, flexible corner tool, knives, mud holder, sander.*

dry well: In plumbing, a pit or hole in the ground which is lined with stone in such a way that liquid effluent or other sanitary wastes will leach or percolate into the surrounding soil. See Fig. 214.

dry wood: Any timber from which the sap has been removed by seasoning.

ducts: In building construction, metal pipes, usually round or rectangular in shape, for distributing warm air from the heating plant to the various rooms or for conveying air from air-conditioning devices. In electricity, a space in an underground conduit to hold a cable or conductor; also, a ventilating passage for cooling an electrical machine.

dumb-waiter: A small elevator, usually operated by hand, for moving small supplies or, in some cases, food between floors.

duplex apartment: A building with two apartments for separate families.

duplex cable: In electricity, a cable consisting of two insulated conductors which may be twisted or braided together, either with or without a common covering.

duplex lock: A cylinder-type masterkey lock, having two cylinders, both of which control the same bolt, but one working with a change key and the other with a master key, designed to control a series of such locks.

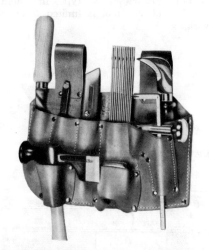

Fig. 213. Drywall tool pouch. (Goldblatt Tool Co.)

164

Keuffel and Esser Co.

Fig. 215. The dusting brush is a desirable accessory for the draftsman.

duplex-headed nail: See *double-headed nail.*

durability: In masonry, any construction which has the capacity to stand long and hard usage. The quality of hardened concrete to withstand long period of use, despite the weather, chemical attacks, or human and mechanical traffic.

dust mask: Protective mask worn when working in areas with high dust density.

dust-tight construction: Any construction which is so close in structure it will not admit the passage of dust; dustproof construction.

dusting: The appearance of a powdery material at the surface of a newly hardened concrete slab.

dusting brush: In architectural drafting, a brush used for removing eraser crumbs dust and graphite particles from the drawing surface. See Fig. 215.

Dutch arch: In masonry, a brick arch which is flat at both the top and bottom, constructed with ordinary bricks which are not worked to a wedge shape but are laid so as to slope outward from the middle of the arch. See *French arch,* page 208.

Dutch bond: In masonry, a bond having the courses made up alternately of headers and stretchers. Same as *English cross bond.* See *typical bonds,* Fig. 73, page 60.

Dutch colonial: A type of early architecture with a gable or gambrel type roof which flared over the eaves. The gambrel roof was adopted during the 18th Century. The Dutch colonial, however, was typified by a steep gable roof. Fig. 216 shows a Dutch colonial with a gambrel roof.

Fig. 216. "Dutch Colonial" with a New York or Flemish type *gambrel* roof. Note the Dutch door with the "bull's eye" lights in the upper half. This is the David Desmarest house located in New Milford, New Jersey, built about 1681. (Historic American Building Survey, Library of Congress, Washington, D.C.)

165

Dutch door: A door divided horizontally, so the lower section can be closed and fastened while the upper part remains open; commonly used on barns.

Dutch-door bolt: A door lock designed to fasten both the upper and lower halves of a dutch door. See *Dutch door.*

dutchman: In carpentry, an odd piece inserted to fill an opening or to cover a defect.

dwarf partition: A wall which does not extend from the floor to the ceiling.

dwarf rafter: A rafter which has been cut shorter than the common rafter, yet serves the same purpose; the same as a *jack rafter.* See Fig. 483, page 371.

dwarf wall: A term applied to any low wall such as a parapet or *fire wall;* also, a retaining wall; a *toe wall.*

dwelling: A building designed or used as the living quarters for one or more families.

E

ear: In plumbing, a projection on a metal pipe, by means of which the pipe may be nailed to a wall. See *crossette,* page 133.

early English period: A period in the history of building without definite limits but beginning early in the thirteenth century when architectural design, as well as structural methods, became more refined. Masonry joints were less conspicuous, arches more pointed, windows were longer but more narrow, and decorative features, becoming less grotesque, were consequently more pleasing in appearance.

early wood: See *springwood,* page 421.

earth: The grounded side of an electrical circuit or machine. Same as *ground.* Also, the soil built upon by or removed for structures, as in *earth sample, heavy earth mover,* etc.

easement: In architecture, a curved member used to prevent abrupt changes in direction as in a baseboard or handrail. In stairway construction, a triangular piece to match the inside string and the wall base

where these join at the bottom of the stairs. Also, the strips of land just inside the paralleling boundaries that must be left free of construction.

eaves: That part of a roof which projects over the side wall; a margin or lower part of a roof hanging over the wall; the edges of the roof which extend beyond the wall. See Fig. 217.

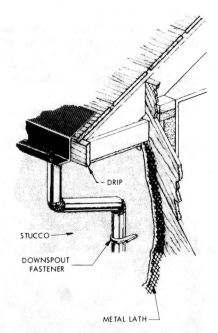

Fig. 217. Eave projection. (Keystone Steel & Wire Co.)

eaves board: A strip of wedge-shaped wood, used at the eaves of a roof to back up the first course of shingles, tiles, or slates; also used along valleys to keep the water from seeping under the shingles; used along gables to prevent rain water from dripping over the edges; a *tilting fillet.*

eaves trough: A gutter at the eaves of a roof for carrying off rain water.

eccentric fitting: In plumbing, a type of fitting in which the center line is offset.

echinus: In the Greek Doric order, the rounded molding supporting the abacus of the capital; also found in a modified form in the Ionic order. Sometimes embellished with ornamental designs, such as the *egg and dart molding*. See Figs. 218, 223, and 230.

Fig. 218. Echinus-ovolo.

economizer: A device used on furnace boilers, consisting of a bank of tubes or pipes through which the boiler feed water is pumped. The water in these pipes absorbs the heat that has passed the furnace flues. Thus the heat which would otherwise be wasted is used to preheat the feed water before it enters the boiler.

economy brick: A *solid masonry unit* whose nominal dimensions (Which include allowance for the mortar joint used with it) are usually 4 " x 8" and are thus related to the 4" modular system.

economy wall: In masonry, a brick wall four inches thick covered with a blanket of back mortaring. The wall is strengthened at intervals with vertical pilasters having brick corbeling which supports the floors and roof. This provides a four-inch outside reveal for windows and doors, with every window and door frame bricked in.

edge: In carpentry, that part of a board across which the thickness is measured; also, the thin cutting side of a tool, as the edge of a saw.

edge, blind: In sheet metal, an edge used to cover nail heads and the raw edges of sheet metal when sheets must be nailed to a wooden surface, such as in covering a door with metal. (Also called *false edge* and *dutchman*.) See Fig. 219.

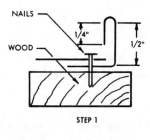

STEP 1

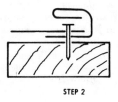

STEP 2

Fig. 219. Blind edge.

edge, capped: In sheet metal, an edge used when the ordinary edge was forgotten or, more often, when a sheet metal object is cut down and a raw edge is exposed that must be covered. It is a strip of metal bent and slipped over the raw edge of the metal. Generally, the cap is held in place by tack soldering, though it is sometimes riveted or bolted. See Fig. 220.

edge grain: Lumber in which the annual rings or grain forms an angle of 45 degrees or more with the surface of the piece. Same as *vertical grain*.

Fig. 220. Capped edge.

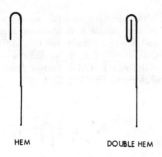

HEM   DOUBLE HEM

Fig. 221. Hem edges.

edge, hem: In sheet metal, a simple bend on the edge of the meal. See Fig. 221. A *double hem edge* is a simple hem done twice. It provides much greater strength than the single hem. (See Fig. 221, right.)

edge joint: In carpentry, a joint formed by uniting the edges of two boards or surfaces making an angle or corner. See *joint,* page 251.

edge roll: A decorative molding used in furniture making; the design is of Greek origin.

edge toenailing: A method of joining board surfaces by driving the nails at a slant so the heads of the nails will be concealed. See *toenailing,* page 455.

edger: In concrete flatwork, a special tool used to round off the edges of slabs and steps. Edging compacts and strengthens the edge, preventing chipping.

edging: In concrete flatwork, the finishing of the outside edges of slabs, sidewalks, steps, etc., into a convex arc. Edging compacts and strengthens the edge and prevents chipping. Also: A term used in cabinetmaking where small solid squares are set on the edge of a table top which is veneered. The *edging* serves as a protection to the veneer.

edging board: Usually the first board cut from a log after the *slab cut.*

edifice: A structure or building. Usually the term is applied only to large structures which are distinguished as an architectural masterpiece, such as a cathedral or church.

efficiency: The ratio which a joint, a machine, or a structure or structural part bears to some standard used for comparison.

efflorescence: A white, powdery substance, also called a *bloom,* which forms on masonry surfaces, particularly brick walls. It is caused by calcium carbide in the mortar. May be removed with builder's acid. See Fig. 222.

Fig. 222. Efflorescence on a recently constructed brick wall. (Masonry Building)

effluent: In plumbing, liquid sewage discharge from a septic tank or sewage disposal plant, after having passed through any stage in its purification.

egg-and-anchor enrichment: A decorative feature carved on a molding, resembling eggs alternating with another form of ornament resembling an anchor; used to enrich the ovolo.

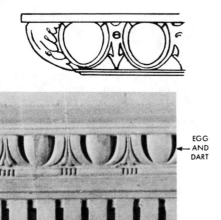

PLASTER CORNICE

Fig. 223. Egg and dart molding.

Fig. 224. Elastic knife. (Goldblatt Tool Co.)

egg-and-dart molding: A decorative molding with a design composed of an oval-shaped ornament alternating with another ornament in the form of a dart. See Fig. 223.

egg-and-tongue ornament: An egg-shaped ornament alternating with another in the form of a tongue; used to enrich the ovolo. Called, also, *egg-and-dart* or *egg-and-anchor*. See Fig. 223.

elastic: The ability of hardened concrete, steel, or wood members to return to size and shape after deformation under load.

elastic knife: A plasterer's tool made of highly flexible carbon steel, made in 5″ and 6″ widths. Used for trimming back the browning at beads, grounds, etc. See Fig. 224.

elbow: In pipe work of any kind, a short fitting connecting two pipes at a right angle. See Fig. 620, page 473. Also called *ell*. In electrical work, the elbow is sometimes fitted with a removable cap. A sheet metal elbow for duct work is shown in Fig. 268, page 203.

elbow board: In carpentry, a term applied to a window board beneath a window on the inside or interior.

elbow catch: A type of lock commonly used on cupboard doors. It has a hook on one end to engage a staple or strike, with the other end bent at a right angle to provide a means of releasing the catch. See Fig. 225.

Fig. 225. Elbow catch.

electric eye: A popular, nontechnical term used in referring to any of the various types of photoelectric cells.

electric hand sander: Electrically powered hand sanders with interchangeable abrasive attachments for various on-the-job finishing purposes.

169

electric handsaw: Portable, electrically powered saws are available with interchangeable blades and other attachments, for various building jobs, including masonry cutting and tuck pointing, as well as wood cutting, trimming, etc.

electric heater: A heating unit consisting of a resistance wire which becomes hot as the current flows through it.

electric horsepower: The equivalent of one horsepower in electrical energy, which is 746 watts.

electric radiant heat: A method of heating, utilizing the energy of electric current. It has gained usage through the reduction in cost of electric current. Additional insulation is necessary in homes using electric heat, since electric heat is pure energy, and heat losses are expensive. There are four electric heating systems: electric cables buried in plaster or dry wall ceilings; conductive rubber ceiling panels; radiant glass panels (conductive metal fused into glass panels acts as a path for the current); and baseboard and wall convectors. Regardless of the system used, all forms of resistance heat produce 3,412 British Thermal Units per kilowatt hour. Use of electric heating systems is said to allow builders to begin finishing operations faster. Also immediate heat is available to speed painting, plastering, etc., in inclement weather.

electrician's hammer: Long nosed used by electricians. Useful if nails should be required inside the back of an outlet box. See Fig. 226.

electrode: Thin metal rod, as shown in Fig. 227, coated with a special substance and used as a filler to join the metal to be welded.

electrolier: A hanging electric fixture holding lamps which can be lighted separately or all at once.

electrolier switch: An electric switch which controls the lamps of an electrolier.

electronic glue gun: An instantaneous curing glue gun, with its own electronic heat unit, for synthetic thermosetting rosin adhesives. The gun is lightweight and portable, eliminates nailing, and filling of nailheads and hammer marks on many jobs; makes possible on-the-job gluing of wall paneling, laminates for cabinets or counters, and hardwood flooring.

elements: The simple principles of any system or art; in architecture, the elements of geometry are used in making designs and plans in all construction work, including ornamental features, such as the tracery in a decorated window.

elephant trunk: An articulated tube or chute used in concrete placement.

elevation: A geometrical drawing or projection on a vertical plane showing the external upright parts of a building. Drawings of building walls made as though the observer were looking straight at the wall. See Fig. 228. Also, the vertical angle between a surveyor's line of sight toward a higher object and a horizontal line from his point of observation.

Fig. 227. These three electrodes are coated except for small portions at the lower right, where they are gripped by the electrode holder.

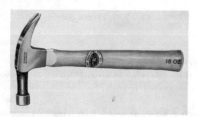

Fig. 226. Electrician's hammer. (Champion DeArment Tool Co.)

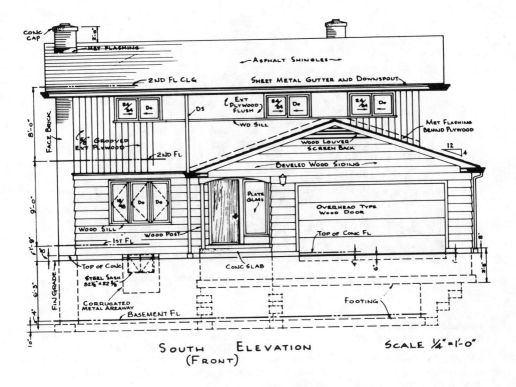

CONC CAP

MET FLASHING

— ASPHALT SHINGLES —

— 2ND FL CLG

SHEET METAL GUTTER AND DOWNSPOUT

FACE BRICK

8'-0"

EXT PLYWOOD FLUSH

DS

WD SILL

MET FLASHING BEHIND PLYWOOD

GROOVED EXT PLYWOOD

2ND FL

WOOD LOUVER SCREEN BACK

12   4

BEVELED WOOD SIDING

9'-0"

PLATE GLASS

OVERHEAD TYPE WOOD DOOR

WOOD SILL

WOOD POST

1ST FL

TOP OF CONC FL

TOP OF CONC

STEEL SASH

CONC SLAB

FIN GRADE

6'-3"

CORRUGATED METAL AREAWAY

BASEMENT FL

FOOTING

SOUTH   ELEVATION
(FRONT)

SCALE ¼"=1'-0"

Fig. 228. Building elevation.

elevator: In a building, a cage or platform enclosed in a vertical shaft and used for conveying persons or goods from one floor level to another.

Elizabethan: In building, refers to a style of architecture prevailing in England during the time of Queen Elizabeth I or about 1550-1600. This style was much along the lines of the Tudor but with certain features emphasized so that they have come to be regarded as characteristic of the Elizabethan type, even though they were used to some extent by the builders of the Tudor houses. The combination of exposed timber framework and stucco or brickwork on the exterior of the buildings was developed, during the Elizabethan era, to a high state of perfection. Half-timbered exterior treatment has come to be considered characteristic of this style. This is true to such an extent that another name for the Elizabethan is *English Half-Timbered* style. Fig. 229 illustrates a house built in the Elizabethan tradition.

ell: An addition to a building at right angles to one end or an extension of a building at right angles to the length of the main section; in plumbing, a name applied to a short pipe shaped like the letter **L**.

ellipse: The path of a point the sum of whose distances from two fixed points is a constant; a conic section formed by an oblique plane passing through a right circular cone.

171

Fig. 229. Elizabethan or English half-timbered style.

ellipsoid: A solid of which every plane section is an ellipse or a circle.

elliptical: A closed shape formed by a curve of constantly varying radii, having two axes at right angles one of which is always larger than the other; pertaining to, or having the form of, an *ellipse.*

elliptical arch: In architecture, an arch having an *intrados* in the form of an ellipse. Sometimes called a *circular arch.*

elliptical stairs: A stairway having steps which, in plan, are arranged so as to form an ellipse or an elongated circle. See Fig. 563, page 426.

embattled: Furnished with battlements used as a decorative feature.

embattlement: The same as *battlement;* furnished with battlements; to form with square indentations, as an *embattled molding.*

emblazon: Embellish with heraldic or armorial designs.

embossed: Ornamental designs raised above a surface; figures in relief, as a head on a coin; decorative protuberances.

embrasure: An opening in a wall with sides flaring outward, as the recess of a door or window; a loophole; a lookout; an opening in a battlement between the raised portions, sometimes called a *crenel.*

emery: An impure corundum stone of a blackish or bluish gray color used as an abrasive. The stone is crushed and graded and made into emery paper, emery cloth, and emery wheels.

emery cloth: A cloth used for removing file marks and for polishing metallic surfaces. It is prepared by sprinkling powdered emery over a thin cloth coated with glue.

emery wheel: A wheel composed mostly of emery and used for grinding or polishing purposes. It is revolved at high speed.

emissivity: The rate at which particles of electricity or heat are radiated from an object.

emulsion: A mixture of liquids which are insoluble in one another; in wood preservation a mixture of creosote or other oils and water or solution of a salt in water.

enamel: A type of paint or varnish that dries to a hard, glossy surface. Also, a smooth, glossy or semi-glossy hard finish.

enameled brick: In masonry, brick with an enamel-like or glazed surface.

encarpus: A sculptured ornament in imitation of a festoon of fruits, leaves, or flowers, or other objects hanging between two points.

encased knot: A defect in a piece of wood where the growth rings of the knot are not intergrown and homogeneous with the growth rings of the piece in which the knot is encased.

encaustic: Relating to the burning in of colors, applied to painting on glass, tiles, brick, and porcelain; any process by which colors are fixed by the application of heat.

enclosed fuse: In electricity, a fuse placed inside an insulated tube to prevent the ignition of gas or dust.

enclosed stairway: A stairway which is enclosed by, and separated from, hallways and living units by means of walls or partitions and made accessible to such hallways or living units by means of a door or doors.

enclosure wall: Any nonbearing wall, either exterior or interior, of skeleton construction which is anchored to columns, piers, or floors but is not necessarily erected between columns or piers.

end: That part of a board along which its width may be measured; also, across which the thickness may be measured; the extreme limits of a piece of lumber.

end-grain: In woodworking, the face of a piece of timber which is exposed when the fibers are cut transversely.

end joint: A joint formed by the bringing together of the ends of two pieces of boards; a *butt joint* as opposed to an *edge joint.* See *joinery of boards,* page 251.

end-lap joint: A joint formed at a corner where two boards lap. The boards are cut away to half their thickness so that they fit into each other. They are halved to a distance equal to their width, and when fitted together the outer surfaces are flush. See Fig. 329, page 251.

end thrust: In building, a pressure exerted in the direction of the end of a structural member, such as a girder, beam, truss, or rafter.

end view: In architectural drawing, an elevation view of either end (left or right) of a building or object drawn in the vertical plane. Usually called the *side view.*

endive scroll: In furniture making, an ornate carved-leaf design; often used in woodwork.

engaged: Attached; especially a circular column built one-third or one-quarter into a wall, the remainder projecting beyond and free from the wall face.

engaged columns: Columns or pilasters partly embedded in a wall. Also called *embedded columns.*

engineers' brick: A *solid masonry unit* whose nominal dimensions, which include allowance for the mortar joint designed for use with it, are 4″ x 3⅕″ x 8″.

English bond: In brickwork, a form of bond in which one course is composed entirely of *headers* and the next course is composed entirely of *stretchers,* the header and stretcher courses alternating throughout the wall; a type of bond especially popular for use in a building intended for residential purposes. See *brick bonds,* Fig. 73, page 60.

English cross bond: A form of bond similar to old English bond. It is used where strength and beauty are required. Same as *Dutch bond.* See *brick bonds,* Fig. 73, page 60.

engrailed: Indented with curved lines or small concave scallops.

enrichment: Adornment; embellishing plain work by adding ornamental designs.

ensemble: The whole, all parts considered together; the entire effect, as of a completed work of art where each part is considered only in its relation to the other parts.

entablature: In classic architecture, that part of the building which rests horizontally upon the columns and consists of the cor-

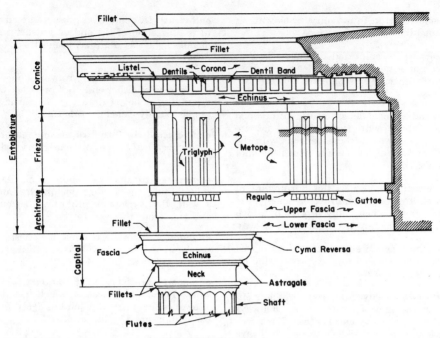

Fig. 230. Entablature.

nice, frieze, and architrave. The height of the entablature, divided into one hundred parts, establishes a scale which may be used in determining the proper proportions of all parts of the order. See Fig. 5, page 4, and Fig. 230.

entail: In architecture, carving in relief; intaglio; carved figures or patterns.

entasis: A swelling or outward curve along with an inward taper in the vertical profile of the shaft of a column.

entasis of a column: The swelling or outward curve of the shaft of a column to avoid the hollow appearance which would result if the column were made absolutely straight with no bulge.

enthalpy: The heat content or total heat of a substance per unit mass. Expressible in Btu per pound.

entrained air: Microscopic air bubbles intentionally incorporated in mortar or concrete during mixing.

entrance switch: An electric switch to which the wires entering a building are connected.

entrapped air: Air voids in concrete which are not purposely entrained.

entresol (en'ter-sol): A low story between two higher stories; usually between the ground floor and the first floor. The same as *mezzanine floor.*

entry: A hallway or entrance to a building.

epistyle: The lowest member of an *entablature;* the *architrave.* See Fig. 230.

epoxy plastics: These *thermoset* plastics have excellent adhesion properties, good resistance to chemicals, heat, and weather, a slow burning rate, and maximum use temperatures of from 200° to 280°F., used for adhesives, laminates, chemical exhaust ducts, and printed circuit boards.

equivalent direct radiation: Abbreviation *EDR.* In steam heating, the amount of heating surface expressed in square feet, which will deliver 240 Btu per hour, under the design operating conditions; in hot-water heating, the amount of heating surface, expressed in square feet, which will deliver 150 Btu per hour, under the design operating conditions. But one square foot of *EDR* does not imply 144 square inches of heater surface but means a heat delivery of 240 (or 150) Btu per hour for each *EDR* of a given radiator or convector.

erasers: These are a necessary part of the architectural draftsman's equipment. They are available in the prismatic form or in the stick variety. Probably the stick type is the most convenient for the majority of jobs. The number of erasers required by the draftsman depends upon the type of drawing. Usually three kinds of erasers are used: hard, soft, and gum. The soft eraser removes light lines, smudges, etc., while the harder eraser (no grit) removes heavy, stubborn lines. The gum type eraser is especially suited for removing construction lines, smudges, or finger prints.

erasing shield: In drawing, a thin metal shield used when erasing to avoid erasing the surrounding work. See Fig. 231.

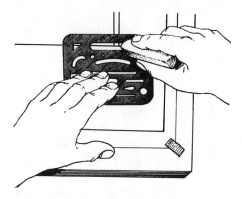

Fig. 231. The erasing shield is used to protect adjacent lines.

erecting: Raising and setting in an upright position, as the final putting together in perpendicular form the structural parts of a building.

escalator: A stairway consisting of a series of movable steps, or corresponding parts, joined in an endless belt and so operated that the steps or treads ascend or descend continuously. Commonly used in large department stores and transportation terminal buildings. Sometimes called *moving staircase.*

esconson: A jamb shaft in the inside arris of a window jamb.

escutcheon: In architecture, a metal shield placed around a keyhole to protect the wood; also a metal plate to which a door knocker is attached. Such plates are sometimes ornately decorated. Also the plate surrounding an ordinary light switch on a wall.

escutcheon pin: A decorative nail having a round head, used in fastening ornamental and/or protective metal plates to wood.

espagnolette: A kind of fastening for a French casement window, usually consisting of a long rod with hooks at the top and bottom of the sash and turned by a handle. Also, a decorative feature on corners of Louis XIV furniture.

essex board measure: A method of rapid calculation for finding board feet; the essex board-measure table usually is found on the framing square conveniently located for the carpenter's use. See Fig. 232.

estimating: Calculating the amount of material needed, the amount of labor to fabricate or do the work, and the approximate evaluation of the finished product.

estimating description: General information concerning the estimate which the estimator will use throughout his calculations. It will contain information about the owner, the architect, the engineer, square feet of roof, walls, and lot, general information about the structure, and details about the various construction elements.

etching: A process by which designs or pictures are engraved on glass or metal plates by means of linen eaten or corroded with the use of a strong acid.

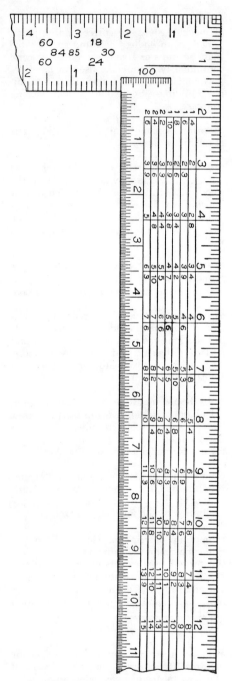

Fig. 232. Essex board measure table.

eustyle: Denoting an arrangement of columns having an intercolumniation or space between column shafts of two and one-fourth diameters.

evaporation rate: Rate at which bleed water is evaporated from the surface of a concrete slab. The time in which a unit quantity of moisture is absorbed by the contacting air.

evaporative cooler: An air conditioner which cools the air by the effect of water evaporation. Outdoor air is drawn through a moistened filter pad in a cabinet, and the cooled air is then circulated throughout the house. Used in regions with relatively low humidity.

even pitch: A term applied to a roof having an equal pitch, or a slope, which is the same throughout its entire length.

evolute: A curved wavelike scroll often used as a decorative feature on a frieze molding.

excavation: A cavity or hole made by digging out of earth.

excavation line: A line, indicated by a string or heavy cord stretched between batter boards, showing where the excavation is to be made for the foundation walls of a new building.

excess chalking: In painting, a condition due to the application of too many coats of paint or lacquer to a heavy porous undercoating or to a lack of proper percentage of binder to pigment.

exedra: A raised, semicircular or elliptical platform with seat facing toward the center; often used in public places as a memorial.

exit: A way from a living unit to the exterior at street or grade level, including doorways, corridors, stairways, ramps, etc.

expanded metal lath: Sheets of metal which are slit and drawn out to form openings on which plaster is spread. See Fig. 375, page 283.

expanded shale: A type of lightweight aggregate used to produce structural lightweight concrete.

expansion: In terms of fresh or hardened concrete, the swelling or stretching of the concrete due to heat of hydration, or, more especially, due to weather conditions, such as the freezing of excess water within the concrete.

expansion bit: A boring tool which has one or more cutting edges so arranged as to allow for a radial adjustment, making it possible to bore holes of different-sized diameters with the same tool. Also called *expansive bit.* See Fig. 59, page 50.

expansion bolt: In building, a bolt equipped with a split casing which acts as a wedge, often used when attaching timbers to concrete or brick work. See Fig. 286, page 218.

expansion joint: In concrete work a control joint. See *contraction joint,* page 119, *control joint,* page 119. See Fig. 233. In plumbing, a device used to overcome the motion of expansion and contraction in pipes due to change in temperature. In steam and hot-water heating systems, the *expansion joints* are of the sliding-sleeve type or the *sylphon* bellows type. The latter is preferable on low-pressure systems up to 15 pounds pressure.

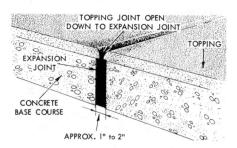

Fig. 233. Expansion joint.

expansion pipe: In a domestic system of heating, a pipe carried up from the hot-water tank to a point above the level of the cold-water tank, where the open end of the pipe is bent over, so, in case the water boils, any water or steam forced out may discharge into the cold-water tank.

expansion sleeve: In building construction, a device consisting of a type of sleeve placed around pipes to provide ample clearance space for their expansion or contraction when they pass through masonry walls or floors.

expansion strip: A soft, resilient material used to fill the void provided for the expansion and contraction of any two adjacent substances. Use of the expansion strip in conjunction with glass blocks is shown in Fig. 286, page 218.

expansion tank: In a hot-water system, a tank joined to the hot-water cylinder, but above it, to allow for the expansion of the heated water. Often the cold-water feed tank is used for this purpose. See *expansion pipe.*

expansive bit: A type of auger bit having a cutting blade which can be adjusted for boring various sizes of holes. See Fig. 59, page 50.

expletive: In masonry, a stone which is used to fill a cavity.

exposed: In construction, any wiring, piping, or other normally concealed equipment that is run exposed along a wall or ceiling.

exposed aggregate: A special concrete finish in which attractive aggregates at the surface are exposed to create interesting and beautiful effects.

exposed joint: In masonry, a mortar joint on the face of a brick or stone wall, above the ground level.

extender: In painting, a substance, which usually is an inert material, added to paint to give it body or to serve as an adulterating medium.

extension: In electricity, a length of cable or lamp cord fitted with a plug and a socket, in order to extend a lamp or other electric device farther than the point where it was originally connected. An object or structure that is prolonged or extended from the original.

extension bolt: A vertical catch, or bolt, in an accessible position at the top or bottom of a door. It consists of an extension rod

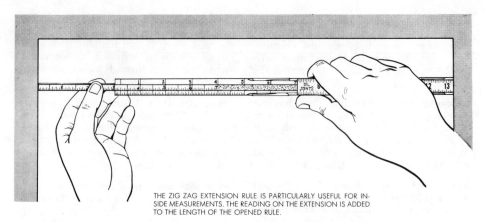

THE ZIG ZAG EXTENSION RULE IS PARTICULARLY USEFUL FOR IN-
SIDE MEASUREMENTS. THE READING ON THE EXTENSION IS ADDED
TO THE LENGTH OF THE OPENED RULE.

Fig. 234. How extension rulers are used. (Stanley Works)

terminating in a knob or thumb piece inserted through a hole bored in the thickness
of the door.

extension rule: A carpenter's rule, used for
taking measurements between jambs when
fitting doors. See Fig. 234.

exterior: The outer surface or part, as in
building the *exterior* of the structure or the
exterior wall.

exterior door frame: The frame in which
a door swings in the outside wall of a
building.

exterior finish: In building construction,
the outside finish which is intended primarily to serve as a protection for the interior of the building and for decorative
purposes. It includes the cornice trim,
gutters, roof covering, door and window
frames, water tables, corner boards, belt
courses, and wall covering.

exterior-protected construction: A type of
building construction in which the exterior
walls, fire walls, and party walls are of an
incombustible material. These walls are
self-supporting and the interior structural
framing is wholly or partly of wood or similar material.

exterior trim: The finish material applied
to the outside of a building which adds to
the pleasing appearance of the structure. It
includes trim for cornices, gutters, gables;
also the roof ridge corner boards, belt
courses, and the finish around door and
window openings.

exterior wall: Any outer wall serving as a
vertical enclosure of a building except a
common wall.

external vibrator: See *vibrator,* page 472.

extra-fine threads: These are designated as
UNEF and are used for threaded parts
which require a fine adjustment, such as
bearing retaining nuts, adjusting screws,
and for thin-walled tubing and thin nuts
where maximum thread engagement is
needed.

extra heavy: In plumbing, when applied to
pipe, designates one which is thicker than
standard pipe.

extrados: The exterior curve in an arch or
vault. See Fig. 137, page 108.

extruded: Thrust, forced, or pressed out.
Formed into desired shape by ejecting
through a shaped opening.

eye: In architecture, the opening at the top of a *cupola;* also, the center of the *roll* or *volute* of an Ionic capital, Fig. 1, page 1. In tools, the opening in the head of an implement to receive the handle, as the *eye* of a hammer. See *adze eye,* Fig. 9, page 7.

eyebolt: A bolt which is provided with an eye, or hole, instead of the ordinary head. The eye receives the pin, hook, or stud which takes the pull of the bolt.

eyebrow dormer: A low dormer in a roof over which the roof is carried, in a wave line similar to the arch or ridge, over an eye. See *dormer,* page 152; also *ventilating eyebrow,* page 471.

eye of dome: The opening at the top of a dome.

eye of volute: The circle in the center of a *volute.* See Fig. 1, page 1.

eye splice: See *cable attachments,* page 80.

F

FHA: Federal Housing Authority.

fabric: In building construction, a term often applied to the walls, floors, and roof of a building; also, the framework of a structure.

fabricating: Shop work on reinforcing steel, such as cutting, bundling, tagging.

facade: The entire exterior side of a building, especially the front; the face of a structure; the front elevation or exterior face of a building.

face: The plane of a board upon which the width and length may be measured, or the widest plane; also, in lumber dressed only on one side, the finished side is called the *face.* In construction work, the principal side or front of a wall or building; also, the exposed vertical surface of an arch.

facebrick: The better quality of brick such as is used on exposed parts of a building, especially those parts which are prominent in view. See Fig. 85, page 69.

faced wall: A masonry wall in which one or both sides are faced with a different ma-
terial from the body of the wall but with the facing and body so bonded they will exert action as a unit under the weight of a load. See *wall,* page 474.

face hammer: A heavy hammer having flat faces, with one blunt end and one cutting end; used for rough dressing of blocks of quarried stone.

face joint: In masonry, a joint between the stones or brick in the face of a wall. Since it is visible, the joint is carefully struck or pointed.

face mark: In woodworking, a mark placed on the surface of a piece of wood to indicate that part as the face, according to which all other sides are dressed true.

face measure: The measurement across the face of any wood member or piece, exclusive of any solid mold or rabbet. The width of any piece of lumber not including the tongue or lap.

face mix: In masonry, a mixture of stone dust and cement sometimes used as a facing for concrete blocks in imitation of real stone.

face mold: In architectural drawings, the full-size diagram, scale drawing, or pattern of the curved portions of a sloping handrail. The true dimension and shape of the top of the handrail are given in the drawing; in building, a *templet* used as a pattern for shaping the face of wood, stone, or other building material. See *templets,* Fig. 588, page 449.

face nailing: To nail perpendicular to the initial surface or to the pieces joined.

face of arch: In building, the exposed vertical surface of an arch. See Fig. 235.

face of hammer: That part of the head of a claw hammer striking a nail which is being driven into wood. See Fig. 127, page 101.

face of square: The side of a framing square on which the name of the manufacturer is stamped.

face plate: In a marking gage, that portion, usually of metal, which is pressed against the edge of a piece of wood while it is being marked.

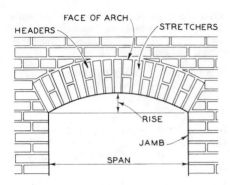

Fig. 235. Face of an arch.

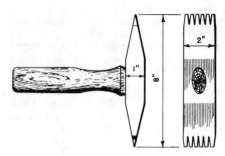

Fig. 236. Facing hammer.

face putty: The putty which is formed in the angle of a sash after the glass has been laid in the rabbet. See *putty,* page 352.

face puttying: The process of applying putty to the face of a window sash. This is done by inserting the glass in the rabbet provided for it and securely wedging the glass where necessary to prevent its shifting in position. Glazing points are then driven into the wood to keep the glass firmly sealed. The rabbet is next filled with putty which should be beveled back against the sash and *muntins* by means of a putty knife.

face side: In carpentery, that side of a piece of wood on which the *face mark* is made. See *face mark.*

face size: That portion of the dressed or finished piece exposed to view when it is in place.

face string: In a staircase, the outermost string, often of superior material, and separate from the *roughstring* which it conceals in a wooden stair. Same as *outer string.*

face tier: In masonry, the outside tier of exterior brick walls and chimneys of residences, where a high grade of face brick is commonly used. See *face brick.* See Fig. 37, page 32.

face veneer: The veneer sheet on the upper side of a plywood panel.

face wall: The front wall of a building.

facette: In architecture, a projecting flat surface between adjacent *flutes* in a column.

facia: See *fascia,* page 182.

facing hammer: In masonry, a special type of stone hammer used for dressing the surface of stone or cast-concrete slabs. See Fig. 236.

factor of safety: The number which results from dividing the ultimate strength of a material by the actual unit stress on a sectional area. In structural design, it is the number designating the overload safety capacity. For example, a pressure vessel designed to withstand a pressure of 10 pounds per square inch may actually withstand a pressure of 50 pounds per square inch. Therefore, the *factor of safety* is 5.

factory: A term applied loosely to every building in which goods, wares, and merchandise are manufactured; a building, usually with its equipment, where workmen are employed in the manufacture of articles by machinery; any building the whole or greater portion of which is used for manufacturing purposes.

factory lumber: Graded lumber intended to be cut up for use in additional manufacture. Such lumber is used pricipally in window sashes, doors, and door frames, in different types of millwork, and in furniture factories. See *lumber,* page 274; *shop lumber,* 401.

180

facure: A plain facing of varying width defined by angles or moldings upon each side, as in the *architrave* of the classic entablature.

Fahrenheit: A temperature scale so graduated that the freezing point of water is 32 degrees and the boiling point is 212 degrees.

faience: Glazed terra-cotta blocks used as facing for buildings or fireplaces. Glazed plastic mosaic is known as *faience mosaic* and is used for ornamental floors.

failure: In carpentry construction, the inability of a structure or materials to endure and fulfill the purpose for which they were selected and designed. The nonperformance of any structure under designed load.

false arch: In building, a structural member having the appearance of an arch, though not of arch construction.

false header: In masonry, a half brick as is sometimes used in *Flemish bond;* in framing, a short piece of timber fitted between two floor joists, as shown in Fig. 237.

false rafter: A short extension added to a main rafter over a cornice, especially where there is a change in the roof line.

false set: The rapid development of rigidity in a freshly mixed portland cement paste, mortar, or concrete. This condition can be heated and plasticity regained by further mixing without the addition of water. *Premature stiffening, hesitation set, early stiffening,* and *rubber set* are terms referring to the same phenomenon. **False set** is the preferred designation.

falsework: Framework, usually temporary, such as bracing and supports used as an aid in construction but removed when the building is completed.

fan tracery: The complicated decorative tracery of fan vaulting; tracery which rises from the capital of a corbel and diverges like the folds of a fan, spreading over the surface of a vault; a mode of roofing used in the perpendicular style, in which the vault is covered by ribs and veins of tracery.

fan window: A fanlight; a window shaped like a fan with radiating sash bars, semicircular or semielliptical in form. Often occurs over doorways. A term also applied to the topmost part of a window which is hinged for opening.

fanlight: A fan-shaped window, with sash bars radiating like the ribs of a fan, located over a door or window; a *fan window.* Loosely, any window over a door or window.

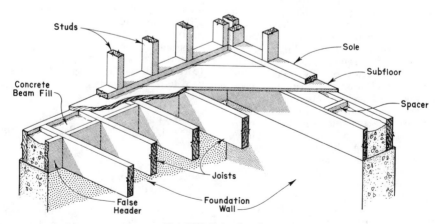

Fig. 237. False header.

fasces: A bundle of rods bound together having an ax among them with its blade projecting; used as an ornamental feature in architecture.

fascia: The flat, outside horizontal member of a cornice placed in a vertical position. A long, flat member or band in the entablature of columns or other parts of a building or at the edge of a bridge beam, especially a horizontal division of an architrave. See Fig. 78, page 63; Fig. 131, page 103; Fig. 230, page 174, and Fig. 241, page 185.

fast-joint butt: A hinge which has the pin riveted or otherwise fastened, holding the two parts of the hinge together permanently.

fastener: In building construction, any device, such as a nail, screw, bolt, or dowel pin used to hold structural members together; also, a latch, lock, barrel bolt, or any other contrivance for securing doors and windows.

fastening tools: A tool which applies greater force and control to the insertion of fasteners than hand-hammer methods alone. Placing the fastener in a narrow channel or slot, open at one end of the tool, force produced in a larger area is concentrated on the fastener from the other end, thus driving the fastener into the desired surface with speed and accuracy, leaving no hammer marks. Fastening tools may be activated by a hand-hammer blow, by release of a spring, or by pneumatic (compressed air) hammer action. One of these can be positioned for roof or floor nailing by means of a foot stirrup, thus eliminating all bending. The above are usually called nailing machines and used for fastening wood. More powerful tools for fastening steel and concrete are activated by exploding powder in a cartridge (as stud drivers), by gasoline (these are used for driving heavy spikes and can be self-contained); by electricity (as impact wrenches and electric hammers). Tackers of the hammer, gun, and air types operate on the same principles, using a bent wire staple, instead of the usual nail or screw, to fasten thin construction material to walls or other surfaces. Many fastening tools have automatic,

magnetic fastener feed devices. See *hammer fasteners, nailers, nailing machines, power driven fasteners* and *staplers.*

fat lime: A quicklime, made by burning a pure, or nearly pure, limestone, such as chalk; used especially for plastering and masonry work. Also called *rich lime.*

fat mortar: In masonry and plastering, a mortar containing a relatively high proportion of cementitious material, particularly lime, producing a rich, easily workable mixture.

faucet: Any device for controlling the flow of a liquid drawn from a fixture attached to the end of a pipe, having a spout and valve; the enlarged or socket end of a pipe at a spigot-and-socket joint; a *tap* or *cock.* Sometimes called a *spigot.*

favus: A Latin word meaning *honeycomb;* in architecture, a term applied to a square detail resembling the cells in a honeycomb.

feather: A small piece or strip of wood which is inserted in the grooved edge of two pieces of board or plank to make a joint; also, to join structural pieces by means of a *tongue-and-groove joint.*

feather joint: In carpentry, a joint made between two boards with squared edges butted together, each board having a plowed groove into which a common tongue is fitted.

featheredge: Anything which tapers off to a thin, featherlike edge, as a tool for carpentry work, a brick for masonry work, or a special type of weatherboarding. Also, a plastering tool used to straighten angles (corners) in the finish coat. It may also be used to produce putty coat screeds for cornice. See Fig. 238.

featheredge brick: A brick which is used especially for arches, similar to a *compass brick.*

featheredged board: A weatherboard of tapering thickness, always placed with the thick edge downward.

featheredged coping: In masonry, a coping stone which slopes in one direction on its top surface.

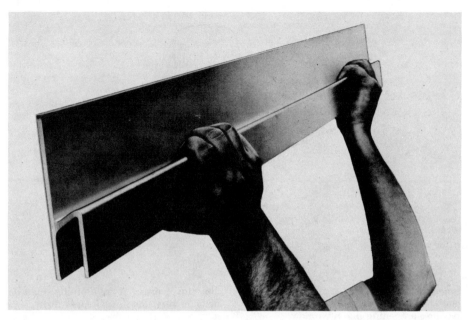

Fig. 238. Magenesium featheredge. (Goldblatt Tool Co.)

feathering: In architecture, the enriching of an opening by use of foils formed by cusps arranged in trefoils, quatrefoils, or similar decorative designs. See *foil,* page 201. In sheet metal, a riveted seam is placed over the stake, and the edges are flattened together or featheredged with a mallet as shown in Fig. 239.

feed pipe: In plumbing, a main-line pipe which carries a supply directly to the point where it is to be used or to secondary lines; also, a pipe supplying feed, as water to a boiler. Also called *feeder.*

feeder: In wiring, any conductor of a wiring system between the service equipment and the branch circuit overload or connecting primary equipment in an electric power system. In plumbing, a *feed pipe.*

felt: A fibrous material composed of hair, roots, or other vegetable fibers, treated to make it watertight; used for soundproofing and as underlining for roofs.

felt-and-gravel roof: A type of roof made of a roofing material composed of felt saturated with asphalt, then surfaced with so-called *mineral aggregates* or gravel.

felt papers: Sheathing papers used on roofs and side walls of buildings as protection against dampness; also as insulation against heat, cold, and wind. *Felt papers* applied to roofs are often infused with tar, asphalt, or chemical compounds.

female plug: A threaded fitting or adapter, having two, sometimes three, orifices, which is screwed into an electric light socket to provide an outlet for the current.

fence: In carpentry, an attachment used as a guide on a steel square in roof framing and stair building; also, a guard attached to any wood-cutting tool or machine for controlling the location and extent of a cut.

fender wall: A low brick wall supporting the hearthstone to a ground-floor fireplace.

Fig. 239. Feathering a riveted seam.

fenestral: A window opening closed with cloth or translucent paper instead of glass; having an opening like a window.

fenestration: The arrangement of windows and doors in a building; in an architectural composition, the design and proportion of windows as a decorative feature.

ferrule: In plumbing, a kind of connection between a water main and a service pipe, consisting of a metallic sleeve, calked or otherwise joined to a side opening in the pipe. The opening is fitted with a screwed plug giving access for inspection and cleaning of the interior of the pipe. In carpentry, the metal chisel, screw driver, or other similar tool, at the end where the *tang* enters. A metal cap placed at the end of a post for strength or protection.

festoon: In architecture and furniture, a decorative feature of carved work representing a garland or wreath of flowers or leaves or b oth.

fiberboard: A type of building board made by reducing fibrous material, such as wood, cane, or other vegetable fibers, to a pulp; then reassembling the fibers into large sheets or boards; used extensively for insulating buildings against heat or cold.

fiberboard knife: A tool specially designed for cutting fiberboard. See Fig. 240.

fiberglas fabric: A reinforcing material made of very fine flexible glass fiber.

fiber glass: A material made from spun glass which is used for insulation and structural sheets and forms.

fiber saturation point: In wood, the point at which all the free water has been evaporated and the walls of the fibers, or cells, begin to lose their moisture; sometimes defined as the condition in which the cell cavities are empty but the cell walls are fully saturated with water. Usually taken as approximately 30 percent moisture content (m.c.) based on over-dry weight.

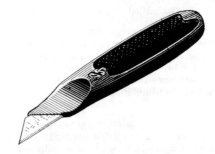

Fig. 240. Fiberboard knife.

fibrous plaster: Prepared plaster slabs, produced by coating canvas with a thin layer of gypsum plaster.

field tile: A type of porous tile which is placed around the outside of a foundation wall of a building to absorb excess water and prevent seepage through the foundation.

field weld: A weld that is done *in the field* during the assembly of parts.

fielded panel: A panel molded, raised, or sunk with either a wide, flat surface or divided into smaller panels.

figure: In carpentry, mottled, streaked, or wavy grain in wood; also, the pattern formed by peculiar or abnormal arrangement of the elements within the tree. To mark or adorn with a pattern or design.

file: A tool, with teeth, used principally for finishing wood or metal surfaces. Common files are from 4 to 14 inches in length. The width and thickness are in proportion to the length. In cross section, the *file* may be rectangular, round, square, half round, triangular, diamond shaped, or oval. Single-cut files have parallel lines of teeth running diagonally across the face of the file. The double-cut files have two sets of parallel lines crossing each other. Single-cut files have four graduations — rough, bastard, second cut, and smooth; double-cut files have an added finer cut known as *dead smooth.*

fill: Material such as soil, gravel, sand, etc., used to bring the subgrade to the desired level, or the same type of material used to replace soft or unwanted soil dug out of the subgrade.

filler: A composition used for stopping up nail holes, blemishes, checks, cracks, pores, and grain of the wood before applying finish, such as stain, varnish, or paint; also, any plate or other piece used to fill in a space between two parts of a structure.

filler coat: A term used by painters when referring to the first coating of paint, varnish, or other similar materials; applied to woodwork to fill the pores of the wood and make a smooth surface for the finish coat; also, the paint used for the first coat. Sometimes called *priming* or *priming coat.*

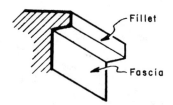

Fig. 241. Fillet and fascia.

fillet: In classical architecture, a narrow vertical band or *listel* separating two surfaces meeting at an angle; a flat molding between two other moldings, the space between flutings in a shaft or column; also, a term applied to a concave junction formed where two structural members meet; a *reglet.* See Fig. 230, page 174, and Fig. 241.

fillet weld: A weld made in the interior angle where the members meet at a right angle. See Fig. 242.

filleted joint: See *joinery of boards,* page 251.

filling in: The process of filling in the open center of a wall between the face and back. This is done to weatherproof and soundproof walls.

fillister: A rabbet or groove, as the groove on a window sash for holding the putty and glass; in mechanical work, the rounded head of a cap screw slotted to receive a screw driver. Also, a plane used for cutting grooves.

fillistered joint: A kind of rabbet joint made by cutting a groove in a piece of structural timber into which a tongue, on an adjoining piece, is slipped to form a joint.

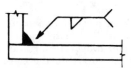

Fig. 242. A fillet welded joint and symbol.

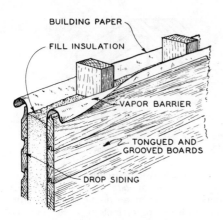

Fig. 243. Fill type insulation.

fill-type insulation: A loose-fill insulation material which is poured in place from bags or is hand packed between framing members. The pneumatic method of application is used in some cases. See Fig. 243.

fin: In heating, a section of sheet metal externally fixed to a steam or hot water coil to increase the radiation surface. The fins may be flat or deformed to increase the heating area.

fine aggregates: The sand in the concrete mix, which ranges from the largest size of ¼ inch down to much smaller sizes except for dust particles.

fineness modulus: A numerical value indicating the measure of fineness of an aggregate; obtained by dividing by 100 the sum of the percentage residue remaining on each of a series of ten sieves with openings ranging from 1.5 inches to 0.0058 inches.

fines: As concrete is troweled, a mixture of cement paste and the fine aggregate are brought to the surface to help seal any small holes. This mixture is called the fines.

fine stuff: In plastering, a paste made by slaking pure lime with water. After the excess water evaporates or is drained off, the paste is worked to the consistency of cream which is then used for plastering purposes.

fine-textured wood: Lumber or wood having small closely spaced pores.

fine threads: This is designated as *UNF* and used extensively on bolts and nuts employed in the automotive and aircraft industries where greater resistance to vibration is required or where greater holding strength is necessary.

finial: A decorative detail that adorns the uppermost extremity of a pinnacle or gable. An ornamental device capping a gable or spire.

finish: In carpentry, the wood materials used in the joiner work, such as doors and stairs. Also, other fine work required to complete a structure, especially the interior, such as casings, baseboards, moldings, etc. See *finish carpenter, finishing.*

finish carpenter: A highly skilled carpenter to install paneling, trim, and other finished surfaces, usually in the interior.

finish casing: The finish material around the exposed portion of a door or window opening, as opposed to the *blind casing.*

finish coat: In plastering, the final coat of plaster which gives a wall a smooth, even surface. See Fig. 579, page 438. Sometimes called *hard-finished white coat.* See *white coat,* page 480.

finished string: In architecture and building, the end string of a stair fastened to the rough carriage. It is cut, mitered, dressed, and often finished with a molding or bead.

finish floor: A floor, usually of high-grade material, laid over the subfloor. The *finish floor* is not laid until all plastering and other finishing work are completed. Also called *finished floor.* See Fig. 189, page 149, and Fig. 258, page 198.

finish flooring: Any material suitable for a *finish floor;* hardwoods, such as oak and maple, are commonly used for finish floor. Also, other materials, including tiles, linoleum, terrazzo, and mosaics.

finish grade: Surface elevation of lawn, drive, or other improved surfaces after completion of grading operations.

finish grinding: The final process of manufacturing portland cement; the clinkers are crushed to a fine powder which is called portland cement.

finish hardware: All of the exposed hardware in a house, such as door knobs, door hinges, locks, and clothes hooks.

finishing: In carpentry, the final workmanship performed on a building, such as the adding of casings, baseboards, and ornamental moldings. In concrete flatwork, the tooling of the surface to produce the desired appearance of the concrete; otherwise, the leveling, smoothing, and compacting of concrete surfaces. In plastering, application, smoothing, and texturing of *finish coat.*

finishing lime: Lime used in making lime putty for finishing plaster coat.

finishing sawhorse: One of a pair of trestles which carpenters use to support lumber while it is being planed, sawed, nailed, or otherwise prepared for constructional work. See Fig. 499, page 384.

finishing tools: In concrete flatwork, special tools used to level, smooth, groom, etc., the surface of fresh concrete. See: *bullfloat, darby, edger, float, groover, jointer, screed, trowel.*

finishing varnish: A liquid preparation designed to form a hard, lustrous coating for a wood finish when a highly glossed surface is desired.

finish nails: These are available in lengths from 2*d* to 20*d*. The head is barrel shaped and has a slight recess in the top. These nails are used for finished work where the final appearance is of importance, such as trimming in buildings, cupboards, and cabinets, as are any nails with small heads. The small head is intended to be sunk into the wood with a nail set. See *penny,* Fig. 419, page 320, for sizes.

finish size: In building, the measurement of any wood part over all, including the solid mold or rabbet.

fireback: The back lining or wall of a fireplace or furnace. Same as *chimney back.*

fire barriers: In building construction, fire-resisting doors, enclosed stairways, and other similar obstructions for preventing the spread of fire in a building.

fire blocks: Short pieces of wood, or blocks, nailed between joists or between studding to serve as bracing and, in case of fire, to stop drafts and prevent the spread of the fire to other parts of the building. See *block bridging,* page 53.

firebox: combustion chamber of a heating unit.

firebrick: Any brick which is especially made to withstand the effects of high heat without fusion, usually made of *fire clay* or other highly siliceous material. See Fig. 85, page 69; Fig. 245.

fire clay: Clay which is capable of being subjected to high temperature without fusing or softening perceptibly. It is used extensively for laying *firebrick.*

firecut: An angular cut at the end of a joist which is anchored in a masonry wall. In the event of fire, the joist will collapse without forcing the wall to fall outward. See Fig. 244.

fire-division wall: A solid masonry wall for subdividing a building to prevent the spread of fire but one not necessarily extending continuously from the foundation through all the stories and through the roof; also, a wall of reinforced concrete which is more or less fire resistant, tending to restrict the spread of fire in a building.

firedog: One of a pair of metal devices for supporting wood in a fireplace. Same as *andiron.*

fire door: In building construction, a door made of fire-resisting material which is slow burning or difficult to ignite.

fire escape: A stairway, usually of steel, attached to the outside of a building to provide a means of escape, in case of fire, for persons within the building.

187

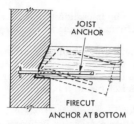

Fig. 244 The joist anchor is attached at the bottom. Dashed line shows how joist would fall without breaking the wall.

fire hazards: In building construction, any source of risk or danger from fire, such as the improper installation of wires for an electric-lighting system, the use of combustible material around a fireplace or other source of heat; also, open spaces between floor joists or between studding, which may create a draft and cause fire to spread to different parts of the building.

fire partition: A wall designed to prevent or restrict the spread of fire or to provide an area of refuge in case of fire.

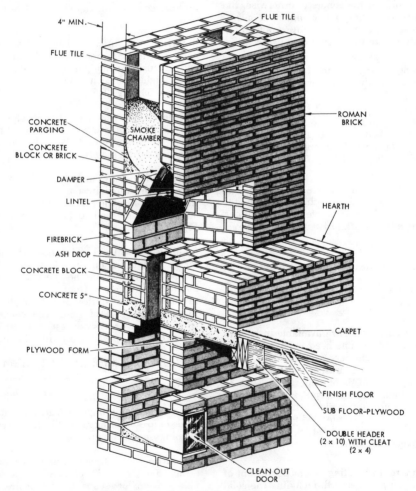

Fig. 245. Fireplace details and nomenclature.

fireplace: A hearth; usually an unclosed recess in a wall in which fuel is burned for the purpose of heating the room into which it opens. A pictorial cross section of a fireplace and chimney is shown in Fig. 245.

fireplace, prefabricated: These are free-standing metal units complete in themselves: the hood, damper, chimney pipe, hearth, base, grate, and screen are included. No masonry work is required since these fireplaces attach to wall or stand free. See Fig. 246.

Fig. 246. A free-standing fireplace may complement the decór of the room.

fireplace throat: In fireplace construction, the opening leading from the fireplace into the smoke chamber of the chimney; the passageway from the fireplace to the flue. See Fig. 245.

fireplace unit: A metal form, whose front rim is usually covered by the fireplace facing. The form often includes a special heating chamber, in addition to firebox, throat damper, downdraft shelf, and smoke chamber. Cool air entering the heating chamber through an inlet near the floor is heated and returns to the room or to adjacent rooms through registers, thus increasing the heating capacity of the fireplace. See Figs. 246, 247.

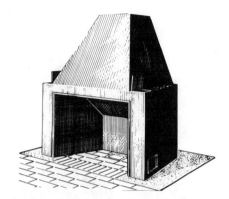

Fig. 247. Fireplace unit.

fireproof: To build with fire-resistive materials in order to reduce fire hazards and to retard the spread of fire; to cover or treat with an incombustible material.

fireproofing: The process of enclosing structural members with a material or combination of materials so as to make them fire-resistive: such as fireproofing structural steel by spraying on insulating materials (see Fig. 12, page 11) or encasing steel with concrete or lath and plaster. See Fig. 248. Also, the chemical treatment of wood to make it fire resistant. Any material used in the process of fireproofing a building or any of its structural members, Fig. 248.

fireproofing machine: A machine used to spray insulating fibers directly onto steel beams and metal decking. See Fig. 12, page 11.

fireproof structures: Buildings which are constructed of materials which are not readily combustible and have fire-resisting qualities. Such buildings will resist fire but, strictly speaking, are not *fireproof*, as any structural material will be damaged by fire if the heat is of sufficient intensity. Hour ratings are given as to how long a material or structure will withstand fire. See *fire-resistance ratings*.

fireproof trim: In building construction, any finish or trim consisting of relatively incombustible materials.

fire resistance: Ability to prevent or retard for a certain time the passage of fire, excessive heat, or hot gases.

189

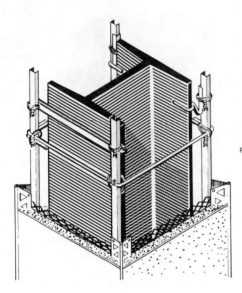

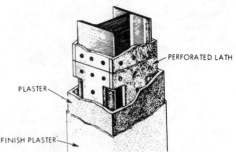

Fig. 248. Fireproofing structural steel construction. (Left) Metal lath and plaster is used. (Top right) Gypsum board and plaster is used. (Bestwall Gypsum Co.)

fire-resistance ratings: Time in hours (or major fraction of an hour) that a material or construction will withstand fire exposure.

fire-resistive: In the absence of a specific ruling by the authority having jurisdiction, the term *fire-resistive* is applied to all building materials which are not combustible in temperatures of ordinary fires and will withstand such fires without serious impairment of their usefulness for at least one hour.

fire-retardant chemical: A chemical used to reduce flammability or to retard spread of fire.

fire separation: A construction of specified fire resistance separating parts of a building.

fire stops: Blocking of incombustible material used to fill air passages through which flames might travel in case the structure were to catch fire; any form of blocking of air passages to prevent the spread of fire through a building. Various methods of constructing for fire stopping are shown in Fig. 249.

fire tower: A name applied to a stairway which is enclosed with fire-resistive construction and is entered by way of a bal-

cony, vestibule, or other arrangement of fire-resistive construction at each floor level; so designed that smoke is prevented from entering the stairway.

firewall: Any wall built for the purpose of restricting or preventing the spread of fire in a building; a wall of solid masonry or reinforced concrete which subdivides a building to prevent the spread of fire. Such a wall begins at the foundation of the building and extends continuously through all stories to, and above, the roof. See *wall*, page 474.

fire window: A window which has its frame, sash, and glazing designed to restrict the spread of fire.

firmer tools: In woodworking, the tools commonly used on the workbench, such as the ordinary chisels and gouges.

first story: The story next above the cellar when a building has a cellar and no basement; the story next above the basement when a building has a basement; the story of which the floor is the first above the ground level in a building with neither cellar or basement. Other stories above the first story are numbered in regular succession counting upward.

fish bellied: A term applied to a structural member such as a beam, girder, or joist which bends downward, bulging out like a fish's belly.

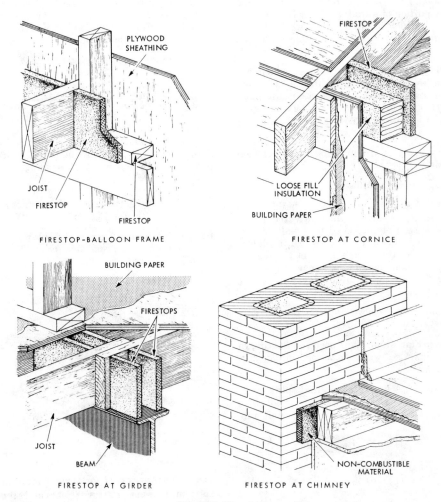

Fig. 249. Fire stop.

fished joint: A joint commonly used when a structural piece must be lengthened. The joint is made by placing a second piece end to end with the first one; then covering the juncture with two additional pieces which are nailed or bolted on opposite sides of the joint. These pieces are called *fish plates* and may be wood or metal. See Fig. 329, page 251, *fished and keyed joint.*

fish plate: In carpentry, a short piece of board or metal used to hold a *fished joint* together. See Fig. 559, page 422.

fish tape: Flexible steel tape which is run through electrical conduit and the wires are attached and pulled through. Also called a *snake*. See *vacuum and blower fish line system,* page 469.

fitment: In carpentry and furniture making, any portion of a wall, room, or built-in furniture which is fitted into place, including chimney pieces, wall paneling, cabinets, and cupboards.

fittings: Manufactured devices which are used to join pipe sections; the job of joining or installing pipe in the system; any piece of sheet metal ductwork of a heating or air conditioning system other than the straight joints or sections.

fixed beam: A structural beam having fixed ends.

fixed light: A window which does not open.

fixture: An attachment to a building; in electricity, a device which is wired inside and is securely attached to a wall or ceiling, used to hold electric lamps; in plumbing, any of the various parts of the plumbing system installed permanently in a building, as the bathtubs, lavatory basins, and toilets.

fixture wire: An insulated stranded wire used for wiring fixtures.

flags: Flat, stone slabs used for flooring or paving. Also called *flagstones or flagging.* See Fig. 250.

flagstone: A kind of stone that splits easily into flags or slabs; also, a term applied to irregular pieces of such stone split into

slabs from 1 to 4 inches thick and used for walks or terraces. A pavement made of stone slabs is known as *flagging.* See Fig. 250.

flamboyant: A name applied to a type of architecture characterized by waving, flamelike curves, as the tracery of windows. This was a French-Gothic type of architecture prominent about 1450-1530.

flame spread: The propagation of flame over a surface.

flange: The two wide projections across the ends of the web of a beam or similar shape or extending at right angles from the ends of the web of a channel. W beam or S beam in structural steel. See Fig. 120, page 94. Also, some types of insulation materials are provided with flanges for fastening purposes. See Fig. 251. Also, the flat rim on end of a cast iron pipe, fitting, or valve provided with holes which permit bolting points together. See Fig. 252.

flanged insulation: Blanket and bolt insulation with flanges on each side for attaching to rafters or studs. See Fig. 251.

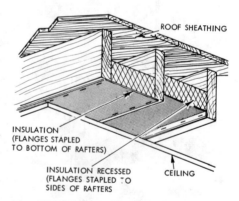

Fig. 251. Methods of installing flexible insulation between rafters. (National Forest Products Assoc.)

flange pipe: A wide variety and size of pipes provided with flanges at ends to attach to other pipes or connections. In many cases cast iron pipes are cast with flanges. See Fig. 252.

Fig. 250. Flagstones.

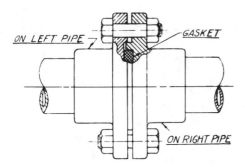

Fig. 252. A flanged fitting.

flange union: In plumbing, a pair of flanges threaded onto the ends of two pipes which are to be joined. When the pipes are joined, the flanges are bolted together.

flank: In architecture, the side of an arch.

flanking in: Applying a thick layer of putty and plaster.

flap valve: A type of nonreturn valve made in the form of a hinged flap or disc, sometimes faced with leather or rubber; used for low pressures.

flare: An operation performed on the end of copper tubing to widen the mouth before it is joined to another piece.

flash set: The rapid development of rigidity in a freshly mixed portland cement paste, mortar or concrete, usually with the evolution of considerable heat, which rigidity cannot be dispelled nor can the plasticity be regained by further mixing without addition of water; also referred to as *quick set* or *grab set.*

flashing: Sheet metal strips or plastic film used to prevent leakage over windows, doors, etc., and around chimneys and roofs; or any rising projection, such as window heads, cornices, and angles between different members or any place where there is danger of leakage from rain water or snow.

These metal or plastic pieces are worked in with shingles of the roof or other construction materials used. See Figs. 253 and 254.

flat: In architecture, a platform, usually horizontal in character, as the deck of a roof which has steep sides, or any roof of which the slope does not exceed more than about one foot of rise in twenty feet.

flat arch or jack arch: A type of construction in which both the outside of an arch and the underside of the arch are flat. See Fig. 324, page 247.

flat building: A building usually of two or more stories, having separate self-contained apartments or flats, with each flat having its own street entrance or with an entrance from an outside vestibule on the level of the first floor.

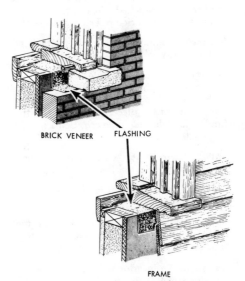

Fig. 253. Flashing, either plastic or metal, is required wherever water may seep into the building.

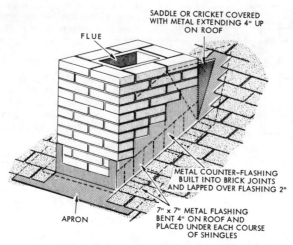

Fig. 254. Flashing around a chimney is turned into the mortar joints and carried under the shingles for 4″.

flat carving: A type of carving where the design is left flat by cutting away only the background.

flat coat: In painting, the first coat of paint applied to a finished wood surface, also called *filling coat.* See *filler coat,* page 185.

flat cost: In building, the cost of labor and material only.

flat grain: A term used to describe softwood lumber in which the annual growth rings are at an angle of less than 45 degrees with the surface of the piece. In hardwoods, this lumber is called *plain sawed.* See Fig. 434, page 330.

flat-head wire brad: A wire nail used as a wood fastening in light construction.

flat molding: A thin, flat molding used only for finishing work.

flat-nose pliers: A specialized hand tool useful in forming and/or grasping small shapes.

flat paint: An interior paint that dries to a flat or lusterless finish.

flat plate: A *flat slab* without *drop panels* or column capitals.

flat roof: A roof with just enough pitch to provide for drainage of rain water or melting snow.

flat skylight: Any skylight which has only enough pitch to carry off rain water or water from melting snow.

flat slab: A type of concrete floor construction which provides a flat surface for the bottom of the slab. A concrete slab reinforced in two or more directions with *drop panels* but generally without beams, with or without column capitals.

flat spots: In painting, spots which lack gloss on a finished surface and indicate porous undercoat or improper surfacing.

flat surface: In painting, a surface presented by a flat coat.

flatting: In veneering, a process of flattening out buckled veneers; also, a finish given to painting which leaves no gloss.

flatwise: In building construction, a term used when referring to studding placed so the lath is nailed to the flat side instead of on the edge.

flatwork: Concrete slabs, such as floors, walks, patios, highways, etc.

194

flaw: A defect in a wood member, or any other structural part, which may eventually cause failure of a building or any part of it.

fleam: A term used in woodworking to indicate the angle of bevel of the edge of a saw tooth with respect to the plane of the blade.

fleche: A slender spire rising above the intersection of the nave and transepts of a large church building or a cathedral; a spire in which the sanctus bell is hung.

Flemish bond: A bond consisting of *headers* and *stretchers* alternating in every course, so laid as always to break joints, each header being placed in the middle of the stretchers in courses above and below. See *brick bonds,* Fig. 73, page 60.

Flemish garden bond: In masonry, a bond consisting of three stretchers alternating with a header, each header being placed in the center of the stretchers in the course above and below.

fleur-de-lis: A conventional design, somewhat resembling the iris, much used as a decorative ornament; the royal insignia of France.

flexibility: The ability to readily change from one use to another.

flexible cable: A cable consisting of insulated, stranded, or woven conductors in electrical work. A holding, hoisting, or hauling cable made up of steel wire strands.

flexible conduit: A nonrigid conduit made of fabric, plastic or a metal strip wound spirally.

flexible cord: In electricity, an insulated conductor consisting of stranded wire.

flexible corner tool: A plastering tool similar to a wide blade *angle plow* (Fig. 23, page 20) but for tighter, more perfect corners.

flexible curves: In drafting, a flexible guide used for drawing *long* curves. They are bent to fit the desired curve. See Fig. 255.

flexible insulation: A type of insulation which may be made of fluffy mineral wool, fibrous slag, glass, rock, or processed vegetable or animal fibers. One-surface asphalt-impregnated paper can serve as a vapor barrier. Flexible insulation comes in blankets, quilts, or bolts for various installation conditions. See Fig. 49, page 41; Fig. 62, page 52; and Fig. 251. See *insulation,* page 243.

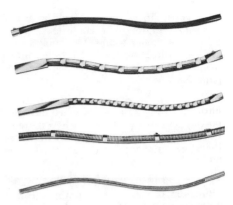

Fig. 255. Flexible curves may be adjusted for any long curve. (Frederick Post Co.)

flexible shower arm: A rigid pipe is connected to the water source by a ball pivot, while a second ball pivot connects the shower head to the other end. This enables the shower to be lowered to heights suitable for children or the varying requirements of adults, in addition to minimizing splash and doubling as a faucet.

flexural strength: The measured resistance to bending forces.

flier: Any single one of a flight of stairs whose treads are parallel to each other; a stair tread that is of uniform width throughout its length.

flight of stairs: A series of steps between floors of a building; a single flight of stairs may be broken into two flights by means of a landing.

flitch: A piece of timber of a size greater than 4x12 inches. It is intended for reconversion; also, a thick piece of lumber which has bark (wane) on one or more edges.

flitch beam: In building, a built-up beam formed by an iron plate sandwiched in between two timber beams, the whole being securely bolted together. Also called *flitch girder* and *sandwich beam*. See Fig. 94, page 76.

flitch girder: A combination beam composed of two or more joists which have between them steel plates ¼ inch or more in thickness. Bolts are used to hold the joists and steel plates together. See Fig. 94, page 76.

float: A tool (not a darby), usually of wood, aluminum, or magnesium, used in finishing operations to impart a relatively even (but not smooth) texture to an unformed fresh plaster or stucco wall or used to smooth finish concrete flatwork. Also, a tool or block used by masons for polishing marble. Fig. 256 illustrates a wood float being used on a plaster wall.

Fig. 256. Rough floating a plaster wall using a wood float.

float coat: In cement work, a term frequently applied to the mortar-setting bed which is put on with a float; also, a term applied to a coat of finishing cement, sometimes called *float finish* which is put on with a float.

float time: A term used in the *critical path method* of scheduling construction to indicate slack time in the schedule. The amount of time that a job can be delayed without affecting a "critical job".

float trap: In a steam-heating system, a type of valve which is set in motion by means of a hollow metal float which is arranged so that steam will be held but condensation and air may pass.

float valve: In plumbing, a valve using a hollow ball floating on the surface of water, to shut off the supply at the intake, as in a toilet tank.

floated coat: In plastering, the second coat of plaster; the coat applied over the *scratch coat*.

floater: A tool used to smooth and finish cement work. See *float*.

floating: The process of spreading plastering, stucco, or cement on the surface of walls to an equal thickness by the use of a board called a *float*. In concrete finishing, an intermediate step usually done after edging and jointing and before trowelling. If a coarsely textured surface is desired, floating may be the final step.

floating foundation: In building construction, a special type of foundation made to carry the weight of a superstructure which is to be erected on swampy land or on unstable soil. Such a foundation consists of a large, raftlike slab composed of concrete, reinforced with steel rods or mesh.

floating partition: A partition which rests on a floor between two joists and parallel to the joists.

floating screed: In plastering, the first strip of plaster laid on for any particular coat. The *screed* serves as a guide for the thickness of the remainder of that coat.

floatstone: In masonry, a type of stone used by bricklayers to smooth gauged brickwork. See *rubbing stone,* page 377.

flood lights: A battery of lamps of high brilliancy, equipped with reflectors to supply a strong light.

floor: In architecture and building, different stories of structure are frequently referred to as floors; for example, the *ground floor,* the *second floor,* and the *basement floor;* also, that portion of a building or room on which one walks.

floor arch: In architecture, a flat or segmental arch between floor beams; also, an arch having a flat *extrados.*

floor chisel: An all-steel chisel with an edge measuring from 2 to 3 inches in width; used especially for removing floorboards.

floor drain: A plumbing fixture used to drain water from floors into the plumbing system. Such drains are usually located in the laundry and near the furnace and are fitted with a deep seal trap. See Fig. 257.

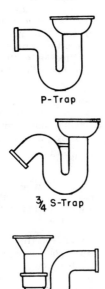

P-Trap

¾ S-Trap

Combination Trap

Fig. 257. Floor drains.

floor framing: In building construction, the framework for a floor, consisting of sills and joists; also, the method used in constructing the frame for a floor, including the joists, sills, and any floor openings. See Fig. 258.

floor-framing plan: An architectural drawing which shows how the various members of a floor frame are to be installed, as the placing of sills and joists, and the method of reinforcing joists around floor openings.

floor furnace: A heating unit specially adapted for small homes which have no basements or cellars. This type of furnace is installed directly underneath the floor of a room. It is used extensively in regions which have mild climates.

floor furring: Furring strips of wood laid over a subfloor construction, when electrical conduits and piping are to be laid on top of the under floor or subfloor.

floor hinge: A pivot-door hinge designed to be placed in or on a door. Usually installed along with a door spring and a door check.

floor joist: The timbers used to support the body of the floor frame to which the flooring is nailed. The sizes of joists commonly used are 2x8 and 2x10 inches. See Fig. 258.

floor lining: A layer of paper, felt, or similar material laid between the subfloor and the finish floor. A term sometimes erroneously applied to the blind or subfloor. See Fig. 258.

floor load: The total weight on a floor, including dead weight of the floor itself and any live or transient load. Permissible loading may be stated in lbs./sq.ft.

floor plan: An architectural drawing showing the length and breadth of a building and the location of the rooms which the building contains. Each floor has a separate plan. A *floor plan* is a *plan view* of a horizontal section taken at some distance above the floor, varying so as to cut the walls at a height which will best show the construction. The cut will cross all openings for that story. Fig. 259 shows a typical *basement plan.* (Symbols used by architects on floor plans are shown in Fig. 372, pages 280 and 281.)

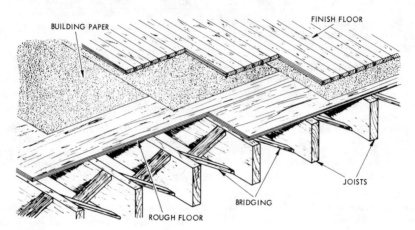

Fig. 258. Floor-framing details.

floor plug: In electricity, a plug-in device placed in the floor to connect a flexible conductor to a circuit terminal.

floor sander: A machine for surfacing floors with sandpaper; also called *sanding machine.*

floor ventilation: The free movement of cross currents of air beneath a building. This circulation is obtained by providing vents and other openings in the foundation walls.

flooring: In building construction, any material used for laying a floor or floors.

floriated: Having floral ornaments; decorated with floral designs, as floriated capitals of columns. One of the parts of the classic Corinthian and Composite capitals.

floury: A soil texture in which the materials are quite fine and resemble flour.

floweret: A small flower, a floret; used in architectural decoration.

flue: An enclosed passageway, such as a pipe or chimney for carrying off smoke, gases, or air. See Fig. 245, page 188.

flue lining: Fire clay or terra cotta pipe, either round or square, usually obtainable in all ordinary flue sizes and in two-foot lengths. It is used for the inner lining of chimneys with brick or masonry work around the outside. Flue lining should run from the concrete footing to the top of the chimney cap. See Fig. 245, page 188, and Fig. 260.

fluidity: A substance which is fluid or capable of flowing; the opposite of solidity. The ability to change shape without resistance while retaining the same volume.

fluing: A term applied to window jambs which are splayed.

fluing arch: An arch in which the opening at one end is less than at the other end, so the arch flares outward like a funnel. See *splayed arch,* page 419.

fluorescent lighting: Electrodes are sealed into each end of a glass tube, and a mercury vapor arc between them generates ultraviolet radiation, which is absorbed by a fluorescent powder coating the inside of the tube and released as visible light.

flush: The continued surface of two contiguous masses in the same plane; that is, surfaces on the same level.

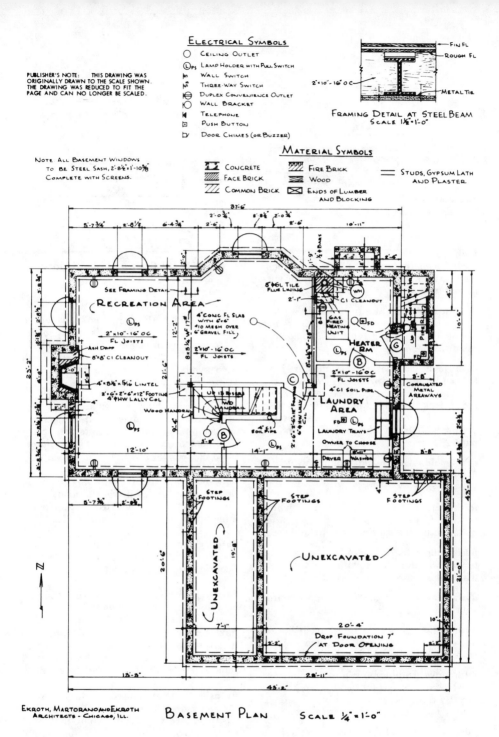

PUBLISHER'S NOTE: THIS DRAWING WAS ORIGINALLY DRAWN TO THE SCALE SHOWN. THE DRAWING WAS REDUCED TO FIT THE PAGE AND CAN NO LONGER BE SCALED.

Fig. 259. Typical basement plan.

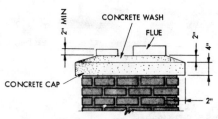

Fig. 260. The flue lining projects 2″ above the concrete cap.

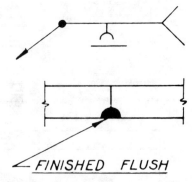

Fig. 261. The flush weld with U groove.

flush bolt: A door bolt which is installed behind a plate designed either for attachment to the surface or to be set into the surface of a door.

flush door: A door of any size, not paneled, having both surfaces flat. Flush doors are frequently of various types of *hollow core* construction.

flush joint: In masonry, a mortar joint formed by cutting surplus mortar from the face of a wall. If a rough texture is desired, the surface of the joint may be tapped with the end of a rough piece of wood after the mortar has slightly stiffened. See Fig. 330, page 252.

flush mold: An applied molding which is finished flush with, or below, the surface of stiles or rails.

flush plate: A door plate of any type which is made to be set into the wood, or other material, flush with the face of the door.

flush receptacle: A type of lamp socket, the top of which is flush with the wall into which the socket is recessed.

flush siding: Tongue-and-groove boards which are laid flush on sidewalls.

flush switch: In electricity, a push button or key switch, the front of which is flush with the wall into which it is recessed.

flush valve: In plumbing, a valve by means of which a fixture is flushed by using water directly from the water-supply pipes or in connection with a special flush tank.

flush weld: A weld that is flush to the level of the pieces to be joined; there is no build-up for reinforcing or strengthening the

weld. Fig. 261 (bottom) shows a typical flush weld. The flush weld is called for by a straight line in connection with the weld symbol. Fig. 261 (top) shows the flush weld symbol used with the symbol for a U groove weld.

flute: A channel, or grooved section, as one of the concave channels used to decorate the columns in classical architecture. Such ornamented columns are said to be *fluted*. See Fig. 230, page 174.

flute reamer: A tool for removing the burrs or any sharp edges inside the mouth of a pipe. The reamer is inserted in a brace for a few turns in reaming. See Fig. 262.

fluted column: In architecture, a column decorated with concave channels or grooves. See Fig. 230, page 174.

fluting: Decorated with grooves or channels, as a fluted column. See *flute*.

flux: Acid or rosin fluid or paste applied to metal surfaces to remove oxide film in preparation for soldering, brazing, and some types of welding operations.

fly ash: A manufactured product used in making hydraulic cement. Otherwise, soot electrostatically collected from industrial smoke stacks. Also used in lightweight concrete (such as *cinder block*) as an aggregate. (See *cinder concrete*, page 99.)

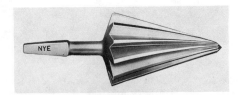

Fig. 262. Spiral flute reamer. (Nye Tool & Machine Works)

Fig. 263. Folding rule. (Lufkin Rule Co.)

fly rafter: In building construction, a decorative board covering the projecting portion of a gable roof; a *bargeboard*.

flyer: In stair building, a straight step; same as *flier*.

flying bond: In bricklaying, a bond formed by inserting a header course at intervals of from four to seven courses of stretchers.

flying buttress: A type of masonry structure in which a detached buttress or pier at a distance from a wall is connected to the wall by an arch or portion of an arch.

flying disk: A type of ornament used to decorate furniture. It is of Egyptian origin and is in the form of a disk with wings.

fog spray: See *fogging*.

fogging: A process of moist curing concrete very similar to sprinkling except for the fact that a special nozzle is used to scatter a fine mist-like spray over the slab.

foil: A rounded, leaflike architectural ornamentation used especially for window decoration, sometimes consisting of three divisions, sometimes of four, and known as *trefoil* and *quatrefoil*.

foil back: Blanket or batt insulation with one surface faced with metal foil. Foil serves as a heat reflector and vapor barrier.

folding rule: Rule used for measuring. Also called a *zigzag rule*. See Fig. 263.

folding stair: A stairway which folds into the ceiling, used for access to areas of a building not in general use. Such a stairway uses only limited space while in use. It is fixed by means of hinges at its uppermost end, while the lower end is provided

with any of various catches which fasten the stairway when folded. Quite often the underside of such a stairway is finished so as to match the ceiling area into which it is folded. See Fig. 264.

foldstir mixer: The foldstir is used to mix drywall mud, acoustic, and exposed aggregate materials. It lifts, folds, and blends the materials so they are thoroughly lump-free. See Fig. 265.

foliage: An architectural ornament representing leaves, flowers, or branches; the distribution of ornamental leaves on various parts of buildings.

Fig. 264. Folding stair.

201

Fig. 265. Foldstir mixer. (Goldblatt Tool Co.)

Fig. 266. Foot bolt. (Stanley Works)

foliated: To ornament with foils or foliage; that is, decorated with a leaf design.

foliation: Ornamentation with foils, such as trefoil, quatrefoil, or other leaf forms given to an arch; also, ornamentation by use of foliage.

foot: In building, the seat of a rafter, the bottom of a column, the lowest step of a staircase. In furniture making, the lowest supporting member of a piece of furniture; the termination of the leg of a table, chair, or other piece.

foot bolt: A bolt which is designed for attaching to the bottom of a door. Usually such a bolt is controlled by a trigger which holds the bolt against a spring. Release of the trigger allows the spring to slide the bolt into a locking position. See Fig. 266.

foot cut: In carpentry, the cut at the lower end of a rafter to fit against the wall plate. Same as *seat cut*. See *bird's mouth,* page 50; Fig. 483, page 371.

footing: A foundation as for a column; spreading courses under a foundation wall; an enlargement at the bottom of a wall to distribute the weight of the superstructure over a greater area and thus prevent set-

tling. *Footings* are usually made of cement and are used under chimneys and columns as well as under foundation walls. See Fig. 267.

footing beam: In roofing, the tie beam for the roof.

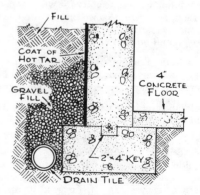

Fig. 267. Footing.

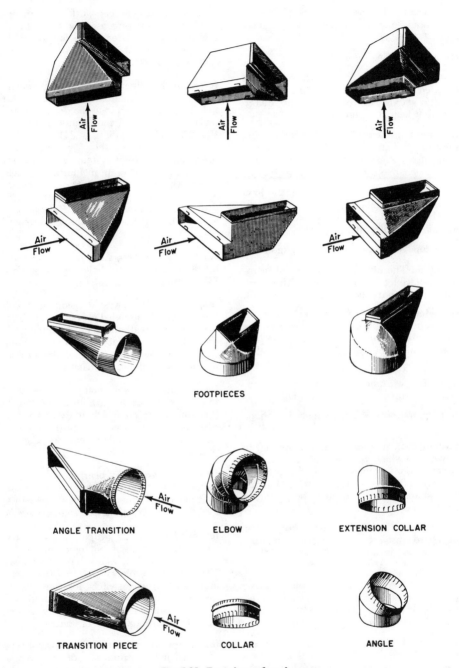

FOOTPIECES

ANGLE TRANSITION   ELBOW   EXTENSION COLLAR

TRANSITION PIECE   COLLAR   ANGLE

Fig. 268. Footpieces for pipes.

footing forms: Forms made of wood or steel for shaping and holding concrete for footings.

footing stop: See *form stop.*

footpace: A landing in a staircase; also, an elevated platform or a predella on which an altar stands. A term formerly applied to the front hearth of a fireplace.

footpieces: In heating and air-conditioning systems, fittings made in standard stock sizes used where pipes or stacks must twist or change direction. See Fig. 268.

foot plate: In framing a building, the lowest horizontal timber of a partition or wall to which the studding is nailed. Same as *mudsill.* See *soleplate,* page 415.

force cup: See *plumber's friend,* page 340.

forced fit: The fitting of a structural member in place by means of force, with the result that the parts become joined as a unit.

fore plane: In carpentry, a bench plane 18 inches in length, intermediate between the jointer plane, which is larger, and the jack plane, which is smaller.

foreman: An overseer who is in charge of a group of workmen and usually is responsible to a superintendent or manager.

forming machine: A machine used to shape metal.

forming tool: A term frequently applied to any device which will facilitate a mechanical operation; a tool especially designed for a particular type of work with its cutting edge shaped like the form to be produced on the work.

form lumber: In form building, any lumber or boards used for shaping and holding green concrete until it has set and thoroughly dried. Also called *form boards.*

form oil: A non-staining oil, sprayed or painted on the inside of the form and used as a bond breaker between the fresh concrete and the form.

form panel layout: Plan showing how the various foundation form panels are to be located and what size panels are to be used. See Fig. 269. See *forms.*

form stop: In concrete work, a term applied to a device consisting of a plank nailed to a 4x4; placed in the forms to hold the wet concrete at the end of a day's pouring. See Fig. 271.

forms: In building construction, an enclosure made of either boards or metal for holding green concrete to the desired shape until it has set and thoroughly dried. See Fig. 270 and Fig. 445, page 341.

formwork: The total system of support for freshly placed concrete including the mold or sheathing which contacts the concrete as well as all supporting members, hardware, and necessary bracing. *Falsework* is also used with essentially the same meaning.

Forstner bit: In carpentry, a type of brace-bit used to sink blind holes in timber. See Fig. 59, page 50.

foundation: The lowest division of a wall for a structure intended for permanent use; that part of a wall on which the building is erected; usually that part of a building which is below the surface of the ground and on which the superstructure rests.

foundation bolt: Any bolt or device used to anchor structural parts of a building to the foundation on which it rests; used to hold machinery in position on its foundation. Also called *anchor bolt.* See Fig. 17, page 17.

foundation wall: Any bearing wall or pier below the first tier of floor joists or beams; that portion of an enclosing wall below the first-floor construction. See *wall,* page 474.

four-way switch: A switch used in house wiring when a light or lights are to be turned on or off at more than two places. Thus, for three places, use two three-way and one four-way switch; for four places, use two three-way and two four-way switches—an additional four-way switch for each additional place of control.

fox wedge: A wedge used in a special type of mortising where the end of a tenon, dowel, or other piece is notched beyond the mortise, then split and a wedge forcibly

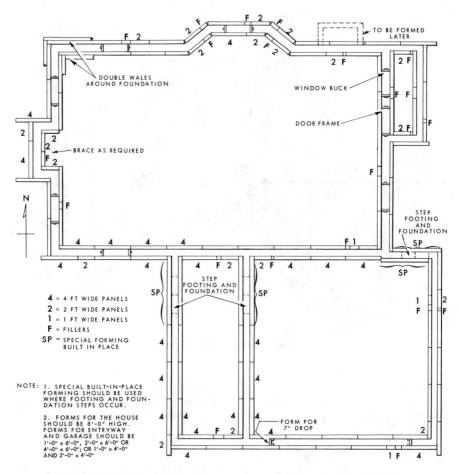

Fig. 269. A panel layout helps the carpenter save time as he erects the forms.

driven in to prevent withdrawal. This wedge enlarges the joint, fastening the end of the tenon in the hole or mortise which holds the joint firm and immovable. This type of wedge is also called *foxtail wedging* or *fox wedging.*

foxtail saw: A saw similar to a tenon saw, used for cutting dovetails; a *dovetail saw.*

foxtail wedge: In carpentry, a wedge for expanding the split end of a dowel pin, a tenon, or other wood piece, so as to fasten the end in a hole or mortise and to prevent withdrawal of the piece.

foyer: An anteroom or lobby, especially of a theater; entrance hallway.

fraction: Any part as distinct from the whole; any part of a unit, as, in mathematics, a *decimal fraction.*

fracture: In masonry, the breaking apart or separation of the continuous parts of a wall of brick or stone caused by a sudden shock or excessive strain.

frame: In carpentry, the timber work supporting the various structural parts, such

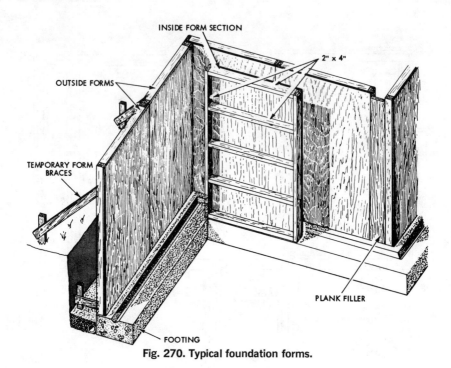

INSIDE FORM SECTION

2" x 4"

OUTSIDE FORMS

TEMPORARY FORM
BRACES

PLANK FILLER

FOOTING

Fig. 270. Typical foundation forms.

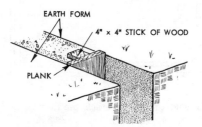

EARTH FORM

4" x 4" STICK OF WOOD

PLANK

Fig. 271. Form stop.

as windows, doors, floors, and roofs; the woodwork of doors, windows, and the entire lumber work supporting the floors, walls, roofs, and partitions.

frame construction. Building using wood structural members. See *construction, frame,* page 117.

frame high: In masonry, the level at which the lintel or arch of an opening is to be laid; also, the height of the top of window or door frames.

frame house: One in which the form and support are constructed of framed timbers; then sheathed with clapboards or shingles, or the frame may be filled in with brick or plaster. See *half-timbered,* page 229.

frame of a house: The framework of a house which includes the joists, studs, plates, sills, partitions, and roofing; that is, all parts which together make up the skeleton of the building.

frame pulley: A box which contains a sheave for carrying a sash cord; designed for installation in a window frame.

framework: The frame of a building; the various supporting parts of a building fitted together into a skeleton form.

framing: The process of putting together the skeleton parts for a building; the rough lumber work on a house, such as flooring, roofing and partitions.

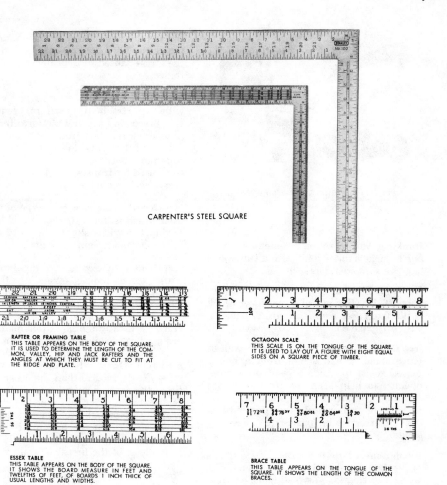

CARPENTER'S STEEL SQUARE

RAFTER OR FRAMING TABLE
THIS TABLE APPEARS ON THE BODY OF THE SQUARE. IT IS USED TO DETERMINE THE LENGTH OF THE COMMON, VALLEY, HIP AND JACK RAFTERS AND THE ANGLES AT WHICH THEY MUST BE CUT TO FIT AT THE RIDGE AND PLATE.

OCTAGON SCALE
THIS SCALE IS ON THE TONGUE OF THE SQUARE. IT IS USED TO LAY OUT A FIGURE WITH EIGHT EQUAL SIDES ON A SQUARE PIECE OF TIMBER.

ESSEX TABLE
THIS TABLE APPEARS ON THE BODY OF THE SQUARE. IT SHOWS THE BOARD MEASURE IN FEET AND TWELFTHS OF FEET, OF BOARDS 1 INCH THICK OF USUAL LENGTHS AND WIDTHS.

BRACE TABLE
THIS TABLE APPEARS ON THE TONGUE OF THE SQUARE. IT SHOWS THE LENGTH OF THE COMMON BRACES.

Fig. 272. Framing square and common tables on the square. (Stanley Works)

framing sawhorse: An X-shaped frame designed to hold rough lumber or logs during the process of sawing. See *sawhorse,* Fig. 499, page 384.

framing square: In building construction, a right angle tool, usually of steel, used for measuring structural material for house framing, roof framing, and stair building. Also called *steel square.* See Fig. 272.

framing-square gage: A device attached to a framing square to secure accuracy when laying out framing material. See Fig. 273. They come in pairs and are used on the framing square to mark off different rises and runs for stringers, in stair construction, and also for rafter layout. They are available in two different styles.

frank: In carpentry, to join or frame together, as molded sash bars, by mitering to the depth of the molding; then squaring by cutting off the rest of each abutting piece or finishing with a mortise-and-tenon joint. See *mortise-and-tenon joint,* page 294.

Fig. 273. Framing square gages.

franking: The operation of notching a *sash bar* to make a miter joint with a transverse bar. See *sash bars,* page 382.

free end: The end of a beam which is unsupported, as that end of a cantilever which is not fixed. See *cantilever joists,* page 84, Fig. 107, page 85.

free-standing vertical sunshades: A wall or fence standing a few feet from a house, placed so as to shade a wall or window opening to help keep the interior of the building cool during warm weather. When louvered or open in style, they do not block out breezes while providing necessary shade.

freemason: A term formerly applied to one of a class of skilled stone masons who worked in freestone as distinguished from an unskilled mason who worked only with rough stone.

freestone: Any stone, as a sandstone, which can be freely worked or quarried; used for molding, tracery, and other work required to be executed with the chisel. Any stone which cuts well in all directions without splitting.

freeze-thaw cycle: The cycle of freezing, melting, freezing, melting, etc. In most climates, pavement (and other concrete construction) will freeze in the night and thaw during the day when the sun hits the surface. If protection is not provided, such as air entrainment, the back and forth of freezing and thawing weather may eventually destroy the concrete.

freeze-thaw test: A test devised to measure the durability of a soil-cement sample to the stress caused by repeated freezing and thawing.

freight elevator: In a building, an elevator with an extra heavy platform, reinforced side braces to keep the platform from tipping, extra rigid car frames, and additional guide-rail brackets to anchor the guide rails more securely to the building structure; used for transferring freight from one story level to another.

French arch: In masonry, a type of bonded arch which is flat at both top and bottom, having the bricks sloping outward from a common center. Same as *Dutch arch.*

French door: In architecture, a pair of doors with glazed panels extending the full length of the door, serving as both door and window; a *French window.*

French Provincial: Adaptations of original designs from France, the French Provincial or Formal French, make use of the *mansard roof.* One of the slopes is lower and more nearly vertical than the other. Sometimes the more nearly horizontal slope is replaced with a flat roof. Fig. 274 shows an example. Note the characteristic slight curve outward at the bottom of the slope where the eaves overhang the walls, nearly at the level of the first-floor ceiling.

French roof: In architecture, a roof having two slopes on each side; a *curb roof.* Also called *mansard roof* (see Fig. 368, page 277). Fig. 274 is an example.

French window: A long, double-sash casement window with the sashes hinged at the sides and opening in the middle. The window extends down to the floor and serves as a door to a porch or terrace.

French-window lock: A mortise-knob lock having a minimum backset; used on windows or doors with narrow stiles, especially French windows.

freon: *Freon* is a trademark applied to a group of gas refrigerants; used extensively in air-conditioning systems because of its nontoxic and nonflammable properties.

Fig. 274. House in French Provincial style, with recessed doorway.

fresco: A term applied to the process of painting on wet plaster. Sometimes incorrectly used in reference to dry painting on plastered walls or ceiling.

fresh-air inlet: In plumbing, a connection made to a house drain above the drain trap, leading to the outside atmosphere, for the purpose of admitting fresh air into the drainage system to dispel the foul gases.

fresh concrete: Concrete that has just been mixed and is still in a mud-like, fluid mass.

fret: Ornamental interlaced relief work characterized especially by its interlocked angular lines. An example of extremely decorative fretwork is that on the Greek Parthenon. See Fig. 275.

fret saw: A narrow, tapering saw used to cut curves; also called *compass saw*.

fretwork: In architecture, any decorative work cut with a *fret saw;* also, ornamental openwork or work in relief.

friable: A term applied to any material which is easily crumbled or reduced to a powder.

friction: Resistance to relative motion set up between particles of two moving surfaces in contact with each other.

friction catch: A device consisting of a spring and plunger contained in a casing, or a diamond-shaped spring metal tongue

Fig. 275. Frets.

that engages a like-shaped socket; used on small doors or articles of furniture to keep them tightly closed but not locked. See Fig. 276.

Fig. 276. Friction catch.

friction tape: For electrical purposes, a tape coated with a black adhesive compound; used as insulation on wire joints.

frieze: The middle portion of an entablature; that is, the part immediately above the architrave and below the cornice; sometimes ornamented with sculpture. See Figs. 5 and 137. A horizontal member connecting the top of the siding with the soffit of the cornice or roof sheathing. See Fig. 78, page 63, Fig. 159, page 125, Fig. 5, page 4, and Fig. 137, page 108.

frilled: An ornamental edging on furniture such as a *frilled* C *scroll;* a term used to refer to any scroll which has added decorative carving along its projecting edges.

frithstool: In some early churches, a seat, usually of stone, placed near the altar as a sacred refuge for anyone who claimed the privilege of sanctuary within them.

frog: A depression, such as a groove or recess, in one or both of the larger sides of a brick or building block, thus providing a key for the mortar at the joints, and, also, effecting a saving in the weight of the material. A name also applied to a part of a carpenter's plane. See Fig. 435, page 331.

front: Any face of a structure, particularly the face containing the principal entrance.

front-door lock. A lock which is designed for use on entrance doors. Such a lock usually contains a dead bolt and a dead latch, with the dead bolt controlled from the outside by a key and from the inside by a knob or key. The latch bolt is controlled by a key on the outside and by the door knob on the inside.

front elevation: In architectural drawings, the front view of a building.

front-entrance door: Any exterior door specially designed to close a front entrance or doorway. A variety of designs for exterior front doors are shown in Fig. 187, page 147.

front hearth: That portion of a hearth which projects into a room, extending beyond the chimney breast. Formerly called the *footplace*.

front of lot: That part of a lot, or plot of ground, bordering on a street or highway. In case of a corner lot, the owner usually designates which edge is to be considered as *the front of the lot*.

front view: In architectural drawings, the view of the front of a building; also called *front elevation*. See Fig. 228, page 171.

frontal: A pediment over a door or window.

frontispiece: A pediment over a door or window; the principal front of a building.

frost line: The depth which frost penetrates into the earth; varies in different parts of the country. Footings or the foundation should go below the frost line.

full frame: Mortised-and-tenoned frame, in which every joint was mortised and tenoned; rarely used today.

full pitch: In roof framing, a term applied to a roof with a pitch having a rise equal to the width of the span of the roof.

full-size details: In architectural drawing, a design which is drawn to full size of the object shown.

fur: A term applied to the process of applying narrow strips of wood, known as *furring strips,* to floor joists or other parts of a building. See *furring,* Fig. 277.

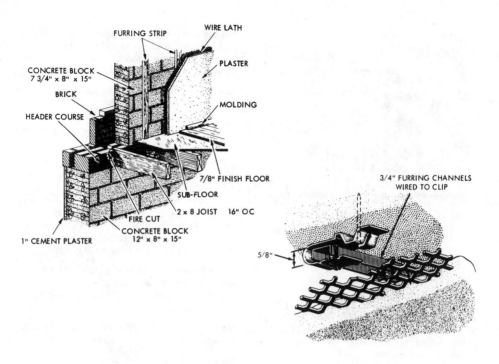

Fig. 277. Furring strips used for wall (left) and for ceiling (right). (Right: U.S. Gypsum Co.)

furnace: An apparatus in which heat is generated and maintained by the combustion of fuel; a heating plant.

furniture: A term formerly applied to the metal trimming around doors, windows, and other similar parts of a building; in this country, a term now commonly applied to *builders' hardware,* including any embellishments, such as locks, door and window bolts, fastenings, and hinges.

furred: The providing of air space between the walls and plastering or subfloor and finish floor by use of wood strips, such as lath or 1x2's nailed to the walls in a vertical position. Walls or floors prepared in this manner are said to be *furred.*

furring: The process of leveling up part of a wall, ceiling, or floor by the use of wood or metal strips; also, a term applied to the strips used to provide air space between a wall and the plastering. See Fig. 277.

furring strips: Flat pieces of lumber or metal used to build up an irregular framing to an even surface, either the leveling of a part of a wall or ceiling. The term *furring strips* or *furrings* is also applied to strips placed against a brick wall for nailing lath, to provide air space between the wall and plastering to avoid dampness. See Fig. 277.

fuse: A safety device for protecting electrical apparatus against the effect of excess current or to prevent overloading a circuit. It consists of a short length of conducting metal which melts at a certain heat and thereby breaks when an excess current flows through it. Most fuses cannot be reused if burned out (blown). Some are renewable, however. See also *circuit breaker,* page 99.

fuse block: In electricity, an insulated block designed to hold fuses.

Fig. 278. Fuse box or distribution panel.

fuse box: A term sometimes applied to a distribution fuse board or service panel when it is enclosed in a box. See Fig. 278. Also called *load center panelboard* or *main control center*.

fuse clip: The spring holder for a cartridge-type fuse.

fuse cutouts: An insulated block with fittings for holding fuses.

fuse link: A length of fuse wire for refilling fuses; the necessary, or fusible, part of a cartridge fuse.

fuse plug: A fuse mounted in a screw plug which is screwed into the fuse block like a lamp in a socket.

fuse strip: A length of ribbon fuse as distinguished from a wire fuse.

fuse wire: A wire made of an alloy which melts at a comparatively low temperature.

fusestat: In electricity, a special type of plug fuse with a time lag and an adapter that makes it impossible to bridge the fuse with a penny. Also called "S" fuse.

fusetron: In electricity, a special type of fuse with a time lag that will carry the current of motors without opening the circuit; they permit an overload for a limited time. Also called *fusestat*.

fusible link: A link on the holding device of a fireproof door or window that breaks (by melting) when subject to extreme heat, allowing the door or window to close.

fust: In architecture, the shaft of a column or pilaster.

G

gable: The end of a building as distinguished from the front or rear side; the triangular end of an exterior wall above the eaves; the end of a ridged roof which, at its extremity, is not returned on itself but is cut off in a vertical plane which above the eaves is triangular in shape due to the slope of the roof. See Fig. 279.

gableboard: A board placed along the sloping edge of a gable roof, covering the timbers that project over the gables. Same as *bargeboard*.

gabled towers: Towers finished with gables in the place of parapets.

gable end: An end wall with a *gable*. See Fig. 279.

gable molding: The molding used as a finish for the gable end of a roof.

gable roof: A ridged roof that slopes up from only two walls. A gable is the triangular portion of the end of a building from the eaves to the ridge. See Fig. 279.

gable wall: A wall surmounted by a *gable*. See Fig. 279.

gable window: A window with a gable or having its upper part shaped like a gable; a gable in or under a window.

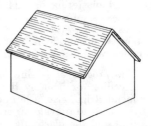

Fig. 279. Gable roof.

gablet: A small gable-shaped architectural ornament over a niche, buttress, or other opening.

gage: A tool used by carpenters to strike a line parallel to the edge of a board. See *dividers,* page 145. Also a uniform standard for wire diameters and for the thickness of metal plates. See Fig. 15, page 14. See also *gage, sheet metal.*

gage board: In stair building, a board used as a marker for the treads and risers on a stringer for housing; also called *templet;* a *pitch board.* See Fig. 433, page 329.

gage lines: In steel construction, lines parallel to the length of a member on which holes for fasteners are placed. The gage distance is the normal distance between the gage line and the edge or back of the member.

gage, sheet metal: Sheet metal thickness is usually specified by gage number. Gages commonly used range from 32 to 10, in increments of 2, with the gage number decreasing as the thickness increases. Thus, gages from 32 to 22 (or .0097 in. to .0299 in.) are considered *light gage,* from 20 to 16 (or .0359 in. to .0598 in.) are *medium gage,* and 14 to 10 (or .0749 in. to .1345 in.) are *heavy gage.*

gain: The notch or mortise where a piece of wood is cut out to receive the end of another piece of wood.

gallery: An elevated floor, or platform, equipped to increase the seating capacity of auditoriums in churches, theaters, and other large audience rooms. Projecting from the interior wall of a building, usually the *gallery* is supported by columns below, but sometimes it is hung on supports from above. In some cases supports are provided both above and below.

gallet: A splinter of stone chipped off by chiseling. Also called a *spall.*

galleting: In rubble work, a term applied to the process of filling in the coarse masonry joints of fresh mortar with small stone chips or gallets. Same as *garreting.*

galvanizing: A coating of zinc applied to iron or steel to prevent rusting.

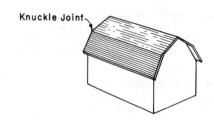

Fig. 280. Gambrel roof.

gambrel roof: A type of roof which has its slope broken by an obtuse angle, so that the lower slope is steeper than the upper slope; a roof with two pitches. See Fig. 280.

ganged forms: Prefabricated panels joined to make a much larger unit (up to 30 x 50 ft.) for convenience in erecting, stripping, and reusing; usually braced with wales, strongbacks, or special lifting hardware.

gangway: In building, a temporary footway made of planks and used as a passageway by workmen on a construction job.

gantry: A spanning framework, as a bridgelike portion of certain cranes.

garage: A building or enclosure designed or used primarily for motor vehicles.

garden bond: A type of masonry construction consisting of three stretchers in each course followed by a header. However, this bond may have from two to five stretchers between headers.

gardenwall bond: In bricklaying, a bond formed by stretchers with headers inserted at intervals of several courses only; also called *flying bond.*

gargoyle: A water spout, often terminating in a grotesquely carved head, projecting from the gutter of a building discharging rain water clear of the wall. The head may be either human or animal with open mouth through which the water gurgles. The noise made by the passing water probably suggested the name *gargoyle* or *gurgoyle.*

garnet paper: An abrasive paper used for polishing and finishing surfaces of woodwork. The paper is prepared by covering one side with glue and a reddish abrasive material.

garret: That part of a house built in the space immediately under a sloping roof. The same as *attic*.

garret window: A skylight so arranged that the glazing lies along the slope of the roof.

garreting: In masonry, a term applied to the process of pressing small splinters of stone into the joints of coarse masonry. Also called *galleting*.

gasket: In plumbing, plaited hemp or cotton yarn wound around the spigot end of a pipe at a joint. The hemp or cotton is forced into the socket of the mating pipe to form a tight joint.

gas log: An imitation log, consisting of a hollow perforated device, used as a gas burner in a fireplace.

gas metal-arc welding (MIG): This welding process (Mig) uses a continuous consumable wire electrode. The molten weld puddle is completely covered with a shield of gas. The wire electrode is fed through the torch at pre-set controlled speeds. The shielding gas is also fed through the torch. See Fig. 281. See *gas shielded arc welding*.

Fig. 281. High temperature electric arc melts advancing wire electrode into a globule of liquid metal. Wire is fed mechanically through the torch. Arc heat is regulated by conditions pre-set on the power supply. (Linde Co.)

gasoline portable tools: Saws, hammers, drills, etc., operated by gasoline, which are used where electric power is not available.

gas pliers: In plumbing, stout pliers having narrow jaws whose gripping faces are concave with the edges notched like teeth; to provide a secure grip on small pipe or round objects.

gas-shielded arc welding: There are two general types. *gas tungsten-arc (Tig)* and *gas metal-arc (Mig)*. Both welding processes can be semi-automatic or fully automatic. These processes are rapidly gaining recognition as being superior to the standard metallic arc. Both the arc and molten puddle are covered by a shield of gas. The shield of gas prevents atmospheric contamination, producing a sounder weld.

gas tungsten-arc welding (TIG): In this process a virtually non-consumable tungsten electrode is used to provide the arc for welding. See Fig. 282. In Tig welding, the electrode is used only to create the arc. It is not consumed in the weld. In this way it differs from the regular shielded metal-arc process, where the stick electrode is consumed in the weld. See *gas-shielded arc welding*.

gas vent: A chimney designed and approved for use of gas-burning appliances only.

gas welding equipment: Equipment used to control and direct the heat on the edges of metal to be joined, while applying a suitable metal filler to the molten pool. The intense heat is obtained from the combustion of gas, usually acetylene and oxygen.

gate valve: A valve consisting of a brass casting into which is fitted a brass gate. The gate is lifted and lowered by means of a screw stem which is operated by a cast-iron wheel handle. A slight pressure of the hand turns the handle. See Fig. 283.

gauged arch: In masonry, an arch constructed with special bricks which have been cut with a bricklayer's saw, then rubbed to the exact shape required for use in an arch where the joints radiate from a common center.

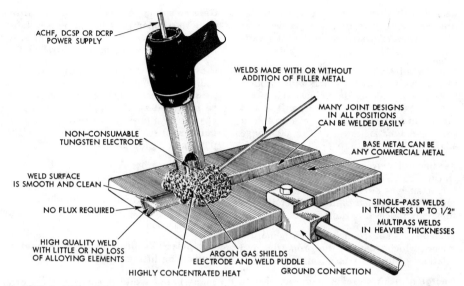

ACHF, DCSP OR DCRP POWER SUPPLY

WELDS MADE WITH OR WITHOUT ADDITION OF FILLER METAL

MANY JOINT DESIGNS IN ALL POSITIONS CAN BE WELDED EASILY

NON–CONSUMABLE TUNGSTEN ELECTRODE

BASE METAL CAN BE ANY COMMERCIAL METAL

WELD SURFACE IS SMOOTH AND CLEAN

NO FLUX REQUIRED

SINGLE–PASS WELDS IN THICKNESS UP TO 1/2"

MULTIPASS WELDS IN HEAVIER THICKNESSES

HIGH QUALITY WELD WITH LITTLE OR NO LOSS OF ALLOYING ELEMENTS

ARGON GAS SHIELDS ELECTRODE AND WELD PUDDLE

HIGHLY CONCENTRATED HEAT

GROUND CONNECTION

Fig. 282. In TIG welding, a non-consumable tungsten electrode is used. It is surrounded by a shield of inert gas. (Linde Co.)

gauged brick: In masonry, bricks which have been cut with a bricklayer's saw, then rubbed to the desired shape. When used in an arch, the joints of *gauged brick* radiate from a common center.

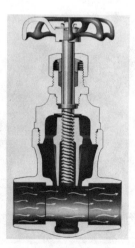

Fig. 283. Gate valve.

gauged mortar: In plastering, any mortar mixed with plaster of paris to make it set more quickly; also called *gauged stuff*.

gauged stuff: In plastering, a mortar made by mixing lime putty with plaster of paris to hasten setting; used for cornices and moldings. Also called *gauged mortar*.

gauging: In masonry, cutting brick or stone to make them uniform in size. In plastering, the mixing of plaster of paris with mortar to effect a quick setting.

gauging plaster: A plaster mixed with finish lime to make lime putty for the finish coat of plaster. The initial strength and the proper setting time of the lime putty is determined by the gauging plaster.

gazebo: A summer house; a cupola on a residence roof; a balcony enclosed with windows.

geodesic: Made of light, straight, structural elements largely in tension, as a geodesic dome; the shortest line between two points on a mathematically derived surface.

geometrical: Pertaining to geometry; figures consisting of regular lines, curves, and angles; conforming to the rules of geometry.

geometrical stair: A winding stair which returns on itself with winders built around a well. The balustrade follows the curve without newel posts at the turns. It is also known as a *spiral stair*. An example of a *geometric stair* is shown in Fig. 563, page 426.

geometrical tracery: A term applied to tracery consisting of simple symmetrical forms, such as circles, trefoils, and quatrefoils whose perimeters are distinct though they may touch at certain points.

geometry: That branch of mathematical science which treats of the properties and relations of lines, surfaces, and solids.

Georgian architecture: A name applied to the type of architecture prevailing in England during the reigns of the four Georges (1714-1830); also, a name applied to a similar type of architecture much used in America during the same period, although now more commonly called *Colonial* or *Old Colonial*. Fig. 284 illustrates a Georgian type of house.

German siding: A type of weatherboarding with the upper part of the exposed face finished with a concave curve and the lower portion of the back face rebated.

gesso (jes'so): A hard, fine surface, especially one prepared for use in painting or for making bas-reliefs. Such a surface can be produced by the application of plaster of paris or a pasty mixture of whiting prepared with size or glue; used as a basis for painting or gilding.

gillmore needle: A device used to determine time of setting of hydraulic cement.

gimlet: A small tool with a handle attached at right angles to the *bit;* used for boring holes in wood.

gin poles: Vertical guyed pole used for supporting lifting tackle.

gingerbread work: A gaudy type of ornamentation in architecture, especially in the trim of a house.

girder: A large, supporting horizontal member used to support walls or joists; a beam, either timber or steel, used for supporting a superstructure. See Fig. 285. See also: Figs. 16, 41, 54, 77, 82, 94.

Fig. 284. Georgian style house.

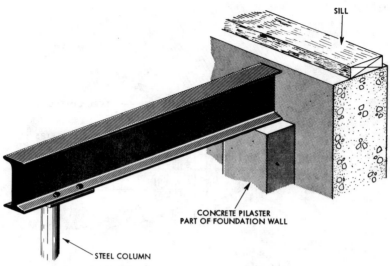

SILL

CONCRETE PILASTER
PART OF FOUNDATION WALL

STEEL COLUMN

Fig. 285. A girder is supported by a pilaster.

girder supports or girder posts: Columns placed so they will support a girder or beam.

girt: A horizontal member used in braced frame construction that carries the second floor joists. Also: The same as girth; the circumference of round timber.

girt strip: A board attached to studding to carry floor joists; a ledger board.

girth: The circumference of any circular object; the distance around a column.

glacial gravel: "Clean" gravel left by a glacier as it retreats. It is a non-graded material, since it has no fines.

glass block: A hollow, glass, building brick having the advantage of admitting light with privacy, insulating against the passage of sound, but not safe to use in a load-bearing wall. Sometimes called *glass brick.* A *glass-block* panel in a brick wall is shown in Fig. 286.

glass cutter: A cutting implement, usually consisting of a diamond or a small rotary wheel set in a handle; used to cut glass to size; any device for cutting glass to size.

glass paper: A paper used as an abrasive and for polishing purposes. It is made by first coating paper with glue, then sprinkling pulverized glass over the glue.

glass stop: A molding which is used to secure glass in doors or window sash.

glass-wool insulation: A kind of insulating material composed of glass fibers which are formed into lightweight blankets of uniform thickness, fastened securely to heavy paper. Usually, the paper is of the asphalt-treated or vapor-barrier type. See *blanket insulation,* page 51.

glassy slag: A term commonly applied to slag particles, whose surfaces are predominantly of a smooth, vitreous nature.

glaze: The process of installing glass panes in window and door frames and applying putty to hold the glass in position.

glazed: Equipped with window panes; the process of placing glass in windows, doors, and mirrors is known as *glazing.*

217

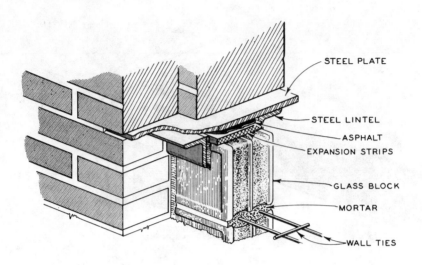

STEEL PLATE

STEEL LINTEL

ASPHALT

EXPANSION STRIPS

GLASS BLOCK

MORTAR

WALL TIES

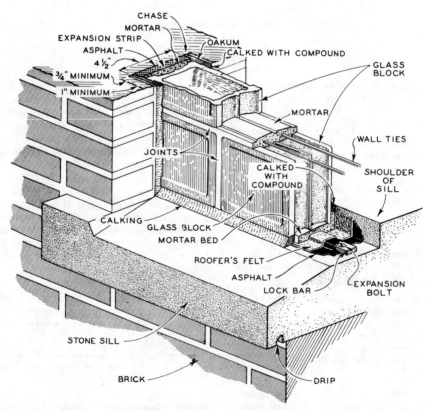

CHASE

MORTAR

EXPANSION STRIP

ASPHALT

OAKUM

CALKED WITH COMPOUND

$4\frac{1}{2}$"

GLASS BLOCK

$\frac{3}{4}$" MINIMUM

1" MINIMUM

MORTAR

WALL TIES

JOINTS

CALKED WITH COMPOUND

SHOULDER OF SILL

CALKING

GLASS BLOCK

MORTAR BED

ROOFER'S FELT

ASPHALT

LOCK BAR

EXPANSION BOLT

STONE SILL

BRICK

DRIP

Fig. 286. Glass block panel.

glazed brick: Building brick prepared by fusing on the surface a glazing material, brick having a glassy surface.

glazed doors: Doors which have been fitted with glass and usually having a pattern or lattice of woodwork between the panes.

glazed tile: A type of masonry tile which has a glassy or glossy surface. A special type of tile unit employed in the construction of residences, barns, and other buildings. Such tiles have their exposed surfaces treated to add to their appearance, to give color, and to make them more resistive to weathering and the action of acids. Also called *face tile.*

glazement: In building, a facing material which gives a glazed waterproof surface; used for concrete or brickwork construction.

glazier: A workman whose business is that of cutting panes of glass to size and fitting them in position in frames for doors or windows.

glazier's chisel: A type of knife made like a chisel and used to apply putty when glazing windows or doors.

glazier's points: Triangular or diamond-shaped points cut from sheet metal; now commonly they have bent flanges so they may be installed easily. They are used by glaziers for holding window panes in place while putty is applied. The points also serve to hold the glass in position until the putty hardens or sets.

glazier's putty: In building, a mixture of whiting and linseed oil and sometimes including white lead forming a plastic substance used for fixing panes of glass into frames. Same as *painter's putty.*

glazing: Placing glass in windows, doors, and mirrors. Also: the filling up of crevices in the surface of a grindstone or emery wheel with minute abraded particles detached in grinding. In plumbing, the process of passing a hot iron over the lead of a *wiped joint* in order to produce a smooth, finished surface.

glazing bead: In building construction, a convex molding, or bead, nailed into a sash rebate to hold a pane of glass in position; used instead of putty. See *bead,* page 43.

glazing brads: Triangular or diamond-shaped pieces of metal, with or without flanges, used to hold panes of glass in position while the putty is applied. See *glazier's points.*

glazing color: In painting, a covering of transparent wash on a ground coat of paint.

glitter guns: Glitter guns are used to apply glitter (dry colored particles) to wet acoustic plaster. See Fig. 287.

Fig. 287. Glitter gun.

globe valve: In plumbing, a kind of valve in which a disk which is operated by a screw and a hand wheel seats on a circular opening; so installed that pressure is applied on the underside of the seat. See Fig. 288.

gloss: A paint or enamel that contains a low proportion of pigment and dries to a sheen or luster. Painters use the terms *high, enamel,* or *mirror* to indicate the highest gloss or luster; and *semigloss, eggshell,* and *flat* to indicate decreasing degrees of gloss in the order given.

219

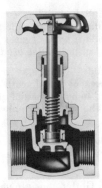

Fig. 288. Globe valve.

glue: An adhesive substance, obtainable on the market in dry or liquid form. There are approximately eight general types of glue commonly used: liquid glue, casein glue, animal glue, epoxy resin, blood albumin glue, vegetable glue, synthetic resin glue, and cellulose cement and rubber compounds. The properties, uses, and methods of application of the different types of glue vary, and the selection of a glue depends upon such factors as the rate of setting, water resistance, and tendency to stain wood as well as the strength factor. Clamping is usually required for a strong bond.

glue injector: A metal syringe with small, pointed nozzle for injecting glue into a joint or through a very small hole.

glue water: Gelatin soaked in water used to retard plaster used for sticking ornaments.

glyph (glif): In architecture, an ornamental channel or groove; a short, vertical groove.

gooseneck: Something curved like the neck of a goose, such as an iron hook or other mechanical contrivance bent or shaped like a goose neck; the curved or bent section of the handrail on a stair.

gorgerin (gor′jer-in): The necklike part of a column, a feature forming the junction between a shaft and its capital; the neck of a capital or the space between the neck moldings. Also called *necking*. See Fig. 5, page 4.

Gothic: In architecture, a particular type and style of classic ornamentation.

Gothic arch: A type of arch, usually high and narrow, coming to a point at the center at the top, especially one with a joint instead of a keystone at the apex.

Gothic stonework: A type of stonework used in a style of architecture which prevailed in western Europe from about 1160 to 1530. An example of this stonework is shown in Fig. 289.

Fig. 289. Gothic stonework.

Gothic style: A name applied to a style of architecture prevalent in western Europe from the 12th to the 16th century. This style of architecture was characterized chiefly by the pointed arch and the comparatively great height of many of the buildings. An example of Gothic stonework is shown in Fig. 289.

gouge: A cutting chisel which has a concavo-convex cross section or cutting surface.

grade: In building trades, the term used when referring to the ground level around a building. Also: the slope of a site or finished slab. In highway construction, the prepared surface in a highway system on which the base or sub-base is placed. In lumber, any of the quality classes into which lumber is segregated for marketing and construction purposes.

grade beam: A reinforced concrete beam, usually at ground level, which provides support for the walls of a building. The beam may be in contact with the earth but it is supported by footings, piers, or caissons.

grade level: The level of the ground around a building. The final or finished elevation of the ground surface, whether to be cut or filled.

grade line: The level of the ground at the building line. Same as *grade level.*

grade marks: A marking rolled onto the bar to identify the grade of steel. See *bar number,* page 37.

grade of steel: The means by which a design engineer specifies the strength properties of the steel he requires in each part of a structure, generally using ASTM designation to distinguish them.

grader: A gasoline operated vehicle with a large blade underneath, used for grading and leveling the ground.

gradient: The degree of inclination of a surface, road, or pipe, usually expressed in percent.

grading: Filling in around a building with rubble and earth, so the ground will slope downward from the foundation at an angle sufficient to carry off rain water. A completed foundation wall before *filling* is begun is shown in Fig. 35, page 31. In concrete, the amount, size, and distribution of aggregates within the concrete so large size aggregate can be used with a suffiicient amount of smaller aggregates to fill in the spaces between the larger ones.

gradual load: The gradual application of a load to the supporting members of a structure, so as to provide the most favorable conditions possible for receiving the stress and strain which these members will be required to carry when the building is completed.

graduate: To mark with degrees of measurement, as the division marks of a scale; the regular dividing of parts into steps or grades.

graduation: The process of separating a unit of measure into equal parts; also, one of the division marks or one of the equal divisions of a scale.

grain: In woodworking, a term applied to the arrangement of wood fibers; working a piece of wood longitudinally may be either with or against the grain; a cross-section, or transverse, cut of wood is spoken of as *cross grain.*

graining comb: A comb-like tool made of steel or leather used for obtaining grain effects in wood finishing.

granite: An igneous rock composed chiefly of feldspar but containing also some quartz and mica; used extensively in construction work and for monuments. It is extremely hard and will take a high polish.

granular: Soil texture, having a resemblance to sugar, where all the particles are of one size, for example, dune sand.

granulated cork: Chips and waste pieces of cork ground into small particles and used as a low-temperature insulating material.

granulated slag: The product of rapid cooling of molten blast-furnace slag, resulting in a mass of friable, porous grains most of which are under one-half inch in size. See *air-cooled slag,* page 11.

graph: A diagram illustrating ideas, or presenting a system of related facts, by means of dots joined by curved or straight lines. Graphic diagrams are made on paper ruled into small squares, prepared especially for the purpose, and known as *graph paper.* In architectural drawing, elevation views and floor plans are made on *graph paper.*

grating: A framework or gratelike arrangement of bars either parallel or crossed; used to cover an opening.

gravel: Gravel varies from about one quarter inch up to three inches.

gravel fill: Crushed rock, pebbles, or gravel deposited in a layer of any desired thickness at the bottom of an excavation, the purpose of which is to insure adequate drainage of any water. See Fig. 63, page 52.

221

gravel strip: A strip of material nailed around the edges of a graveled roof to prevent the gravel from rolling off and to add a finished appearance to the roof. Same as *slag strip.*

gravity water system: Any water system in which flow occurs under the natural pressure due to gravity.

grease trap: In plumbing, an interceptor, or trap, placed in the drain or waste pipe to prevent waste grease from passing into the sewer system where it will eventually cause trouble in the plumbing. See Fig. 290.

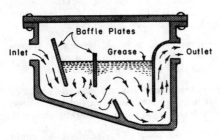

Fig. 290. Grease trap.

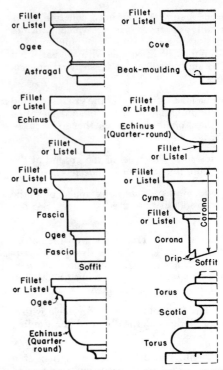

Fig. 291. Molding outlines for Greek architecture.

Greco-Roman architecture: A type of architecture in which the Greek style was modified by influence of the Roman. Sometimes called an *architecture of the beam and column,* in which the lintel which was used pure and unmixed by the Greeks was forced into union with the arch by the Romans.

Greek architecture: A term commonly applied to the three Greek orders—Doric, Ionic, and Corinthian. Various types of moldings are used on the capital of the different orders. Typical molding outlines are shown in Fig. 291. See *order,* page 305.

Greek fret: A geometrical, repeating ornament, used to decorate a fascia, band, or frieze.

green: Not fully seasoned. Freshly sawed lumber or lumber that has not been kiln or air dried.

green brick: In masonry, a molded clay block before it has been burned in preparation for building purposes.

green lumber: Boards cut from green logs; lumber which has not yet been seasoned or dried. Defined as lumber having a moisture content in excess of 19 percent.

green mortar: A term sometimes applied to mortar before it has set firmly.

green wood: A term used by woodworkers when referring to timbers which still contain the moisture, or sap, of the tree from which the wood was cut. Lumber is said to be *seasoned* when the sap has been removed by natural processes of drying or by artificial drying in a kiln.

greenhouse effect: A hot, dry condition created by the hot sun under plastic sheets which are covering a concrete slab for curing purposes.

grid: In structural work, the plan layout for any given building.

grillage: A framework of heavy timbers or beams laid longitudinally and crossed by similar beams laid upon them, for sustaining walls to prevent irregular setting.

grillage foundation: In building, a foundation formed of a framework of sleepers and crossbeams of timbers or steel beams superimposed on a layer of concrete; used for structures erected on marshy land or where the soil contains quicksand.

grille: A grating or openwork barrier, usually of metal but sometimes of wood, used to cover an opening, or as a protection over the glass of a window or door, or over a duct opening. A *grille* may be plain but often it is of an ornamental or decorative character.

grillwork: In building, a heavy framework of crossed timbers or beams, used for foundations in soft soil; any work constructed so as to resemble a *grille;* also, a plain or ornamental openwork construction of wood or metal serving as a protective screen. Same as *grillage.*

grind: To reduce any substance to powder by friction or crushing; to wear down or sharpen a tool by use of an abrasive, such as a whetstone, emery wheel, or grindstone; to reduce in size by the removal of particles of material by contact with a rotating abrasive wheel.

grinder: Any device used to sharpen tools or remove particles of material by any process of grinding.

grindstone: A flat, rotating stone wheel used to sharpen tools or wear down materials by abrading or grinding. *Grindstones* are natural sandstone.

groin: In architecture, the curved line or edge formed by the intersection of two vaults.

groin arch: In the later styles of groining, the cross rib which passes at right angles from wall to wall dividing the vault into bays or travees.

groin ceiling: A name applied to a ceiling of a building composed of oak ribs, the spandrels of which are filled in with narrow, thin strips of wood.

groin centering: When groining without ribs, during the erection of the vaulting, the whole surface is supported by centering. When groining with ribs, only the stone ribs are supported by timber ribs during the progress of the work.

groined: A term applied to the curved intersection of two vaults meeting each other at any angle.

groined vaulting: The intersecting or crossing of two stone, brick, wood, or plaster vaults so they form a projecting solid angle which grows more obtuse at the top; a system of covering a building or passageway with intersecting stone vaults.

groin point: The arris or line of intersection of two vaults where there are no ribs.

groin rib: A rib occupying the place of a groin and concealing the groin point or joints where the spandrels intersect.

groins, Welsh, or underpitch: When the cross or transverse vaults which are run from the windows are lower than the main longitudinal vault of any groining, this system of groining usually is called either *Welsh groining* or *underpitch groining.*

grommet: A metal eyelet used principally in awnings or along the edges of sails.

groove: A channel, usually small, used in woodworking and building for different purposes which sometimes are practical but often merely decorative.

groover: A tool for cutting joints in fresh concrete. It is usually about 6 inches long and 2 to 4 inches wide, with flat bottom surface like a trowel but with a ridge in the center to form a groove. See Fig. 292.

grooving: In sheet metal, a grooving machine is used for grooving longitudinal seams in cylinders. This machine completes the seam by grooving and flattening in one operation of the carriage.

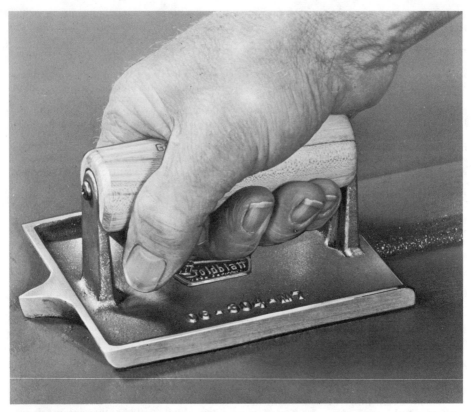

Fig. 292. A groover is used for making joints in concrete flatwork. Also called a *jointer*. (Gold-blatt Tool Co.)

grotesque: An absurdly fantastic style of decorative work and ornamentation found in ancient buildings.

grotto: An artificial cavern-like recess or structure; also, a cave.

ground: One of the pieces of wood flush with the plastering of a room, to which moldings and other similar finish material are nailed. (See Fig. 293.) The *ground* acts as a straight edge and thickness gage to which the plasterer works to insure a straight plaster surface of proper thickness. Also, the side of an electrical circuit or machine which is connected to the earth. In painting, the first coat of paint applied as a basis for succeeding coats.

ground beam: In building construction, a horizontal timber on or near the ground, used to support the superstructure and to steady the framework. These supports may be of iron, stone, or steel. They distribute the load, which they support, over the ground; also called *sleepers*.

ground casing: In building construction, the blind casing of a box-window frame. See *blind casing*, page 52.

ground color: A special product for covering bad spots on a stained surface, giving it a uniform, dull, yellow finish in preparation for the application of a new coat of varnish stain.

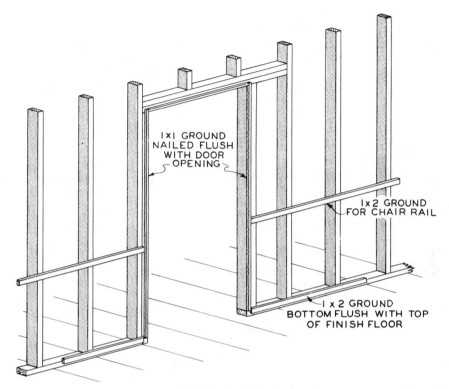

I×I GROUND
NAILED FLUSH
WITH DOOR
OPENING

I×2 GROUND
FOR CHAIR RAIL

I×2 GROUND
BOTTOM FLUSH WITH TOP
OF FINISH FLOOR

Fig. 293. Grounds.

ground course: A horizontal course, usually of masonry, next to the ground.

ground floor: Usually the main floor of a building; the floor of a house most nearly on a level with the ground; that is, the first floor above the ground level.

ground joist: A joist which is blocked up from the ground.

ground line: In building construction, the ground level or natural grade line from which measurements for excavating are taken. In perspective drawing, the intersection of the *ground plane* and the *picture plane.* See *perspective drawing,* page 322.

ground plan: A drawing or plan view of a horizontal section of a building showing the foundation with the layout of rooms, such as location of walls, partitions, doors, and windows on the ground floor, usually shown at window height.

ground plane: In perspective drawing the plane on which the observer stands and on which the object rests. See *perspective drawing,* page 322.

ground wall: In building, the foundation wall; the wall on which a superstructure rests.

ground water: In plumbing, a term applied to water naturally contained in, or passing through, the ground or subsoil.

225

grounds: Pieces of wood or metal embedded in, and flush with, the plastering of walls to which moldings, skirting, and other joiner's work is attached. Also used to stop the plastering around door and window openings; surfaces prepared as a background for decorative features such as scrolls, frets, and figures. A method of framing *plaster grounds* to give them value is shown in Fig. 293.

groundsill: In architecture, the lowest member of the framework of a structure; a timber which supports a superstructure; a *ground plate.*

grouped columns: When three or more columns are placed upon the same pedestal, or otherwise closely associated, they are said to be *grouped columns;* two columns placed together are called *coupled columns.*

grout: A mortar made so thin by the addition of water it will run into joints and cavities of masonry; a fluid cement mixture used to fill crevices.

grouting: The process of injecting cement grout into foundations and decayed walls for reinforcing and strengthening them. Also called *cementation.*

growth ring: The growth put on by a tree in a single year.

grozing iron: In building, a tool used by plumbers for finishing soldered lead joints; also, a tool used for cutting glass.

grub saw: In building, a type of handsaw for cutting building stone, especially marble.

guilloche (gi-losh′): A decorative architectural feature composed of a bandlike ornamentation. This band is made up of interlacing curved lines arranged so as to form wavy motifs with a circular opening at the center of each motif. This open space is filled with a round ornament which further enhances the extravagance of this ornate design. See Fig. 294.

gum: Resin extruded by trees. Sometimes found in lumber as pockets, seams, small patches, or streaks.

gum arabic: A white or colorless powder, soluble in water, obtained from the gum of

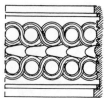

Fig. 294. Example of guilloche or woven band.

certain varieties of acacia; sometimes used in mixing transparent paints.

gum bloom: In paint, a transparent haze or lack of normal gloss caused by the use of an incorrect reducer.

gunite: A construction material composed of cement, sand or crushed slag, and water mixed together and forced through a cement gun by pneumatic pressure. Sold under the trademark *Gunite.*

gusset: A brace or angle bracket used to stiffen a corner or angular piece of work.

gusset plate. A plate used to connect members of a truss together or to connect several steel members at a joint.

gutta (plural guttae): In architecture, one of a series of droplike ornaments, or cone-shaped pendants, used in the decoration of the Doric entablature. See Figs. 5, page 4, and Fig. 230, page 174.

gutter: A channel of wood or metal at the eaves or on the roof of a building for carrying off rain water and water from melting snow.

gutter bolt: A securing bolt in a cast-iron gutter between the spigot and the socket ends at a joint.

gutter bracket: Metal brackets used to support hanging gutters.

guy: A wire, rope, chain, or similar support for a structure. See *guy rope.*

guy rope: A galvanized rope which consists of six strands of seven wires, each covering a hemp core; used to hold a structure in a desired position.

gypsum: A mineral, hydrous sulphate of calcium. In the pure state, gypsum is colorless. When part of the water is removed by a slow heating process, the product becomes what is known as *plaster of paris;* used extensively for decorative purposes. Commonly used as a core in sheets of *drywall.*

gypsum board nails: Nails used for applying both rock lath and gypsum board. They come in 1 inch to 1¾ inch lengths. See Fig. 295.

Fig. 295. Gypsum board nail.

gypsum lath: A plaster base made in sheet form composed of a core of fibered gypsum, faced on both sides with paper.

gypsum wallboard: Gypsum wallboard is commonly used in the interior of a house in *drywall construction.* (Drywall is a wall applied without the use of mortar or plaster.) Panels are composed of a gypsum rock base sandwiched between two layers of special paper. Insulating panels with an aluminum backing are available and standard fire resistant panels (with a base of gypsum rock mixed with glass fibers) are common. Panels may be either unfinished or finished. Vinyl finishes with various permanent colors and textures are available.

H

hack: An unworkmanlike manner of cutting work; rough cutting of any kind.

hack saw: A narrow, light-framed saw used for cutting metal; a fine-toothed, narrow-bladed saw stretched in a firm frame. It may be operated either by hand or by electric power. See Fig. 296.

haft: The handle of any thrusting or cutting tool such as a dagger, knife, sword, or an awl.

Fig. 296. Hacksaw. (Stanley Works)

hairpins: In steel construction, light hairpin-shaped reinforcing bars.

half-back bench saw: A cutting tool in which a stiffening bar extends over only a portion of the blade length, combining the action of both the handsaw and the backsaw.

half bat: A term applied to one half of a building brick.

half hatchet: The half hatchet is a heavy-duty combination hatchet and hammer. See Fig. 297. It is used to chop off hardened plaster, and it is used to do other heavy work.

Fig. 297. Half hatchet.

half lap: A joint formed by cutting away one half of the thickness of the face of one timber and one half of the thickness of the back of the other, so when the two pieces are put together the outer surfaces are flush. See *halving.*

half-lap joint: A jointing of two pieces by cutting away the thickness of each piece so that the pieces fit together with the surfaces flush.

227

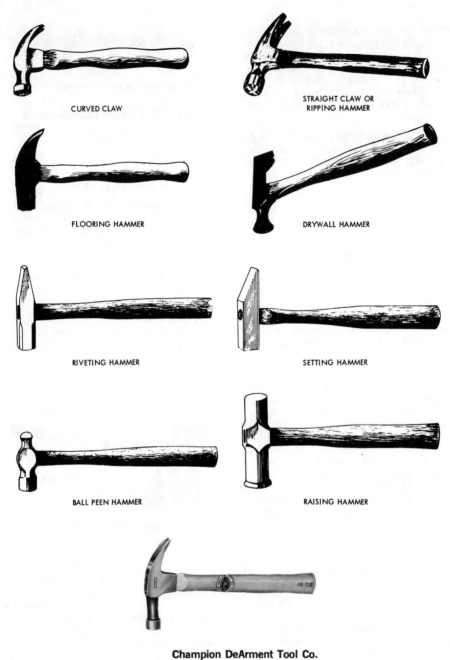

CURVED CLAW

STRAIGHT CLAW OR
RIPPING HAMMER

FLOORING HAMMER

DRYWALL HAMMER

RIVETING HAMMER

SETTING HAMMER

BALL PEEN HAMMER

RAISING HAMMER

18 OZ

Champion DeArment Tool Co.

ELECTRICIAN'S HAMMER

Fig. 298. Common types of hammers.

half-pitch roof: A roof having a pitch which has a rise equal to one half the width of the span.

half-round: A name given to a molding which is a half round in section.

half-round file: A tool which is flat on one side and curved on the other; however, the convexity never equals a semi-circle.

half section: A sectional view drawing which terminates at the center line, showing an external view on one side of the center line and on the other side an interior view.

half story: An attic in a pitched-roof structure having a finished ceiling and floor and some side wall.

half-timbered: A term applied to any building constructed of a timber frame with the spaces filled in, either with masonry or with plaster on laths.

halving: The joining of two pieces of timber by cutting out half of the thickness of each piece, so that one may be let into the other: a junction of two pieces of wood members by letting one into the other. A modification of a halved splice is shown in Fig. 559, page 422.

hammer: A tool used for driving nails, pounding metal, or for other purposes. Though there are various types of hammers used for a variety of purposes, all hammers are similar in having a solid head set crosswise on a handle. See Fig. 9, page 7, and Fig. 298.

hammer fasteners: Pins and threaded studs may be set directly into concrete, building block, and light gauge steel by the use of a specially designed hammer and fastener holder. See Fig. 299.

hand brace: Hand-operated tool, commonly used with a wood bit, to bore holes. It is also used to turn a conduit reamer in deburring conduit. See Fig. 300.

hand drill: A hand-operated tool used for drilling holes. See Fig. 301.

hand file: A tool used in finishing flat surfaces. See *file*, page 185.

Fig. 299. Hammer fastening tool.

Fig. 300. Hand brace. (Stanley Works)

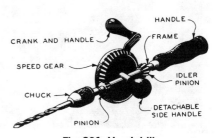

Fig. 301. Hand drill.

229

hand groover: In sheet metal work, a hand tool for cutting grooves. See Fig. 302.

Fig. 302. Hand groover.

hand lever punch: In sheetmetal work, a hand tool for punching holes. See Fig. 303.

handrail: Any railing which serves as a guard; a rail which is intended to be grasped by the hand to serve as a support, as on a stairway or along the edge of a gallery. See Fig. 561, page 562.

handrail bolt: A rodlike metal bolt which is threaded for a nut at both ends; used for bolting together the mating surfaces of a butt joint, such as that between adjacent surfaces of a *handrail.*

handrail wreath: The curved section of a stair rail. See *wreath,* page 489.

handsaw: Any ordinary saw operated with one hand; that is, a one-handled saw, either a ripsaw or a cross-cut saw used by woodworkers. See Fig. 304.

hand screw: A clamp with two parallel jaws and two screws used by woodworkers; the clamping action is provided by means of the screws, one operating through each jaw.

hand tools: Any tools which are operated by and guided by hand.

hangar: A shelter or shed for housing aircraft.

hanger: A drop support, made of strap iron or steel, attached to the end of a joist or beam used to support another joist or beam. See *joist hangers,* page 254, and *stirrup,* page 432. A hanger for supporting soil branches is shown in Fig. 305. In plastering, wire hangers are used to support *suspended ceilings.* In concrete masonry, support used to help hold reinforced concrete joist. In electrical construction, support outlets.

Fig. 303. Hand lever punch. (Whitney Metal Tool Co.)

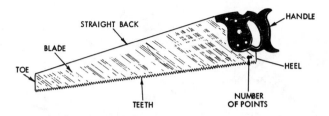

Fig. 304. Straight back handsaw.

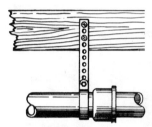

Fig. 305. Hanger for soil branch.

hanger bearing: A shaft bearing which is supported by a hanger.

hanger bolt: A bolt used for attaching hangers to woodwork; it consists of a lag screw at one end with a machine-bolt screw and nut at the other end.

hanging buttress: A buttress used chiefly as a decorative feature and applied only in the decorated and perpendicular styles; one not rising from the ground but supported on a corbel or in some similar manner.

hanging gutter: A sheet-metal gutter shaped in cross section like a half-moon. It is attached to the eaves of a roof by means of metal straps or cast-iron hangers. Also called *half-moon gutter* or *half-round hanging gutter.* See Fig. 374, page 283.

hanging scaffold: This is a suspended scaffold supported by cables or metal straps. See Fig. 306.

hanging stile: A term applied to that *stile* of a door to which the hinges are secured; the upright of a window to which the casements are hinged.

Hanoverian Period: An era in the history of the architecture in western Europe during the eighteenth century, when there was little change in style except for a general decline in artistic design. About the middle of the century a revival took place when interest was renewed in Gothic art.

hardboard: Pressed wood panel. Some hardboards are manufactured for use as lap siding in 8 inch or more widths and in lengths up to 16 feet. Hardboard panels are commonly used in the interior of a house over gypsum board for decorative effect. Hardboards are produced with several different surface patterns, such as tile, embossed, striated, and grooved patterns. Pegboard is another form.

hardened concrete: Concrete that has changed from a fluid, mushy state to a rock-like mass through the process of hydration.

hardener: A chemical (including certain fluosilicates or sodium silicate) applied to concrete floors to reduce wear and dusting.

hard fiber: A material produced by compressing a number of sheets of paper together tightly, which makes it a good insulator.

hard finish: In building, a smooth finishing coat of hard, fine plaster applied to the surface of rough plastering.

231

Fig. 306. Plasterer applying matrix coat for exposed aggregate, using hanging scaffold. (Ceram-Traz Corp.)

hardpan: A cemented or compacted layer in soils, often containing some proportion of clay, through which it is difficult to dig or excavate.

hardware: In building construction, fastenings which permit movement of parts, even when these parts are held together securely. Fastenings, commonly known as *builders' hardware,* include hinges, catches, lifts, locks, and similar devices.

hardwood: The botanical group of broad-leaved trees, such as oak, maple, basswood, poplar, and others. The term has no reference to the actual hardness of the wood. *Angiosperms* is the botanical name for hardwoods.

harmonize: A pleasing arrangement of structural parts so as to form a harmonious whole.

harsh: In concrete masonry, a stony, gritty-feeling concrete that is difficult for finishers to trowel smoothly.

hasp: A hinged-metal strap designed to pass over a staple and secured by a peg or padlock.

hatch: A small door for closing an opening in the floor, as a trap door; also, the cover for an opening leading to the roof or to an attic of a building.

hatchet: A small hand tool with a short handle; used for splitting or rough-dressing of lumber or timbers. See Fig. 307.

232

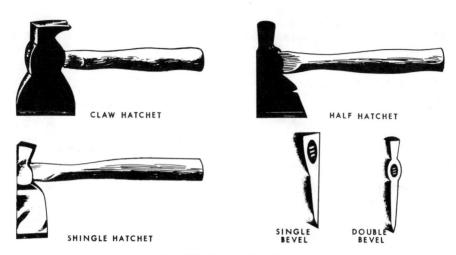

CLAW HATCHET   HALF HATCHET

SHINGLE HATCHET   SINGLE BEVEL   DOUBLE BEVEL

Fig. 307. Types of hatchets.

hatchet iron: In plumbing, a special kind of copper bit which, when heated, may be used as a soldering iron.

hatching: Parallel lines drawn closely together for the purpose of shading or to indicate a section of an object shown in a drawing.

hatchway: An opening covered by a hatch, or trap door, to provide easy access to an attic or cellar; any opening in a floor, ceiling, or roof which makes it possible to pass from one story to another; the opening on ships for passage from one deck to another.

haunch: In architecture, either side of an arch between the crown, or vertex, and the impost where the arch rests on the top of a pier or wall; the shoulder of an arch.

haunched mortise and tenon: See Fig. 329, page 251.

hawk: In plastering, a small, square aluminum or magnesium board used to carry plaster or mortar; held by a central handle attached to its under surface. See Fig. 308.

H bar: In structural work, a steel bar shaped like an I bar, but having wider flanges.

H beam: An H-shaped steel beam.

Fig. 308. Applying first coat on gypsum lathing using hawk and trowel.

head: The topmost member of a door or window frame, as a lintel; the upper end of a vertical timber; the capital of a column. See Fig. 190, page 150.

head casing: Outside casing or trim over a window opening which serves as a stop for the wall covering. The *head casing* is usually topped by a *drip* which throws rain water away from the wall. See Fig. 190, and Fig. 443, page 340.

head jamb: A term sometimes applied to the horizontal top member of a door or window frame. It is also called a *yoke*. See Fig. 190, page 150.

head joint: A vertical joint which joins brick at their ends. See Fig. 37, page 32.

header: In building, a brick or stone laid with the end toward the face of the wall. Also one or more pieces of lumber used around openings to support free ends of floor joists, studs, or rafters and transfer their load to other parallel joists, studs, or rafters; framing member over a window or door opening (Fig. 167, page 131). A structural member placed at right angles to the majority of framing members in a wall, floor, or roof.

header bond: A form of bond in which all courses are laid as headers; used for walls or partitions 8 inches thick.

header course: In a masonry wall surface, a visible row of bricks which is composed entirely of headers. See Fig. 162, page 126.

header-high: In masonry, when a portion of a wall has been laid up to the point where headers are necessary, the wall is said to be *header-high*.

header joist: In carpentry, the large beam or timber into which the common joists are fitted when framing around openings for stairs, chimneys, or any openings in a floor or roof; placed so as to fit between two long beams and support the ends of short timbers. See Fig. 80, page 64.

heading bond: In masonry, a bond formed by courses of headers; also called *header bond*.

heading course: In masonry, a course of headers only; same as a *header course*. See Fig. 162, page 126.

heading joint: In carpentry, a joint of two or more bonds, at right angles to the grain of the wood; in masonry, a joint between two *voussoirs* in the same course.

headroom: The vertical space in a doorway; also, the clear space in height between a stair tread and the ceiling or stairs above. See Fig. 309.

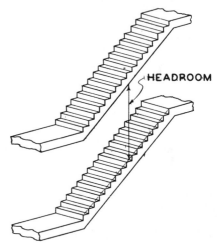

Fig. 309. Headroom.

headway: Clear space in height, as in a doorway, under an arch or girder, or over a stairway. Same as *headroom*. See Fig. 309.

hearth: The floor of a fireplace; also the portion of the floor immediately in front of the fireplace. See Fig. 245, page 188.

heartshake: In lumber, a defect consisting of cracks or splits at the heart of a log. In cross section, these splits appear to radiate starlike from the center of the timber and are sometimes called *star shakes*. They may be due to decay at the heart of the tree from which the log was cut, or they may be caused by too rapid seasoning or drying of the log. See Fig. 310.

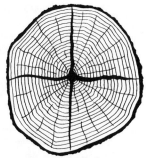

Fig. 310. Heartshake.

heartwood: The wood at the center of a log or tree surrounding the *pith*. The heartwood is surrounded by the *sapwood*. See Fig. 24, page 21.

heat-actuated fire door: A fire door designed to shut automatically under the action of smoke or heat.

heat ducts: Tunnels or similar openings which are located under the concrete slab and through which heating pipes run.

heat gain: An increase in temperature within a structure due to the transmission of heat from the outside through doors, windows, walls, ceilings, floors, and infiltration.

heat insulation: In building construction, material used on walls, floors, or ceiling to prevent heat from passing through these parts of the structure. Mineral wool and felt paper are types of material often used for this purpose.

heat losses: A decrease in temperature within a structure due to the transmission of heat from the inside through doors, windows, walls, ceilings, floors, and infiltration.

heat of hydration: Heat evolved by chemical reactions with water, such as that evolved during the setting and hardening (hydration) of portland cement.

heat pump: A type of heating and air-conditioning installation in which house heat in summer is drawn out and released into the outside air. In winter, the same refrigerant concentrates heat collected from the natural heat of the outside air or from earth or water. It may be used with either a hot water or forced warm air system.

heated concrete: Concrete that has been heated for placing during cold weather.

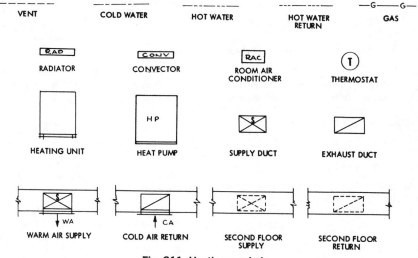

Fig. 311. Heating symbols.

heater: Any appliance for heating a room or building, as a steam radiator, stove, or furnace; also, a portable stove for heating a room or rooms.

heating and ventilating symbols: In heating, standardized symbols used on architectural drawings to indicate the various items connected with a heating or ventilating system. Fig. 311 illustrates typical heating symbols.

heating plant: Any system for heating a building, including a furnace, boiler, pipes, and fixtures. *Symbols* used by a draftsman on architectural drawings, to indicate the various items connected with a heating or ventilating system, are shown in Fig. 311.

heating unit: In electricity, that part of a heating appliance through which the current passes and produces heat.

heavy joist: In woodworking, a timber measuring between 4 and 6 inches in thickness and 8 inches or over in width.

heavyweight concrete: A type of concrete produced from heavyweight aggregates and weighing around 385 pounds per cubic foot; used in the construction of radiation shields in laboratories and medical installations.

heel: That part of a timber, beam, rafter, or joist which rests on the wall plate.

heel of a rafter: The end or foot that rests on the wall plate.

heel plate: Gusset plate at the main support of a roof truss.

height: In reference to an arch, the perpendicular distance between the middle point of the chord and the intrados. Sometimes called the *rise*. See Fig. 235, page 181.

height board: In stair building, a board used to gauge the height of the *treads* and *risers* of a timbered stairway.

height of building: The number of stories in a building, including the basement but not including the cellar; also, more specifically, the vertical distance between the highest point of the roof and the mean grade of the natural ground adjoining the building. Building codes require more restricted definitions of the height of a building.

helix; pl. helices: Any spiral ornament, especially a small *volute* or twist under the *abacus* of the Corinthian capital.

helve: The handle of a tool such as a hammer, hatchet, or ax.

hempseed oil: An oil obtained from the seed of the hemp plant. When fresh, the oil is light green, but when allowed to stand it becomes brownish yellow; used in paints and varnishes.

herringbone: In masonry, a pattern used in brickwork where the brick in alternate courses is laid obliquely in opposite directions forming a design similar in appearance to the spine of a herring; a zigzag pattern used in brickwork; in flooring, material arranged diagonally.

herringbone ·bond: In masonry, the arrangement of bricks in a course in a zigzag fashion, with the end of one brick laid at right angles against the side of a second brick.

herringbone bridging: A system of fixing short struts diagonally between floor joists to add stiffness to the floor. Also called *cross bridging* or *diagonal bridging*.

herringbone strutting: In carpentry, a system of short struts, placed diagonally in pairs, crossing one another between adjacent floor joists. Also called *herringbone bridging*.

hewing: Dealing cutting blows with an ax or other sharp instrument for the purpose of dressing a timber to a desired form or shape.

hexastyle: A structure having six columns across the front; a portico, or façade, having six columns in front.

hick joint: In masonry, a mortar joint finished flush with the surface of the wall.

hickey: A type of portable conduit-bending tool with a side opening jaw. A self-adjusting conduit *hickey* known as the *boss* is suitable for rigid conduits only. Fig. 312 shows a *hickey* being used to bend conduit.

Fig. 312. Proper position for bending of conduit. (Photo by Charles S. Anderson, Electrical Industry Training Center, Fraser, Mich.)

high chairs: A manufactured device used to hold up the welded wire fabric at approximately one-half the thickness of the concrete slab during the time of placing.

high discharge truck: A ready mix truck that discharges concrete from the high end of a tilted drum.

high-early cement: A type of portland cement known as Type III, which sets or hardens to its full strength during a shorter period of time than the other types of portland cement. It is frequently used when the temperature is below freezing.

high gloss: A term applied to a paint which dries with lustrous, enamel-like finish.

high-limit control: A temperature-operated switch used for warm air, hot water, or steam systems which prevents the system from overheating. The control stops the stoker or burner in coal stoker, gas, and oil heating systems and turns on a damper motor to slow the fire in hand-fired furnaces and boilers at maximum safe temperatures.

hinge: A movable joint upon which a door turns; a mechanical device consisting primarily of a pin and two plates which may be attached to a door and the door frame to permit the opening and closing of the door. Hinges are used also on gates and other places where movable joints are desired.

hinge strap: A plate, usually ornamented, designed to be placed on the surface of a door, with one end against the knuckle of a butt to give the appearance of a *strap hinge.*

hip: The external angle formed by the junction of two sloping sides of a roof.

hip knob: A ball, finial, or other ornament placed on the top of the hip of a roof; an ornament between the bargeboards of a gable or on the apex; a decorative feature at the intersection of the *hip rafters* and the *ridge.*

hip rafters: Rafters which form the hip of a roof as distinguished from the common rafters. A *hip rafter* extends diagonally from the corner of the plate to the ridge and is located at the apex of the outer angle formed by the meeting of two sloping sides of a roof whose *wall plates* meet at a right angle. See Fig. 483, page 371.

hip roll: An ornamental strip of metal, composition roofing, tile, or wood for covering and finishing a *hip*.

hip roof: A roof which rises by inclined planes from all four sides of a building. The line where two adjacent sloping sides of a roof meet is called the *hip*. See Fig. 313.

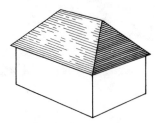

Fig. 313. Hip roof.

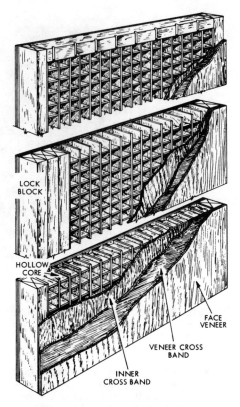

Fig. 314. Hollow core flush door.

hips: Those pieces of timber or lumber placed in an inclined position at the corners or angles of a hip roof. See Fig. 483, page 371.

hob: A level projection at back or side of an open fireplace on which a pot can be placed to be kept warm.

hold-down clamp. A clamp designed for mounting on a surface, such as a workbench, for holding work in place.

hollow concrete blocks: A type of precast concrete building block having a hollow core.

hollow core door or wall: A faced door or wall with a space between the facings which is occupied by a structure consisting of air or insulation filled cells, made of wood, plastic, or other suitable material.

Hollow core constructions have special fire, temperature, and sound insulating properties as well as being lightweight and strong. See Fig. 314.

hollow masonry unit: A masonry unit whose cross-sectional area in any given plane parallel to the bearing surface is less than 75 percent of its gross cross-sectional area measured in the same plane. Voids exceed 25 percent cross-sectional area.

hollow newel: The well hole in a winding stair. See *solid newel,* page 416.

hollow-newel stair: A winding stairway having a wellhole in the middle. Also called an *open-newel stair.* See Fig. 563, page 426.

hollow punch: A small hand-tool of steel, of any desired diameter, used for cutting

238

disks (when an edge is ground on the inside) and circles (when an edge is ground on the outside) in sheet metal and other thin materials. See Fig. 455, page 351.

hollow tile: Clay tile made in a variety of forms and sizes; used for decorative purposes and as a building material for both exterior walls and partitions.

hollow wall: In masonry, a wall constructed of brick, stone, or other materials, having an air space between the outside and inside faces of the wall. Also called *cavity wall.*

homogeneous: of the same kind, similar.

hone: A smooth stone used to give a sharp, keen edge to a cutting tool. The *hone* may be used dry or be moistened with oil or water. See *oilstone,* page 302.

honeycomb: A cell-like structure. Concrete that is poorly mixed and not adequately puddled, having voids or open spaces, is known to be *honeycombed.*

honeycomb core: A structure of air cells, resembling a honeycomb, often made of paper, which is placed between plywood panels, sometimes replacing studs. This type of wall construction provides lighter, prefabricated walls with excellent insulating properties. See *hollow core door or wall.*

honeycomb slating: In building, a method of laying slates so that one diagonal is horizontal. Similar to *drop-point slating,* except that the tiles have their bottom corners removed.

honeycombing: Checks that occur in the interior of a piece of wood. They usually occur along the wood range.

honeysuckle: A kind of architectural ornament suggested by the flower of the same name, commonly used on a decorated frieze; also called *anthemion.* See Fig. 315.

hood: In building, a caplike projection as a canopy over casement windows to give protection, in addition to the *drip cap;* a cover fitted to the top of a chimney to prevent a down draft; also, a projecting cover as for a hearth.

Fig. 315. Honeysuckle ornament.

hood mold: A term applied to the projecting molding over the head of an *arch* over a window or door opening, whether inside or outside, and forming the outermost member of the *archivolt;* a dripstone or weather molding.

hook: A semi-circular (180 degree) or a 90 degree turn at the free end of a bar to provide anchorage in concrete. For stirrups and column ties only, turns of either 90 degrees or 135 degrees are used.

hook-and-butt joint: In carpentry, a type of joint especially formed for resisting tension. See *scarf joint,* Fig. 506, page 387.

hook-and-eye fastener: In building, a type of fastener used on doors or windows. It consists of a wire hook which drops into a staple or loop made of wire. See Fig. 316.

hook and thimble: See *cable attachments,* page 80.

hook strip: A horizontal band of interior wood finish to which metal clothes hooks are attached; usually found in clothes closets.

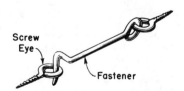

Fig. 316. Hook and eye fastener.

hopper frame: A window frame having superimposed fanlights opening inward; especially used in hospitals; hence, also called *hospital light.*

hopper joint: See Fig. 330, page 252, for an illustration of this joint.

hopper light: A window sash having hinges on its lower edge; so arranged that the window will open inward.

hopper window: A window in which each sash opens inward on hinges placed at the bottom of each sash.

horizon line: In perspective drawing, a real or imaginary line in the distance where the earth and sky meet and at the eye level of the viewer. See *perspective drawing,* page 322.

horizontal: On a level; in a direction parallel to the horizon. For example, the surface of a still body of water is *horizontal* or level.

horizontal construction joint: The joining of fresh concrete on hardened concrete on a horizontal level.

horizontal lock: A lock having its major dimension along a horizontal line.

horse: In building and woodworking, a trestle; one of the slanting supports of a set of steps to which the treads and risers of a stair are attached; a kind of stool, usually a horizontal piece to which three or four legs are attached, used as a support for work; a braced framework of timbers used to carry a load.

horsepower: A unit of power or work. An electrical horsepower is equal to 746 watts.

horsepower hour: The amount of power performed by 746 watts in one hour.

hose bib: A water faucet which is threaded so a hose may be attached; a *sill cock.*

hot: A term in plastering that means a surface is extremely dry and, therefore, has excessive suction.

hot glue: Any glue used in a hot form, such as dry glue which requires heating before it can be used.

hot-water heating: A system of heating a building by means of hot water circulating through pipes, coils, and radiators placed in the rooms for that purpose.

hot weather concreting: The process of preventing the rapid loss of moisture from the concrete during the hot months of summer (temperatures ranging above 73 degrees F).

housed: A piece of lumber fitted into a second piece, such as a *housed joint.* See *housed stair,* Fig. 317.

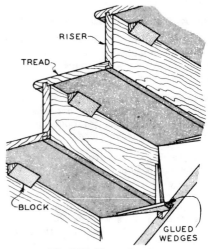

Fig. 317. Housed stair.

housed brace: A diagonal supporting member, the ends of which are mortised into the pieces to be strengthened. See Fig. 329, page 251.

housed joint: A joint made by cutting out a space in the end of a piece of wood to receive the tongue cut on another piece to which the first piece is to be attached; any fitted joint, such as one made with a mortise and tenon.

house drain: The system of horizontal pipes inside a building which extends to, and connects with, the house sewer. All soil, waste, and leader stacks, and sometimes floor drains, as well as the yard area, are connected to the *house drain.* Also commonly called *building drain.*

housed stair: A staircase in which the stringers are grained, or *housed,* to receive the ends of the treads and risers, as in *closed-string stairs.* See Fig. 317.

housed string: A stair string with horizontal and vertical grooves cut on the inside to receive the ends of the risers and treads. Wedges covered with glue often are used to hold the risers and treads in place in the grooves. See Fig. 318.

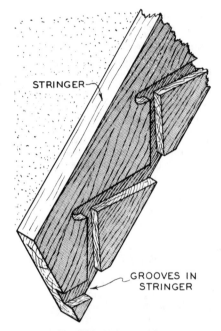

Fig. 318. Housed string.

house models: See *models,* page 288.

house sewer: That part of the drainage system which extends from the building line to the main sewer in the street. Also called *building sewer.*

house slant: In plumbing, a term applied to a sewer connection which is shaped like a T or a Y; used to receive the connection of a house sewer.

house trap: A device for preventing the sewer gases from entering a building.

housing: A part cut out of one member to receive another. In carpentry, the jointing of two timbers by fitting the entire end of one piece into a *gain* or blind mortise cut in the other piece, as the fitting of treads and risers into the stringer of a *closed-string stair.* See Fig. 318.

hub: In plumbing the enlarged end of a pipe which is made to provide a connection into which the end of the joining pipe will fit. In surveying, the corner stakes used to lay out the building lines and to set elevations.

humidifier: A device for maintaining desirable humidity conditions in the air supplied to a building.

humidify: To make more humid by any process which will increase the density of water vapor within a given space.

humidifying: The process of increasing the amount of moisture in air, usually to prevent air from becoming too dry for health or easy breathing.

humidity: The amount of moisture in the air or the water vapor within a given space.

humus: A dark, organic material in soils produced by the decomposition of vegetable or animal matter.

hydrated lime: The material which remains after a chemical reaction due to the contact of quicklime and water. The same as *slaked lime.*

hydration: The chemical reaction between cement and water causing the cement paste to harden and to bind the aggregates together to form mortar or concrete.

hydraulic: To harden under (or with) water. All portland cements are hydraulic cements.

hydraulic jack: A lifting device operated by a lever from the outside and put into action by means of a small force pump, through the use of a liquid, such as water or oil.

hydraulic joint: In plumbing, a type of joint used in large water mains where sheet lead is forced tightly into the bell of a pipe by the hydraulic pressure of a liquid.

241

hydraulic lime: A lime which will harden under water.

hydraulic mortar: In masonry, a mortar which will harden under water; used for foundations or any masonry construction under water.

hydraulic pressure: The resistance resulting when a quantity of water or other liquid is forced through a small orifice.

hydraulic valve: In the construction of hydraulic elevators, a valve used to regulate the distribution of water in the cylinders.

hydrocal: A special molding plaster that develops two to three times the strength and hardness of regular molding plaster.

hydrochloric acid: A very strong liquid acid that is commonly used in industry for cleaning purposes.

hydronic system: Forced hot water system.

hydrostone: A special plaster that develops six to eight times the strength of regular plaster. It is used for industrial casting and pattern making.

hygroscopic water: A film of moisture surrounding each soil particle. Varies with the relative humidity.

hypotenuse: That side of a right triangle which is opposite the right angle.

hypotrachelium: In the Doric order, the junction of the capital and the shaft, marked by a bevel or cut around the lower edge of the capital block; the necking of a column or the space between two neck moldings; also called *necking*. See *gorgerin*, Fig. 5, page 4.

I

I-beam: A structural iron beam with a cross section similar to the letter I. Now called *S* beam.

ichnography: The drawing of ground plans; the art of making a ground plan; a horizontal section of a building or other object drawn so as to show its true dimensions according to a geometric scale.

illustration: In architectural drawing, a diagram or picture which helps to make clear the design or plans for a building.

impermeability: The quality or state of not permitting passage (as a fluid).

impost: The uppermost member of a column, pillar, pier, or wall upon which the end of an arch rests. Sometimes called *chaptrel*. See *column*, Fig. 137, page 108.

improved land: Building sites which have water and sewage connections available and access to streets and telephone, gas, and electrical services.

in antis: When two columns stand between two antae in a portico, the columns and, by extension, the portico are said (in Latin) to be *in antis*.

incise: To cut or carve; to cut marks as in the process of engraving.

inclined plane: A surface inclined to the plane of the horizon; the angle which it makes with the horizontal line is known as the *angle of inclination*.

increaser: In pipe work of any kind, a coupling with one end larger than the other. See Fig. 112, page 89. In plumbing, the increaser is used at the top of the vent stack as a means of preventing vapor from freezing and clogging the stack in severe climates.

indirect lighting: A system of illumination in which the desired lighting effect is secured by throwing the light against the ceiling or some other surface, from which it is reflected and diffused in the room.

industrial waste: In plumbing, a term applied to the liquid waste which results from the various processes employed in industrial plants or establishments.

inert-gas metal-arc welding: A special type of (electrical) arc welding in which a consumable bare electrode is fed into a weld at a controlled rate while a continuous blanket of inert gas shields the weld zone from the atmosphere. It is a process that produces high quality welds at high welding speeds without the use of flux or the need for post-welding cleaning.

inert materials: Materials that do not enter into a chemical reaction, such as hydration; the aggregates within the concrete mix.

inhibitor: A material used to reduce corrosion of metals imbedded in concrete.

initial set: Mortar that has the appearance of being set but is still in the plastic state.

inlaid parquet: In architecture, a floor covering of hardwood blocks of fancy woods, inlaid in fancy patterns on an ordinary floor boarding, to which the pieces are secured with glue or some other form of suitable adhesive.

inlaid work: A decorative design laid in the body of a surface by setting in small pieces of material different from the material used in the ground work.

inlay: To decorate with ornamental designs by setting in small pieces of material in the body of a piece of work which is made of different material from the inlaid pieces; also, the designs so made.

inserts: Devices buried in concrete to receive a bolt or screw to support shelf angles, machinery, etc.

inside angle tool: In masonry, an *angle float* used for shaping inside corners.

inside calipers: In shopwork, a type of calipers having the points at the ends of the legs turned outward instead of inward so the tool can be used for gauging the inside diameters.

inside casing: Interior trim around a window or door, consisting of dressed boards, molding, or other specially prepared finish material. In buildings constructed of fire-resistive material, the inside casings should be of incombustible material or a combination material having fire-resistive qualities equal to that of fire-proofed wood. See Figs. 189 and 190, pages 149 and 150.

inside corner trowel: Trowel used to finish inside corners. See *trowel,* page 461.

inside stop: In building, a strip of wood, usually with a bead or molding on one edge, used for holding window sash in place. Sometimes called a *bead stop.*

inside trim: In building, the finishing for the interior of the building, especially around window and door openings, such as casings. See *inside casing.* See Fig. 189, page 149, and Fig. 190, page 150.

inside wiring: Wiring for electric lights or electric appliances inside a residence or other building.

inspector: One who checks work performed by someone else for the purpose of passing judgment on the quality and quantity of what has been accomplished.

insulating concrete: A type of concrete produced from lightweight aggregates and weighing only 20 to 70 pounds per cubic foot; used as insulation to provide protection from the heat, cold, fire, and sound.

insulating glass: Two panes of glass separated by an air space and sealed around the edges. See *double glazing,* page 153.

insulating resistance: In electricity, the resistance offered by an insulating material to the flow of an electric current through it.

insulating tileboard: A board made from the same basic stock as insulating board but in smaller squares and rectangular patterns. Usually, the edges are beveled. It is most frequently used for covering ceilings.

insulation: Any material used in walls, floors, and ceilings to prevent heat transmission. This may be in the form of board, pellets, or encased dead air. Fig. 319 illustrates various types and techniques of insulation. Also: in electrical wiring material used to protect a conductor.

insulation blanket: A blanket-like covering used to keep concrete warm while curing in cold weather.

insulation board: Any type of building board used in construction work to prevent the passage of heat, cold, or sound through walls or floors. Fig. 320 illustrates the application of insulation board on the exterior of a house.

insulator: In electricity, any device which serves as a nonconductor, usually made of glass or porcelain.

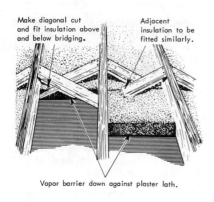

Make diagonal cut and fit insulation above and below bridging.

Adjacent insulation to be fitted similarly.

Vapor barrier down against plaster lath.

CEILING JOISTS (over heated areas)

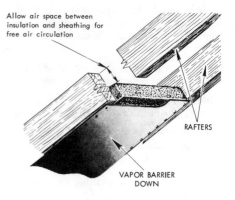

Allow air space between insulation and sheathing for free air circulation

RAFTERS

VAPOR BARRIER DOWN

RAFTERS (pitched roof)

Provide louvers or other permanent vents above insulated area

VENT

LIVING SPACE

VAPOR BARRIERS

VENTILATION

VAPOR BARRIER UP

Either vapor permeable asphalt felt, wood strips or lacing wire, to hold insulation against flooring.

CEILING JOISTS (over unheated areas)

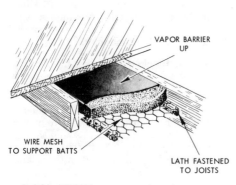

VAPOR BARRIER UP

WIRE MESH TO SUPPORT BATTS

LATH FASTENED TO JOISTS

FLOOR JOISTS (over unexcavated areas)

CONTINUOUS INSECT SCREEN

FURRING

If free air circulation parallel to rafters cannot be provided, install furring and insert screen as shown.

RAFTERS (flat roof or ceiling)

Fig. 319. Techniques for insulating various areas using batts and blankets. (Insulation Board Institute)

intaglio: A sculpture or carving in which the figures are sunk below the general surface, such as a seal the impression of which in wax is in bas-relief.

intake: A place where water or air is taken into a pipe, conduit, or machine.

intake belt course: In building, a belt course with the molded face cut so that it serves as an intake between the varying thicknesses of two walls.

intarsia: A decorative design, produced by inlay work in wood; used extensively during the fifteenth century by Italian furniture makers.

Fig. 320. Applying insulating board. (Celotex Corp.)

integral: Elements which act together as a unit, such as concrete joist and slab. Concrete members may be made integral by bond, dowels, or being cast in one piece.

intercepting sewer: In plumbing, a type of collecting sewer constructed of poured concrete and placed at varying depths in the ground. The depth depends upon the natural contour of the soil.

intercolumniation: A system of spacing between columns; the clear space between columns; the distance from column to column.

interior: The inside of a room, house, or other structure.

interior door jamb: The lining or surrounding case into which, and out of which, a door closes and opens, consisting of two upright pieces, or jambs, and a head. See Fig. 189, page 149.

interior finish: A term applied to the total effect produced by the inside finishing of a building, including not only the materials used but also the manner in which the trim and decorative features have been handled.

interior stairway: A stairway within the exterior walls of a building.

interior trim: The finishing of the interior of a building, such as the casings, baseboards, and stairs. Sometimes called *inside finish*.

interior wiring: In electricity, wiring for illumination or for electric equipment placed on the inside of a building.

interlaced arches: Arches which usually are circular and so constructed that their archivolts intersect, appearing to be interlaced.

interlocked grain: Wood in which the fibers are inclined in one direction in a number of rings of annual growth, then reversed gradually and inclined in the opposite direction in succeeding growth rings; then reversed again.

internal friction: Resistance to sliding within the soil mass.

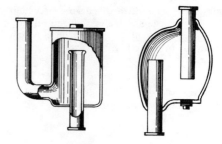

Fig. 321. Internal partition traps.

internal-partition traps: In plumbing, a type of trap which forms its seal by means of an internal partition. Two types of *internal-partition* traps are shown in Fig. 321.

interpolate: To go between given or stated terms, thereby approximating a location between fixed points.

interrupted arch: A pediment in the form of an arch with the central portion cut away.

intersect: To cross, as two diameters of a circle which cut across each other; to cut through or into.

intersection: The point where two intersecting lines cross each other.

intrados or soffit: The under surface or interior curve of an arch. See Fig. 137, page 108.

inundation batching: Measurement of the volume of sand immersed in water. This method eliminates errors in measurement of volume caused by bulking of sand due to moisture.

inverse: Reversed in position, direction, or tendency; inverted.

invert: In plumbing, the lowest portion of the inside surface of the cross section of any drain pipe or sewer conduit which is not vertical.

inverted arch: In masonry, an arch where the keystone is located at the lowest point of the arch.

invisible hinge: A type of door hinge which is mortised into place in such a way that

Fig. 322. Invisible hinge.

when the door is closed the hinge is out of sight. Sometimes called a *secret hinge*. See Fig. 322.

involute: A curve such as would be described by the unwinding of a string from a cylinder.

ionic: Pertaining to a classic Greek type of architecture characterized by the scroll-like ornaments of the capital. See *order,* page 305.

ionic order: A style of architecture developed by the Ionians. This type of architecture is distinguished especially by the scroll which is the most important decorative feature of the capital which surmounts the columns. See *order,* page 305.

iron expansion shield: A type of shield used with an anchor bolt for securing wood structural parts to a masonry wall. See Fig. 18, page 17.

ironwork: A term applied to the use of iron for ornamental purposes. Elaborately designed ornamentation in ironwork was used for hinges, door knockers, and escutcheons in the architecture of the Middle Ages.

irregular-coursed: In masonry, rubble walls built up in courses of different heights.

irregular curve: An instrument, made of wood, hard rubber, or celluloid, used by draftsmen for drawing curves other than arcs or circles. Also called, *French curve.* Fig. 323 illustrates a typical curve. Irregular curves come in a variety of sizes and shapes to produce practically every kind of curve.

irregular pitch: In roof framing, a roof which does not have the same rise per foot run throughout.

isolation joint: A separation in concrete work used to completely isolate one part of a concrete slab or structure from another.

isometric drawing: A drawing which resembles a perspective drawing, differing, however, in that its lines all run parallel instead of to a vanishing point. All horizontal lines are drawn at an angle of 30°, all vertical lines remain vertical, and all dimensions are accurate on the 30° angle lines and the vertical lines. A type of *axonometric projection.* See Fig. 422, page 323.

J

jack: A portable machine used for lifting heavy loads through short distances with a minimum expenditure of effort or power. In electricity, the terminal of two lines on a switchboard of a telephone exchange.

jack arch: An arch which is flat instead of rounded. This type of arch is sometimes called a *French arch.* See Fig. 324.

Fig. 323. Irregular curve.

JACK ARCH FOR OPENINGS OVER 22 INCHES

Fig. 324. Jack arch.

jacking up: The lifting or raising of a heavy object or a structure by means of a mechanical device known as a *jack.*

jack plane: A bench plane, appropriately named for a beast of burden often called upon to do the hardest and roughest kind of work. The *jack plane,* likewise, is called upon to do the hardest and roughest work on a piece of timber as it first comes from the saw. This plane is the one used to true up the edges and rapidly prepare the rough surface of a board for the finer work of the smoothing planes. See Fig. 325.

Fig. 325. Jack plane for rough work and preliminary smoothing. (Stanley Works)

jack rafter: A short rafter of which there are three kinds. (1) The *hip jack* which runs from the rafter plate to the hip rafter. (2) The *valley jack* which extends from the valley rafter to the ridge of the roof. (3) The third type of jack rafter is the *cripple jack,* which may be classified into *hip valley cripple* and *valley cripple.* Neither one of these cripple jack rafters touches the ridge or the plate. The *hip valley cripple* extends between the valley and the hip rafters. When the ridges of the two roofs are on different levels, the *valley cripple jack* is framed from the supporting valley rafter to the valley of the addition. *Jack rafters* are used especially in hip roofs. See Fig 326.

jackscrew: A mechanical device operated by a screw, used in lifting weights and for leveling work.

jack timbers: In building construction, timbers which are used in a narrowing situation, as in a *hip roof* where certain rafters have to be shorter than the other rafters. Also called *cripple timbers.*

jack truss: In architecture, a secondary truss used in a hip roof when the roof does not have its full section or by reason of its location the truss is cut short.

jalousie window: A window consisting of narrow pieces of glass opening outward to admit air but exclude rain. The window appears similar to a venetian blind.

jamb: In building, the lining of an opening, such as the vertical side posts used in the framing of a doorway or window. See Fig. 189, page 149, and Fig. 190, page 150.

jamb post: In carpentry, a vertical member at the side of a door opening.

jamb shaft: In architecture, a column, which may be either free or engaged, used as a decoration for the jamb of a door or window opening, especially in classical architecture. Sometimes called an *esconson.*

jambstone: In architecture, a stone which is set in an upright position at the edge of a wall opening, such as for a door or window, so one of the faces of the stone forms a part or all of a jamb.

jedding ax: In masonry, an ax having one flat face and one pointed peen. See *cavil,* page 190.

jerkin head: In building construction, a term applied to the end of a pitched roof when shaped like a gable but having the upper portion sloping backward like a hip.

jetting out: The projecting of a construction member from the face of a wall for supporting a load, as a *corbel.*

jetty: In building, any overhanging or projecting part, as a *bay window.* Same as *jutty.*

jeweling: In furniture making, the carving of an ornament on a surface to resemble a jewel.

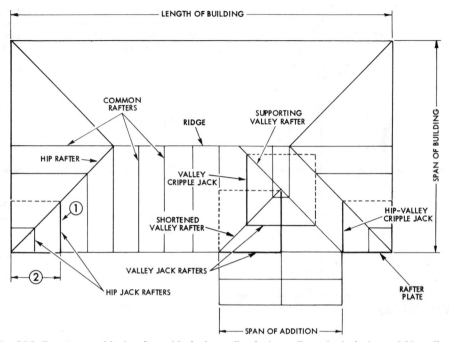

LENGTH OF BUILDING

COMMON RAFTERS

RIDGE

SUPPORTING VALLEY RAFTER

SPAN OF BUILDING

HIP RAFTER

VALLEY CRIPPLE JACK

①

SHORTENED VALLEY RAFTER

HIP-VALLEY CRIPPLE JACK

②

VALLEY JACK RAFTERS

HIP JACK RAFTERS

RAFTER PLATE

SPAN OF ADDITION

Fig. 326. Four types of jack rafters: hip jacks, valley jacks, valley cripple jacks and hip-valley cripple jacks.

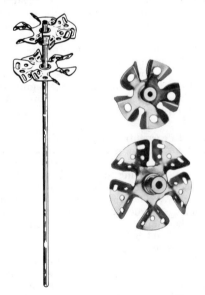

Fig. 327. Jiffler mixers. (Goldblatt Tool Co.)

jib door: A door which is flush with the wall; a disguised door which carries and continues the general decorations of the wall.

jiffler mixers. Jiffler mixers are used to mix drywall mud and exposed aggregate materials. See Fig. 327. The upper wheel cuts the material downward, and the lower wheel cuts the material upward, thus creating a counter flow to disperse lumps quickly. The jiffler mixers can be used with a ⅜″ or ½″ drill (450 to 1200 RPM).

jiffy mud and resin mixers: This type mixer is used by the plasterer to mix drywall joint cement or epoxies. See Fig. 328. These paddles should be used with a ¼″ or ½″ drill with recommended speed of 450 to 650 rpm.

jig: A contrivance which rotates and holds a piece of material and guides the tools while the work is being performed. They are used in the manufacture of components and trusses.

249

Fig. 328. Jiffy mud and resin mixers. (Goldblatt Tool Co.)

jig saw: In woodworking, a type of saw with a thin, narrow blade to which an up-and-down motion is imparted either by foot power or by mechanical means.

job mixing: To mix concrete on the job either by hand or by a machine mixer.

jog: In building, any change or irregularity in the direction of a line or surface.

jogged: Any piece of material which has either projections or depressions; a notched construction member.

joggle: A projection, or shoulder, to receive the thrust of a brace; also, a key, or projecting pin, set in between two joining surfaces for the purpose of reinforcing the joint.

joggle beam: A built-up beam with the various members secured by joggling.

joggle joint: In masonry, or stonework, a joint in which a projection on one member fits into a recess in another member to prevent lateral movement.

joggle piece: A vertical timber tie connecting the apex of a triangular truss with the base or tie beam. The joggle piece supports one end of a brace or strut by a shoulder or joggle. Same as *joggle post*.

joggle post: Any post made of timbers joggled together; a vertical timber tie joining the ridge and tie beam of a roof, with struts supporting the middle points of the main rafters and bearing upon the enlarged foot of the joggle post. The purpose of the joggle post is to prevent the sagging of the tie beam in the middle. Also called *joggle piece* and *king post*.

joggle tenon: A short tenon usually at the lower end of a post which it holds in position. Same as *stub tenon*.

joggle truss: A roof truss formed with a joggle post or *king post*.

joggle work: Masonry in which slipping between the courses of stones is prevented by the use of joggles.

joiner: A craftsman in woodworking who constructs joints; usually a term applied to the workmen in shops who construct doors, windows, and other fitted parts of a house or ship.

joinery: A term used by woodworkers when referring to the various types of joints used in woodworking. Wood joints commonly used in timber framing, in edge joining of boards, and other forms of woodworking are shown in Fig. 329.

joint: In carpentry, the place where two or more surfaces meet; also, to form, or unite, two pieces into a *joint;* to provide with a *joint* by preparing the edges of two pieces so they will fit together properly when joined. Wood joints commonly used in cabinet construction and for interior trim are shown in Fig. 330. In masonry, the mortar bond between individual masonry units. In concrete work, a groove or separation in a concrete slab or structure used to control cracking and movement, to isolate one part of a structure from another, or to joint parts of a slab or structure into a rigid unit.

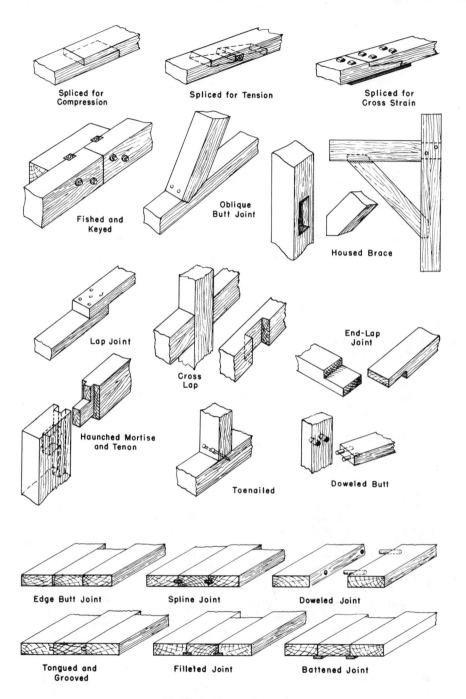

Fig. 329. Joinery of boards.

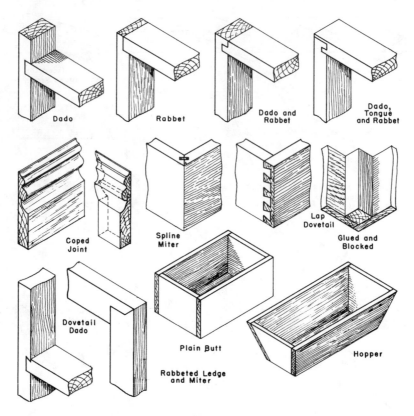

Fig. 330. Joints.

Joint Apprenticeship and Training Committee (JATC): This is a group, equally representative of management and labor, established to carry out the development and administration of apprenticeship and journeyman training programs. The Committee may represent labor-management interests at the National, State, or local level. The Joint Apprenticeship and Training Committee or the Joint Apprenticeship Committee (JAC) has the delegated power to set the local standards consistent with the basic requirements established by the National Committee. The apprentice, when he signs the indenture agreement, agrees to live up to all its provisions and, in turn, is protected by its rules and regulations. The JAC also established the curriculum for the related classroom work plus supervising the on-the-job training the apprentice receives. When an apprentice completes his training, the JAC notifies the Bureau of Apprenticeship, and this agency issues a completion certificate.

joint bolt: In stair building, a type of bolt which is threaded for a nut on both ends; used to hold two pieces of a handrail together. Also called *handrail bolt.*

joint cement: A powder that is mixed with water and used for joint treatment in gypsum-wallboard finish. Often called *spackle,* mixtures may be purchased already prepared.

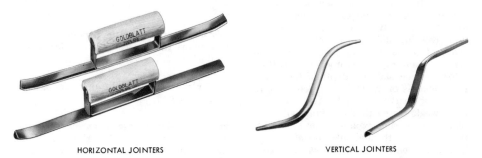

HORIZONTAL JOINTERS   VERTICAL JOINTERS

Fig. 331. Jointers used in brick and concrete block work. (Goldblatt Tool Co.)

jointer: In masonry, a flat steel tool used by bricklayers to form the various types of mortar joints between the courses of bricks upon the face of a wall in pointing, as the V, the concave, and weather joints. Fig. 331 shows two types of jointers, for *horizontal* joints (Fig. 331, bottom left) and for *vertical* joints (Fig. 331, bottom right). Fig. 331, top, shows how the tool is used. In cement masonry, a jointer or *groover* is used for making joints in concrete flatwork. See Fig. 292, page 224. Also: a woodworking machine used for squaring edge of boards and for planing surfaces on pieces of wood.

jointer plane: A large bench plane used chiefly for long work and for final truing up of wood edges or surfaces for joining two pieces of wood; an iron or wood plane suitable for all kinds of plane work and especially adaptable for truing large surfaces required in furniture making. See Fig. 332.

Fig. 332. Jointer plane, largest of the carpenter's planes, is intended for use on the work bench. (Stanley Works)

jointing: In masonry, the operation of making and finishing the exterior surface of mortar joints between courses of masonry units. (See Fig. 331). Fig. 333 shows the two types of joints commonly used. Also, in concrete masonry, the process of cutting into a concrete slab to a depth of 1/4 to 1/5 the thickness of the slab at spacings of 10 to 15 feet apart in order to create a structural weakness so that cracking will take place here during expansion and contraction instead of throughout the slab; this is known as *control jointing*. See also *construction joint,* page 117, and *isolation joint,* page 247.

FLUSH   V-TOOLED

Fig. 333. Jointing.

joint runner: In plumbing, an incombustible material used as packing in the bottom of the socket of a pipe. Commonly used for holding molten lead in the bell of a lead joint to prevent running or spread of the lead when it is poured. See *spigot-and-socket joint,* page 418.

joint wiping: to spread by wiping; to form a joint between lead pipes by applying solder in repeated increments individually spread and shaped with pads of greased cloth.

joist: A heavy piece of horizontal timber, to which the boards of a floor or the lath of a ceiling are nailed. Joists are laid edgewise to form the floor support. See Fig. 41, page 35, Fig. 82, page 65, and Fig. 258, page 198.

joist anchor: Device used to anchor the ends of joists to masonry walls. See Fig. 244, page 188.

joist chairs: In cement masonry, bent or welded wire supports which hold and space the two bars in the bottom of a concrete joist.

joist hangers: A steel or iron stirrup used to support the ends of joists which are to be flush with the girder. See Fig. 334.

joist plan: Drawing showing where each joist is located.

joist schedule: In cement masonry, a table giving the quantity and mark of the joists; the quantity, size, length, bending details of bars and usually the quantity of joist chairs in each concrete joist.

Fig. 334. Joist hangers.

journeyman: A workman who has learned his trade by serving an apprenticeship. A term usually applied to a skilled workman who is able to command the standard wage rate of a mechanic in his particular trade.

jumbo: Traveling support for forms, commonly used in tunnel work.

jumbo brick: A brick larger than standard size, usually 4″ x 4″ x 12″, including mortar joint.

jumper: A temporary connection made around part of an electric circuit.

junction box: In electrical work, a box in a street distribution system where one main is connected to another main; also, a box where a circuit is connected to a main. See Fig. 461 (B), page 356.

jut: In building, a term applied to any part of a structure which projects outward as a *jut window.*

jutty: In building, any projecting part as a wall or window. Also called *jetty.*

jut window: In architecture, a window which projects from the main wall of a building, as a *bay window* or *bow window.*

K

Keene's cement: A quick-setting, white, hard-finish plaster which produces a wall of extreme durability. It is doubly calcined, and almost all the water from the gypsum

rock has been removed. There are two types: regular (slow setting) and quick setting. Keene's is a high-strength, white plaster used with slaked lime and is the only gypsum plaster that can be retempered. It is used most commonly with lime and sand for a float or sprayed finish.

keeper: In building, the strike plate of a door lock; the socket which is fitted to a door jamb to house the bolt of the lock when the door is in a closed position.

kellastone: In architecture, a stucco with crushed finish.

kentish tracery: A peculiar form of cusping consisting of two cusps close together or what might be called a *split cusp.*

kerf: A cut made with a saw.

kerfing: The process of cutting grooves or kerfs across a board so as to make it flexible for bending. *Kerfs* are cut down to about two-thirds of the thickness of the piece to be bent. An example is found in the bullnose of a stair which frequently is bent by the process of kerfing.

kevel: A stonemason's hammer, used for breaking and dressing stone.

key: In building, a wedge for splitting a tenon in a mortise to tighten its hold; a strip of wood inserted in a piece of timber across the grain to prevent casting; also, a wedge of metal used to make a dovetail joint in a stone; a hollow in a tile to hold mortar or cement; the plastering forced between laths for holding the rest of the plaster in place; a groove made in cement footings for tying in the cement foundation of a structure; the rough surface on the reverse side of a veneer for holding the glue. A *footing key* is shown in Fig. 267, page 202.

key console: In architecture, a console placed at the crown of an arch intersecting the archivolt. An Ionic key console is shown in Fig. 335.

keyed mortise and tenon: A joint with extended tenon, pierced to receive a tapered key which serves to draw the joint up tightly. Frequently used without glue for massive furniture and for "knocked-down" parts which are to be assembled in position.

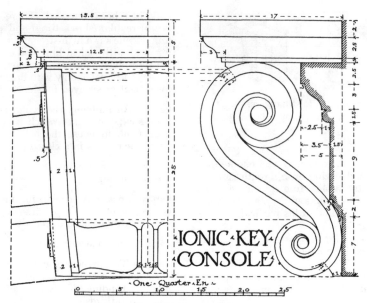

Fig. 335. Key console.

keyhole saw: A small handsaw of a special type with a thin, tapering blade designed for cutting a small circle or other small opening, such as a keyhole. They are used to enlarge holes and to notch structural frame members for cables and conduits and are often sold in sets called *nests*. See Fig. 336.

keystone: The wedge-shaped piece at the top of an arch which is regarded as the most important member because it binds, or locks, all the other members together. The position of a keystone is shown in Fig. 337.

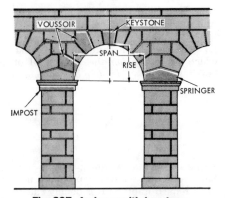

Fig. 336. Keyhole saw. (Stanley Works)

keying: In furniture making, a process used for strengthening miter joints.

key plate: A door plate which may be either plain or ornamented, having one or more keyholes, but without a knob socket. It is designed for attachment to the face of a door.

Fig. 337. Archway with keystone.

keyway: A recess or groove in one lift or placement of concrete which is filled by concrete of the next lift, giving shear strength to the joint. A groove formed in concrete to cause it to interlock with another slab or structure which has a projection on it called a key. Also: The opening in a cylinder lock to receive the key and guide it in contradistinction to the open keyhole of a common lock.

kicker: A piece of wood (block or board) attached to a formwork member to take the thrust of another member; sometimes called a cleat.

kick plate: A metal plate, or strip, placed along the lower surface of a door to prevent the marring of the finish by shoe marks.

kiln: A large oven or heated chamber for the purpose of baking, drying, or hardening, as a *kiln* for drying lumber; a *kiln* for baking brick; a lime *kiln* for burning lime.

kiln-dried: A term applied to lumber which has been dried by artificially controlled heat and humidity to a satisfactory moisture content.

kiln-dried lumber: Lumber which has been dried in kilns or ovens instead of through the natural process known as *air drying* or *seasoning*. The time required for kiln drying ranges from two days to six weeks, depending upon the thickness and grade of the lumber.

kiln-dried wood: Wood from which the moisture has been removed by means of hot air and heated for the purpose in large ovens or kilns.

kilo: A prefix placed before a word to indicate a number one thousand times that indicated by the word.

kiloampere: One thousand amperes.

kilovolt: One thousand volts.

kilowatt: A measurement of electricity containing 1000 watts.

kilowatt-hour: A measurement of electricity which equals 1000 watt hours.

king closer: In masonry, a closer used to fill an opening in a course larger than a half brick. A *king closer* is about three-fourths the size of a regular-sized brick.

king post: In a roof truss, the central upright piece against which the rafters abut and which supports the tie beam. See Fig. 338.

king-post truss: Truss used in roof framing. See Fig. 338.

kip: One thousand pounds.

kit: A box in which tools are stored and carried.

kite winder: A stair step used at the angle of a change in direction of a stairway; so-called from its triangular shape which somewhat resembles a kite. See *winders,* page 483.

knee: A piece of lumber bent in an angular shape either naturally or artificially to receive and relieve the strain of a weight on another piece of timber.

Fig. 338. The king post truss is a small truss with plywood gusset plates nailed and glued in place.

knee brace: In building construction, a member placed across the inside of an angle in a framework to add stiffness to the frame, especially at the angle between the roof and wall of the building.

knee walls: Partitions of varying length used to support roof rafters when their span is so great that additional support is required to stiffen them.

kneeler: In masonry, a stone cut to provide a change in direction, as in the curve of an arch.

knife switch: A switch which opens or closes an electric circuit by means of a thin blade which makes contact between two flat surfaces or short blades to complete the circuit.

knives, plastering: Knives used by plasterers are of two types. One has a straight edge and the other a slightly concave shearing edge bowed in .050″ to allow build-up of material in the center while removing it at both ends. Fig. 339 shows both types. These knives are used by the plasterer to cover nail heads and little nicks in the boards. Blades are 4″, 5″, and 6″ wide.

Fig. 339. Plasterer's knives: left, concave knife; right, straight knife. (Goldblatt Tool Co.)

knob: A projecting handle, usually round, for operating a lock.

knob or **knot:** An ornamental floral design carved on a corbel or on a boss.

knob-and-tube wiring: In electricity, a system of concealed wiring which was one of the earliest methods used for wiring houses while they were being built. It is the oldest type of electrical installation which meets requirements of the National Electrical Code. Today this method is not approved by many local codes and is rarely installed due mainly to high labor costs, as compared to other methods. Knob-and-tube wiring has a definite advantage for installations in damp or wet locations and also in buildings where certain corrosive vapors exist. Temporary installations—for example, fair grounds and construction jobs—can be more readily served by knob-and-tube wiring. Fig. 340 illustrates this type of wiring.

knob insulator: A porcelain knob to which electric wires may be fastened.

knob lock: A lock for a door with both a spring bolt, which is operated by a knob, and a dead bolt operated by a key. See Fig. 341.

knob, porcelain: A postlike ceramic insulator used in stringing single strand electric wire in a system (not permitted by many of the local city codes) known as "open wiring" or "knob and tube wiring." See Fig. 340.

knob rose: A round plate or washer which forms a doorknob socket; designed for fastening to the face of a door.

knob shank: The projecting stem on a knob with the hole or socket which fits the spindle.

knocked down: Construction material, as for a house, which is complete in its various parts, delivered to a job unassembled but cut and ready for reassembling.

knot: In lumber, a defect caused by a broken branch or limb embedded in the tree and which has been cut through in the process of lumber manufacture. Knots are classified according to size, form, quality, and frequency of occurrence.

knuckle: The part of a butt or hinge which encloses the hinge pin.

knuckle joint: The joint at the center break in a gambrel roof. Also called a *curb joint.* See Fig. 280, page 213.

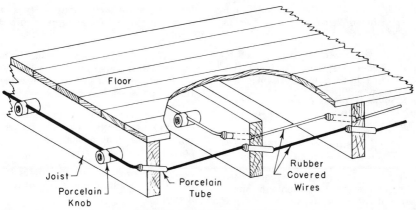

Fig. 340. Knob-and-tube wiring.

Fig. 341. Knob and Lock Set.

knurl: To finish a piece of work, by roughing or milling the surface to allow for a better grip, as on the head of a thumb screw.

kraft paper: A type of strong brown paper used extensively for wrapping purposes and as a building paper.

L

label: A molding or dripstone over a door or window, especially one which extends horizontally across the top of the opening and vertically downward for a certain distance at the edges.

label stop: In architecture, a type of boss or finish at each end of a window sill or door sill.

label terminations: Carvings on labels which terminate near the springing of the windows. In early Norman architecture,

often these carvings were stiff floral knots or grotesque figures of birds or animals. In later periods the carvings on labels became more decorative, sometimes consisting of ornamental bunches of flowers or the heads of noted persons.

laced valley: In building, a valley formed in a tile roof by interlacing tile-and-a-half tiles across a valley board.

lacing: Horizontal brace between shoring members.

lacing course: In masonry, a course of brickwork built into a stone wall for bonding and leveling purposes.

lacquer: Any of certain natural varnishes that dries by evaporating; a varnish consisting of a solution of shellac in alcohol, used in varnishing metalwork, sometimes used on wood.

lacquer work: Any metalwork or wood coated with lacquer as a preventive against tarnishing from the atmosphere or from handling; also, any decorative work which is coated with lacquer in imitation of enamel.

lacunar: Pertaining to *lacuna*. In architecture, a ceiling or the under surface of a cornice formed of sunken compartments.

259

lacunaria: A paneled ceiling, so-called from the *lacuna* or sunken compartments composing it.

ladder: A series of steps or rungs used for climbing, sometimes permanently attached to a structure but usually portable.

ladder hook: A metal projection used to secure a ladder to a ledge or to the ridge of a roof.

lag: In architecture, one of the narrow cross strips in the centering of an arch.

lag bolt: A bolt having a wrench head, usually square or hexagonal in shape, threaded at the lower end like a lag screw, and used for the same purpose as a lag screw. See *bolts,* Fig. 72, page 59.

lag expansion shield: Holding device used with a lag bolt. There is no nut in this anchor. The lag bolt screws itself further in as it is tightened. See Fig. 342.

Fig. 342. Lag expansion shield.

lag screw: A heavy wood screw with a square head. Since there is no slot in the head, the screw must be tightened down with a wrench. See *lag bolt,* Fig. 72, page 59.

lagging: In architecture, the narrow wood strips nailed to the ribs of arch centers to form the immediate supporting surface for the arch until the mortar has time to set. Also: heavy sheathing used in underground work to withstand earth pressure.

laid to the weather: The amount of shingle or siding exposed to the weather.

laitance: An accumulation of fine particles on the surface of freshly poured concrete caused by an upward movement of water through the concrete. This can be caused by too much mixing water, by excessive tamping, or by vibration of the concrete.

lally column: A metal pipe sometimes filled with concrete. Used to support girders or beams.

laminate: In home construction, the building up with layers of wood, each layer being a lamination or ply; also, the construction of plywood.

laminated: Any construction built up out of thin sheets or plates which are fastened together with glue, cement, or other similar adhesive.

laminated arches: Arched rafters formed by nailing or gluing thin strips of wood together.

laminated rafter: A rafter built up of plies or laminations which are joined and held together with glue or with mechanical fastenings.

laminated wood: An assembly of pieces of wood with the fibers or grain in each piece parallel to the fibers of the other pieces. The wood is built up of plies or laminations and joined together with glue or with some mechanical fastenings. This is in contrast to plywood, where the grain of the various layers alternate crosswise, with the grain on the two exposed faces parallel.

lamp circuit: In electricity, a branch circuit supplying current to lamps only and not to motors.

lamp cord: In electricity, two flexible insulated wires twisted together and used to carry the current from the outlet box to the lamp sockets.

lamp dimmer: In electricity, an adjustable resistance connected in a lamp circuit in order to reduce the voltage and the brightness of the lamp.

lamp holder: In electricity, receptacle into which the base of a *lamp bulb* is inserted connecting the lamp to the circuit. Also called *lamp socket.*

lamp socket: A receptacle into which the base of an electric light or lamp bulb is inserted. Same as *lamp holder.*

lanai: Hawaiian for "porch"; a covered walkway.

lancet: A name applied to either a *lancet arch* or a *lancet window*.

lancet arch: A sharply pointed arch with a greater rise than an equilateral arch having the same span.

lancet window: A high, narrow window terminating at the top in a lancet arch.

landing: A platform introduced at some location on a stairway to change the direction or to break the run.

landing newel: A post at the landing point of a stair supporting the handrail.

landing platform: A landing or platform in a flight of stairs. See *landing.*

landing tread: In building, a term used when referring to the front end of a stair landing. The method of construction usually provides the front edge with a thickness and finish of a stair tread while the back has the same thickness as the flooring of the landing.

lantern: An open structure of light material upon a roof to give light and air to the interior; a cupola, or towerlike member, crowning a larger structure either for ornamental purposes or to admit light and air; the chamber containing the light at the top of a lighthouse; sometimes, a cage or open chamber of rich architecture.

lantern light: A relatively small lantern or raised skylight.

lap: To cross over, as a board which extends over a second board. In masonry, the distance one brick extends beyond or over another. Also: joining of two reinforcing bars by lapping them side by side; similarly, the side and end overlap of sheets or rolls of welded wire fabric. Also, the length of overlap of two bars, usually measured in bar diameters.

lap dovetail: A dovetail joint in which the dovetail tenons are shorter than the thickness of the piece containing the mortises. This is used in drawer construction to avoid having the joint show on the face of the drawer.

lap joint: The overlapping of two pieces of wood or metal. In woodworking, such a uniting of two pieces of board is produced by cutting away one-half the thickness of each piece. When joined, the two pieces fit into each other so the outer faces are flush. See *end-lap joint,* Fig. 329, page 251.

lap siding: The siding used for finishing the exterior surface of a house or other structure. See *bevel siding,* Fig. 531, page 403.

lap weld: A lap weld is a weld where two pieces are overlapped, one member over another, and held in place until the welding operation fuses the two members together.

large knot: In woodworking, any sound knot measuring more than 1½ inches in diameter. See *sound knot,* page 416.

latch: A device for fastening a door. It usually consists of a movable bar which is secured to the door and falls into a hook or catch on the frame of the door.

latch bolt: In a lock, a bolt with a beveled head, moved by a spring when it is retracted in contact with the strike.

lateral: Proceeding from or to, or situated at a side; at right angles to the height or length; pertaining to the side. A diagonal bracing member.

lateral thrust: In masonry, the pressure of a load which extends to the sides.

lath: Metal mesh which is fastened to structural members to provide a base for plaster. In older residential structures wood strips were used. An example of metal lath is shown in Fig. 375, page 283.

lathe: In shopwork, a mechanical device used in the process of producing circular work for wood or metal turning.

lathe work: In woodworking or in metal work, the *lathe work* includes practically all branches of production by turning or boring, which commonly is done in the lathe.

lathing: In architecture, the nailing of lath in position; also a term used for the material itself.

Fig. 343. Lathing hatchets. (Goldblatt Tool Co.)

lathing hammer: A hammer which has a hatchet blade; used for trimming and nailing lath.

lathing hatchet: Tool used to cut and nail rocklath or to nail metal lath. See Fig. 343.

lattice: Any open work produced by interlacing of laths or other thin strips.

latticework: Any work in wood or metal made of lattice or a collection of lattices.

laundry chute: A duct or square chute through which soiled clothes are conveyed from the bathroom or kitchen to the laundry. Also called *clothes chute.*

laurel: In classical architecture, a decorative feature consisting of a laurel-leaf motif; sometimes used on moldings. See Fig. 344.

Fig. 344. Laurel.

lavatory: A basin for washing the hands and face; any room equipped with running water, drain, and fixed bowls or basins for washing.

laying out: The process of marking out material to full size for a piece of work which is to be performed.

laying out excavation lines: The process of establishing the outside foundation lines for a building. See *batter board,* Fig. 51, page 42.

layout: A diagram or working plan marked plan marked out during the process of developing a pattern for a particular construction. Determining the exact placement of the structure on the plot by defining the outer edges of the foundation with stakes and twine.

layout tee: In carpentry, a convenient device used for laying out the various cuts of rafters, including side cuts, ridge, bird's-mouth, and tail cuts. A handy layout tee is shown in Fig. 345.

leaching: Subjecting to the action of percolating water or other liquid in order to separate the soluble components; to dissolve out by the action of a percolating liquid.

leaching cesspool: In plumbing, any cesspool which is not watertight and permits waste liquids to pass into the surrounding soil by percolation.

leaching trenches: In plumbing, trenches which carry waste liquids from sewers. Such trenches may be constructed in gravelly or sandy soils which permit the liquids to pass into the surrounding soil by percolation; or the trenches may be dug in firm ground to the required depth and then be filled with broken stones, gravel, and sand, as shown in Fig. 346.

lead: In masonry, end or corner of a brick structure which is laid up prior to completing the courses; a part of a wall built as a guide for the laying of the balance of the wall.

lead-capped nail: A specialized fastening designed for use on metal-covered roofs. When driven through metal, the lead-capped nail will make a leak-proof joint.

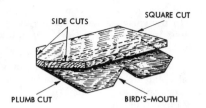

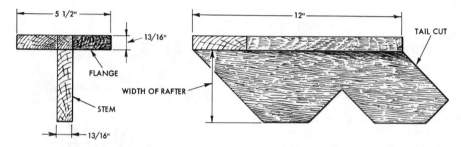

Fig. 345. A layout tee is a device used for making rafter cuts.

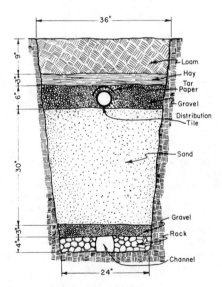

Fig. 346. Leaching trench.

which purpose it is run into a mortise in the stone.

leaded joint: Joint made in piping by ramming calking (usually oakum) in the opening between the bell and spigot, followed by hot lead. See Fig. 347.

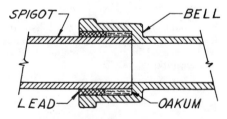

Fig. 347. Leaded bell and Spigot joint.

leaded light: A sash in which the lights are held together with lead or zinc bars.

leader: In plumbing, a pipe or *downspout* which carries rain water from the gutter to the ground or to a sewer connection; in

lead dot: In building, a dowel, or peg of lead used to fasten sheet lead to the upper surface of a coping or cornice, for

263

a heating system, a pipe which conducts warm air from the furnace to the various rooms which are to be heated. In dimensioning, an indicator for notes; an arrow which points to something to identify it.

leader head: An ornamental enlargement at the top or head of a leader, or conductor, for receiving rain water in large volume at a narrow opening where a gutter is not practical.

lead-flat: In building, a term applied to a flat roof formed of sheet lead laid on boarding and joists. See *flat roof,* page 194.

lead joint: In plumbing, a term usually applied to the forming of a joint between successive lengths of large water pipes. This is done by pouring molten lead into the annular space between a bell and spigot and then making the joint tight by calking.

lead nail: A small copper-alloy nail used to secure sheet lead to a roof.

lead paint: Any ordinary paint in which white lead is used as a base.

lead plug: In masonry, a connecting piece of cast lead which binds together adjacent stones in a course. This plug is formed by running molten lead into channels cut in the jointing faces.

lead screw anchor: Device used for anchoring to a wall. See Fig. 348.

lead shield: An anchor, consisting of a shell or case of lead, for an expansion bolt or screw. See *anchors,* Fig. 18, page 17.

lead wool: In masonry, a specially prepared lead fiber consisting of fine threads which is used in place of molten lead in making pipe joints.

Fig. 348. Lead screw anchor.

leads: Short lengths of insulated wires which conduct electric current to and from a device or appliance.

leaf and dart: An ornamental design composed of a water plant and arrows used to decorate the *ogee.* See Fig. 349.

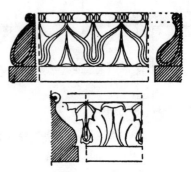

Fig. 349. Leaf and dart.

leak: In building, an opening, such as a crack, crevice, or hole in a roof, by means of which water from rain or snow can enter the structure; also, in plumbing, an opening in a pipe which permits gas or fluid to escape.

lean mortar: In masonry, a mortar that lacks cementitious materials and may be weak, harsh, and difficult to spread.

lean-to: A small building or extension of a larger building having a single-sloped roof whose rafters pitch or lean against another building or against a wall; a crude shelter with a single-pitched roof leaning against two posts or trees.

lean-to-roof: The sloping roof of a room having its rafters or supports pitched against and leaning on the adjoining wall of a building.

leaves: The sliding, hinged, or detachable parts of a folding door, window shutters, or a table top.

ledge: In architecture, any shelflike projection from a wall.

ledged door: In building, a door made by nailing boards on battens or on large cleats.

ledger: A board used in balloon framing to tie the studs together and to act as a support for the joists. Also called ribbon board or strip.

ledger strip: A strip of lumber nailed along the bottom of the side of a girder on which joists rest. When joists are to be flush with the top of the girder, they must be notched sufficiently to fit over the *ledger strip* and still rest on a plane even with the topside of the girder.

ledgers: The horizontal pieces of timber fastened to the vertical uprights of the scaffolding raised around a building during the process of erection; the ledgers support the putlogs on which the flooring boards of the scaffolding are laid.

leg: Either of the sides of an angle iron, one of whose legs is usually shorter than the other (see Fig. 20, left, page 19); one of the limbs of a pair of compasses or dividers (see Fig. 75, page 62); either side of a triangle as distinguished from the base, or in a right triangle, from the hypotenuse.

length: In the measurement of an object, the greatest dimension or distance from end to end, as distinguished from breadth and thickness.

lengthening bar: A metal bar attached to a compass in order to increase the radius.

let into: Notched.

lettering: In architecture, the forming of letters in accordance with a style generally accepted by architects. Architectural lettering differs from mechanical lettering in the freedom of its style. Examples of architectural lettering are shown in Fig. 350.

Fig. 350. Lettering samples.

lettering pens: In architectural drafting, specially designed pens. To obtain the best results in architectural lettering, the proper type of pen must be used.

level: A device, also known as a *spirit level,* consisting of a glass tube nearly filled with alcohol or ether, leaving a movable air bubble. This device, protected by a metal or wood casing, is used for determining a point, or adjusting an object, in a line or plane perpendicular to the direction of the force of gravity. When centered, the bubble indicates the line of sight to be truly horizontal. A slight tilting of the *level* at either end will cause the bubble to move away from center, indicating a line which is not horizontal. An example of a *spirit level* obtainable in either wood or metal is shown in Fig. 351.

lever: A rigid bar which turns on a fulcrum or axis wherein exist two or more other points where forces are exerted.

L-head: The top of a shore formed with a braced horizontal member projecting on one side forming an inverted L-shaped assembly.

lierne: In Gothic vaulting, a short connecting rib.

lierne rib: In a groined vault, any rib which does not spring from the shaft or wall but crosses the spandrel from one boss or intersection of the main ribs to another producing star-shaped patterns.

lierne vault: Vaulting which is divided into panels by the use of *lierne ribs.*

Fig. 351. Level.

level man: The surveyor who has charge of the leveling instrument.

leveling instrument: A leveling device consisting of a spirit level attached to a sighting tube and the whole mounted on a tripod; used for leveling a surface to a horizontal plane. When the bubble in the level is in the center, the line of sight is horizontal. Also called a *builder's level.* See Fig. 352.

leveling rod or leveling staff: A rod or staff with graduated marks for measuring heights or vertical distances between given points and the line of sight of a *leveling instrument.* The different types of leveling rods in common use are the *target rods* read only by the rodman and the *self-reading rods,* which are read directly by the men who do the leveling. Fig. 353..

lift: An enclosed platform made to ascend or descend in a vertical shaft or framework; used for transferring persons, goods, or vehicles from one floor level to another; an *elevator.* Also: In concrete work, a layer of concrete placed in a wall form; the dimension from the top of one placement of concrete to the top of the next placement, for example, an *8 inch lift.*

lift slab: Floor construction in which slabs are cast directly on one another. Each slab is lifted into final position by jacks on top of the columns. Floors are secured at each floor level by column brackets or collars.

light: A window pane; a section of a window sash for a single pane of glass.

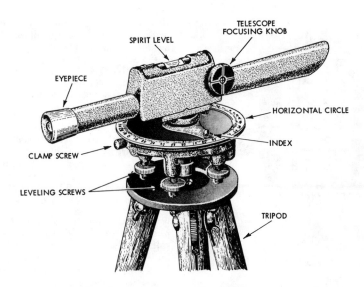

Fig. 352. The level is an accurate instrument used for determining points in a horizontal plane. (David White Instruments, Div. of Realist, Inc.)

Fig. 353. A leveling rod must be held firmly in a vertical position.

light cut: A term used by woodworkers when referring to a cut where the shavings removed are thin and narrow.

light load: In electricity, a load that is less than the usual or normal load on the circuit.

lighting fixture: In electricity, an ornamental device fastened to the outlet box which has sockets for holding lamps.

lighting panel: In electric wiring, a metal box in which fuses are located wherever it is necessary to change the size of the wire. Such a cabinet is usually mounted in a wall with the plate flush with the finished plastered surface. Also called a *panelboard.* See Fig. 354. Also, see *fuse box,* Fig. 278, page 213. See also *distribution panel,* page 144.

lightning rod: One of a system of metal rods extending from above the highest point of a building to the ground, thus protecting the building from damage by lightning. Also called *lightning conductor.*

lights: The openings or pieces of glass in an opening.

267

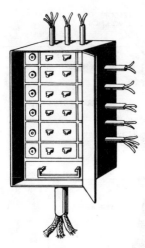

Fig. 354. Lighting panel.

lime-burning: The process of producing lime by the burning of limestone. See *calcining,* page 82.

lime mixers: These are used by the plasterer to mix lime and are similar to kitchen mixers in construction, although they are larger. They come in sizes of "one bag" or "three bags". They are constructed of a drum which holds the material to be mixed and a steel shaft to which several impellers are fastened. See Fig. 355.

Fig. 355. Lime mixer. (Goldblatt Tool Co.)

lime paste: The material produced when water is mixed with quicklime. The same as *slaked* lime.

lime putty: A mixture of gauging plaster and finish lime; used for the finish coat of plaster. See *gauging plaster,* page 215.

limestone: A type of stone used extensively for building purposes, especially in the better grade of structures. *Limestone* is composed largely of calcium carbonate originating usually from an accumulation of organic remains, such as shells, which yield lime when burned. Therefore, this stone is also used extensively as a source of lime.

limewash: Lime slaked in water and applied with a brush or as a spray. Sometimes salt is added to make it adhere better, and bluing may be added to give a white tone. It is used chiefly as a wall covering. See *whitewash,* page 481.

limit switch: A switch which opens an electric circuit when a device such as an electric lift has reached the end of its travel course.

lineal foot: Pertaining to a line one foot in length, as distinguished from a square foot or cubic foot.

linear: Resembling a line or thread; narrow and elongated; involving measurement in one direction; pertaining to length.

linear measure: A system of measurement in length; also known as *long measure:*

12 inches (in.)	= 1 foot (ft.)
3 feet	= 1 yard yd.)
16½ feet	= 1 rod (rd.)
320 rods	= 1 mile (mi.)
5280 feet	= 1 mile

line drop: In electricity, the loss in voltage in the conductors of a circuit due to their resistance.

line level: A bubble level designed to hook on a string. It is used in leveling a string line. Used when laying foundations, tile pipe, determining grades, or for other similar work. See Fig. 356.

line of direction: An imaginary line extending from the central corner of the object that touches or is nearest the picture plane.

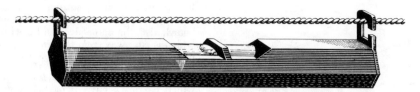

Fig. 356. Line level.

line of traverse: A line that passes across, through, or over.

line of sight: In perspective drawing, the imaginary lines which extend from the viewer's eye to the object. Also called *visual rays.* See *perspective drawing,* page 322.

line pipe: In plumbing, a test pipe having recessed and taper-thread couplings.

lineman: A man who erects or works on an electric transmission line.

linen fold: A carved decoration used on panels, consisting of shallow moldings almost covering the panel; named from a supposed resemblance to folded linen. Also called *linen pattern* and *linen scroll.*

linen pattern: A form of decorative ornament suggesting the convolutions of rolled or folded linen. Also called *linen scroll* and *linen fold.*

linen scroll: In architecture, a type of decoration used for ornamentation of panels, characterized by rolls or convolutions.

lining: The covering for the interior of a building as opposed to *casing,* which is the covering for the exterior. Also, in plastering, the setting of dots to a line on the sides of a beam to produce a finished product that is true in width, depth, and straightness.

link: A measure of length of 7.92 inches. The link is associated with the Gunthers chain in survey measurement. One hundred links make a chain or 66 feet.

link and thimble: See *cable attachments,* page 80.

linoleum: A composition material made of solidified linseed oil, gums, cork dust, and pigments, laid on burlap as a backing; used extensively as floor covering and for other interior finish purposes.

linseed oil: A yellowish drying oil obtained from linseed (the seeds of flax); used extensively in paints, either raw or boiled.

lintel: A piece of wood, stone, or steel placed horizontally across the top of door and window openings to support the walls immediately above the openings. Examples of steel and stone lintels are shown in Fig. 357.

lip: A term used by carpenters when referring to the cutting edge of a tool.

lip molding: A small, convex molding which hangs like a lip, especially used as a finish around cupboard drawers.

lip strike: A metal part which contacts with the lip of another part of a fastener, as the lip of a sash lock.

lip union: In plumbing, a particular type of union which has a lip for preventing the gasket from being squeezed into the pipe so as to obstruct the flow.

liquid glue: Any glue used in a cold form, taken directly from the container and applied without heating. Same as *cold glue.*

liquid limit: The point of moisture content at which a soil material changes from a solid to a liquid state.

liquid membrane-forming compound: A liquid that is uniformly sprayed on fresh

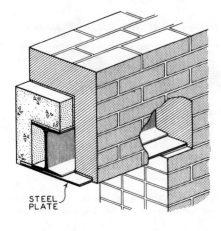

STEEL PLATE

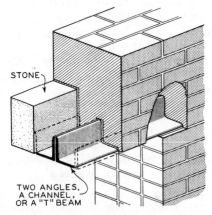

STONE

TWO ANGLES,
A CHANNEL,
OR A "T" BEAM

Fig. 357. Lintel.

concrete either by hand-operated or power-driven spray equipment. Once on the concrete, this liquid forms into a very thin covering that seals in the moisture of the concrete.

list: In architecture, a narrow band separating two structural members; in carpentry, a narrow strip of wood such as sapwood which is cut from the edge of a board.

listel: A small, square molding often used in conjunction with a larger member; a list or narrow *fillet*. See Fig. 230, page 175.

listing: In carpentry, cutting or trimming the sapwood from the edge of a plank or board; also, the name given to the sapwood which is cut away from the edge of a board or plank.

live: In electricity, a conductor or circuit which carries a current or has a voltage on it.

live load: The moving load or variable weight to which a building is subjected, due to the weight of the people who occupy it; the furnishings and other movable objects as distinct from the *dead load* or weight of the structural members and other fixed loads; the weight of moving traffic over a bridge as opposed to the weight of the bridge itself. *Live load* does not include wind load or earthquake shock.

load: In electricity, the work required to be done by a machine; also, the current flowing through a circuit.

load-bearing walls: Any wall which bears its own weight as well as other weight; same as a supporting wall. Also called *bearing wall*.

load center: A *distribution panel*. Also called: *panel, panelboard, main control center* and *switchboard*.

loam: Commonly, though incorrectly, any earth or soil. More specifically, a soil constituted of a friable mixture of varying quantities of clay, sand, and organic matter.

lobes: Projections, especially when of a rounded form.

local vent: In plumbing, a pipe or similar connection which serves to convey foul air from a room or from a plumbing fixture to the outer air.

locate: To establish or determine a fixed position in a particular situation or spot.

lock: A contrivance for securing a door in position when closed, consisting of a bolt operated by a key or some other combination.

lock bar: A strip of steel, usually $1\frac{1}{4}''$ square, fastened to the sill of an opening for a glass block panel, the purpose of

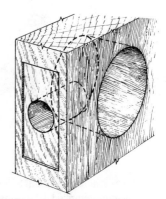

Fig. 358. Cylindrical lock sets for heavy duty exterior use. (Yale & Towne Mfg. Co.)

which is to provide an anchor for the mortar bed. See Fig. 286, page 218.

lock cap: The top piece or removable lid of a lock; also called *lock cover.*

lock case: The box or enclosure of a lock containing the bolts and mechanism.

lock cover: The removable lid of a lock. Same as *lock cap.*

lock, cylindrical: Cylindrical lock sets are sturdy, heavy duty locks, designed for maximum security for installation in exterior doors. See Fig. 358.

lock, mortise: An ordinary *mortise lock* is illustrated in Fig. 359. More elaborate mortise locks are made with cylinder locks, with a handle on one side and a knob on the other side or with handles on both sides. This type of lock is used principally on front or outside doors.

Fig. 359. Mortise lock. (Yale & Towne Mfg. Co.)

lock nut: A type of secondary nut used on a bolt to prevent the first nut from turning; also a nut which locks when tightened.

lock rail: In building, the horizontal piece of a door to which the lock is fastened.

lock seam: In sheet metal, the joining of two surfaces in the same plane in which the edges to be united are folded back for a suitable distance, the folds interlocked, and the joint then pressed tight.

lock set: A term used to designate a complete lock with all the trim, including knobs, escutcheon plates, and screws.

lock stile: That stile of a door to which the lock is attached. Same as *locking stile.*

lock, tubular: Tubular lock sets are used mainly for interior doors, for bedrooms, bathrooms, passages, and closets. They can be obtained with pin tumbler locks in the knob on the outside of the door and turn button or push button locks on the inside. See Fig. 360.

locking stile: The vertical section of a door to which the lock is fastened.

loft: An attic; the uppermost room in a house, especially if in the roof; a gallery in a church to accommodate the organ and

271

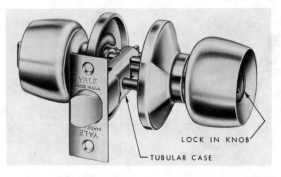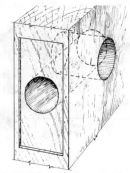

LOCK IN KNOB

TUBULAR CASE

Fig. 360. Tubular lock set is installed by drilling 2 holes ond mortising lock face. Locks of this type are supplied for several different applications. (Yale & Towne Mfg. Co.)

choir singers, known as the *organ loft* or the *choir loft;* the highest floor of a warehouse or business building; the space in a barn directly beneath the roof commonly used for storing hay and called the *hay loft.*

log: A rough, unshaped piece of tree trunk; also, a squared and dressed timber used for construction purposes.

log-cabin siding: An exterior-wall finish, used principally on summer cottages, consisting of a kind of siding which has been machined to produce the appearance of logs; hence, giving the building a rustic log-cabin effect.

loggia: In architecture, a roofed arcade, or gallery, usually within the body of the building at the height of the second story, or higher, with one side open to the air, making an open-air room.

long-and-short work: In masonry, a method of forming angles of door and window jambs in rubble walls by laying stones horizontally alternating with stones set on end, the upright stones usually being longer than the horizontal stones.

long float: A plasterer's trowel, which is of such great length as to require two men to handle it. See *float,* page 196.

longitudinal: Pertaining to length.

longitudinal joint: In building construction, a joint which fastens two pieces of timber together, in the direction of their length.

longitudinal section: In shopwork and drawing, a lengthwise cut of any portion of a structure; also, pertaining to a measurement along the axis of a body.

longitudinal wires: The wires of welded wire fabric which run lengthwise.

long-nose pliers: These are generally used for making eyelets in wires for screw terminations and positioning objects in tight places. See Fig. 361.

long screw: In plumbing, a nipple six inches in length, having one thread much longer than the ordinary thread.

lookout: A short member used to support the overhanging portion of a roof. See Fig. 131, page 103.

Fig. 361. Long-nose pliers. (Champion De Arment Tool Co.)

loop: A narrow window or opening in a wall, such as a staircase for admitting light, or in a barn to admit air for ventilation. Same as *loophole*.

loop or **circuit vent:** In plumbing, the extension of a horizontal soil pipe beyond the connection at which liquid wastes from a fixture enter the pipe. Usually the extension is vertical directly beyond its connection to the soil or waste pipe. The base of the vertical portion of the vent may be connected to the horizontal portion of the soil or waste stack between the fixtures which are connected to the pipe. See Fig. 362.

loophole: A small or narrow opening, as in a wall or parapet, for looking through or for admitting light and air; an opening in the wall of a building, narrow on the outside and splayed within, from which arrows or darts might be discharged on an enemy. Often *loopholes* are in the form of a cross and usually have round holes at the ends.

loose butt hinge: A butt hinge in which one leaf may be lifted from the other. For example, a door hung on this type of hinge can be removed easily.

loose-fill insulation: A fill insulation which may be fibrous, granular, or powdered.

loose-joint butt: A hinge having a single knuckle on each half, one of them with the pin and the other with a corresponding hole, permitting separation of the two parts of the butt. See Fig. 363.

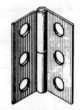

Fig. 363. Loose-joint butt.

loose knot: In woodworking, a term applied to a knot which is not held in position firmly by the surrounding wood fibers; such a knot is a severe blemish in a piece of lumber, making the board unfit for first-class work.

loose-pin butt: A butt having a hinge pin which can be withdrawn to allow separation of the two parts of the butt.

lot: As used in building codes, one of the smaller portions of land into which a village, town, or city block is divided or laid out; a parcel of land or subdivision of a town or city block, described by reference to a recorded plot or by definite boundaries; also, a portion of land in one ownership, whether plotted or unplotted, devoted to a certain use or occupied by a building or group of buildings united by a common interest and with the customary accessories. If two or more lots are occupied by a building or group of buildings as a unit of property, such a plot usually is considered as a single lot.

lot line: A building term referring to the line which bounds a plot of ground described as a *lot* in the title to a property.

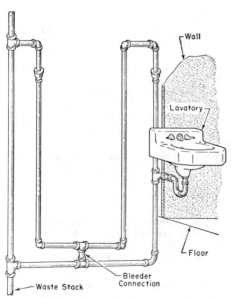

Fig. 362. Looped vent.

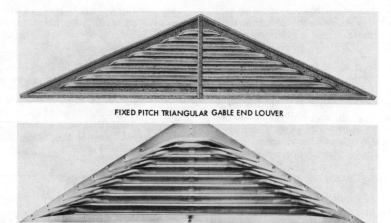

FIXED PITCH TRIANGULAR GABLE END LOUVER

ADJUSTABLE TRIANGULAR GABLE END LOUVER
Fig. 364. Louvers. (H. C. Products Co., Princeville, Illinois)

louver: An opening for ventilating closed attics or other used spaces; also, a louver board. A slatted opening for ventilation in which the slats are so placed as to exclude rain, light, or vision. See Fig. 364.

louver boards: In architecture, a series of overlapping sloping boards or slats in an opening so arranged as to admit air but keep out rain or snow.

lozenge: In architecture, a term applied to any diamond-shaped ornament or design, as a *lozenge molding;* also, a name applied to a window having diamond-shaped panes of glass. A geometric figure having four equal sides with two acute angles and two obtuse angles.

lozenge molding: An ornamental molding used in Norman architecture, characterized by diamond-shaped ornaments resembling a lozenge.

lucarne (lu-karn'): A small, vertical window projecting from the slope of a roof; same as *dormer window.*

lug sill: In building, a term applied to a window sill in a brick or stone wall, where the sill extends beyond the width of the window opening, with the ends of the sill set in the wall.

lugs: In carpentry, an extension of the stile of a window beyond the meeting rails. *Lugs* usually are sawed ornamentally on the inside of the stile; in electricity, terminals placed on the end of conductors to enable the wire to be attached or detached quickly. Also: A projecting part used to hold or grip something; lugs on a reinforcing bar.

lumber: Any material, such as boards, planks, or beams cut from timber to a size and form suitable for marketing.

lumber blemish: Though not classified as a defect, a *blemish* is any imperfection which mars the appearance of wood.

lumber, boards: Yard lumber less than 2 inches thick and 2 or more inches wide.

lumber defect: As the term is used in the trade, a *defect* is an irregularity occurring in or on wood that will tend to impair its strength, durability, or utility value.

lumber, dimension: Yard lumber from 2 inches to but not including 5 inches thick and 2 or more inches wide. Includes joists, rafters, studding, plank, and small timbers.

lumber, dressed size: The dimensions of lumber, after shrinking from the green dimension and after planing, usually ⅜ inch

274

Fig. 365. Machine expansion shield.

less than the nominal or rough size. For example, a 2 by 4 stud actually measures 1⅝ by 3⅝ inches.

lumber, matched: Lumber that is edge-dressed and shaped to make a close tongue-and-groove joint at the edges or ends when laid edge to edge or end to end.

lumber, shiplap: Lumber that is edge-dressed to make a close rabbeted or lapped joint.

lumber, timbers: Yard lumber 5 or more inches in least dimension. Includes beams, stringers, posts, caps, sills, girders, and purlins.

lumber, yard: Lumber of those grades, sizes, and patterns which are generally intended for ordinary construction, such as framework and rough coverage of houses.

lump lime: Lime commonly known as *quicklime* produced by burning limestone in a kiln.

lunette: A lunette is a crescent-shaped opening in a vault or barreled ceiling, usually to provide a window or a recess for decorative effect.

luthern: In building, a vertical window set in a roof, as a *dormer window.*

M

machine bolt: A rodlike type of metal bolt, having a wrench head, usually square or hexagonal in shape, with threads on the lower end for attaching a nut. See bolts, Fig. 72, page 59.

machine drawing: A drawing of a machine or parts including notes and dimensions.

machine expansion shield: This takes a machine bolt and is used in heavy construction. There is a tapered nut in the bottom

which locks when the bolt is tightened and thereafter will be securely anchored even if the bolt is removed. The smaller sizes are for ¼ inch bolts and the larger ones for up to 1 inch bolts. See Fig. 365.

machine rating: In electricity, the amount of load, or power, a machine can deliver without overheating.

machine screws: For the assembling of metal parts, *machine screws* are used. These screws are made regularly in steel and brass with the four types of heads: *flat, round, oval,* and *fillister.* See Fig. 366. The same style can be obtained also in the Phillips recessed heads. Sizes are designated as to length in inches from ⅛ of an inch to 3 inches and as to diameter from 1/16 of an inch to ⅜ inch or more. The number of threads per inch may vary, depending upon the standard used. Machine screws are used to fasten butt hinges to metal jambs, lock cases, and door closers to their brackets. They are available with both coarse and fine threads.

made ground: In building construction, a portion of land, or ground, formed by filling in natural or artificial pits with rubbish or other material.

mahlstick: In painting, a slender stick of wood padded at one end with a ball of cloth

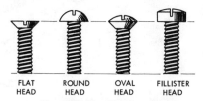

| FLAT HEAD | ROUND HEAD | OVAL HEAD | FILLISTER HEAD |

Fig. 366. Machine screws.

or leather; used by painters to steady and support the hand using the brush. Sometimes spelled *maulstick.*

main: In electricity, the circuit from which all other smaller circuits are taken.

main beam: In floor construction, one of the principal beams which transmits loads direct to the columns.

main control center. *See control center, main,* page 119.

main couple: In building construction, the principal truss in a timber roof.

main rafter: A roof member extending at right angles from the plate to the ridge. Same as *common rafter.*

main tie: In building construction, the lower tensional member of a roof truss which connects the feet of the principal rafters.

male plug: The two- and sometimes three-prong connector used to establish an electrical circuit.

malleable: Capable of being extended or shaped by hammering or by pressure with rollers.

mallet: A small maul, or hammer, usually made of wood or rubber; used for driving another tool, such as a chisel. Also used for other purposes. See Fig. 367.

malm (mam): In brickmaking, an artificial marl produced by mixing clay and chalk in a wash mill. The product is used as clay in the manufacture of brick.

malm bricks: In masonry, bricks which are made from marl or *malm.* See *malm.*

malm rubber: In brickwork, a soft form of *malm brick,* which is capable of being worked, by cutting or rubbing, into special shapes.

manhole: A hole, usually with a cover, large enough for a man to creep through to gain access to a sewer, drainpipe, an electric conduit, a steam boiler, or other similar places when it is necessary to make repairs.

manhole in conduit: In electricity, an opening or chamber placed in a conduit run, large enough to admit a man to splice or join cables.

manipulation: The process of performing work by the skillful use of the hands.

mansard roof: A roof with two slopes on all four sides, the lower slope very steep, the upper slope almost flat; frequently used as a convenient method of adding another story to a building. See Fig. 368.

mantel: The ornamental facing around a fireplace, including the shelf which is usually attached to the breast of the chimney above the fireplace.

Fig. 367. Mallet.

Fig. 368. Mansard roof.

Fig. 369. Marking gage.

mantle: In building construction, the outer covering of a wall surface when the outer surface is of different material from the inner surface.

manufactured aggregates: The after-product of industrial furnaces and used as aggregates in the concrete mix; slag and cinders.

marble: Any limestone capable of taking a high polish; used extensively for both interior and exterior finish of buildings. Because of the wide range of colors from white to dark gray and brown, *marble* is much used in architectural work for decorative purposes.

marble dust: Pulverized limestone used in making putty.

marbling: The process of painting a wood surface so that it will resemble marble.

margin: In building construction, the exposed width of each slate in coursed work; also, the flat surface of stiles or rails in paneled framing.

margin draft: In ashlar work, a smooth surface surrounding a joint.

margin lights: In building, narrow panes of glass near the edges of a window sash.

margin of safety: An allowance for any defects in material or workmanship when designing a piece of material to sustain a certain load. It is found by dividing the ultimate strength of a material by the actual unit stress on a sectional area. Same as *factor of safety.*

margin trowel: In plastering, a small triangular trowel used for cleaning the plastering trowel and for small plastering jobs. See trowels.

marginal bars: Glazing bars arranged in windows so as to divide the glazed opening into a large central part bordered by narrow panes at the edges.

marigold window: In architecture, a circular window having radial bars; also called *rose window;* same as *Catherine wheel.*

marking awl: A sharp-pointed steel instrument used for laying out work, especially on hardwood.

marking gage: A tool used by carpenters for scribing a line parallel to the edge of a piece of work. See Fig. 369.

marking knife: In furniture making, a knife used as a marking awl, particularly on softwoods.

marking out: In building construction, the laying out of boundaries and levels for a proposed piece of work.

marks: A series of letters, numbers, or a combination of both used to designate (a) the parts of a structure or (b) the identity of a bent bar.

marquee: A permanent hood which projects over an entrance to a building and is not supported by posts or columns.

marquetry: Inlaid work in furniture, where an ornamental surface is built up with thin-shaped pieces of variously colored hardwoods or other materials to form a design.

marquise: In building, a projecting canopy over the entrance to a building. See *marquee.*

mason: A workman skilled in laying brick or stone, as a *bricklayer,* a *stonemason.*

masonry: A term applied to anything constructed of stone, brick, tiles, cement, concrete, and similar materials; also, the work done by a mason who works in stone, brick, cement, tiles, or concrete.

masonry arches: Arches, usually curved, thrown across openings in a masonry wall for providing support for the superimposed structure. The arches may be constructed of such material as stone blocks or brick put together in a particular arrangement, so a complete masonry arch will resist the pressure of the load it carries by a balancing of certain thrusts and counterthrusts.

masonry cement: A type of portland cement used predominantly by bricklayers because of special qualities of workability and water retention.

masonry nail: A hardened-steel nail of specialized design, used for fastening wood, etc., to masonry work. See Fig. 370.

Fig. 370. Masonry nail.

masonry saw: Portable, electrically powered hand saw, similar in design to all-purpose *electric hand saw.* Designed specifically for cutting masonry, this saw has a variety of masonry blade choices, including diamond and abrasive blades. Is available for on-the-job use or for the shop. See Fig. 371.

masonry wall: Any wall constructed of such material as stone, brick, tile cement blocks, or concrete, put in place by a mason. See *wall,* page 474.

mason's lime: The lime which is used by masons when making mortar for masonry work.

mason's rules: Special rules graduated in either "course" sizes for laying up courses or in modular 16″ spacings.

master-keyed lock: A lock which is one of a series, each one of which may be operated by two keys, a master key which will operate all of them, and individual keys which operate individual locks only.

master switch: In electrictity, a switch which controls the operation of other switches or contact switches.

master time value chart: A tabulation of each building operation including planning, design, land acquisition, and financing as well as actual building steps. The estimated time for completion of each operation is shown on the chart.

masterpiece: Any piece of lumber finished with superior skill and used as a pattern by which duplicate pieces are cut.

mastics: Mastics, or pasty type cements, are being used more and more for installing wallboard, paneling, and certain kinds of flooring. The mastics on the market are quite diverse. Some are thick pastes and can be used where there is no moisture problem. Others are waterproof and can be used on concrete floors and in kitchens, laundries, and bathrooms. Some require a hot application. Usually these are handled by specialists who have the equipment to heat the mastic and keep it in a fluid condition during use. Many mastics come in cans ready for use and need only to be applied.

mat: A large footing or foundation slab used to support an entire structure. Also, a grid of reinforcing bars.

mat sinking: A depression or sinking in a floor at the entrance door to provide for a fiber mat; same as *mat well.*

mat well: A term applied to a low-level area in an entranceway to provide for a fiber mat. See *mat sinking.*

matched boards: Boards which have been finished so as to hold a tongue-and-groove joint securely in place; also boards finished with a rebated edge for close fitting.

Fig. 371. Masonry saw. (Skil Corp., Chicago, Ill.)

matched joint: In carpentry, a joint made with tongue-and-groove material.

matched lumber: Any lumber which has been edge dressed and shaped to make a close tongue-and-groove joint on the edges or ends when laid edge-to-edge or end-to-end. See *dressed and matched,* page 158.

matched roof boards: Sheathing boards which have a tongue on one edge and a corresponding groove on the other edge or *tongue-and-groove* boards. See *open cornice.*

material: In carpentry, anything used in the process of constructing a new building, such as lumber, plastering, builders' hardware, and other structural *stuff.*

material symbols: In architecture, various standardized symbols used by architects and builders to designate the different kinds of materials to be used in the construction of a new building. See Fig. 372. See also *symbols and abbreviations.*

matrix: In the case of mortar, the cement paste in which the fine aggregate particles are embedded; in the case of concrete, the mortar in which the coarse aggregate particles are embedded.

matted: A term used in furniture making when referring to the rough background of carved oak.

maul: A heavy hammer or club used for driving stakes or piles; also, a heavy mallet or mace; any of various types of heavy hammers used for driving wedges, piles, or stakes.

maximum demand: In electricity, the greatest load on a system occurring during a certain interval of time.

maximum density: The highest unit weight to which a material can be compacted.

meager lime: In building, a lime in which the impurities are in excess of 6 percent. See *poor lime,* page 346.

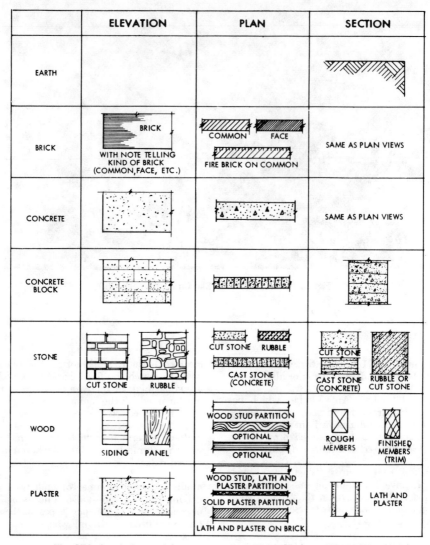

Fig. 372. Symbols used for common materials shown on blueprints.

mean horizontal candle power: The average candle power measured on a horizontal plane in all directions from the lamp filament.

mean spherical candle power: In electricity, the average candle power of a lamp

measured in all directions from the center of the lamp.

measurement: A dimension found by determining the length, breadth, and thickness of structural material by use of some device, such as a ruler or gage; also, the size

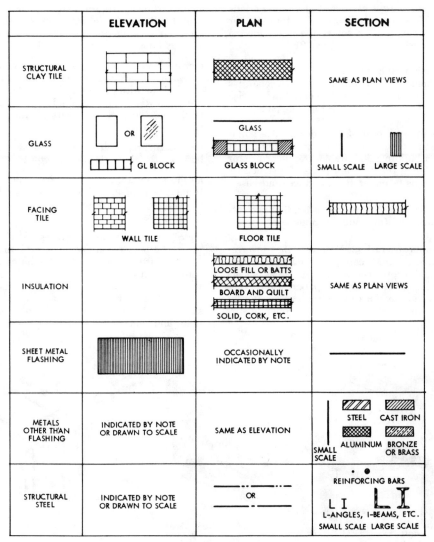

Fig. 372. Con't.

of an area or the capacity of a system ascertained by means of suitable instruments or apparatus.

mechanic: Pertaining to a handicraft, or one skilled in some manual art; also, a skilled workman who makes repairs or as-

sembles machines; a skilled worker with tools or machines.

mechanical force: Pressure put on concrete by the weight of materials or objects resting on it or pushing against it.

medullary rays: In a cross section of wood, the *wood rays* composed of bands of cells which extend radially from the pith or center of the log across the grain toward the bark. See Fig. 24, page 21.

meeting rail: The strip of wood or metal forming the horizontal bar which separates the upper and lower sash of a window. See *check rail,* page 95. See Fig. 198, page 154.

member: A part of an order or of a building; a column or a molding; a definite part of a building, an entablature, a cornice, or molding; the different parts of a structure, such as beams, rafters, cornice, and base.

membrane: A thin skin or film that protects a material from outside influences.

membrane curing: A process that involves either a liquid sealing compound or a non-liquid protective coating (such as sheets of plastic or waterproof paper). Both types function as films to restrict evaporation of mixing water from the fresh concrete surface.

mending plate: A steel strip of any convenient dimensions, drilled and countersunk for flathead screws and bolts, used in repairing or strengthening wood structures such as house screens, etc. See Fig. 373.

mensuration: The process of measuring, especially that branch of mathematics which deals with the determining of length, area, and volume; that is, finding the length of a line, the area of a surface, and the volume of a solid.

meros: In architecture, the plain surfaces between the channels of a *triglyph.*

mesh: In building construction, any material consisting of a network formed by the crossing of wires or strings. See *welded wire fabric,* page 479.

metal arches: Plastering arches for doorways or other arched openings, readymade for standard 2x4 partitions, eliminates the construction of curved wooden forms and the forming of corner beads around these curves. Such arches are made of heavy sheet metal having a surface of alternate holes and solid metal for plaster keying.

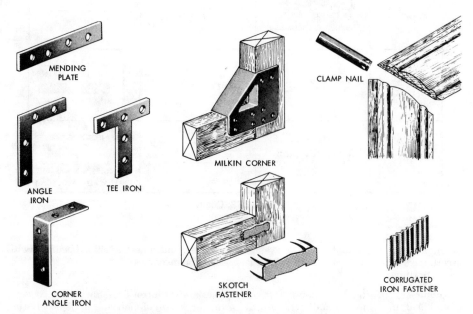

Fig. 373. Metal fasteners used in cabinetmaking and other light construction work.

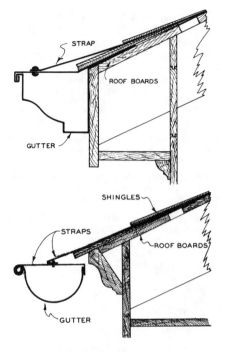

Fig. 374. Metal gutters.

metal conduit: In electricity, iron or steel pipes in which electric wires and cables are installed. Two types are in general use: thin wall and rigid.

metal deck: A sheet metal roofing for flat roofs.

metal fasteners: In carpentry, a type of fastener used for light construction work. See Fig. 373.

metal finishing: Pertaining to the final step in metalwork when a metal piece is given either a dull or glossy finish.

metal gutters: A type of attached gutter, prefabricated of sheet metal; usually obtainable in two styles, as shown in Fig. 374.

metal lath: Sheets of metal which are slit and drawn out to form openings on which plaster is spread. Same as *expanded metal lath.* See Fig. 375.

metal strip: A term sometimes applied to metal flashing used on water tables or around chimneys to prevent water seeping into the roof or walls. See *belt course,* Fig. 55, page 46.

Fig. 375. Expanded metal lath with a ¾″ raised rib. (National Gypsum Co.)

metal studs: Metal studs have long been used in light commercial and industrial construction, and they are also increasingly being used in residential construction. Metal studs are usually either webbed or hollow. Ordinary channel iron may also be used. See *stud,* page 439.

metal ties: In masonry, a type of steel tie which is coated with portland cement and used to bond two separate wall sections together in cavity-type walls. Typical metal ties, commonly used, are shown in Fig. 376.

metal trim: Any decorative feature made out of pressed-metal sheeting, such as metal strips around door or window openings.

metal valley: A V-shaped valley or gutter between two roof slopes, lined with pieces of lead, zinc, copper, or sheet metal to prevent the leaking of water in gutters, over doors and windows, around chimneys, or any rising projection where there is danger of leakage from rain water or snow.

metal wall ties: A metal wire or strip used to bond two separate walls together.

metallic insulation: A metal, such as aluminum, which is processed into thin sheets having bright and shiny surfaces. The heat, when striking such a surface, is reflected back and does not pass through to the other side.

metalwork: Any ornamental feature shaped out of metal, such as ironwork.

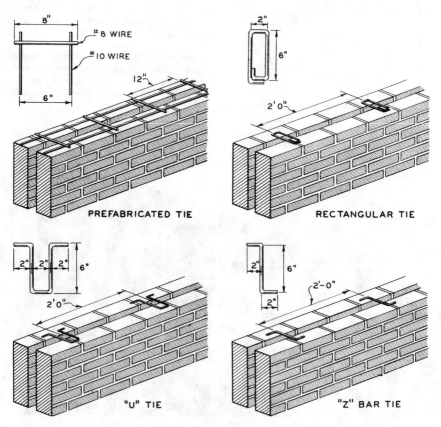

PREFABRICATED TIE

RECTANGULAR TIE

"U" TIE

"Z" BAR TIE

Fig. 376. Metal ties.

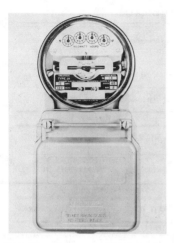

Fig. 377. Electric meter. (Sangamo Electric Co.)

meter: In electricity, a measuring instrument which records and indicates a certain value of electric current. See Fig. 377. Also: A measure in the metric system equal to 39.37 inches.

meter stop: In plumbing, a device placed on a water service-pipe to serve as a controlling stop for the building installation. See Fig. 378.

metope: In the Doric frieze, one of the square spaces, either decorated or plain, between two *triglyphs*. See Fig. 230, page 174.

metric system: Measuring system used throughout most of the world based on the centimeter-gram-second (CGS), as opposed to the *English system* used in the United States based on the foot-pound-second.

Table 2 lists factors for converting units from metric to English, while Table 3 lists factors for converting from English to metric units.

To convert a quantity from *metric* to *English* units:

1. Multiply by the factor shown in Table 2.
2. Use the resulting quantity "rounded off" to the number of decimal digits needed for practical application.
3. Wherever practical in semi-precision measurements, convert the decimal part of the number to the nearest common fraction.

To convert a quantity from *English* to *metric* units:

1. If the English measurement is expressed in fractional form, change this to an equivalent decimal form.
2. Multiply this quantity by the factor shown in Table 3.
3. Round off the result to the precision required.

Relatively small measurements, such as 17.3 cm, are generally expressed in equivalent millimeter form. In this example, the measurement would be 173 mm.

mezzanine: A low story between two higher stories, usually a gallerylike floor midway between the main floor and the next floor above it.

mezzo-relievo: Sculpture in which the relief is between alto-relievo and bas-relief; middle relief, which is intermediate between high relief and bas-relief.

microinch: A measure of one millionth of an inch.

micron: A unit of length; one-thousandth of a millimeter or one-millionth of a meter.

mid-wall column or shaft: A column or shaft standing about midway between the front and back of a wall which is thicker than the diameter of the column or shaft which supports it. The term *mid-wall shaft* is sometimes applied to a shaft dividing the lights of a belfry window.

Fig. 378. Meter stop.

285

TABLE 2 CONVERSION OF METRIC TO ENGLISH UNITS

LENGTHS:		WEIGHTS:	
1 MILLIMETER (MM)	= 0.03937 IN.	1 GRAM (G)	= 0.03527 OZ (AVDP)
1 CENTIMETER (CM)	= 0.3937 IN.	1 KILOGRAM (KG)	= 2.205 LBS
1 METER (M)	= 3.281 FT OR 1.0937 YDS	1 METRIC TON	= 2205 LBS
1 KILOMETER (KM)	= 0.6214 MILES	**LIQUID MEASUREMENTS:**	
AREAS:		1 CU CENTIMETER (CC)	= 0.06102 CU IN.
1 SQ MILLIMETER	= 0.00155 SQ IN.	1 LITER (= 1000 CC)	= 1.057 QUARTS OR 2.113 PINTS OR 61.02 CU INS.
1 SQ CENTIMETER	= 0.155 SQ IN.	**POWER MEASUREMENTS:**	
1 SQ METER	= 10.76 SQ FT OR 1.196 SQ YDS	1 KILOWATT (KW)	= 1.341 HORSEPOWER
VOLUMES:		**TEMPERATURE MEASUREMENTS:**	
1 CU CENTIMETER	= 0.06102 CU IN.	TO CONVERT DEGREES CELSIUS TO DEGREES FAHRENHEIT, USE THE FOLLOWING FORMULA: DEG F = (DEG C X 9/5) + 32.	
1 CU METER	= 35.31 CU FT OR 1.308 CU YDS		

SOME IMPORTANT FEATURES OF THE CGS SYSTEM ARE:

1 CC OF PURE WATER = 1 GRAM. PURE WATER FREEZES AT 0 DEGREES C AND BOILS AT 100 DEGREES C.

TABLE 3 CONVERSION OF ENGLISH TO METRIC UNITS

LENGTHS:		WEIGHTS:	
1 INCH	= 2.540 CENTIMETERS	1 OUNCE (AVDP)	= 28.35 GRAMS
1 FOOT	= 30.48 CENTIMETERS	1 POUND	= 453.6 GRAMS OR 0.4536 KILOGRAM
1 YARD	= 91.44 CENTIMETERS OR 0.9144 METERS	1 (SHORT) TON	= 907.2 KILOGRAMS
1 MILE	= 1.609 KILOMETERS	**LIQUID MEASUREMENTS:**	
AREAS:		1 (FLUID) OUNCE	= 0.02957 LITER OR 28.35 GRAMS
1 SQ IN.	= 6.452 SQ CENTIMETERS	1 PINT	= 473.2 CU CENTIMETERS
1 SQ FT	= 929.0 SQ CENTIMETERS OR 0.0929 SQ METER	1 QUART	= 0.9463 LITER
1 SQ YD	= 0.8361 SQ METER	1 (US) GALLON	= 3785 CU CENTIMETERS OR 3.785 LITERS
VOLUMES:		**POWER MEASUREMENTS:**	
1 CU IN.	= 16.39 CU CENTIMETERS	1 HORSEPOWER	= 0.7457 KILOWATT
1 CU FT	= 0.02832 CU METER	**TEMPERATURE MEASUREMENTS:**	
1 CU YD	= 0.7646 CU METER	TO CONVERT DEGREES FAHRENHEIT TO DEGREES CELSIUS, USE THE FOLLOWING FORMULA: DEG C = (DEG F – 32) X 5/9.	

midget trowel: See *trowel,* page 461.

mil: One-thousandth part of an inch or .001 inch.

mildew: A mold or discoloration on wood caused by parasitic fungi.

mill: In steel construction, to plane the end of a member by means of a rotary planer or milling machine.

mill scale: A rust layer that develops on reinforcing steel during the time of hot rolling in the steel mill.

millimeter: A measure of one thousandth of a meter, or .03937 inches.

millwork: In woodworking, any work which has been finished, machined, and partly assembled at the mill.

millwright: A workman who designs and sets up mills or mill machinery; also, a mechanic who installs machinery in a mill or workshop.

mineral admixture: Admixtures containing inorganic substances such as pozzolans or fly ash which are used to reduce cement requirements, heat build-up, and expansion of concrete.

mineral aggregate: In masonry work, an aggregate consisting of a mixture of broken stone, broken slag, crushed or uncrushed gravel, sand, stone, screenings, and mineral dust.

mineral wool: A type of material used for insulating buildings, produced by sending a blast of steam through molten slag or rock; common types now in use include: rock wool, glass wool, slag wool, and others.

minute of arc: A measure used by architects to find the proportion of a column; one sixtieth of a degree. See *module,* page 290.

miscellaneous iron: Steel items such as lintel angles, inserts, plates, form braces, spreaders, and other structural shapes attached to or embedded in reinforced concrete.

miter: The joining of two pieces at an evenly divided angle, as the joint in the corner of a picture frame. See Fig. 330, page 252.

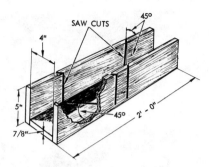

Fig. 379. Miter box.

miter box: A device used by a carpenter for guiding a handsaw at the proper angle for cutting a miter joint in wood. The carpenter usually makes his own *miter box* on the job, Fig. 379.

miter cut: In carpentry, a cut made at an angle for joining two pieces of board so cut that they will form an angle.

miter plane: A tool used for any type of utility work where a joint is made without overlapping of the boards, as in butt or miter joints.

miter rods or joint rods: In plastering, miter rods are pieces of metal from 2″ to 24″ long, 4″ wide, and $\frac{1}{16}$″ thick. Miter rods are used to form and shape joints and miters in cornice work. Fig. 380 illustrates a miter or joint rod being used with a pointing trowel to form a straight line down a cornice miter.

miter saw: A relatively long hacksaw having fine teeth and a stiffening piece along the upper edge or back. Often used in adjustable metal miter boxes. See *tenon saw,* page 449.

mitering: The joining of two pieces of board at an evenly divided angle; joining two boards by using a miter joint. See Fig. 330, page 252.

mix design: The process of selecting proportions of cement, water and fine and coarse aggregates to produce concrete that is workable and meets the specifications for its intended use.

Fig. 380. Cutting a straight line through the intersection.

mix water: The water in freshly mixed sand-cement grout, mortar or concrete, exclusive of any absorbed by the aggregate.

mixed grain: Any combination of edge grain and flat grain.

mock rafter: In the construction of an open cornice, a short piece of timber used to give the appearance of a real rafter. Usually it is sawed so as to give a decorative effect. Also called *rafter studs* or *rafter ends*.

modeling tools: See *small tools,* page 410.

models: In architecture, models are a supplementary means of checking the graphical description shown on the plan, elevations, and perspective. They aid in the visualization of the finished appearance of the proposed structure and its room arrangement. Usually, models are built to a small scale and incorporate as much detail as possible to achieve a realistic effect. Fig. 381 shows a display model.

modified wood: Wood processed to impart properties different from those of the original wood.

O'DELL, HEWETT, AND LUCKENBACH, ASSOCIATES, ARCHITECTS; BIRMINGHAM, MICHIGAN

Fig. 381: This figure shows a display model of the Oakland County Courthouse, Michigan. Note the use of scale model figures and automobiles in the foreground.

modillion: In classic architecture, an ornamental block or bracket placed under the corona of the cornice.

modular: A structural system designed to have the parts fit together on a grid of a standard module. See *modular measure.*

modular brick: Brick which are designed for use in walls built in accordance with the modular dimensions of four inches.

modular construction: Any building construction in which the size of the building materials used is based upon a common unit of measure, known as the *modular dimension.* Also: a complete room or part of a house with all piping and fixtures installed. See *modular measure.* Fig. 382 illustrates modular construction.

modular dimensions: Building material and equipment, based upon a common unit of measure of 4 inches, known as the module.

This *module* is used as a basis for the *grid* which is essential for dimensional coordination of two or more different materials. Fig. 383 illustrates four-inch modular application.

modular masonry: Masonry construction in which the size of the building material used, such as brick or tile, is based upon common units of measure, known as the *modular dimensionals.*

modular measure: Considerable confusion has resulted in the use of the terms *module, modular measure,* and *modular construction.* The term *modular measure* relates to a simplified dimensional system which coordinates building layout to stock unit sizes of building materials. A *module* in this sense is a 4-inch unit generally thought of as a cube. *Modular construction* is a system of building with prefabrication units which are called *modules.* Each "box" is a module and may be a complete kitchen or

289

Fig. 382. Modules are three-dimensional building units which can be positioned on the foundation. (National Homes Corporation)

bathroom or even a half of a house. The modules are delivered to the job and installed with a crane or slid into position.

module: A unit of measurement commonly established at 4 inches. A complete part of a building assembled in a shop, such as a bathroom or kitchen. See Fig. 384. (Fig. 382 also illustrates a module being installed.)

modulus of elasticity: The ratio of normal stress to corresponding strain for tensile or compressive stresses below the proportional limit of the material; referred to as "elastic modulus," "Young's modulus," and "Young's modulus of elasticity"; denoted by the symbol E.

modulus of rupture: A measure of the ultimate load-carrying capacity of a beam and sometimes referred to as "rupture strength". It is calculated for apparent tensile stress in the extreme fiber of a transverse test specimen under the load which produces rupture.

moist cure: Curing of concrete in an area at a selected temperature (usually 23.0 ± 1.7 C or 73.4 ± 3.0 F) and relative humidity of at least 98% or more.

moisture barrier: Any material which is used to retard the passage or flow of vapor or moisture into walls and thus prevent condensation within them. Also called a *vapor barrier.*

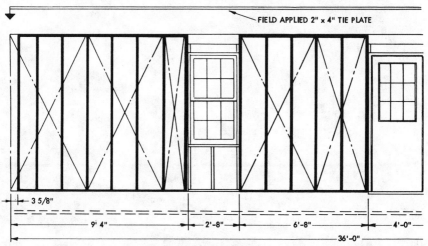

Fig. 383. "Unicom" panels are made in units which are multiples of 4 inches in width.

moisture content in wood: The amount of moisture in wood, usually expressed as percentage of the dry weight of wood; abbreviated as MC.

moisture expansion: In building, the increase in volume of a material from the absorption of moisture. See *bulking,* page 76.

moisture gradient: A condition of graduated moisture content between the inner and outer portions of a material, such as wood, due to the loss or absorption of moisture. See *fiber saturation point,* page 184.

moisture proofing: A term applied to the process of making a material resistant to change in moisture content, especially to the entrance or absorption of moisture or vapor.

mold: Device used in plastering to contour cornices, miters, and other surfaces. Fig. 385 illustrates the use of a simple cornice mold.

molded belt course: A type of construction used to protect the lower part of a wall which is covered with two different kinds of material. Such a belt course is formed by placing blocks of wood, cut to the required shape, at intervals against the outside wall to support a molding placed where the two materials meet. See Fig. 55, page 47.

molding: A strip of wood or metal, either plain or curved, formed into long, regular channels or projections, used for finishing and decorative purposes. See Fig. 640, page 488. *Molding* can be bought in many different sizes and shapes.

molding cap: A molding used at the top of a door or window trim to relieve its plainness.

molding plane: A small tool used in furniture making for cutting molding into various sizes, shapes, and widths.

molding plaster: This is a selection of calcined gypsum ground very fine. It has a very fine powdery form which brings out details in ornamental trim, cornices, and cast work. For running cornices, slaked lime is added for plasticity and as a lubricant for the template.

moldings, ornamental: Moldings enriched with decorative designs are of a great variety of patterns; included among the most common are: *chevrons* or *zig-zag, egg and dart, leaf and dart, dogtooth, honeysuckle, guilloche.*

molly expansion anchor: A type of metal fastener, consisting of a bolt encased in a shell which expands, wedging itself into a

291

Fig. 384. A bathroom module is hoisted to its position in a motel building (top). A module is rolled to its final position in the building (bottom). (The American Group Incorporated)

Fig. 385. Final run of the mold to finish the cornice.

hole drilled to receive it; used principally for securing structural wood parts to a concrete or masonry wall. See *anchors*, Fig. 18, page 17.

monial: A vertical bar between window lights or screens. The same as *mullion*.

monolith: A single detached block of stone, especially one of large size shaped into a column or monument; a shaft or column cut out of a single block of stone and not built up of drums.

monolithic: Pertaining to a hollow foundation piece constructed of masonry, with a number of open walls passing through it. The wells are finally filled with concrete to form a solid foundation. A term applied to any concrete structure made of a continuous mass of material or cast as a single piece.

montriglyphic: The mode of intercolumniation which, in the Doric order, requires the spaced use of one triglyph and two metopes in the entablature above; or, as is said of the usual intercolumniation of the Doric entablature, having only one triglyph to the portion of the frieze over the space between two columns. See Fig. 5, page 4.

mop board: In building, a finishing board covering the edge of a plastered wall where the wall and floor meet. Same as *baseboard*.

mortar: In masonry, a pasty building material, composed of sand and lime, or cement mixed with water, which gradually hardens when exposed to the air. *Mortar* is used as a joining medium in brick and stone construction.

mortar bed: A thick layer of plastic mortar in which is seated any structural member, such as a brick. See Fig. 386.

mortar board: In masonry, a small square board with a handle underneath, on which a mason holds his mortar. Same as *hawk*, Fig. 308, page 233.

mortar box: In plastering, a box in which plaster or mortar is mixed.

mortar color: Any special pigment which is used to color mortar. The colors commonly used for this purpose include black, buff, chocolate, green, and red.

mortar cube: A 2-in. cube composed of 1 part cement and 2.75 parts sand by weight. The sand is a graded Ottawa silica sand,

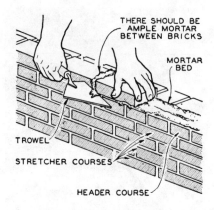

Fig. 386. Laying a brick in a mortar bed.

Fig. 387. Mortise lock. (Sargent and Co.)

and the water requirement is determined experimentally.

mortar joints: Joints which represent a wide range of types in finishing the mortar in stone or brick work. See *weathered joint, flush joint, exposed joint, struck joint, concave joint,* and *V joint.* See, also, Fig. 333, page 254.

mortar mixer: A machine which mixes mortar by means of rotating paddles in a drum. Usually these machines are power-driven, and sometimes a large one is mounted on the back of a truck. The truck-mounted machine mixes the mortar as it travels to the job and also transports the mortar to various locations where needed on the job.

mortar sand: A type of sand that contains only very small particles, used especially for the mortar when laying bricks; sand that will all pass through a #8 sieve (eight openings per linear inch).

mortar staining: Splatterings of fresh or hardened cement paste.

mortise: In woodworking, a cavity cut in a piece of wood, or timber, to receive a tenon, or tongue, projecting from another piece; for example, a mortise-and-tenon joint.

mortise and tenon: A joint made by connecting two pieces of wood; the projecting part of one piece fits into the corresponding cutout on the other piece.

mortise bolt: A bolt housed in a mortise in a door flush with the edge of the door.

mortise chisel: A tool used in wood working for cutting mortises; a heavy-bodied chisel with a narrow face.

mortise gage: A carpenter's tool consisting of a head and bar containing two scratch pins which may be adjusted for scribing parallel lines for cutting mortises to whatever width may be desired.

mortise joint: A joint made by a mortise and tenon.

mortise lock: A lock made to fit into a mortise in the edge of a door. A *mortise lock* is shown in Fig. 387.

mortising machine: A carpenter's tool used for cutting mortises in wood, either by using a chisel or a circular cutting bit.

mosaic: A combination of small colored stones, glass, or other material so arranged as to form a decorative surface design. Usually the various pieces are inlaid in a ground of cement or stucco.

mosaic work: In building, a design formed of inlaid work on plaster with the use of small irregular-shaped fragments of marble, glazed pottery, or glass; also, small cubes called *tessrae* are used for this type of work. See *mosaic.*

motion study: In masonry, a term applied to a study of the movements made by workmen in performing certain operations. Such a study is made with the purpose of increasing the efficiency of mechanics by eliminating all unnecessary motions.

mount: A fitted piece used to strengthen a structural member, designed so as to also add a decorative feature.

M roof: In architecture, a type of roof formed by the junction of two common gable roofs, with a valley between them, so the sections represent the letter M.

mucking: The adjusting of steel bars during placement of concrete.

mud: In plastering, a special plaster with additives to control setting and hardness; used to fix joints in drywall and to cover nail holes. Sometimes used to patch plaster cracks.

mud holder: In plastering, the mud holder is a hawk 12″ x 6″ with a lip on one side and a handle fastened to the underside. The plasterer uses this to carry mud to his work. See Fig. 388.

mud mixer: In plastering, a portable, electric mixer used for mixing *mud*. They come in sizes of "one bag" or "three bags". The mud mixer's impellers are shaped so as to blend the mixes without drawing too much air into the mix. Similar to a *lime mixer*.

mudsill: The lowest sill of a structure, as a foundation timber placed directly on the ground or foundation.

mud slab: A 2- to 6-in. layer of concrete below structural concrete floor or footing over soft, wet soil.

mullion: In architecture, the division between multiple windows or screens. Sometimes this term is confused with *muntin*. (See Fig. 634, page 484.)

multifoil: A decorative feature, or leaf ornament, having more than five divisions applied to foils in windows.

Fig. 388. Mud holder. (Goldblatt Tool Co.)

muntin: The small members that divide glass in a window frame; vertical separators between panels in a panel door. (See Fig. 637, page 484.)

N

nail: A slender piece of metal pointed at one end for driving into wood and flat or rounded at the other end for striking with a hammer; used as a wood fastener by carpenters and other construction workers. The sizes of nails are indicated by the term *penny* (d), which originally indicated the price per hundred but now refers to the length. Although the sizes of nails may vary as much as $\frac{1}{8}$ to $\frac{1}{4}$ inch from that indicated, the approximate lengths as sold on the market are:

    4d nail = $1\frac{1}{4}$ inches
    6d nail = 2 inches
    8d nail = $2\frac{1}{2}$ inches
  10d nail = 3 inches
  20d nail = 4 inches
  60d nail = 6 inches

Nails are divided into two general types: wire and cut nails. Nails are specified as to size (penny), type (wire or cut), type of head, point and shank, and type of coating. *Common nails* (Fig. 389) are available from 2d to 60d in length. As their name implies, they are the most commonly used kind of nail and usually will be supplied if no other specification is made. They are used when the appearance of the work is not important, for example, in the framing-in of houses and building of concrete forms.

Finish nails (Fig. 389) are available in lengths from 2d to 20d. The head is barrel shaped and has a slight recess in the top. As the name implies, these nails are used

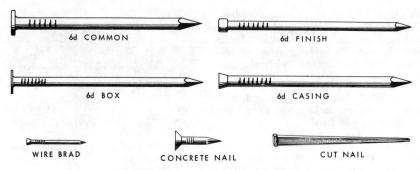

Fig. 389. Commonly used types of nails.

for finished work where the final appearance is of importance, such as trimming in buildings, cupboards, and cabinets, as are any nails with small heads. The small head is intended to be sunk into the wood with a nail set.

Roofing nails (Fig. 390) are not specified by the penny system. They are available in lengths from ¾ inch to 2 inches and have large heads.

Shingle nails (Fig. 390) are sized from 3d to 6d. They are used for cedar shingles and have thin shanks with small heads. Two nails are used for each shingle.

For different types of nails, nailheads, nail points, and nail shanks, see Figs. 389 to 393. See also *annular, box, clout, common, concrete, double head, finish, gypsum board, masonry, ratchet, roofing,* and *shingle nails.*

nailer, air: An automatic air operated ma-

chine which drives large nails at a greater rate of speed than hand nailing. See Fig. 394.

nail-glued roof truss: A glued truss with plywood gusset plates that uses nails to hold it together, only until the glue dries. A few hours after assembly, the strength of the truss bonds depend on the glue alone. Grade A casein glue is applied with a specially designed spreader to members whose design specifications must be followed exactly to get proper stresses. This truss requires no special joining or cutting and is stronger than conventional truss designs, showing less deflection under test loads.

nailhead molding: An enrichment suggestive of nailheads, consisting of a series of low, four-sided pyramids. A simple form of dogtooth ornament.

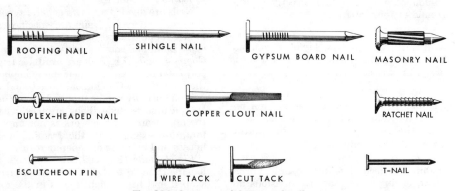

Fig. 390. Some special types of nails.

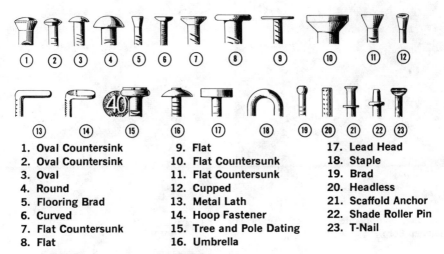

1. Oval Countersink	9. Flat	17. Lead Head
2. Oval Countersink	10. Flat Countersunk	18. Staple
3. Oval	11. Flat Countersunk	19. Brad
4. Round	12. Cupped	20. Headless
5. Flooring Brad	13. Metal Lath	21. Scaffold Anchor
6. Curved	14. Hoop Fastener	22. Shade Roller Pin
7. Flat Countersunk	15. Tree and Pole Dating	23. T-Nail
8. Flat	16. Umbrella	

Fig. 391. Different types of nail head available.

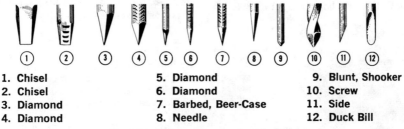

1. Chisel	5. Diamond	9. Blunt, Shooker
2. Chisel	6. Diamond	10. Screw
3. Diamond	7. Barbed, Beer-Case	11. Side
4. Diamond	8. Needle	12. Duck Bill

Fig. 392. Different types of nail points.

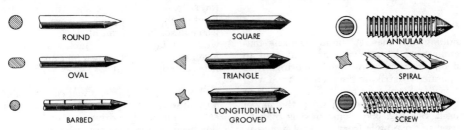

Fig. 393. Different types of nail shanks available.

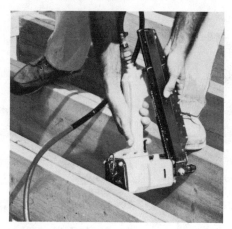

Fig. 394. Air-operated nailer. (Duo-Fast Fastener Corp.)

nailing block: A nailing base for material, usually a small block of wood.

nailing clips: Nailing clips are sometimes used to connect joists to steel beams and channels. This type of clip comes in various sizes to fit the steel beam used. Fig. 395.

Fig. 396. Nailing machines used for flooring. (Duo-Fast Fastener Corp.)

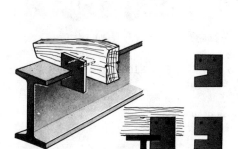

Fig. 395. Nailing clips.

nailing machines: A manual nailing machine used for applying underlayment to floors and for laying finish flooring. It is operated by striking the plunger knob with a mallet. Staples up to 1⅛ to 1¾ inch long may be used, depending upon the model used. See Fig. 396. Some models may be used to drive nails from 1¼ to 2 inches in length.

nailing strips: Pieces of wood such as furring strips to which lath or ceiling material, or plaster grounds, or flooring may be nailed. See *furring strips,* page 211.

nail pops: Where small areas of plaster directly over nail heads pop off, exposing the nail head.

nail puller: Any small punch bar suitable for prying purposes, with a V-shaped or forked end which can be slipped under the head of a nail for prying it loose from the wood; also, a mechanical device provided with two jaws, one of which serves as a leverage heel for gripping a nail and prying it loose from a board.

nail punch: A carpenter's tool consisting of a small steel rod, tapering almost to a point at one end; used to drive in a nail so that the head is sunk beneath the surface of the wood. See *nail set.*

nail set: A tool usually made from a solid bar of high-grade tool steel, measuring about 4 inches in length; used to set the heads of nails below the surface of wood. One end of the tool is drawn to a taper, and the head is so shaped there is slight possibility of the device slipping off the head of a nail. Both ends are polished, body machine knurled. See Fig. 397.

Fig. 397. Nail set.

naked wall: In plastering, a term applied to a wall which is lathed ready for the plastering; an unplastered, lathed wall.

National Association of Home Builders (NAHB): This is an organization of large and small builders of single family and multi-family dwellings.

National Electrical Code (NEC): A set of standards covering the design and manufacture of electrical devices and materials and the manner of their installation. All wiring should conform with the NEC and local codes as well.

natural aggregates: Sand, gravel, or crushed stones that are obtained from quarries or gravel pits.

natural beds: The surface of stone as it lies in the quarry. In stratified rocks, if the walls are not laid in their natural bed, the laminae, or scales, separate.

natural cement: A cement made from a natural earth requiring but little preparation; similar to hydraulic lime.

natural finish: A transparent finish which does not seriously change the original color or grain of the wood.

natural foundation: In building, a foundation in soil which requires no preparation, as the driving of piles to make an effective foundation for supporting the structure it is to carry.

natural grade: The elevation of the original or undisturbed surface of the ground.

natural seasoning: A term applied to the process of seasoning lumber by exposure to air. Cut timbers are stacked to permit free circulation of air around each timber.

nave: The main portion of a church; that is, the central part extending from the choir between the side columns back to the main entrance.

neat cement: In masonry, a pure cement uncut by a sand admixture.

neat plaster: A term applied to plaster made without sand.

neat work: In masonry, the brickwork above the footings.

nebule: In architecture, a term applied to an ornamental molding consisting of an overhang band characterized by a wavy lower edge.

neck: In architecture, that part of a column immediately below the capital and directly above the astragal at the head of the shaft. See Fig. 230, page 174.

neck mold: In architecture, a molding placed around the neck of the shaft of a column where the shaft joins the cap; also called neck molding. See Fig. 79, page 64.

neck of hammer: That part of the *head* of a claw hammer between the *poll* and the *cheek*. See Fig. 127, page 101.

necking: In architecture, any narrow molding encircling a column near the head, between the stop of the shaft and the projecting part of the capital; also called *gorgerin*. See Fig. 5, page 4.

needle: In building construction, a term applied to a short stout timber, steel, or iron beam which is passed through a wall horizontally to support the end of a shoring timber.

299

needle bath: In plumbing, a term applied to a type of bathroom fixture having pipes which are perforated and arranged in such a manner that sprays of water will strike a bather from practically every direction; often used in connection with a shower bath.

needle beam: In building, a horizontal timber, such as a beam or girder, on which a wall rests when needles are used to shore a building while it is being repaired; also called *needle girder*.

neoclassic architecture: Pertaining to a revival of classic style, beginning with the Italian Renaissance of the fifteenth century; the architecture of modern times, especially that which is studied from Greco-Roman examples.

nest of saws: A set of saw blades intended for use in the same handle, which is detachable. Such a collection of thin, narrow-bladed saws usually consists of one or more compass saws and a keyhole saw designed primarily for cutting out small holes, such as keyholes. See Fig. 336, page 256.

net absorption: In lumber, the amount of preservative left in the wood after the treating operation is completed.

network: In electricity, a number of electrical circuits and distribution lines which are interconnected for distribution of electrical energy.

new wood: A term used to indicate wood which has never before been finished nor worked by tools.

newel: In architecture, an upright post supporting the handrail at the top and bottom of a stairway or at the turn on a landing; also, the main post about which a circular staircase winds; sometimes called the *newel post*. See Fig. 561, page 424.

newel cap: An ornamental finish placed on top of a newel post.

newel drop: A decorative finish at the lower end of a newel post, above ground level.

newel joints: The joints which connect the newel post with the handrail of a stair.

newel post: The principal post at the foot of a stairway or a secondary one at a landing; the lowest or first step of stairs at the point where the handrail starts or is received; the upright post which supports the string and handrail. See Fig. 561, page 424.

newel stair: A term applied to a stairway which has newels at the angles to receive the ends of the string. Also, spiral stairs having the inner or smaller ends of the treads engaged in a solid core.

niche: A niche is a recess or hollow in a wall formed to hold various decorative figures and at one time was popular as a telephone receptacle. The niche may be semi-circular, elliptical, or practically any shape desired.

night bolt: A door lock having a spring bolt which cannot be operated from the outside except by use of a key. It is operated from the inside with a knob. It is fitted with a device which prevents operation from either side.

night latch: A door lock having a bolt which is operated with a key on the outside and with a knob on the inside but is fitted with a device for preventing operation from either side. Same as *night bolt*.

nippers: Nippers (also called end cutting pliers) are small pincers used for holding, breaking, or cutting. See Fig. 398. Two types of nippers are used. One has solid jaws; the other has removable jaws which can be replaced after wear.

nipple: In plumbing, a short length of pipe threaded externally at both ends, for fitting into and connecting two lengths of internally threaded pipes.

nogging: In masonry, the filling in with bricks of the spaces between timbers, such as studding in walls and partitions.

Fig. 398. Nippers.

noiseproof: A term applied to a building or room which has been insulated so that the walls, floors, and ceilings are resistant to noise or sound. The same as *soundproof*.

nominal: Approximate; not actual.

nominal size: The commercial size given a piece of lumber, or other material, by the trade other than its actual size. For example, the actual size of a 2 x 8 board is $1\frac{1}{2}''$ x $7\frac{1}{4}''$.

nonbearing partition: A wall which divides a space into rooms and does not carry the load of the floor or floors above.

nonbearing wall: One which supports no vertical load except that of its own weight. See *wall,* page 474.

noncombustible materials: Any material which does not burn or is incombustible; hence, has fire-resistive properties.

nook shaft: A shaft or column set in the nook or recess of a jamb; differing from an *angle shaft* in standing free and, therefore, usually is larger.

normal weight concrete: The type of concrete we are most familiar with; commonly used for sidewalks, pavements, etc., and weights around 140 to 160 pounds per cubic foot.

Norman brick: A *solid masonry unit* $2\frac{1}{4}''$ x $3\frac{5}{8}''$ x $12''$. See Fig. 85, page 69.

Norman style: A Romanesque style of architecture introduced and fully developed in England after the Normans had established themselves there. Plainness and massiveness are the chief characteristics of the style practiced by the Normans. The pillars were very massive and often were built up of small stones like brickwork. The arches, doorways, and windows were semicircular.

northlight roof: A type of pitched roof having unequal slopes of which the steeper slope is glazed and so arranged as to receive only light from the north, as an artist's studio.

nose-and-miter: In stair building, a return nosing which is mitered onto the tread of an open stair.

nose key: A wedge for spreading the edges of a tenon into a dovetail which holds the joint together. Same as *fox wedge*.

nose plate: In builders' hardware, a small metal plate which surrounds the nose of a cylinder lock.

nosing: That portion of the stair tread that extends beyond the face of the riser. See Fig. 561, page 424.

nosing strip: In stair building, a type of nosing matching the nosing of the stair treads; used around the wellhole.

notch: A crosswise rabbet at the end of a board.

notchboard: In stair building, the board which receives the ends of the steps in a staircase. Sometimes called a *housed stringer*.

notching: In carpentry, a method of joining scantlings or other timbers by cutting notches, usually at the ends, then overlapping or interlocking the notched pieces to form a joint.

novelty flooring: In carpentry, flooring laid in unusual or strange patterns.

novelty siding: In carpentry, a drop siding which has an unusual design, as a *German siding*.

nulling: In Jacobean architecture, a type of decorative detail carved on friezes and moldings; quadrant shaped in section.

O

oakum: Hemp or untwisted rope used for calking joints. See Fig. 105, page 83.

obelisk: A four-sided shaft of stone, usually monolithic, tapering as it rises and terminating in a pyramid at the apex.

oblique drawing: A drawing in which all lines in the front face are shown in their true lengths and in their true relations to one another. Lines not in the plane of the front face, nor perpendicular to it, are drawn at any convenient angle other than 90 degrees. See Fig. 421, page 322.

oblique joint: A joint in which one of the members has a beveled cut where it butts against the other; a beveled butt joint. Also called an *oblique butt joint*.

oblique perspective: See *three-point perspective,* page 452.

obscuration: In painting, the covering of a surface with an opaque paint or finishing material; also, the covering power of a paint or enamel.

O.C. On Center: Measurement from the center of one building member to another, as spacing of joists or studs.

octagon: A polygon having eight angles and consequently eight sides.

octagon scale: A rafter-framing table usually found on the tongue of a steel framing square; used for laying out an octagon. Also called *octagon table.* See Fig. 570, page 431.

octastyle: In architecture, a term applied to a structure having eight columns in front, as a temple or portico. Also spelled *octostyle.*

odeum: In architecture, a small gallery or hall used for musical or dramatic performances; in ancient Greek, a small roofed theater.

offset: A term used in building when referring to a set-off such as a sunken panel in a wall or a recess of any kind; also, a horizontal ledge on a wall formed by the diminishing of the thickness of the wall at that point.

offset pipe: In pipe work of any kind, a section of pipe which leads around some obstacle. See Fig. 112, page 89.

ogee: A molding with an S-shaped curve formed by the union of a concave and convex line; that is, a cyma recta or cyma reversa. See Fig. 174, page 136.

ogee arch: A type of arch which has a compound curve, partly concave and partly convex; a term applied to both arches and moldings. See *cyma,* Fig. 174, page 136.

ogive: In architecture, a diagonal rib crossing a Gothic vault; a term used in furniture making when referring to a pointed arch.

ohm: The unit of electrical resistance. The current in an electric circuit is equal to the pressure divided by the resistance. This is known as Ohm's law.

oil bloom: In painting and lacquer work, an iridescent appearance usually due to the polishing or rubbing of a surface with a material containing free oil which floats to the surface of the film.

oil varnish: In wood finishing, a varnish containing a drying oil such as linseed, china wood, cotton seed, poppy seed, soya bean, castor oil, or tung oil. The hardening process takes place slowly through oxidation.

oilslip: A term used by woodworkers when referring to a small unmounted oilstone held in the hand while they sharpen the cutting edges of gouges.

oilstone: A fine-grained whetstone, the surface of which is moistened with oil, for sharpening tools.

old English bond: In masonry work, a bond consisting of alternating courses of stretchers and headers, with a *closer* laid next to the corner bricks in every course of headers. See *English bond,* Fig. 73, page 60.

old wood: A term applied to wood which has been worked by tools previously and is again being used for some other purpose.

on center: A term used in taking measurements, meaning the distance from the center of one structural member to the center of a corresponding member (O.C.), as in the spacing of studding, girders, joists, or other structural members. Same as *center to center* (C to C).

one-fourth pitch: In roof framing, a roof pitch which has a rise equal to one-fourth the width of the span.

one-half pitch: in roof framing, a roof pitch having a rise which is equal to one-half the width of the span.

one-point perspective: A form of pictorial drawing with two principal axes parallel to the picture plane forming only one vanishing point. See Fig. 421, page 322.

one-third pitch: In roof framing, a roof pitch which has a rise equal to one third of the width of the span.

one-way floor and roof system: In reinforced concrete construction, one of two major classes of floor and roof systems. The one-way system includes a *solid slab* supported by reinforced girders which run parallel in one direction supported by columns. See Fig. 399. There may also be intermediate beams at right angles to the girders. A *one-way joist floor,* also called a *one-way ribbed floor,* with narrow beams or joists closely spaced is a variation. See Fig. 400. The one-way joist floor is constructed using steel pans to form the voids in the floor or may use structural clay or other tile units between the ribs. One-way systems are versatile to meet the needs of many different loading problems and are relatively easy to calculate. The floor and beams are poured to make a monolithic structure. Still another variation of the one-way system makes use of *precast pretensioned floor units.* (See Fig. 451, page 348.) See also *two-way floor and roof system,* page 466, for the other major system.

onyx marble: A variety of marble which takes a high polish and is valuable as a building stone.

open-corner fireplace: A fireplace of which two adjacent sides are open. Important factors which differ from conventional fireplace construction considerations are flue capacity and cross draft. A ¼″ steel plate usually supports the corner overhang, extending back beyond the corbeled abutment. Angle iron and plate rest on the cap of a steel column.

open cornice: A cornice in which the rafter overhang is exposed in contrast to the *closed cornice.* See Fig. 401.

open grain: A term which painters commonly apply to wood having large pores. Also called *coarse textured.*

open mortise: A slot cut in the end of a piece of wood, open at both edges and one end; a term applied to a type of joint which has an open slot cut in the end of one piece to accommodate a tenon cut on the end of another piece.

open-newel stair: In stair building, a stairway laid out so as to use two landings, with a short flight of steps between them, and newel posts at the angles. Also called *hollow newel stair.*

open-planning millwork: Some millwork stock includes special profiles for use in large window area and open modular planning constructions, where framing members are often used as finish members.

open socket: See *cable attachments,* page 80.

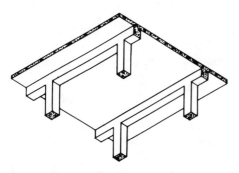

Fig. 399. Solid slab construction.

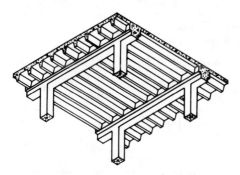

Fig. 400. One-way joist construction.

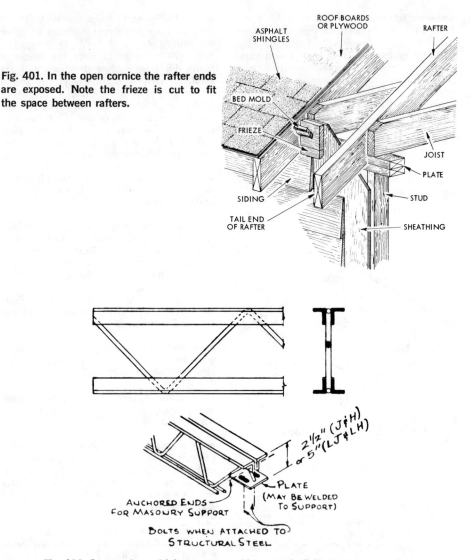

Fig. 401. In the open cornice the rafter ends are exposed. Note the frieze is cut to fit the space between rafters.

Fig. 402. Open web steel joists support wide spans in light steel construction.

open stairway: A stair which has one or both sides open to a room or hall. A balustrade or handrail is commonly used on the open side or sides. Stairways, in ascending, sometimes change from an open to a closed stairway near the top; a stairway with no walls on the sides as opposed to a *closed stairway.*

open-string stairs: Stairs which are so constructed that the ends of the treads are visible from the side, as opposed to *closed-string stairs*. See Fig. 561, page 424.

open valley: In roof framing, a valley where the shingles are laid back two inches from the *splash rib* of the metal flashing which covers the joint where two sloping roofs meet.

open web joist: A joist made up of light metal members and bars. See Fig. 402.

open-web studs: Studs made of open-web steel, which permit pass-through of plumbing pipes and vents, electrical conduit, without notching or cutting. Studs snap into place in base and ceiling runners. See *stud,* page 439.

open-well stair: A stairway of two or more flights enclosing a clear, vertical, open space between the outer sides of the flights.

open wiring: Electric wires fastened to surfaces by the use of porcelain knobs; a circuit supported by insulators. Wiring which is not concealed.

openwork: Any type of construction which shows openings through the substance of which the surface is formed, especially ornamental designs of wood, metal, stone, or other materials.

optimum moisture: The moisture content (in percentage) at which soil can be compacted to maximum density.

orange peel: In painting, a term applied to a pebble effect in sprayed coats of paint or lacquer similar to the peel of an orange. This is caused by too much air pressure, holding the gun too close to the surface, spraying lacquer which is cooler than room temperature, or using a thinner which dries too quickly and prevents the proper flow of the solids.

order: A type of column and its entablature considered as a unit of style in architecture, such as those used by the ancient Greeks: Doric, Ionic, and Corinthian, each distinguished by its particular style of entablature. For capitals of different orders of classical architecture see Fig. 403.

order of an arch: One ring of stones or bricks in an arch. An arch is said to be of *several orders* if the arch consists of a number of concentric rings.

orders of architecture: Classical architecture includes five orders, three used by the ancient Greeks—Doric, Ionic, and Corinthian—and two added by the Romans—Tuscan and Composite.

ordinary construction: A term usually applied to construction in which the exterior walls are of masonry, or of reinforced concrete, with the interior structural elements wholly or partly of wood.

organic materials: Substances that came originally from living plants or animals. These include fats, petroleum products, sugars, coal, wood, etc. All of these contain the chemical element carbon.

oriel: In architecture, a window projecting from the outer face of a wall, especially an upper story, and supported by brackets or corbels.

oriel window: A window or group of windows projecting from the main line of an enclosing wall of a building and carried on brackets, corbels, or a cantilever.

orientation: The direction which a building faces.

orifice: A small opening, as at the end of a vent pipe or any similar mouthlike aperture.

ornament: In architecture and furniture making, any decorative detail added to enhance the beauty or elegance of the design.

ornamental facing: Principles of integrated design gaining wide acceptance are resulting in greater variety in the use of construction units, in ornamental pattern effects for inside and outside walls. Some of the materials include tile, specially cast and ornamented concrete block, brick, logs, wooden boards, cast-iron grilles, and pebble mosaic. Spacing and positioning are varied to produce unusual effects which help to integrate the appearance, function, and surroundings of the structures.

ornamental slating: In building construction, a slating material which has a decorative pattern or diamondlike arrangement.

ornamental tools: See *small tools,* page 411.

305

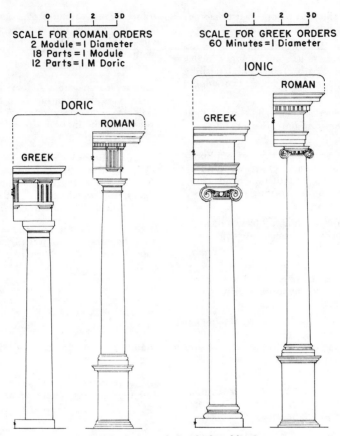

Fig. 403. Orders of classical architecture.

ornamentation: In masonry, a design formed by the laying of stone, brick, or tile so as to produce a decorative effect.

orthograph: In architecture, a drawing which shows an elevation view of a building or a part of a building. See *orthographic projection.*

orthographic projection: In architecture, the arrangement in a drawing of the various views of a building, or sections of a building, so the projecting lines are perpendicular to the plane of projection. See Fig. 404.

orthography: In the building trade, a geometrical elevation of a structure which is represented as it actually exists and in perspective as it would appear to the observer.

orthostyle: In architecture, the placing of a series of columns in a straight row.

OSHA: Occupational Safety and Health Act of 1970.

outer string: In a staircase, the string farthest from the wall.

outlet: A point in an electric wiring system where current is drawn to supply a lighting fixture or appliance. See Fig. 405. Also: an opening serving to direct the discharge of a liquid.

outlet box: A metal box placed at the end of a conduit system where electric wires are joined to one another and to the fixtures. See Fig. 406.

306

CORINTHIAN

ROMAN

GREEK

TUSCAN
ROMAN

Fig. 403. Orders of classical architecture. (Cont'd.)

outline: A line which marks or bounds the outside of a figure or object; a sketch or drawing showing a contour line.

out-of-center: In carpentry work, a term applied to a structural member which is not properly centered.

out-of-plumb: In construction work, a term used when referring to a structural member which is not in alignment but true.

out-of-true: In shopworking and the building trade, a term used when there is a twist or any other irregularity in the alignment of a form; also, a varying from exactness in a structural part.

out-of-wind: In masonry, to be free of hollows or bulges in a wall.

outrigger: A projecting beam used in connection with overhanging roofs. A support for rafters in cases where roofs extend two or more feet beyond the walls of a house.

outside architrave: Pieces of finished lumber placed around a window opening to serve as a stop for the outside wall covering. Also called *outside trim*. See *outside casing*.

outside casing: Pieces of finished lumber placed around the outside of a window opening to serve as a stop for the outside

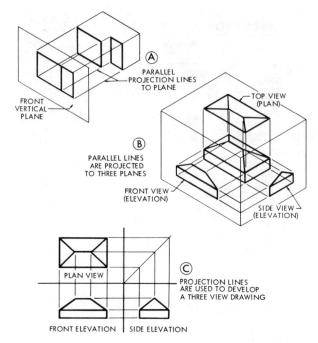

Fig. 404. Orthographic projection: A three view drawing is visualized from a pictorial representation.

wall covering. Sometimes called *outside trim* or *outside architrave.* See Fig. 198.

outside corner trowel: This trowel is constructed the same as the inside corner trowel except in reverse. Its size is 6" long, 2½" wide. This is an ideal tool for freehanding arrises for exposed aggregates. See *trowels,* page 461.

outside foundation line: A line which indicates the location of the outside of the foundation wall for a new building. See *batter board,* Fig. 51, page 42.

outside gouge: In woodworking, a type of gouge where the bevel is ground on the convex or outside face.

outside studding plate: A plate, either the sole or the double top plate, of an exterior wall. Usually it is the same size as the studding in the wall.

over-all: In the building trades, a term used to designate the total or outer dimension of any material used in the construction process. See *over-all width.*

over-all width: The total width of a piece of dressed-and-matched or shiplapped lumber, including the width of the tongue or lap. The amount of such lumber required to cover a given area should not be computed on the basis of the over-all width, since the tongue or lap is the means of joining the pieces and does not cover any surface.

overburden: Loose earth covering a building site.

overflow pipe: In plumbing, a pipe provided to carry off excess water from a tank; also, an emergency outlet for a tank.

Fig. 405. Electrical outlets and symbols.

Fig. 406. Making a splice in a ceiling outlet box with insulated wire connector. (Minnesota Mining and Manufacturing Co.)

overgraining: In painting, a term used when referring to a coat of graining color, usually mixed with beer as a drier; applied over grating work so as to produce shades across it.

overhand work: In masonry, work performed on the outside of a wall from a scaffold constructed on the inside of the wall.

overhang: The projection of a roof or upper story of a building beyond the wall of the lower part, as the *overhang* of a roof. See *shade line* for the overhang width, page 399.

overhanging eaves: A type of roof in which the rafters and roofing extend two or more feet beyond the exterior face of a building. Often used for ornamental effect and to guard against snow and rain. The wide overhang of such eaves permits freer use of window walls. They cast a large shadow area, preventing direct sunlight from entering the room, while allowing sufficient natural illumination.

overhaul: The process of repairing a building or machine by removing damaged or worn-out parts and replacing such parts with new material.

overhead: Indirect expenses that are not connected with a particular job. These include record keeping expenses, office rent, telephone expenses, advertising, legal services, office salaries, automobile expenses, taxes, and so on.

overhead door: A door which may be mounted on a sliding track or pivoted canopy frame, which moves upward to an overhead position when opened. Such doors may be manually operated or may be impelled by a variety of power mechanisms and are commonly used as garage doors. See *roll-up doors,* page 370; *tilt-up doors,* page 453.

overlaid veneer: A sheet of veneer overlaid and bonded on one or both sides with paper, metal, etc.

overload: In electricity, more than a normal amount of electric current flowing through a device or machine or a load greater than the device or machine is designed to carry.

overloading: In building, placing too heavy a load on a beam, column, or floor.

oversize brick: Modular brick related to the 4-inch module, every 12 inches in height; size 2½″ x 3½″ x 7½″.

ovolo: A convex molding, forming or approximating in section a quarter of a circle; a quarter-round molding.

oxter piece: In carpentry, a piece of timber which is used in ashlaring.

oxyacetylene welding: A type of gas welding in which cylinders containing compressed oxygen and acetylene are fed separately through a torch so designed that the mixture of gases can be regulated to produce flames of various temperatures. Essentially this type of welding is manual and limited to low-volume applications of considerable range.

oylet: A small hole or perforation; an eyelet.

P

packaged chimney: A complete prefabricated chimney unit, usually made of metal, which comes in a range of specifications and types, Fig. 407. Some are equipped with real or simulated brick or masonry housings and are coupled with prefabricated fireplace units (such as those shown in Figs. 246 and 247), page 189.

packing: In masonry, the process or operation of filling in a double or hollow wall; also, any material used in the operation of filling or closing up a hollow space as in a wall. See *furring,* page 211.

pad stone: In building, a stone *template;* a stone placed in a wall under a girder or other beam to distribute the weight or pressure of the load above; also, a lintel of stone spanning a doorway and supporting joists. See *template,* page 449.

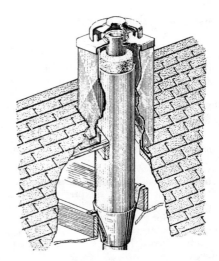

Fig. 407. Packaged chimney unit.

padding: In welding, a process often used in building up worn surfaces of shafts, wheels, and other machine parts. The operation consists of depositing several layers of beads, one on top of the other.

pagoda: In furniture making, a small towerlike decorative feature on cupboards and cabinets, used by Chippendale and other furniture designers of the eighteenth century, under oriental influence; also a towerlike temple, or memorial structure, of several ornate stories, frequently seen in India, China, and Japan.

pailing: Form sheathing which runs vertically.

paint: In building, a pigment, usually colored, mixed with oil and applied to a wall surface as a preservative or for decorative purposes.

paint base: Zinc, or any other similar material used as a base for paint.

paint drier: The most commonly used paint driers are composed of lead and manganese. The use of too much drier in paint may become harmful, but a limited amount of drier often serves a good purpose.

paint thinner: Heavy-bodied paints may be thinned by the addition of turpentine or petroleum spirits in order to make application of the paint easier. On account of the lower cost, petroleum spirits are often used instead of turpentine.

painted glass: Colored glass used to produce decorative effects, as in picture windows.

painter's putty: In building, a plastic substance composed of a mixture of whiting and linseed oil, sometimes including white lead; used for fixing panes of glass in window frames; also used to fill nail holes and defects in wood before applying paint or enamel.

pair: In building construction, to match two similar objects on opposite hands.

palladian window: A window composed of a main window having an arched head and on each side a long narrow window with a square head.

palmette (pal-met'): A conventional ornament of ancient origin, of floral design somewhat resembling a palm leaf, and consisting especially of radiating petals springing from a calyxlike base; closely related to the Egyptian lotus and Greek anthemion; the honeysuckle ornament much used to enrich moldings and other architectural features. See Fig. 315, page 239.

pan: In half-timbered work, a panel of brickwork or lath and plaster; any large division of an exterior wall, such as the space between upright and horizontal timbers in a frame structure where the surface is to be filled with boards, brickwork, or lath and plaster. Also, in carpentry, a recess bed for the leaf of a hinge.

pane: One of the different pieces of glass in a window; the same as *light;* also, a division or compartment of a plane surface or a flat space on one side of a building.

panel: A piece of wood or other material forming a portion of a wall, ceiling, or other surface. The panel may be raised or recessed. In industrialized construction, a

two-dimensional *component* (Fig. 408). (See also Fig. 383.) In plastering, a *coffer.* Also, the part of a truss that is repeated throughout the span.

panelboard: The term applied to an upright board to which the fuse box and switches controlling the electric system are attached; a *control center* or *lighting panel.* See also *panel box.*

panel box: A box in which electric switches and fuses for branch circuits are located. See *lighting panel,* page 267; *control center,* page 119.

panel door: A door made up of horizontal and vertical wood members and sunken panels. See Fig. 187, page 147.

panel forms: Foundation forms made from plywood sheets. See Figs. 269 and 270, pages 205 and 206.

panel heating: A method of heating a building by using units or coils of pipes concealed in special panels or built in the wall or ceiling plaster. Also called *concealed heating.*

paneling: A surface which is either sunken or raised and surrounded by a border or frame of wood; to make into panels. In interior finish, plywood sheets or joined boards used for covering interior walls.

panel strip: A term used in the building trade when referring to a molded strip of wood or metal used to cover a joint between two sheathing boards forming a panel; also, a strip of any kind of material used in the framing of panels.

pan floor: In concrete joist floor construction, a series of concrete joists or small beams joined together at the top with a thin slab. See Fig. 409. See also *two-way floor and roof system,* page 466.

pan forms: Pan-like metal or fiberglass structures used as forms for the bottom side of concrete floors. Reinforcing bars are placed in the recesses between the pans, which, when filled with concrete, become, in effect, floor joists. See Fig. 409.

pantile: A type of roofing tile with straight lengthwise lines, but curved in cross section, laid so that the joint between two

Fig. 408. Two-dimensional components are assembled complete with windows, doors, and interior and exterior wall finish.

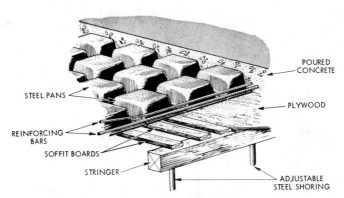

STEEL PANS

REINFORCING BARS

SOFFIT BOARDS

STRINGER

POURED CONCRETE

PLYWOOD

ADJUSTABLE STEEL SHORING

Fig. 409. Metal pans used for concrete floor construction.

concave tiles is covered by a convex tile; also, a type of tile in which there is both a concave and convex portion; this tile is laid so that the convex portion overlaps the rim of the concave portion of an adjoining tile; also, a gutter tile.

pan-tread: A stair tread formed by placing concrete in a steel pan.

313

paper building: Papers, felts and similar sheet materials used in buildings, as for wall and roof construction as a protection against air and moisture passage. Also called *sheathing paper.*

paper, drafting: Paper used for finished drawings, either in sheets or rolls.

paper hanging: The process of decorating the interior surface of a wall by covering it with wallpaper.

paperhanging: To use an excessively thin coat of mortar.

parallel: Lines (straight or curved), planes, and surfaces lying side by side, extending in the same direction, and equally distant from each other at all points. The parallels of the earth's surface, though appearing on a small map as straight parallel lines, are in reality *curved parallel lines.*

parallelogram: A four-sided plane figure whose opposite sides are parallel; hence, equal.

parapet: In architecture, a protective railing or low wall along the edge of a roof, balcony, bridge, or terrace.

parapet gutter: In building construction, a gutter placed behind a parapet wall.

parapet wall: That portion of any exterior wall, party wall, or fire wall which extends above the roof line; a wall which serves as a guard at the edge of a balcony or roof. See Fig. 410. See *wall,* page 474.

parge coat: In masonry, a coarse coat of plasterwork applied over masonry as a protection or for a decoration, Fig. 411. Also, a base coat or protective coat for damp-proofing. See Fig. 245, page 188.

parget: To cover with plaster; also plaster, whitewash, or rough cast for covering a wall.

pargeting: A term used by architects when referring to the decoration of a room with plaster work or stucco in relief, such as raised ornamental figures; also, plastering on the inside of flues which gives a smooth surface and improves the draft.

parging: Thin coat of cement plaster used to smooth rough masonry walls. See *fireplace,* Fig. 245, page 188. Also: a horizontal layer of mortar between the tiers of a multi-wythe wall. See Fig. 411.

paring: A term used by wood turners when referring to a method of wood turning which is opposed to the scraping method commonly employed by patternmakers.

paring chisel: A type of long chisel employed by patternmakers for slicing or paring cuts in wood so as to make a smooth surface which is difficult to obtain when cutting directly across the grain.

paring gouge: A woodworker's bench tool with its cutting edge beveled on the inside, or concave face, of the blade.

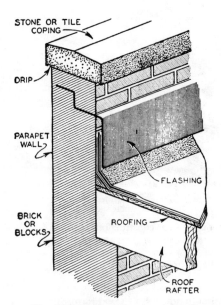

STONE OR TILE COPING

DRIP

PARAPET WALL

FLASHING

BRICK OR BLOCKS

ROOFING

ROOF RAFTER

Fig. 410. Section of a parapet wall.

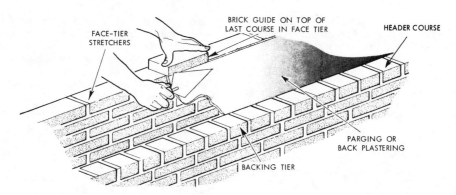

FACE-TIER
STRETCHERS

BRICK GUIDE ON TOP OF
LAST COURSE IN FACE TIER

HEADER COURSE

PARGING OR
BACK PLASTERING

BACKING TIER

Fig. 411. Parging.

parquetry: An inlaid pattern of various designs in wood; used especially for floors and for decorative features in furniture.

particleboard: A processed wood usually made into panels; it is made from dry wood particles which are bonded together by pressure and heat with a resin bond.

parting bead: The strip or *bead* which separates the upper and lower sash of a window. The *bead* is set into a groove in the jamb about one half of its width. Also called *parting strip.*

parting slip: A thin piece of wood used to separate two adjoining members as in a sash window; one of the thin strips let into the pulley stile to keep the sashes apart. The thin piece of wood inserted in the window box to separate the weights. Sometimes called *wagtail.* See *parting strip.*

parting stop: In a double-hung window frame, a piece of wood which separates the top from the bottom sash.

parting strip: A piece of wood (vertical) separating the upper and lower sash in a double hung window. See Fig. 198, page 154.

parting tool: A narrow-bladed turning tool used by woodworkers for cutting recesses, grooves, or channels.

partition: An interior wall, separating one portion of a house or building from another; usually a permanent inside wall which divides a house into various rooms. In residences, often partitions are constructed of studding covered with lath and plaster or drywall; in factories, the partitions are made of more durable materials, such as concrete blocks, hollow tile, brick, or heavy glass.

partition cap: The top plate or head of a partition wall; the upper horizontal timber which is nailed to the upper end of partition studding. Also called *partition head.*

partition plate: A term applied by builders to the horizontal member which serves as a cap for the partition studs and also supports the joists, rafters, and studding.

partition studding plate: A plate, either the sole or double top plate, for a partition wall. It should be the same dimensions as the studding for that wall. The lineal feet required for the sole and double-top plate will be three times the length of the partition.

partition studs: A series of slender wood or metal structural members placed as supporting elements in walls and partitions; usually 2x4 inches in size.

partition wall: Any interior wall which separates a building into rooms or compartments; an interior nonbearing wall entirely supported at each story by the beams or

315

girders of a skeleton frame; also, a masonry wall commonly found in factories, business-office buildings, and other large structures for subdividing an enclosed space into separate compartments.

party wall: In architecture, a term used when referring to a wall on the line between adjoining buildings in which each of the respective owners of the adjacent buildings share the rights and enjoyment of the common wall. See *wall,* page 474.

pass: In welding, each layer of beads deposited on the base metal.

pass-through: An opening in a kitchen wall used for passing dishes to and from the dining room.

patching: In plastering, repair and alteration of a plaster job. Patching should be done with well-aged putty and enough gauging plaster to insure a hard, well-bonded patch.

patera: A rounded ornamental feature usually in bas-relief worked into friezes; also, a round decorative ornament in relief on furniture.

patio: An outdoor paved court partially or entirely surrounded by rooms or other parts of a house; used for outdoor dining or living.

pattern: A model intended to be used as a copy for anything which is to be reproduced or imitated. A specimen of anything which is to be copied.

pattern-maker's saw: A small handsaw with a thin blade designed especially for accuracy in cutting patterns or for cabinetmaking.

patterned lumber: Lumber that is shaped to a pattern or to a molded form, in addition to being dressed, matched, or ship-lapped or any combination of these workings.

pavement: In building, an interior floor of ornamental tiles or colored bricks; a floor paved with concrete, bricks, or wood blocks, such as a factory floor.

paver: Mobile equipment used to place and finish a concrete pavement. The equipment, which runs on wheels or crawler treads, usually consists of a mixer, screws, or conveyors for distributing the concrete, screeds, and power trowels. Several machines that travel over the roadbed in succession are often used. This assemblage of equipment is called a paving train.

pavilion: A partially enclosed structure, usually roofed, for shelter purposes at the seaside, in parks, or other places where people gather for amusement or pleasure. Sometimes a *pavilion* is adorned with ornamental designs intended to add a decorative feature to a landscaped park or garden.

pavilion roof: A roof with equal hips on all sides; also, a roof which, in plan, forms a geometrical figure of more than four straight sides.

peavy: A *peavy* is similar to the *cant hook* except that it has a point set into the lower end of the handle as illustrated in Fig. 412. See *cant hook,* page 84.

Fig. 412. The peavy is used mainly on water, where the point serves as a pike.

pebble dash: In the building trade, a term used for finishing the exterior walls of a structure by dashing pebbles against the plaster or cement.

pebble dashing: In plastering, a rough finish given to a wall by coating it with plaster onto which small stones and liquid lime are thrown while the plaster is still soft.

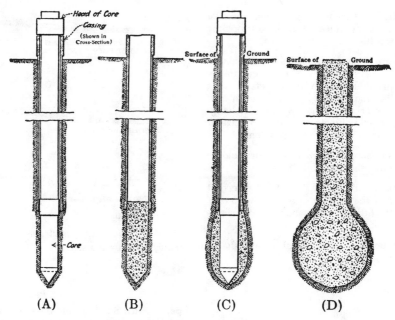

Fig. 413. Pedestal Pile.

peck: A term applied to spots of decay in cedar or cypress wood; pitted or channeled areas or pockets of localized decay. Timber or wood containing such defects is designated as *pecky*.

pecky: Timber which shows signs of decay. See *peck*.

pedestal: A support for a column or statue; also, a name given to the base of smaller objects such as a vase. Examples of the use of piles as supports for pedestals are shown in Fig. 413.

pediment: In classic architecture, a triangular member resembling a gable, crowning the front of a structure, especially over a portico; usually low in height as compared with the width of its base. See Fig. 414.

peen: The end of a hammer or sledge opposite to that of the hammering face. Sometimes spelled *pean* or *pane*.

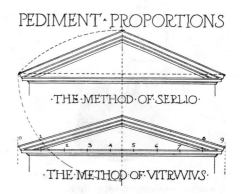

Fig. 414. Pediment.

peen hammer: A hammer of various designs, used especially by metal workers and by stone masons. Sometimes this hammer has two opposite cutting edges and is roughly toothed to facilitate the cutting of stone or the breaking of brick. See Fig. 298, page 229.

317

peg: In furniture making, a small piece of wood used in place of nails for holding parts together.

pegboard: Board with holes evenly spaced over its entire surface. May be cut to desired size and used to line closets or hang on walls. Hooks placed in the holes at convenient intervals provide facilities for hanging household objects of almost any size or shape, simplifying storage problems.

pellet molding: A narrow band or molding enriched with small flat disks.

pelmet: In building, a short head placed at the top of the interior of a window to conceal the fitting from which the curtains hang.

pencil pointer: Mechanical pencil sharpener. See Fig. 415.

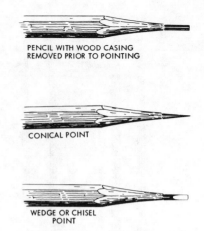

PENCIL WITH WOOD CASING REMOVED PRIOR TO POINTING

CONICAL POINT

WEDGE OR CHISEL POINT

Fig. 416. Two basic pencil points are commonly used by draftsmen.

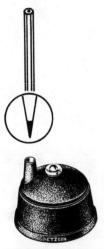

Fig. 415. A mechanical pencil pointer saves the draftsman considerable time.

pencil points: Two types of pencil points are commonly used by draftsmen: the conical point and the wedge or chisel point. See Fig. 416. The conical point is probably the most widely used but it does require pointing more frequently than the wedge.

pencil rods: Small, round bars used as temperature reinforcement in a slab or round wires used as hangers for suspended ceilings.

pencils: A pencil is the usual means of recording information on the drawing medium. Pencils are graded by hardness. This is indicated by a number and a letter stamped on one end of the pencil. Fig. 417 shows pencils in their general hardness classifications with line samples of different pencil grades. Pencils used by the draftsman or designer are wood-cased or held in mechanical lead holders. (See Fig. 418.) Probably the main advantage of the mechanical lead holder is that the weight and length of the pencil are always the same.

pendant: A hanging ornament, on roofs and ceilings, used extensively as a decorative feature in the later style of Gothic architecture.

pendant posts: A term applied to timbers which hang down the side of a wall from the plate in hammer-beam trusses and which receive the hammer braces; a post set against the wall and resting on a corbel or other solid support which holds up the ends of a collar beam or any part of a roof.

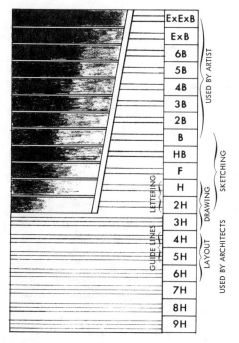

Fig. 417. Different pencil grades produce different line widths. The harder the pencil the thinner the line.

Fig. 418. Mechanical lead holders eliminate the pencil sharpening problem. The two basic types, spring chuck (top) and screw chuck (bottom), are shown above. (Koh-I-Noor)

pendative: In architecture, a spherical triangle formed by a dome which springs from a square or polygonal base.

pendentive bracketing: Bracketing which springs from the rectangular walls of an apartment upward to the ceiling and forming the horizontal part of the ceiling into a circle or ellipse. See *cove bracketing,* page 127.

pendentives: A term applied to the vaulted portions supporting the angles of a domed cupola; an arch which cuts off internally the corners of a square building so the superstructure may become an octagon or dome; that part of a groined vault springing from a single pier or corbel.

penetrating: That which has the power to pass into or through something, as in wood finishing; a penetrating stain is one that forces its way below the surface into the fibers of the wood. In welding, the depth of fusion from the surface of the base metal to the bottom of the bead.

penny: A system of designating nail sizes. The term originated in England and formerly indicated the price per hundred. Abbreviated as *d.* Fig. 419 illustrates nail sizes. See also *nail,* page 295.

pent roof: A roof like that of a penthouse, attached to and sloping from a wall of a building in one direction only.

pentagon: Has five equal sides.

pentastyle: A structure having five columns across the front, as a temple or portico.

penthouse: A room, apartment, or any type of dwelling built on the roof of another building; also, a room built on the roof of a building to cover a stairway, to house elevator machinery, water tanks, or ventilating apparatus or to provide working space above the elevator sheaves.

perch: A solid measure used for stone work, commonly $16\frac{1}{2}$ ft. x $1\frac{1}{2}$ ft. x 1 foot, or $24\frac{3}{4}$ cu. ft. However, the measure for stone varies according to locality and custom, sometimes $16\frac{2}{3}$ cu. ft. being used for solid work.

perforated board: *Pegboard.*

pergola: A structure which is open to the sky, since its roof is composed only of girders and cross rafters; usually supported on posts or piers and arranged in parallel rows, sometimes in a circular or other geometric ground plan.

perimeter heating: A system of heating in which ducts radiate from a central plenum chamber and release warm air through registers located along the outer walls.

319

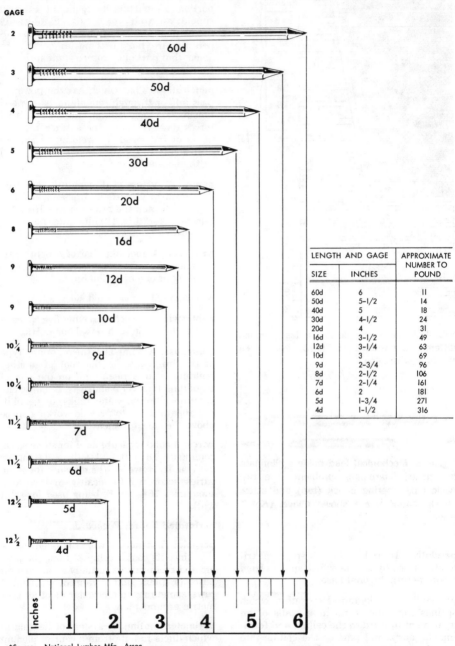

*Source: National Lumber Mfg. Assoc.

Fig. 419. Commonly used nails: Size, gage, and number per pound.

LENGTH AND GAGE		APPROXIMATE NUMBER TO POUND
SIZE	INCHES	
60d	6	11
50d	5-1/2	14
40d	5	18
30d	4-1/2	24
20d	4	31
16d	3-1/2	49
12d	3-1/4	63
10d	3	69
9d	2-3/4	96
8d	2-1/2	106
7d	2-1/4	161
6d	2	181
5d	1-3/4	271
4d	1-1/2	316

320

peripheral: At the outside; external.

peripteral: A style of structure which has a row of columns on all sides; peristylar.

periptery: Any temple or edifice surrounded by a peristyle; a peripteros.

peristyle: A range of columns together with their entablatures; also, a complete system of roof-supporting columns encircling a building or court.

perling: A supported piece of timber which is placed under rafters to prevent them from sagging, between where they rest on the wall and ridgepiece or ridgepole.

perlite: A type of lightweight aggregate used to produce insulating concrete.

perm: The unit of measurement of the water vapor permeance of a material. Value of one perm is equal to one grain of water vapor per square foot hour per inch of mercury vapor pressure difference.

permeability: A characteristic of substances that allows the passage of fluids.

permeability agent: An admixture used to make hardened concrete more watertight.

perpend: In masonry, a header brick or large stone extending through a wall so that one end appears on each side of the wall and acts as a binder.

perpendicular: A line or plane which meets another line or plane at right angles.

perpendicular style: A name applied to a style of architecture in which a large proportion of the principal lines of the tracery intersect at right angles; the third and last stage of the English Gothic style of architecture; the last of the pointed or Gothic type; also called *florid style.* Same as *rectilinear style.*

perron: An architectural term referring to an out-of-door stairway leading to the first floor of a building; a name sometimes applied to the platform upon which an entrance door opens, together with the flight of steps leading up to it; also, a flight of stairs, as in a garden, leading to a terrace or upper story.

perspective: The representation of an object on a plane surface so it will have the same appearance as when viewed from a particular location. In perspective drawing, the observer assumes he is viewing all objects through a transparent *picture plane* (an imaginary plane) upon which the object is projected. See Fig. 420 for an illustration of this concept and others discussed. The point from which the observer sights is called the *station point* and the plane on which he stands (and on which the object rests) is the *ground plane.* The intersection of the picture plane and ground plane is

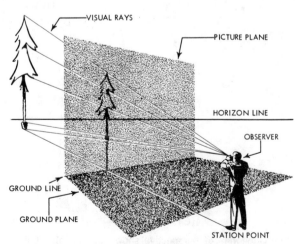

Fig. 420. This figure illustrates the basic concepts and terminology used in perspective.

called the *ground line*. The lines which extend from the viewer's eye to the object are the *visual rays* or *lines of sight*. Each perspective drawing contains a *horizon line:* This is a real or an imaginary line in the distance at *the eye level of the viewer*. The *vanishing points* are the points on the horizon line where the lines of the object meet. A perspective drawing gives a view as seen from only *one* station point (eye view). The perspective types are illustrated in Fig. 421. See *perspective drawing*.

perspective drawing: The representation of an object on a plane surface, so presented as to have the same appearance as when seen from a particular viewpoint. Perspective drawings may be classified into three categories: (1) *parallel* or one-point, (2) *angular* or two-point, and (3) *oblique* or three-point. Each type may be used to a particular advantage. See Fig. 421.

pert (program evaluation and review technique): A method similar to the *critical*

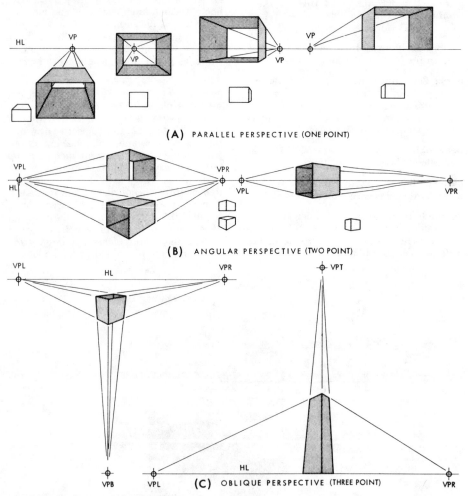

Fig. 421. These three categories of perspective show how the object lines converge at the vanishing point(s).

path method; used in governmental and manufacturing management applications.

phantom drawing: Usually refers to some "dotted in" part added to a drawing to show the relation, method of connection, assembly, etc., of or to the project being drawn.

phase. The type of power available, either single-phase or three-phase. Only single-phase is available in some residential and rural areas. Three-phase is used for heavy power consumers, like factories.

Phillips head screw: A type of screw having a cross slot cut in the head for driving or removing the screw. A special type screwdriver, known as the *Phillips head screwdriver,* is used to drive or remove this type of screw. See Fig. 515, page 395.

pH paper: pH stands for *potential Hydro*gen. A pH of 7 is neutral (the value of water); pH of 0 to 7 indicates acidity; and 7 to 14 indicates alkalinity.

piazza: In architecture, an enclosed court, arcade, or colonnade of a building; in the United States, an exterior entrance covered with a separate roof, as a veranda or porch of a house.

pick test: Rough estimate of the hydration of cement in a sample by careful picking with a relatively sharp instrument such as a dull ice pick.

picket: A stake or narrow board, sharpened at the top, used in making fences; also, sometimes called a *pale.*

pictorial view: In drawing, a view represented as in a picture; in building, a view illustrated by pictures or drawings. Also called *pictorial drawing.* Fig. 421 illustrates pictorial drawing made in perspective. An *isometric drawing* and an *oblique drawing* are also pictorial views. See Fig. 422 for an illustration of an *isometric drawing.* See also *oblique drawing,* page 301.

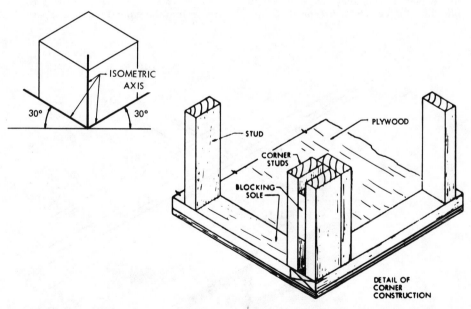

Fig. 422. Isometric Drawing: Three axes are laid out first; full measurements are used along each axis and any line parallel to one of the main axis. This type of pictorial view is often used to show details of construction.

picture mold: A narrow molding, fastened to an interior wall, used for hanging pictures, which are suspended from the molding by means of fine wire and a metal hook.

picture plane: In perspective drawing, an imaginary plane upon which the object is projected. See *perspective drawing*.

picture rail: An ornamental, grooved molding or rail, around the interior walls of a room near the ceiling, provided for hanging pictures. Same as *picture mold*.

picture window: A large window whose bottom ledge is not more than waist high, which includes a dominant fixed sash area, though movable sash may also be enclosed by the frame. The fixed sash area is usually wider than it is high.

pier: One of the pillars supporting an arch; also, a supporting section of wall between two openings. A masonry or concrete column (or isolated foundation member) used to support foundations, floor structures, or other structural members. The diameter of a pier is usually less than 2 feet; over 2 feet a pier is commonly called a *caisson pile*. Fig. 423 illustrates a typical pier.

pier arch: An arch carried by piers, especially any of the side arches of the nave of a basilican church with piers; the nave arcades, as the arches between the nave and aisles of a church.

pigment: An insoluble coloring substance, usually in powder form, which is mixed with oil or water to make paints.

pike pole: An implement, equipped with a sharp metal point, used for holding poles, such as telephone or telegraph poles, in an upright position while planting or removing them.

pilaster: A rectangular column attached to a wall or pier for stiffening. Structurally a pier, but it is treated architecturally as a column with a capital, shaft, and base. See Fig. 424 which illustrates a pilaster constructed of concrete block.

pilaster strip: A pilaster of slender proportion in any way; a pilaster mass of slight projection without a cap.

pile: A large timber, steel member, or precast concrete shaft with a steel casing driven into the ground for the support of a

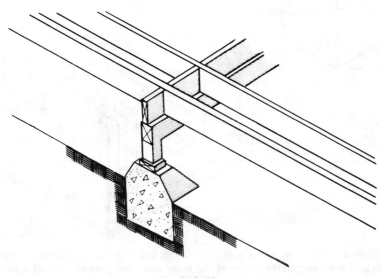

Fig. 423. Pier.

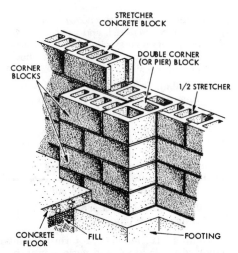

Fig. 424. Pilasters are added to basement walls to provide increased strength. When pilasters are used with concrete block they are tied into the wall by alternating the pattern on each level.

structure or a vertical load. Frequently *piles* are made of the entire trunk of a tree.

pile cap: A structural member placed on the top of a pile and used to distribute loads from the structure to the pile.

pile driver: A machine for driving piles; usually a high vertical framework with appliances attached for raising a heavy mass of iron which, after being lifted to the top of the framework, is allowed to fall, by the force of gravity, on the head of the pile, thus driving it into the ground.

piling: A structure made of piles.

pillar: An upright shaft or column, of stone, marble, brick, or other materials, relatively slender in comparison to its height. Used principally for supporting superstructures but may stand alone as for a monument.

pilot hole: Any hole made in a piece of wood to guide a screw. The hole may be made with any type of boring tool, such as a gimlet or auger bit, hand drill, or brad awl.

pilot lamp: A small lamp connected to an electric circuit, such as a switchboard, to indicate that the circuit is alive and a circuit switch or other device has operated.

pilotis: Stilt-type columns that are used to provide an open area such as a promenade or arcade in a building Such an area may be glass enclosed but the columns are visible.

pin: In carpentry, a piece of wood used to hold structural parts together, as a small peg or wooden nail. Steel piece used for connecting members of a truss or the ends of two spans together.

pincers: A jointed tool with two handles and a pair of jaws used for gripping and holding an object.

pinch bar: A type of crowbar, or lever, on one end of which a pointed projection serves as a kind of fulcrum; used especially for rolling heavy wheels. See *wrecking bar,* page 489. Also called *ripping bar* or *wrecking bar.* See Fig. 425.

Fig. 425. Pinch bar.

pin knot: A term used by woodworkers when referring to a blemish in boards, consisting of a small knot of 1/2 inch or less in diameter.

pin members: The tenons in a dovetail are called pin members.

pinholing: In painting, a defect in a sprayed-paint surface caused by holes due to bubbles which persist until the film has dried. The bubbles may be caused by draughts, sealed air pockets, moisture or oil in the air lines, porous undercoatings, difference in temperature between the surface being sprayed and the lacquer itself, or the bubbles may be caused by the use of a thinner which dries too quickly.

pinnacle: In architecture, a tall, pointed, relatively slender, upright member usually terminating in a cone-shaped spire; used as a decorative feature on a buttress or in an angle of a pier; also, a slender ornament as on a parapet or any turret-like decoration.

pintles: These are used to transfer loads of columns on upper floors through intervening beams and girders to metal *column caps* as illustrated in Fig. 426. The pintle serves as a base for the column on one floor and is used to avoid problems of shrinkage that would cause trouble due to uneven or unequal seasoning in the timbers used.

pipe: There are five basic kinds of pipe used today: (1) steel and wrought iron pipe, (2) cast iron pipe, (3) seamless brass and copper pipe, (4) copper tubing, and (5) plastic pipe. The common types of pipe

joints are: screwed (threaded), bell and spigot, flanged, soldered, and welded. Each of these has its own symbol. Fig. 427 illustrates the basic symbols when used to show a 90° elbow. See also Fig. 112, page 89.

pipe coupling: In plumbing, a short collar consisting of a threaded sleeve used to connect two pipes.

pipe cutter: In plumbing, a tool used for cutting steel or wrought-iron pipes. The curved end of the tool partly encircles the pipe and carries one or more cutting disks. As the tool is rotated around the pipe, a screw regulates the feed of the cutter.

pipe die: In plumbing, a screw plate used for cutting threads on pipe.

pipe fittings: In plumbing, a term used in reference to ells, tees, and various branch connectors used in connecting pipes. See Fig. 428. See also Fig. 112, page 89, and Fig. 427.

pipe hangers: In plumbing, a term applied to various types of supports, such as clamps and brackets, for soil pipes. For method of fastening such supports in place, see Fig. 429.

pipe, soil: A pipe which conveys to the building drain or sewer the discharge of one or more water closets and/or discharge of any other fixture which receives fecal matter, with or without discharge from other fixtures.

pipe threads: There are two standard forms of pipe threads: *Regular* and *Dryseal*. Regular pipe thread is the standard for the plumbing trade. Dryseal pipe thread is the standard for automotive, refrigeration, and hydraulic tube and pipe fittings, lubrication fittings, and drain cocks.

pipe trowel: In plastering, a trowel used behind fixtures and between pipes. See Fig. 430.

pipe vise: There are two kinds of pipe vises used in the plumbing trade — the hinged-side type with V jaws for small pipes and the chain type used for large pipes. Fig. 118, page 93, illustrates a chain type pipe vise.

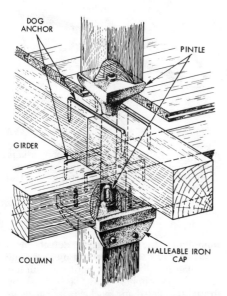

DOG ANCHOR

PINTLE

GIRDER

COLUMN

MALLEABLE IRON CAP

Fig. 426. Pintle transfers the load from upper column to a malleable iron cap.

pipe vise stand: In plumbing and electrical wiring, a stand for holding pipe so it may

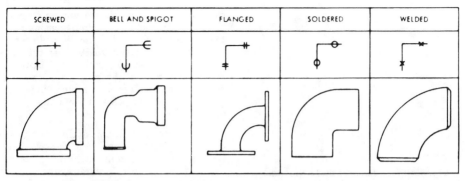

SCREWED	BELL AND SPIGOT	FLANGED	SOLDERED	WELDED

Fig. 427. Pipe joints and symbols for a 90° elbow.

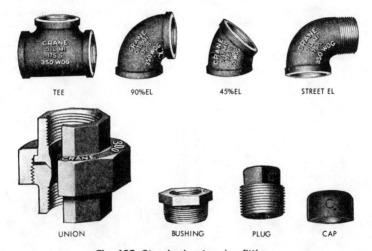

TEE   90%EL   45%EL   STREET EL

UNION   BUSHING   PLUG   CAP

Fig. 428. Standard water pipe fittings.

be worked on, cut, bent, reamed, etc. See Fig. 431.

pipe, waste: A pipe which conveys liquid or liquid-borne waste, free of fecal matter.

pipe, water riser: A water supply pipe that extends vertically, a full story or more, to convey water to branches or fixtures.

pipe weights: There are ten different weights of pipe available, designated by Schedule — such as Schedule for standard pipe and Schedule 80 for extra strong.

Double extra strong is also available. The OD (outside diameter) would remain the same for different weights of pipe while the ID (inside diameter) would decrease for the heavier pipe. Consistency of OD has the advantage that different weights of pipe can be connected with the same size connectors.

pipe wrench: Ten to fourteen inch wrench used to hold conduit or pipe and to tighten fittings on. See Fig. 432.

327

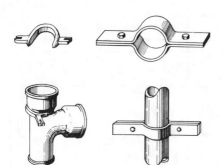

Fig. 429. Pipe hangers and supports.

pique: In furniture making, a type of inlay which is of French origin.

pitch: The incline of the rafters expressed as a ratio of rise to run. In plumbing, the slope of a floor toward a drain (in inches per foot). In steel construction, spacing between rivet centers. Also, the center to center spacing between turns of a spiral. In row lumber, a resinous substance consisting of a fusible residue of tars. It occurs naturally in asphalt. (It is used in plumbing and for numerous purposes in building construction.)

pitch board: In building, a thin piece of board, cut in the shape of a right-angled triangle, used as a guide in forming work. When making cuts for stairs, the *pitch board* serves as a pattern for marking cuts; the shortest side is the height of the riser cut, and the next longer side is the width of the tread. See Fig. 433.

pitch of a roof: The angle, or degree, of slope of a roof from the plate to the ridge. The pitch can be found by dividing the

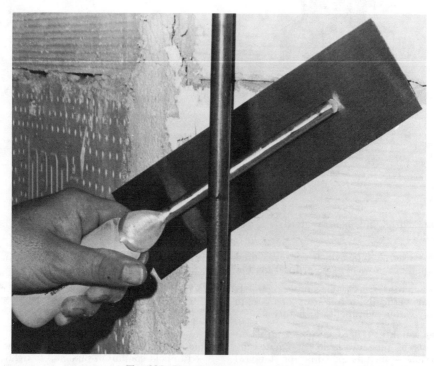

Fig. 430. Plasterer using a pipe trowel.

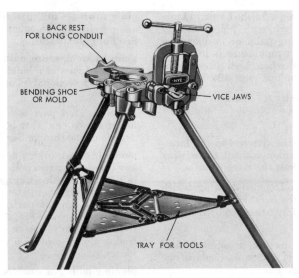

Fig. 431. Portable pipe vise stand and bender. (Nye Tool & Machine Works)

height, or rise, by the span; for example, if the height is 8 feet and the span 16 feet, the pitch is 8/16 equals 1/2; then the angle of pitch is 45 degrees.

pitch pocket: In lumber, a well-defined opening between rings of annual growth. Usually such pockets contain more or less pitch in either liquid or solid form.

pitch triangle: A right triangle whose horizontal base is always 12″ in length (run), whose hypotenuse is parallel to the roof incline, and whose altitude (rise) is expressed in inches.

pitching piece: A horizontal timber located at the top of a staircase with one end wedged into the wall to support the upper end of the rough string. Same as *apron piece.*

pith: The central core of a log. The *pith* is surrounded by the *heartwood.*

pith knot: In woodworking, a term used when referring to a blemish in boards, consisting of a small knot with a pith hole not more than 1/4 inch in diameter.

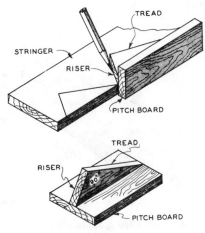

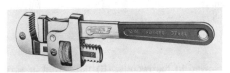

Fig. 432. Pipe wrench (Crescent Tool Co.)

Fig. 433. Pitch board.

329

pitting: In painting, a finished, sprayed surface disfigured by small holes; usually caused by spraying paint or lacquer in a room where the temperature is less than 65°F., especially when high pressure is applied. See *pinholing,* page 325.

pivoted casement: A casement window which has its upper and lower edges pivoted.

placing: Putting the concrete in the forms where it is to harden without segregating the aggregates from the cement paste.

placing drawings: Detailed drawings which give the size of the bars, location, spacing, and all other information required by the ironworker.

plafond: In architecture, a ceiling formed by the underside of a floor, particularly one of an elaborate design.

plain concrete: A concrete mixture which does not contain more than two-tenths of one percent of reinforcement.

plain rail: Meeting rails which are of the same thickness as the balance of the window. It is the opposite of a *check rail.*

plain-sawed grain: Another term for *flat-grain lumber;* generally used in reference to hardwoods. See *flat grain,* page 194. See also: *quarter sawed grain,* page 453. Fig. 434 illustrates wood cuts.

plain sawing: Cutting wood so the saw cuts are parallel to the squared side of a log. See *flat grain,* page 194.

plan: In architecture, a diagram showing a horizontal view of a building, such as floor plans and sectional plans. See Fig. 259, page 199.

plancier: That part of a cornice directly under the corona; that is, the soffit or underside of the corona. See Fig. 78, page 63.

plane: In woodworking, a flat surface where any line joining two points will lie entirely in the surface. Also, a carpenter's tool used for smoothing boards or other wood surfaces. The various parts of a carpenter's plane are shown in Fig. 435. Fig. 436 illustrates common planes used in the building trades. See also *block plane,* page 54, and *router,* page 376.

planing mill: An establishment equipped with woodworking machinery for smoothing rough wood surfaces, cutting, fitting and matching boards with tongued-and-grooved joints; a woodworking mill.

planing-mill products: Any lumber which has been worked to pattern, such as flooring, siding, and ceiling.

plank: A long, flat, heavy piece of timber thicker than a board; a term commonly applied to a piece of construction material 6 inches or more in width and more than 1 inch thick.

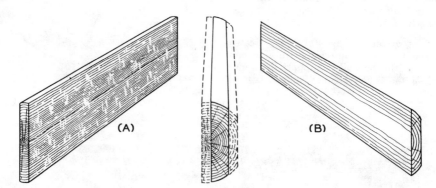

Fig. 434. (A) Edge grain in softwood and quartersawed in hardwoods; (B) flat-sawed in softwoods and plain sawed in hardwoods. (U.S. Forest Products Laboratory)

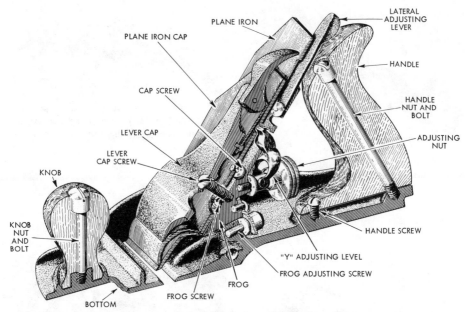

Fig. 435. Parts of a plane.

plank and beam construction: A system of construction currently used in one-story buildings in which post and beam-framing units are the basic load-bearing members. Fewer framing members are needed, leaving more open space for functional use, for easier installation of large windows, and more flexible placing of free standing walls and partitions. It is also adaptable for prefabricated modular panel installation. Wide roof overhangs, for sun protection, and outdoor living areas are simpler to construct when this framing system is used. Posts and beams may be of wood, structural steel, or concrete. Ceiling heights are higher for the same cubage, and it is reported that building is faster and cheaper. Roof deck can double as finished ceiling in the post, beam, and plank variation of the system. Problems include the necessity for extra insulation, difficulty in concealing wiring and duct work, and the necessity for extra care in the choice of materials and in planning. See Fig. 437.

plank lumber: A wide board, usually more than one inch thick, laid with its wide dimension horizontal and used as a bearing surface.

plank truss: Any truss work constructed of heavy timbers such as planking in a roof truss or in a bridge truss.

plan shape: A plan shape is the basic pattern on which a house is laid out. Most commonly used plan shapes are the square, rectangle, T, L, H, U, and split-level patterns. T, L, H, and U plan shapes roughly follow the shape of the alphabet letter by which they are indicated. See *split-level,* page 419.

planter box: A container constructed in various shapes, designed to hold growing plants.

planting: Sticking or gluing plaster cornice pieces or ornaments in place.

plan view: In architectural drawing, a floor plan or top view of a horizontal section

331

Jointer plane. Largest of the carpenter's planes (20″ to 24″) is intended for use on the work bench. (Stanley Works)

Jack plane for rough work and preliminary smoothing; 14″ length is common. (Stanley Works)

Low-angled steel block plane; operated with one hand. (Stanley Works)

Duplex rabbet plane for planing into corners. (Stanley Works)

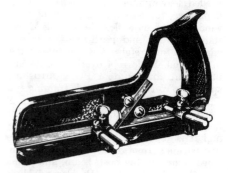

Smooth plane, usually smaller than jack plane. (Stanley Works)

Grooving plow plane used for cutting grooves, as for weatherstripping.

Fig. 436. Planes.

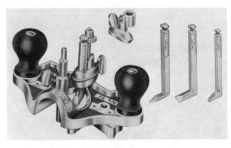

Router plane used for surfacing grooves. (Stanley Works)

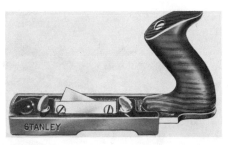

Fiberboard bevel plane. (Stanley Works)

Bull-nose rabbet plane for working close into corners. (Stanley Works)

Forming plane used on wood, plastics, leather, soft metals, fiber composition boards. (Stanley Works)

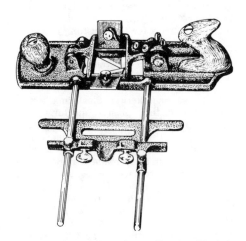

Fiberboard grooving plane. (Stanley Works)

Portable power plane. (Skil Corp.)

Fig. 436. Planes. (Cont'd)

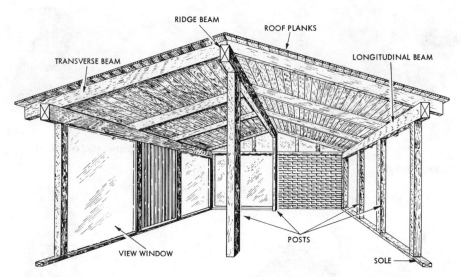

Fig. 437. Plank and beam framing requires careful placement of posts and beams. The roof planks must be strong enough to span the distance between beams.

taken at a distance above the floor, varying so as to cut the walls at a height which will best show the construction. Such a plan is drawn as though we were looking down into the rooms. Also called *floor plan.* See Fig. 259, page 199.

plaster: Any pasty material of a mortar-like consistency used for covering walls and ceilings of buildings. Formerly, a widely used type of plastering composed of a mixture of lime, sand, hair, and water. A more durable and popular plastering is now made of portland cement mixed with sand and water.

plaster arch: Any untrimmed plaster opening. See *metal arches,* page 282.

plaster base: Any foundation material to which plaster is to be applied, such as wood lath, metal lath, woven-wire fabric, and plasterboard.

plaster ceiling panel: A section of a ceiling made so as to give the appearance of being depressed or raised by furring on the joints before lathing is done.

plaster cove: A term usually applied to a cove between a sidewall and ceiling, made

by nailing rough-sawn cove brackets against each stud and the corresponding ceiling joist. Lathing is continuous from the sidewall to the ceiling. Usually such coves are made on a 15-inch radius.

plaster grounds: In building, strips of wood nailed to walls to serve as guides for the plasterer. The strips are sometimes used as nailing strips for the finishing material.

plaster lath: Thin, narrow strps of wood nailed to ceiling joists, studding, or rafters as a groundwork for receiving plastering.

plaster mortar mixer: In plastering, a machine for mixing plaster mortar. Most mortar mixers have rotating paddles enclosed in a drum-shaped container. The paddles are made of steel with a leading edge and an extension made of hard rubber which can be replaced when worn. The purpose of the rubber blades is to allow the paddles to compress against the sides of the drum while turning, thus keeping the drum clean. When mixing has been completed, the drum can be tilted so the mortar can be poured easily into a wheelbarrow or mortar box or hopper of a pumping machine. Fig. 438 shows the plaster

334

Fig. 438. Plaster mortar mixer. (Gilson Brothers Co.)

mortar mixer with the drum in a tilted position.

plaster of paris: A term commonly applied to calcined gypsum. The name is derived from extensive deposits of gypsum found in the neighborhood of Paris.

plaster return: A plastering term used to describe the return of the plastered wall around such areas as window or door openings. The usual wood trim is omitted.

plaster wainscot cap: A band of interior trim covering a horizontal joint, usually at a point where the plaster wainscoting and float finish meet in kitchens and bathrooms. The term is sometimes wrongly used when referring to a *chair rail.*

plasterboard: A rigid, insulating board made of plastering material covered on both sides with heavy paper. See *gypsum,* page 227 and *drywall,* page 162.

plasterboard nail: A short, heavy nail with a large head, designed for use in the installation of plasterboard. See Fig. 390, *gypsum board nails,* page 227.

plastering knife: See *knives, plastering,* page 258.

plastering machine: A motor-powered, portable pump which feeds plaster into a hose by a worm drive mechanism at the bottom of a hopper. An auxiliary hose feeds compressed air into the main hose, forcing the plaster through the hose, out the nozzle, and onto the surface to be plastered without the use of hawk or trowel. See Fig. 439.

plasterer's knives: These knives are used by the plasterer to cover nail heads and little nicks in the boards. Blades are 4", 5" and 6" wide. See *knives, plastering,* page 258.

plasterer's putty: A putty paste made of pure slaked lime strained through a fine sieve. See *fine stuff,* page 186.

Fig. 439. Plastering machine. (Essick Div. of A-T-O Inc.)

plasterer's rubber sponge: The plasterer's rubber sponge is oval shaped to fit the hand and is made of pure sponge rubber. This tool is ideal for texture floating curved surfaces.

plasterwork: Work done with or in plaster, especially plastering used as finishing of any architectural construction, as the plastering of the walls and ceilings of a room.

plastic anchors: Plastic anchors are now being commonly used for light load. These are similar in appearance to the *lead screw anchors*. Sheet metal screws are used to expand the anchor.

plastic concrete: Fresh concrete that can be moved and molded into any shape; concrete that has not hardened or set.

plastic tile: Lightweight tile units made of various plastics, available in a variety of shapes and sizes. Such tile is in general use in moderately priced homes. They are used as wall or counter top coverings in much the same manner that *ceramic tile* is used. The tile is fastened to walls and counter tops with a mastic, creating durable, decorative, and dirt-resistant surfaces. The shape and size of these units may vary

with the individual manufacturer, especially trim units, but some of the more common shapes are shown in Fig. 440.

plastic veneers: Flexible plastic films with adhesive backs used to cover various surfaces on which a fine finish is desired.

plastic window lights: Made of resin and glass fiber, the panes diffuse light and are resistant to breakage.

plastic wood: A manufactured plastic material used extensively for filling cracks and defects in wood.

plasticity: A complex property of material involving a combination of qualities of mobility and magnitude of yield without breaking apart.

plastics: A term applied to a chemically produced, synthetic substance which may be molded and shaped by heat or pressure or both. Plastic materials are used extensively in the building industries and for numerous domestic purposes.

plat: A plan, map, or chart of a city, town, section, or subdivision indicating the location and boundaries of individual properties.

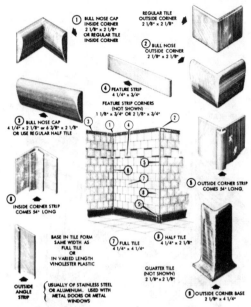

① BULL NOSE CAP
INSIDE CORNER
2 1/8" x 2 1/8"
OR REGULAR TILE
INSIDE CORNER

REGULAR TILE
OUTSIDE CORNER
2 1/8" x 2 1/8"

② BULL NOSE
OUTSIDE CORNER
2 1/8" x 2 1/8"

④ FEATURE STRIP
4 1/4" x 3/4"

FEATURE STRIP CORNERS
(NOT SHOWN)
1 1/8" x 3/4" OR 2 1/8" x 3/4"

③ BULL NOSE CAP
4 1/4" x 2 1/8" or 6 3/8" x 2 1/8"
OR USE REGULAR HALF TILE

⑧ OUTSIDE CORNER STRIP
COMES 54" LONG.

⑥ INSIDE CORNER STRIP
COMES 54" LONG

BASE IN TILE FORM
SAME WIDTH AS
FULL TILE
OR
IN VARIED LENGTH
VINOLESTER PLASTIC

⑦ FULL TILE
4 1/4" x 4 1/4"

⑨ HALF TILE
4 1/4" x 2 1/8"

QUARTER TILE
(NOT SHOWN)
2 1/8" x 2 1/8"

OUTSIDE
ANGLE
STRIP

USUALLY OF STAINLESS STEEL
OR ALUMINUM. USED WITH
METAL DOORS OR METAL
WINDOWS

⑤ OUTSIDE CORNER BASE
2 1/8" x 4 1/4"

Fig. 440. Plastic tile units.

plate glass: A polished, high-grade glass cast in the form of a plate, or sheet, used principally in high-priced structures. A sheet of glass usually thicker and of a better quality than ordinary window glass; also with a smoother surface free from blemishes.

plate rail: A narrow, shelflike molding attached to the interior of a wall for supporting decorated pieces of chinaware, especially plates.

plate tracery: A type of tracery developed in the twelfth century, consisting of a series of decorative patterns cut through a flat plate of stone. This became the parent of all later forms of tracery.

plate: A term usually applied to a 2x4 placed on top of studs in frame walls. It serves as the top horizontal timber upon which the attic joists and roof rafters rest and to which these members are fastened. See Fig. 41, page 35; Fig. 82, page 65; and Fig. 441. A *sill plate:* Plate on top of foundation wall which supports floor framing. A *wall plate :* Plate at top or bottom of wall or partition framing. A *rafter or joist plate:*

platform: A horizontal and usually flat surface, commonly higher, rarely lower, than the adjoining floor or ground, as a depot platform, the stage of a theater, the elevated part of the floor of a church or other public building where the speaker stands while addressing an audience.

platform framing: A type of construction in which the floor platforms are framed independently; also, the second and third floors are supported by studs of only one story in height. Also called *Western framing.* See Fig. 441.

platform stairs: A stairway having landings, especially near the top or bottom; a stairs with flights rising in opposite directions,

Plate at top of masonry or concrete wall supporting rafter or roof joist and ceiling framing. Also, a flat piece of steel used in conjunction with angle irons, channels, or S beams in the construction of lintels.

plate cut: In carpentry, the cut at the lower end of a rafter, where the rafter fits against the plate. Also called *seat cut* or *foot cut.* See *bird's-mouth,* Fig. 483, page 371.

337

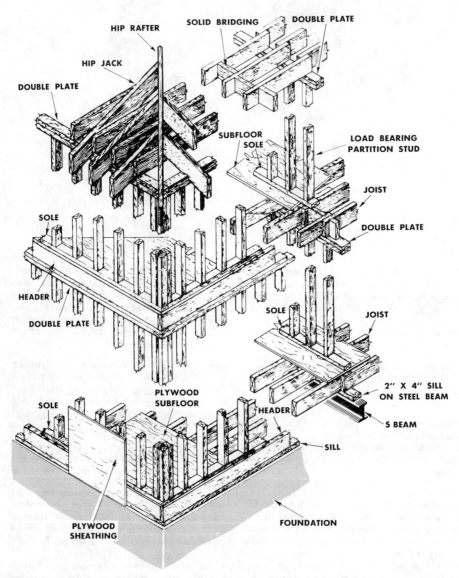

HIP RAFTER

SOLID BRIDGING

DOUBLE PLATE

HIP JACK

DOUBLE PLATE

SUBFLOOR
SOLE

LOAD BEARING
PARTITION STUD

JOIST

DOUBLE PLATE

SOLE

HEADER

DOUBLE PLATE

SOLE

JOIST

SOLE

2" X 4" SILL
ON STEEL BEAM

S BEAM

PLYWOOD
SUBFLOOR

HEADER

SILL

SOLE

PLYWOOD
SHEATHING

FOUNDATION

Fig. 441. Platform (or western) framing is popular because it can be erected quickly and easily. The rough floor provides a platform for the workman.

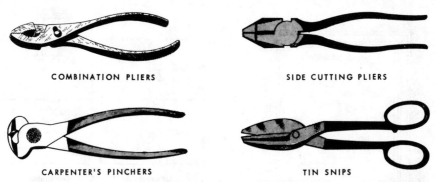

COMBINATION PLIERS   SIDE CUTTING PLIERS

CARPENTER'S PINCHERS   TIN SNIPS

Fig. 442. Pliers, pincers and snips.

arranged with landings but without a well-hole. Also called *dog-legged stairs.*

plenum: An air compartment maintained under pressure and connected to one or more distributing ducts.

plenum system: A system of air conditioning in which the air forced into the building is maintained at a higher pressure than the atmosphere.

pliers: A small, pincerlike tool having a pair of long, relatively broad jaws which are roughened for gripping and bending wire or for holding small objects. Sometimes pliers are made with nippers at the side of the jaws for cutting off wire. Different types of *pliers* in common use are shown in Fig. 442. See *diagonal, long nose, side cutting, slip joint pliers.*

plinth: The lowest square-shaped part of a column; a course of stones as at the base of a wall. See also *plinth block.*

plinth block: A small block slightly thicker and wider than the casing for interior trim of a door. It is placed at the bottom of the door trim against which the baseboard or mopboard is butted. See Fig. 443.

plot: A parcel of land consisting of one or more lots which is described by a recorded plat. See *plot plan.*

plot plan: A plan showing the size of the lot on which the building is to be erected, with all data necessary before excavation for foundation is begun.

plot survey: This includes the lengths of property lines, angles, street names, building restriction lines, north reference, and other related boundary items. The plot survey may include contour lines giving the elevations which must relate to the foundation plan.

plow: A carpenter's grooving plane, which has an adjustable fence and is capable of being fitted with various irons for cutting grooves; a term often used when referring to the work done by a cutting tool, such as *plowing out a rabbet* with a rabbet plane or *plowing out a groove.*

plug: In plumbing, a threaded fitting used to close the end of a valve, union, or coupling. In electrical work, either of two members, usually designated as male and female, used in establishing a circuit. See *male plug,* page 276, and *female plug,* page 183.

plug weld: In welding, when two overlapping pieces are welded together by a weld that passes through a hole in one of the members and fuses the two parts together. When the hole is elongated, the term used is *slot weld,* and when the hole is round the term used is *plug weld.* See Fig. 444. The number in the weld symbol calls for the depth of filling. Omission indicates filling is complete.

plum: In masonry, a large, undressed stone which, together with other similar stones, is used in mass concrete to form footings for walls. When plum stones are used, less concrete is required.

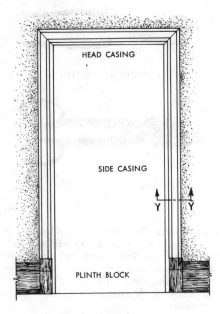

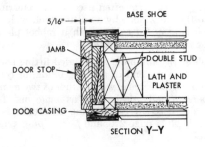

SECTION Y—Y

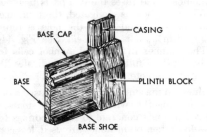

Fig. 443. Plinth block.

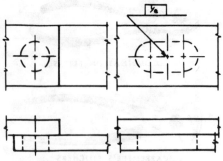

Fig. 444. Plug and slot welds.

plumb: True according to a plumb line; perpendicular; vertical; to true up vertically, as a wall, by use of a plumb line.

plumb and level: A well-finished hardwood or metal case containing a glass tube with bubble set lengthwise for testing accuracy of horizontal planes and lines; also containing a second glass tube with bubble set crosswise for testing accuracy of vertical lines and perpendicular walls. A *level.* See Fig. 351, page 266.

plumb bob: A weight attached to a line used to test perpendicular surfaces for trueness to establish vertical lines or to locate a point. Also, to test or adjust with a plumb line. See Fig. 445.

plumb cut: The cut at right angles to the seat or level cut. The plumb cut is shown in Fig. 586, page 447, as used at the bird's mouth. Also, the cut on the rafter at the ridge line.

plumb line: A strong, heavy string or cord with a weight on one end. It is used to establish a perpendicular line. See Fig. 445. Also: in roof framing, any line that is vertical when the rafter is in position on the roof. See *seat cut,* page 394.

plumb rule: A narrow board having a plumb line and bob on one end. It is used for establishing vertical lines.

plum stone: Large, undressed stone embedded in concrete to form footings for walls. The use of plum stones, where practical, saves in the amount of concrete required.

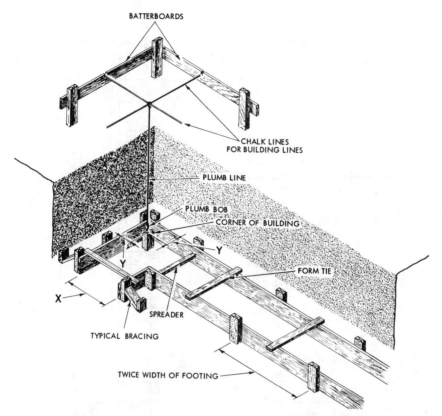

Fig. 445. Plumb bob used to locate the corner of a building when placing footings.

plumber's friend: A plumber's *force cup.* A rubber plunger, with wooden handle, which is used on plumbing fixtures in order to clear stoppages. Also called a *plumber's helper;* a *plunger.*

plumbing diagram: Drawing showing layout, pipe runs, and sizes of the plumbing system. See Fig. 446.

plumbing symbols: Standardized symbols used, instead of written instructions, on architectural drawings or blueprints to designate the location of pipes, drains, and cleanouts. For list of such symbols, see Fig. 447. See also Fig. 427, page 327.

plunger: A device which is used to remove stoppages in plumbing fixtures. A *plumber's friend.*

ply: One thickness of any material used for building up of several layers, as roofing felt or layers of wood in laminated woodwork.

plywood: A building material consisting of two or more thin sheets of wood glued together with the grain of adjacent layers, usually at right angles to each other. See Fig. 448.

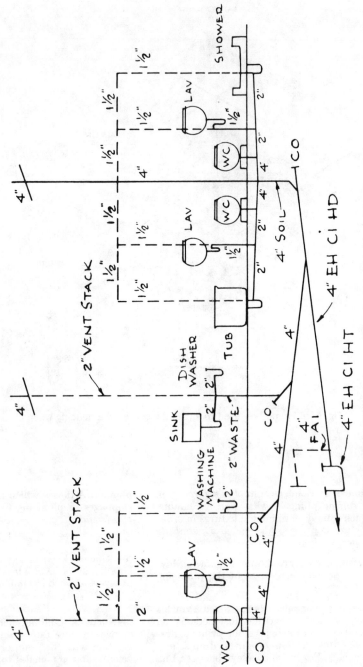

Fig. 446. A plumbing diagram is sometimes included in the working drawings.

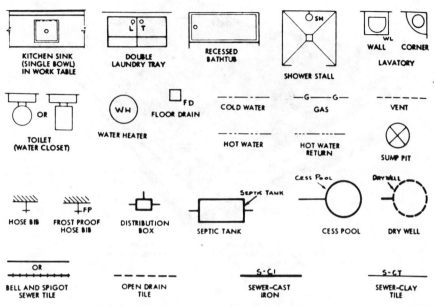

Fig. 447. Common plumbing symbols.

plywood grades: Grade marking of plywood to show the quality and uses of plywood panels. Fig. 449 illustrates typical plywood grade marking. The designation "Group 2" (Fig. 449) refers to the type of wood. Under the softwood commercial standard there are four groups of wood types. The designation A-C refers to the quality of wood on the front veneer and back veneer. The softwood commercial standard lists four common grades: A, B, C and D. A grade is smooth and paintable; neatly made repairs are permissible. This is the best grade commonly found in residential construction. (The highest grade, N grade, is used for cabinet work where natural finishes are desired.) B grade is a solid veneer in which some repair plugs are permitted. C grade and D grade permit more defects and faults with knotholes, splits, and repairs of varying degrees. In addition to these common grades, other special grades are also used.

pneumatic: In building, a term applying to any machine or tool which is powered or driven by compressed air.

pneumatically applied concrete: See *shotcreting,* page 402.

pock marks: In painting and lacquer work, air bubbles trapped in a porous surface coat and which show up as defects when the surface is sanded. These bubbles may be due to applying too much spray or using too much pressure, or the combination of the two may be the cause of this condition. See *pitting,* page 330.

pocket: In carpentry, a hole in a pulley stile through which the counterpoise weights are passed into the box of a window sash and frame.

pocket butt: A hinge designed for three-ply inside shutters. Each leaf of the butt is bent at a right angle near its center. The *pocket butt* is used on the third leaf of a shutter to allow it to enter and leave its pocket without jamming.

pocket door: A door which slides into a pocket in the wall when opened.

343

This opened view of a plywood panel shows how the wood grain of the plies runs in opposing directions to each other to counteract weakness with the grain.

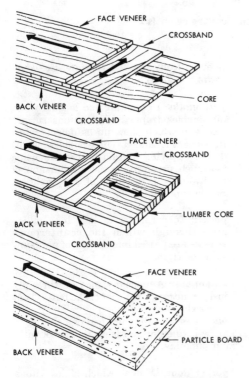

FACE VENEER

CROSSBAND

BACK VENEER

CORE

CROSSBAND

VENEER CORE: The most common plywood uses an all veneer core. The number of plies depends on the use. The more plies the greater strength.

FACE VENEER

CROSSBAND

BACK VENEER

LUMBER CORE

CROSSBAND

LUMBER CORE: The core consists of lumber strips, one to four inches wide, edge glued together. Lumber cores with face wood on all four edges may be ordered.

FACE VENEER

BACK VENEER

PARTICLE BOARD

PARTICLE BOARD CORE: The core is made of wood flakes and chips bonded together with resin to form a mat. Three to five ply panels, one-fourth inch or more in thickness, are common.

Fig. 448. Types of plywoods.

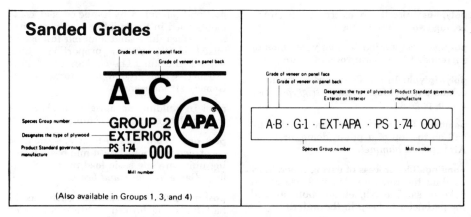

Fig. 449. Plywood marking. (American Plywood Assoc.)

pocket level: A small level used to level or plumb small or difficult to reach surfaces. Also called a *torpedo level*.

pointed ashlar: In stonework, face markings on a stone made with a pointed tool.

pointed style: In architecture, the style characterized by the pointed arch.

pointed work: In masonry, a rough finish on the face of a stone produced by dressing off rough projections with a pointed tool. See *pointed ashlar.*

pointing: A term used in masonry for finishing of joints in a brick or stone wall.

pointing trowel: A small hand instrument used by stone masons or bricklayers for pointing up joints or for removing old mortar from the face of a wall. They are small enough to be used in places where the larger trowels will not fit. They are also used to clean tools and to handle small pats of material in many plastering operations. See *trowel,* page 461.

polarized outlet: A special purpose outlet which supplies 240 V; used with heavy equipment, high wattage appliances, and tools.

pole: A long, circular section of timber, with a relatively small circumference, having a breast-high diameter of about 12 inches or less.

pole derrick: A small, portable derrick guyed by ropes. Sometimes referred to as a *monkey.*

pole piece: A term sometimes applied to the ridgepole of a roof.

pole plate: The horizontal, roof-framing member which supports the feet of the common rafters at the bird's-mouth directly over the wall of the building. The *pole plate* rests on the tie beam or bottom chord of a truss similar to the king-post truss when purlins are used to support the roof rafters. See Fig. 456, page 352.

poll: The blunt end of a hammer; the part which is used for driving nails, as opposed to the *peen* end. Fig. 127, page 101.

polyethylene film: Large, plastic sheets used as a vapor barrier, for water proofing, and to cover fresh concrete so it may cure.

polygon: A geometric figure, usually plane and usually closed, having many angles, especially more than four, and as many sides as angles.

polyphase: In electricity, a current having more than one phase. A single alternating current is called a *single-phase current,* while several currents differing in phase are said to be *polyphase currents* or *multiphase currents.*

345

polyphase circuit: In electricity, a circuit having two or three phases.

polystyle: Supported by many columns or surrounded by several rows of columns.

polytriglyph: In the Doric order, an intercolumniation of four or more *triglyphs.* See Fig. 5, page 4.

pommel: In architecture, an ornamental ball on the top of a pillar, dome, or finial. Also spelled *pummel.*

ponding: The process of curing concrete by flooding the concrete slab with water. (A dyke of sand, earth, etc., is built around the perimeter to keep in the water.)

pool trowel: See *trowel,* page 461.

poor lime: In building, a lime containing more than 15 percent impurities; sometimes called *meager lime.*

poorly reacting sands: Certain sands found to contain an organic compound which interrupts the process of hydration.

poor mortar: Mortar mixture containing less cementing material than normal.

popout: The breaking or chipping away of small portions of a concrete surface due to internal pressure.

poppy heads: In architecture, an ornament often elaborately carved at the top of the ends of benches or pews.

porcelainize: To coat with a ceramic material.

porch: A covered entrance to a building, projecting from the main wall with a separate roof; also, a type of veranda which often is partially enclosed.

porch lattice: A network panel made by crossing lattice to screen the underside of a porch which does not have a continuous foundation.

porosity: The ratio, usually expressed as percentage, of the volume of voids in material to the total volume of the material.

portable: Anything which may be removed from place to place easily, as portable animal pens or portable houses for human beings.

portland cement: A hydraulic cement, commonly used in the building trades, consisting of silica, lime, and alumina intimately mixed in the proper proportions, then burned in a kiln. The clinkers or vitrified product, when ground fine, form an extremely strong cement.

post: In building, an upright member in a frame; also, a pillar or column.

post and beam construction: A system of construction in which post and beam framing units are the basic load-bearing members. Same as *plank and beam.*

post and pan: A term sometimes applied to half timbering formed of brickwork or of lath and plaster panels. See *post* and *petrall.*

post and petrall: Half timbering formed of lath and plaster panels or of brickwork. Same as *post and pan.*

post-tensioned concrete: The same as prestressed concrete except for the fact that the wires are tensioned on the job after the concrete has hardened by running the wires through ducts provided for this purpose. Post-tensioned concrete can be either precast or cast at the job.

pounce: The fine powder sometimes applied to the surface of tracing linen to facilitate inking.

powder-driven fastener: A special tool which drives metal pins by means of an explosive cartridge. Usually used to fasten wood or other materials to concrete. See Fig. 450.

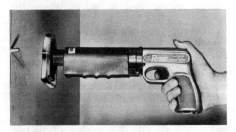

Fig. 450. Powder-driven fastener: pin has just been driven squarely in place with a powder charge. (Ramset Fastening System)

power: In electricity, the rate at which work is done. In direct-current circuits, power in watts equals volts times amperes $(W = E \times I)$. The electrical unit is the *watt*.

power factor: In electricity, the ratio of the true power (watts) to the apparent power (volts × amperes); the cosine of the angle of lag between the alternating current and the voltage waves.

power hammer: Portable electric, pneumatic, and self-contained gasoline-driven hammers using a vibratory action principle. They accommodate such tools as chisels, frost wedges, solid drill steel, clay spades, tampers, diggers, asphalt cutters, ground rod drivers, offset trimming spades, plug and feathers, etc. They are used for removing defective brick from walls, hardened putty from steel sash, and mortar for repointing; for vibrating concrete wall forms, cutting wood, drilling holes in tile floors, digging holes for posts or sewers, and many other applications.

power panel: In electric wiring for motors, a metal box in which fuses are located when it is necessary to change the size of the wires. See *control center, distribution panel, lighting panel, load center, panelboard, panel box.*

power plant: The generators, machines, and buildings where electrical power or energy is produced.

pratt truss: A special type of construction used in both roof and bridge building in which the vertical members are in compression and the diagonals are in tension.

pre-apprenticeship training: Preliminary training given to prepare the student for apprenticeship.

precast concrete: Concrete structures, such as beams, columns, wall panels, pipes, etc., which are batched, placed, and cured at a factory and delivered to a job site. Fig. 451 illustrates a precast concrete unit. See *tilt slab wall unit,* page 453.

prefabricate: To construct or fabricate all the parts, as of a house, at the factory in advance of selling so that the final construction of the building consists merely of assembling and uniting the standard parts.

prefabricated construction: A building so designed as to involve a minimum of assembly at the site; usually comprising a series of large units or panels manufactured in a factory. See Fig. 408, page 313, and Fig. 452.

prefabricated houses: Houses prepared in sections in a shop before material is brought to the building site, where it is assembled in a relatively short time. See Figs. 408, 452.

prefabricated modular units: Units of construction which are prefabricated on a measurement variation base of 4" or its multiples and can be fitted together on the job with a minimum of adjustments. See Fig. 452.

preferred and critical angles: In stair building, the *preferred angle,* for the slope of a stairs and the slope which provides the greatest degree of safety, is between 30 and 50 degrees. An angle of slope of 75 degrees or more is known as a *critical angle.*

prefinished: Material, such as doors, moldings, cabinets, and paneling, which has been painted or stained and varnished in the shop.

preglazed: Describes window sash delivered to the job with glass installed and puttied in place.

prehung doors: Doors that are delivered to the site already hung in the frame.

preliminary study model: In architecture, a model used as an aid to study structure in regard to mass, space, and general form.

preservative: When referring to wood, any substance which is applied to, or injected into, wood to protect it from attack by fungi, insects, or marine animals.

pressed brick: A high-grade brick which is molded under pressure, as a result of which it has sharp edges formed by the meeting of two surfaces and a smooth face, making it suitable for exposed surface work.

pressed wood: In carpentry, a panel manufactured from wood fibers by the use of heat and pressure.

pressure reducing: In steam heating systems, a device used to reduce steam pres-

Fig. 451. Precast reinforced concrete facing units are transported to the job and then lifted and fastened in place at the Mutual Benefit Building in Philadelphia. (Medusa Portland Cement Co.)

Fig. 452. Modules are three-dimensional building units which can be positioned on the foundation. (National Homes Corp.)

sure where boilers are operated at high pressure, as for power purposes.

prestressed concrete: Preliminary stresses are placed in a structure member before a load is applied. Concrete is usually prestressed by imbedding a high strength steel wire in tension in a concrete member.

prick punch: In sheet metal work, a punch used to punch holes through sheet metal for making profiles and also to outline profile patterns through blueprints onto sheet metal when making cornice molds. See Fig. 455.

primary colors: The three primary colors are red, yellow, and blue; the secondary colors are orange, green, and violet.

prime contractor: The contractor who takes responsibility for the entire project. He may build all of the building himself or have subcontractors build the entire building, or he may build part of it and subcontract the rest.

primer: First coat of paint or similar substance which is applied to a surface; a priming paint.

priming: The first coat of paint put on for sizing and preserving wood.

priming coat: The first, or ground, coat of paint applied to wood to fill the pores of the surface. The priming paint is mixed with turpentine to make it thinner than normal consistency

349

priming paint: In painting, the first, or ground, coat of paint applied to a piece of woodwork to fill the pores of the wood and to make a hard, opaque surface. See *priming*.

princess posts: In architecture, additional posts on each side of *queen posts* in buildings which have relatively large spans; posts which give additional support to the queen posts.

principal: In architecture, the most important member in the construction which supports the roof covering for a building; a *roof truss*.

principal meridian: The term *principal meridian* refers to *lines running north and south* and converging at the poles. These serve as reference positions for east and west measurements. Townships or a range of townships will be referred to by principal meridian lines.

profile: An outline drawing of a section, especially a vertical section through a structural part; that is, a contour drawing.

projected: Continued or extended; delineated or carried out according to any system of correspondence between the points of a figure and the points of the surface on which the delineation is made.

projecting belt course: A masonry term used when referring to an elaboration of a plain band course or cut-stone work projecting beyond the face of a wall for several inches.

projection: In architecture, a jutting out of any part or member of a building or other structure. The horizontal distance from the face of a wall to the end of a rafter.

projector: A line used in view development. It is usually drawn perpendicular to a plane of projection.

projet: A plan or project; a projected or finished presentation of a design problem; a proposed design when developed beyond the stage of a sketch.

promenade tile: In masonry, unglazed machine-made tile. Same as quarry tile.

property: A lot or plot, including all buildings and improvements thereon.

property line: A recorded boundary of a plot.

property title: A document stating right to ownership; a deed, especially of real estate. This is a court recorded item.

proportional dividers: Dividers used for enlarging or reducing line or for dividing any distance into a number of equal points. One side of the dividers is marked to obtain the desired number of divisions for lines. Circles may also be divided. The series of divisions for circles are marked 'circle'. See Fig. 453.

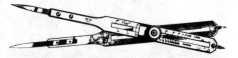

Fig. 453. Proportional dividers are helpful for quickly enlarging, reducing, or dividing distances. (Keuffel and Esser Co.)

proportioning: Selecting the relative amounts of ingredients, that is, the ratio of one ingredient to another.

prostyle: Pertaining to a portico in which the columns stand out entirely in front of the walls of the building to which it is attached; usually this is a four-columned portico; also, a term applied to a prostyle building.

protractor: A mathematical instrument used in plotting and drawing for laying off and measuring angles on paper.

psi: Pounds per square inch; the compressive strength of concrete is measured in psi's.

pteroma: In a classical temple, or any similar columnar structure, the enclosed space between the wall of the cella and the solid wall behind the portico, including the stoa, portica, and the stylobate.

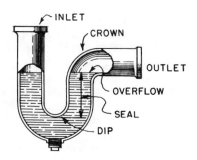

Fig. 454. P Trap.

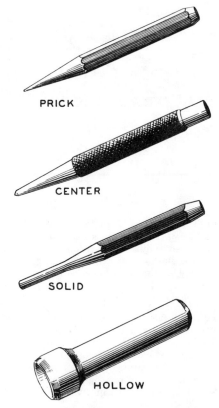

Fig. 455. Punches.

p trap: In plumbing, a type of trap used in sanitary pipes, shaped like the letter P, having an almost horizontal outlet. See Fig. 454.

puddle: A mixture of sand, clay, and water worked while wet to form a substance impervious to water; to make loose dirt firm and solid by turning on water.

puddle sticks: A hand tool used for consolidating fresh concrete; this tool resembles a sidewalk ice scraper but has a longer hanger.

pugging: A coarse kind of mortar used for packing or covering and laid between floor joists to prevent the passage of sound; mortar used to deaden sound; also called *deadening*.

pull: A drawer pull.

pull box: In electricity, a metal box placed in a long run of conduit, or where a number of conduits make a sharp bend, to help in pulling in the conductors, or for the purpose of distributing the conductors.

pull switch: In electricity, a snap switch located in the ceiling of a room; usually operated by a chain or cord extending down into the room. Also called *ceiling switch* or *chain-pull switch*.

pulverize: To break up into small parts.

pulvinated: In architecture, a term applied to a structural member which is swelled or curved convexly, as a frieze with a bulging face; called a *pulvinated frieze*.

pumice: Finely powdered volcanic glass used for polishing.

punch: A steel driving tool used principally for making indentations or holes. See Fig. 455.

puncheon: A short, upright piece of framing timber; a short post or stud giving intermediate support to a beam, especially in trussed partitions; also, a roughly dressed slab of a split log used as flooring.

purlin post: In heavy-timber framing; a post placed beneath a purlin to support it and to prevent sagging.

purlins: Horizontal timbers supporting the common rafters in roofs, the timbers spanning from truss to truss. See Fig. 456.

351

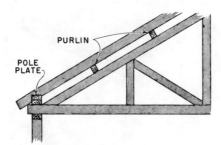

Fig. 456. Purlins.

push plate: A metal plate fastened on the surface of a door to protect the door from wear and soiling, as a result of its being pushed by persons when opening it. In public buildings and business houses, usually the word *push* is a part of the face design of the *push plate*.

push-pull rule: A type of rule made of rigid flexible steel which serves both as a rule and as a measuring tape. It can be used in restricted places where other scaling devices cannot enter. When not in use, the blade is coiled into a light, compact case which can be carried in a vest pocket. See Fig. 457.

putlog: A crosspiece in a scaffolding, one end of which rests in a hole in a wall; also, horizontal pieces which support the floor-

ing of scaffolding, one end being inserted into *putlog* holes; that is, short timbers on which the flooring of a scaffolding is laid.

putty: A type of cement usually made of whiting and boiled linseed oil, beaten or kneaded to the consistency of dough, and used in sealing glass in sash, filling small holes and crevices in wood, and for similar purposes.

putty coat: A common finish coat in plastering; a *smooth coat*. It can be worked to a smooth, straight, hard surface, and it is well suited to all types of surface treatments. Sometimes called a white coat, hardcoat, creamcoat, or smooth coat.

putty in plastering: A cement consisting of lump lime slacked with water to the consistency of cream and left to harden by evaporation until it becomes like soft putty. It is then mixed with sand or plaster of Paris and used for a finishing coat.

PVC (vinyl) pipe: In plumbing, vinyl piping used in all parts of the plumbing system. See Fig. 458. Also used for electrical conduit.

Q

quadrangle: In architecture, an open court or space in the form of a parallelogram, usually rectangular in shape, partially or entirely surrounded by buildings, as on a college campus; also, the buildings surrounding the court.

quadrant: An instrument usually consisting of a graduated arc of 90 degrees, with an index or vernier; used primarily for measuring altitudes. Sometimes a spirit level or a plumb line is attached to the *quadrant* for determining the vertical or horizontal direction.

quadrilateral: A polygon having four sides and four angles.

quality: Peculiar property or power of anything; also, grade or degree of goodness.

quarrel: A small square or diamond-shaped member, as a pane of glass, especially when set diagonally; same as *quarry*.

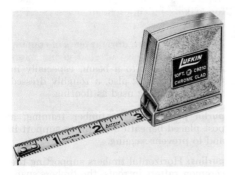

Fig. 457. Push-pull rule. (Lufkin Rule Co.)

Fig. 458. PVC pipe is lightweight and easy to install. It can be preassembled readily. (B. F. Goodrich Chemical Co.)

quarry: A diamond-shaped pane of glass; same as quarrel; also, a small square stone or tile.

quarry-faced masonry: Squared stone as it comes from the quarry, with split face, only squared at joints; having the face left rough as when taken from the quarry, as building stone; masonry built of such stone.

quarrying: A process of digging or blasting from the earth raw materials that make up portland cement.

quarry-stone bond: In masonry, a term applied to the arrangement of stones in rubblework.

quarry tile: In masonry, a name given to machine-made, unglazed tile. Also called *promenade tile.*

quarter bend: A bend, as of a pipe, through an arc of 90 degrees.

quarter round: A type of molding which presents a profile of a quarter of a circle.

quarter-sawed grain: Another term for *edge-grain lumber,* used generally in hardwoods. See *edge grain,* page 167. See Fig. 434, page 330. See *plain sawed grain,* page 330.

quarter sawing: The sawing of logs lengthwise into quarters, with the saw cuts parallel with the medullary rays; then cutting the quarters into boards, as in making quartered oak boards.

quatrefoil: In architecture, a single decorative feature consisting of an ornamental unit in the form of a four-leaved flower.

Queen Anne arch: A type of combination arch, consisting of a central semi-circular arch having side camber arches carried from the same springings. See *Venetian arch,* page 471.

353

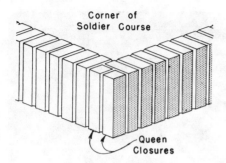

Corner of
Soldier Course

Queen
Closures

Fig. 459. Queen closure.

queen bolt: A long bolt of steel or iron serving in a roof truss in place of a *queen post.* Same as *queen rod.* See Fig. 460.

queen closure: A half brick made by cutting a whole brick in two lengthwise; also, a half brick used in a course of brick masonry to prevent vertical joints falling above one another. Sometimes spelled *closer.* See Fig. 459.

queen post: One of the two vertical tie posts in a roof truss or any similar framed truss. Sometimes a steel or iron rod is used in place of a *queen post.* Such a rod is known as a *queen rod.* See Fig. 460.

queen-post roof: A timber roof having two queen posts but without a king post. See *queen post,* Fig. 460.

queen-post truss: A truss in which the tie beams are supported by two posts called *queen posts.* See Fig. 460.

queen rod: A long, steel or iron rod serving in a queen truss as a queen post. See *queen bolt.* See Fig. 460.

queen truss: A truss framed with queen posts; that is, two vertical tie posts, distinguished from the king truss which has only one tie post. See Fig. 460.

quicklime: The solid product remaining after limestone has been heated to a high temperature. The process of producing lime is known as *lime-burning.*

quick sweep: In architecture, a term applied to circular work which has a relatively small radius.

quirk: A small groove, or channel, separating a bead or other molding from the adjoining members; also, an acute angle between moldings or beads.

quirk bead: A bead molding separated from the surface on one side by a channel or groove. A *double quirk bead* refers to a molding with a channel on each side of the beads.

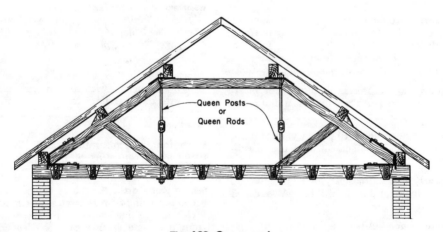

Queen Posts
or
Queen Rods

Fig. 460. Queen post.

quirk molding: An architectural term usually applied to a molding which has a small groove, although sometimes the term is used in reference to a molding with both a convex and a concave curve separated by a flat portion.

quoins: In architecture, large squared stones set at the angles of a building. In stone masonry, often the *quoins* are made of stones much larger than those in the remainder of the wall; in brickwork, sometimes the *quoins* are of large squared stones.

quotation: A statement of the price for which a specified product or service will be supplied.

R

rab: In plastering, a stick or beater used for mixing hair with mortar.

rabbet: In woodworking, a term used in referring to a groove cut in the surface or along the edge of a board, plank, or other timber, so as to receive another board or piece similarly cut. See Fig. 190, page 150.

rabbet joint: A joint which is formed by fitting together two pieces of timber which have been rabbeted. See Fig. 330, page 252.

rabbet plane: In carpentry, a type of bench plane used for cutting or rabbeting in trimming dados, moldings, and grooves. *Rabbet planes* used for planing into corners are shown in Fig. 436, page 332.

rabbeted lock: In building, a lock which is fitted into a recess cut in the edge of a door.

raceway: In electricity, any channel which is designed expressly for and used only for holding wires or cables. Fig. 461 illustrates the use of a raceway.

racked: In carpentry, a term applied to a temporary timbering, braced so as to stiffen it against deformation.

racking: In laying a stone or brick wall when workmen approach a corner where two walls meet, they step back the end of each course so it is shorter than the course below it. This procedure is known as *racking*. The workmen can then tie in their courses in the easiest manner, and the junction of the walls does not form a vertical line which might cause cracking, owing to uneven settlement of the different parts.

rack saw: In carpentry, a saw having wide teeth.

radial: Pertaining to rays of radii; shooting out or radiating from a center, like rays.

radial bar: A device made by attaching a point and pencil to a wooden bar which is then used for striking large curves.

radial saw: A circular saw which hangs from, and slides back and forth on, a horizontal arm or beam which is supported by a vertical post at the rear of the saw table. The horizontal arm pivots from side to side to allow for angle cuts. The saw, and the motor which usually hangs with it, can be tilted to cut bevels. See Fig. 462.

radiant heating: A system in which a space is heated only by the use of pipe coils or electric resistance wires placed in the floor, ceiling, or walls.

radiating brick: In masonry, a brick which tapers in at least one direction, so as to be especially useful for curved work, as in building arches. Sometimes called *radius brick.* See *compass brick,* page 111.

radiation: The transfer of heat through space by wave motion or rays; also, the energy rays from the sun.

radiator: A heating unit which transfers heat by radiation; usually fed by hot water or steam.

radius: A straight line radiating from the center of a circle or sphere to the circumference; the semidiameter of a circle or sphere.

radius bent: Reinforcing bars bent to a radius larger than that specified for standard hooks; a bar curved to fit into circular walls, as the horizontal bar in a silo.

radius tool: In masonry and cement work, a finishing tool used for shaping curved sections which must be smooth and true.

raft or mat foundations: Foundation system where the building structure is sup-

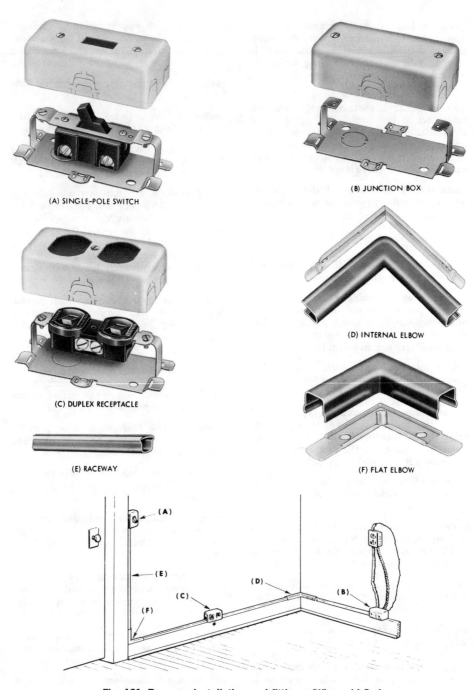

(A) SINGLE-POLE SWITCH

(B) JUNCTION BOX

(C) DUPLEX RECEPTACLE

(D) INTERNAL ELBOW

(E) RACEWAY

(F) FLAT ELBOW

Fig. 461. Raceway installation and fittings. (Wiremold Co.)

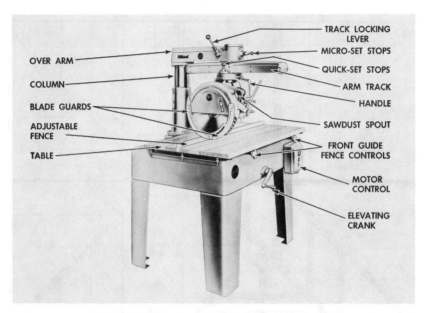

Fig. 462. Radial saw and parts. (Rockwell Mfg. Co.)

ported upon a system of continuous concrete beams or slabs.

rafter: A sloping roof member that supports the roof covering which extends from the ridge or the hip of the roof to the eaves. There are five basic types of rafters: (1) The *common rafter* is cut to fit the ridge board at the top and a top plate on a wall for the bottom cut. (2) The *jack rafter* also fits on a top plate of a wall with the high end having a double slant cut to fit the hip rafter. (3) The *hip rafters* are the long rafters from the corner of the building to the end of the ridge board. (4) The *valley rafter* serves the intersection of two roof surfaces that come together as the inside of the V. (5) The *cripple rafter* has double slant cuts on each end. See *roof members.* See Figs. 463 and 483. See also *hip rafters,* page 238, and *jack rafter,* page 248.

rafter or joist plate: Plate at top of masonry or concrete wall supporting rafter or roof joist and ceiling framing. See *plate,* page 337.

rafter plate: In building construction, the framing member upon which the rafters rest. See Fig. 483, page 371.

rafter table: A table found on the face of the blade, or body, of the best-grade steel framing squares. The table gives directly the length per foot of run for a large variety of common rafters. See Fig. 464.

rag felt: In building construction, a type of heavy paper composed of rags impregnated with asphalt; used in the manufacture of waterproofing membranes, and for making asphalt shingles and other types of composition roofing, such as asphalt roofing.

raggle: In masonry, a manufactured building unit provided with a groove into which metal flashing is fitted. *Raggle* is used especially around parapet walls, or in connection with water tables, to prevent leaking where flashing is applied to a masonry wall. Also, a term applied to a groove made in stone to receive adjoining material.

rag work: In masonry, a term applied to any kind of rubble work made of small, thin stones.

rail: A horizontal bar of wood or metal used as a guard, as the top member of a balustrade; also, the horizontal member of a

357

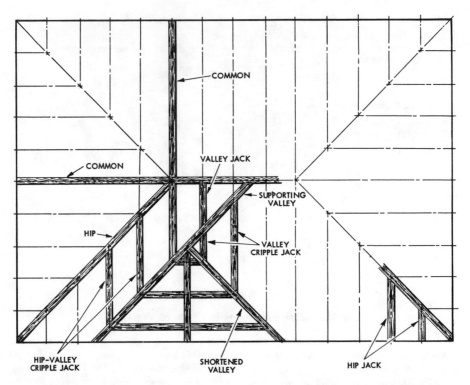

Fig. 463. Rafters are named according to their position in the roof and their cuts.

			14	13	
LENGTH OF MAIN RAFTERS PER FOOT OF RUN	21.63		18.44	17.69	
LENGTH OF HIP OR VALLEY RAFTERS PER FOOT OF RUN	24.74		22.00	21.38	
DIFFERENCE IN LENGTH OF JACKS — 16 INCHES ON CENTERS	28.84		24.585	23.588	
DIFFERENCES IN LENGTH OF JACKS — 2 FEET ON CENTERS	43.27		36.38	35.38	
SIDE CUT OF JACKS	6-11/16		7-13/16	8-1/8	
SIDE CUT OF HIP OR VALLEY	8-1/4		9-3/8	9-5/8	

Fig. 464. Unit-length rafter table on face of framing square.

door or window sash. See Fig. 189, page 149, and Fig. 198, page 154.

rail bolt: In stair building, a bolt which is threaded for a nut on both ends; used for fastening stair rails; a stair bolt. Also called *handrail bolt.*

railing: A handrail of a stair including the balusters and newels. See Fig. 561, page 424.

rainwater pipe: A pipe which conveys rainwater from a roof to the drain. Same as *downspout.*

raised grain: A roughened condition of the surface of dressed lumber—the hard summerwood is raised above the softer springwood but not torn loose from it.

raised mold: An applied molding which partially covers, or which extends above, the face or surface of stiles or rails.

raised table: In architecture, an elevated or projecting member on a flat surface which is large in proportion to the projection.

raising: In painting and lacquer work, a wrinkled or blistered condition on a finished surface. This defect is caused by the reaction of lacquer solvents on unoxidized oil in an oil-base undercoater or by the application of lacquer over old paint or varnish.

raising hammer: A hammer having a rounded face used in lifting or raising sheet metal. See Fig. 465.

Fig. 465. Raising hammer.

raising plate: In building construction, a horizontal timber resting on part of a structure and supporting a superstructure. See *wall plate,* page 475.

rake: The inclined portion of a cornice; also, the angle of slope of a roof rafter, commonly spoken of as the *rake of the roof.*

raked joint: In brick masonry, a type of joint which has the mortar raked out to a specified depth while the mortar is still green.

rake molding: A gable molding with a longer face than that of the eaves molding. The face of the *rake molding* is worked out so it will line up with the eaves molding. See Fig. 466.

rake or raking bond: In masonry, a method of laying the courses of brick in an angular or zigzag fashion, as is often seen in the end walls of Colonial houses. See *herringbone bond,* page 236.

rake out: In masonry, the removal of loose mortar by scraping, in preparation for pointing of the joints.

raking: Moldings with the arrises inclined to the horizon. In masonry, headers laid diagonally, either with all headers parallel or in a plan forming a herringbone pattern, in which case it is known as *herringbone bond.* Also: a sloping brace for a shore head. See *raking shore.*

raking bond: In masonry, a type of bond characterized by diagonal headers which may be parallel to each other, or they may be arranged in a herringbone pattern.

raking cornice: In architecture, a type of cornice especially designed as a decorative feature for the slant sides of a pediment.

raking course: In masonry, a course of bricks laid diagonally between the face courses of a specially thick wall for the purpose of adding strength to the wall.

raking shore: In carpentry, a heavy inclined timber, one end of which rests on the ground while the other end presses against a wall to which temporary support is to be given.

rammed earth construction: A type of building construction in which the exterior walls

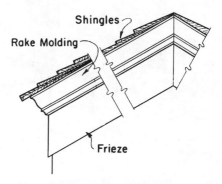

Fig. 466. Rake molding.

are bearing walls composed of a controlled combination of sand, clay, coarse aggregate, and moisture. The mixture is compacted by pressure into forms.

rammer: In building construction, a term applied to an instrument which is used for driving anything by force, as stones or piles, or for compacting earth. In concrete work, a kind of "stomper" used to pack concrete by removing the air bubbles.

ramp: A short bend, slope, or curve usually in a vertical plane where a handrail, coping, or similar element changes direction; also, a sloping roadway or passageway.

ramp and twist: In masonry, a term used when referring to work in which a surface both twisting and rising has to be, or is, produced.

rampant: A term applied to an arch or vault which springs from one level of support and rests at the other side on a higher level; an arch whose abutments spring from an inclined plane.

rampant arch: In building, an arch whose abutments are not in the same horizontal line.

rance: A timber or piece of lumber placed in an oblique position against a wall or building to serve as a temporary prop or support. Same as *shore.*

ranch style architecture: A one-story house of rambling type originating in the warmer climates of the west. The roof is low-pitched. The plan is geared to outdoor living with rooms frequently arranged around a court. See Fig. 467.

random: A haphazard course without definite aim or direction; also, without method or system. Odd sizes of materials taken together are spoken of as *random sizes.* A manner of laying stones so they do not follow a regular pattern.

random ashlar: In masonry, a type of ashlar construction where the building blocks are laid apparently at random but actually are placed in a definite pattern which is repeated again and again. See *ashlar,* Fig. 30, page 28.

random bond: A type of masonry in which the stones are not laid in any regular pattern but are laid as a hit-and-miss bond.

Fig. 467. The ranch-type house may assume many plan shapes and may be designed to fit problem lots. The casual appearance of its design gives a feeling of openness.

random joints: A term used in furniture making when pieces of veneer are joined without special attention being given as to whether or not the various pieces are of equal widths.

random shingles: Shingles of different widths banded together; often these vary from 2½ inches to 12 inches or more in width.

random widths: A term used by lumber dealers when referring to material which is of varying widths, as *random shingles* which are of different widths.

random work: Any type of work done in irregular order, as a wall built up of odd-sized stones.

range: Refers to a *row of townships* north and south and numbered successively 1, 2, 3, etc., either north or south from a reference position.

range masonry: Squared stone laid in horizontal courses of even height. Same as *rangework.*

ranged rubble: Masonry built of rough fragments of broken stone, or unsquared or rudely dressed stones, irregular in size and shape. See *rubblework,* page 378.

ranger: A horizontal bracing member used in form construction. Also called a *whaler* or *waler.*

rangework: Squared stone laid in horizontal courses of even height; same as *coursed ashlar;* also known as *ranged masonry.*

rasp: A coarse file or a filelike tool which has coarse projections for reducing material by a grinding motion instead of by cutting. See Fig. 468.

rat stop: A type of construction for a masonry wall which provides protection against rats by stopping them when they attempt to burrow down along the outside of the foundation.

ratchet bit brace: A carpenter's tool consisting of a bit brace with a ratchet attachment which permits operation of the tool in close quarters. See Fig. 469.

ratchet drill: A hand drill which is rotated by a ratchet wheel moved by a pawl and lever.

ratchet hoist: Device for lifting loads. Some-

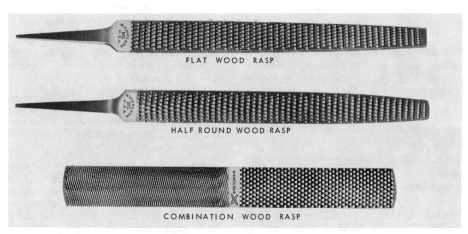

FLAT WOOD RASP

HALF ROUND WOOD RASP

COMBINATION WOOD RASP

Fig. 468. Rasps. (Nicholson File Co.)

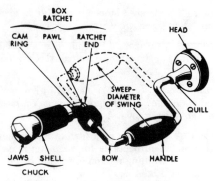

Fig. 469. Ratchet brace and parts.

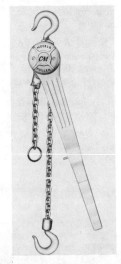

Fig. 470. A ratchet-type puller, for lifting or pulling loads in any position. (Chisholm-Moore Hoist Div. of Columbus McKinnon Corp.)

times called a ratchet puller or "come along". See Fig. 470.

ratchet nail: A special type of annular nail used for nailing into metal studs to hold drywall and gypsum lath. See Fig. 390, page 296.

ratchet wheel: A wheel with angular teeth on the edge, into which a pawl drops or catches to prevent a reversal of motion.

rating: In electricity, the capacity or limit of a load of an electrical machine expressed in horsepower, watts, volts, or amperes.

ratio: The relation between two similar magnitudes in respect to the number of times the first contains the second, either integrally or fractionally, as the *ratio* of 3 to 4 may be written 3:4 or 3/4.

rawlplug anchor: A special type of anchor for bolts and screws; used to secure structural wood parts to masonry or concrete walls. See anchors, Fig. 18, page 17. Fig. 471 illustrates how anchor is installed.

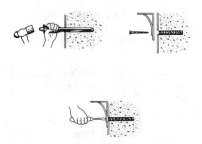

Fig. 471. Rawlplug anchor.

ready-mix concrete: Concrete delivered to the job site already mixed.

ream: The process of smoothing the surface of a hole and finishing it to the required size with a *reamer*.

reamer: Device for removing burrs or sharp edges inside the mouth of a pipe. See *flute reamer,* Fig. 262, page 201. Also, a tool used for finishing holes which have been drilled in wood or metal.

rear arch: An arch which carries the inner thickness of a wall, when the face of the exterior is carried in some other way, as when a door or window piece is designed in an elaborate manner, leaving one-half or more of the thickness of the wall to be supported apart from it.

rebar: A contraction for *reinforcing bar,* commonly used in the building trades.

rebate: A woodworking term used when referring to a recess in or near the edge of one piece of timber to receive the edge of another piece cut to fit it; that is, a rabbet groove.

receptacle: In electricity, a device placed in an *outlet box* to which the wires in the conduit are fastened. House fixtures plug into the receptacle. See Fig. 461 C, page 357.

receptacle outlet: An outlet where one or more receptacles are installed. See Fig. 461 C.

receptacle plug: In electricity, a device which enables a quick electrical connection to be made between an appliance and a receptacle.

recess: An indention in the surface of a room as an alcove or bay window.

recess bathtub: A *bathtub* built into a recess or alcove as a permanent fixture.

reciprocating: Moving with an alternating backward and forward movement.

rectangular tie: A heavy wire fabrication shaped in the form of a rectangle, usually about 2x6 inches. See Fig. 376, page 284. Such ties are used to bind together the two separate wall sections of a cavity wall, the ends of each tie being embedded in the horizontal mortar joint of both tiers at intervals of 24".

reducer: A fitting which has one opening of a smaller diameter used to reduce the size of pipe in the line. See Fig. 112, page 89.

reducing valve: A valve set to maintain a minimum pressure of steam in a heating system. Should the pressure in the system fall below the setting, the valve automatically opens, feeding water to the boiler until the pressure in the system again reaches the setting point. Used now with steam radiant heating systems.

reeding: A general, architectural term applied to various kinds of ornamental molding; for example, a small convex or semicylindrical molding resembling a reed; also, a set of such moldings as on a column; any

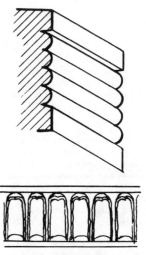

Fig. 472. Reeding.

ornamentation consisting of such moldings. See Fig. 472.

reel and bead molding: An ornamental molding in which flattened disclike parts alternate, singly or in pairs, with elongated rounded bodies called *beads* or *olives.* See *bead and reel molding,* Fig. 52, page 43.

reel fixture: A light fixture which is suspended from a concealed reel of wire, permitting the light source to be raised and lowered at will.

reflective insulation: Foil-surfaced insulation whose insulating power is determined by the number of its reflective surfaces and which must be used in connection with an air space. This type of insulation also acts as a vapor barrier.

reflector: A device consisting of a bright, polished surface so shaped that light or heat falling upon it will be directed to the place desired.

refractory brick: Brick that can withstand great heat without softening.

refrigerant: A substance suitable as a working agent in a refrigerator and which produces a refrigerating effect by its absorption of heat while expanding or vaporizing.

register: A fixture through which conditioned air flows.

reglet: In architecture, a flat, narrow molding used to separate structural members such as panels; a molding turned to form frets and knobs or other ornamental features. A groove in a wall to receive flashing. In carpentry, a molding used to cover joints between boards.

regula: In the Doric order of architecture, the flat block from which the small cone-shaped pendants, or *guttae,* drop. See Fig. 230, page 174.

reinforced concrete: Concrete in which steel reinforcing bars are embedded to provide added strength. See Figs. 139, 451 and 473.

reinforced concrete beams: Girders or beams made of concrete which has been strengthened by the use of reinforcing steel bars. See Fig. 473.

reinforced concrete column: Column with concrete reinforced with steel bars. See Fig. 139, page 110.

reinforced concrete construction: A type of building in which the principal structural members, such as floors, columns and beams, are made of concrete, which is poured around isolated steel bars, or steel meshwork, in such a way that the two materials act together in resisting force. Fig. 474 shows reinforcement for a typical concrete floor. See also Figs. 139, 451 and 473.

reinforced T beams: Concrete beams shaped like the letter T are strengthened with steel bars inserted in the concrete while it is in a plastic condition. See Fig. 473.

reinforcing: The steel bars or fabric used to strengthen concrete slabs, beams, or columns.

reinforcing bars: Steel bars imbedded in concrete to increase its ability to withstand bending and stretching. Sometimes called *rebars.*

related trades: The different or allied trades whose work is necessary for the completing of a project.

relative humidity: A measurement of the amount of moisture present in the air; expressed in percentage.

relieving arch: Any arch, strut, or piece built over a lintel, as of a door, or over another arch not strong enough to carry the load of the superstructure, for relieving or distributing the weight of the load. Same as *discharging arch.*

relievo: The projection of figures or other ornamental work from a background; relief work; the same as *rilievo.*

renaissance: In architecture, a style of structural ornamentation which follows the medieval, originating in Italy in the fifteenth century.

rendering: A term used in perspective drawing meaning to finish with ink or color to bring out the effect of the design.

rendu (ran'du): A finished design problem artistically expressed.

renewable fuse: In electricity, an enclosed fuse so constructed that the fusing material can be replaced easily.

repairs: Any labor or materials provided to restore, reconstruct, or renew any exist-

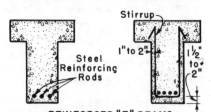

REINFORCED RECTANGULAR BEAMS

REINFORCED "T" BEAMS

Fig. 473. Reinforced beams.

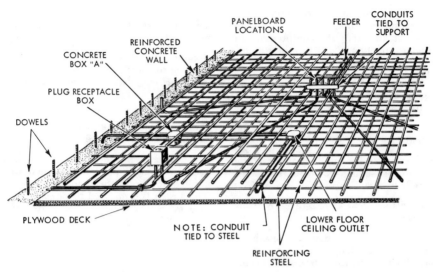

Fig. 474. Reinforcing bars in place for a concrete reinforced floor.

ing part of a building, its fixtures, or appurtenances.

replacing: The renewing or restoring to a former place or condition, as the renewing of parts of a building which have been damaged or impaired by use or the elements.

reshoring: Temporary vertical support for forms or completed structure, placed after original shoring support has been removed.

resins (natural wood): A sticky yellow or brown substance that flows from certain plants and trees, especially the pine and fir.

resistance welding: The fusing together of metals by heat and pressure. If two pieces of metal are placed between electrodes which become conductors for a low voltage and high amperage current, the materials will, because of their own resistance, become heated to a plastic or semi-solid state. To complete the weld, the current is interrupted before pressure is released, thereby allowing the weld metal to cool for solid strength.

resonator: Any device or acoustic enclosure, such as a resonance box, a pipe, or cavity,

for increasing the power of sound. See *acoustic jars,* page 3.

respond: An engaged pilaster forming a pair with another, as a half column supporting an arch, a colonnade, or arcade; a corbel used as a respond or a pilaster backing a free column.

retaining wall: Any wall erected to hold back or support a bank of earth; any wall subjected to lateral pressure other than wind pressure; also, an enclosing wall built to resist the lateral pressure of internal loads.

retarder: An admixture used to slow the setting process in concrete or mortar. Used occasionally during hot weather.

retempering: The addition of water and remixing of concrete or mortar which has started to stiffen.

reticulate: In furniture making, to divide, mark, or construct so as to form a network.

reticulated: In masonry, work in which the courses are arranged like the meshes of a net; work constructed or faced with diamond-shaped stones or of stones arranged diagonally.

365

return: The turn and continuation of a molding, wall, or projection, in an opposite or different direction; the continuation in a different direction of the face of a building, or any member, as a colonnade or molding.

return bend. A fitting or a pipe shaped like the letter U.

return head: A head appearing both on the edge and face of a piece of work.

return nosing: In the building of stairs, the mitered, overhanging end of a tread outside the balusters. See Fig. 561, page 424.

return register: Vent that returns cold air to be warmed.

reveal: In architecture, that part of a jamb or vertical face of an opening for a window or doorway between the frame and the outside surface of a wall; also, a term sometimes applied to the entire jamb or vertical face of an opening.

reversed door: A door which opens in the direction opposite to that considered *regular*. A room door opening inward is *regular,* and one opening outward is a *reversed door.* Cupboard doors opening outward are *regular.*

revetment: A concrete facing to protect a wall—usually from erosion by water.

revolution: The turning or revolving of a body on its axis until it makes a complete circle, as the *revolution* of a shaft.

revolving shelf: Sometimes called a lazy susan, this shelf revolves to provide easy access to the total shelf area. It is often placed in a closet, especially in the ordinarily unusable inner corners where two cabinets meet each other at right angles.

rhomboid: A parallelogram whose angles are oblique and only the opposite sides are equal.

rhombus: An equilateral parallelogram whose angles are oblique.

rib: A plain or molded arched member which forms a support for an arch or vault; a decorative feature, resembling a rib, on the surface of a vault or ceiling; a project-

ing piece or molding upon the interior of a vault, or used to form tracery in ornamental work.

ribbon: A narrow board used in balloon framing to tie studs together and serve as a support for joists. Also called *ledger.* See Fig. 41.

ribbon strip: A board which is nailed to studding for carrying floor joists. Same as *ribbon.* See Fig. 41, page 35.

rice brush: In plastering, a brush usually used for acoustic plasters. The material is applied to the surface and straightened. This brush is then used to punch the surface evenly to create a textured surface. Also called a *stippling brush.* See Fig. 475.

Fig. 475. Rice brush or stippling brush.

rich lime: A quicklime, which is free from impurities, used especially for plastering and for masonry work. Also called *fat lime.*

rich mortar: Mortar mixture contains a large portion of cementing material.

ridge: The intersection of two surfaces forming an outward projecting angle, as at the top of a roof where two slopes meet. The highest point of a roof composed of sloping sides. See Fig. 483, page 371.

ridge board: A horizontal timber at the upper end of the common rafters, to which these rafters are nailed. In house construction, usually the *ridge board* is a 1x6 piece. See *ridge,* Fig. 483, page 371.

ridge capping: The covering of wood or metal which tops the ridge of a roof.

ridge course: The last or top course of slates or tiles on a roof; cut to length as required.

ridge covering: The covering applied over the ridge of a roof to protect the intersection of the sloping roof surfaces. See *ridge capping.*

ridge cut: The cut of a rafter for a gable roof.

ridge fillet: In architecture, a ridge between flutes of a column or other depressions.

ridge pole: The horizontal member or timber at the top of a roof which receives the upper ends of the rafters.

ridge rib: A rib forming the ridge in a vaulted roof.

ridge roll: A strip of sheet metal, composition roofing, tiling, or wood used to cover and finish a roof ridge; also, a *ridgepiece,* or rounded section, over which a lead flashing is secured as a covering for the roof ridge.

ridge roof: A roof whose end view is a gable and whose rafters meet in an apex.

ridge stop: A strip or piece of sheet lead which is shaped over the junction between a roof ridge and a wall; used when a watertight joint must be made where the two run into each other.

ridge tiles: Tiles used to cap the ridge of a roof.

ridge ventilator: A raised section on a roof ridge provided with vents which admit air currents.

ridgepiece: A timber member laid horizontally along the ridge of a roof to protect the intersection of the two roof slopes. Same as *ridge pole.*

ridging: Material for making or covering the ridges of roofs.

rigging: Handling of rope, chain and steel cable.

right angle: An angle formed by two lines which are perpendicular to each other; that is, the lines represent two radii that intercept a quarter of a circle; hence, a 90-degree angle.

right-hand door: If the door swings from you and the hinges are at your right hand, when you face the door from the outside, it is called a *right-hand door.* If the door swings toward you, then it is known as a *reverse right-hand door.*

right-hand lock: A door lock constructed for a right-hand door.

right-hand stairway: Stairs where the handrail is to your right as you ascend the stairs. See Fig. 561, page 424.

right-hand tool: A tool designed for the use of a right-handed person, as opposed to a *left-hand tool,* which is made for a left-handed person.

right line: The shortest distance between two points; that is, a straight line.

rigid conduit: Non-flexible steel tubing used to carry electrical conductors.

rim: A term used when referring to articles of hardware designed to be applied to the face of doors and windows; in contra-distinction to items designed to be mortised into the wood.

rim latch: A door lock designed to be screwed to the face of a door, in contra-distinction to a *mortise lock.*

rime: A rung of a ladder.

ring rot: A term used with reference to lumber in which decay or rot follows the rings of annual growth.

ring shake: A separation of the wood between the annual growth rings of a tree.

ripping: In woodworking, the sawing or splitting of wood lengthwise of the grain or fiber.

ripping bar: A steel or wrought-iron bar having one end slightly bent with a chisel-shaped tip; used for prying purposes. The

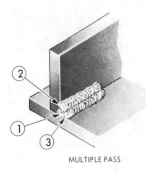
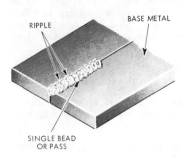

Fig. 476. Ripples.

other end, which is curved gooseneck fashion, is split and used for pulling nails. Sometimes called *wrecking bar, claw bar,* or *pinch bar.* See Fig. 425, page 325.

ripping size: The required width of stock or material to produce any given finish size; usually 1/4 inch over finished size.

ripple: In welding, the shape of the deposited bead caused by movement of the rod. See Fig. 476.

riprap: In masonry construction, broken stones or other similar material, thrown together loosely and without definite order, for a sustaining bed where a foundation wall is to be formed on soft earth or under deep water.

ripsaw: A saw having coarse, chisel-shaped teeth used in cutting wood in the direction of the grain. See Fig. 477.

rise: (Roof) The vertical distance between the plate and the ridge. (Stair) The total height of a stair. Also, the vertical distance between the springing of an arch and the highest point of the intrados (Fig. 235), page 180.

rise and run: A term used by carpenters to indicate the degree of incline.

rise of an arch: In architecture, the vertical distance from the center of the span of an arch, in the springing line, to the center of the intrados. See Fig. 235, page 180.

riser: A vertical board under the tread of a stair step; that is, a board set on edge for

connecting the treads of a stairway. See Fig. 561, page 424. In electricity, vertical conduits containing wires or cables which run from floor to floor of a building and supply electric current to the various floors. In steam heating, a vertical pipe for the purpose of supplying steam for heating an upper room or rooms. See, also, *riser pipe.*

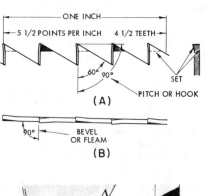

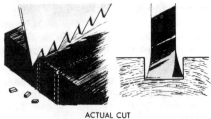

ACTUAL CUT

Fig. 477. Ripsaw teeth which cut like a gang of chisels in a row.

riser pipe: In building, a vertical pipe which rises from one floor level to another floor level, for the purpose of conducting steam, water, or gas from one floor to another.

rivet set: A tool which is specially designed for shaping a head on a rivet. See Fig. 479.

riveting hammer: An instrument consisting of a head, usually of steel or iron, attached to a handle crosswise, and used for beating sheet metal and driving rivets or nails. See Fig. 298, page 228.

rivets: Bolts or pins made of soft metal, used to fasten two metal plates, or a metal plate and a piece of wood, together. Different types of rivet heads are shown in Fig. 478. The four most common types are the tinners', flathead, roundhead and countersunk head. Tinners' and flathead rivets are used in most jobs of fabrication. The countersunk head is used when a flush surface is desired and the roundhead when exceptional strength is required.

rockpockets: An area in concrete that is made up primarily of coarse aggregates without enough mortar or cement paste.

rococo: A style of architectural ornamentation prevalent in Europe during the seventeenth and eighteenth centuries; a florid, ornate type of decoration characterized by curved lines in imitation of shells, foliage, and scrolls massed together.

rod: A polelike stick of timber used by carpenters as a measuring device for determining the exact height of risers in a flight of stairs; sometimes called a *story rod*. Also: a measurement of sixteen and one half feet.

rodding: In plastering, straightening the plaster surface between *grounds* and *screeds*.

roll: In architecture, in the Ionic order, the rounding end of the volute which rolls up on itself. See Fig. 1.

roll-capped: A term applied to ridge tiles finished with a roll or cylindrical projection along the apex.

rolled-strip roofing: In building, a type of composition roofing put up in rolls for the market; a term applied to any roofing material which comes from the dealers in rolls. An example of asphalt *rolled-strip roofing* is shown in Fig. 480.

rolling scaffold: This is a scaffold on wheels that permit it to be moved.

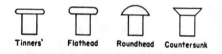

Tinners'   Flathead   Roundhead   Countersunk

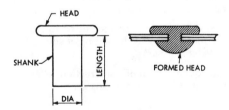

Fig. 478. Rivets.

Fig. 479. Rivet set.

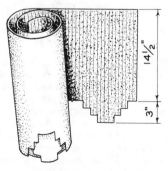

Fig. 480. Rolled-strip roofing.

Fig. 481. Bending EMT on the floor. (Republic Steel Corp.)

roll type hand benders: Tool used for bending EMT (electrical metallic tubing). They have high supporting sidewalls to prevent flattening or kinking of the tubing and a long arc that permits the making of 90° bends in a single sweep without moving the bender to a new position along the tubing. There are different makes of benders with bending marks to follow for precision bending. These marks are molded into the shoe, with directions to add or subtract a dimension from a total bend figure. See Fig. 481.

roll-up doors: Constructed in horizontally hinged sections and usually made of wood, these doors are equipped with springs, tracks, counterbalancers, and other hardware which roll the sections into an overhead position clear of the opening. They are often motor-operated with manual, radio, or magnetic driver controls and are commonly used on garages. See *tilt-up doors,* page 453.

rolok: See *rowlock,* page 376.

Roman brick: A *solid masonry unit* whose nominal dimensions are 2″ x 4″ x 12″. The nominal dimensions vary from the specified dimensions by the addition of the thickness of the mortar joint with which the unit is designed to be laid but not more than ½ inch. The specified dimensions of Roman brick are 1⅝″ x 3⅝″ x 11⅝″. Roman brick is sometimes made 16 inches or more in length to suit various construction needs. See Fig. 85, page 69.

Romanesque: A term applied to a style of architecture which developed in western Europe between the Roman and Gothic styles. It is characterized especially for lavish ornamentation, the decorative use of arcades, and for the rounded arch and vault.

roof: The external covering of a house or other buildings. See Fig. 482

roof boards: Boards laid on a roof frame to provide a foundation and an undercovering for the shingles or other materials, such as slate and tiles.

roof dormer: A small window projecting from a roof slope.

roof framing: In building, the process, or method, of putting the parts of a roof, such as rafters, ridge, and plates, in position. The location and names of the various roof members are shown in Fig. 483.

roof guard: A contrivance fitted to a sloping roof to prevent the sliding of snow. Also called *snow guard.*

roof gutter: In roof construction, a gutter built at the eaves for carrying away rain water.

roofing: Material used for covering of the exterior of the upper part of a building to make it watertight.

roofing nail: A short, heavy nail with a large head, designed for use in attaching asphalt shingles, etc., to a roof. See Fig. 390, page 296.

roofing terms: In roof framing, the terms, or names, given to the different parts of a roof. See Fig. 483.

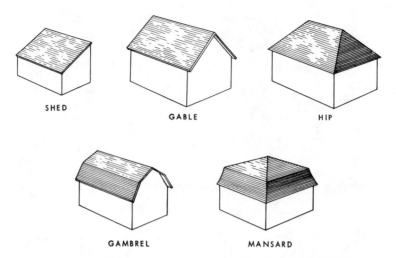

Fig. 482. Five basic styles of roofs are used in present day building.

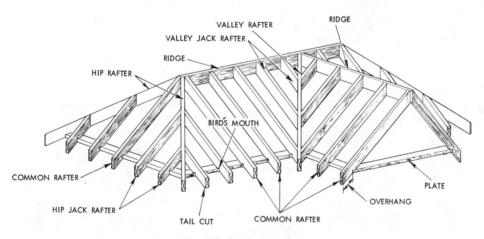

Fig. 483. Roof members.

roof leader: In plumbing, the portion of a storm-drainage system between the storm drain and the *roof terminal.*

roof members: In building construction, the various parts or members which compose a roof, as the framing members. The names of important *roof members* are given in Fig. 483.

roof pitch: In roofing construction, the slope or inclination of a roof. It is given as a fraction: $\frac{1}{3}$, $\frac{1}{4}$, etc., and represents the coordinates of an angle. Two conditions are always available in the size of a building; the *span,* which is the width that the roof covers, and the *rise,* which is the height of the roof slope. In other words we can

371

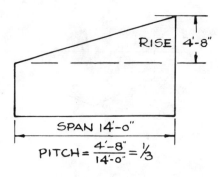

$$PITCH = \frac{4'-8''}{14'-0''} = \frac{1}{3}$$

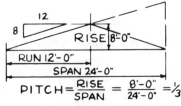

$$PITCH = \frac{RISE}{SPAN} = \frac{8'-0''}{24'-0''} = \frac{1}{3}$$

Fig. 484. Roof pitch.

say that the pitch of a roof is *rise over span*. Fig. 484, top, illustrates this principle. The gable roof, which pitches on two sides, introduces another term, *run*. Run is one half the span. The gable roof gains its full rise at half the span. See Fig. 484, bottom. The pitch, however, is still the span (twice the run) divided into the rise. Fig. 484, bottom, shows a slope of 8 over 12. This means that for every 12″ (or foot) of run there is an 8″ rise. (The 12 is used because of the convenience in using the framing square.) In the 8″ rise to 12″ run of Fig. 484, bottom, the pitch would be ⅓ (span divided into the rise). Fig. 485 shows representative roof pitches.

roof sheathing: Boards which are nailed on roof rafters and over which shingles or other roof covering is laid.

roof terminal: The upper end of a soil pipe, usually consisting of a cast-iron pipe which extends about 18 inches above the surface of a roof. In cold climates, roof terminals are designed to resist closure by frost. Two

different types of roof terminals are shown in Figs. 486 and 487.

roof ties: Construction members, such as boards or planks, fastened to rafters above the plate line and set at regular intervals to prevent walls and roof from spreading. Same as *collar beams*.

rooftree: The ridgepole of a roof; the beam in the angle of a roof.

roof truss: The structural support for a roof, consisting of braced timbers or structural iron fastened together for strengthening and stiffening this portion of a building. Typical roof trusses in common use are shown in Fig. 488. See also *W truss*, page 489.

room divider: A temporary curtain wall such as a *folding partition*, or a permanent partition, which may or may not reach from floor to ceiling, as a bookcase or cabinet with planter box. These partitions serve to block off activity areas in a room, for various needs, while providing for flexibility of function.

room door lock: A type of knob lock used on doors which lead from corridors or hallways into rooms. Also called *inside door lock*.

rope knots: The building tradesman should know several basic knots. Figs. 489 and 490 show a number of common knots in rope. The square knot should be used in rope of the same size in order to hold. The granny, which looks somewhat similar, can easily be confused with the square knot. However, it will not hold a heavy strain. The thief knot, also, will not hold strain. If both ends are not visible, it cannot be told from a square knot, but a careful observation of the parts of the rope carrying the load will show the difference. The bowline and timber hitch are basic knots every building tradesman should understand fully. The bowline will not slip, and it has the advantage that it can be untied even after having been subjected to considerable strain. This knot will hold if emergency demands tying a knot in steel cable.

rose: In building, a decorative metal plate, or escutcheon, fastened to a door and containing a socket for receiving and guiding the shank of a door knob. Though the *rose*

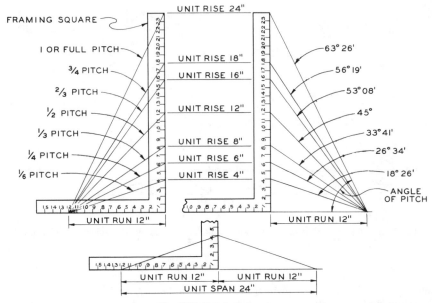

Fig. 485. Roof pitches.

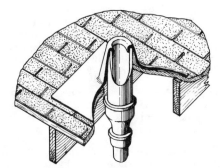

Fig. 486. Increased roof terminal.

may be oblong or square, usually it is circular in shape.

rosette: In architecture, any rounded ornament resembling a rose in the arrangement of its parts; any circular roselike unit of ornamentation with mullions or tracery radiating from the center; also, a decorative unit similar to a roundel filled with leaflike ornaments.

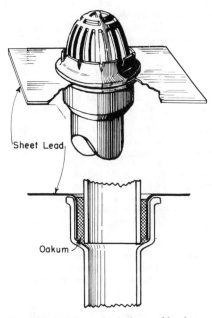

Fig. 487. Roof terminals for roof leaders.

373

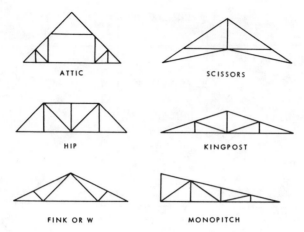

Fig. 488. The trussed roof rafter has several basic shapes each designed for a particular purpose.

rosette: In electricity, a device which permits a drop cord to be attached to a ceiling outlet or fixture.

rose window: A circular window decorated with ornamental designs similar to those found in the head of a Gothic window or in some ornate styles of vaulting; also, an ornamental circular window adorned with roselike tracery or mullions radiating from the center.

rosin: An amber-colored product which exudes from pine trees, as a gum. It is used extensively as a soldering flux and in varnishes; also used as a drier in paints.

rot: In plastering, improperly cured plaster that had remained wet too long, causing the gypsum to break down and become weak.

rottenstone: A decomposed, brittle limestone from which the calcium carbonate has been removed by the solvent action of water. Marketed in the form of a fine powder and used in the polishing of varnished surfaces.

roughcast: A term used in the building trade for a kind of plastering made of lime mixed with shells or pebbles and applied to the outside of buildings.

rough coat: The first coat of plastering applied to a wall surface.

rough floor: A subfloor serving as a base for the laying of the *finished floor* which may be of wood, linoleum, tile, or other suitable material. See *floor framing,* Fig. 41, page 35, and Fig. 258, page 198.

rough flooring: Materials used for rough floors, usually square-edged lumber size 1x6, though dressed-and-matched boards or shiplap is sometimes used. Rough flooring may be laid either straight or diagonal. See Fig. 41, page 35 and Fig. 258, page 198.

rough hardware: All of the concealed hardware in a house or other building, such as bolts, nails, and spikes which are used in the construction of the building.

rough-hewn: Timbers or lumber with a rough, uneven surface made by trimming with an axe or adz; sometimes used for decorative effect.

roughing-in: In building, a term applied to doing the first or rough work on any part of the construction, as roughing-in plastering, plumbing, and stairs.

rough lumber: Lumber that has *not* been dressed (surfaced) but which has been sawed, edged, and trimmed at least to the extent of showing saw marks in the wood on the four longitudinal surfaces of each piece for its entire length.

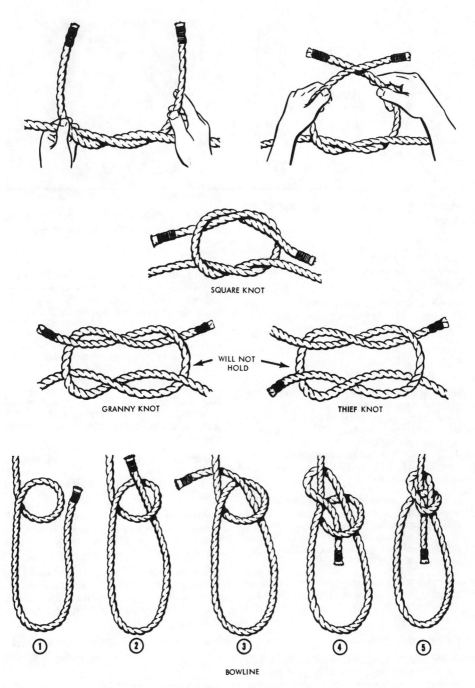

SQUARE KNOT

WILL NOT
HOLD

GRANNY KNOT　　　　　　　THIEF KNOT

① ② ③ ④ ⑤

BOWLINE

Fig. 489. Knots used in rigging. (Dept. of the Army)

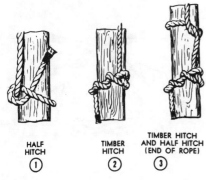

Fig. 490. Knots used in rigging. (Dept. of the Army.)

Fig. 491. Portable router equipped with hinge butt template kit. (Black & Decker Mfg. Co.)

rough opening: An unfinished window or door opening; any unfinished opening in a building.

rough rubble: In masonry, a wall composed of unsquared field stones laid without regularity of coursing but well bonded.

rough sill: In a frame wall, the short plate or header which forms the base of a rough opening for a window.

rough work: In building construction, the work of constructing the rough skeleton of a building; the rough framework, including the boxing and sheeting. The *rough work* may include making the rough frames for doors and windows and any similar work done in a factory and later moved to the building site ready for installing.

roughstring: In wide, wooden staircases, an intermediate support for the treads of the stairs between the wall string and the outer string. It consists of a board notched out to fit the steps and is sometimes called a *carriage piece.*

rout: A term in woodworking for cutting or gouging out material with a tool called a *router,* which is a special type of smoothing plane.

routed: See *mortised.*

router: A two-handled woodworking tool used for smoothing the face of depressed surfaces, such as the bottom of grooves or any other depressions parallel with the sur-

face of a piece of work. See Fig. 436, page 332. Fig. 491 illustrates a power router being used. Different shaped bits are used to make the desired cut. See Fig. 492.

routing: The cutting away of any unnecessary parts that would interfere with the usefulness or mar the appearance of a piece of millwork.

rowlock: In masonry, a term applied to a course of bricks laid on edge. Also, the end of a brick showing on the face of a brick wall in a vertical position. See Fig. 162, page 126.

rowlock arch: In architecture, an arch in which the *voussoirs* are arranged in separate concentric rings, each ring forming an arch.

rowlock-back wall: In masonry, a wall whose external face is formed of bricks laid flat in the ordinary manner, while the backing is formed of bricks laid on edge.

rubbed effect: A dull finish produced by rubbing a varnished or shellacked surface with powdered pumice stone and water, mixed to the consistency of cream and applied on a felt pad.

rubbed joint: A type of joint formed by rubbing together two wood surfaces coated with glue.

rubber gloves: In plastering, the plasterer uses rubber gloves when applying cornice

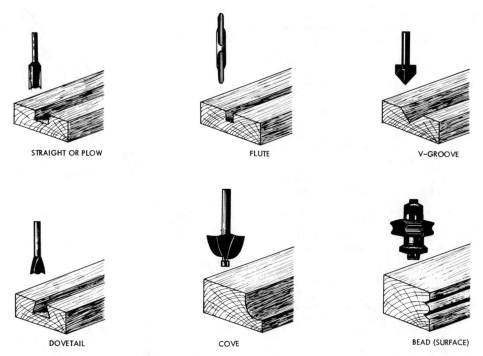

STRAIGHT OR PLOW   FLUTE   V-GROOVE

DOVETAIL   COVE   BEAD (SURFACE)

Fig. 492. Typical router bits and common cuts.

plaster and similar work. They protect his hands from lime burns, permitting him to manually feed the cornice mold or "stick ornament" (apply ornamental work). The thick "gauntlet" type of glove is preferred because it wears well and can be quickly removed from the hand with a jerking motion.

rubber tape: An adhesive elastic tape made from a rubber compound; used extensively in electrical work for insulating purposes.

rubber test plug: In plumbing, a rubber plug used to seal all connections serving as floor drains before testing the house drain with water.

rubbing stone: In masonry, a stone used by bricklayers to smooth bricks which are designed for some particular purpose in a structure, as in a *gaged arch.*

rubbing varnish: A term applied to a varnish rubbed down to form a smooth foundation for the second coat called *finishing*

varnish. If a rubbed effect is desired, the finishing varnish is not needed.

rubble: Rough, broken stones or bricks used to fill in courses of walls or for other filling; also, rough broken stone direct from the quarry.

rubble arch: An arch constructed of undressed stone and cement mortar; also called a *rustic arch.*

rubble ashlar: Squared stones with rubble backing.

rubble concrete: In masonry work, a form of concrete reinforced by broken stones, especially that used in massive construction, such as solid masonry dams; also, masonry construction composed of large stone blocks set about six inches apart in fine cement concrete, and faced with squared rubble or ashlar. See *rubblework.*

rubble masonry: Masonry walls built of unsquared or rudely squared stones, irregular

377

in size and shape; also, uncut stone used for rough work, such as for backing of unfinished masonry walls.

rubblework: Masonry built of rough fragments of broken stones, or unsquared or rudely dressed stones, irregular in size and shape. When only the roughest irregularities are removed, it is sometimes called *scabbled rubble,* and when the stones in each course are roughly dressed to almost a uniform height it is often called *ranged rubble.* See *scabble,* page 386.

rubrication: The coloring, especially in red, of a background by use of enamel or paint.

rudenture: Same as *cabling.* Commonly used in relief without flutings, as the purpose is to give greater solidity to the lower part of a shaft and secure the edges.

rule joint: In woodworking, a pivoted joint where two flat strips are joined end to end so that each strip will turn or fold only in one direction; an example is the ordinary two-foot folding rule used by carpenters and other woodworkers.

ruling pen: In drawing, a pen used for straight lines and curves which are not arcs or circles. Sometimes called *line pen.* See Fig. 493.

run: In plumbing, a part of a pipe or fitting that continues in the same straight line as the direction of flow. *Roof:* the horizontal distance between the outer face of the wall and the ridge of the roof. See *roof pitch,* page 371. *Stairs:* the horizontal distance from the face of the first or upper riser to the face of the last or lower riser.

rung: A bar connecting the two side posts of a ladder and serving as a step.

running bond: In masonry, a form of bond used largely for internal partition walls in which every brick is laid as a stretcher, with each vertical joint lying between the centers of the stretchers above and below, making angle closers unnecessary. Same as *stretcher* or *stretching bond.* See, also, *chimney bond,* page 97.

running dog: A classic ornamental molding used in a frieze or band and resembling the wave ornament. Also called *Vitruvian scroll.* See Fig. 494.

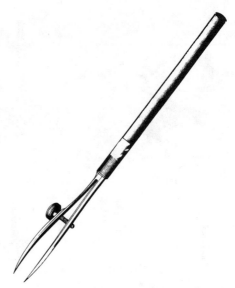

Fig. 493. Ruling pen.

running or stretcher bond: The surface of the wall is made up of stretchers which break joint at the center with a header on each alternate course at the corner.

run of rafter: In building, the horizontal distance from the face of a wall to the ridge of the roof. This distance is represented by the base of a right-angled triangle, with the length of the rafter represented by the hypotenuse of the triangle.

run of stairs: A term used when referring to the horizontal part of a stair step without the nosing; that is, the horizontal distance between the faces of two risers or the horizontal distance of a flight of stairs. This is found by multiplying the number of steps by the width of the treads. If there are 14 steps, each 10 inches wide, then 14 × 10 equals 140 inches, or 11 feet 8 inches, which is the *run of the stairs.*

Fig. 494. Running dog molding.

run of work: A term used in reference to a steady run of jobs following one another in rapid succession; also applied to a type of job which calls for the repeated production of a quantity of the same kind of article.

rusticated: Pertaining to the treatment of the surface of a stone wall, where separate blocks are left with a rough-hewn surface projecting from the line of the joints, which are deeply recessed in chamfered or rectangular grooves and whose width is emphasized.

rusticated ashlar: In masonry, ashlar work in which the face stands out from the joints where the arrises are beveled. The face may be finished smooth or rough or be tooled in various ways.

rustication: In building and masonry, the use of squared or hewn stone blocks with roughened surfaces and edges deeply beveled or grooved to make the joints conspicuous.

rustication strip: A strip of wood or other material attached to a form surface to produce a groove or rustication in the concrete.

rustic beveled work: Masonry in which the face of the stones is smooth and parallel to the face of the wall. The angles are beveled to an angle of 135 degrees with the face of the stone so that when two stones come together on the wall the beveling forms an internal right angle.

rustic frosted work: Masonry in which the margins of the stones are reduced to a plane parallel to the plane of the wall, the intermediate parts having an irregular or frosted appearance.

rustic joint: In masonry, a sunken joint between building stones.

rustics: In masonry, bricks which have a rough-textured surface, often multi-colored.

rustic siding: A type of siding which has shiplap joints similar to drop siding.

rustic vermiculated work: Masonry in which the intermediate parts between the joints are so worked as to have the appearance of being worm-eaten.

rustic work: In masonry, cutting the face of stone so as to present a rough surface in imitation of nature; a building having the surface roughly finished with the joints deeply chamfered, or sunk, so they will be conspicuous; work in which the horizontal and vertical channels are cut in the joinings of stones, which, when placed together, form an angular channel at each joint. See *rustication.*

rust joint: In plumbing, a watertight joint between adjoining lengths of guttering or pipes, in which some oxidizing agent is employed either to cure a leak or to withstand high pressure. Such a joint is formed by packing the socket with a mixture of iron filings, crushed sal ammoniac, and sulphur.

S

saddle: The ridge covering of a roof; also, the metal covering of a roll on a metal-covered roof; any portion of a roof or other surface constructed in a manner suggesting or corresponding in position to a rider's saddle; a horizontal piece set on top of a post to diminish the supported span of a beam; a strip of thin board covering the floor joint on the threshold of a door. Same as *cricket.* See Fig. 165, page 130.

saddleback roof: A roof with a slope on both sides, as one which has a ridge and two gables; also, a tower having a gable roof. See *saddle roof.*

saddle bars: Slender, horizontal bars of iron passing from mullion to mullion of a window and often through the whole window from side to side, to which the lead panels of a glazed window are secured. Sometimes the window lights are further strengthened by upright bars forged on the saddle bars and known as *stanchions.*

saddle board: The finish of the ridge of a pitch-roof house. Sometimes called comb board.

saddle roof: A roof constructed so that any portion of it is suggestive of a saddle, one having a ridge terminating in two gables. Also called *cricket.* See Fig. 165, page 130.

safe carrying capacity: In the building industry, a term used with reference to construction of any piece or part so it will carry the weight or load it is designed to

Fig. 495. Safety hasp.

Fig. 496. Portable belt sander. (Porter-Cable Machine Co.)

support without breaking down; in electricity, the maximum current a conductor will carry without becoming overheated.

safety hasp: A fastening device having a slotted plate which fits over a staple to which the *hasp* is secured by the use of a padlock or peg. See Fig. 495.

safety switch: In electricity, a knife switch enclosed in a metal box. The switch is opened and closed by a handle on the outside.

sag: To droop or settle downward, especially in the middle, because of weight or pressure; also, the departure from original shape, a dragging down by its own weight, as a sagging door.

sagging: The bending in the middle of a beam or other body, either by a load placed upon it or by its own weight.

salamander: A type of temporary heater used on construction sites.

salient: Pointing or projecting outward, as a salient angle, an angular projection from a wall commanding a length of wall on each side of it.

sand: A term loosely applied to fine gravel, grains of quartz, or other minerals resulting from the disintegration of rock.

sander, electric: Portable sanding machine with interchangeable abrasive attachments for various on-the-job finishing purposes. Abrasive surface may be either on a spinning disk, a rotating continuous belt, or a vibrating plane surface. See Fig. 496.

sanding: In carpentry, the operation of finishing wood surfaces, such as floors, with *sandpaper* or some other abrasive. Often this finishing is done with a *sanding machine* which has a revolving disk faced with *sandpaper.*

sandpaper: An abrasive paper, made by coating a heavy paper with fine sand or other abrasives held in place by some adhesive such as glue; used for polishing surfaces and finishing work. Different minerals are used as cutting agents for making abrasive tools. Three of these used in their natural state are: *garnet, emery,* and *quartz,* which is commonly called *flint.* Examples of abrasives manufactured by an electric-furnace process are *silicon carbide,* trademarked *Carborundum,* and aluminum oxide. (The abrasive minerals are shaped and bonded to form abrasive tools, such as whetstones and grindstones.) Abrasive papers come in sheets 9x11 inches or in rolls measuring from 1 inch to 27 inches in width and up to 50 yards in length. The 27-inch width is used principally on machines and on belt or drum sanders. The abrasive paper also comes in *open coat* where the abrasive particles are separated and cover only about 50 to 70 percent of the surface. The *closed coat* has the abrasive particles close together covering the entire surface of the paper or cloth backing. The comparative grit numbers for various abrasive papers are shown in Table 4. To remove tool marks, by hand sanding on bare wood, use garnet paper ranging from *medium,* No. ½ and 0 to *fine,* No. 3/0 or 4/0, for the finished surface. The coarseness of sandpaper originally was designated as #3 for very coarse to 7/0 for very fine. This designation of abrasives is still in practice

TABLE 4. APPROXIMATE COMPARISON OF GRIT NUMBERS

ARTIFICIAL*	GARNET	FLINT	GRADE
400–10/0	—	—	
360	—	—	
320–9/0	—	7/0	
280–8/0	8/0	6/0	Very fine
240–7/0	7/0	5/0	
220–6/0	6/0	4/0	
		3/0	
180–5/0	5/0	—	
150–4/0	4/0	—	
		2/0	Fine
120–3/0	3/0	—	
		0	
100–2/0	2/0	—	
		½	
80–0	0	—	
		1	Medium
60–½	½	—	
50–1	1	1½	
		2	
40–1½	1½	—	
		2½	Coarse
36–2	2	—	
30–2½	2½	3	
24–3	3	—	
20–3½	3½	—	
16–4	—	—	Very Coarse
12–4½	—	—	

* Includes *silicon carbide* and *aluminum oxide*.

today. However, the more modern method is to designate the coarseness by the size of the screen through which the abrasive must pass in the manufacturing process. When a screen with 280 openings per square inch is used, the paper is designated as 280. Due to difference in hardness of some of the abrasives; it will be noted that a coarser grade of flint paper is used to bring about the same result as with garnet or artificial papers. For example, an 8/0 garnet paper is the same in coarseness as 280-8/0 artificial paper, but it would require a 6/0 flint paper to give the same results.

sand plate: A flat, steel plate or strip welded to the legs of bar supports for use on compacted soil.

sandstone: A building stone, usually quartz, composed of fine grains of sand cemented together with silica, oxide of iron, or carbonate of lime. *Grindstones* are made of sandstone in its natural state.

sandwich beam: A built-up beam composed of two joists with a steel plate between them. The joists and plate are held together by bolts. Same as *flitch beam*. See *built-up beams*, Fig. 94, page 76.

sandwiched girder: In building construction, a girder having a steel or iron plate sandwiched into it by placing the steel or iron between two timbers which are then bolted together. Same as *flitched girder*. See Fig. 94, page 76.

sandwich panel: Panel made of two sheets of plywood facing glued over a honeycomb core. See *stressed skin panels,* page 436.

sanitary sewer: In plumbing, an underground pipe or tunnel for carrying off domestic wastes as a sanitary measure.

sanitary shoe: In carpentry, a type of *base shoe* molding having a concave surface which eliminates sharp angles in which dust and dirt can collect.

sanitary tee: A soil pipe fitting with a side outlet to form a tee shape. See Fig. 112, page 89.

sap: In wood plants, the watery circulating fluid which is necessary to their growth.

sap streaks: Streaks showing through a finished wood surface which contains sapwood. Such streaks must be *toned out* in order to secure a uniform finish.

sapwood: The wood just beneath the bark of a tree; that is, the young softwood consisting of living tissues outside the heartwood. See Fig. 24, page 21.

sash: The frame in which window lights are set. See Fig. 497.

sash balance: In double-hung windows, a device usually operated with a spring, designed to counterbalance the window sash without the use of weights, pulleys, and cord. See Fig. 498.

sash bars: In building, the strips which separate the panes of glass in a window sash.

sash center: A term applied to a bearing for a transom light or other sash which turns on a horizontal axis; usually consists of two plates, one with a pin and the other with a socket for receiving the pin.

sash door: Any door which has the upper portion glazed.

sash fast: A fastening for two window sash, especially at the meeting of the sash at their rails. Same as *sash holder.*

sash holder: Any device for holding two window sash together at the rails. See *sash fast.*

sash lift: Usually a metal hook, plate, or bar attached to a sash as an aid in raising and lowering the window.

sashless window: Panes of glass which slide along parallel tracks in the window frame toward one another, to leave openings at the sides, are used as windows; also, fixed pane sashless windows are often used for picture windows as well as other purposes.

sash lift and lock: A sash lift equipped with a locking lever which contacts with a strike in the window frame.

sash lock: A device for holding two window sash together at the rails. Same as *sash fast.*

sash pin: A heavy-gauge barbed headless nail or pin used to fasten the mortise-and-tenon joints of window sash and doors.

sash plane: A plane having a notched cutter used by carpenters for trimming the inside of window-sash frames and door frames.

sash plates: A pair of plates, one with a pin and the other with a socket, used as bearings for a transom light or other sash turning on a horizontal axis.

sash stop: In window framing, a small strip of wood, such as a beaded molding, used for holding a sash in place. The same as a stop bead. Also called window stop.

saturated: To be thoroughly soaked to capacity.

saturated felt: A felt which is impregnated with tar or asphalt.

saw: In building, a carpenter's tool used for cutting wood. It consists of a steel blade with teeth and a handle; the same as *handsaw.* See: *backsaw, bandsaw, coping saw, crosscut saw, dovetail saw, hacksaw, keyhole saw, radial saw, rip saw, table saw.* See also: *saw, power.*

saw arbor: The spindle or shaft on which a circular saw is mounted.

saw bench: A table or framework for carrying a circular saw.

sawbuck: A buck, a sawhorse.

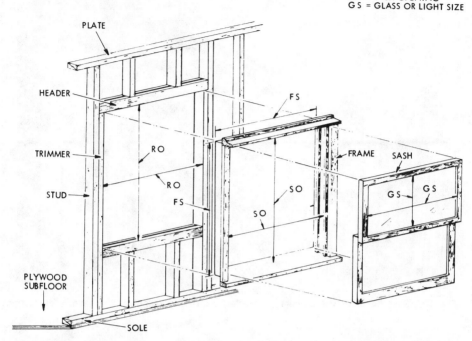

RO = ROUGH OPENING
FS = FRAME SIZE
SO = SASH OPENING
GS = GLASS OR LIGHT SIZE

Fig. 497. This drawing shows how the sash fits into the frame and how the frame fits into the rough opening.

saw butted: Trimmed by a saw on both ends.

saw gullet: The throat at the bottom of the teeth of a circular saw.

saw gumming: Shaping the teeth of a circular saw. Usually a grinding process.

sawhorse: A rack or frame for holding wood while it is being sawed; also, the ordinary trestle on which wood or boards are laid by carpenters for sawing by hand. See Fig. 499.

saw kerf: In carpentry, a groove or channel made by a saw when cutting lumber. Such a groove is made especially for the purpose of bending boards around corners.

saw, power: Electrically powered saws which are available with interchangeable blades and other attachments for various building jobs, including masonry cutting as well as wood and metal cutting, trimming, etc. Figs. 500 and 501 illustrate two common types of portable power saws. Stationary power saws are also used by the building tradesman. These include the circular table saw, the radial saw, and the band saw. The *circular table saw* uses a circular blade up to 16 inches in diameter and is mounted on a table. See Fig. 585, page 447. The *radial saw* has many of the characteristics of a table saw but differs in one important respect. The material being cut always remains in the same place, while

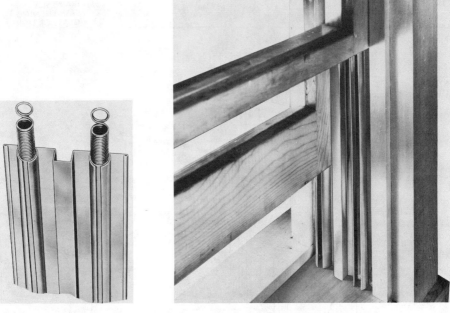

Fig. 498. Sash balances use springs to counterbalance the weight of the sash. (Zegers Inc.)

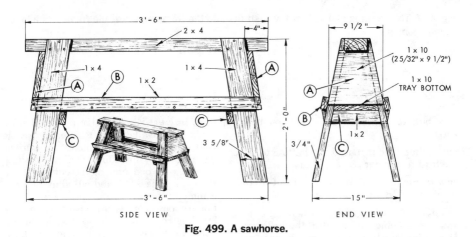

SIDE VIEW   END VIEW

Fig. 499. A sawhorse.

it is the saw itself that moves. See Fig. 462, page 357. The *bandsaw*, Fig. 42, page 36, is mainly used for cutting curved surfaces or for cutting contours.

saw set: An instrument used for giving set to saw teeth. See Fig. 502.

saw teeth: On a saw blade, the cutting

Fig. 500. Ripping fence used with a portable power saw. (Miller Falls Co.)

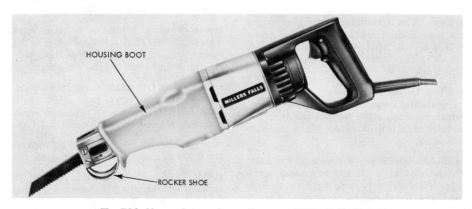

Fig. 501. Heavy duty reciprocating saw. (Miller Falls Co.)

points which are formed by filing. For examples of saw teeth, see Fig. 169, page 132, and Fig. 477, page 368.

saw-toothed skylight: In architecture, a term applied to a skylight roof with its profile shaped like the teeth of a saw.

saw-tooth roof: A roof which is formed of a number of north light trusses. When viewed from the end, such a roof presents a serrated or toothed profile similar to the teeth of a saw.

sawyer: One whose occupation is that of sawing wood or other material; sometimes used in a restricted sense meaning one who operates one of several saws.

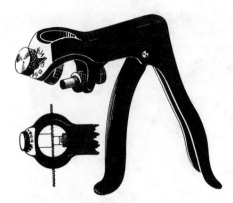

Fig. 502. Saw set.

S beam: A steel beam with short flanges used in structural work. Formerly called I beam.

scab: Short piece of lumber nailed over a splice or joint to add strength or prevent slippage or movement.

scabble: The dressing down of the roughest irregularities and projections of stone which is to be used for rubble masonry. A stone ax or scabbling hammer is used for this work.

scaffold height: In masonry, the distance between the various stages of scaffolding, which represents the height within which a bricklayer can carry on his work with efficiency.

scaffolds: These are wood or metal platforms used to work above ground level. Fig. 503 shows a wooden light trade scaffold. Fig. 504 shows an example of a metal scaffold. See: *hanging scaffold, rolling scaffold, swing stage scaffold, trestle scaffold.*

scagliola: An imitation of ornamental marble, consisting of a base of finely ground gypsum mixed with an adhesive, such as a hard cement, and variegated on the surface while in a plastic condition, with chips of marble or with colored graphite dust. When this mixture is hardened, it is finished with a high polish and used for floors, columns, and other interior work.

scale: An instrument with graduated spaces for measuring. Scales are used for measuring distances full size, as well as laying out distances to scale. The term "laying out" or "drawing to scale" indicates that an object may be drawn on the sheet full size, enlarged, or reduced. Almost all scales have from two to eleven graduated faces that enable the draftsman to reduce or enlarge a distance to fit within the limits of the drawing sheet. Scales may be open divided with units marked (Fig. 505, top) along the entire length of the face of the scale, but with only the end units subdivided into inches and fractions of an inch. A fully divided scale (Fig. 505, bottom) has equal divisions and subdivisions carried the full length of the scale face with continuous numbering. Only one kind of a division can be made on a face. Scales are made in a variety of shapes. Flat scales are usually preferred by draftsmen. The triangular shapes, Fig. 201, page 157 are commonly used by the architect. Table 5 gives the most commonly used standard scales found on the architect's scale. Almost any combination of scales can be obtained with divisions suitable to the work at hand.

scaled drawing: A plan made according to a scale, smaller than the work which it represents but to a specified proportion which should be indicated on the drawing.

scale details: In architectural drawings, details which are drawn to a scale smaller than full size, as one-fourth inch equals one foot or one-half inch equals one foot.

scaling: Local flaking or peeling away of the outer surface of concrete or mortar.

scalp: To remove a small portion of the surface of a material, usually $1/8$ to $3/4$ inches scraped off the top.

scamillus: In architecture, a small groove separating the necking of a column from the shaft in the Greek Doric order; in the Ionic and Corinthian orders, a kind of second plinth or block below the bases; usually without moldings and of a smaller size than the pedestal.

scantling: A piece of framing lumber of comparatively small dimensions; for example, a 2x4 stud.

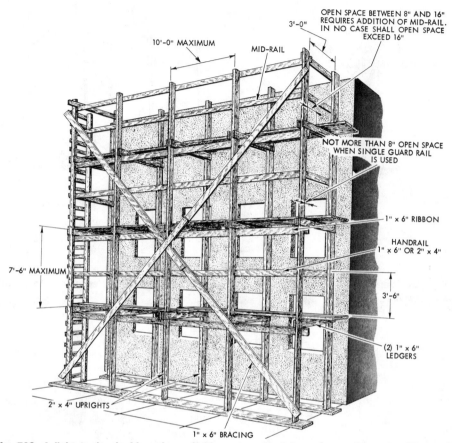

OPEN SPACE BETWEEN 8" AND 16" REQUIRES ADDITION OF MID-RAIL. IN NO CASE SHALL OPEN SPACE EXCEED 16"

3'-0"

10'-0" MAXIMUM

MID-RAIL

NOT MORE THAN 8" OPEN SPACE WHEN SINGLE GUARD RAIL IS USED

1" x 6" RIBBON

HANDRAIL 1" x 6" OR 2" x 4"

3'-6"

7'-6" MAXIMUM

(2) 1" x 6" LEDGERS

2" x 4" UPRIGHTS

1" x 6" BRACING

Fig. 503. A light trade, double pole scaffold must meet state code requirements. (State of California, "Construction Safety Orders.")

scarf joint: The joining of two pieces of timber by notching and lapping the ends, then fastening them with straps or bolts. See Fig. 506.

scarfing: The joining by overlapping and bolting of two pieces of timber transversely, in such a manner that the two pieces appear as one. See *scarf joint.*

scarifier: In plastering, a tool to scratch the surface of unset materials so the next coat will have sufficient bond. See Fig. 507. Also *scratcher,* page 390.

schedule: Table or list of working drawings giving number, size, and placement of similar items. See *beam schedule, column schedule, door schedule, window schedule.* Fig. 68, page 56, shows a *door schedule.*

scissors truss: In architecture, a type of truss used in roof framing; so named from its resemblance to a pair of scissors. Often it is used for supporting roofs over hallways and in construction of church roofs. See Fig. 508.

sconce: A decorative bracket projecting from a wall for holding candles.

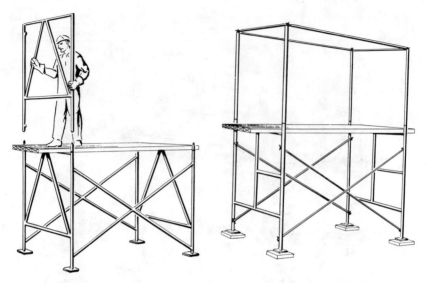

Fig. 504. Prefabricated metal frames and diagonal braces are assembled quickly to provide safe scaffolds.

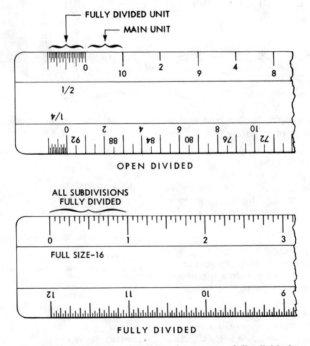

Fig. 505. Scale graduations may be open or fully divided.

TABLE 5. STANDARD SCALES

STANDARD SIZES COMMONLY USED ON ARCHITECTURAL DRAWINGS		
WHEN DRAWING IS:	TO PRODUCE A DRAWING IN WHICH:	INDICATION ON SCALE FACE IS:
FULL SIZE	12" ON DRAWING EQUALS 12" ON OBJECT	12"
1/4 SIZE	3" ON DRAWING EQUALS 12" ON OBJECT	3"
1/8 SIZE	1 1/2" ON DRAWING EQUALS 12" ON OBJECT	1 1/2"
1/12 SIZE	1" ON DRAWING EQUALS 12" ON OBJECT	1"
1/16 SIZE	3/4" ON DRAWING EQUALS 12" ON OBJECT	3/4"
1/24 SIZE	1/2" ON DRAWING EQUALS 12" ON OBJECT	1/2"
1/32 SIZE	3/8" ON DRAWING EQUALS 12" ON OBJECT	3/8"
1/48 SIZE	1/4" ON DRAWING EQUALS 12" ON OBJECT	1/4"
1/64 SIZE	3/16" ON DRAWING EQUALS 12" ON OBJECT	3/16"
1/96 SIZE	1/8" ON DRAWING EQUALS 12" ON OBJECT	1/8"
1/128 SIZE	3/32" ON DRAWING EQUALS 12" ON OBJECT	3/32"

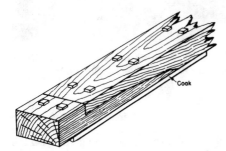

Fig. 506. Scarf joint.

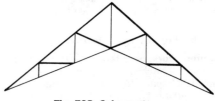

Fig. 508. Scissors truss.

Fig. 507. Scarifier or scratcher.

sconcheon arch: That portion of the side of an opening from the back of the reveal to the inside face of the wall and which usually forms a rebate in the masonry in which the wooden frame is set. Same as *rear arch*.

scoring: To mark with lines, scratches, and grooves across the grain of a piece of wood with any kind of steel instrument, for the purpose of making the surface rough enough to make it a firmer joint when glued.

scotch: In masonry, a tool resembling a small pick with a flat cutting edge, used for trimming brick to a particular shape. Same as *scutch*.

scotia: A concave molding as at the base of a pillar or column; so called because of the dark shadow it casts. From the Greek word *skotia* meaning *darkness*. See Fig. 509.

SCR brick: A *solid masonry unit* whose greater thickness permits the use of a single wythe in construction. Its nominal di-

389

Fig. 509. Scotia.

mensions, which vary from the specified dimensions by the addition of the thickness of the mortar joint with which the unit is designed to be laid (but not more than ½ inch), are 6″ x 2⅔″ x 12″. See Fig. 85, page 69.

scrabbled rubble: See *rubblework*, page 378.

scraffeto work: Scraffeto is an Italian word meaning scratched and has come back into use in reference to work involving layers of colored mortar. While the layers are still wet, they are scored to produce various novelty effects or imitation brick, stone, or wood.

scraper: A flat, thin steel blade used to pare a wood surface which is being given a final dressing or finish.

scratch awl: A tool used by shopworkers for marking on metal or wood. It is made from a sharp-pointed piece of steel. See *awl*, Fig. 33, page 30.

scratch coat: The first coat of plaster, which is scratched to afford a bond for the second coat. Fig. 510 shows a scratch coat being applied.

scratcher: In plastering, a tool used to scratch marks in a cement surface or the first coat of plaster in order to provide a grip for succeeding coats so they will adhere more satisfactorily. See *scarifier*, Fig. 507.

scratch work: A kind of surface decoration in which two finishing coats of contrasting colors are applied one on top of the other. Before the top coat has set, portions are removed according to some design or pattern, thus exposing the coat below. Same as *sgraffito*.

Fig. 510. Applying the scratch coat. (Dahlhauser; Keystone Steel & Wire Co.)

screed: In cement masonry flatwork, the wood or metal straightedge used to strike off or level newly placed concrete. Also the leveling strips or formwood which establishes the surface of the concrete by drawing a straightedge (screed) over their surface. See Fig. 511. Fig. 512 illustrates a mechanical screed. In plastering, narrow bands of mortar which are plumbed, leveled, or built up between dots (small spots of plaster set plumb with the grounds or level on a ceiling) to function as guide lines upon which the straightedge may ride when rodding the mortar on walls or ceilings. (Fig. 513.) The strips usually are about 8 inches wide with a thickness of two coats of plaster, serving also as thickness guides when applying the remainder of the plastering. Also sometimes a strip of wood to act as a guide for plaster or concrete work (called *grounds*).

screed chairs: In reinforced concrete formwork, supports used to fix the depth of a slab and to hold the screeds.

screed coat: In plastering, a coat of plaster laid level with the screeds. See *screed*.

screeding: In concrete flatwork, leveling a concrete surface; *striking off*. In plaster-

Fig. 511. Screeding freshly placed concrete. Both the leveling device used and the formwork for the cement are called screeds. (Portland Cement Association)

ing, straightening the plaster surface; *rod-ding.*

screed strip: In plastering, a strip of plaster laid on the surface of a wall to serve as a guide for the thickness of the coat of plaster which is to be applied later.

screen molding: A small, flat molding used to cover the staples and edge of screen wire where it is nailed to the wood.

screenings: In masonry, when mixing mortar, the coarse part of the sand, such as pebbles, which does not run through the screen.

screw: A mechanical device used to unite wood or metal parts in structural work. It consists of a helix wound around a cylinder. Screws are of several varieties. Figs. 514 and 515 illustrate different types of common wood screws. Fig. 516 illustrates common metal screws.

screw anchor: A metal shell, much like that used with an *expansion bolt,* which expands and wedges itself into the hole drilled for it. Also, like the expansion bolt, it is used to fasten light work to masonry construction. See *lead screw anchor,* page 264; *raw-plug anchor,* page 362.

Fig. 512. A power-vibrated mechanical screed. (Stow Manufacturing Co.)

screw chuck: A contrivance for holding work in a wood-turning lathe, with a projecting screw as live center.

screw clamp: A woodworker's clamp consisting of two parallel jaws and two screws; the clamping action is obtained by means of the screws, one operating through each jaw.

screw eye: A screw with the head shaped into a completely closed ring or circle, *forming* a loop or eye. See Fig. 316, page 239.

screw hole plugs: In woodworking, plugs that are used to fill screwhole entrance after screw has been recessed in hole.

screw jack: A lifting device which is actuated by means of a square-threaded screw.

screw nail: A fastening device with a slotted head, designed for use where great holding power is required. It is driven in place, removed with a screw driver. See Fig. 393, page 297, and Figs. 514 and 515.

screwdriver: A woodworker's tool used for driving in or removing screws by turning them. The tool is made of a well-tempered steel bar or rod flattened at one end to fit into the slots of screw heads. The steel bar is then fitted into a handle made of tough wood reinforced to prevent splitting. See Fig. 517. Fig. 518 illustrates a portable electric screwdriver. See *spiral ratchet screwdriver,* page 418.

scribe: To mark or rule a faint line on wood with a sharp knife or scriber.

scriber: A carpentry tool consisting of a compass of pressed steel with a pencil in

Fig. 513. Forming horizontal screed.

one leg or end and a metal point in the other leg; used to draw a line to mark the irregularities of a surface in fitting cabinets or other trim members to the wall or floor. See Fig. 519. See *dividers, carpenter's,* page 145.

scribing: Marking and fitting woodwork to an irregular surface.

scrim: A name given to a kind of tape made of any coarse material, usually a low-grade linen tow; used to reinforce the joints of plaster board and to cover the joints of building boards before plastering is applied.

scroll: In furniture making, an ornamental design resembling a partially unrolled scroll of paper; also, any ornamental feature characterized by free-flowing curves. See *volute,* Fig. 1.

scroll saw: A thin-bladed saw used for cutting curved designs.

scrollwork: In architecture, any decorative feature suggestive of an unfolding parch-

ment roll. An example is the capital of the Greek Ionic order. See Fig. 403, page 306.

scrub board: A finishing board placed around a room next to the floor to protect the wall finish. Same as *baseboard.* Also called *mopboard.*

sculpture: In architecture, decorative features carved from wood, stone, marble, or other similar materials.

scupper: An outlet in the wall of a building for drainage of overflow of water from a floor or flat roof; an opening in outside or court walls to permit water to drain off from automatic sprinklers or, in case of fire, from the fire hose.

scutch: In masonry, a bricklayer's cutting tool used for dressing and trimming brick to special shapes. It resembles a small pick and is sometimes called a *scotch.*

scutcheon or escutcheon: In carpentry, a term applied to a metal shield used to protect wood, as around the keyhole of a door;

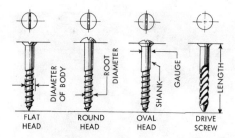

Fig. 514. Common styles of wood screws.

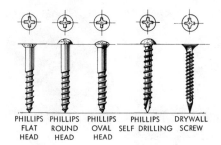

Fig. 515. Common styles of Phillips screws.

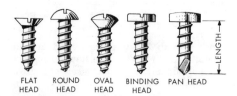

Fig. 516. Common metal screws.

also, a metal plate of a decorative character.

scuttle: A small opening, furnished with a lid or cover, in a ceiling or roof, the purpose of which is to provide access to the other side.

seal: In plumbing, the presence of water in the lower section of the U of a trap, the purpose of which is to prevent noxious gases and/or odors from finding their way from the sewage system into the residence or other structure being served. See Fig. 454, page 454.

sealant: A liquid, usually clear, which is painted on wood, concrete, and masonry to prevent the entry of moisture.

seamer: A small, hand tool used to make seams or joints in sheet metal. See Fig. 520.

seams, sheet metal: Method of joining edges of sheet metal. For lighter sheet metal, mechanical joints are used. See Fig. 521. In medium and heavy gage metal, a riveted or welded seam is used.

seasoning: In lumber, the evaporation or extraction of moisture from green or partially dried wood or lumber, either by natural (air dried) or artificial (kiln dried) means.

seasoning of lumber: A term used by woodworkers when referring to the drying out of green lumber. The drying process may be accomplished naturally by allowing the lumber to dry in the air while sheltered from the weather under a shed, or the wood may be dried artificially in an oven or kiln specially prepared for that purpose.

seat cut: In roof framing, any line that is horizontal when the rafter is in proper position; also called a *level line* or *plate cut*. Same as *foot cut*. See *plumb line,* page 341.

seat of a rafter: The horizontal cut on the bottom end of a rafter which rests on the top of the plate.

second-growth timber: The timber which has grown up after the removal by any means of all or a large portion of the first growth or previous stand.

secondary beam: In floor construction, a beam carried by main beams and transmitting loads to them.

secondary color: In painting, a color produced by mixing two or more primary colors, as the colors obtained by mixing red, yellow, and blue pigment together, in pairs. Red and yellow make orange; yellow and blue make green.

seconds: In masonry, bricks which are similar to cutters but having a slightly uneven color. See *cutter,* 136.

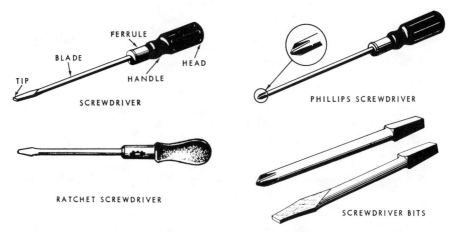

Fig. 517. Types of screwdrivers in common use.

Fig. 518. Portable power screwdriver. (Black and Decker Mfg. Co.)

Fig. 519. Scriber.

secret dovetail: A mitered housing joint in which dovetails and pins fit into each other. The same as a *blind miter.*

secret nailing: In carpentry, driving nails in such a way that the holes are concealed. Also called *blind nailing.*

Fig. 520. Seamer.

section: A part of a building cut vertically or horizontally so as to show the interior or profile. Fig. 522 illustrates a typical wall section. A section is also a basic land unit of one square mile (640 acres). A land section is divided into 36 parts. The top row of sections within a township is numbered from right to left—1 through 6. The second row is numbered from left to right 7 through 12. Continuing in this order, section 36 will be found at the lower right corner of the township, or the southeast corner.

sectional elevation: In architectural drawing, a cross-section view of a building showing the details of the construction.

sectional view: A type of drawing sometimes called *section,* intended to clarify details of construction. In making a sectional view, or section, the exposed cut surface of the materials is indicated by "section lin-

395

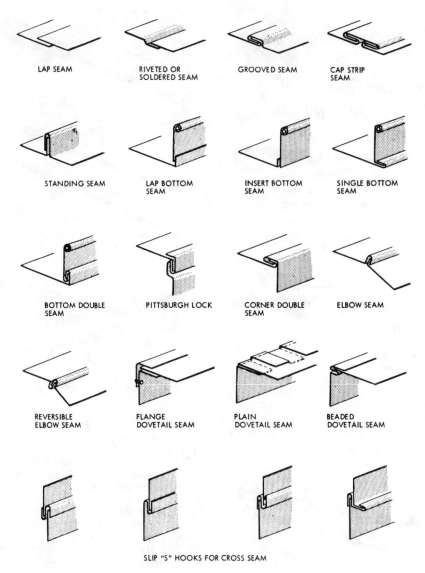

LAP SEAM

RIVETED OR SOLDERED SEAM

GROOVED SEAM

CAP STRIP SEAM

STANDING SEAM

LAP BOTTOM SEAM

INSERT BOTTOM SEAM

SINGLE BOTTOM SEAM

BOTTOM DOUBLE SEAM

PITTSBURGH LOCK

CORNER DOUBLE SEAM

ELBOW SEAM

REVERSIBLE ELBOW SEAM

FLANGE DOVETAIL SEAM

PLAIN DOVETAIL SEAM

BEADED DOVETAIL SEAM

SLIP "S" HOOKS FOR CROSS SEAM

Fig. 521. Mechanical sheet metal seams.

ing" or "crosshatching" with uniformly spaced fine lines or other symbols. Hidden lines and details beyond the cutting plane are omitted unless required for the necessary description of the object. A *section view* further aids in the study of construc-

tion work by supposing some portion of the construction cut away, or the building entirely cut through so as to exhibit a cross section of the walls, showing the heights of the internal doors and other apertures; also showing the heights of the stories, thickness

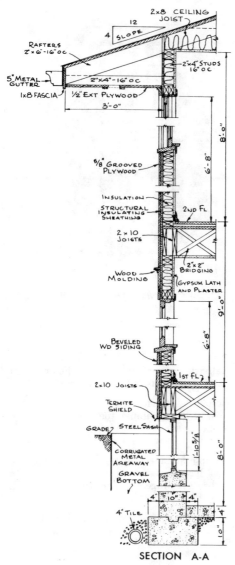

SECTION A-A

Fig. 522. Typical wall section.

the portion of a circular plane bounded by a chord and an arc; for example, the diameter of a circular plane divides the plane into two equal segments.

segmental: Relating to, or of the nature of, a segment or part of a whole, especially of a circle, as a segmental arch.

segmental arch: A type of masonry construction where the curve of an arch, though an arc or segment, is always less than a semicircle. See Fig. 27, page 24.

segregate: The tendency of coarse aggregates in fresh concrete to separate from the cement paste and fine aggregates and to settle to the bottom.

segregation: The differential concentration of the components of mixed concrete, resulting in nonuniform proportions in the mass.

select lumber: In carpentry, boards with few defects and suitable for fine finished work.

self-drilling snap-off anchor: The fastener itself drills the hole and is then snapped off and left in place. The insertion of a screw expands the fastener to give a secure hold. See *snap off anchors,* page 412.

self-faced: In masonry, a term applied to stone, such as flagstone, which splits along natural cleavage planes and does not require dressing.

self-supporting walls: In building construction, walls which support their own weight but do not carry the weight of the floors or the live load. In such construction, columns are used to support the weight of the floors and to give additional stiffness to the walls. Also called *self-sustaining walls.*

semichord: One-half the length of any chord of an arc.

semicircle: A segment of a circle which is bound by the diameter and one-half of the circumference.

semicircular: A term used with reference to an object or a structural feature which has the form of one-half of a circle.

of the floors, and other dimensions. See Fig. 522.

segment: Any portion of a whole which is divided into parts; as, when an apple is cut into quarters, each quarter is a *segment.* In geometry, a term specially applied to

semicircular arch: In architecture, a type of masonry construction where the curve of an arch, that is the intrados, forms a half circle.

sepia: A color—brownish red in hue.

septfoil: A decorative foliation consisting of seven lobes.

septic tank: A tank in which sewage is kept in order to cause disintegration of organic matter by bacterial action.

series circuit: In electricity, a circuit in which the same current flows through all the devices.

serration: A formation resembling the toothed edge of a saw.

service drop: The feed wires from the power company lines to the secondary rack on the customer's building. Also called *service conductors.*

service ell: In plumbing, an elbow having an outside thread on one end.

service entrance: The place where the service conductors are run into a building.

service pipe: In building, a pipe which connects a structure with a water or gas main.

service connections: In electricity, the wiring from the distributing mains to a building; *service conductors.* See *service drop.*

service switch: The main switch which connects all the lamps or motors in a building to the service wires. See Fig. 523.

service tee: In plumbing, a tee having inside threads on one end and on the branch, but having outside threads on the other end of the run.

service wires: The wires which connect the wiring in a building to the outside supply wires, *service conductors.*

set: In woodworking, a term applied to a small tool used for setting nail heads below the surface of a piece of work; also, a term used in connection with the adjusting of some part of a tool, as to *set* saw teeth, or to *set* a plane bit. See *nail set,* page 299. In masonry when plaster or concrete is properly hardened.

Fig. 523. Service switch. (I.T.E. Imperial Corp.)

setback: A specified minimum distance that a structure must be located from a lot line.

setoff: A ledge formed by the upper part of a wall being thinner than the lower part. Same as *offset.* Also, a horizontal line showing where a wall is reduced in thickness.

setting hammer: A type of hammer-like tool having a grooved or hollowed-out face used as a swage when riveting sheet metal. See Fig. 524.

setting time: The time required for freshly mixed concrete or mortar to harden.

Fig. 524. Setting hammer.

settlement: A term used in the building industry for an unequal sinking or lowering of any part of a structure, which may be caused by the use of unseasoned lumber, by skimping in material, by the weakness of the foundation, or settlement of earth.

sewage: Any waste material carried away by a sewer. Also called *sewerage.*

sewer: In plumbing, a pipe or closed channel for carrying away sewage, storm water, or waste water from industrial plants for sanitary purposes.

sewer gas: A self-generated combustible gas which collects in sewer pipes and tanks. It has a slow rate of flame propagation.

sewer pipe: A conduit or pipe for carrying off water or sewage.

sewer trap: A device in a sewer system which prevents sewer gas from entering a branch pipe leading to a building.

sgraffito: The decoration of a wall surface by laying on two coats of contrasting finishing colors, one on top of the other. Before the upper coat has set, parts are removed according to some pattern, usually by a scratching process. Thus, by revealing the coat of a different color beneath, a decorative design can be worked out.

shackle and thimble: *See cable attachments,* page 80.

shade line: Line that divides the shaded from the unshaded parts of a window, determined by amount of overhang, location of house, and position of the window. Used in calculating heat loss and heat gain. See Fig. 525.

shaft: The part of the column extending from the capital to the base. Same as *body.* See Fig. 230, page 174. See *column,* Fig. 137, page 108.

shake: A defect in timber such as a fissure or split causing a separation of the wood between the annual growth rings. See *wind-shake,* Fig. 635, page 485.

shakes: Hand split wood shingles.

shank: That part of a tool by which it is attached to the handle or socket.

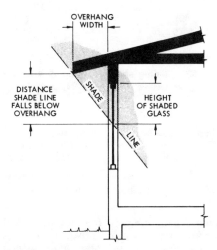

Fig. 525. The shade line is based on the latitude, width of overhang and location of window.

shear: Shear is caused by opposing forces that almost meet head on. It may be *perpendicular* or *parallel* to the grain. In timber construction, shear perpendicular to the grain is called *vertical shear* since usually it occurs in a vertical direction near loaded bearing surfaces. See Fig. 526. In their calculations, most designing engineers consider vertical shear as a type of compression stress, since crushing of the wood fibers occurs. Usually shear stress parallel to the grain is called *sliding shear.* As Fig. 527 shows, this stress is cased by loads which force sections of a member to slide across one another. Although sliding shear usually occurs in bending, Fig. 528 shows how it can occur in an upright post that was not properly squared at the ends. See also *simple beam,* Fig. 532, page 404.

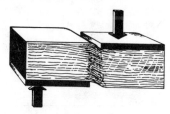

Fig. 526. Vertical shear in wood is a shearing that is perpendicular to the grain.

Fig. 527. Sliding shear in wood is a shearing stress that is parallel to the grain.

shearhead: Assembled steel unit in the top of the columns of flat slab or flat plate construction to transmit loads from slab to column.

shear plate: A timber connector. See Fig. 595, page 455.

shear reinforcement: Reinforcement designed to resist shearing forces; usually consisting of stirrups or truss bars bent and located as required.

shear strength: The measured resistance to twisting forces.

shear wall: A wall designed to resist forces resulting from wind, blast, or earthquake.

shears: A tool having two heavy steel blades for cutting metal used in building construction. Portable electric shears are often used.

sheathed cable: In electricity, a wire or cable which is protected from injury by an outside covering.

sheathing: Fiberwood, gypsum board, plywood, or flat wood boards that cover the outside of a building's wood superstructure. See Fig. 69, page 57, and Fig. 320, page 245.

sheathing paper: Insulating paper which is applied between the sheathing and outer wall of a building to prevent wind infiltration. Same as *building paper*.

shed: A one-story structure for shelter or storage, often open on one side. It may be attached to another building but frequently stands apart from other structures. See Fig. 529.

shed roof or **lean-to:** A roof having only one slope or pitch, with only one set of rafters which fall from a higher to a lower wall, like a pent roof; a wing or extension with a lean-to roof. See Fig. 529.

sheet-metal screws: Self-tapping screws used in sheet-metal work. See Fig. 516. The larger sizes are driven into clean-punched or drilled holes, but in lighter metal only pierced holes are necessary for starting the screws. These screws come in lengths ranging from $\frac{1}{8}$ of an inch to 2 inches, with diameters ranging from a No. 2 to No. 14 screw gage. This type of screw is used to fasten two pieces of metal together without riveting or soldering. The pan head metal screw shown in Fig. 516 has a self-drilling point and is used for fastening metal studs to metal, such as metal stud runner.

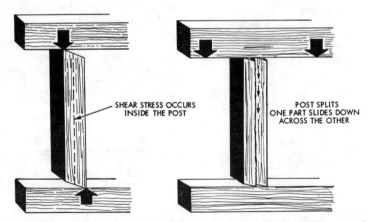

SHEAR STRESS OCCURS
INSIDE THE POST

POST SPLITS
ONE PART SLIDES DOWN
ACROSS THE OTHER

Fig. 528. Sliding shear can occur in a post if the ends are not square. In the post shown here (left), the arrows indicate a vertical load. The post splits (right) in reaction to the load.

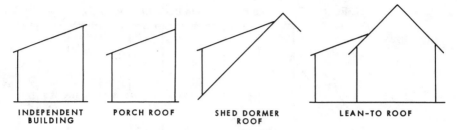

INDEPENDENT BUILDING   PORCH ROOF   SHED DORMER ROOF   LEAN-TO ROOF

Fig. 529. Shed roofs have several applications.

sheeting: In construction work, a term synonymous with *sheathing*.

shelf angles: Angles attached to the face of a building to support masonry or wall facing materials.

shellac varnish: A type of varnish used extensively in wood finishing. Usually it is made by dissolving flake shellac in alcohol.

shim: In building construction, a thin piece of material, such as wood or stone, used to fill in, as when leveling a structural stone or other member. Usually such a piece is tapered and so designed that it can be removed when its purpose has been served; a term sometimes applied to a shingle which has one side thicker than the other.

shingle lap: A type of lap joint in which the sections joined are tapered so the bottom of each section laps or fits over the top of the section below.

shingle nails: These are sized from 3d to 6d. They are used for cedar shingles and have thin shanks with small heads. Two nails are used for each shingle. See Fig. 390, page 296. See *penny,* page 320 for size.

shingles: Thin pieces of wood or other material, oblong in shape and thinner at one end, used for covering roofs or walls. The standard thicknesses of wood shingles are described as 4/2, 5/2-1/4, and 5/2, meaning, respectively, 4 shingles to 2 inches of butt thickness, 5 shingles to 2¼ inches of butt thickness, and 5 shingles to 2 inches of butt thickness. Lengths may be 16, 18, or 24 inches. Wood shingles may be bought in random or dimension widths. A diagram for different shingle exposures is shown in Fig. 530.

shingling hatchet: A type of carpenter's hatchet used for installing shingles. Fig. 307, page 233.

shiplapped lumber: Lumber that has been worked or rabbeted on both edges of each piece to provide a close lapped joint by fitting two pieces together. Used for *siding.* See Fig. 531.

shoe: A small molding on the order of a quarter round, nailed next to the floor on baseboards. Also, the short, bent portion of a downpipe which directs water away from the wall. In heavy timber construction, a metal plate used at the bottom of heavy timber columns. See Fig. 138, page 109.

shoe mold: For interior finish, a molding strip nailed to the baseboard close to the floor; also called *base shoe.* See Fig. 47, page 39.

shooting board: A board with a stop attached to one end against which a piece of board is braced while the ends are finished with a plane.

shop lumber: Lumber which is graded for use in further manufacturing. It is graded on the basis of the percentage of the area which will produce a limited number of cuttings of a specified or given minimum size and quality.

shore: A piece of lumber placed in an oblique direction to support a building temporarily; also, to support as with a prop of stout timber or with a device of steel or wood designed for this purpose. A shore may be placed in an oblique, vertical, or

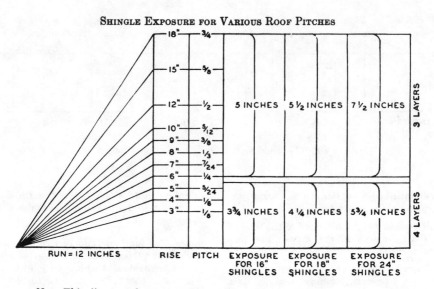

Note: This diagram shows at a glance the weather exposure to be used for various roof pitches. For example, if a roof has a rise of 8 inches in a run of 12 inches, it can be seen that this is ⅛ pitch and that an exposure of either 5 inches, 5½ inches, or 7½ inches should be employed, depending upon the length of the shingles used.

Fig. 530. Shingle exposures.

horizontal position. Also: Temporary supports for concrete framework.

shoring: The use of timbers to prevent the sliding of earth adjoining an excavation; also, the timbers and adjustable steel or wooden devices used as bracing against a wall or under decking for temporary support.

short: In electricity, a contraction for short circuit.

short circuit: In electricity, an accidental connection of low resistance joining two sides of a circuit through which nearly all the current will flow. Also called *short*.

short length: A term used by woodworkers when referring to lumber which measures less than 8 feet in length.

shotcreting: Pneumatic placing of concrete. The concrete is forced at high velocity through a nozzle onto a prepared surface. Widely used for large structures with curved surfaces, such as swimming pools,

reservoirs, architectural roofs, etc., where ordinary forming techniques would be difficult and expensive.

shoulder: The edge of a highway used for emergency stopping.

shoulder box: A *toolbox* in which a workman carries his small tools.

show rafter: An architectural term applied to a short rafter which may be seen below the cornice; often an ornamental rafter.

shrink: A term applied to the natural contraction of lumber which has not been properly dried and seasoned.

shrinking: The contracting of material used in construction work. In building, allowance must be made for contraction, as well as expansion, of structural members.

shutters: A protective covering for the outside of a window; a type of door with louvers designed for shutting out light; used

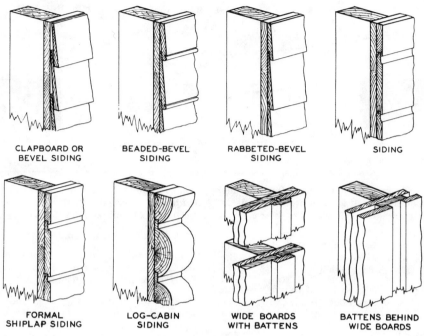

| CLAPBOARD OR BEVEL SIDING | BEADED-BEVEL SIDING | RABBETED-BEVEL SIDING | SIDING |

| FORMAL SHIPLAP SIDING | LOG-CABIN SIDING | WIDE BOARDS WITH BATTENS | BATTENS BEHIND WIDE BOARDS |

Fig. 531. Wood sidings.

on either the inside or outside of a window; sometimes called *window blind.*

side: In architecture, usually the longitudinal walls are called the *sides,* and a view of one of the longer walls is known as a *side elevation.*

side cut: In building construction, the beveled edge of hip, jack, valley, and cripple rafters. The same as *cheek cut.* Also: In lumber, when the pith is not enclosed in a piece.

side-cutting pliers: Used for cutting wire and for stripping wire by crushing insulation directly behind the hinge. In electrical work the handles can be used to tap in the outlet box knockouts and remove them with the plier gripping jaws also. See Fig. 442, page 339.

siding: The outside finish on a house, generally wood, plastic overlaid wood, vinal, hardboard, aluminum, asphalt, asbestos concrete, or steel. Fig. 531 illustrates typical wood siding. See also *bevel siding,* page 48, *drop siding,* page 161, *shiplapped lumber.*

siding shingles: Any of various kinds of shingles, some especially designed, which can be used as the exterior sidewall covering for a structure.

silica brick: In building, a refractory material made from quartzite bonded with milk of lime; used where resistance to high temperature is desired.

sill: The lowest member beneath an opening, such as a window or door. Also, the horizontal timbers which form the lowest members of a frame supporting the superstructure of a house, bridge, or other structure. See Fig. 41, page 35.

sill anchor: In building construction, a bolt embedded in a concrete or masonry foundation for the purpose of anchoring the sill to the foundation. Sometimes called a *plate anchor.* See *anchor bolt,* Fig. 80, page 64.

403

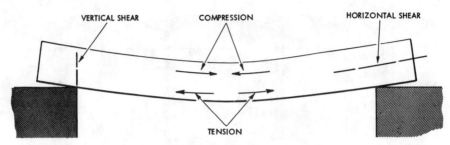

Fig. 532. Stresses in a simple beam.

sill cock: In plumbing, a water faucet which is placed at about sill height on the outside of a building. Sometimes called *hose cock* or *bib*.

sill high: The distance from the ground level to the window sill. In masonry, the height from floor to sill.

sill plate: Plate on top of foundation wall which supports floor framing. See *plate,* page 337.

simple beam: Beam supported at each end (two points) without bending restraint at either end. See Fig. 532.

simple cornice: A type of cornice construction which consists only of a *frieze* and *molding*.

single-pitch roof: In building, a roof which slopes only one way, as a *lean-to* or *shed roof*. See Fig. 529.

singlepole switch: An electric device for making or breaking one side of an electric current.

sinkage: In architecture, a sinking or depression, as a *mat sinking*.

sink bib: A device such as a stopcock used for starting and stopping the flow of water into a kitchen sink; a *bib nozzle*.

sinking: In architecture, a recess cut below the general surface of the work; a depression. In painting, a condition due to a porous undercoating which causes the color to sink in, resulting in flat or semi-gloss spots.

siphon trap: In plumbing, a trap fitted to water closets and sinks, having a double bend like an S on its side, the lower bend containing the water seal which prevents the reflux of foul odors and gases.

site: Location of a building.

sizing: Working a material to the desired size. Material applied to a surface to seal it before painting or finishing.

skeleton construction: A type of building in which all external and internal loads and stresses are transmitted to the foundations by a rigidly connected framework of metal or reinforced concrete. The enclosing walls are supported by the frame at designated intervals, usually at each story.

sketch: In architecture, a freehand drawing of a building, or some part of a building, such as a plan sketch or an elevation sketch. See Fig. 533.

skew: Twisted to one side; slanting.

skew arch: An arch in which the axis is not at right angles with the face which is inclined so as to form an oblique angle with the axis; an arch whose face is not at right angles with the jambs.

skew chisel: A woodworking tool with a straight cutting edge, sharpened at an angle; used in wood turning.

skew nailing: A carpentry term referring to the driving of nails on a slant or obliquely. See *toenailing, page 455.*

skewback: A sloping surface against which the end of an arch rests; that is, the course of masonry against which the end of the arch abuts.

Fig. 533. Finished elevation sketch.

skim coat: In plastering, the finishing coat consisting of *fine stuff* to which fine white sand may be added. The surface is finally polished to a glazed finish with a trowel. Sometimes called *troweled stucco.*

skinning knife: In electrical work, a knife with a curved blade used for reaching around wires and cables to cut and remove insulation. See Fig. 534.

skintled brickwork: In masonry, an irregular arrangement of bricks with respect to the normal face of a wall. The bricks are set in and out so as to produce an uneven effect on the surface of the wall; also, a rough effect caused by mortar being squeezed out of the joints.

skip: In masonry, a scoop-like hopper usually used with small portable mixers or paving equipment for charging aggregates and cement into the mixer drum. The skip lowers to accept materials and is raised to allow the materials to slide into the drum. Also, in carpentry, a defect in lumber due to an area on a piece that failed to surface when the board was planed.

skirt: In architecture, the border or molded piece under a window stool; commonly called *apron;* also, a *baseboard.* The same as *skirting.*

skirting: The same as baseboard; that is, a finishing board which covers the plastering where it meets the floor of a room.

skirting board: A term applied to the board used to cover the plaster of a wall where it meets the floor. The same as *baseboard* or *mopboard.*

skotch fasteners: Devices used for making or strengthening any type of wood joint. The curved prongs draw both sides of a joint firmly together. Skotch fasteners are available in three sizes. Fig. 535.

skylight: An opening in a roof or ceiling for admitting daylight; also, the window fitted into such an opening.

slab: A flat area of concrete. In residential construction, the slab is usually set on a fill of crushed rock; in southern areas where frost penetration is not appreciable or common the slab may rest directly on the earth. Fig. 536 illustrates a slab placed on a fill with a perimeter wall foundation or rim wall carried below the front line. Fig. 537

Fig. 534. Skinning knife. (Champion DeArment Tool Co.)

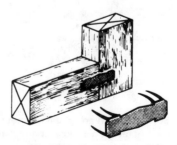

Fig. 535. Skotch fastener.

illustrates a floating slab foundation. For reinforced concrete slabs, see Figs. 399, 400, 409. Also, a steel plate used as a column base. Also, a term applied to the outside piece cut from a log.

slab bolster: In reinforced concrete, bar support with corrugated longitudinal wire and supporting legs, used to support bottom slab bars.

slab cut: First cut from a log made before the first board cut is made.

slab, on-grade: See Figs. 536, 537.

slab schedule: In reinforced concrete, a list of reinforcement for each slab.

slab spacer: In reinforced concrete, bar support with straight longitudinal top wire and supporting legs spaced to match the spacing of slab bars which they support.

slabbing: In building construction, the process of squaring a timber.

slabjacking: To force grout under a slab to return it to its original place and to stabilize the sub-base.

slack: Loose fitting; a looseness in a structural member which must be removed to insure proper construction; a looseness as in the belt of a pulley which must be tightened before power is applied.

slag: A by-product of smelting ore such as iron, lead, or copper. A type of lightweight aggregate used to produce structural lightweight concrete.

slag cement: An artificial cement made by first chilling slag from blast furnaces in water, then mixing and grinding the granulated slag with lime, a process which produces a cement with hydraulic properties.

slag concrete: A concrete in which blast-furnace slag is used as an aggregate. Relatively light in weight, *slag concrete* is used in almost every type of construction and is also valued because of its fire-resistant properties as well as for its insulating qualities against cold and sound.

slag plaster: A plaster made of granulated slag, valuable as an acoustic plaster because of its superior absorbent properties.

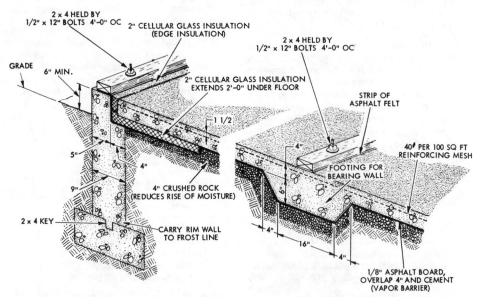

Fig. 536. In northern areas, the perimeter wall in a basementless house extends two feet under the floor to prevent heat loss and moisture penetration. Note the insulation at the perimeter of the slab.

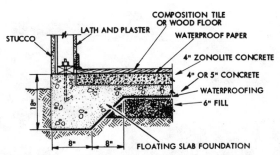

Fig. 537. In southern areas a floating slab foundation for a basementless house is used. Note how the foundation splays inward to to give additional support.

slag strip: In roofing, a strip of wood nailed around the edges of a graveled roof to give the edge a finish and to prevent the gravel from rolling off the roof. Also called *gravel strip*.

slaked lime: A crumbly mass of lime formed when quicklime is treated with water. Same as *hydrated lime*.

slaking: The process of hydrating quick-lime into a putty by combining it with water.

slamming stile: A term used in carpentry when referring to the upright strip at the side of a door opening against which the door slams or against which it abuts when closed; also, the strip into which the bolt on the door slips when the lock is turned.

sledge: A heavy hammer having a long handle, usually wielded with both hands and used for driving posts or other large stakes.

sleeper: A heavy beam or piece of timber laid on, or near, the ground for receiving floor joists and to support the superstructure; also, strips of wood, usually 2x2, laid over a rough concrete floor to which the finished wood floor is nailed. See Fig. 538.

sleeper clips: Sheet-metal strips used to anchor wood flooring to concrete. See Fig. 538. See also *anchors,* Fig. 18, page 17.

sleeve: A tube or tubelike part fitting over or around another part. In building, a pipe used to provide openings for the installation of electric and plumbing services. Used particularly in solid concrete floors through which the services must pass. Also called *sleeve chase*. See Fig. 539.

sleeve chase: See *sleeve.*

slicing cut: The cutting of material with a sliding movement in order to remove only thin pieces or slices.

slicker: Flat metal or wooden board used to smooth plaster. The slicker is used in place of the *darby* and is preferred by some plasterers because it can be bent slightly while it is being floated over the mortar and can be handled at a better angle to the surface. See Fig. 540. It is sometimes called a shingle.

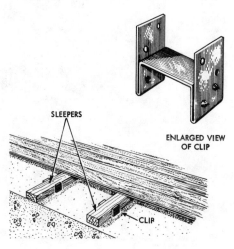

Fig. 538. Sleepers with sleeper clips.

Fig. 539. Sleeves through a concrete floor.

Fig. 540. Plasterer using slicker to smooth brown coat.

sliding-door lock: A lock designed for use on a sliding door having hookshaped bolts to fit the strike.

sliding doors: Doors hung from an overhead track on which the panels are wheeled into a special recess at the sides to clear the opening. A related construction operates on a scissors type suspension attached to the narrow strip of wall at the inner end of the recess and to that edge of the door which first enters the recess when it is pushed.

sliding sash: A window in which the sashes slide along parallel tracks in the frame toward one another. See Fig. 541.

Fig. 541. Sliding sash window.

sling: Short lengths of wire rope, with a spliced eye at each end or a spliced eye at one end and a hook at the other used to encircle a hood for hoisting purposes. See Fig. 542.

slip-form: Also referred to as "sliding form". A form which moves, usually continuously, during placing of the concrete. Movement may be either horizontal or vertical.

slip-form paver: A machine that moves along a prepared roadbed forming a ribbon of pavement as it goes. The consistency of the concrete is such that it does not change form after being placed. The slip-form paver finishes the surface of the concrete as it goes along.

slip joint: In masonry, especially in brickwork, type of joint made where a new wall is joined to an old wall by cutting a channel or groove in the old wall to receive the brick of the new wall. This method of joining the two walls forms a kind of telescopic, nonleaking joint.

slip mortise: A mortise which is made in the end of a construction member. Same as *slot mortise.*

slip newel: A three-sided newel which fits on the free end of a partition wall.

slip sill: In the building trade, a term applied to a simple sill consisting of a stone slab just as long as the window is wide and fitting into the walls between the window jambs. The *slip sill* differs from the *lug sill,* which is longer than the width of the window opening and is *let in* to the wall on each side. See *lug sill,* page 274.

slip stone: An oilstone used in wood turning and wood patternmaking for sharpening gouges. The small wedge-shaped stone has rounded edges and can be conveniently held in one hand when whetting a tool.

slope: Incline of roof—used particularly to designate incline of trussed roofs. Expressed as a ratio of horizontal distance to vertical rise or fall. For example, a horizontal distance of 2 feet to 1 foot rise would be expressed as a ratio of 2 to 1 or 2:1.

slot mortise: A mortise which is made in the end of a construction member. See *slip mortise.*

slotted angles: Lengths of steel angle, prepunched with many slots. Some are made specially for shelving; others are used for framework in utility structures. No drilling, riveting, or welding is required, since pieces are bolted together through the slots.

slow drying: In painting, when a finishing coat of paint, enamel, or other material does not dry within the time specified by the manufacturer, the indications are that either the surface was not clean and dry, the wrong type of reducer was used, or the drying conditions were not normal.

slump: In concrete work, the relative consistency or stiffness of the fresh concrete mix.

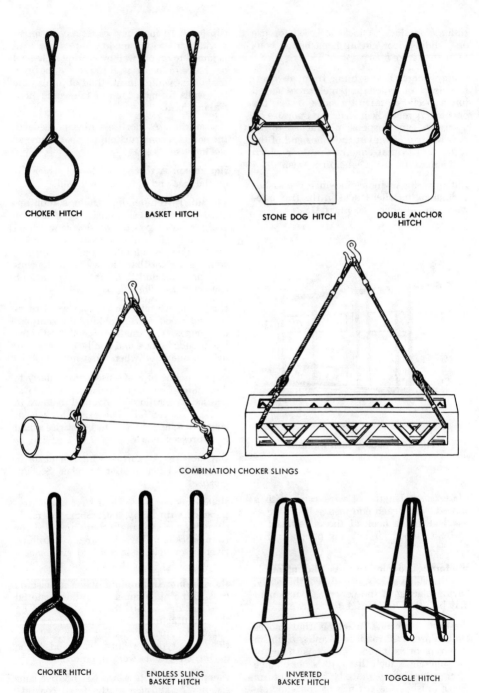

CHOKER HITCH

BASKET HITCH

STONE DOG HITCH

DOUBLE ANCHOR HITCH

COMBINATION CHOKER SLINGS

CHOKER HITCH

ENDLESS SLING BASKET HITCH

INVERTED BASKET HITCH

TOGGLE HITCH

Fig. 542. Hitches used with slings. (Dept. of the Army.)

slurry: A mixture of water and any finely divided insoluble material, such as portland cement, slag, soil in suspension.

small tools: In plastering, small tools are used in pointing the joints when erecting cast ornamental work. They are also used to finish the final intersection of a miter in cornice work. They are also used for any work that requires a fine, small-sized tool. See Fig. 543. Sometimes these are called *modeling tools* or *ornamental tools*.

smoke chamber: The slanting area above the wind shelf, and below the flue, of a fireplace. See Fig. 245, page 188.

smoke pipe: In building construction, a pipe for carrying smoke either to a smoke flue or to the open air.

smoke shelf: In fireplaces, a projection at the bottom of the smoke chamber used to prevent down-rushing air currents from forcing smoke into the room. See Fig. 245, page 188.

smooth coat: In plastering, a *putty coat.*

smooth plane: See Fig. 436, page 332.

snake: In plumbing, a coil spring which can be inserted into a drain for cleaning. In electrical wiring, a flexible steel tape used to pull wire through conduit; a *fish tape.*

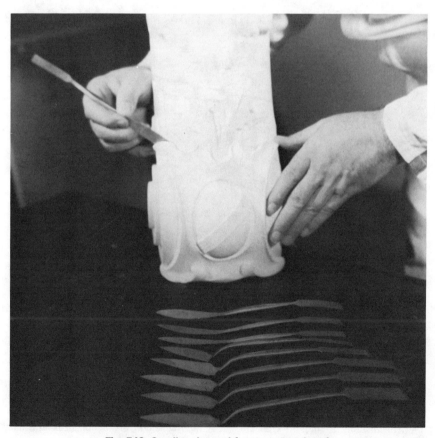

Fig. 543. Small tools used for ornamental work.

snap-off anchor: Self drilling anchor which is broken off after drilling and left in place so a bolt may be screwed in. See Fig. 544.

snap tie: A concrete wall form tie, the end of which can be twisted or snapped off after the forms have been removed. See Fig. 545.

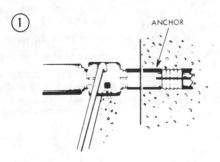

The drill is self-cleaning. Cuttings pass through the core and holes in the chuck head.

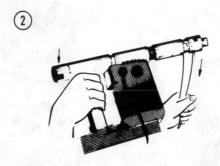

Snap off chucking end of anchor with a quick lateral strain on the hammer.

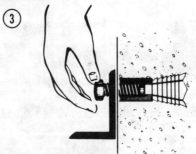

The anchor is now ready to serve as an internally threaded steel bolt hole to support any bolted object.

Fig. 544. Installation of snap-off type anchor. A wide selection of anchor sizes and lengths is available. (Phillips Drill Co.)

snapping lines: Guide lines made by use of a chalked cord which is held taut, then raised near the central point and allowed to snap onto the surface of a roof or floor to provide a guide for laying shingles or flooring. See *chalk line,* Fig. 119, page 93.

sneck: A small stone used to fill in between larger stones, as in rubble-work masonry; also, a term sometimes applied to the laying of a rubble-work wall, or *snecked wall.*

snecked masonry: A term applied to rubble walls in which the stones are roughly squared but of irregular sizes and not arranged in courses.

snips: A scissors-like hand tool, hand shears, used for cutting sheet metal. See Fig. 546.

snow guard: Any device used to prevent snow from sliding off a sloping roof. Same as *roof guard.*

socket: In plumbing, that portion of a pipe which for a short distance is enlarged to receive the end of another pipe of the same diameter. The joint thus made is secured by calking. Same as *bell* or *hub.* In electrical wiring, what a bulb screws into.

socket chisel: A woodworker's tool of great strength and with sharp cutting edges on each side. Usually the upper end of the shank terminates in a socket into which the handle is driven. In the best quality tools of this type, the blade and socket are forged in one piece with no welded socket.

socketing: The joining of structural members by wedging one piece of wood into a cavity in another piece.

socle: An architectural term applied to a projecting member at the base of a supporting wall or pier or at the bottom of a pedestal or column.

soffit: The underside of any subordinate member of a building, such as the under surface of an arch, cornice, eave, beam or stairway. See Fig. 547 for an example using a beam.

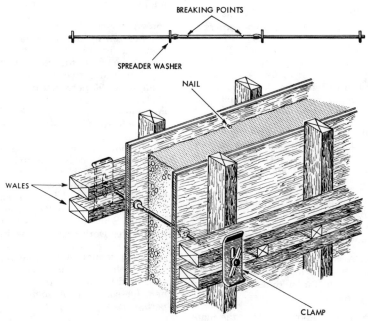

Fig. 545. Snap ties provide a means of spacing the walls at the proper distance apart and also clamping the whole assembly together.

413

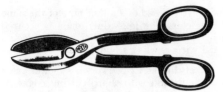

Fig. 546. Snips.

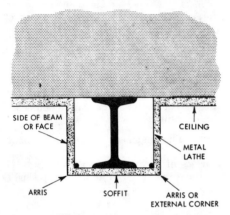

SIDE OF BEAM OR FACE

CEILING

METAL LATHE

ARRIS   SOFFIT   ARRIS OR EXTERNAL CORNER

Fig. 547. Soffit, sides (also known as faces or cheeks) and arrises or external corners of a beam.

soffit vent: An opening in the underside of a roof overhang, which acts as a passageway into the house for air currents.

softwood: Wood from a group of trees which have needles or scalelike leaves commonly referred to as *confers,* including cedars, pines, and firs popularly known as *evergreens.*

soil-cement: A hard, durable material made by mixing a specified amount of cement with soil and water, compacting to specified density and allowing to cure.

soil pipe: A vertical drain pipe conveying waste matter from a water closet to the drainage system of a building. Same as *soil stack, waste stack.*

soil stack: In a plumbing system, the main vertical pipe which receives waste material from all fixtures. See *soil pipe.*

414

soil vent: The portion of a soil stack which is above the highest fixture waste connection to it.

solar orientation: The position of a house and the arrangement of its surfaces and openings, with reference to the amount of sun admitted to, and excluded from, various functional areas of the house. Experiment and research are developing simplified means of calculating these effects with respect to climate, season, and time of day. If solar orientation factors are carefully considered, the amount of heating, air conditioning, and insulation needed in a house can be minimized.

solder: A metal or metallic alloy (tin and lead) which is used, when melted, to join metallic surfaces. Usually with a flux (as rosin, borax or zinc chloride) to cleanse the surfaces. Common solder has the least percent of tin; it has the highest melting point. It is used most frequently in plumbing work and for splicing the covering of lead cables. Fine solder has the greatest percent of tin. Fine and medium solders have lower melting points and are used for electrical work.

solder, commercial bar: Is identified by numbers giving the percentage of tin and lead. The first number is the percentage of tin contained in the alloy. For example, 30/70 indicates that the bar of solder is made up of 30 percent tin and 70 percent lead. Alloy designated 50/50 is called half-and-half and is sometimes labeled that way. It is preferred for most sheet metal jobs.

solder gun: An electrically heated device designed to speed soldering operations. Heating element reaches operating temperature in approximately three seconds by pressing operating trigger. Element need not be heated continually during serial operations. Some have small spotlight which illuminates work surface. See Fig. 548.

soldering copper: A tool having a copper bit or bolt with a pointed wedge-shaped end; used by sheet-metal workers and tinners for soldering. A *soldering iron, coppering bit.*

soldering iron: A tool used for uniting two portions of metals or metallic alloy by

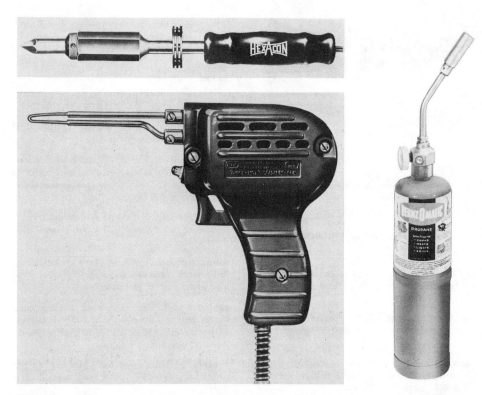

Fig. 548. Soldering iron, soldering gun and torch. (Hexacon Electric Co.; Wen Products, Inc.; Otto Bernz Co., Inc.)

means of another metal or alloy. See *soldering copper*. See Fig. 548.

soldering torch: Propane torch used for soldering. See Fig. 548.

solderless connector: An insulated wire nut which is screwed onto the ends of wires to be connected. A cone-shaped spiral spring inside the nut presses the skinned wires together, replacing solder. See Fig. 549.

soldier: In masonry, that side or face of a brick which shows on the face of the wall in a vertical position. See *soldier course*. Fig. 162, page 126.

soldier course: In masonry, a term applied to a course of bricks where the bricks are laid so they are all standing on end. See Fig. 162, page 126.

sole: The horizontal member placed on the sub-flooring upon which the wall and partition studs rest. Also called *soleplate*. See Fig. 441, page 338, and Fig. 550.

solepiece: See *soleplate*.

soleplate: The lowest horizontal member of a wall or partition which rests on the rough floor, to which the studding is nailed. See Fig. 441, page 338, and Fig. 550. Same as *solepiece* and *sole*.

solid bearing: The support underneath a beam which is supported along its entire length.

solid bridging: Bridging, usually wood, which fills the space between joists.

solid masonry unit: A masonry unit whose cross-sectional area in every plane parallel

415

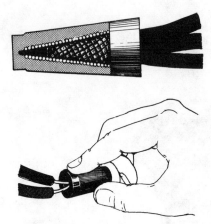

Fig. 549. Solderless connector.

to the bearing surface is 75 percent or more of its gross cross-sectional area measured in the same plane.

solid newel: The center post of a winding stair, as distinct from a *hollow newel.*

solid punch: A small hand tool of steel, of any useful diameter, employed, for example, in starting a bolt out of a hole, etc. See Fig. 455, page 351.

sommer: In a floor or partition, a horizontal timber or principal beam into which smaller joists and studs are framed. See *summer* and *breastsummer.*

soot pocket: In chimney construction, an extension of a flue opening to a depth of 8 or 10 inches below the smoke pipe entrance.

The pocket thus formed prevents soot from collecting in the smoke pipe.

sound: Free of decay.

sound knot: A term used in woodworking when referring to any knot so firmly fixed in a piece of lumber that it will continue to hold its position even when the piece is worked; also, is solid across its face and hard as the wood encircling it.

soundproofing: The application of deadening material to walls, ceilings, and floors to prevent sound from passing through these structural members into other rooms.

sound transmission class: A method of rating acoustic efficiency of various wall and floor systems.

sound transmission loss: The reduction in the sound between two stated points, usually expressed in decibels.

southern colonial: Type of architecture found in the Old South; usually 2 stories with an elaborate entrance using turned or paneled posts. See Fig. 551.

spackle: Mixture used for patching plaster or for joint treatment in gypsum-wallboard finish; *joint cement.*

spading: The compacting with a spade or shovel of newly placed concrete against the forms to prevent the formation of voids on the surface.

spall: A fragment or chip of stone or brick, especially bad or broke brick; in masonry, to reduce an irregular stone block to ap-

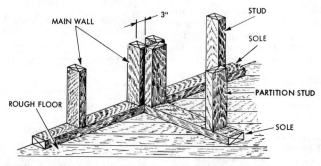

Fig. 550. The sole goes under wall studs and partition studs and over rough flooring.

Fig. 551. The Southern Colonial is earmarked by large elaborate entrances using turned or paneled posts. The Dr. R. H. Richardson house, built in 1835 at Athens, Alabama, is still used as a residence.

proximately the desired size by chipping with a stone hammer. See *gallet,* page 213. Also spelled *spawl.*

span: The distance between the abutments of an arch or the space between two adjoining arches. The distance between the wall, or rafter, plates of a building. The distance between wall supports; distance between structural supports such as walls, columns, piers, beams, girders, etc.

span roof: A common pitched roof consisting of two sloping sides having the same inclination, meeting in one ridge with eaves on both sides.

spandrel: The space between the exterior curve of an arch and the enclosing right angle; or the triangular space between either half of the extrados of an arch and the rectangular molding enclosing the arch. See Figs. 45, 137. The part of wall between the head of one window and the sill of another window above it.

spandrel beams: Marginal or edge beams; a beam in an exterior wall.

spandrel wall: A wall erected on the extrados of an arch to fill the spandrels.

span of a roof or **arch:** The clear space or distance between two supporting members, as the supporting walls or piers.

spanpiece: A *sparpiece,* or the collar beam of a roof.

spark arresters: See *arresters,* page 26.

sparpiece: The horizontal beam connecting the rafters of a collar-beam roof. Same as *spanpiece.*

specifications: Written instructions to the builder containing information about the materials, style, workmanship, and finish for the job. When there is a difference between the specifications and the plans, the specifications take precedence.

specific gravity: The ratio of the weight of any volume of a substance to the weight of an equal volume of some other substance; taken as a standard, usually water for sol-

417

ids and liquids, and air or hydrogen for gases.

specific heat: The quantity of heat required to raise the temperature of one pound of any substance 1° F. (expressed in B.t.u.).

specs: A short term for "specifications".

spigot: In plumbing, the plain end of a pipe which enters the enlarged end of the next pipe to form a joint between the two lengths; the plug or peg used to close the vent in a pipe. A term sometimes applied to a *faucet* or *cock.* See *tap,* page 448.

spigot-and-socket joint: In plumbing, each length of cast-iron pipe is made with a plain or spigot end of one length fitting into the enlarged or socket end of the next length. The joint is made tight by calking. See *bell-and-spigot joint,* page 46.

spike: In the building trade, a term commonly applied to a large-sized nail usually made of iron or steel, used as a fastener for heavy lumber. Also, in masonry, to add gypsum to cement mortar.

spike grid: A timber connector. See Fig. 595, page 455.

spike knot: In woodworking, a knot sawed lengthwise; also called *splay knot.*

spile: A small peg or wooden pin used to close an opening or vent; a *spigot.*

spindle: In furniture making, a slender rod, resembling a spinning-wheel spindle, used for a brace or support, as in the backs of chairs.

spiny: Sharply serrated; pointed; referring to certain forms of the Greek *acanthus.* See Fig. 2, page 2.

spiral: Anything which winds continuously round and round a fixed point as a center,

such as the coil of a watch spring; also, a similar coil not in the same plane, as the conelike formation of a univalve sea snail or periwinkle. In furniture making, a decorative feature designed to resemble or suggest the coiled structure of a nautilus or ammonite shell. Also: a continuously coiled bar or wire.

spiral grain: A type of growth in which the fibers take a spiral course about the bole of a tree instead of the normal vertical course. The spiral may extend either in a right-handed or left-handed direction around the trunk of a tree.

spiral ratchet screwdriver: A type of screwdriver that drives a screw when it is pumped up and down. Different size bits, including a Phillips screwdriver bit, are available. It is most useful for the rapid tightening of screws. It is especially practical where many screws are to be used at one time, as in the application of butts to doors. It can be steadied by holding the revolving chuck sleeve with the free hand. Screws can also be removed by changing the ratchet shift to the opposite direction. See Fig. 552.

spiral stairs: A staircase which is circular in plan, consisting entirely of winders or wedge-shaped steps. See Fig. 563, page 426.

spire: In architecture, a tapering tower or roof; any elongated structural mass shaped like a cone or pyramid; also, the topmost feature of a steeple.

spirit level: An instrument used for testing horizontal or vertical accuracy of the position of any structural part of a building. The correct position is indicated by the movement of an air bubble in alcohol. See *level,* Fig. 351, page 266.

splash block: A small, masonry block laid with the top close to the ground surface to

Fig. 552. Spiral ratchet screwdriver.

receive drainage of rain water from the roof and carry it away from the building.

splat: A strip of wood used as a cover for joints between adjacent sheets of building board.

splay: An inclined surface, as the slope or bevel at the sides of a door or window; also, to make a beveled surface or to spread out or make oblique; an angle greater than 90°. See Fig. 553.

splayed: Spread out, extended, or beveled; having an oblique angle or bevel causing a flare outward, as a *splayed arch.*

splayed arch: An arch with the opening at one end larger than the opening at the other end, so the intrados face is conical or funnel-shaped. Also called *fluing arch.*

splayed brick: A purpose-made brick having one side beveled off.

splayed grounds: Grounds having the edges undercut or rebated and shaped like dovetails, providing a key for holding the plaster to the wall in cases where the grounds also serve as screeds. See *ground,* page 224.

splayed skirting: A skirting board having its top edge beveled or chamfered. See *skirting,* page 405.

splay end: The end of a brick which is opposite the end laid squarely by rule.

splay knot: In lumber, a knot which has been cut through lengthwise. Same as *spike knot.*

splice: A joint where two pieces of wood are connected by overlapping them. A weaving together of two pieces of rope. Also: Connection of one reinforcing bar to another by lapping, welding, mechanical couplings, or other means. The lap between sheets or rolls of welded wire fabric.

splice box: An iron box in which cable connections and splices are made.

spline: In building construction, a thin, flat piece of wood used for various purposes, such as between two pieces of heavy subflooring where a loose tongue takes the place of a tongue-and-groove joint; also, sometimes used as a means of stiffening a

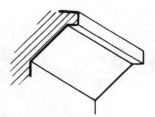

Fig. 553. Splay.

miter joint (Fig. 330, page 252), or it may be used as a fillet within a groove created by two joining rabbets.

spline miter: A miter *joint* strengthened by a feather (thin strip of wood) inserted in matching grooves (splines) cut on the joining faces. See Fig. 330, page 252.

splines: Metal keys used to secure ceiling tile together.

split: A lengthwise separation of wood due to a tearing apart. Usually a split occurs across the rings of annual growth, extending from one surface through the piece of timber to the opposite surface or to an adjoining surface.

split bolt connector: In electrical wiring, mechanical device used to splice two cable ends together. See Fig. 554.

split level: In residential construction, a house which in one part is one story and in another adjacent part two story. A house in which two or more floors are usually located directly above one another, and one or more additional floors, adjacent to them, are placed at a different level. Also called a *bi-level* or *tri-level.* See Fig. 555.

split loading: Method of charging a mixer in which the solid ingredients do not all enter the mixer together. Cement and sometimes different sizes of aggregate may be added separately.

split ring: A metal device used at joints in wood trusses to keep the members in position. See Fig. 556.

split shakes: A type of shingle split by hand. See *shakes,* page 399.

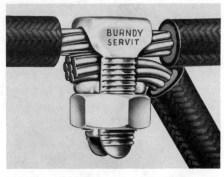

Fig. 554. Split bolt connector. (Burndy Corp.)

Fig. 556. Split ring connectors give strength by distributing the stress over a greater area. (Timber Engineering Co.)

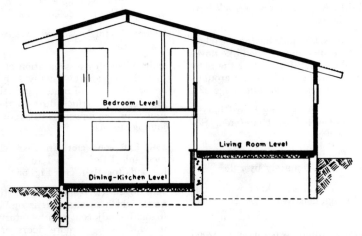

Fig. 555. Section through the split-level house. (Donald H. Drummond; David Runnels, Architect)

splitting: In painting, when a painted or lacquered surface is sanded too much or with too much force, the old film will be fractured, and, when a new coat is applied, the solvents will penetrate into the old film. The sanding scratches will then open up, resulting in what usually is called splitting.

splocket: A short, wedge-shaped piece of wood nailed on the upper side of a common rafter near the lower end, at a flatter pitch, thus forming a break in the roof near the eaves. Same as *sprocket*.

spokeshave: A cutting tool or plane with a transverse blade set between two handles. This device is especially suitable for dressing rounded pieces of wood of small diameter, such as spokes or other similarly curved work. See Fig. 557.

sponge rubber float: In plastering, a tool replacing the carpet float. This plasterer's finishing tool is rectangular in shape. It has a handle on one side, and the other side is covered with a sheet of sponge rubber for producing a fine sanded finish on plaster

Fig. 557. Spokeshave for curved surfaces. (Stanley Works)

work. The rubber is not affected by lime and water and lasts longer than the carpet surface.

spongy wood: In carpentry, a soft wood, which is unsuitable for construction work.

spontaneous combustion: An instantaneous bursting into flames in a substance, or combination of substances, due to the evolution of heat through the chemical action of its own constituents, as the instant burning of oily rags in an unventilated pile of rubbish.

spot weld: Spot weld refers to pieces held together by spots rather than a complete seam (continuous weld). Spot can also be called *tack weld* and be used to hold pieces together for further welding operations.

spot zoning: An action by the municipality changing the intended use of land in a particular area; for example, changing one lot in an area zoned for single family dwellings to a lot for a business.

spread footing: A footing whose sides slope gradually outward from the foundation to the base. See Fig. 537, page 407.

sprig: In woodworking, a term applied to a small brad with no head; also, one of the small triangular-shaped pieces of tin or zinc used for holding a pane of glass in a window sash.

springback: Property of sheet metal to resist bending and then to partially recover its original shape after it is bent.

springer: In architecture, a stone or other solid piece of masonry forming the impost of an arch; that is, the topmost member of a pillar or pier upon which the weight of the arch rests. See Fig. 337, page 256.

spring hinge: A joint with a spring built into it, used for self-closing doors, such as screen doors.

springing: A line through the point where an extrados of an arch meets the abutment of a pier.

springing line: A line across the span of an arch passing through the points where the arch intersects with the *skewbacks*.

spring latch: A type of door latch which fastens with a spring. See Fig. 558.

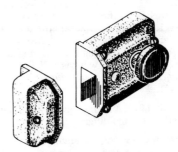

Fig. 558. Spring latch.

springwood: The part of the annual growth ring that is formed during the early part of the season; usually weaker than *summer wood*.

sprinkler system: In building, an arrangement of overhead pipes equipped with sprinkler heads or nozzles. In case of fire, these nozzles automatically release sprays of water for extinguishing the fire.

sprinkling: The process of curing concrete by uniformly spraying water over concrete by use of a water hose and nozzle.

sprocket: A small wedgeshaped piece of wood nailed to the upper surface of the foot of a common rafter, in cases where the latter overhangs the wall to form a projecting eaves to the roof, and providing a break in the slope of the roof near the eaves. Also called *splocket*.

sprung molding: In carpentry, a term applied to a curved molding.

spud wrench: This is similar to a monkey wrench; used primarily on large, square nuts on plumbing fixtures.

421

spur: A sharp-pointed, carpenter's tool used for cutting veneer.

spur center: A term used by woodworkers when referring to the center used in the headstock of a woodturning lathe.

square: The multiplying of a number by itself; also, a plane figure of four equal sides, with opposite sides parallel, and all angles, right angles. Shingles for the trade are put up in bundles so packed that 4 bundles of 16- or 18-inch shingles, when laid 5 inches to the weather, will cover a *square* 10 by 10, or 100 square feet, and three bundles of 24-inch shingles will also cover a *square.* An instrument for measuring and laying out work is called a *framing square.* See also *steel square,* Fig. 570, page 431.

square and flat: A frame having a flat panel and without a molding.

square and rabbet: A small molding or ridge forming a ring, as on a capital; same as *annulet.*

square bolt: A bolt mounted on a plate with a projecting frame to hold the bolt in place and to guide it. A bolt similar to a barrel bolt except the *square bolt* is square or flat. See *barrel bolt,* Fig. 46, page 38.

squared splice: In carpentry, a type of spliced joint specially designed to resist tension. The pieces to be joined are cut to fit into each other and reinforced with a fish plate which holds them together securely, as shown in Fig. 559.

square joint: A joint which is formed between the squared ends of two jointing

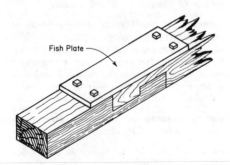
Fish Plate

Fig. 559. Squared splice.

pieces which meet but do not overlap, being without tongues, dowels, or other fittings. See *straight joint,* page 434.

square measure: The measure of areas in square units.

144 square inches (sq. in.)	= 1 square foot (sq. ft.)
9 square feet	= 1 square yard (sq. yd.)
30¼ square yards	= 1 square rod (sq. rd.)
160 square rods	= 1 acre (A.)
640 acres	= 1 square mile (sq. mi.)
36 square miles	= 1 township (twp.)

square root: A quantity of which the given quantity is the square, as 4 is the *square root* of 16, the given quantity.

square up: A term applied to the planing of a board, or other piece of stock, so that both faces are smooth, both edges and both ends are straight and level, and all corners are right angles.

squaring: In building, the operation of making the corners of a structure conform to the lines of a perfect right angle.

squeezed joint: A joint formed by squeezing together two wood surfaces coated with glue.

squinch: A small arch built across an interior corner of a room for carrying the weight of a superimposed mass such as the spire of a tower.

squinch arch: An arch, lintel, or corbeling built across an angle of a tower to support a superimposed mass, as an octagonal spire or drum resting upon a square tower.

squint brick: In masonry, a brick which has been shaped or molded to a special desired form; a purpose-made brick.

squint window: In roof construction, a type of small dormer which provides a lookout.

stabbing: In masonry, a term used when referring to the process of making a brick surface rough in order to provide a key for plasterwork.

stack: In architecture, a large chimney usually of brick, stone, or sheet metal for carrying off smoke or fumes from a furnace; often a group of flues or chimneys embodied in one structure rising above a roof. Also: The vertical main of soil, waste, or vent piping system.

stack bond: See *bonds,* Fig. 73, page 60.

stack partition: A partition wall which carries the stack or soil pipe; sometimes constructed with 2x6 or 2x8 studs and continuous from first floor to attic lines.

stack vent: Extension of a waste or soil stack above the highest horizontal drain which is connected to the stack.

staff: In architecture, a strip of wood placed on an external angle formed by two plastered surfaces to protect the finish plaster against damage. When a *staff* is of an ornamental design it is commonly called an *angle staff.*

staff bead: In the building trades, a term applied to a strip of molding inserted between the masonry of a wall and a window frame, for protection against the weather.

stagger: To set in rows, as the placing of nails, screws, or rivets, with one row alternating with the spaces of another row; also, to arrange structural parts in an uneven line, as the staggering of joints.

staggered partition: In building, a type of construction used to soundproof walls. Such a partition is made by using two rows of studding, one row supporting the lath and plaster on one side of the wall, and the other row supporting the lath and plaster on the other side of the wall. The two sides are separated by a lining of felt paper or other sound-deadening material. See Fig. 560.

staggered screeds: Wood screeds (2″ x 4″), embedded in mastic, are staggered below flooring, instead of subflooring, to provide nailing surface for floor boards.

staggered splices: Splices in bars which are not made in the same line.

staging: In building construction, the same as scaffolding; that is, a temporary structure of posts and boards on which the workmen stand when their work is too high to be reached from the ground.

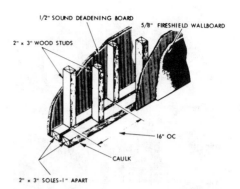

Fig. 560. Double stud wall separates the two wall surfaces completely. (National Gypsum Co.)

stain: A discoloration that penetrates the wood fiber of a piece of lumber and of any color other than the natural color of a piece in which it is found. A *stain* is classed as *light, medium,* or *heavy* and generally is blue or brown; also, a term applied to a wood finish which does not obscure the grain of the wood.

stained glass: A colored glass used for decorative purposes, as in windows.

stainless steel: A hard, tough steel which retains polish; an alloy of steel which contains a high percentage of chromium, sometimes with the addition of nickel or copper.

stair: One step in a flight of stairs. Also called a *stairstep.* Fig. 561 illustrates two basic types of stair construction.

stair carriage: A stringer which supports the steps on stairs. See Fig. 561.

stair flight: A run of stairs or steps between landings. See Fig. 563.

stair hall: The stairs, stair landings, hallways, or other portions of the public hall through which it is necessary to pass when going from the entrance floor to the top story of a building.

423

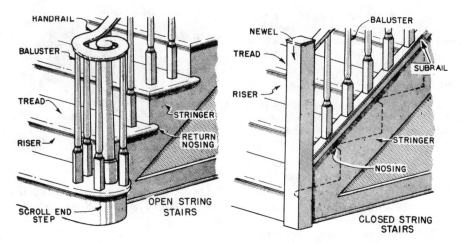

Fig. 561. Open and closed string stairs.

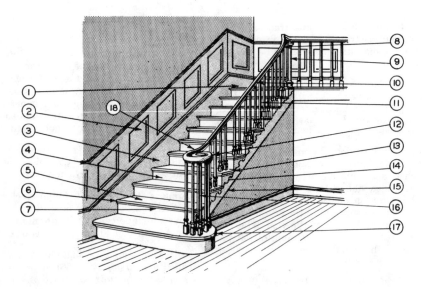

1. Landing	10. Handrail
2. Raised-panel dado	11. Baluster
3. Closed stringer	12. Volute
4. Riser	13. End nosing
5. Tread	14. Bracket
6. Tread housing	15. Open stringer
7. Cove molding under nosing	16. Starting newel post
8. Goose neck	17. Bull-nose starting step
9. Landing newel post	18. Concave easement

Fig. 562. The tradesman should know the names of the parts of a staircase.

stair horse: One of the inclined supports of a flight of stairs.

stair landing: A platform between flights of stairs, or at the termination of a flight of stairs. See *Straight Flight Stair with Landing,* Fig. 563.

stair rise: The vertical distance from the top of one stair tread to the top of the one next above it. See *riser,* Figs. 561 and 562.

stair riser: The vertical part of a stair step. See *riser,* Figs. 561 and 562.

stair rod: A name given to a metal rod used for holding a stair carpet in place between the tread of one step and the riser of the next step above; especially useful when stone steps are carpeted. A lightweight stair rod is sometimes called a *stair wire.*

stair treads: The upper horizontal boards of a flight of steps. See Figs. 561 and 562.

stair well: A compartment extending vertically through a building and in which stairs are placed.

stairbuilder's truss: A term applied to a pair of crossed beams used to support the landing of a staircase.

staircase: A flight of steps leading from one floor or story to another above. The term includes landings, newel posts, handrails, and balustrades. See Fig. 561. Fig. 562 gives further stair terminology.

stairs: In building, a term applied to a complete flight of steps between two floors. *Straight run stairs* lead directly from one floor to another without a turn. Typical designs for stairs which change direction are shown in Fig. 563.

stairs, box: Stairs built between walls, usually with no support except the wall strings.

stake: In sheet-metal work, a small anvil which is designed to fit into a hole in a bench top or into a stake holder fastened to the bench. *Bench stakes* are of various forms, each designed for a specific purpose. See Fig. 564. Also: A length of wood, pointed on one end, that is driven into the ground to support forms, screeds, or string lines.

staking out: A term used for the laying out of a building plan by driving stakes into the ground showing the location of the foundation. To insure a clean edge when excavating, the stakes are connected with strong cord indicating the building lines. See *batter boards,* Fig. 51, page 42.

stanchion: An upright bar, prop, or support as in a window where upright iron bars pass through the eyes of the saddle bars to steady the lead lights. See *saddle bars,* page 379.

standard brick: In masonry, common brick, size $2\frac{1}{4}''$ x $3\frac{3}{4}''$ x $8''$. Permissible variables are, plus or minus, $\frac{1}{16}''$ in depth, $\frac{1}{8}''$ in width, and $\frac{1}{4}''$ in length.

standard knot: In lumber, a knot $1\frac{1}{2}$ inches or less in diameter.

standard modular brick: Brick designed in accord with the standard $4''$ module. (See *modular dimension standards.*) Modular dimensions are the *actual* dimensions plus the thickness of the mortar joint. For a $4''$ x $4''$ x $8''$ modular unit using a $\frac{3}{8}''$ mortar joint, the actual size of the brick would be $3\frac{5}{8}''$ x $2\frac{1}{4}''$ x $7\frac{5}{8}''$.

standee: In reinforced concrete construction, a term used in some localities to designate a special bar bent to a U-shape with 90 degree bent legs extending in opposite directions at right angles to the U-bend. It is used as a high chair resting upon a lower mat of bars and supporting an upper mat.

standing finish: In architecture, that part of the interior fittings of a building, including openings, base, etc.

standing panel: In building, a door panel whose height is greater than its width.

staple: A U-shaped metal fastener used to fasten paper, tiles, insulation, etc., to framework or other backing material. Various kinds and sizes of staples are now commonly being used in both pneumatic and manually operated staplers. Many of these are used in building construction. Often the type of point determines the use. Fig.

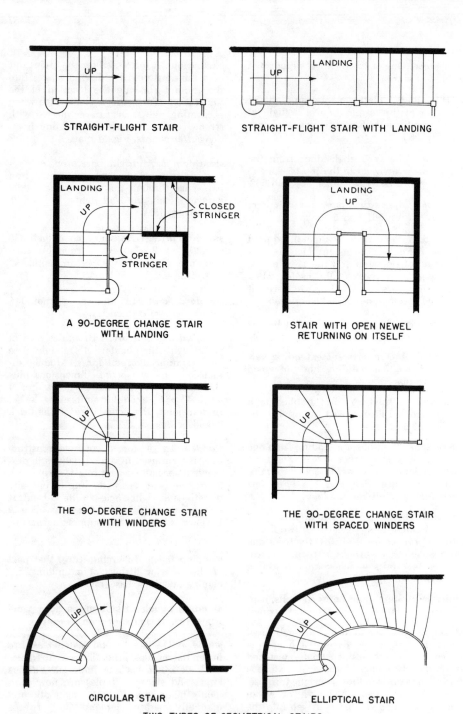

STRAIGHT-FLIGHT STAIR

STRAIGHT-FLIGHT STAIR WITH LANDING

A 90-DEGREE CHANGE STAIR
WITH LANDING

STAIR WITH OPEN NEWEL
RETURNING ON ITSELF

THE 90-DEGREE CHANGE STAIR
WITH WINDERS

THE 90-DEGREE CHANGE STAIR
WITH SPACED WINDERS

CIRCULAR STAIR

ELLIPTICAL STAIR

TWO TYPES OF GEOMETRICAL STAIRS

Fig. 563. Types of stairs.

426

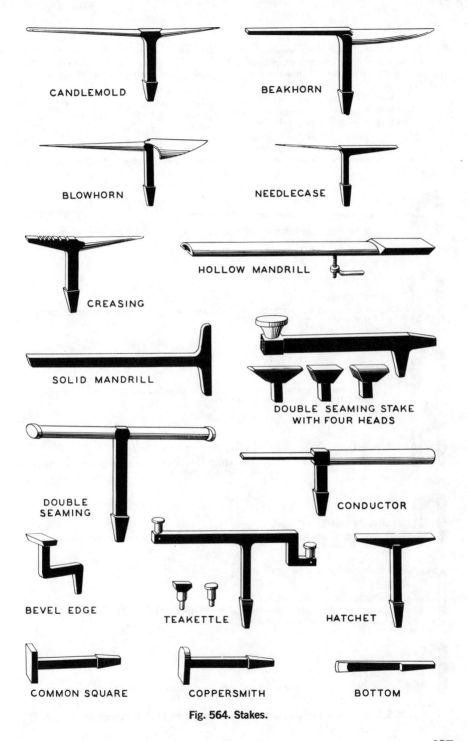

CANDLEMOLD

BEAKHORN

BLOWHORN

NEEDLECASE

CREASING

HOLLOW MANDRILL

SOLID MANDRILL

DOUBLE SEAMING STAKE
WITH FOUR HEADS

DOUBLE
SEAMING

CONDUCTOR

BEVEL EDGE

TEAKETTLE

HATCHET

COMMON SQUARE

COPPERSMITH

BOTTOM

Fig. 564. Stakes.

565 illustrates the types of points that staples may have. Steel, aluminum, bronze, and other metals are used to make staples. Steel, however, is most commonly used. A galvanized finish is available. Some staples are acid etched. Staples are available with various coatings, such as cement, nylon, paint, etc. The crown width, the length, the type of point, and the wire gage varies. Crown width commonly varies from ⅜ of

an inch to 1 inch. Length commonly varies from ½ of an inch to 2 inches. The wire gage is commonly 14 or 16 gage.

stapler: A device for applying staples. The stapler may be mechanical (Fig. 566) or air operated (Fig. 567). The air-operated stapler is capable of driving staples into hard materials at a high rate of speed.

star dryvin anchor: A type of *expansion*

CHISEL

CHISEL POINT KEEPS STAPLE LEGS PARALLEL TO DEPTH OF ENTIRE LEG LENGTH. RECOMMENDED FOR GRAINY WOODS AND PLYWOODS.

INSIDE CHISEL

INSIDE CHISEL POINT FOR OUTWARD CLINCHING AGAINST STEEL PLATE AFTER PENETRATING THROUGH MATERIAL BEING STAPLED.

SPEAR

SPEAR POINT PROVIDES GOOD PENETRATION IN EVEN DENSITY MATERIALS. POINT WILL BE DEFLECTED IF IT STRIKES AN OBSTRUCTION.

DIVERGENT

DIVERGENT POINT IS BEST FOR WALLBOARD APPLICATION. AFTER PENETRATION, LEGS DIVERGE TO ALLOW USE OF LONGER LEG STAPLES IN THIN MATERIAL.

OUTSIDE CHISEL

OUTSIDE CHISEL POINT FOR INWARD CLINCHING AFTER PENETRATING THROUGH MATERIAL BEING STAPLED.

OUTSIDE CHISEL DIVERGENT

OUTSIDE CHISEL DIVERGENT POINT HAS EXCELLENT PENETRATION QUALITIES. LEGS DIVERGE, THEN CROSS, LOCKING STAPLE IN POSITION.

CROSSCUT CHISEL

CROSSCUT CHISEL POINT PENETRATES WELL, CUTS THROUGH CROSS GRAIN WOOD, KEEPS LEGS STRAIGHT AND PARALLEL. FOR GENERAL NAILING OR TACKING USES.

Fig. 565. Various types of staple points. (California State Department of Education)

Fig. 566. Stapler. (Duo-Fast Fastener Corp.)

Fig. 567. Air-operated stapler. (Duo-Fast Fastener Corp.)

anchor used for securing wood structural parts to a masonry or concrete wall. See *anchors,* Fig. 18. Lengths range from ⅞ inch to 3½ inches. The shield holds the fixture, while the nail expands the lead wrapper on the bottom end. See Fig. 568.

star expansion bolt: A bolt or screw having a shield of two semicircular parts which spread apart as the bolt is driven into the shield. Used for securing structural wood parts to a masonry wall.

star shake: A defect in wood appearing as cracks or splits, radiating from the center of an end view of a log or timber, and due to the lumber being cut green and drying too rapidly. A defect similar to *heart shake,* which is caused by decay. See Fig. 310, page 235.

starling: A protection about a bridge or pier made by driving piles close together to form an enclosure.

starting board: In form building, the first board nailed in position at the bottom of a foundation form.

starting newel: A post at the bottom of a staircase for supporting the balustrade. See Fig. 561.

starting step: The first step at the bottom of a flight of stairs. See Fig. 561.

starting strip: In roofing, the first strip of composition roofing material applied to a roof. See Fig. 569.

starved joint: A glue joint where the adhesive has been forced out by excessive clamping pressure.

stationary mixer: A mixer that remains at a ready-mix plant and is not moved from one job site to another.

station point: In perspective drawing the point from which the observer sights. See *perspective drawing,* page 322.

staves: The supports or stems holding up ornamental portions of the leafage on the Corinthian and Composite capitals.

stay: In carpentry, a strut or brace.

steam trap: A self-acting device or trap into which water from the condensing of steam passing through pipes is allowed to drain and which automatically ejects the

Fig. 568. Star dryvin expansion device.

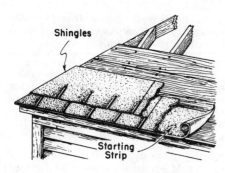

Fig. 569. Starting strip.

water without permitting the escape of steam.

stearate: A salt of stearic acid, a white fatty acid such as tallow.

steel forms: Removable pieces of steel which hold wet concrete in desired shapes for casting foundations, footings, and window frames on the spot. Some foundation formwork comes with interlocking modular hardware. Steel forms are said to last indefinitely, produce a clean, accurate face, and to be easier to set up and clean than wooden forms.

steel-frame construction: A type of building in which the structural members are of steel or are dependent on a steel frame for support.

steel square: An instrument having at least one right angle and two or more straight edges; used for testing and laying out work for trueness. A term frequently applied to the large framing square used by carpenters. See Fig. 570. Three parts of a steel square bear names: the *tongue* is the shorter arm, the *blade* is the longer of the two arms, and the *heel* is the meeting place of the two arms.

steel tape: A flexible steel tapeline or ribbon of steel used for measuring. When not in use, the tape coils up in a case made for that purpose. The steel tape is used to measure distances longer than is possible with the six-foot folding rule. Two sizes are in general use: 50′ and 100′ lengths. See Fig. 571.

steel wire gage: A system of designating the diameters of wires and sheets of non-ferrous metals, such as aluminum, brass, and copper, by numbers ranging from 7/10 (0.49 in.) to 50 (0.0044 in.). Also known as Washburn and Moen, American Steel and Wire Co., and Roebling Wire Gages.

steel wool: A mass of fine steel threads matted together and used principally for polishing and cleaning surfaces of wood or metal.

steeple: A church tower usually surmounted by a spire; any lofty tower-like structure topped by a tapering superstructure such as a spire.

stench trap: A trap for shutting off or carrying off foul air or gas from drain pipes or sewers. Same as *air trap*. See Fig. 13.

step: In stair building, the combination of a riser and a tread; also, one application of a framing square when laying out stair horses. In roof framing, one application of the steel framing square when laying out rafters; also called *stepping off rafters*.

stepped footings: If a house is built on sloping ground, the footings cannot all be at the same depth; hence, they are stepped.

stepped ramp: A series of steps connected by ramps on a slope. Also called *ramped steps*.

stepping off rafters: Finding the exact length of a rafter by laying off unit lengths by the application of a framing square. Each unit thus marked is called a *step*.

stereobate: The lower part or base of a building consisting of masonry visible above the ground level and distinguished from stylobate by the absence of columns; that is, a *stereobate* is a masonry platform without columns, while a *stylobate* is a masonry platform supporting columns or on which columns rest.

sticker: In woodworking, a machine used for making molding. See *sticker machine*. Also, boards used to separate layers of lumber to allow air to circulate.

sticker machine: A machine for molding wood rods; also used for making molding; a *sticker*.

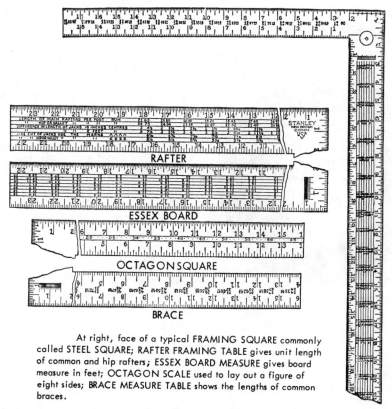

At right, face of a typical FRAMING SQUARE commonly called STEEL SQUARE; RAFTER FRAMING TABLE gives unit length of common and hip rafters; ESSEX BOARD MEASURE gives board measure in feet; OCTAGON SCALE used to lay out a figure of eight sides; BRACE MEASURE TABLE shows the lengths of common braces.

Fig. 570. Steel square.

sticking: The molded edge machined on the rails of a door around the panels or lights. In plastering, the setting of ornament into a prepared plaster bed; a special sticking plaster is used. Fig. 572 illustrates ornament stuck into the bed. See *stuck molding,* page 439.

stiffener: In architecture, any steel angles, bars, rods, or other types of material secured to structural members to strengthen joints and to prevent buckling in any part of the building.

stile: In carpentry, one of the vertical members in a door or sash into which secondary members are fitted. See Fig. 189, page 149.

stillson wrench: The pipe wrench which is commonly used by plumbers; named for its inventor.

stilted: In architecture, any member raised above its usual level; as an arch having its springing raised above the apparent impost; hence, called a *stilted arch.*

stilted arch: An arch having its springing line raised above the apparent impost; one which does not spring immediately from the apparent imposts but is raised above them by intervening courses or members.

stilt house: A house which is constructed on stilts above the ground. Used mostly in hot, moist regions and on very uneven ground level sites. Provides breeze passage underneath, protection from insects, and space for car.

431

Fig. 571. Steel tape. (Lufkin Rule Co.)

stilts: In many parts of the country, stilts are being used by the plasterer in place of low scaffolding. There are basically two types: adjustable and unadjustable. Fig. 573 illustrates the use of stilts.

stippling: In plastering, to form a rough texture using a *stippling brush.* Fig. 574 illustrates one technique.

stippling brush: A soft brush used to give texture in plaster. Also called a rice brush. See Fig. 574.

stirrup: In building trades, a term applied to any stirruplike drop support attached to a wall to carry the end of a beam or timber, such as the end of a joist. *Stirrups* or *hangers* may also be suspended from a girder as well as from a wall. Same as *hanger.* See *joist hanger, stirrup,* Fig. 334, page 255, for an illustration of a stirrup. Also: in reinforced concrete construction, a support used to hold the bars. See Fig. 575.

stock: Any timber, boards, or other wood members from which anything is constructed; lumber of any kind.

stonecutter's chisel: A stonemason's tool used for dressing soft stone. Also called *tooth chisel.*

stonemason: In building, one who builds foundations and walls of stone.

stool: In architecture, a term applied to the base or support of wood at the bottom of a window, as the shelflike piece inside and extending across the lower part of a window opening. See Fig. 198, page 154.

stoop: A raised entrance platform, with steps leading up to it, at the door of a building; sometimes the term is applied to a porch or veranda.

Fig. 572. Ornament bed, showing how space is allowed for sticking material.

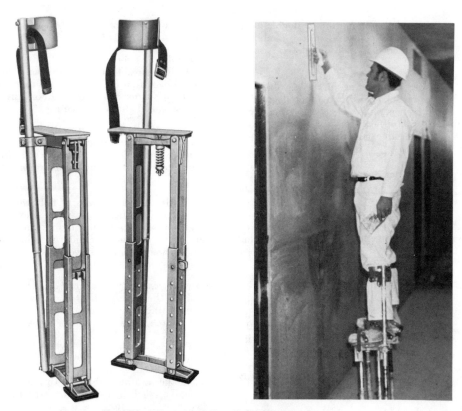

Fig. 573. Adjustable stilts. (Left: Goldblatt Tool Co.)

STIPPLING BRUSH

Fig. 574. Texture formed with stippling brush. Another quite different effect may be formed by moving the brush in a circular motion.

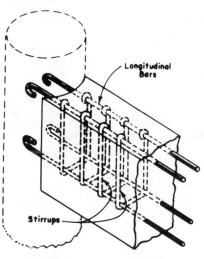

Longitudinal Bars

Stirrups

Fig. 575. Stirrups, reinforced concrete.

stop: Inside molding on a double-hung window which is fastened to the jamb and holds the bottom sash in place. Also, a *doorstop.*

stopcock: In plumbing, a type of valve consisting of a body with a tapered opening into which a plug of corresponding taper is fitted. The flow can be turned on or off by turning the plug through an arc of 90 degrees.

stopped miter. A miter and butt joint used when the pieces being joined are not of the same thickness.

storm cellar: A cellar or cave designed to afford protection against violent wind storms such as cyclones and tornadoes, which often occur on the Great Plains of the United States. Same as *cyclone cellar.*

storm door: An extra outside or additional door for protection against inclement winter weather. Such a door also serves the purpose of lessening the chill of the interior of a building, making it easier to heat, and also helps to avoid the effects of wind and rain at the entrance doorway during milder seasons.

storm drain: A drain which receives the discharge of waste water from storms as excess surface water but not sewage. See *storm sewer.*

storm sash: An additional sash placed at the outside of a window for protection against the severe weather of winter.

storm sewer: A sewer designed to carry away water waste from storms, as clear water or surface water but not sewage. A storm sewer usually terminates in a river, dry run, lake, or natural drainage basin. See *storm drain.*

storm window: A window placed outside an ordinary window for additional protection against severe winter weather. Also called *storm sash.*

story: That part of a building included between the upper surface of any floor and the upper surface of the next floor or roof above.

story pole: A pole or rod cut to the proposed clear height between finished floor and ceiling. Often the *story pole* is marked with minor dimensions, as for door trims, etc. Also called *story rod.* See Fig. 576.

story rod: A rod or pole cut to the proposed clear height between finished floor and ceiling. The *story rod* is often marked with minor dimensions, as for door trims, etc. Also called *story pole.* See Fig. 576.

stove bolt: A special type of bolt with a nut. Formerly such bolts were provided with a coarser thread pitch than a machine bolt. However, the only difference now is that, without a nut, a stove bolt is called a *machine screw.*

straight arch: A type of arch construction in which the intrados is straight but with its joints radiating as in a common arch. See *flat arch,* page 193.

straightedge: A bar of wood or metal with the edges true and parallel; used for testing straight lines and surfaces; that is, gaging the accuracy of work. In masonry, a long-handled tool used for smoothing plaster or concrete.

straight-flight stairs: A stairway consisting of a flight unbroken by turns. See Fig. 563.

straight-grained wood: In timber, when the fiber of the wood runs parallel with the axis of the stem or branch, the lumber cut from such wood is said to be *straight-grained.*

straight jacket: In building construction, a term applied to a stiff timber fastened to a wall to hold it in a rigid position and to reinforce the wall.

straight joint: A continuous floor joint running transverse to the length of the boards; a joint formed between the squared ends of two pieces which meet but do not overlap. In masonry, a continuity of vertical joints in brickwork resulting in unsound construction because there are no bricks at this point to support the load the wall must carry. See *square joint,* page 422.

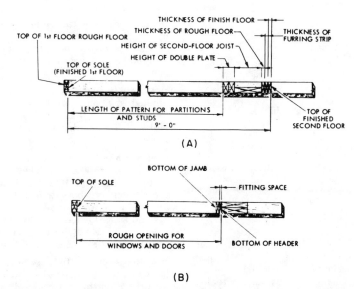

Fig. 576. Story pole or rod. (A) The master stud pattern indicates various heights. These measurements are transferred to the studs. (B) Information for window and door headers is also marked on the master stud pattern.

straight-peen hammer: A hammer having one end of the head wedge-shaped, with a rounded edge. This peening edge is parallel with the handle of the hammer.

straight-shank: A term applied to a tool, such as a drill, having a round, parallel shank used in self-centering chucks.

straight-shank drill bit: A type of drill bit used for boring holes in which either screws or nails are to be driven.

straight tee: In plumbing, a tee which has all openings of the same size. See *bullhead tee,* page 77.

straining arch: A type of construction which is arch-shaped to resist end thrust, as of a *flying buttress.*

straining beam: In building construction, a short piece of timber in a truss; used for holding the ends of struts or rafters in place; also called a *straining piece.*

straining piece: A short piece of timber used to hold the ends of struts and rafters in place; same as *straining beam.*

straining sill: In building, a *straining beam* on the tie beam of a truss to resist the pressure at each end of the foot of a diagonal strut.

stranded wires: In electricity, wires or cables composed of a number of smaller wires twisted or braided together.

strap: A strap of metal, usually steel, of any required dimensions used to attach, secure, or otherwise fasten one object to another. An example of the use of the strap is shown in Fig. 374, page 283.

strap hinge: A hinge having one or both plates longer than the plates of a *butt hinge.* It is designed for fastening to the surface of a heavy door or gate. See Fig. 577.

strap pipe hanger: In plumbing, a pipe hanger consisting of a metal strap or band nailed or screwed to the ceiling or a rafter and slung around a suspended pipe. See Fig. 305, page 231.

strapping: A term sometimes applied to

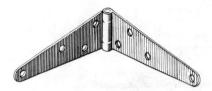

Fig. 577. Strap hinge.

battens fastened to the internal faces of walls as a support for lath and plaster.

strapwork: A narrow fillet or band which is crossed, folded, or interlaced in a decorative design.

streaking: Light and dark streaks which occur in spray coats of paint or lacquer caused by not lapping the wet edges of the spray or by using a spray nozzle that is out of line or adjustment.

stress grading: The strengths of different woods are determined by laboratory tests. In bending, for example, these tests determine exactly how much loading is necessary to deflect a beam to its proportional limit, beyond which the beam bends at a faster rate than the rate of increase in the loading. The stress caused by this loading is called the fiber stress at proportional limit.

stressed skin: In frame construction, the outer surfaces of panels used for floors and roof decks. The skins have structural value. In steel construction, the extra finish of steel structures designed so it serves to help support the structure.

stressed-skin panels: These consist of facings, normally plywood, glued on the two sides of an inner structural framework made of lumber. This type of construction acts as a unit and the load or stress on the panel is distributed by the internal framework. Insulation is sometimes added to the stressed-skin panel within the framework. They are usually delivered to the job as a ready-made unit. Stressed-skin panels are used in floor, wall, and roof construction. They are commonly made in 4'x8' units, though larger lengths for roofing are used. See Fig. 578.

stresses: Stresses are the forces on a member caused by loads. The four basic types of stresses are *torsion, compression, tension,* and *shear.* See *simple beam,* Fig. 532, page 404.

stretcher: In masonry construction, a term applied to a course in which brick or stone lies lengthwise; that is, a brick or stone is laid with its length parallel to the face of the wall.

stretcher bond: In masonry, a bond which consists entirely of stretchers, with each vertical joint lying between the centers of the stretchers above and below, so that angle closers are not required. This type of bond is used extensively for internal partition walls which have a thickness of a single tier of brick. See Fig. 73, page 60.

stretching course: In masonry, a row of bricks with only their sides visible as a part of the wall surface; a course made up entirely of stretchers. Also called a *stretcher course.* See Fig. 73, page 60.

stretchout: In sheet metal work, laying the flat sheet out with the pattern before forming.

strike: A metal piece fastened to a door frame into which the bolt of a lock is projected for holding the door securely in place. See *lip strike,* page 269.

strike block: In carpentry, a plane shorter than a jointer, used for fitting a short joint.

strike-off: In concrete work, the process of filling the forms evenly with fresh concrete by removing excess concrete or the process of bringing the concrete to grade within the forms; this is done by a straight-edged piece of wood or metal (also known as a strikeoff) by means of a forward sawing movement or by a power operated tool for this purpose. This process is also known as straight-edging or *screeding.*

strike plate: In building, the part of a door lock which is fastened to the jamb. Sometimes called a *striking plate* or a *keeper.*

striking off: See *screeding,* page 391.

striking plate: A metal piece or plate screwed to the jamb of a door case in such a position that, when the door is being closed, the bolt of the lock strikes against,

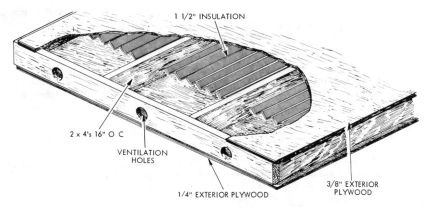

1 1/2" INSULATION

2 x 4's 16" O C

VENTILATION
HOLES

1/4" EXTERIOR PLYWOOD

3/8" EXTERIOR
PLYWOOD

Fig. 578. Stressed skin panels for roof decking.

and rubs along, the metal plate and finally engages in a hole in the plate.

string: In building trades, a term applied to the inclined member which supports the treads and risers of a stair. Also called a *stringer*. See Figs. 561 and 562, page 424.

string board: A board or built-up facing used to cover the ends of the steps in a staircase; a board placed next to the well-hole in wooden stairs so as to hide the true string. The *string piece* is the board or piece placed beneath the treads and risers for a support; hence, the string piece forms the support of the stairs.

string course or **sailing course:** In building, a horizontal band forming a part of the design, consisting of a course of brick or stone, projecting from a wall, for decorative purposes, or to break the plain effect of a large expanse of wall surface.

string line: A line laid between stakes to indicate the shape and elevation of flat-work or structure.

stringer: A long, heavy, horizontal timber or reinforced concrete beam resting on vertical supports and supporting joists. Also, the inclined member which supports the treads and risers of a stair. See *string*. See Figs. 561 and 562, page 424.

strip: In the building trades, a term applied to a narrow piece of wood, relatively long, and usually of a uniform width. The yard lumber known to the trade as *strips* is less than 2 inches in thickness and less than 8 inches in width. Also used when referring to the breaking or tearing of the threads of a bolt or nut. In reinforced concrete construction, bands of reinforcing bars in flat slab or flat plate construction.

stripping: This involves applying wood strip to the sides of a beam to develop the soffit and arrises. In concrete work, the removal of forms from hardened concrete.

strongback: A frame attached to the back of a form to stiffen or reinforce it; additional vertical wales placed outside horizontal wales for added strength or to improve alignment; also called stiffback.

struck joint: In masonry, a mortar joint which is formed with a recess at the bottom of the joint. The *struck joint* is used chiefly for interior-wall surfaces, since it is inferior for outside joints because of its lack of weather-resisting qualities. The recess at the bottom allows water from rain or snow to seep into the wall and it is not recommended.

structural clay tile: A term applied to various sizes and kinds of hollow and practically solid building units, molded from surface clay, shale, fire clay, or a mixture of these materials, and laid by masons.

structural glass: A vitreous finishing material used as a covering for masonry walls.

437

It is available in rectangular plates which are held in position by a specially prepared mastic in which the plates are embedded.

structural lightweight concrete: A strictly structural type of concrete used in the production of buildings, bridges, etc.; weighs around 85 to 115 pounds per cubic foot.

structural lumber: Lumber, sometimes termed *structural timber,* is 5 inches or more in both thickness and width. It is graded according to its strength and to the use which is to be made of an entire piece. Such lumber is used principally for bridge or trestle timbers, for car and ship timbers, for ship decking, and for framing of buildings.

structural timber: See *structural lumber.*

structure: An edifice, especially one of large size or imposing appearance; any kind of building; any construction composed of parts arranged and fitted together in some way, as a bridge or dam.

strut: In carpentry, any piece fixed between two other pieces to keep them apart, as a member which is designed to resist pressure or compressive stress endwise in a frame or structure. A secondary member in a truss. Also, a short column.

strut tenon: A term applied to a piece of wood or iron, or some other member of a structure, designed to resist pressure or weight in the direction of its length; used on a diagonal piece, usually on heavy timbers, as a timber extending obliquely from a rafter to the king post. See *king post,* page 257.

Stuart architecture: The style of architecture prevailing in England from approximately the accession of Charles I to the reign of William and Mary; also known as *Jacobean architecture.* This style of construction and decoration was most prominent during the early seventeenth century and was a continuation of the Elizabethan, with more freedom in the use of the classical orders.

stub mortise: In carpentry, a mortise which does not pass entirely through a timber.

stub tenon: In woodworking, a term applied to a tenon cut to fit a *stub mortise;* in heavy timber framing, a short tenon used at the lower end of a post to prevent its slipping out of position. Also called a *joggle tenon.*

stucco: Any of various plasters used as covering for walls; a coating for exterior walls in which cement is largely used; any material used for covering walls and put on wet, but when dry becomes exceedingly hard and durable. Fig. 579 shows a typical stucco job done over metal lath.

stuck: In carpentry, a term applied to any work which is accomplished by running it through a *sticking machine.*

Fig. 579. Proper construction for stucco on metal reinforcement. Note how the mesh is embedded in the scratch coat because it is held away from the waterproof paper by spacing nails. Total thickness of the three coats should be approximately 1″. (Portland Cement Association)

stuck molding: A type of molding made by running a piece of board through a *sticker machine* to bring the edge to a desired form. A molding shaped on solid material, as a trim molding cut on the edge of a board with a *sticker*. In masonry, a molding built to a form on the floor or on a table and *stuck* in position when finished. See *sticking*, page 431.

stud: In building, an upright member, usually a piece of dimension lumber, 2x4 or 2x6, used in the framework of a wall or partition. On an inside wall, the laths are nailed to the studs. On the outside of a frame wall, sheathings nailed to the studs. The height of a ceiling is determined by the length or height of the studs. See Fig. 41, page 35, and Fig. 441, page 338. Metal studs are also commonly used today. Fig. 580 illustrates one type of metal stud. See also *webbed metal studding*, page 479.

studding: In building, the dimension lumber from which *studs* are cut. Sometimes the term *studding* is also applied to the pieces which have been cut for *studs*.

stud walls: A stud wall consists of verticals spaced 16″ on centers (or sometimes 24″ O.C.) between top and bottom plate. Stud walls include, or can include, window shapes and headers and can be preassembled and moved into position.

stuff: In carpentry, wood or timbers sawed or manufactured for use in building construction, as *dimension stuff*.

stump tracery: In the late German Gothic style of architecture, tracery in which the molded bar in its convolutions appears to pass through itself, then is cut off short in such a way that at the end of each similar stump a section of the molding is seen.

stylobate: A continuous base or platform of flat coping supporting a row of columns. Usually the ancient Greek temples had three or four steps around the entire struc-

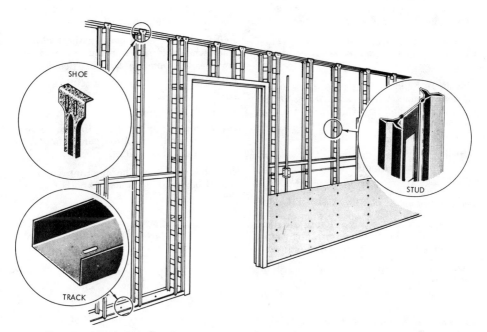

Fig. 580. Metal stud construction using hollow metal studs. (National Gypsum Co.)

ture with the base of the columns resting on the top step. This is known as the *stylobate.*

subbase: In architecture, the lowest part of a structural base which consists of two or more horizontal members, as the base of a column; also, a *baseboard.*

subcasing: In door and window framing, a concealed casing used as a rough frame over which the *finish-casing* material is applied. Also called *blind casing.*

subcontractor: A contractor who has contracted to construct a part of a structure; such as plumbing, plastering, foundation, or any other part.

subfloor: In carpentry, a term applied to a flooring of rough boards laid directly on the joists and serving the purpose of a floor during the process of construction on the building. When all rough construction work is completed, the finish floor is laid over the subfloor. See Figs. 41 and 550.

subflooring: Any material used for a subfloor which is beneath the finished floor. Often an inferior grade of lumber or softwood is used for subflooring.

subgrade: The soil prepared and compacted to support concrete slab or structure.

subrail: In building a closed string stair, a molded member, called a *subrail* or *shoe,* is placed on the top edge of the stair string to receive and carry the lower end of the balusters. See Fig. 561, page 424.

subsill: In building, the part of a window sill which comes directly against the main sill and serves as a *stop* for blinds and screens; also, a secondary door sill which rests on the *mudsill.*

substructure: The lower portion of a structure forming the foundation which supports the superstructure of a building.

suction: In plastering, a term applied to the manner in which certain types of plastering material *pull* when worked with a trowel; adhesive quality.

summer: In building, a large horizontal timber or stone; the lintel of a door or window; a stone forming the cap of a pier or column to support an arch; a girder; the principal timber or beam which carries the weight of a floor or partition.

summertree: A principal floor timber or beam; a horizontal, longitudinal timber used in framing. Same as *summer* or *sommer.*

summerwood: The part of the annual growth ring that is formed during the summer; usually stronger than *springwood.*

sump: A pit or depression in a building where water is allowed to accumulate; for example, in a basement floor to collect seepage, or a depression in the roof of a building for receiving rain water and delivering it to the downspout. A device used for removing water from such a depression is known as a *sump pump.*

sump pump: A pump used to remove water from a sump pit sunk in the basement floor.

sunk fillet: In architecture, a term applied to a *fillet* which is produced by cutting a groove in a plane surface. See Fig. 581.

sunk molding: Any molding recessed below the level of adjoining surfaces.

sunk panels: A term used in the building trade when referring to panels recessed below the surrounding surface. See *coffer,* page 105.

sunlit glass: Glass that is not screened from the sun's rays.

sunshades: A shelter from the sun, built with wood and tarpaulins or any other type of strong cloth coverings.

supercolumniation: The superimposition of one order of columns above another order.

Fig. 581. Sunk fillet.

superimposed: Laid above something else, as one order of columns placed on top of another.

superposition: Placing one thing above another, as the use of a lighter column order for the second story of a building placed above a heavier order used for the first story.

superstructure: The framing above the main supporting level or substructure, as a foundation wall.

surbase: In architecture, a molding above a base, as that immediately above the baseboard of a room; also, a molding or series of moldings which crown the base of a pedestal.

surbased arch: An arch with a rise that is less than one-half of its span; or an arch having the curve center or centers below the springing line or imposts.

surface: To finish or make even and smooth by planing, as lumber; also, to give a particular kind of surface to interior work by polishing, varnishing, or the use of some other method to produce a smooth finish.

surfaced lumber: Lumber which is dressed by running it through a planer.

surface hinge: A hinge having one or both of the plates longer than butt-hinge plates. See *strap hinge,* Fig. 577, page 436.

surface imperfections: In painting, when fine crazing or hairline checks appear on a painted, enameled, or lacquered surface after a finish coat has dried thoroughly, such an imperfection indicates a shrinkage of the undercoats. Sometimes this defect presents itself where a new finish coat is applied over an old finish that has crazed or checked.

surfacing of lumber: In woodworking, symbols are used to indicate how lumber has been surfaced, as S1E, surfaced on one edge, S1S, surfaced on one side; S2S, surfaced on two sides, and so on.

surfactant: Wetting agent.

survey of lot: In building, a plan or map of a building lot showing the elevations and character of the ground surface on which a house is to be erected. See *plot survey,* page 339.

surveying: That branch of applied mathematics dealing with the science of measuring land, the unit of measure being the surveyor's chain, with 80 chains equal to 1 mile.

suspended ceiling: A ceiling suspended from the structural ceiling above. See Fig. 582.

swage: In carpentry, a tool used for various purposes but especially used to set the teeth of saws instead of using a *saw set.* In sheet-metal work, a hand tool used to shape material to the desired form.

swale: A drainage channel formed by the convergence of intersecting slopes.

sway brace: Diagonal bracing used to resist wind or other lateral forces; also *X-brace.*

sweating: Condensation of moisture on a cool surface.

sweat joint: In plumbing, a type of joint made by the union of two pieces of copper tubing which are coated with solder containing tin. The pipes are pressed together and heat applied until the solder melts.

sweatout: Condition when plaster stays wet and will not set.

sweep: In architecture, a term applied to a curving structural member, as the *sweep* of an arch; also, a curved wall or stairway.

Sweet's Architectural Catalog File: Architectural catalog file on building products, systems, and engineering.

swell: Bulge; referring to the slight increase in the size of a column between the base and the neck.

swing stage scaffold: This is a scaffold supported from above, using ropes and pulleys which permit it to be raised or lowered as needed. This type of scaffold is used on exterior work. See Fig. 583.

switch: In electricity, a device for closing, opening, or changing the connections of a circuit in which it is placed. See Fig. 405, page 309, and Fig. 461, page 356 for an illus-

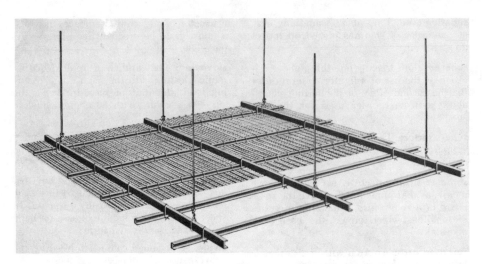

Fig. 582. Suspended ceiling, using hangers, carriers, and furring channels. (Inland Steel Products Co.)

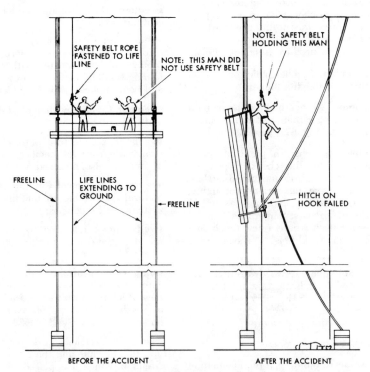

Fig. 583. Swing stage scaffold safety devices. (National Safety Council)

tration of a switch with its symbol. Fig. 584 also illustrates two common switches and their symbols.

switchboard: The panel or supports upon which are placed the switches, rheostats, and meters for the control of electrical machines and systems.

switch box: Metal box in which an electrical switch is installed. See Fig. 461, page 356.

swivel: A device used as a coupling which allows either half of a mechanism to rotate independently of the other half.

symbols and abbreviations: A symbol is an abbreviation standing for the name of something which is indicated by some mark, character, letter, figure, or a combination of any such characters. Typical symbols used to designate building materials are shown in Fig. 372, page 280. Abbreviations commonly used on elevations and plan views are shown on pages 444, 445, and 446.

symmetrical: Pertaining to any plane or solid body or figure which is well-proportioned, with corresponding parts properly balanced and harmonious in all details; anything which exhibits symmetry in size, form, and arrangement of its parts.

systyle: An intercolumniation in which the columns stand only two diameters apart, or three diameters on center.

T

tabernacle work: The rich, ornamental work or tracery used in tabernacles or canopies over a tomb; also decorative work over stalls, seats, the head of niches, and in the carved screens of cathedrals or churches;

an architectural design in which tabernacles form the characteristic feature.

table: In carpentry, the insertion of one timber into another by alternate projections or scores from the middle; same as *coak*. In architecture, a flat surface on a wall, usually raised, as a *stringcourse,* especially a projecting band of stone or brick where an offset is required. See *water table,* Fig. 625, page 478.

table saw: This tool employes a circular saw blade up to 16 or more inches in diameter. The axis of the saw can usually be tilted from the vertical; that is, it has a tilting arbor. The blade may be raised or lowered, and the blade is protected by a safety blade guard (splitter). There are various circular *saw blades* available for the table saw. The ones commonly used are the crosscut, rip, combination, and hollow ground. Fig. 585 illustrates a table saw.

tabling: In masonry, the forming of a type of horizontal joint by arranging various stones in a course so they will run into the next course, hence preventing them from slipping; in carpentry, the shaping of a projection on a piece of timber so it will fit into a recess prepared to receive it in another timber.

tack: A relatively short fastening device with a large head, used for securing linoleum and rugs to floors, etc. See Fig. 390, page 296.

tacking: This is the process of melting small drops of solder at intervals along a seam for the purpose of holding it in place until it is properly soldered.

tackle: A construction of blocks and ropes, chains, or cables used for hoisting purposes in heavy construction work. Often spoken of as *block and tackle.*

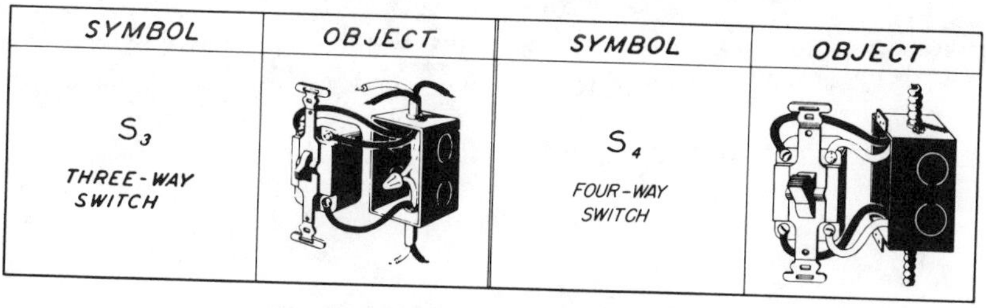

SYMBOL	OBJECT	SYMBOL	OBJECT
S_3 THREE-WAY SWITCH		S_4 FOUR-WAY SWITCH	

Fig. 584. Switches and their symbols.

ABBREVIATIONS COMMONLY USED ON ELEVATIONS

Aluminum	AL	Length Over All	LOA
Asbestos	ASB	Level	LEV
Asphalt	ASPH	Light	LT
Basement	BSMT	Line	L
Beveled	BEV	Lining	LN
Brick	BRK	Long	LG
Building	BLDG	Louver	LV
Cast Iron	CI	Low Point	LP
Ceiling	CLG	Masonry Opening	MO
Cement	CEM	Metal	MET. or M
Center	CTR	Molding	MLDG
Center Line	℄ or CL	Mullion	MULL
Clear	CLR	North	N
Column	COL	Number	NO. or #
Concrete	CONC	Opening	OPNG
Concrete Block	CONC B	Outlet	OUT
Copper	COP	Outside Diameter	OD
Corner	COR	Overhead	OVHD
Detail	DET	Panel	PNL
Diameter	DIA or ⌀	Perpendicular	PERP
Dimension	DIM.	Plate Glass	PL GL
Ditto	DO.	Plate Height	PL HT
Divided	DIV	Radius	R
Door	DR	Revision	REV
Double-Hung Window	DHW	Riser	R
Down	DN or D	Roof	RF
Downspout	DS	Roof Drain	RD
Drawing	DWG	Roofing	RFG
Drip Cap	DC	Rough	RGH
Each	EA	Saddle	SDL or S
East	E	Scale	SC
Elevation	EL	Schedule	SCH
Entrance	ENT	Section	SECT
Excavate	EXC	Sheathing	SHTHG
Exterior	EXT	Sheet	SH
Finish	FIN.	Shiplap	SHLP
Flashing	FL	Siding	SDG
Floor	FL	South	S
Foot or Feet	' or FT	Specifications	SPEC
Foundation	FND	Square	SQ or □
Full Size	FS	Square Inch	SQ IN. or □"
Galvanized	GALV	Stainless Steel	SST
Galvanized Iron	GI	Steel	STL
Gauge	GA	Stone	STN
Glass	GL	Terra Cotta	TC
Glass Block	GL BL	Thick or Thickness	THK or T
Grade	GR	Typical	TYP
Grade Line	GL	Vertical	VERT
Height	HGT or H or HT	Waterproofing	WP
High Point	H PT	West	W
Horizontal	HOR	Width	W or WTH
Hose Bibb	HB	Window	WDW
Inch or Inches	" or IN.	Wire Glass	W GL
Insulating (Insulated)	INS	Wood	WD
Length	LGTH, LG or L	Wrought Iron	WI

ABBREVIATIONS COMMONLY USED ON PLAN VIEWS

Access Panel	AP	Concrete Floor	CONC FL
Acoustic	ACST	Conduit	CND
Acoustical Tile	AT	Construction	CONST
Aggregate	AGGR	Contract	CONT
Air Conditioning	AIR COND	Copper	COP
Aluminum	AL	Counter	CTR
Anchor Bolt	AB	Cubic Feet	CU FT
Angle	∠	Cut Out	CO
Apartment	APT	Detail	DET
Approximate	APPROX	Diagram	DIAG
Architectural	ARCH	Dimension	DIM
Area	A	Dining Room	DR
Area Drain	AD	Dishwasher	DW
Asbestos	ASB	Ditto	DO.
Asbestos Board	AB	Double-Acting	DA
Asphalt	ASPH	Double Strength Glass	DSG
Asphalt Tile	AT	Down	DN
Basement	BSMT	Downspout	DS
Bathroom	B	Drain	D or DR
Bath Tub	BT	Drawing	DWG
Beam	BM	Dressed and Matched	D & M
Bearing Plate	BRG PL	Dryer	D
Bedroom	BR	Electric Panel	EP
Blocking	BLKG	End to End	E to E
Blueprint	BP	Excavate	EXC
Boiler	BLR	Expansion Joint	EXP JT
Book Shelves	BK SH	Exterior	EXT
Brass	BRS	Finish	FIN.
Brick	BRK	Finished Floor	FIN. FL
Bronze	BRZ	Firebrick	FBRK
Broom Closet	BC	Fireplace	FP
Building	BLDG	Fireproof	FPRF
Building Line	BL	Fixture	FIX.
Cabinet	CAB.	Flashing	FL
Calking	CLKG	Floor	FL
Casing	CSG	Floor Drain	FD
Cast Iron	CI	Flooring	FLG
Cast Stone	CS	Fluorescent	FLUOR
Catch Basin	CB	Flush	FL
Cellar	CEL	Footing	FTG
Cement	CEM	Foundation	FND
Cement Asbestos Board	CEM AB	Frame	FR
Cement Floor	CEM FL	Full Size	FS
Cement Mortar	CEM MORT	Furring	FUR
Center	CTR	Galvanized Iron	GI
Center to Center	C to C	Garage	GAR
Center Line	℄ or CL	Gas	G
Center Matched	CM	Glass	GL
Ceramic	CER	Glass Block	GL BL
Channel	CHAN	Grille	G
Cinder Block	CIN BL	Gypsum	GYP
Circuit Breaker	CIR BKR	Hardware	HDW
Cleanout	CO	Hollow Metal Door	HMD
Clean Out Door	COD	Hose Bib	HB
Clear Glass	CL GL	Hot Air	HA
Closet	C, CL or CLO	Hot Water	HW
Cold Air	CA	Hot Water Heater	HWH
Cold Water	CW	I Beam	I
Collar Beam	COL B	Inside Diameter	ID
Concrete	CONC	Insulation	INS
Concrete Block	CONC B	Interior	INT

Iron	I
Jamb	JB
Kitchen	K
Landing	LDG
Lath	LTH
Laundry	LAU
Laundry Tray	LT
Lavatory	LAV
Leader	L
Length	L, LG or LNG
Library	LIB
Light	LT
Limestone	LS
Linen Closet	L CL
Lining	LN
Linoleum	LINO
Living Room	LR
Louver	LV
Main	MN
Marble	MR
Masonry Opening	MO
Material	MATL
Maximum	MAX
Medicine Cabinet	MC
Minimum	MIN
Miscellaneous	MISC
Mixture	MIX
Modular	MOD
Mortar	MOR
Moulding	MLDG
Nosing	NOS
Obscure Glass	OBSC GL
On Center	OC
Opening	OPNG
Outlet	OUT
Overall	OA
Overhead	OVHD
Pantry	PAN.
Partition	PTN
Plaster	PL or PLAS
Plastered Opening	PO
Plate	PL
Plate Glass	PL GL
Platform	PLAT
Plumbing	PLBG
Porch	P
Precast	PRCST
Prefabricated	PREFAB
Pull Switch	PS
Quarry Tile Floor	QTF
Radiator	RAD
Random	RDM
Range	R
Recessed	REC
Refrigerator	REF
Register	REG
Reinforce or Reinforcing	REINF
Revision	REV
Riser	R
Roof	RF

Roof Drain	RD
Room	RM or R
Rough	RGH
Rough Opening	RGH OPNG
Rubber Tile	R TILE
Scale	SC
Schedule	SCH
Screen	SCR
Scuttle	S
Section	SECT
Select	SEL
Service	SERV
Sewer	SEW.
Sheathing	SHTHG
Sheet	SH
Shelf and Rod	SH & RD
Shelving	SHELV
Shower	SH
Sill Cock	SC
Single Strength Glass	SSG
Sink	SK or S
Soil Pipe	SP
Specification	SPEC
Square Feet	SQ FT
Stained	STN
Stairs	ST
Stairway	STWY
Standard	STD
Steel	ST or STL
Steel Sash	SS
Storage	STG
Switch	SW or S
Telephone	TEL
Terra Cotta	TC
Terrazzo	TER
Thermostat	THERMO
Threshold	TH
Toilet	T
Tongue and Groove	T & G
Tread	TR or T
Typical	TYP
Unexcavated	UNEXC
Unfinished	UNF
Utility Room	URM
Vent	V
Vent Stack	VS
Vinyl Tile	V TILE
Warm Air	WA
Washing Machine	WM
Water	W
Water Closet	WC
Water Heater	WH
Waterproof	WP
Weather Stripping	WS
Weephole	WH
White Pine	WP
Wide Flange	WF
Wood	WD
Wood Frame	WF
Yellow Pine	YP

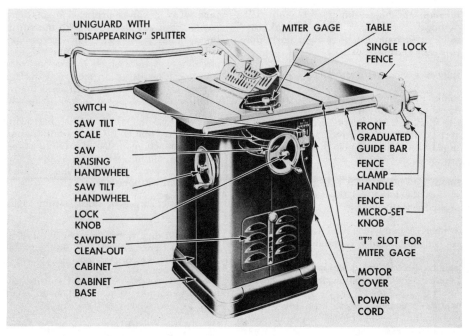

Fig. 585. Circular table saw and parts. (Rockwell Mfg. Co.)

tacky: *Sticky,* as a tacky adhesive.

taenia: In Doric architecture, a fillet or flat band between the architrave and the frieze.

tail: In building, the lower end of a rafter, as the *overhang*. Also called *lookout* or *tail piece*. In masonry, the part of a stone step which is built into a wall.

tail bay: In architecture, one of the main divisions or bays of a framed roof or floor which is next to the end wall, so its joists rest with one end on the wall and the other end on a girder; also, the space under a floor between a wall and the nearest girder.

tail beam or **tail joist:** Any timber or joist which fits against the header joist.

tail cut: In building, the cut of the lower end of a rafter or *overhang* which is some-times trimmed or cut so as to give an orna-mental effect. Typical examples of *tail cuts* are shown in Fig. 586.

tailing: In building construction, any pro-jecting part of a stone or brick inserted in a wall.

tail joist: Any building joist with one end fitted against a header joist.

tailpiece: A relatively short beam, joist, or rafter supported in a wall on one end and by a header on the other end.

take off: The preparation of a list of ma-terials taken from the plans and specifica-tions giving the kind of material, the num-ber, size, weight, volume, or other unit.

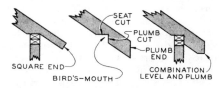

Fig. 586. Tail cut.

take-up: In shopworking, any equipment or device provided to tighten or take up slack or to remove looseness in parts due to wear or other causes.

tally stick: See *board rule,* page 57.

tambour: In architecture, one of the cylindrical or nearly cylindrical blocks of which the shaft of a column is composed; also, a vertical wall, either circular or polygonal in plan, carrying a cupola or dome; a ceiled vestibule.

tamp: To pound down with repeated light strokes the loose soil thrown in as filling around a wall.

tamper: A hand tool used for compacting the subgrade before concrete is placed. It is usually a square iron or steel plate with about a 4-foot wooden handle attached perpendicularly to the flat surface.

tampered concrete pipe: Pipe formed by compacting freshly placed concrete with repeated blows.

tandem: One behind another.

tang: The shank or piece forming the extension of a tool, such as a knife, file, or chisel; which connects with the handle; that portion of a cutting tool which is driven into the handle or *haft.* See *auger bit,* Fig. 59, page 50.

tangent: A term applied to straight lines, curves, or surfaces which touch at a single point but do not intersect.

tangent-sawed: A term applied to a method of cutting lumber whereby a log is sawed lengthwise, in regular succession, by parallel cuts. Also called *bastard-sawed.*

tap: Tool for cutting the thread of an internal screw; a hole made in tapping (as one in a fitting) to furnish connection for a branch pipe, faucet, valve, or hole. Hole which is drilled into the water main into which is inserted a corporation valve to receive the water service pipe from the building. Also a peg or spile used to close a vent, as a spigot. Same as *faucet* or *cock.*

tape: Any flexible narrow strip of linen, cotton, or steel marked off with measuring lines similar to the scale on a carpenter's rule. Usually the tape is contained in a circular case into which it can easily be rewound after using. In electrical work, a narrow strip of treated cloth used for insulating purposes. See *steel tape,* page 430.

taper: Anything which has a narrowing form toward one end; the gradual diminution or reduction in size of any object, especially a column, which gradually grows narrower toward the top; to narrow gradually toward a point.

tarpaulins: Canvas or other strong cloth, made waterproof.

taut: Anything tightly drawn until it is tense and tight, with all sag eliminated as a rope, wire, or cord pulled *taut.*

T bevel: A woodworker's tool used for testing the accuracy of work cut at an angle such as a beveled edge. See Fig. 587.

tee: In pipe work of any kind, a fitting used in connecting pipe lengths, one of which is to be fixed as a branch of the other; also, a fitting for connecting pipes of unequal sizes or for changing the direction of a pipe run. See Fig. 112, page 89 and see *bullhead tee,* page 77.

tee iron: A reinforcing device stamped from sheet metal, then drilled and countersunk, used for strengthening light wooden construction such as window screens, etc. See Fig. 373, page 282.

telamones: Male figures used to support columns or pilasters; same as *atlantes.*

telltale: Any device designed to indicate movement of formwork.

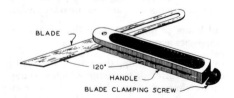

Fig. 587. T bevel.

temperature bars: Steel rods placed horizontally in concrete slabs for prevention of cracks, due to temperature changes, drying, etc., parallel to the reinforcing rods. The rods are the same physically as reinforcing rods and usually are laid at right angles to and almost in the same plane as reinforcing rods.

template: A gage, commonly a thin board or light frame, used as a guide for forming work to be done. In steel construction, a pattern used to locate the centers of holes in members. In architectural drafting, guides used for drawing. These are used for drawing lines, circles, symbols, fixtures, furniture, etc., in both plan and elevation. Templates save time and simplify much drafting. Fig. 588 illustrates a template used in architectural drafting.

templet: A short piece of timber under a beam in a wall to distribute the pressure of a load; also, a beam spanning an aperature, as a doorway and supporting joists. A mold or pattern used by masons for cutting or setting work. See *template.*

tenacious: Holding fast.

tenon: In carpentry, a piece of lumber or timber cut with a projection or tongue on the end for fitting into a mortise. The joint formed by inserting a tenon into a mortise constitutes a so-called *mortise-and-tenon joint.*

tenon saw: In woodworking, any small backsaw used on the bench for cutting tenons.

tensile strain: A stretching, straining, or pulling in a longitudinal direction; the reverse of crushing strain.

tensile strength: In structural work, the strength necessary to enable a structure or structural member to resist a *tensile* strain or pulling strain. See *tensile strain.*

tensile stress: The stress or strain to which a structure or structural member is subjected when in *tension.* See *tension.*

tension: A pulling or stretching force, the opposite of compression, which is a crushing strain. See Fig. 56, page 48, and Fig. 532, page 404.

terminal: In carpentry, the extremity of any structural part, especially the finish

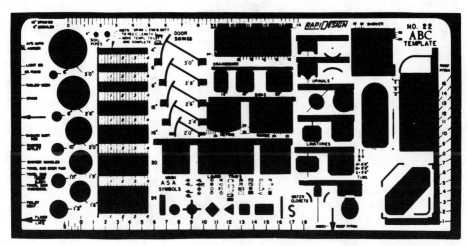

EUGENE DIETZGEN COMPANY, CHICAGO, ILLINOIS

Fig. 588. Templates aid the draftsman and designer in drawing circles, fixtures, symbols, etc.

of a newel post or standard; also, a carving used for decorative purposes at the end of some structural member such as a pedestal.

terminals: Connections to which wires can be fastened.

termites: Wood-devouring insects, which eat the woodwork of a structure and utterly ruin the building. Sometimes called *white ants,* because they resemble ants in general appearance and in their habits of living in colonies.

termite shield: A protective shield made of noncorrodible metal, placed in or on a foundation wall, or other mass of masonry, or around pipes entering a building, to prevent passage of termites into the structure. See Fig. 589.

terrace: An elevated level surface of earth supported on one or more faces by a masonry wall or by a sloping bank covered with turf.

terra cotta: A clay product used for ornamental work on the exterior of buildings; also used extensively in making vases and for decorations on statuettes. It is made of hard-baked clay in variable colors with a fine glazed surface.

terrazzo: A type of Venetian marble mosaic in which Portland cement is used as a matrix. Though used in buildings for centuries, *terrazzo* is a modern floor finish, used also for bases, borders, and wainscoting as well as on stair treads, partitions, and other wall surfaces.

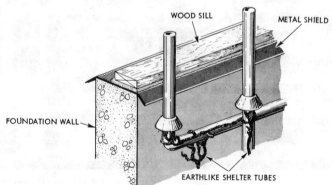

Fig. 589. Termite shields are placed over the concrete and masonry walls and also on pipes.

terrazzo flooring: A term used in the building trades for a type of flooring made of small fragments of colored stone, or marble, embedded irregularly in cement. Finally, the surface is given a high polish.

tesselated: Formed of cubes of stone, marble, glass, or other suitable materials (tessera) arranged in a checkered pattern as in mosaic floors and pavements.

tessera: Any one of the small square pieces of marble, stone, tile, or glass used in mosaic work, such as in floors or pavements.

tetrastyle: Consisting of four columns or having four columns across the front, as a *tetrastyle building.*

texture float: In plastering, a tool, such as a carpet or cork float, used for texturing plaster. See *float,* page 196.

textured finish: In concrete work, a coarser final finish than that achieved by troweling. It may be for decorative purposes or for safety, as for a skidproof floor or sidewalk.

T head: Top of a shore formed with a braced horizontal member projecting on two sides forming a T-shaped assembly.

T hinge: A type of joint with an abutting piece set at right angles to a strap, thus forming a T-shaped hinge; used mainly on outside work such as barn doors and gates. See Fig. 590.

thermal conductance: The time rate at which heat flows through a unit area of a substance of a given size and shape, per unit temperature difference. The common unit is B.t.u. per hour, square foot, and Fahrenheit degree.

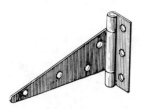

Fig. 590. "T" Hinge.

thermal conductor: Any material which transmits heat readily by means of conduction.

thermal radiation: The transmission of energy by means of electromagnetic waves of relatively long length. Radiant energy of any wave length may, when absorbed, become thermal (heat) energy and result in an increase in the temperature of the absorbing body.

thermal stress: Internal stress caused by heat.

thermal unit: Any unit chosen for the calculation of quantities of heat; that is, a unit of measurement used as a standard of comparison of other quantities of heat, such as B.t.u. (British thermal unit).

thermostat: An instrument, electrically operated, which automatically controls the operation of a heating or cooling device by responding to changes of temperature.

thermostatic: In steam-heating systems, a device which drains air and condensation from a radiator without allowing steam to escape. The discharge valve is operated by means of a diaphragm filled with a volatile liquid which causes a rapid expansion or contraction.

thickness: In lumber, the distance across the edge of a board or piece of timber; the distance through a timber.

thimble: In building, a term applied to a metal lining for a chimney or furnace pipe.

thimble in eye: See *cable attachments,* page 80.

thin-walled conduit: In electricity, a thin-walled raceway of circular cross section, which is constructed for the purpose of pulling in or withdrawing a wire after it has been installed. Also called *electrical metal tubing* (E.M.T.).

thinner: A volatile liquid, such as turpentine, used to thin paint.

tholobate: A substructure on which a dome or cupola rests.

thread escutcheon: A small key plate made in the shape of an outline of the keyhole.

three point perspective: The three principal axes of an object are inclined to the picture plane; therefore requiring three vanishing points. See *perspective,* Fig. 421, page 322.

three-prong plug: In electricity, a plug with three contact prongs, two for the main circuit and one for the ground connection. Used on power equipment. See Fig. 591.

three-way switch: A switch used in house wiring when a light (or lights) is to be turned on or off from two places. A three-way switch must be used at each place. Fig. 584, page 443.

three-wire circuit: In electricity, a circuit using a neutral wire in which the voltage between outside wires is twice that between neutral and each side. A 240v circuit.

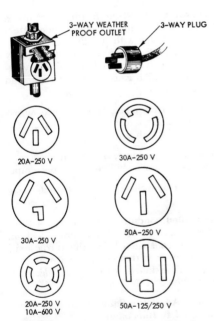

Fig. 591. Approved electrical outlets (receptacles), commonly used for 220 volt tools and equipment. (Amperage and voltage are given on a metal plate attached to the motor of the tool.)

threshold: In building construction, a term applied to the piece of timber, plank, or stone under a door. See Fig. 190, page 150.

throat: The part of a house chimney between the fireplace and the smoke chamber which contracts in ascending and through which smoke rises from the hearth or combustion areas. Also, a groove or channel on the underside of a stringcourse, coping, or other projection of a wall to prevent rain water from running back toward the wall. See *fireplace,* Fig. 245, page 188.

through shake: A separation of wood between annual growth rings, extending between two faces of timber, similar to a *windshake.* See Fig. 635, page 485.

through stone: In stone masonry, a term applied to a stone which extends through a wall forming a bond. Also called *bondstone.*

through tenon: A joint made with tenons on the end of the rails; mortised or tenoned through and showing on the outside of the stile.

thrust: The outward pressure of equal horizontal or diagonal forces, as of an arch against an abutment, due to the loading carried by it, or of a rafter against a supporting wall.

thumb plane: In woodworking, a term sometimes applied to a small plane not more than 4 or 5 inches in length with a bit about 1 inch in width.

thumb screw: A screw with its head so constructed that it can be turned easily with the thumb and finger.

thurm: In cabinetmaking, working with saw and chisel across the grain so as to produce patterns, especially in upright work, like those produced by turning.

tie: In architecture, anything used to hold two parts together, as a post, rod, or beam. In *masonry veneer,* a metal strip used to tie the masonry wall to the wood sheathing. In *concrete formwork,* devices used to tie the two sides of a form together. See *anchors,* page 17; *metal ties,* page 284.

tie bars: Bars at right angles and tied to main reinforcement to keep it in place; bars extending across a construction joint.

tie beam: A timber used for tying structural parts together, as in the roof of a building. Any beam which ties together or prevents the spreading apart of the lower ends of the rafters of a roof. A *collar beam.*

tie piece: In building, a timber which connects two structural members and holds them together, as a *tie beam.*

tie rod: In building, a steel rod used to hold structural parts together; a rod used to tie a truss in position and hold it there.

tie wire: In form building, a wire used to hold forms together so they will not spread apart when concrete is poured into the forms. Also, in reinforced concrete construction, wire used to secure intersections of reinforcing bars for the purpose of holding them in place until concreting is completed.

tier: In building, a row, or one or more rows, of anything placed one above another, as a *tier* of beams.

tight coat: Very thin plaster coat.

tile: A building material made of fired clay, stone, cement, or glass used for floors, roofing, and drains; also made in varied ornamental designs for decorative work. See *plastic tile,* page 336. See Fig. 592.

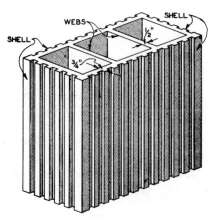

Fig. 592. Tile-shell and web.

tile floors: Floors covered with tiles made of different materials, such as baked clay, terra cotta, glass, cement, and asbestos cement.

tile hanging: A term applied to the hanging of tile on a vertical surface, such as a wall to protect the wall against dampness. See *weather tiling,* page 479.

tile roof: A roof covered with tiling designed especially for the purpose. See *pantile,* page 312.

tile setting adhesives: Specially formulated glues or mastics used instead of mortar bed for tile setting. They are said to be clean, waterproof, less expensive, and faster.

tilting mixer: A cement mixer with a drum which can be tilted. The materials are fed in when the discharge opening of the drum is raised and the mixture is discharged by tilting the drum.

tilt slab wall unit: In reinforced concrete construction, a precast unit. Unit is first cast horizontally on the deck with window and door opening in place and then tilted up into its vertical position. See Fig. 593.

tilt-up construction: A method of constructing walls, and sometimes floors, by pouring concrete or putting wooden walls together in flat panels and when completed moving them to location at a building site, where they are tilted into permanent place. See Fig. 593 for an example.

tilt-up doors: Usually consisting of a rigid panel of sheet steel, aluminum, or wood, these doors are equipped with springs, tracks, counterbalances, and other hardware which pull the door clear of the opening to an overhead position. They are often motor-operated with manual, radio, or magnetic driver controls and are commonly used on garages. See *roll-up doors,* page 370.

timber: In building, a term sometimes applied to a piece of sawed lumber with a cross-section over 4x6 inches. Strictly speaking, *timber* is growing trees.

timber building: A method of building construction in which the principal members are of stout timbers and the walls are formed by filling the spaces between the wood members with plaster. See *half-timbered,* page 229.

453

Fig. 593. A tilt slab wall unit is first cast horizontally on the deck, and then tilted up into its vertical position.

timber carrier: Device for carrying timbers or heavy building members. The hooks grip a log or timber firmly so that it can be lifted by the two men using the carrier. Normally, two teams of two men each are used to carry a log. Also called lug hooks and come-alongs. See Fig. 594.

timber connectors: Metal or wood rings and dowels used to tie adjacent structural members together. The *connectors* are placed in precut holes or grooves in the timber-fram-

ing members; then the members are drawn together and held firmly in place by bolts. See Fig. 595.

timbers: Lumber measuring five inches or more in the smallest dimension.

tinker's dam: In plumbing, a small dam made to enclose a spot which is to be flooded with solder.

tin snips: A cutting instrument, such as the ordinary hand shears, used by sheetmetal

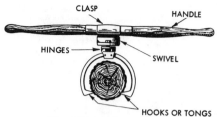

Fig. 594. Timber carrier.

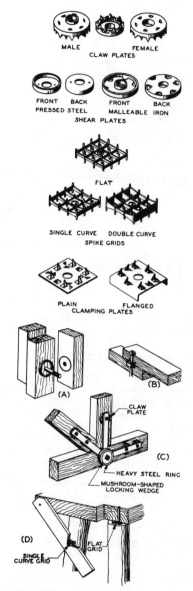

workers, lathers, plasterers, etc. See Fig. 442.

T iron: Metal device used as a fastener in light construction. See Fig. 373.

title block: In architectural drafting, the outlined space usually in the lower right corner, or in a strip form across the bottom of a drawing, containing name of company, title of drawing, scale, date, and such other information as may be considered necessary. See Fig. 596.

T joint: In plumbing, an ordinary threeway pipe fitting, where one branch is at right angles to the other two and midway between them. In welding, where the edge of one member is welded to the surface of another to form a joint shaped like a T.

toe: In building construction, the part of a rafter which does not project over the plate, as the point opposite the heel of the foot cut of the rafter.

toe hold: A piece of board nailed to a sloping roof to prevent the workmen from slipping off the roof. Also spelled *toe holt.*

toe wall: A low retaining wall, built at the foot of an embankment slope to prevent any tendency of the earth to spread or slip; a *dwarf wall.*

toed: In carpentry, a term applied to a structural member which has been secured to another member by the driving of the nails obliquely, or toenailed, as in Fig. 329.

toeing: In carpentry, the driving of nails or brads obliquely; also, to clinch nails so driven. See Fig. 329, page 251.

toenailing: The driving of a nail, spike, or brad slantingly to the end of a piece of

Fig. 595. Timber connectors used in conjunction with bolts, and methods of installation. (A) Method of assembling shear plate; (B) Joining wood to wood with claw plate; (C) Siemens-Bauunion hinge-connector assembly; (D) Use of single curve and flat grids.

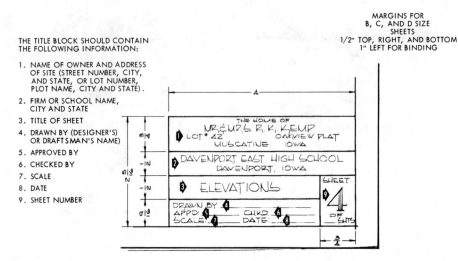

THE TITLE BLOCK SHOULD CONTAIN
THE FOLLOWING INFORMATION:

MARGINS FOR
B, C, AND D SIZE
SHEETS
1/2" TOP, RIGHT, AND BOTTOM
1" LEFT FOR BINDING

1. NAME OF OWNER AND ADDRESS
   OF SITE (STREET NUMBER, CITY,
   AND STATE, OR LOT NUMBER,
   PLOT NAME, CITY AND STATE).
2. FIRM OR SCHOOL NAME,
   CITY AND STATE
3. TITLE OF SHEET
4. DRAWN BY (DESIGNER'S)
   OR DRAFTSMAN'S NAME)
5. APPROVED BY
6. CHECKED BY
7. SCALE
8. DATE
9. SHEET NUMBER

Fig. 596. This title block may be used for architectural working drawing on B, C, or D size sheets.

lumber to attach it to another piece, especially as in laying a floor, to avoid having the heads of the nails show above the surface. See Fig. 329, page 251.

toggle bolt: A bolt having a nut with a pivoted, flanged, winglike anchor on one end. The wings close against a spring when the nut is passed through the constricted passage of a hole bored in a wall. After emerging from the hole, the wings open into a T position, anchoring the bolt to the wall. See *anchors,* Fig. 18, page 17.

tongue: A projecting rib cut along the edge of a piece of timber so it can be fiitted into a groove cut in another piece. See Fig. 329 *tongue and groove,* page 251.

tongue and groove: In carpentry, a joint made by joining two pieces of timber, one having a tongue cut in the edge, the other having a groove to receive the corresponding tongue; a term also applied to material prepared for fitting together with *tongue-and-groove joints.* See Fig. 329, page 251.

tongue-and-groove boards: Boards having their edges treated with a groove in one edge and a tongue on the other edge, so any two boards will fit together tightly. Sometimes called *matched boards.*

tongue-and-groove lumber: Any lumber, such as boards or planks, machined in such a manner that there is a groove on one edge and a corresponding tongue on the other. See *dressed and matched,* page 158.

tongue-and-lip joint: In carpentry, a term applied to a tongue-and-groove joint for boards; the board has a tongue and a bead which serves to conceal the joint.

tongue of framing square: The short, narrow part of a square which is at right angles to the body or blade.

toolbox: A box or chest in which a tradesman keeps his tools.

tool brush: In plastering, tool brushes are used to apply water to small places and to brush out miters, ornamental work, etc. Two sizes are generally used. They are 1" round sash type and 1½" flat, long-handled type. A good quality paint brush is ideal as a tool brush.

tool case: A relatively small *toolbox* in which a tradesman carries his tools; a hand box.

tooled joints: In masonry, mortar joints which are specially prepared by compressing and spreading the mortar after it has

456

set slightly. *Tooled joints* present the best weathering properties and include the *weathered joint,* V joint, and *concave joint.* See Fig. 333, page 254.

tooth chisel: A chisel especially designed for cutting stone. Same as *stonecutter's chisel.*

toothing: In masonry construction, the allowing of alternate courses of brick to project toothlike and provide for a good bond with any adjoining brickwork which may follow.

top cut: In carpentry, the cut at the upper end of a rafter, as the comb cut; also called *plumb cut.*

topography: The relief figures or surface configuration of an area.

topping: A mixture of cement, sand, and water, used in creating the finished surface of concrete work such as walks and floors. See Fig. 233, page 179.

topping joint: In concrete finishing, a space or break of about ⅛″ made at regular intervals, particularly over expansion joints, to allow for contraction and expansion in the topping layer of sidewalks, driveways, and similar structures. See Fig. 233.

top plate: In building, the horizontal member nailed to the top of the partition studding.

torpedo level: See *pocket level,* page 343.

torque wrench: Measures and indicates the amount of turning and twisting force which is applied in tightening a nut or bolt.

torsion: Torsional stress is the result of twisting. See Fig. 597. Of the four types of stresses, torsion is the least important in timber construction. It does occur but in amounts that are negligible if the other types of stresses are provided. See *compression, tension* and *shear.*

torus: In architecture, a type of molding with a convex portion which is nearly semicircular in form; used extensively as a base molding. See Fig. 598.

Fig. 597. Torsional stress, the result of twisting a length of wood.

total run: The sum of all treads in a stair.

to the weather: The projection of shingles or siding beyond the course above.

tower bolt: A door or sash bolt made to slide in a cylindrical socket or barrel. Same as *barrel bolt.* See Fig. 46, page 38.

township: A basic unit of *six miles square* or an area of thirty-six square miles.

T plate: A T-shaped metal plate commonly used as a splice; also used for stiffening a joint where the end of one beam abuts against the side of another.

trabeate, trabeated: A term applied to a type of architecture designed or constructed of horizontal beams or lintels, as a flat, unvaulted ceiling or an unarched doorway; the principle of post and lintel construction as distinguished from the vaulted or arched type.

trabeated system: In building construction, a system in which the load or weight of a wall over an opening, such as windows and doors, is supported by straight beams or lintels.

Fig. 598. Torus.

trace: To make sketches, drawings, or designs on tracing paper or on tracing linen for reproduction, as for blueprinting.

tracery: An architectural term applied to any delicate ornamental work consisting of interlacing lines such as the decorative designs carved on panels or screens; also, the intersecting of ribs and bars, as in rose windows and the upper part of Gothic windows; and decorative design suggestive of network.

traces: The point where a line pierces a transparent plane (plane of projection or picture plane). See *perspective,* page 321.

tracing: Sketches or drawings made on transparent paper for reproduction.

tracing paper: Thin, semi-transparent relatively inexpensive paper on which drawings are made for blueprinting.

trade-union: A combination of tradesmen organized for the purpose of promoting their common interests in regard to wages, hours of work, safety measures, unemployment compensation, and other benefits.

trammel: An instrument used for drawing arcs or radii too great for the capacity of the ordinary compass; a *beam compass* with adjustable points attached to the end of a bar of wood or metal used by draftsmen and shopworkers for describing unusually large circles or arcs. See Fig. 599. In plastering, a cross-shaped figure used for laying out moldings.

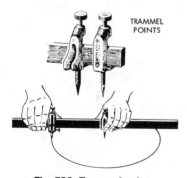

TRAMMEL POINTS

Fig. 599. Trammel points.

transept: In architecture, the transverse section of a cruciform church structure; either of the two arms of such a church building.

transformer: An apparatus used to increase or decrease the voltage. There are two types—*step-up* and *step-down.*

transit: A surveyor's instrument used by builders to establish points and elevations. The transit operates in both the horizontal and vertical planes. See Fig. 600.

transition piece: A sheet metal device shaped to form a transition from one shaped duct to another shaped duct.

transit-mixed concrete: Ready-mix concrete that is completely mixed in a truck mixer either at the ready-mix plant or on the way to the job site.

transit mixer: A truck chassis on which is mounted a drum which is capable of mixing concrete.

transmission: The passage of sound through walls and ceilings of floors of adjoining rooms.

transom: A term used in building for any small window over a door or another window.

transom bar: A crossbar of wood or stone which divides an opening horizontally into two parts.

transverse wires: The wires of welded wire fabric which run width-wise.

trap: A bend or dip in a water pipe, so arranged as to be always full of water, in order to imprison air within the pipe and to prevent offensive odors backing up the pipes. See Fig. 177, page 139.

trap door: A covering for an opening in a floor, ceiling, or roof; usually such a door is level, or practically so, with the surface of the opening which it covers.

travelers: Wires that connect terminals between two electrical switches. See Fig. 601.

traverse: Any horizontal member or lateral structure such as a railing or a transom; a barrier; also, a loft of communication, a

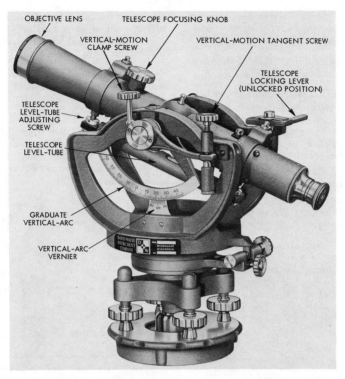

Fig. 600. The transit-level can be used to line up stakes or to plumb walls when adjusted in the transit position. The angle of elevation from a horizontal plane can be measured. (David White Instruments, Div. of Realist, Inc.)

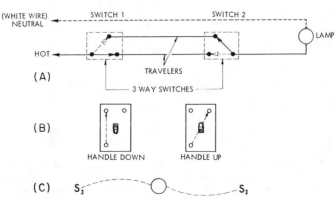

Fig. 601. (A) Wiring diagram for 3-way switch; (B) 3-way switch contact positions. The lamp is off; throwing either switch will cause it to go on. (C) Architectural plan symbols for 3-way switches, used, for example, for a hallway or a room with switches at two doors.

cross gallery; planing across the grain of wood, as *traversing* a floor by planing cross-wise of the boards.

tread: The horizontal portion of the step. See Figs. 561 and 562, page 424.

treenail: A wooden peg or pin used to hold a *mortise-and-tenon joint* together. Usually such a pin is cut from dry, compressed wood so that when damp it will swell and tighten the joint. Also called a *drawbore pin.* Sometimes spelled *trenail.*

trefoil: In architecture, an ornamental three-lobed unit resembling in form the foliage of an herb whose leaf is divided into three distinct parts, such as the common varieties of clover.

tremie: A chute for placing concrete under water consisting of a tube with removable sections and a funnel for receiving the concrete. The bottom of the tube is always immersed in the concrete, being gradually raised as the form is filled. See Fig. 602.

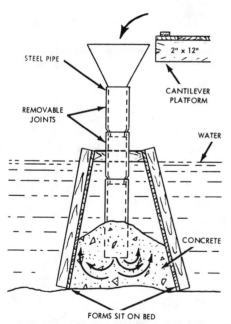

Fig. 602. Placing concrete under water with a tremie.

trestle scaffold: A braced framework, usually consisting of a horizontal beam supported at each end by a pair of spreading legs which serve as braces.

trial mix: A small batch of concrete that is used to select the best proportions of materials or to test the proportions calculated for a mix.

triangle: A geometrical figure having three sides and three angles; also, a thin, flat, right-angled, triangular instrument made of celluloid, wood, or metal; used by draftsmen. See Fig. 603.

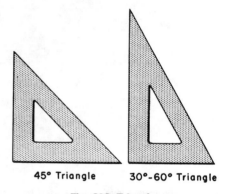

45° Triangle   **30°-60° Triangle**

Fig. 603. Triangle.

triangular scale: A draftsman's three-faced measuring device having six graduated edges. On one edge is shown a scale of full-sized measurements, while on the other edges are shown various reductions in scale. Also called *architect's scale.* See Fig. 201, page 157.

triangular truss: A popular type of truss used for short spans, especially for roof supports.

triglyphs: A structural member in a Doric frieze consisting typically of a rectangular block with two vertical grooves, or glyphs, and two chamfers, or half grooves, at the sides, which together count as a third glyph. See Figs. 5 and 230 (page 174).

trim: In carpentry, a term applied to the visible finishing work of the interior of a building, including any ornamental parts

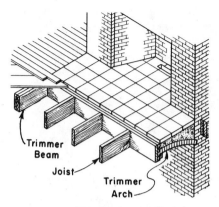

Fig. 604. Trimmer arch.

of either wood or metal used for covering joints between jambs and plaster around windows and doors. The term may also include the locks, knobs, and hinges on doors. Also: the exterior finish around openings.

trimmer: The beam or floor joist into which a header is framed. See Fig. 604.

trimmer arch: A comparatively flat arch, such as may be used in the construction of a fireplace. A trimmer arch is shown in Fig. 604.

trimmer beam: Usually two joists spiked together around a fireplace opening in floor framing.

trimmer joist: The member around an opening or side parallel with common joists and carrying the header joists.

trimmer tail: The trimmer nearest to the wall into which joist ends are secured.

trimming joist: A timber or beam which supports a header.

triptich: A wood reredos consisting of three compartments side by side, with painted or carved pictures on each panel or compartment; a picture serving as an altarpiece with a central panel and two flanking panels which fold over the central panel. Also spelled *triptych*.

trisect: To divide into three equal parts.

trowel: A flat steel tool, of various sizes and shapes, used to spread and smooth plaster, mortar, or concrete. A trowel has three parts. They are called the *blade,* the *mounting* and the *handle.* Commonly used trowels are shown in Fig. 605. The *common trowel* is used for smoothing concrete or plaster. *Pointing trowels* are used for many purposes. They are small enough to be used in places where the larger trowels will not fit. They are used to clean tools and to handle small pats of material in many plastering operations. The *margin trowel* is used to apply and trowel-up material in narrow places, such as between moldings that are run closely together. In plastering, specialized trowels, such as those shown in Fig. 606 are also used. An *outside corner trowel,* the reverse of the *inside corner trowel,* Fig. 606D is also used.

troweler, power: A machine operated by one man, designed to do a complete job of concrete finishing. Generally, gasoline powered, the power source, which is mounted

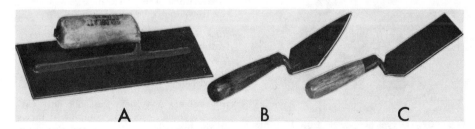

Fig. 605. Common trowels: (A) trowel, (B) pointing trowel and (C) margin trowel.

461

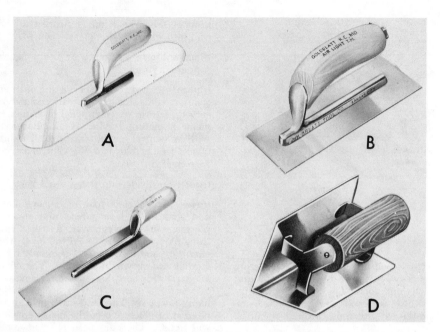

Fig. 606. Specialized plastering trowels: (A) pool trowel, (B) midget trowel, (C) pipe trowel, and (D) inside corner trowel.

Fig. 607. A typical power trowel. (Stow Manufacturing Co.)

vertically to the ground, turns troweling blades which are mounted radially on a central shaft. The pitch of the troweling blades is adjustable while the machine is in operation, allowing continual use on varying surfaces. Due to the circular swath of the troweler, hand finishing is generally necessary in corners and along walls. See Fig. 607.

troweling: To smooth and compact the surface of fresh plaster or concrete by strokes of a trowel. Fig. 608 shows a trowel being used to finish a plaster wall. Fig. 609 shows the troweling of concrete flatwork.

truck agitator: A vehicle used to carry freshly mixed concrete from the point of mixing to that of placing; this truck merely agitates the fresh concrete, which was mixed before being placed in the truck.

truck-mixer: A vehicle that not only carries the ready-mix but completely mixes all the ingredients either at the ready-mix plant or on the way to the job site.

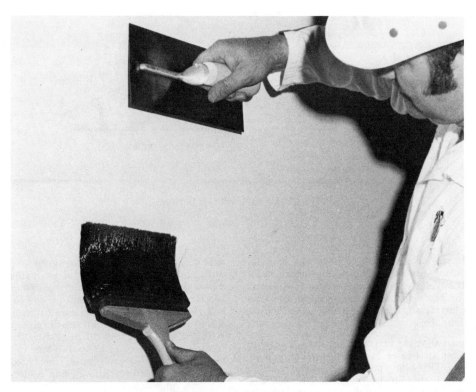

Fig. 608. Troweling finish surface.

Fig. 609. Steel troweling. Note the use of kneeboards. (Portland Cement Association)

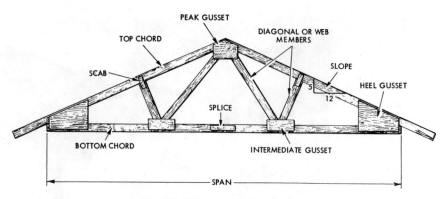

Fig. 610. W truss with terminology.

truss: A combination of members, such as beams, bars and ties, usually arranged in triangular units to form a rigid framework for supporting loads over a span. Fig. 610 illustrates a typical W truss used in residential construction.

truss clips: A clip connector used in assembling trusses or in joining lumber end to end. Depending on the size of the connector, each clip has an effective holding power of 20 to 60 nails. They are galvanized or made from a non-rusting material. See Fig. 611.

trussed beam: An architectural term applied to a beam stiffened by a truss rod.

trussed-wall opening: A wall opening, such as for a door or window, where the framing is trussed to support a concentrated load carried above the opening.

trussed rafter: A roof truss which serves to support the roof and ceiling construction.

truss rod: A tie rod in a truss, or a diagonal rod for trussing a wooden beam.

try square: A tool used for laying out right angles and for testing work for squareness. See Fig. 612.

T-square: The *T-square* is used for drawing horizontal and parallel lines. It is also used as a guide for triangles in drawing vertical and inclined lines. *T-squares* vary in length from 18″ to 60″. See Fig. 613.

tubing: Tubing commonly comes in copper, brass and bronze and is used for conveying steam, gases, liquids, etc. The hot water heating system in a house and other general plumbing features make use of tubing. There are four weights or classes of tubing: K, L, M and O. These range in strength from K extra-heavy to O light. There are two basic fastening procedures: the flared tube with appropriate fittings, and soldering with appropriate fittings.

Fig. 611. Truss clips have an effective holding power of 20 to 60 nails. (Panel Clip Co.)

Fig. 612. Try square.

tuckpointing: In masonry, the repairing of worn or damaged mortar joints by raking out the old mortar, replacing with fresh mortar.

Tudor arch: An obtusely pointed, four-centered arch characteristic of the reign of the Tudors (1485-1603).

Tudor style: In building, the architectural style prevailing in England during the reign of the Tudors, especially during the

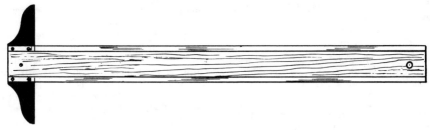

Fig. 613. T square.

tubular lock: A rim lock with a fixed tube containing the tumblers, which are attached to the lock case. See Fig. 614.

tubular scaffolds: Scaffolds for interior and exterior construction work made of tube steel. These scaffolds are light weight, offer low wind resistance, and are easily dismantled. They are obtainable in several strengths for varying heights and types of work.

period from Henry VIII to Elizabeth; a style characterized by flat arches, shallow moldings, and extensive paneling. The latest style of English Gothic.

tumble home: To incline inward from the greatest breadth, as the sloping in of a column or building toward the top; a term derived from shipbuilding, referring to the sloping in of the sides of a vessel above the water line and as they near the top of the boat.

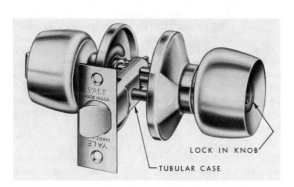

LOCK IN KNOB
TUBULAR CASE

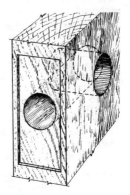

Fig. 614. Tubular lock set is installed by drilling 2 holes and mortising lock face. Locks of this type are supplied for several different applications. (Yale & Towne Mfg. Co.)

tunnel vault: A vault semicylindrical in form having parallel abutments and with the same section throughout. Also called *barrel vault.* See *barrel arch,* Fig. 45, page 38.

turn tread: A tread or step usually triangular in plan, forming a step at the change in direction of a stair. See *winders,* page 483.

turnbuckle: A type of coupling between the ends of two rods, used primarily for adjusting or regulating the tension in the rods which it connects. It consists of a loop or sleeve with a screw thread on one end and a swivel at the other or with an internal screw thread at each end.

turning gouge: In woodworking, a tool used for roughing down woodwork in a lathe. The widths of gouges vary from ¼ to 1½ inches.

turpentine: The distilled sap of the longleaf pine. Used in the mixing of paint to make it spread easier.

Tuscan: Pertaining to one of the five classic orders of architecture; distinguished especially by the plain column and the absence of decorative detail.

tusk tenon: In carpentry, a tenon which is strengthened by one or more tusklike projections, or steps, on the underside.

twelfth scale: A scale which divides the inch into 12 parts instead of 16; found usually on the back of the *framing square* along the outside edge. In this scale, one inch equals one foot. The *twelfth scale* makes it possible to reduce layouts to 1/12 of their regular size and to solve basic right triangle problems.

twist: A defect in lumber consisting of a form of warp resulting in distortion caused by the turning or winding of the edges of a board.

twist bit: In woodwork, a tool used for boring holes in wood for screws. A tool similar to the twist drill used for drilling holes in metal, except that the cutting edge of the *twist bit* is ground at a greater angle.

twist drill: A drilling tool having helical grooves extending from the point to the smooth portion of the shank. This type of drill is made of round stock with a shank

that may be either straight or tapering. It is used for drilling holes in metal. A similar drill used for wood is known as a *twist bit.*

two-point perspective: One principal axis of an object is parallel to the picture plane; therefore, requiring two vanishing points. See *perspective,* page 321.

two-way floor and roof system: In reinforced concrete construction, one of the two major classes of floor and roof systems. In the two-way system, the main reinforcement runs in two directions. A two-way system may be designed using a solid slab supported by beams which run between the columns in both directions. (See Fig. 615.) Another type is called the *flat slab* with the support coming from columns with flared capitals and drop panels to distribute the load over a greater area. (See Fig. 616.) For lighter floor loads, such as those for apartment houses or office buildings, a two-way slab is designed without column capitols or drop panels. (See Fig. 617.) This is called *flat-plate* construction. Increased reinforcement is necessary at columns because of the shear stress caused by the transfer of the load to the small area of the column. The great advantage of this system is the thin floor and unobstructed ceiling which results in a saving in the floor-to-floor height. There is one more two-way system which is very popular called the *waffle flat plate.* It is, in reality, a two-way grid of narrow beams with the voids formed by steel pans regularly spaced. (See Fig. 618.) Each of these one- and two-way slabs and supporting members, except those using precast members, are poured to make a monolithic unit with the reinforcing bars suspended at the exact location to provide for the forces of tension, compression, and shear. The various floor and roof systems discussed in the preceding paragraphs each has its own design problems in the use and size of reinforcing bars, shapes of members, and thicknesses of slabs. See also pan *floor, pan forms.* (See *one-way floor and roof system* for the other major system.)

tympanum: In architecture, a term often used interchangeably with *pediment,* although, strictly speaking, it is the recessed, usually triangular, space enclosed between

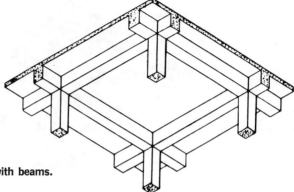

Fig. 615. Flat slab construction with beams.

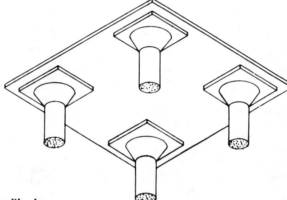

Fig. 616. Flat slab construction with drop panels.

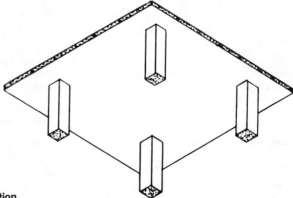

Fig. 617. Flat plate construction.

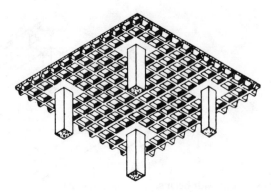

Fig. 618. A waffle flat plate construction uses a two-way joist system formed with the use of steel domes or "pans."

the horizontal and sloping cornices of a *pediment*. See *pediment,* page 317. See Fig. 5.

U bolt: An iron bar bent into a U-shaped bolt, with screw threads and nuts on each end. Often called a clip, as a spring clip on an automobile.

ultimate stress: When a load is increased on a structural member, such as a beam, girder, or post, the highest point of stress sustained by the member just before it falls and breaks is called the *ultimate stress.*

unbalanced back-flow valve: In plumbing, a type of valve which remains closed until a flow of sewerage strikes the gate. A fresh-air pipe must be provided to admit air into the system when this type of valve is used. See *back-flow valve,* page 31.

undercoater: Any common flat wall paint manufactured as a base coat for enamel or any prepared paint used as a base for enamel.

undercut: To cut away material on the underside so as to leave an overhanging portion, as moldings having a section which overhangs, giving a deep hollow or dark shadow beneath.

underlayment: Floor covering of plywood or fiberboard used to provide a level surface for carpet or other resilient flooring.

unified thread series: This thread is similar to the former *American National thread*

except that the principal differences relate to the application of allowances, the variation of tolerances with size, and differences in the amounts of pitch diameter tolerances for external and internal threads. In the UNC, UNF, and UNEF thread series, the number of threads per inch (pitch) varies with the diameter of the shaft or hole.

union: In plumbing, a connection or coupling for pipes. See Fig. 428, page 327.

union joint: In plumbing, a pipe fitting in which two pipes are joined so they can be disconnected without disturbing the pipes themselves.

unit length rafter table: A table which appears on the blade of the *framing square*. It gives unit lengths of *common rafters* for seventeen different rises, ranging from 2 to 18 inches. It also gives the unit lengths for *hip* or *valley rafters,* difference in lengths of *jack rafters* set 16 inches on center, jack rafters set 24 inches on center, and the *side cuts* for jack and hip rafters.

unjointed: Concrete slabs which have not been jointed. See *jointing,* page 254.

unsound knot: A term used by woodworkers when referring to a *knot* which is not so solid as the wood in the board surrounding it.

upperbeam bolster: Welded wire support

for the upper layer of bottom bars in beams.

upright: In building, a term applied to a piece of timber which stands upright or in a vertical position, as the vertical pieces at the sides of a doorway or window frame.

upset: In carpentry, the buckling of wood fibers due to crushing of a piece of timber; in machinery, to thicken and shorten a piece of structural metal by hammering on the end, as a heated bar of iron.

utility knife: A cutting knife with a single-edge razor blade held between the two sides of the knife. The size is about 5″ long by 1″ wide and ¾″ thick.

V

vacuum and blower fish line system: In electrical wiring, a device for blowing or vacuuming a fish line through electrical conduit. A *wire pulling rope* is then run through and the wires attached and pulled through. See Fig. 619.

vacuum pump: In a steam-heating system, a centrifugal pump which removes air and

Fig. 619. Vacuuming a fish line through a conduit. (Greenlee Tool Co.)

condensation from the return main of the system, in order to create a vacuum and return the condensate to the boiler or to a receiving tank.

valley: In architecture, a term applied to a depressed angle formed by the meeting at the bottom of two inclined sides of a roof, as a gutter; also, the space, when viewed from above, between vault ridges.

valley board: In building, a board nailed along the top of the valley rafter as a support for a laced valley.

valley flashing: Pieces of lead, tin, or sheet metal worked in with shingles or other construction materials along the valley of a roof.

valley jack: A rafter which fits against a *valley rafter* or onto a *valley board.* See Fig. 463, page 358.

valley rafter: A rafter disposed in the internal angle of a roof to form a *valley* or depression in the roof. See Fig. 463, page 358.

valley roof: A type of roof which has one or more valleys. See *valley.*

valley shingles: In carpentry, shingles which have been cut at the proper angle so they will fit correctly along a *valley.*

valley tile: Trough-shaped building tile made for use in valleys of roofs.

valve: A device for regulating the flow of a liquid or gas in a pipe line.

Van Dyke: A reproduction from a tracing printed by a process which gives a print with dark lines on a white background.

vandyke pieces: In plumbing, the lead pieces or scraps which remain after the cutting out of a stepped flashing.

vanishing points: In perspective drawing the point on the *horizon line* where the lines of the object meet. See *perspective drawing,* page 322.

vapor barrier: Material used to retard the passage of vapor or moisture through walls and thus prevent condensation within them; also called *moisture barrier.*

varnish: In painting, a solution of a resin or resinous gum, in alcohol or oil, applied to a surface to produce a hard, glossy finish, and to protect the underlying coat of paint. Varnishes may be either clear or colored.

vault: In architecture, an arched structure of masonry usually forming a ceiling or roof; also, an arched passageway under ground or any room or space covered by arches.

vaulting capital: The uppermost member, or capital, of a vaulting shaft.

vaulting cell: One of the compartments in a ribbed structure, such as a vault; designed so as to permit the building of one entire section at a time.

vaulting course: A course formed by the springers of a vault which usually are set with horizontal beds, either corbeled out or in projection.

vaulting shaft: A small, upright member placed against a wall to carry vaulting, as a pilaster or column from which a rib, or group of ribs, of the vault springs. A *vaulting shaft* is commonly composed of a cluster of columns or pillars, or it may be a part of a larger pier.

vault rib: One of the curved members of a ribbed arch carrying a vault.

vehicle: In painting, the liquid medium or substance, as oil, with which a pigment is mixed to form a paint.

vellum: Paper used to prepare architectural drawings. Vellums are characterized by their high transparent quality, yet are very durable and non-yellowing. Vellums are manufactured from 100 percent rag stock. See *tracing paper,* page 458.

veneer plaster: In plastering, a classification used throughout the industry to describe any thin application of a monolithic troweled finish to walls and ceilings. There are two systems: One is the use of two coats; the other is the one coat. There are several manufacturers, and each has developed its own particular system.

veneer saw: A circular saw used for cutting veneers.

veneered construction: In building, a method of construction in which a thin layer of marble slabs, or other facing material, is applied to the external surface of steel, reinforced concrete, or frame walls. Two methods of applying brick veneer are shown in Fig. 88, page 71.

veneered wall: A wall with a masonry facing which is not bonded but is attached to a wall so as to form an integral part of the wall for purposes of load bearing and stability. See Fig. 88, page 71.

Venetian arch: A type of pointed arch in which the intrados and extrados are not parallel. See *Queen Anne arch,* page 353.

Venetian dentil: In architecture, one of a series of cubical projections alternating with splayed surfaces, used as a decorative feature.

vent: A small opening to allow the passage of air through any space in a building, as for ventilation of an attic or the unexcavated area under a first-floor construction.

vent flue: A vertical pipe providing an escape for foul gases from a sanitary fixture and leading into the vent stack. Same as *vent pipe.*

vent pipe: A flue or pipe connecting any interior space in a building with the outer air for purposes of ventilation; any small pipe extending from any of the various plumbing fixtures in a structure to the vent stack.

vent shaft: An air duct or shaft for ventilating a room or building. Same as *vent flue.*

vent stack: A vertical pipe connected with all vent pipes carrying off foul air or gases from a building. It extends through the roof and provides an outlet for gases and contaminated air and also aids in maintaining a water seal in the trap.

vent system: A pipe, or pipes, installed in order to provide a flow of air to or from a drainage system; or to provide circulation of air within the system to equalize pressures and ventilate the system and protect trap seals from siphonage and back pressure.

ventilating bead: A piece of board of timber covering about three inches of the movement of the bottom sash of a window, thus allowing for ventilation at the meeting rail while, to all intents and purposes, keeping the bottom of the window closed. Same as *deep bead.*

ventilating brick: A brick which has been cored to provide an air passage for ventilating purposes.

ventilating eyebrow: A low dormer in a roof over which the roofing is carried in a wave line; sometimes used for ventilating attics. See *attic louver,* page 29.

ventilating fan: An electrically driven fan used for circulating air in a room or building.

ventilating flues: The ducts which carry air into a ventilating system.

ventilation: The free circulation of air in a room or building; a process of changing the air in a room by either natural or artificial means; any provision made for removing contaminated air or gases from a room and replacing the foul air by fresh air.

ventilator: A contrivance for replacing foul or stagnant air with fresh air in a room or building.

verge: The edge of tiling, slate, or shingles projecting over the gable of a roof, that on the horizontal portion being called the *eaves.*

verge board: The board under the verge of a gable, sometimes molded. During the latter part of the nineteenth century, often *verge boards* were richly adorned with decorative carving, perforations, and cusps, frequently having pendants at the apex. Often the term *verge board* is corrupted into *bargeboard.*

verge rafter: An exposed rafter on the end of a gable roof. Same as *bargeboard.* See *verge board.*

vermiculated work: In masonry, a type of finish consisting of worm-shaped sinkings,

471

accomplished by a sand-blast process, and intended to give a rustic appearance to a wall or building.

vermiculite: Expanded mica used for loose fill insulation and as aggregate in concrete or plaster.

vertex: In architecture, the highest point of an arch, and the point where the keystone is placed. Sometimes called the *crown* of an arch.

vertex of an angle: The point at which the two lines of an angle meet.

vertical: Pertaining to anything, such as a structural member, which is upright in position, perpendicular to a horizontal member, and exactly plumb.

vertical bar: In a window, a small strip of metal or wood used to separate the glass in a window. It refers only to the upright strips; otherwise, the same as *muntin.*

vertical cut: Any plumb cut; a cut which takes a vertical position when a structural member, such as a rafter, is in place. Also, a cut made by a *vertical saw.*

vertical saw: A cutting tool, such as a circular saw, which operates in a vertical position.

vertical siding: A type of siding consisting of matched boards which are ten and twelve inches wide, or the boards may be of random widths, the joints being either V cut or covered with battens.

vestibule: A small entrance room at the outer door of a building; an anteroom which is sometimes used as a waiting room.

vestibule door: In architecture, a door leading from an entrance room, such as a vestibule, into an adjoining room.

vibrating screed: Used both for leveling and consolidating a concrete slab.

vibrator: In concrete work, a special tool for compacting freshly placed concrete within the forms. The vibrating *head,* which is either pneumatically or mechanically driven, is immersed in the concrete as it is being placed, causing rapid and thorough consolidation.

vice: A term formerly applied to a winding stairway around a column called a *newel;* also the shaft, sometimes of wood but more often of stone, in a spiral staircase. Also spelled *vise.*

view: In architecture, a term applied to a drawing representing a particular viewpoint, as a *front view,* a *side view,* or a *back view.*

vignette: In architecture, a small decorative vinelike ornament.

vinyl plastics: Noncrystalline *thermoplastics* which are tough and strong. They come in all colors, have excellent electrical insulating properties, are self-extinguishing, and have maximum use temperatures of 135° to 200° F. Plasticizers have a tendency to migrate, and colors will darken in sunshine; used for floor and wall tiles, kickboards, flashing, expansion joints, glazing, sprayed coatings, wiring, piping, ducts, siding, and insulation when foamed.

vise: A mechanical device for holding a piece of wood or metal rigid while it is being worked. Usually it consists of two jaws, one fixed and the other movable. The movable jaw is operated by a screw or lever by means of which clamping action is obtained.

vise clamps: False jaws for a vise, used over the face of steel jaws to prevent damage to the piece being worked on.

vise-grip pliers: Adjustable pliers. A screw adjustment in one of the handles makes them suitable for several different sizes. Vise-grip pliers will clamp on an object and stay.

visual rays: In perspective drawing, the imaginary lines which extend from the viewer's eye to the object. Also called *lines of sight.* See *perspective drawing,* page 322.

vitreous: Of the nature of glass. Vitreous tile is ceramic tile baked so as to become very hard and waterproof.

vitrified brick. A paving brick burned to the point of vitrification; then toughened by annealing.

Tee Branch   Y-Branch

Offset   Reducer   Increaser

Square El   Short Curve   Cut Curve

Running Trap   Slant   Cut El

Fig. 620. Vitrified tile.

vitrified tile: In building construction, pipes made of clay baked hard and then glazed so they are impervious to water; used especially for underground drainage. Typical vitrified clay fittings are shown in Fig. 620.

vitruvian scroll: A typical Greek decorative ornament, consisting of a series of spirals somewhat resembling waves; used especially in friezes of the composite order. See *running dog,* page 378.

vitruvian wave: A decorative ornament used on moldings, consisting of a series of wavelike spirals. See *running dog,* page 378.

volt: The unit used in measuring the electrical pressure causing the current to flow. Voltage is electrical pressure. Normally it is supplied to homes in dual voltage 115-230 and 120-240 volts.

volume: The size of any object measured in three dimensions; volume = length × height × width.

volume stability: The maintaining to a minimum the same amount of concrete during and after the hardening period. Because of temperature changes, moisture changes, etc., concrete expands or contracts, which changes the volume of the concrete.

volute: The spiral ornament which appears in both the Ionic and Corinthian orders of architecture. Especially in the Ionic order, of which the chief characteristic and most distinguishing feature is the convolute spiral ornament. See Fig. 1.

volute with easement: The spiral portion of a handrail which sometimes supplants a newel post in stair building. See Fig. 561.

voussoir: In architecture, any one of the wedge-shaped pieces, or stones, used in forming an arch. See Fig. 337. The middle one is called the *keystone.* See *keystone.*

voussoir brick: Building brick made especially for constructing arches. Such brick are so formed that the face joints radiate from a common center.

V roof: Any double-pitched roof, such as a *gable roof.*

V tool: A cutting tool having a V-shaped cutting edge, such as V-shaped chisel for carving out V-shaped grooves.

V tooled joint: In masonry, a mortar joint formed with a special tool similar to that shown in Fig. 331. After excess mortar has been removed, the tool is run along the joint. See Fig. 333, page 254.

W

waffle flat plate construction: In reinforced concrete, a two-way joist system formed with the use of steel domes or pans. See Fig. 618.

waffle slab: A two-way reinforced concrete joist floor with ribs running in both directions. (Named after the waffle-like appearance of the underside of the finished floor.) See Fig. 618.

wagon-headed dormer: A dormer window having the form of a round arch, resembling the end of a covered wagon of pioneer days; a dormer with a roof in the form of a semicylinder, like the cover of a wagon stretched over the bows.

wagon roof: A roof formed by a wagon vault.

wagon vault: A vault of semicircular, or nearly semicircular, cross section and usually with a length considerably greater than its diameter. Same as *barrel vault.*

wagtail: In building construction, a term sometimes applied to a *parting strip; a* small piece of wood used to hold adjoining members apart. See *parting slip,* page 315.

wainscot: A wall covering for the lower part of an interior wall; covering may be of wood, glass, tile, etc.

wainscoting: The material used in lining the interior of walls; also, the process of applying such materials to walls.

wainscoting cap: A molding at the top of a wainscoting.

wales: In concrete formwork, the horizontal timbers on the outside of the form to which the ties are fastened, and which hold the forms in line. Also called *walers* and *whalers.* See Fig. 545.

walking line: In stair building, an imaginary line used, especially where there are winders, in setting out the widths of the treads. Usually this line is taken about 18 inches from the inside of the handrail.

wall: An upright structure of definite dimensions for enclosing space, as a building or room. A wall may be constructed of stone, brick, or other suitable building material. *Bearing wall:* A wall which supports a vertical load in addition to its own weight. *Cavity wall:* A masonry on concrete wall consisting of two wythes arranged to provide an air space within the wall. *Curtain wall:* A wall, usually nonbearing, between piers or columns. *Faced wall:* A combination wall in which the masonry facing and the backing are so bonded as to exert a common reaction under load. *Firewall:* A wall with qualities of fire resistance and structural stability. *Foundation wall:* A wall below, or partly below, grade providing support for the exterior parts of a building. *Masonry wall:* A wall made of masonry units. *Non-bearing wall:* A wall which supports no vertical load other than its own weight. *Party wall:* A wall used jointly by two parties. *Veneered wall:* A wall with a masonry face which is attached to but not bonded to the body of the wall and does not exert a common reaction under load.

wall anchor: In building construction, a type of anchor used to tie the walls to the floors and hold them firmly in position. Also called *wall beam.*

wall beam: In masonry, a metal member or type of anchor fastened to a floor joist to tie the wall firmly to the floor. The anchor extends into the masonry wall, and at the end of the anchor there is some kind of bolt or wall hook, which may be either L-shaped or T-shaped, for holding the anchor in the wall. See *wall anchor.*

wall bearer: In stair building, a timber which is spiked flat against the wall parallel with the pitch of the stairway. The timber is placed about three-quarters of an inch below the back of the steps to give support to the stairs. The steps are then wedged in such a way that the stairway will be straight and will also be well supported.

wall bearing: A wall which supports any vertical load in addition to its own weight, as a *wall-bearing partition;* also, a wall support for a girder or beam.

wall-bearing partition: A partition wall which carries any vertical load in addition to its own weight, such as floor joists and other partitions above it.

wall bed: In building, any one of the various types of beds which fold or swing into a wall or closet when not in use. A type of bed commonly used where the conserving of space is important, such as in apartment buildings.

wall box: A support, usually of cast iron, built into a wall to carry the end of a timber and to provide for its ventilation; a metal box placed in a wall for the electric switches and fuses; also, a frame set in a wall to receive the bearing for a shaft passing through the wall. Sometimes called a *wall frame.*

wall bracket: In building construction, any bracket attached to a wall and used to support a structural member, such as a beam, girder, or joist.

wall chase: A square or rectangular recess in a masonry wall to accommodate pipes, heating ducts, and other similar equipment. See *chase,* Fig. 121, page 94.

wall clamp: A device for holding walls or parts of a double wall together.

wall columns: Columns of steel enclosed in the walls of a building for carrying both the dead and live loads of the floors of the structure in which they are used.

wall coping: The covering course on top of a brick or stone wall; also referred to as *capping.* Where porches or other similar spaces are enclosed with solid walls to the height of the porch railing, the material which is used as a finish is called *coping.*

wall cornice: A kind of coping with a cornicelike finish at the top of a masonry wall; also, a finish for the top of a wall.

wall covering: In building construction, a term applied to any material used to cover either interior or exterior wall surfaces.

wall face: The front or finished surface of the wall of a building; the outside surface of a retaining wall.

wall hanger: In building construction, a support of pressed steel or cast iron, partially built into a wall for carrying the end of a structural timber, when the timber itself is not to be built into the wall.

wall hook: A special type of metal hook or nail which is designed to be set and fixed in a wall as a support for construction members. The hook or nail may be either L-shaped or T-shaped. See *wall anchor,* page 474.

wall iron: A type of metal bracket attached to the exterior wall of a building to serve as a support for downspouts, lightning rods, and other similar features.

wall line: The face line of the main wall of a building. See *building line,* page 74.

wall panel: A nonbearing wall built between the columns or piers of a structure and supported at each story height by girders or beams of a skeleton frame.

wall plate: Plate at top or bottom of wall or partition framing. See *plate,* page 337.

wall spacers: In concrete work, a type of tie for holding the forms in position while the concrete is being poured and until it has set. See Fig. 445.

wall spreader: An accessory, usually fabricated from reinforcing bar to a "Z" or "U" shape, used to separate and hold apart two faces or curtains of reinforcement in a wall.

wall string: In stair building, that string of a staircase which is next to the wall. Also called *wall stringer.*

wall symbols: In building construction, standardized symbols which are used by architects and builders to designate the kind of material to be used for outside walls and for partitions. See Fig. 372, page 280.

wall tie: A device, in any of various shapes, formed of $1/4''$ diameter steel wire, the purpose of which is to bind together the tiers of a masonry wall, particularly those in a hollow wall construction. See Figs. 115, 286 and 376. Also, a contrivance, usually a metal strip, employed to attach or secure a brick veneer wall to a frame building. See Fig. 621.

wall vents: Cavity ventilators used to vent solid or veneer masonry walls. See Fig. 622.

walling: Material used in the construction of a wall for a building; that which serves as a wall; also, the act or process of making the wall for a building.

wallpiece: Any flat piece of timber fastened to a wall as a bearing for the upper end of a prop or shore.

wane: Any defect on the edge or corner of a piece of lumber due to a lack of wood or bark.

warehouse pack: The stiffening or hardening of sacked cement stored for periods of time.

warp: To bend, twist, or turn from a straight line as a piece of lumber, when improperly seasoned, may become curved,

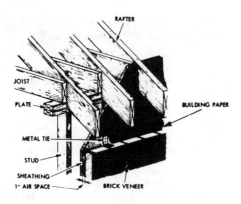

Fig. 621. Metal ties are used to hold the masonry wall to the frame superstructure.

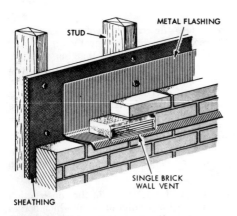

Fig. 622. Brick walls may be vented by wall vents.

twisted, or turned from a straight flat form; a defect or permanent distortion of a timber from its true form; usually caused by exposure to heat or moisture. See Fig. 623.

warped: In woodworking, a term applied to any piece of timber which has been twisted out of shape and permanently distorted during the process of seasoning.

warren truss: A form of girder or truss which consists of upper and lower mem-

bers connected by other members which are inclined alternately in opposite directions. Also called *warren girder.*

wash: In building, the upper surface of material or a construction member which is given a slope outward and downward so it will shed water, as the *wash* of a window sill. Hence, any structure or receptacle shaped so as to receive and carry off water.

washer: A small, metal piece or disc, usually flat, used under a nut to distribute pressure or between jointing members to insure a tight fitting joint.

waste: In construction work, the excess material, such as wood or stone, cut away on any given piece of work; also called *spoil.* In plumbing, material carried away as sewerage.

waste pipe: In plumbing, a pipe for carrying off waste or superfluous fluid; the outlet pipe at the bottom of a lavatory, bathtub, or sink.

waste stack: Vertical pipe that leads from waste pipes to the building drain. A *soil pipe* or *soil stack.*

waste trap: In plumbing, a device designed for use in connection with waste pipes leading from sinks and lavatories to prevent the escape of sewage gas from the *waste pipe.*

water bar: A strip of material inserted in a joint between wood and stone of a window sill to prevent or bar the passage of water from rain or snow.

water closet: A room equipped with toilet fixtures and facilities.

water hammer: A noise which develops in plumbing water supply lines when faucets are turned off because there is no cushion provided for the sudden change in pressure.

water joint: In stonework, a joint protected from rain and snow by sloping the surface of the stone away from the wall, so it will shed water easily.

water level: This is a light (rubber or plastic) hose, usually ⅜″ or ½″ inside diameter. In each end of the hose, a glass tube

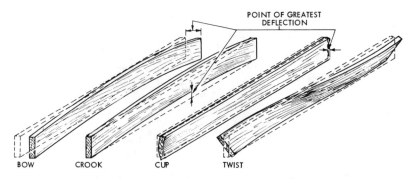

POINT OF GREATEST DEFLECTION

BOW   CROOK   CUP   TWIST

Fig. 623. Various kinds of warp in wood: bow, crook, cup and twist.

about 12″ long is placed. To use the level, place the middle of one glass over the mark that is to be leveled around the room. Hold the other glass at about the same height and at the place where the next level mark is needed. Fig. 624 shows a water level.

water lime: A lime or cement which will harden under water; hydraulic cement.

water main: Water supply pipe in the street which serves as a community pipe.

water of capillarity: In building, the moisture drawn up from the soil into the walls of a building by capillary action.

water of convenience: Water added to the mix over and above the water of necessity to make fresh concrete workable.

water of necessity: Least amount of water required to hydrate cement.

water-pipe fittings: Cast-iron pipes used for conveying water or gas are connected by various types of fittings, consisting of tees, elbows, curves, and other special types.

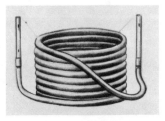

Fig. 624. Water level.

water putty: In woodworking, a powder which, when mixed with water, makes an excellent filler for cracks and nail holes. It is not suitable for glazing purposes.

water reducer: An admixture that maintains the workability of fresh concrete with a reduced amount of water.

water seal: In plumbing, the water contained in a trap to prevent the flow of air, foul odors, or gas from one side of the trap to the other side. See Fig. 454, page 351.

watershed: A projecting sloping member fitted around a building to throw rain water away from the wall. Same as *water table.* See Figs. 55, 625.

water stain: In wood finishing, a stain which consists of coloring matter dissolved in water.

water table: A ledge or slight projection of the masonry or wood construction on the outside of a foundation wall, or just above, to protect the foundation from rain by throwing water away from the wall. Also called a drip cap or drip strip. See Fig. 55, page 47, and Fig. 625, page 476.

waterproof cement: A cement which, when set, is watertight.

waterproofing: Coating with any material that will prevent the passage of moisture or water.

waterproof paper: A special treated paper that retains moisture and is used for curing fresh concrete.

477

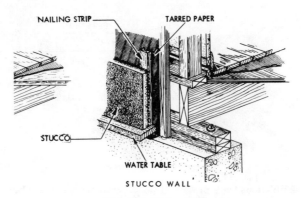

Fig. 625. Water table.

waterstop: In concrete masonry, thin sheet of rubber, plastic, or other material inserted in a construction joint to obstruct the seeping of water through the joint.

watt: The unit of electrical power. Amps × Volts = Watts. For example, 10 amps × 120 volts equals 1,200 watts.

wave ornament: A decorative form of flowing curves, regularly repeated, used by the Greeks in classic architecture; usually a band of frieze.

wavy grain: Wood in which the fibers, when taken collectively, form waves or undulations.

W beam: A steel beam with wide flanges used in structural work. Formerly called *wide flange* beam or WF.

weather: A term applied to any change in the condition of wood, stone, or other building materials due to exposure to the weather.

weather bar: A strip of material, such as galvanized iron, set in the joint between the wood and stone sills of a window to prevent the penetration of water from rain or snow; same as *water bar.*

weatherboards: Boards shaped so as to be specially adaptable for overlapping at the joints to prevent rain or other moisture from passing through the wall; also called *siding.* See Fig. 531, page 403.

weather cap: In electrical work, a metal cap to exclude moisture from an exterior electrical conduit.

weather strip: A piece of metal, wood, or other material used to cover joints around doors and windows to prevent drafts and to keep out rain and snow. A typical weather strip is shown in Fig. 627.

weather tiling: Tiles hung on battens to surface such as a wall. See *tile hanging,* page 453.

weathered: In masonry, stonework which has been cut with sloped surfaces so it will shed water from rain or snow. See *water joint.* In carpentry, a term applied to lumber which has been seasoned in the open air, page 476.

weathered joint: In masonry, a mortar joint formed as a plain cut joint, finished with the trowel after the mortar has slightly stiffened. A water-shedding, low-cost joint. See Fig. 626.

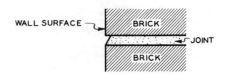

Fig. 626. Weather joint.

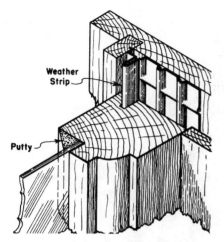

Fig. 627. Weather strip.

weathering: A slope given to the top of cornices, window sills, and various moldings to throw off rain water.

weathertight: In building construction, a type of joint which does not permit the passing through of wind, water, heat, or cold.

web: In steel construction, the wide part of a beam between flanges. Also, a diagonal support member in a truss. (See Fig. 610.) In architecture, a thin plate or panel, as one of the panels in a rib-and-panel vault.

web member: Secondary members of a truss contained between chords. See Fig. 610, page 464.

webbing: In building construction, the relatively slender vertical part or parts of an S beam or built-up girder, such as a box girder, separating the two flanges.

webbed metal studding: Open web steel studs used in partitions. Generally the partitions are non-load bearing and the studs are on 24 inch centers. A channel runner or track is fastened to the floor and to the ceiling with nails, screws, or powder actuated fasteners. The studs are clipped into place. See Fig. 628.

wedge: A V-shaped piece of wood used to produce pressure on a structural member. See Fig. 317, page 240. Also, a V-shaped piece of metal, usually steel, used for splitting wood, rock, or other material. A V-shaped piece of metal driven into the head end of the handle of a hammer to tighten the handle in the eye. See Fig. 127, page 101.

wedge socket: See *cable attachments.*

weephole: In masonry cavity or veneer walls, an opening through the mortar joints at regular intervals to allow for drainage of condensed moisture. See Fig. 629. Also, a drain through retaining walls.

weld: A joint which is formed by welding.

welded wire fabric: Heavy steel wire welded together in a grid pattern; used for reinforcing concrete slabs.

welding joints: Position of two or more members to be joined, as in Fig. 630.

welding plastics: Plastic welding is a combination of heat and pressure. The plastic sheets to be joined and the welding rod are heated with a stream of hot air. The rod is pressed down into the softened plastic "V" joint and fuses with the sheets.

welding position: Location of the piece to be welded. The four main positions are horizontal, flat, overhead, and vertical. See Fig. 631.

welding symbols: Symbols used to designate the desired weld. See Fig. 632.

well: In architecture, an open, unoccupied area bounded on all sides by the walls of a building passing through at least one floor; commonly used to supply light and air for stairways and interior spaces.

well opening: The opening in the floor to permit passage from one floor to another.

wellhole: An open space such as a shaft or well in a building, as for a staircase; also, the open space about which a circular stairs turns.

western framing: In building construction, a method of framing where the studding of each story rests on a sort of sill, as opposed to the *balloon* type of framing. Also called *platform framing.* See Fig. 441, page 338.

479

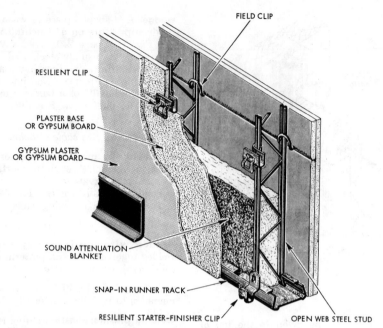

FIELD CLIP

RESILIENT CLIP

PLASTER BASE
OR GYPSUM BOARD

GYPSUM PLASTER
OR GYPSUM BOARD

SOUND ATTENUATION
BLANKET

SNAP-IN RUNNER TRACK

RESILIENT STARTER-FINISHER CLIP

OPEN WEB STEEL STUD

Fig. 628. Open web stud system uses clips to hold gypsum board. (U.S. Gypsum Co.)

wet coverings: Materials such as burlap, sand, earth, hay, straw, cotton mats, etc., used to cure concrete. These materials are effective only if they completely cover the concrete slab and are kept constantly moist.

wet rot: A term used by woodworkers for decay of lumber or wood, due particularly to moisture and warmth.

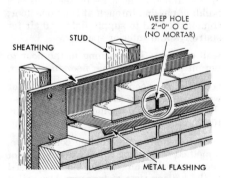

WEEP HOLE
2'-0" O C
(NO MORTAR)

STUD

SHEATHING

METAL FLASHING

Fig. 629. Weep hole.

whaler: A horizontal bracing member used in form construction. Also known as a *ranger* or *waler*. See Fig. 545, page 413.

wheel window: A circular window with mullions or arms radiating from the center, as the spokes of a wheel.

whetstone: A natural or artificial stone used for sharpening the cutting edge of tools.

white coat: In plastering, the hard, white top coat on a plastered wall. Usually this coat consists of a composition of plaster of Paris and lime putty, to which marble dust is sometimes added. Gypsum plasters may be used for hard coatings.

white print: A diazo reproduction process that gives a positive type print (dark lines on a white background).

white spots: In painting, white dots or specks which appear in the final film of paint on a surface. These spots may be

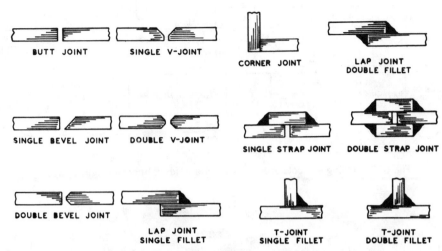

Fig. 630. A variety of joints can be used in welding.

due to the rushing of a job through too hastily or to the sealing in of moisture.

whitewash: A composition for covering walls where frequent applications are necessary. It is prepared by slaking lump lime with about one-third of its weight of water and then adding sufficient water to make a milk.

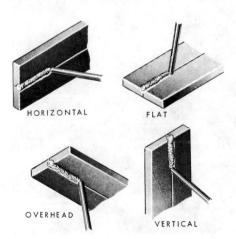

Fig. 631. There are four main welding positions.

whorl: In furniture making, a spiral scroll ornamental design.

wicket: A small door set within a larger door; also, a window or similar opening closed by a grating through which communication takes place, as a cashier's window.

wide flange beam: See *W beam,* page 478.

winches: Basically, these are drums or rollers which are turned by a crank through a system of reduction gears. Many have a gripping piece, called a dog, which engages a tooth on a gear to hold the load in place.

wind: A bend, a turn, a warp, or twist from a straight or parallel line; the warp or twist in a piece of wood is often spoken of as *wind.*

wind beam: A beam used as a wind brace between adjoining roof trusses. See *wind brace.*

wind brace: Reinforcing member, a strut, used as a brace to strengthen a frame or structure against the wind. Fig. 633 shows wind bracing used in a modern skyscraper. Wind braces are also placed at columns to reduce bending of the structure due to high wind forces.

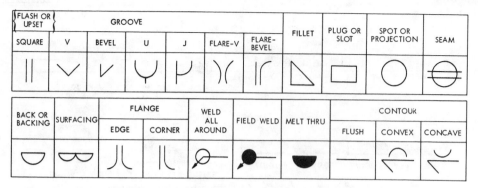

FLASH OR UPSET	GROOVE						FILLET	PLUG OR SLOT	SPOT OR PROJECTION	SEAM
SQUARE	V	BEVEL	U	J	FLARE-V	FLARE-BEVEL				
||	⌵	⌵	Y	Y	)(	℩⌒	◸	▭	○	⊖

BACK OR BACKING	SURFACING	FLANGE		WELD ALL AROUND	FIELD WELD	MELT THRU	CONTOUR		
		EDGE	CORNER				FLUSH	CONVEX	CONCAVE
◡	◡◡	⌐⌐	⌐∟	⌀	●	◗	—	⌒	⌣

Fig. 632. Welding symbols used to designate welds. (American Welding Society)

Fig. 633. A skyscraper 100 stories tall uses heavy windbraces in exterior walls. The John Hancock Building, Chicago. (Progressive Architecture).

wind load: In building construction, the estimated pressure or force exerted upon a structure by the wind, especially the wind pressure which must be provided for when constructing the roof of a building.

winders: Treads of steps used in a winding staircase or where stairs are carried around curves or angles. *Winders* are cut wider at one end than at the other so they can be arranged in a circular form. See Fig. 563, page 426.

winding stair: A circular staircase which changes directions by means of winders or a landing and winders. The wellhole is relatively wide and the balustrade follows the curve with only a newel post at the bottom. See Fig. 563, page 426.

windlass: A device for hoisting weights, consisting usually of a horizontal cylinder turned by a lever or crank. A cable, attached to the weight to be lifted, winds around the cylinder as the crank is turned, thus raising the load to whatever position is desired.

window: An opening in an outside wall, other than a door, which provides for natural light and ventilation. Such an opening is covered by transparent material inserted in a frame conveniently located for admitting sunlight and constructed so that it can be opened to admit air. See *double-hung window,* Figs. 198 and 497.

window apron: In building, a plain or molded finish piece put on to cover the rough edge of plastering below the stool of a window.

window bar: A wood or metal bar in a window, as division between the panes of glass, sometimes called *muntin;* also, a bar for fastening a window or shutter; a bar, usually of metal, across a window to prevent persons going out or coming in through the window.

window casing: A finish or trim for a window opening.

window catch: A lock or fastener for securing a window sash in a fixed position.

window details: In carpentry those parts of the building which pertain to the framing and finishing of the window, including the jamb and head details. In drafting a section taken through the window to show the details of the window. See Fig. 198, page 154.

window frame: The lining for a window opening, including the two side-pulley stiles, the head jamb or yoke, and the sill. See Fig. 497, page 383.

window head: In architecture, a term applied to the upper portion of a window frame. See Fig. 198, page 154.

window jack: A portable platform which fits over a window sill projecting outward beyond the sill; used principally by painters.

window jamb: In architecture, a term applied to the middle portion of a window frame. See Fig. 198, page 154.

window lift: A device attached to a window sash by means of which the window can be raised; also called *sash lift.*

window lock: A fastening device secured to the meeting rails of the sashes of a double-hung window, serving to fasten both sashes in a closed position. Also called *sash lock.*

window opening: Any open space left in a wall where a window is to be placed. See Fig. 497, page 383.

window pull: A handle commonly mounted on a metal plate; designed for attaching to a window sash to facilitate the opening and closing of the window. Also called *sash pull.*

window sash: The frame in which the window lights are set. See Figs. 497 and 634.

window schedule: A table, usually located on elevation drawings, which gives the symbols (number or letter) for each type of window. This code symbol is placed on the work drawing by each particular window. The quantity, type, rough opening dimensions, sash size, and the manufacturer's number are also placed in the window schedule. A "remarks" column gives information unique to each window type, such as the kind of glass, etc. See also *schedule,* page 387.

window seat: A seat built in the recess of a window or in front of a window.

window shutter: A movable covering for a window, to shut out light, give protection, and to add temporary insulation. See *blind,* page 52, and *shutter,* page 402.

window sill: In architecture, a term applied to the bottom portion of a window frame. See Fig. 198, page 154, and Fig. 634.

window space: The area or amount of wall surface taken up by the windows of a room or of a building.

window stool: In a window trim, the nosing directly above the apron; the horizontal member of the window finish which forms a stool for the side casings and conceals the *window sill.*

window stop: In a window frame, a nar-

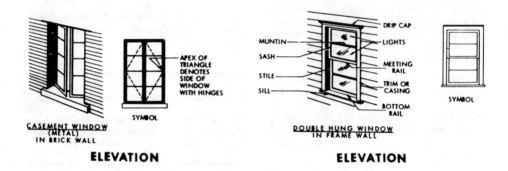

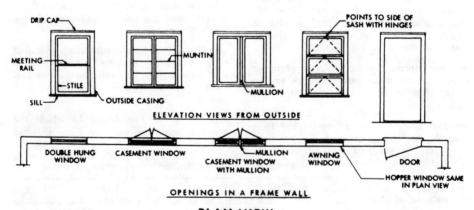

Fig. 634. Window symbols. Many lines are omitted when symbols are drawn. Wood windows have wider sash parts than metal windows. Windows in frame walls have wood trim. Windows in masonry walls have narrow brick mold. The side which has the hinges on swinging windows is indicated by the apex (or point) of a dashed triangle. (Note the swing symbol for a casement window.) A stationary window with no provision for opening is called a "fixed sash window". Locks and hinges on doors are not generally shown.

row, wooden strip which holds the sash in position in the frame.

window symbols: Standardized symbols used by architects and builders to designate the location and types of windows to be installed in a building. See Fig. 634.

window trim: The interior finish of a window opening; also called *window casing.*

window wall: An outside wall of which a large portion is glass. Glass area may consist of one or more windows. A window wall may be made up entirely of windows.

windproof: In building, a type of construction which prevents the passage of wind through joints or materials; the same as *windtight.*

windshake: A defect in wood, so-called because of the belief that it is caused by wrenching of the growing tree by the wind. Since there is a separation of the annual rings from each other around the trunk of the tree, this defect is cuplike in appearance and is sometimes known as *cupshake.* See Fig. 635.

wing: In building, a term applied to a section, or addition, extending out from the main part of a structure.

winning: In brick manufacture, the quarrying or mining of the raw materials.

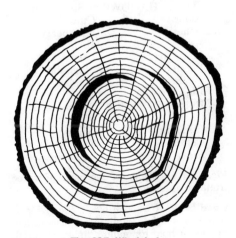

Fig. 635. Windshake.

wiped joint: In plumbing, a joint formed between two pieces of lead pipe. Molten lead is poured upon the joint until the two pieces of pipe are of the right temperature. The joint is then wiped up by hand with a moleskin or cloth pad while the solder is in a plastic condition. See Fig. 636.

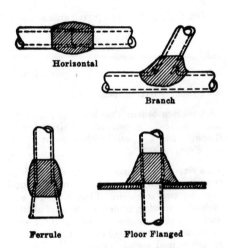

Horizontal

Branch

Ferrule   Floor Flanged

Fig. 636. Wiped joints.

wire brad: A nail with a small head, used on finished surfaces where the head must be concealed. See Fig. 389, page 296.

wire connectors: In electrical wiring, connectors used to join two wires. See Fig. 637. Also called a *wire nut.*

wire gage: A gage used for measuring the diameter of wire or the thickness of sheet metal; usually consists of a notched metal plate having a series of gaged slots of various widths in its edges. The slots are numbered according to the sizes of the wire or sheet metal to be measured. See Fig. 15, page 14.

wire lath: Wire netting used as a plaster base. See *metal lath,* Fig. 375, page 283.

wire mesh: See *welded wire fabric,* page 479.

wire nail: Any one of several types of nails made of wire, especially those used in finishing work.

Fig. 637. Unsoldered pigtail splices are sometimes made before applying wire connectors.

wire nut: See *wire connectors,* page 485.

wire rope: See *cable,* page 80.

wire texture brush: This brush is primarily used to texture cement by dragging it through the applied finishes before it is set. See Fig. 638.

wire ties: Short lengths of wire in various shapes and gages for reinforcing the bond between two members. They may be embedded in mortar, nailed, or twisted around and between masonry, wood, or metal. Wire ties are usually of cement coated steel or galvanized metal.

wiring layout: In drafting, the plans showing the location of electrical outlets, switches, fixtures, and wiring.

Fig. 638. Scoring the surface, using a wire brush.

withe: In masonry, a single vertical wall of brick, a single-brick thick part of a wall. Also spelled *wythe.*

wood: A product of trees used for construction purposes when sawed up into lumber, such as boards, planks, and other similar materials.

Trees commonly cut into lumber and timber products are divided into two broad groups: *hardwood* and *softwood.*

The common commercial softwoods and hardwoods of the United States are:

SOFTWOODS

Cedars and junipers	Larch
Cypress	Pines
Douglas fir	Redwood
White fir	Tamarack
Hemlocks	Spruce
	Yew

HARDWOODS

Alder	Gums
Ashes	Hackberry
Aspen	Hickories
Basswood	Locust
Beech	Magnolia
Birches	Maples
Buckeye	Oaks
Butternut	Sycamore
Cherry	Walnut
Chestnut	Willow
Cottonwood	Yellow
Elms	poplar

Fig. 24, page 21, shows the parts of a tree trunk cross section.

wood brick: A wooden block, the size and shape of a brick; built into brickwork to provide a hold for nailing finish material. A *nailing block.*

wood finishing: In carpentry, preparing a wood surface to receive a finish and applying paint, stain, or varnish; also polishing a surface when certain kinds of finish are desired.

wood chisels. The *socket wood chisel* or *firming chisel* is used in framing and other rough carpentry work and is designed to withstand a great deal of pounding. A cutting edge ranging from 1½ to 2 inches is recommended. For finer work, such as fitting locks, putting on hinges, and for cabinet work, a more delicate *lightweight wood chisel* or *finish chisel* is *needed*. See Fig. 639.

wood flooring: Standard dressed and matched flooring.

wood-frame construction: In building, a type of construction in which the structural members are of wood or are dependent upon a wood frame for support. Same as *frame construction.*

wood gutter: In building construction, an eaves trough built entirely of wood. It may be of one piece or be built up of different pieces.

wood lath: A strip of wood usually measuring four feet in length and one and one-half inches in width; used in the past as a foundation for plaster.

wood moldings: Trim members consisting of moldings which are entirely of wood. Various designs carried in stock by lumber dealers are shown in Fig. 640.

wood patternmaking: In carpentry, making plans for patterns out of wood, as a *rafter pattern.*

wood rays: In a cross section of a log, cells which appear as rays passing radially from the center or heart of the log to the bark. Also called *medullary rays.* See Fig. 24, page 21.

wood screws: Wood fasteners of various types and sizes, ranging from No. 0 to 30 and in length from ¼ inch to 6 inches. Length is measured from largest bearing diameter of head to the point of the screw. Threads extend for seven-tenths of the length, beginning at the point. Screws are made in oval-, round-, and flat-headed types, while gimlet points are standard. Standardized types of screws used in the building trade are shown in Figs. 514 and 515, page 394.

wood turning: The process of shaping pieces of wood or blocks into various forms and fashions by means of a lathe.

wood veneers: Sheets of flexible or rigid wood for surfacing plywood panels and for other uses are available in a wide variety of woods and grains. New adhesives simplify their application and help make installation comparatively inexpensive.

woodwork: Interior fittings of wood, such as moldings and staircases; also, work done in or with wooden objects or parts made of wood.

workability agent: Fly ash, entrained air, or certain organic materials used as an admixture to make fresh concrete easier

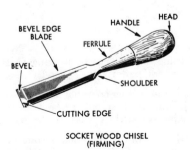

SOCKET WOOD CHISEL
(FIRMING)

LIGHTWEIGHT WOOD CHISEL
(FINISH)

Fig. 639. Wood chisels.

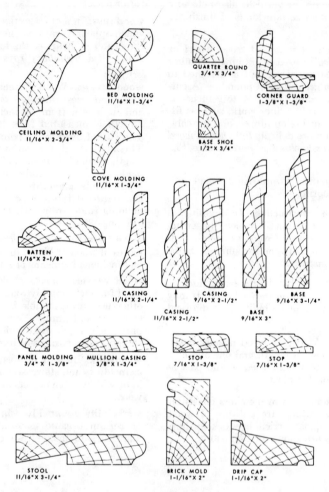

Fig. 640. Wood moldings.

to place, consolidate, and finish with a reduced amount of water.

workable: Fresh concrete that can be easily mixed, placed, and finished.

work edge: In the operation of squaring up a board, the first edge to be finished by planing is called the *work edge.*

worked lumber: Lumber which in addition to being dressed has been matched, shiplapped, or patterned.

work end: In the operation of squaring up a board, the first end to be finished by planing is called the *work end.*

work face: In the operation of squaring up a board, the first board surface to be finished by planing is called the *work face.*

working drawing: A drawing containing all dimensions and information necessary to carry a job through to successful completion.

working edge: In planing a piece of work, one edge is trued square with the *work face* as an aid in truing the other surfaces square. This is known as the *working edge;* same as *work edge.*

workman's compensation law: Under this if a worker suffers an "industrial injury" or illness on the job, he is entitled to compensation payments to partially offset his loss of wages.

wrapping: Reinforcing bars or mesh surrounding a structural steel column or beam to reinforce concrete or plaster fireproofing.

wreath: The curved section of a stair rail, curved in both the vertical and horizontal planes; used to join the side of a newel post to the ascending run of the handrail.

wreath piece: In stair building, the curved section of the handrail string of a curved or winding stair. Any ornamental design intertwined into a circular form.

wrecking bar: A steel bar about ¾ of an inch in diameter and 24 to 30 inches in length, used for prying and pulling nails. One end of the bar is slightly bent, with a chisel-shaped tip, and the other end U-shaped with a claw tip for pulling nails; sometimes called *ripping bar* or *pinch bar.* See Fig. 425, page 325.

wrecking strip: In concrete formwork, small piece or panel fitted into formwork assembly in such a way that it can be easily removed ahead of main panels or forms, making it easier to strip those major form components.

wrench: A tool used to tighten a nut or bolt by the exertion of a twisting strain. See *adjustable wrench.* See Fig. 641.

wrench head: A type of head for a bolt or screw; usually square or hexagonal and shaped so it can be gripped easily by the jaws of a wrench. See *machine bolt,* page 275.

wrinkling: In painting, a wrinkled or gathered film which sometimes appears on a finished surface. *Wrinkling* may be caused by applying heavy coats of paint, by abnormal heating or humidity, or by the application of an elastic film over a surface.

wrought iron: A commercial form of iron which is malleable, tough, and relatively soft and can be easily magnetized; iron metal in its purest form.

W truss: A type of roof truss commonly used for short spans because of the shortness of its struts, which makes it economical and prevents waste. See Fig. 610.

wye: In plumbing, a fitting or branch pipe, either of cast or wrought iron, which has

Pipe Wrench

Monkey Wrench

Open End Wrench

Fig. 641. Typical wrenches.

one side outlet at any angle except a right angle; usually a 45-degree angle unless otherwise specified.

wythe: Single vertical wall of brick. See *withe,* page 486.

X

X-brace: Diagonal bracing. See *wind brace,* page 481. See Fig. 633.

X mark: In carpentry, a mark made by a workman to indicate where certain structural members are to be placed; also, sometimes used to indicate the face side of a structural member.

Y

yardage: A term applied to cubic yards of earth which are excavated. It can be applied, also, to square measure, as *yardage* of plaster.

yard catch basin: A receptacle used to catch surface water which drains from cemented courts, driveways, and dooryards.

yard lumber: The lumber known as *yard lumber* is less than 5 inches in thickness and is intended for general building purposes.

Y branch: In plumbing, a pipe connection shaped like the capital letter Y, used where, for any reason, a change in direction of the pipe is required.

year ring: One of the clearly defined rings in a cross section of a tree trunk showing the amount of annual growth of the tree. Each ring represents one year of growth; also called *growth ring* and *annual ring.* The rings are made up of cells or tubes which convey sap through the tree. Year rings are shown in Fig. 24, page 21.

Y fitting: In pipe work of any kind, a short, specialized section, one end of which branches or divides, usually at an angle of 45°, forming two separate openings resembling the letter Y. In some instances, especially in plumbing, a door or removable plug is fitted in one branch of the Y, and it is used as a cleanout. See Fig. 112, page 89.

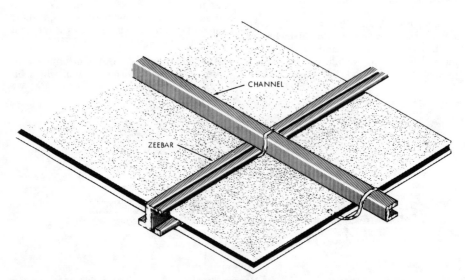

CHANNEL

ZEEBAR

Fig. 642. Supporting tiles during installation. Use temporary clips when possible to provide support for tiles until next zeebar is inserted. This prevents bending of zeebar flange.

yield strength: The load limit to which a steel bar can be stretched and still return to its original length.

yoke: In architecture, a term applied to the horizontal top member of a window frame, the *head*. In plumbing, a Y-shaped fitting for a soil-pipe connection.

Y tile: In plumbing, a Y-shaped tile used in a drain or sewer pipe. See Y branch, page 490.

Z

Z bar: A heavy wire fabrication shaped in the form of the letter Z, usually about four by six inches in size. See Fig. 376. Such ties are used to bind together the two separate sections of a cavity wall, the ends of each tie being embedded in the horizontal mortar joint of both tiers at intervals of 24″. Also, a specially shaped channel iron used for installing ceiling panels, spelled *zeebar* (Fig. 642).

zeebar: Special channel iron used for installing ceiling panels. See Fig. 642.

zigzag molding: A chevron or a series of chevrons; a molding running in a zigzag line. See *chevron,* page 95.

zigzag rule: A measuring device made up in six-inch sections, taking its name from the manner of opening and closing. Also called *folding rule*. See Fig. 263, page 201.

zone controls: A control system which uses two or more thermostats.

zoned heating: Maintaining different temperatures for different areas or zones.

zoning: A term applied to the division of a certain political subdivision into districts which may have different types of regulation. Such a condition is brought about by local ordinance under the police power of a state, granted by specific legislation commonly called an *enabling act*. Zoning laws pertain to the use of land in a particular area.

zonolite concrete: A form of concrete which acts as an insulator.

Legal Terms

A

abstract: A summary of important items in a document, such as a deed to real property. In the building trades, a term applied to a concise, itemized list of quantities and qualities of materials prepared for use in connection with a builder's contract.

abstract of title: A summary of all the successive conveyances upon which a person's title to a piece of land rests, such as deeds, wills, or other legal proceedings.

accrued depreciation: The falling in value of an asset, such as property, during a given period of time or up to a given date. Such depreciation may be due to normal wear and tear, action of the elements, inadequacy, obsolescence, or to other causes. The term is also applied to the difference between the valuation on the date of appraisal and the estimated cost of replacement of the property in new condition.

acreage: An area, or portion of land, which is measured in acres. Land which has been subdivided into city lots is measured in front feet or square feet.

air rights: A privilege, or right, protected by law to build in, occupy, or otherwise use a portion of air space above real property at a stated elevation, in conjunction with definitely located spaces on the ground surface, for the foundation and supporting columns.

amenity: An agreeable situation, or satisfaction, derived from the ownership or occupancy of a property due to its excellent characteristic qualities and agreeable surroundings. When appraising property, the term "amenities" is most often used in connection with satisfactions and considerations which commonly are strongly appealing to prospective buyers for ownership occupany.

amortization: In finance, the extinguishing of a debt by means of a sinking fund; in accounting, a term used when referring to the scheduled liquidation of a long-term debt.

amortized mortgage: A systematic loan reduction plan. Monthly payments are made to retire the mortgage. These payments include interest, payment on principal, taxes, assessments, and insurance premiums.

appraisal: The fixing of a price or value on a property through the process of making estimates and valuations pertaining to the property.

arterial highway: A main thoroughfare which is a primary channel, with tributaries, for vehicular traffic. Also, road or street.

assessed value: An estimated price placed on property by an authorized assessment agency. Usually the assessed value which appears on the assessment roll is considered to be much less than the real value of the property.

assessment: A tax levied against property to meet some specific expense; also a ratification placed upon a property for taxing purposes.

B

balloon-payment mortgage loan: A term applied to a type of mortgage which, by its terms, provides for periodic payments, as partial liquidation of the loan before the date of maturity. Sometimes the balance due at maturity and paid on that date is called the *balloon payment.*

base line: A term applied to a definitely located arbitrary line used for reference-control purposes; also, any imaginary east-and-west line on the earth's surface from which township lines are established.

blight: A term applied to a deteriorating influence or condition which affects the value or use of a property or real estate. A depleted tenement-house district or any type of *hazardous-use unit* may be considered a *blight* on the neighboring real estate or property.

building grade: The ground level, or elevation of a building, established by the authority which has jurisdiction over a particular building for the purpose of regulating the height of such a building.

business district: An area set apart for commercial purposes in a city or town. Often such an area is limited, defined, and regulated by city codes and zoning laws.

C

call loan: A loan which terminates upon the demand of either the borrower or lender; a type of *demand mortgage loan.*

cash tenant: A tenant farmer who pays his rent with cash instead of a share in the crop.

certificate of occupancy: A written statement signed by a building authority, certifying: (1) a structure meets all requirements set forth in existing ordinances, or (2) a structure or designated land area may be used lawfully for specified purposes.

certificate of title: is the assurance that the title to the property is unmistakably in the purchaser's name.

chattel: Any article or item of property, movable or immovable, except real estate or a freehold. *Chattels* are classified as *real* or *personal.* If a chattel includes an interest involving land, as a lease or growing crops, it is known as a *chattel real; a chattel personal* refers only to personal property, such as money, goods, or livestock—sometimes a slave. A *chattel mortgage* is a mortgage on personal property as distinct from a mortgage on *real estate.*

chattel mortgage: A mortgage secured by tangible personal property, as distinct from a real-estate mortgage. See *chattel.*

closing costs: Cost paid by the buyer as a fee charged by the lenders for making the mortgage.

common or joint services: A combination of service systems designed to provide lighting, heating, plumbing, and air conditioning for several families occupying the same building or several buildings.

common passageway: An open space, provided by deed or agreement, between two buildings, affording an unobstructed entranceway or exit "forever".

completion: In the building trade, the act of bringing a structure to that point of construction where it is physically ready for use and occupancy, legally considered a completed condition.

condemnation: A pronouncement by a legally constituted authority, provided with police power, declaring a structure unfit for use or occupancy because of its threatened danger to persons or other property. Also, the judicial exercise of the right of *eminent domain* by the taking over of private property for public use.

construction loan: In the building trades, a loan of money secured by a negotiable paper, such as a bond, promissory note and mortgage, or trust deed. The money obtained through the loan is intended to defray the cost of the building to be erected. Usually the money is advanced to the borrower in specified sums during the progress of construction. After completion of the structure, often such a loan is converted into a term loan.

corner lot: A lot which abuts upon two or more streets or highways at the point of their intersection.

D

dead-end street: A public thoroughfare having one end closed.

debenture: A term often applied to a type of loan bond or unsecured promissory note and is not a specific lien upon the real property of the issuer. Collection of such a loan bond can be made only through ordinary action of law.

deed: A written legal instrument that transfers the title of property from one person to another. *Warranty Deed* is a guarantee by the seller that the title is flawless. *Quitclaim Deed* guarantees nothing—it merely undertakes to transfer the title. The deed has (or presumes to have) properly described the property.

deed restriction: A statement, included in the deed to a piece of land, placing limitations upon the use of property.

demand mortgage loan: A type of loan which is repayable upon the demand of the lender; a *call loan.*

depreciation: A decline in value; reduction of worth.

differential rental: A variable charge in the rate of rent which is not determined by the size and desirability of the living unit but is adjusted according to the ability to pay and the need of each tenant family.

direct-reduction mortgage loan: A type of mortgage loan which provides, by its terms, for the crediting of any payments by the mortgagor: (1) to accrued interest upon the outstanding principal balance as of the date payment is made; and (2) to the outstanding principal balance of the mortgage itself.

E

earnest money: Payment made to the seller, for the purpose of binding the contract, as evidence he is in earnest about buying the property.

easement: In law, a privilege vested or acquired which one person may have in the land of another. Such a right being held by someone other than the owner who holds title to the land. The right or privilege to use land, other than as a tenant, for some specific purpose.

economic rent: In the building trades, a term applied to a rate of rent which is sufficient to cover all costs of maintenance and operation of the building and, in addition, yield a reasonable return on the investment of the owner. In estimating *economic rent,* the life of the building must be taken into consideration.

eminent domain: The right of a sovereign power, such as a state, to condemn and appropriate private property for public use.

encumbrance: Any right or interest in land which diminishes the value of the fee but does not prevent the conveyance of the fee by the owner. *Encumbrances* such as taxes, mortgages, and judgments are known as *liens;* restrictions, reservations, and easements are encumbrances but are not liens.

equity: An interest, commonly expressed in money, which an owner has in property over and above all liens against the property.

escheat: The reverting of land to the state due to the failure of persons who are legally entitled to hold the property.

escrow: Money and papers held by a third party until the conditions in the contract are fulfilled.

estate: A person's possessions or property, consisting of land or buildings or both.

estate in fee simple: An estate of inheritance in land, without limitations to any particular class of heirs, which endures until the extinction of all lineal and collateral heirs of the owner. Such an estate may be freely conveyed by its owner. A term also applied to the longest possible estate.

estate in land: The ownership or interest a person has in land.

estate of freehold: A term applied to any one of the three types of possessory interests a person may have in land, as fee simple, fee tail, and estate for life. The duration of estates of freehold is considered to be indefinite; any other form of an estate is referred to as *less than freehold.*

existing home mortgage: A mortgage secured by a dwelling which has been in existence for one year or more, as of the date of application for the mortgage loan.

F

FHA loans: An FHA loan is *insured by the government* against default. As with the GI loan, a private lending agency grants the loan, but the federal government insures that the *lender* will not lose on the loan. The loan is insured only when *both* the credit standing of the borrower and the construction standards of the house are satisfactory. (The construction is checked periodically by an inspector from the FHA.) These standards enable much larger loans (higher loan to value ratio) to be granted by the lender because of the protection against loss. Thus, smaller down payments are required. The borrower pays an insurance premium of $\frac{1}{2}$ of 1 percent, computed monthly, on the outstanding principal. In addition, an application fee is charged by the FHA. Both "government

type" loans take much longer to obtain due to the extensive investigative measures which must be conducted.

federal savings and loan association: A type of savings, loan, and building association chartered under the Federal Home Loan Bank Act (1932).

fee: An estate of inheritance, either fee simple or fee tail; also, remuneration for services, as a *lawyer's fee.*

fee simple absolute: An estate of indefinite duration and inheritable without conditions or limitations; also, the largest possible interest in property or an estate, subject only to the limitations of *eminent domain,* police power, taxation, and *escheat.*

fee tail: An estate of inheritance which is limited to a particular class of heirs, such as lineal descendants of the person to whom the fee is granted.

first mortgage: A written instrument which has priority claim over all subordinate mortgages or instruments created for the same purpose on the same property.

foreclosure: After a certain number of mortgage defaults, the mortgagee, under the terms of the contract, has the right to sell the property in public auction to regain his investment.

franchise: A particular right or privilege conferred by grant of a sovereign authority, such as the state, upon a corporation or upon an individual.

freehold: A tenure of land or property which is unencumbered by lease and is held in absolute fee simple, limited fee simple, or fee tail.

freeway: A piece of land, similar to a roadway, restricted to use for rapid through traffic.

front of lot: In building, the end of a lot which borders on a street or highway. In case of a corner lot, the owner, with consent of the proper authority, may designate either the end or the side which borders on a street or highway as the front of his property.

frontage: The extent of land along a public highway, a stream, or a city lot; also, the extent of a building along a public street, road, or waterway.

full owner: Anyone having a legal title to a property which is free of encumbrances, such as liens.

G

GI loans: The GI loan is for veterans only. The maximum interest rate and the terms of the loan are controlled by the federal government. The down payment is less than other types of loans and the terms are longer. The government guarantees the lending institution a greater part of the loan in case of default. Private lending institutions make the loan; *the government does not lend the money.*

gore lot: Any lot which is triangular in shape.

government survey: A land survey authorized in 1775 by the Continental Congress and by later congressional acts and conducted in Alabama, Florida, Mississippi and all states west of the Mississippi River (except Texas) or north of the Ohio River. The land thus surveyed was divided into townships approximately six miles square.

ground rent: Money paid as compensation for the right to use improved or unimproved land, for a specified time, as a year or several years.

H

hazardous use units: Any building, or part of a building, designed, intended, or used for the purpose of any occupancy, having contents which are liable to burn rapidly or to cause explosions. The term is also applied to anything which is of a hazardous nature as designated in a building code.

homestead: Land, and the buildings thereon, occupied by the owner as a home. In most states, such a property is protected by statute and is exempt from seizure or attachment to satisfy a judgment rendered in favor of a creditor.

I

improvement: Any change made in a property which tends to increase its value, as the addition of a building for a home or other utility purposes. An *improvement* may be made by drainage and by removing unsightly objects or growths; any act which serves to add utility, beauty, or otherwise increases the value of the property.

improvements on land: Any addition to a site which tends to increase its value or utility, such as the erection of buildings and retaining walls; also the building of fences and driveways.

improvements to land: Buildings or facilities which, though not embraced within the boundaries of a property, add to its value and usefulness, such as water mains, sewers, street lighting, sidewalks, and curbs.

interest: The rent paid for money borrowed.

interior or inside lot: A property, or lot, which is bounded by a street or highway on only one side or end.

J

junior mortgage: A mortgage loan creating a claim subordinate to the claims previously created by a first mortgage on the same property; a second or third mortgage.

L

land: Ground, soil, or any portion of the earth's surface considered as subject to ownership, either public or private. Property which in fact or law is regarded as immovable.

land subdivision: A given area which has been divided into blocks or plots of ground, such as residential, commercial, industrial, or agricultural sites, with suitable streets, roadways, and open spaces. The term is also applied to the process of making such divisions of land areas.

lease: An agreement by which a person conveys real estate for life, or a specified term, for compensation, under certain specified conditions, to another person for use and occupancy.

lessee: A tenant under a lease.

lessor: One who conveys by lease.

lien: A legal charge against property which is made security for the payment of a debt or for the performance of an obligation.

limited fee simple: An estate in fee whose termination is governed by the occurrence of a stated event. The owner of such an estate is given free rights so long as certan conditions obtain.

littoral right: A privilege or legal right attached to land affected by waves or coastal currents, because of its proximity to, or its bordering on, a large body of water, such as a sea or a great lake.

lot: A term usually applied to a relatively small parcel of land which is a subdivision of a block of ground described by reference to a recorded plot and devoted to a certain use or occupied by a building.

lot line: An imaginary line which bounds a property as described in the title to the lot or property.

M

meridian: An imaginary circular line on the earth's surface which passes through the north and south poles and is used as a reference line when measuring longitude.

metes and bounds: A term used to define boundary lines when describing the location of land in terms of directions and distances from one or more points of reference.

monument: When applied to land ownership, a permanent marker, such as a boundary stone, locating a property line or corner.

mortgage: A contract under the terms of which property is conveyed, upon condition, as security for the payment of a debt or for the performance of a duty. A *mortgage* becomes a lien against the property for the same purpose.

mortgage risk rating: A term applied to the process of analyzing the chief factors of risk, which are undertaken when making a mortgage loan, and the rating to the mortgage in accordance with the risk involved in the loan transaction in connection with the insurance of the mortgage.

mortgagee: He who takes or receives a mortgage.

mortgagor: He who gives a mortgage.

N

new-home mortgage: A mortgage loan secured by a home which has been completed within twelve months prior to the date of acceptance of the mortgage or which is in process of construction as of that date or which is to be constructed.

note or bond: A written promise to repay the money borrowed.

O

obsolescence: A term applied to anything which is out of date or no longer current; obsolete. Impairment of a building resulting from a change in the design or from external influences which tend to make the property less desirable for continued use.

occupancy: Acquiring title to a property by taking possession of it; the act of taking over anything which has no owner.

on schedule: Payments which fall periodically on a set date.

owner: In building, one who possesses the legal right or title to a property; also, a firm or corporation having control as the authorized agent of property; a guardian or trustee having a vested or contingent interest in a property.

P

personal property: A term applied to possessions which are movable, such as livestock, household goods, and jewels, or other similar valuable objects; any property not classified as *real property*.

planting strip: A term applied to a narrow piece of land in residential areas, where trees, grass, shrubbery, or flowers may be grown. Usually such a strip of land is located between the sidewalks and a street, roadway, or drive. Sometimes such a strip of land is called a *parking strip,* but this is an incorrect term.

principal meridian: Any one of the established meridians in the United States which serves as the meridian of reference for subdividing public lands, as a meridian from which range lines are established.

property: In a restricted sense, a term usually applied to a plot or parcel of land, with or without buildings or other improvements, the owner of which is protected by law.

property line: An imaginary boundary line between plots of land such as lots or farms. The location of a *property line* is recorded in the legal description of a piece of land.

purchase agreement: Written document which contains all essential terms and conditions of the sale, and the memorandum of agreement between seller and purchaser. This is executed pending examination of the title and performance of other conditions affecting the transfer of property.

purchase-money mortgage: A mortgage covering property accepted by the seller of the property as part payment of the purchase price.

Q

quantity survey: An inventory compiled for the purpose of estimating the amount of materials and labor required to complete a construction operation.

quitclaim deed: A written instrument, or deed, whereby a grantor releases whatever interest he possesses in the property granted without warranty to the grantee.

R

real property: A term applied to and synonymous with *real estate* which includes not only land but also the buildings, fences, sidewalks, and other improvements upon the land whose value would be impaired by the removal of such improvements. *Real property* also includes waters of the earth within the boundaries of the land; likewise minerals and oils in natural deposit beneath the surface of the land.

real property inventory: An itemized list and classification of the real property of a person or estate, showing the amount, character, and condition of such property at a given time; also, an objective listing of the supply, character, and condition of all *real property* in a given area at a certain time.

rear of lot: The edge or border of a lot opposite to the front. In case of a gore or triangular lot, the *rear* is designated by the owner with consent of the authority having jurisdiction over the property.

reserve for depreciation: A sum reserved and charged periodically against income to create a reserve fund for the purpose of offsetting depreciation of fixed assets, carried at values assigned to them before they had suffered the depreciation provided for by the reserve fund.

right of way: A strip of land over which a lawful right of passage exists for the benefit of persons who do not own the land.

riparian right: The legal right of a property owner to use water from a water course bordering on his land; also relates to ownership of soil under the stream.

road: A term commonly applied to a thoroughfare or traffic way for public use, usually a rural passageway without curbs, gutters, and sidewalks.

S

satellite community: A term often applied to a subordinate area located near a metropolitan center or within the influence of a large city but usually having separate laws pertaining to taxation, zoning, building regulations, and restrictions.

second mortgage: Mortgage made on property where a first mortgage already exists. The risks are greater and interest rates are higher. In the case of foreclosure, the holder of the second mortgage cannot collect until the first mortgage holder has been satisfied.

service driveway: A passageway which provides access to buildings or property for vehicular traffic, frequently for delivery of supplies.

share cropper: A term commonly applied to a tenant farmer who pays his rent with a share of the crop which he produces; also, a person who works on a farm but owns no capital. The landlord supplies him with food, housing, tools, seeds, fertilizer, and stock in exchange for his labor, which is paid for with a share of the crop which he produces.

share tenant: A tenant farmer who operates a farm by using his own capital and equipment on land belonging to another person. He pays his rent with a specified share in the products from farm.

squatter's right: A term applied to the privilege, without legal right or arrangement, of occupancy of a property by virtue of a long and continuous use of the land.

straight mortgage loan: A loan secured by a mortgage which provides, by its terms, for the liquidation of the loan by means of a single principal payment at the date of maturity of the mortgage loan.

street: A strip of land reserved for use as a public thoroughfare to provide access to a building or buildings bordering on the land. *Streets* may be called avenues, boulevards, drives, lanes, or roads.

sublease: An agreement which conveys the use and occupancy of a property from a tenant, the lessor, to another person, the lessee. In such a transaction, the lessor is the lessee in the prior lease.

subsistence homestead: A property occupied by the owner, who provides subsistence for himself and family, largely through the cultivation of his own land. Sometimes the term is applied to dwelling property that is located near employment sources, thus enabling the workers in the family to earn a cash income which provides subsistence for the family.

T

tax: A charge levied upon persons or property by the government to defray the cost of services performed for the common benefit.

taxpayer: A term commonly applied to all persons who are liable for the payment of a tax whether or not they pay it.

tenancy: A term usually applied to the temporary occupancy of property by persons other than those in whom the fee title is vested.

tenant's improvement: Any fixed improvements on land or on a structure, installed and paid for by a tenant or lessee. Such improvements become the property of the lessor unless specified agreements are previously made to the contrary.

through lot: A lot which is not a corner lot but has frontage on two public streets or highways.

title: The means whereby the owner has the just possession of his property.

title insurance: Insurance against any defects that may exist in the title prior to the time the title is passed. These defects may come to light at a future transaction.

title search: Investigation conducted to see that the ownership of house is free of liens.

topographical map: In building, a type of plan view which shows the contour of the land, also the existing earth and water features, and the surface characteristics of the tract. Such a map usually shows the elevation of the land above sea level, an important feature when selecting a building site.

township: In the United States, a primary unit of local government of varying character in different parts of the country. In the middle west and northwestern states, a *township* is a subdivision of a county. It is an area included between two adjacent township lines and two adjacent range lines, usually containing 36 square miles.

township line: An imaginary line which is one of a series of lines running due east and west, at six-mile intervals, on the earth's surface. These lines are used for locating and describing parcels of land under government survey.

trust agreement: A written instrument or agreement between the owner of a property and a trustee, whereby the owner transfers legal title and control of the property to the trustee, under conditions set forth in the agreement which vests authority in the trustee to hold, manage, or dispose of the property for the benefit of a third party, known as the *beneficiary.*

trust deed: A written instrument or deed which conveys legal title to a property to a trustee for the purpose of securing a debt or to discharge an obligation while the equitable title remains vested in the trustor.

unearned increment: A property valuation which is increased because of the influence or operations of certain social or economic conditions, rather than because of any efforts or initiative exerted by the owner of the property.

V

vacated street: A public thoroughfare which is abandoned through appropriate official action by a public authority.

value: In real estate, the marketable price, or sum of money, which should be paid in exchange for a property under consideration.

vendee: One who buys; in legal usage often refers to one who buys real estate under a contract of sales which gives the right of possession but does not convey title.

W

warranty deed: A written instrument containing a covenant of warranty, either expressed or implied. The grantor guarantees that the title he undertakes to transfer has not been previously conveyed by him and that it is free from encumbrances except as stated therein. He and his heirs agree to protect and defend the grantee against loss which may be suffered due to the existence of any previous title or interest in the property at the time the deed was executed and not *excepted* therein.

water right: The lawful right of a property owner to a water supply, as for irrigation purposes.

Z

zone: A portion of a city, town, or community set apart for specific purposes, as a *business zone* or a *residence zone.* Definite restrictions are placed upon such areas.

Building Material Sizes

Some of the common material sizes used by the architectural draftsman are given here. For ease of reference they are listed in alphabetical order.

Anchor Bolts

SIZES
3/8" & 1/2" x 6" to 24"
5/8" x 8" to 24"
3/4" x 8" to 24"

Anchor Joists for Masonry Walls

STYLE T	SIZES
	1/8" x 1" x 15" & 20"
	3/16" x 1" x 15" & 20"
	1 1/8" x 1 1/2" x 15" & 20"

STYLE L	
	1/8" x 1" x 15" & 20"
	3/16" x 1" x 15" & 20"
	3/16" x 1 1/2" x 15" & 20"

Area Walls — Window Wells, Metal (16 Gage Galvanized Steel)

DEPTH	WIDTH	HEIGHT
16"	38"	11 1/2"
16"	38"	17 1/2"
16"	38"	23 1/2"
16"	38"	29
16"	38"	35

Ash Dumps

SIZE
4 1/2" x 8"
5" x 8"
7" x 10"

Ash Pit — Clean Out Doors

SIZE
8" x 8"
8" x 12"
12" x 12"
18" x 24"
24" x 30"

Beams, Light Weight, Steel. (See also Discussion of "Structural Steel Shapes")

DEPTH	WEIGHT PER FOOT	WIDTH	WEB THICK.	FLANGE THICK.
6"	4.4 lbs	1 7/8"	1/8"	3/16"
7"	5.5 lbs	2 1/8"	1/8"	3/16"
8"	6.5 lbs	2 1/4"	1/8"	3/16"
10"	9.0 lbs	2 3/4"	3/16"	3/16"
12"	11.8 lbs	3"	3/16"	1/4"

*See also discussion A "Structural Steel Shapes."

Brick Sizes (Modular)*

Nominal Size of Brick in. t h l	Number of Brick per 100 sq ft	Cubic Feet of Mortar: Per 100 Sq Ft, ⅜-in. Joints	Per 100 Sq Ft, ½-in. Joints	Per 1000 Brick, ⅜-in. Joints	Per 1000 Brick, ½-in. Joints
4 x 2⅔ x 8	675	5.5	7.0	8.1	10.3
4 x 3⅕ x 8	563	4.8	6.1	8.6	10.9
4 x 4 x 8	450	4.2	5.3	9.2	11.7
4 x 5⅓ x 8	338	3.5	4.4	10.2	12.9
4 x 2 x 12	600	6.5	8.2	10.8	13.7
4 x 2⅔ x 12	450	5.1	6.5	11.3	14.4
4 x 3⅕ x 12	375	4.4	5.6	11.7	14.9
4 x 4 x 12	300	3.7	4.8	12.3	15.7
4 x 5⅓ x 12	225	3.0	3.9	13.4	17.1
6 x 2⅔ x 12	450	7.9	10.2	17.5	22.6
6 x 3⅕ x 12	375	6.8	8.8	18.1	23.4
6 x 4 x 12	300	5.6	7.4	19.1	24.7

* Modular Brick and Mortar Required for Single Wythe Walls in Running Bond (No allowances for breakage or waste)

Concrete Masonry, Wall Thickness (Codes Vary: Check Requirements)

	Residence			Commercial			Cavity Wall Residence			Cavity Wall Commercial		
Story →	1	2	3	1	2	3	1	2	3	1	2	3
Foundation Basement	8"	8"	8"	8-12"	12"	12-16"	8"	(SOLID) 10"	12"	10"	(SOLID) 10"	12"
1st Story	8"	8"	8"	8-12"	12"	12-16"	10"	10"	10-12"	10-12"	12"	12"
2nd Story		8"	8"		8-12"	12"		10"	20"		10-12"	12"
3rd Story			8"			8-12"			10"			10-12"

Doors, Folding

2'-4", 2'-10" W x 6'-8 1/2" Ht

2'-4", 2'-10", 3'-5"
3'-11", 4'-5", 5'0", 6'0" } W x 6'-8" Ht
7'-1"

3'-11", 4'-5", 5'0", 6'0"
7'-1", 8'-2", 9'-3", 10'-3" } W x 8'0" Ht

Doors, French

1'-6" x 6'-8" x 1 3/8"
2'-0" x 6'-8" x 1 3/8"
2'-6" x 6'-8" x 1 3/8"
2'-8" x 6'-8" x 1 3/8"
2'-6" x 6'-8" x 1 3/4"
2'-0" x 6'-8" x 1 3/4"
3'-0" x 6'-8" x 1 3/4"
3'-0" x 6'-8" x 1 3/8"

Doors, Hollow Metal, Interior and Exterior (1⅜" (A) and 1¾" (B) Thick

2'-0" x 6'-8" (A, B)	3'-0" x 6'-8" (A, B)
2'-0" x 7'-0" (A, B)	3'-0" x 7'-0" (A, B)
2'-0" x 7'-2" (A, B)	3'-0" x 7'-2" (A, B)
2'-4" x 6'-8" (A, B)	3'-4" x 6'-8" (B)
2'-4" x 7'-0" (A, B)	3'-4" x 7'-0" (B)
2'-4" x 7'-2" (A, B)	3'-4" x 7'-2" (B)
2'-6" x 6'-8" (A, B)	3'-6" x 6'-8" (B)
2'-6" x 7'-0" (A, B)	3'-6" x 7'-0" (B)
2'-6" x 7'-2" (A, B)	3'-6" x 7'-2" (B)
2'-8" x 6'-8" (A, B)	3'-8" x 6'-8" (B)
2'-8" x 7'-0" (A, B)	3'-8" x 7'-0" (B)
2'-8" x 7'-2" (A, B)	3'-8" x 7'-2" (B)
	4'-0" x 6'-8" (B)
	4'-0" x 7'-0" (B)
	4'-0" x 7'-2" (B)

Doors, Louver

2'-8 1/2" x 6'-10"	2 Panel
3'-0" x 6'-10"	3 Panel

Doors, Metal, Access

Overall Dimension	Door Size	Wall Opening	Door Thickness
10" x 14"	7 1/8" x 11 1/8"	8" x 12"	1/16"
14" x 18"	11 1/8" x 15 1/8"	12" x 16"	1/16"
18" x 26"	15 1/8" x 23 1/8"	16" x 24"	12 gage
26" x 36"	25 1/8" x 31 1/8"	24" x 32"	12 gage

Doors, Outside Basement

Width	Length	Rise	Steel
3'-11"	4'-10"	2'-0"	12 gage
4'-3"	5'-4"	1'-10"	12 gage
4'-7"	6'-0"	1'-7"	12 gage

Doors, Overhead

8'-0" x 7'-0" x 1 3/8"
8'-0" x 7'-0" x 1 2/4"
8'-0" x 8'-0" x 1 3/4"
9'-0" x 7'-0" x 1 3/4"
16'-0" x 7'-0" x 1 3/4"

Doors, Wood (Interior (I) and Exterior (E)), 1⅜″ and 1¾″ Thick

1'-6" x 6'-6" (I)	2'-6" x 6'-0" (I)	3'-0" x 6'-8" (I, E)
1'-6" x 6'-8" (I)	2'-6" x 6'-6" (I)	3'-0" x 7'-0" (I, E)
2'-0" x 6'-0" (I)	2'-6" x 6'-8" (I, E)	3'-0" x 7'-6" (E)
2'-0" x 6'-6" (I)	2'-6" x 7'-0" (I, E)	3'-0" x 8'-0" (E)
2'-0" x 6'-8" (I)	2'-8" x 6'-0" (I)	3'-4" x 6'-8" (I, E)
2'-0" x 7'-0" (I)	2'-8" x 6'-6" (I)	3'-4" x 7'-0" (I, E)
2'-4" x 6'-0" (I)	2'-8" x 6'-8" (I, E)	3'-4" x 7'-6" (E)
2'-4" x 6'-6" (I)	2'-8" x 7'-0" (I, E)	3'-4" x 8'-0" (E)

Fireplaces, Recommended Sizes

	Location			
	Short Side		Long Side	
Room Size	W	H	W	H
10' x 14'	28"	27"	28"	27"
11' x 16'	28"	27"	32"	27"
	32"	27"	36"	27"
12' x 20'	32"	27"	36"	27"
	36"	27"	40"	27"
12' x 24'	32"	27"	36"	27"
	36"	27"	40"	29"
14' x 28'	36"	27"	40"	29"
	40"	29"	48"	29"
16' x 30'	36"	27"	40"	29"
	40"	29"	48"	29"
20' x 30'	40"	29"	48"	29"
	48"	29"	60"	32"

Flue Lining, Modular

Outside Diameter	Modular Dimension	Thickness*	Inside Area	Length
3 1/2" x 7 1/2"	4" x 8"	1/2"	15 sq in	2'-0"
3 1/2" x 11 1/2"	4" x 12"	5/8"	20 " "	"
3 1/2" x 15 1/2"	4" x 16"	3/4"	27 " "	"
7 1/2" x 7 1/2"	8" x 8"	5/8"	35 " "	"
7 1/2" x 11 1/2"	8" x 12"	3/4"	57 " "	"
7 1/2" x 15 1/2"	8" x 16"	7/8"	74 " "	"
11 1/2" x 11 1/2"	12" x 12"	7/8"	87 " "	"
11 1/2" x 15 1/2"	12" x 16"	1"	120 " "	"
15 1/2" x 15 1/2"	16" x 16"	1 1/8"	162 " "	"
15 1/2" x 19 1/2"	16" x 20"	1 1/4"	208 " "	"
19 1/2" x 19 1/2"	20" x 20"	1 3/8"	262 " "	"

* Minimum wall thickness

Flue Lining, Round

INSIDE DIAMETER	THICKNESS*	LENGTH	AREA INSIDE
6"	5/8"	2' 0"	26 sq. in.
7"	11/16"	2' 0"	37 " "
8"	3/4"	2' 0"	47 " "
10"	7/8"	2' 0"	74 1/2 " "
12"	1"	2' 0"	108 " "
15"	1 1/8"	2' 0"	171 " "
18"	1 1/4"	2' 0"	240 " "
20"	1 3/8"	2' 0"	298 " "

*Minimum wall thickness

Flue Lining, Standard

OUTSIDE	INSIDE	THICKNESS*	AREA INSIDE	LENGTH
4 1/2" x 8 1/2"	3 1/4" x 7 1/4"	5/8"	22 sq. in.	2'0"
4 1/2" x 13"	3 1/4" x 11 3/4"	5/8"	36 " "	"
7 1/2" x 7 1/2"	6 1/4" x 6 1/4"	5/8"	38 " "	"
8 1/2" x 8 1/2"	7 1/4" x 7 1/4"	5/8"	51 " "	"
8 1/2" x 13"	7" x 11 1/2"	3/4"	79 " "	"
8 1/2" x 18"	6 3/4" x 16 1/4"	7/8"	108 " "	"
13" x 13"	11 1/4" x 11 1/4"	7/8"	125 " "	"
13" x 18"	11 1/4" x 16 1/4"	7/8"	168 " "	"
18" x 18"	15 3/4" x 15 3/4"	1 1/8"	232 " "	"
20" x 20"	17 1/4" x 17 1/4"	1 3/8"	279 " "	"

*Minimum wall thickness

Glass Block

NOMINAL	ACTUAL
6" sq	5 3/4" sq
8" sq	7 3/4" sq
12" sq	11 3/4" sq

Gutters, Fir

SIZE	ACTUAL SIZE	LENGTHS
3" x 4"	2 1/2" x 3 1/2"	Up to 20'
3" x 5"	2 1/2" x 4 1/2"	"
4" x 4"	3 1/2" x 3 1/2"	"
4" x 5"	3 1/2" x 4 1/2"	"
4" x 6"	3 1/2" x 5 1/2"	"
5" x 7"	4 1/2" x 6 1/2"	"

Gutters, Ogee Metal Box (Galvanized)*

DEPTH	WIDTH	GAUGE
3 1/2"	3 1/2"	28-29
4 1/4"	4 3/8"	"
5"	5"	"

*10' Lengths

Gypsum Wallboard

Width	Lengths	Thickness	Joist or Stud Spacing
4'	6', 7', 8', 9', 10' 12', 14'	1/2"	16" or 24" OC
4'	6', 7', 8', 9', 10' 14'	3/8"	16" OC
4'	8', 10'	1/4"	16" OC
4'	6', 7', 8', 9', 10', 12', 14'	5/8"	16" or 24" OC

Hardboard

Material	Thickness	Size
Standard Hardboard and Tempered Hardboard	1/8", 3/16" 1/4", 5/16"	4' x 5', 6', 8', 9', 10', 12'

Insulating Board

Product	Sizes	Thickness	Edges
Building Board	4' x 7', 8', 9', 10', 12'	1/2", 3/4", 1"	Sq.
Sheathing	4' x 8', 9', 10', 12', 3' x 8'; 2' x 8'	1/2", 25/32" 1/2", 25/32"	Sq. Long edges fabricated Sq. Edge Short Ends
Thin Board	4' x 7', 8', 9', 10', 12'	1/4"	Sq.
Lath	18" x 48", 24" x 48"	1/2", 1"	Long Edge fabricated
Roof Insulation	23" x 47"	1/2", 1", 1 1/2", 2"	Sq.
Tile Board	12" x 12", 16" x 16", 12" x 24", 16" x 32"	1/2", 3/4", 1"	Fab. Edges
Plank	W 8, 10, 12, 16 x 8', 10', 12	1/2"	Fab. Long Edges

Lath, Metal

TYPE	SIZE	REMARKS
Diamond Mesh Self Furring	27" x 96"	5/16" mesh
Diamond Mesh Stucco Lath	27" x 96" 48" x 96"	5/16" furred 3/8" 1 3/8" furred 3/8"
1/8" Rib Lath	24" x 96" 27" x 96"	1/8" Rib
3/8" Rib Lath	24" x 96" 27" x 96"	3/8" Rib
3/4" Rib Lath	29" x 72" 29" x 96" 29" x 120" 29" x 144"	3/4" Rib – 3 5/8 OC " " " " " "

Lintels, Concrete

Span	With Wall Load One Piece Lintel Size	Reinforcing	Split Lintel Size	Reinforcing	End Bearing
TO -7'	7-5/8" x 5-3/4" x	2 No. 3 (3/8 Dia.) bars	3-5/8" x 5-3/4"	1 No. 3 (3/8 Dia.) bar	8"
7'-8'	7-5/8" x 5-3/4"	2 No. 5 (5/8 Dia.) bars	3-5/8" x 5-3/4"	1 No. 5 (5/8 Dia.) bar	8"
7'-8'	7-5/8" x 7-5/8"	2 No. 3 (3/8 Dia.) bars	3-5/8" x 7-5/8"	1 No. 3 (3/8 Dia.) bar	8"
8'-9'	7-5/8" x 7-5/8"	2 No. 4 (1/2 Dia.) bars	3-5/8" x 7-5/8"	1 No. 4 (1/2 Dia.) bar	12"
9'-10'	7-5/8" x 7-5/8"	2 No. 5 (5/8 Dia.) bars	3-5/8" 7-5/8"	1 No. 5 (5/8 Dia.) bar	12"

Lintels, Concrete, Reinforced (With Wall and Floor Load 75 lb to 85 lb for 20' Span)

Span	Size	Bottom Reinforcing	Top Reinforcing	Stirrups or Webs	End Bearing
3'	7 5/8" x 7 5/8" x	2 No. 4 (1/2" Dia.) bars	None	None	8"
4'	7 5/8" x 7 5/8" x	2 No. 6 (3/4" Dia.) bars	None	3-6 gage	8"
5'	7 5/8" x 7 5/8" x	2 No. 7 (7/8" Dia.) bars	2 No. 3 (3/8" Dia.) bars	5-6 gage	8"
6'	7 5/8" x 7 5/8" x	2 No. 7 (7/8" Dia.) bars	2 No. 4 (1/2" Dia.) bars	7-6 gage	12"
7'	7 5/8" x 7 5/8" x	2 No. 8 (1" Dia.) bars	2 No. 8 (1" Dia.) bars	9 gage	12"

Lintels, Steel (4" Bearing)

MASONRY OPENINGS	ANGLE SIZE
Up to 3'-0"	3" x 3" x 1/2"
3'-0" to 7'-0"	3 1/2" x 3 1/2" x 3/8"
7'-0" to 8'-0"	3 1/2" x 3 1/2" x 1/2"
8'-0" to 10'-0"	5" x 3 1/2" x 1/2"
10'-0" to 11'-0"	4" x 4" x 1/2"
11' 0" to 15' 0"	6" x 4" x 3/8"
15' 0" to 16' 0"	6" x 4" x 1/2"

Lintels, Wood (In Walls Where Roof and Floor Loads Need Not BeSupported)

ROUGH OPENING	NOMINAL SIZE STRUCTURAL MEMBERS
Up to 3'-6"	2 – 2"x 4"
3'-6" to 5'-6"	2 – 2"x 6"
5'-6" to 7'-6"	2 – 2"x 8"
7'-6' to 9'-6"	2 – 2"x 10"
9'-6" to 11'-0"	1 – 1"x 12"

*In walls where roof and floor loads need not be supported.

Lumber, Standard Sizes

Type	Nominal Size		Actual Size	
	Thickness	Width	Thickness	Width
Dimension	2"	2" 4" 6" 8" 10" 12"	1 1/2"	1 1/2" 3 1/2" 5 1/2" 7 1/4" 9 1/4" 11 1/4"
Timbers 4", 6", 8"	4" 6" 8"	4" 6" 8" 10"	3 1/2"	3 1/2" 5 1/2" 7 1/2" 9 1/2"
	6"	6" 8" 10"	5 1/2"	5 1/2" 7 1/2" 9 1/2"
	8"	8" 10"	7 1/2" 7 1/2"	7 1/2" 9 1/2"
Common Boards	1"	2" 4" 6" 8" 10" 12"	3/4" or 25/32"	1 1/2" 3 1/2" 5 1/2" 7 1/4" 9 1/4" 11 1/4"
Shiplap Boards	1"	4" 6" 8" 10" 12"	3/4" or 25/32"	3 1/8" Face 5 1/8" Width 7 1/8" " 9 1/8" " 11 1/8" "
T & G Boards	1"	4" 6" 8" 10" 12"	3/4" or 25/32"	3 1/4" Face 5 1/4" Width 7 1/4" " 9 1/4" " 11 1/4" "
Bevel Siding Thin Thick	1/2" 1/2" 1/2" 1/2" 3/4" 3/4" 3/16"	4" 5" 6" 7" 8" 10" 12"	15/32" 3/16" 15/32" 3/16" 15/32" 3/16" 15/32" 3/16" 3/4" 3/16" 3/4" 3/16" 3/4" 3/16"	3 1/2" 4 1/2" 5 1/2" 6 1/2" 7 1/4" 9 1/4" 11 1/4"

Plywood Sizes

Exterior Widths, Ft	Length, Ft	Thickness, In
2 1/2, 3, 3 1/2, 4	5, 6, 7, 8, 9, 10, 12	3/16, 1/4, 3/8, 1/2, 3/4, 7/8, 1, 1 1/8
4	8, 9, 10, 12	5/16, 3/8, 1/2, 5/8
4	8	5/8, 3/4
Interior 2 1/2, 3, 3 1/2, 4	5, 6, 7, 8, 9, 10, 12	3/16, 1/4, 3/8, 1/2, 5/8, 3/4
4	8, 9, 10, 12	5/16, 3/8, 1/2, 5/8
4	8	1/3, 1/2, 3/16, 5/8, 3/4

Plywood Uses

Thickness	Use
1/4" or 1/2"	Interior Wall, ceiling coverings
1/4", 5/16", 3/8", 1/2"	Wall Sheathing (to be covered)
5/16", 3/8", 1/2", 5/8"	Roof Sheathing (To be covered)
1/2", 5/8"	Sub Floors
3/8", 1/2", 5/8"	Exterior Panels or Siding (Exposed to Weather)

Roofing, Built Up

Roof Slope	Description
1/4" to 4"/ft.	Gravel, Slag, Mineral - 3, 4, or 5 plies felt. Bonded with tar or asphalt and surfaced with mineral, gravel or slag.

Roofing, Wood Shingles

ROOF SLOPE			SHINGLE EXPOSURE		
Pitch	Rise	Run	16"	18"	24"
1/8	3"	12"	3 3/4"	4 1/4"	5 3/4"
1/6	4"	12"			
1/4	6"	12"			
1/3	8"	12"			
1/2	12"	12"	5"	5 1/2"	7 1/2"
5/8	15"	12"			
3/4	18"	12"			

Structural Steel Shape Designations (Hot-Rolled Steel)

New Designation	Type of Shape	Old Designation
W 24 × 76 W 14 × 26	W shape	24 WF 76 14 B 26
S 24 × 100	S shape	24 I 100
M 8 × 18.5 M 10 × 9 M 8 × 34.3	M shape	8 M 18.5 10 JR 9.0 8 × 8 M 34.3
C 12 × 20.7	American Standard Channel	12 ⊏ 20.7
MC 12 × 45 MC 12 × 10.6	Miscellaneous Channel	12 × 4 ⊏ 45.0 12 JR ⊏ 10.6
HP 14 × 73	HP shape	14 BP 73
L 6 × 6 × ¾ L 6 × 4 × ⅝	Equal Leg Angle Unequal Leg Angle	∠ 6 × 6 × ¾ ∠ 6 × 4 × ⅝
WT 12 × 38 WT 7 × 13	Structural Tee cut from W shape	ST 12 WF 38 ST 7 B 13
ST 12 × 50	Structural Tee cut from S shape	ST 12 I 50
MT 4 × 9.25 MT 5 × 4.5 MT 4 × 17.15	Structural Tee cut from M shape	ST 4 M 9.25 ST 5 JR 4.5 ST 4 M 17.15
PL ½ × 18	Plate	PL 18 × ½
Bar 1 ⫠ Bar 1¼ φ Bar 2½ × ½	Square Bar Round Bar Flat Bar	Bar 1 ⫠ Bar 1¼ φ Bar 2½ × ½
Pipe 4 Std. Pipe 4 X - Strong Pipe 4 XX - Strong	Pipe	Pipe 4 Std. Pipe 4 X-Strong Pipe 4 XX-Strong
TS 4 × 4 × .375 TS 5 × 3 × .375 TS 3 OD × .250	Structural Tubing: Square Structural Tubing: Rectangular Structural Tubing: Circular	Tube 4 × 4 × .375 Tube 5 × 3 × .375 Tube 3 OD × .250

AMERICAN INSTITUTE OF STEEL CONSTRUCTION

Ventilators, Brick, Cast Iron or Aluminum

Width	Length	Depth	Net Free Area
2 1/4"	8 1/8"	2 3/4"	8 1/2 sq in
2 1/2"	8"	1/2"	9 sq in
5"	8"	1/2"	19 sq in
5"	12"	1/2"	30 sq in

Ventilators, Masonry Wall

BAR TYPE SIZE	DIAGONAL TYPE SIZE
8" × 8"	8" × 8"
12" × 8"	12" × 8"
16" × 8"	16" × 8"
12" × 12"	12" × 12"
18" × 12"	18" × 12"
24" × 12"	24" × 12"